ICHR Series of Dictionaries of Social, Economic, and Administrative Terms in Indian Inscriptions

Dictionary of Social, Economic, and Administrative Terms in South Indian Inscriptions

'The dictionary is an important landmark in the history of epigraphical studies in India. A comprehensive dictionary like the present one is extremely useful for the scholars doing research in Indian history, particularly south Indian history, using epigraphical sources. The excellent work painstakingly done by K.V. Ramesh and his team deserves great appreciation.'

—**Noboru Karashima**, Professor Emeritus, University of Tokyo

'Medieval Indian inscriptions, and especially south Indian inscriptions are the invaluable treasure for students of Indian history in many countries. But proper understanding of them offers difficulty because, in particular, terms used in them have sometimes different meanings. This dictionary, summarizing all the contexts in which terms were used, will greatly help researchers in their work.'

—**Leonid Alayev**, Professor, Russian Academy of Sciences

'One of the problems facing the students using epigraphical material has been the difficulty in defining the terms occurring in the inscriptions. Although there can be no finality in such matters, the availability of the current knowledge in one place is most desirable. This dictionary will go a long way in providing the much-needed help for historians, scholars of language and linguistics and other aspects of the culture of India.'

—**Kesavan Veluthat**, Professor of History, University of Delhi

'This monumental work fulfils a long-felt need of researchers and students of early and medieval Indian history. This dictionary explains all the important technical vocabulary, giving due importance to the context and time of each usage, in south Indian inscriptions, which constitute the bulk of Indian inscriptions. It is the product of several years of strenuous work of a team of epigraphists headed by the chief editor K.V. Ramesh, who is himself a seasoned epigraphist.'

—**Y. Subbarayalu**, Researcher and Head, French Institute of Pondicherry

Dictionary of Social, Economic, and Administrative Terms in South Indian Inscriptions

Volume I

(A–D)

Edited by

K.V. Ramesh

General Editor

R.S. Sharma

Indian Council of Historical Research

OXFORD

UNIVERSITY PRESS

OXFORD
UNIVERSITY PRESS

Oxford University Press is a department of the University of Oxford. It furthers the University's objective of excellence in research, scholarship, and education by publishing worldwide. Oxford is a registered trademark of Oxford University Press in the UK and in certain other countries

Published in India by
Oxford University Press
YMCA Library Building, 1 Jai Singh Road, New Delhi 110 001, India

First published in 2012

ISBN-13: 978-0-19-808015-2
ISBN-10: 0-19-808015-8

Typeset in Diacritical 10/14
Printed in India at G.H. Prints Pvt. Ltd., New Delhi 110 020

Contents

Foreword

We have before us in this volume, the first fruit of a project that began its life in 1989. The Indian Council of Historical Research (ICHR) had on its agenda from the 1970s a number of projects aiming at the compilation and publication of epigraphic data. That naturally lead to a lexicographic project oriented to epigraphic sources. Irfan Habib, then Chairman of the ICHR, after consultation with former Chairman R.S. Sharma requested K.V. Ramesh, the then Director (Epigraphy), Archaeological Survey of India, to organize a workshop in August 1989 in Mysore as a preparatory step. The Council of the ICHR at a meeting in November 1989 approved the scheme that was shaped in the workshop in Mysore and formed an Advisory Board for the proposed dictionary of social, economic, and administrative terms in Indian inscriptions; the ICHR Chairman was to be the Chairman of the board and R.S. Sharma the General Editor, while the editors would be K.V. Ramesh and K.M. Shrimali. It was decided that the projected volumes covering (1) north Indian, (2) south Indian, and (3) Arabic and Persian inscriptions were to be edited by K.M. Shrimali, K.V. Ramesh, and Irfan Habib respectively. For reasons unknown to us the project was suddenly terminated in 1993 soon after Chairman Irfan Habib demitted office. After a long gap of eleven years, towards the end of 2004, the ICHR decided to revive the project. It was further decided that B.K. Pandeya would be coordinating the project. The editors had the difficult task of picking up lost threads of the project after many years and reconstituting the data pool accumulated earlier. K.V. Ramesh is to be congratulated for having completed the first of the projected series of volumes.

Readers of this volume will recall that in the nineteenth century efforts were made to compile dictionaries of Indian judicial, administrative, and revenue terminology. The most well-known was the *Glossary of Judicial* and *Revenue Terms*, edited by Horace H. Wilson, and published in 1865. As the librarian of the East India Company and the Boden Professor of Sanskrit at Oxford, Wilson had formidable reputation. However, the glossary he compiled had a limited objective. The Court of Directors of the East India Company resolved in August 1842 to have prepared a glossary of words relating to the administration of British India. As Wilson explains in his 'Preface' to the glossary, it aimed to include 'words employed in official documents'. All these documents abound more or less with native terms, which, not in all instances strictly technical, are treated as officially current and therefore in need of interpretation (H.H. Wilson, ed. *Glossary of Judicial* and *Revenue Terms*, first ed. 1855, reprint, Delhi, 1966, p. v). Wilson's glossary excluded terms which were not in use in the nineteenth century. The present project of the ICHR is the first attempt to cover the period up to that, right from early Indian inscriptions up to A.D. 1800.

The scheme adopted by the ICHR covers all inscriptions (except post–A.D. 1500 inscriptions in European languages) in the South Asian region. The range covered by the scheme includes fiscal, commercial, social, relational, legal, educational, administrative terminology, and terms related to organized religious activities and folk culture and life. It is a very comprehensive list of over fifty categories covering all the above subjects. Both in its time-span and range of themes to be covered, the scheme of the present dictionary has a wider range than any attempt of its kind in the past.

The present volume compiled by its editor K.V. Ramesh comprises epigraphic terms in south Indian inscriptions, beginning with letters from A to D, arranged in alphabetical order and on historical principles. K.V. Ramesh would like to state that the meanings given for some entries are of a tentative nature because some words are obsolete and obscure due to lapse of many centuries. Like a true scholar, the editor of this volume has expressed this caveat. I congratulate him for having completed the first part of this work of immense scholarship. I would also thank the coordinator B.K. Pandeya and the data-entry operator G.S. Ravishankar who worked for this project with exemplary commitment. I hope that other volumes, including those edited by other scholars, will be published soon.

New Delhi

Sabyasachi Bhattacharya
Former Chairman
Indian Council of Historical Research

Preface

It is my privilege to present to the world of scholarship this first volume of the *Dictionary of Social, Economic and Administrative Terms in South Indian Inscriptions*. The Indian Council of Historical Research launched this ambitious project of a dictionary of social, economic and administrative terms in the inscriptions of India in 1989. The project was in full swing when it was unfortunately dropped in 1993. It was revived, after eleven long years, under the chairmanship of D.N. Tripathi. This volume, the first of the series covering entries from A to D, of the social, economic and administrative terms in the inscriptions of south India, is now ready.

I need hardly say that a dictionary of this kind cannot be prepared by any single individual. The hard labour of those who prepared the data cards, the diligent work of the editors and the rich fund of experience of the editor, K.V. Ramesh, have all contributed to making this volume what it is. The initiative and leadership provided by my predecessors in this office, particularly Irfan Habib, D.N. Tripathi, and Sabyasachi Bhattacharya lie behind the successful completion of this volume. I should like to place on record the debt of gratitude that the Indian Council of Historical Research owes each one of them. I also take this opportunity to thank the Oxford University Press for publishing this work in record time.

Basudev Chatterji
Chairman
Indian Council of Historical Research

System of Transliteration

K = Kannada, M = Malayalam, T = Tamil, Te = Telugu, Skt. = Sanskrit

K	M	T	Te	Skt.	Roman Transliteration	
ಆ	ആ	ஆ	ఆ	आ	ā	Ā
ಈ	ഈ	ஈ	ఈ	ई	ī	Ī
ಊ	ഊ	ஊ	ఊ	ऊ	ū	Ū
ಋ	ഋ	ഋ	ఋ	ऋ	ṛi	Ṛi
ಏ	ഏ	ஏ	ఏ	ए	ē	Ē
ಓ	ഓ	ஓ	ఓ	ओ	ō	Ō
ಙ	ങ	ங	ఙ	ङ	ṅ	Ṅ
ಞ	ഞ	ஞ	ఞ	ञ	ñ	Ñ
ಡ	ഡ		డ	ड	ḍ	Ḍ
ಣ	ണ	ண	ణ	ण	ṇ	Ṇ
ಂ			ం	ं	ṁ	Ṁ
ಱ	റ	ற	ఱ		r̤	R̤
ೞ	ഴ	ழ			l̤	L̤
		ன			n̤	N̤
ಳ	ള	ள	ళ	ळ	ḷ	Ḷ

Introduction

The project for compiling a multi-volume *Dictionary of Social, Economic, and Administrative Terms* occurring in inscriptions from the ancient period onwards, with the exception of inscriptions in western languages of the post-A.D. 1500 was essentially the brain-child of Irfan Habib, when he was serving as the Chairman of the Indian Council of Historical Research (ICHR). It was to be implemented under the auspices of the ICHR. As a prelude to the project Irfan Habib asked me—I was then Director (Epigraphy) of the Archaeological Survey of India at Mysore—to convene a workshop in which the format and other details of the project could be discussed and finalized. The workshop was held between 25 and 27 August 1989 at Mysore and was attended by a number of well known historians and epigraphists including R.S. Sharma, Romila Thapar, G.S. Gai, K.G. Krishnan, and others. To begin with, it was unanimously decided that the comprehensive *Dictionary of Social, Economic, and Administrative Terms* found in Indian Inscriptions should take into account inscriptions from the earliest times to c. 1800 and that the dictionary itself should be based on historical principles. It was further decided that the area of inscriptions covered by the dictionary should comprise India, Bangladesh, Pakistan, and Afghanistan, south of the Hindu Kush Mountains. It was also decided that inscriptions from outside this area may also be exploited wherever necessary.

Published inscriptions in all languages within this area would be included with the exception of inscriptions subsequent to A.D. 1500 in European languages (Latin, Portuguese, English, Dutch, French, and others). It was further decided that the inscriptions to be included would be of two categories:

(i) Published ones with or without translations and critical notes. Comprehensive coverage of such inscriptions would not pose any problems.

(ii) Unpublished inscriptions: This category would cover un-deciphered inscriptions which have reliable transcripts already prepared. For unpublished inscriptions whose transcripts are not available but are discussed or quoted in a published work, a specific acknowledgement (to be indicated by a suitable symbol) that the original text has not been seen by the compilers or editors will be made.

The workshop took the first major decision that there will be three editors for the following three categories of the dictionaries.

(i) Irfan Habib would be the editor for the dictionary on Arabic and Persian inscriptions.
(ii) K.M. Srimali would be the editor for the dictionary of north Indian inscriptions.
(iii) K.V. Ramesh would be the editor for the dictionary of south Indian inscriptions.

It was also decided that the three categories of dictionaries would be published in separate volumes and not combined together.

Soon after the workshop, meetings were held at the premises of the ICHR, New Delhi, on the *modus operandi* for these dictionaries. It was also decided to provide necessary computer facilities including computer operators for the project. From 1990 to 1993, the work of preparing data cards by different scholars went on in full swing and thousands of cards were prepared for the compilation of the north Indian, Arabic and Persian, and south Indian volumes. Many more cards were yet to be prepared and processed before starting the process of compilation.

As bad luck would have it, the project was suddenly discontinued after the departure of Irfan Habib from the Chairmanship of ICHR in 1993. It was only on 25 November 2004, after a long gap of eleven years, that the then Chairman of ICHR D.N. Tripathi called Irfan Habib, K.M. Srimali, B.K. Pandeya, Shukla and me for a meeting at the ICHR, in which it was decided that the dictionary project should be revived. It was decided that B.K. Pandeya would act as the co-ordinator for the entire project. It was felt that the dictionary project would be a very important tool of research especially for ancient India and that its volumes should begin to come out as early as possible. It was noted that a substantial part of the work of preparing data cards necessary for compiling the dictionary had already been done by 1993. Practically many volumes of the *South Indian Inscriptions series* already published had been covered in data cards with citations extracted from the inscriptions. It was also felt that since the ICHR had already invested a huge sum, it was only fitting that such an investment should bear fruit. Thus, a long forgotten project was once again revived in November 2006 when more data cards were sought, which were to be prepared by the scholars still available. However, an unfortunate fall out of the prolonged discontinuance of this project had resulted in the non-availability of most of the data card preparers.

Restarting the project was not easy. Since most of the data card preparers were no longer available and the preparation of the remaining data cards progressed very slowly, I had to depend upon N.K. Ramaseshan and also G.S. Ravishankar in listing a very large number of entry words, for which there were no data cards. Each word was discussed in detail and included as entry word with its meaning, citation, translation, the dynasty and king, as well as the provenance and date of the inscription. Nevertheless, with the available cards and further additions of entry words for which data cards were not available the compilation of the first volume (A to D) of the *Dictionary of Social, Economic, and Administrative Terms in South Indian Inscriptions* was begun in right earnest.

Main Entries

Terms relating to the following themes are included in the dictionary:

(i) geographical features (for example, words for hill, desert, water, forest, river, stream); proper names of mountains have, however, not been included;

(ii) wildlife of economic importance (for example, wild elephants, game, forestry, forest produce such as lac, wax, silks, basketry, fishing);

(iii) agriculture—cultivable lands, agricultural wastes, soil types, methods and implementations of cultivation, crops, sericulture, semi-agricultural products, fruits and orchards;

(iv) cattle and other domestic animals, poultry;

(v) irrigation, tanks, wells, canals, water wheels, and any other methods of water-lifting;

(vi) agricultural manufacture such as grain-milling, oil-milling, sugar and indigo refining, wine fermentation and distillation;

(vii) mines, quarries and minerals; metallurgy;

(viii) crafts (for example, spinning, weaving, cloth printing, carpentry, masonry. Buildings (architectural terms are not to be included);

(ix) non-craft professions rural and urban;

(x) land transport (for example, carts, chariots, palanquins, pack-animals) roads, bridges, inns and choultries;

(xi) water transport (for example, boats, ships, navigation). Port, harbour (proper names of ports not be included);

(xii) means of communication (for example, relay messengers);

(xiii) peasants (words for, for example, *kshetrakāra, kuṭumbin*, ryot), types of peasants (for example, *kuḍi, uparika*), village labourers, farm servants;

(xiv) rural and urban artisans (for example, carpenters, masons, smiths, potters, oilmen, cobblers), other professionals (for example, prostitutes, courtesans, concubines);

(xv) menials, castes and communities;

(xvi) land tenures (for example, tenancy; superior right-holders, for example, grants, grantees);

(xvii) land measures; grain measures, liquid measures;

(xviii) land tax; other rural imposts, cattle grazing, house taxes;

(xix) forced labour;

(xx) taxes other than land tax such as tax on trade (tolls, customs), tax on houses, on professions and on markets; poll tax;

(xxi) trade, commerce and banking, guilds, mercantile and artisan corporations;

(xxii) coins, their various names, issuances of coins (excluding proper names of issuing kings);

(xxiii) deposits, credits, mortgage, interest, exchange (money changing) rates, bill discounts;

(xxiv) villages, hamlets, cottages;

(xxv) village community;

(xxvi) castes and tribes; groups of castes, other communities, ethnic groups (for example, *śaka, kulika, raṭṭa, karnāṭaka, khaśa, pulinda*), proper names not to be included;

(xxvii) slaves, eunuchs;

(xxviii) servants and attendants; wages;

(xxix) women's status, rights, obligations, *sati*, marriage laws, family organizations;

(xxx) inheritance of property, sales, house owning;

(xxxi) states sovereignty (for example, designations and titles of rulers; selectiveness has been exercised); civil, judicial, police administration, officials, royal households, royal lands (for example, *rājakshētra*);

(xxxii) army officers, soldiers, weapons, warfare, horses, elephants;

(xxxiii) Hierarchical relations, infeudation and sub-infeudation assignments (for example, *jāgīr, manneya*);

(xxxiv) local governing bodies; corporations;

(xxxv) territorial divisions (for example, *āhāra, vishaya, ūr, maṇḍala*);

(xxxvi) agrarian magnates (for example, *rāṇaka, ṭhakura, zameendar*);

(xxxvii) clothing, costumes;

(xxxviii) diet, food habits;

(xxxix) luxury articles (for example, ornaments), mark of status (for example, umbrellas);

(xl) education, educational institutions (for example, *agrahāra, maṭha*);

(xli) writing materials, books, documents, scribes and engravers (proper names have been excluded);

(xlii) health, medicine, medical profession;

(xliii) priests (for example, *brāhmaṇas, śramaṇas, archakas*. Temple organizations; priestly fees;

(xliv) pilgrimages;

(xlv) expiatory rites, suicides;

(xlvi) law, morality (for example, *dharma*), crime and punishment;

(xlvii) charity, gift;

(xlviii) games and amusements;

(xlix) natural calamities (for example, famine, epidemic, flood);

(l) social conflicts, disturbances, revolts (words only, proper names not included);

The main difficulty in the case of south Indian inscriptions is the numerous fiscal terms mentioned in connection with grants made by the donors. For instance, in the case of Tamil inscriptions, a good many of these terms do not lend themselves to easy translation and interpretation while many more translations of such terms offered in this dictionary are only tentative. It must also be pointed out that the same holds good for terminologies and words occurring in early and medieval inscriptions in the other Dravidian languages of Kannada, Telugu, and Malayalam. This problem continues even until the seventeenth century in the case of the inscriptions of the last Vijayanagara rulers and those of their subordinates.

Topographical Problems

In post-independent India, in all the southern states, as in the case of the northern states, many new districts and taluks have been created from out of the old divisions. New names replaced old names of taluks and districts and in many cases there was a reversal to the old names. I have retained, for want of updated information, the names of districts and taluks as given in the published epigraphical volumes.[1] Special care will be taken to obtain latest lists of villages, taluks, and districts in the south Indian states and southern Maharashtra while preparing further volumes of the dictionary.

History of South Indian Inscriptions: An Overview

Of the four major Dravidian languages, Kannaḍa makes its appearance as an epigraphical medium in the middle of the fifth century A.D. followed by Telugu about a century later. The influence of Malayāḷam can be noticed from late eleventh century A.D. in the Tamil inscriptions of the Kēraḷa and adjoining regions, but Malayāḷam inscriptions begin to appear around the fourteenth century A.D. It is only when we take up the chronological history of Tamil epigraphy that scholars find themselves in controversy. In this connection it must be pointed out that, while many scholars stick to the age old theory that there cannot be any pre-Aśokan inscriptions anywhere in India, I and a good number of epigraphists have lent our thoughts to re-examine the evidence available to the contrary. I will briefly record the results of a new probe to extract evidence from early inscriptions which give a different picture. To state briefly the justification for such a probe:

(1) The story of inscriptional palaeographical development all over India, without exception, has been movement from utter or stark simplicity to progressively complex variegation andḥor ornamentation to standardized scripts followed by later decline and degeneration. The last phase could be attributed to the availability of other more easily viable writing materials, chiefly paper.
(2) Similarly, the contents of Indian epigraphical texts have invariably tended to become more detailed and pompous in contrast with their simple beginnings.
(3) It is axiomatic that these palaeographical transformations and transmutations cannot be studied in isolation. On the other hand such studies will have to necessarily take into account the fact that the history of Indian palaeography is inextricably interrelated to the epigraphical language media.

In the background of these unassailable fundamental facts, I will, hopefully convincingly, demonstrate the existence of pre-Aśokan inscriptions through the process of comparison and contrast:
The main features of the Aśokan Brāhmī are

a) its basic consonants being endowed with the inherent *a* vowel value (*ka, cha, ṭa, ta, pa,* and so on);
b) presence of letter forms for soft sounds (*ga, ja, ḍa, da, ba*);
c) presence of aspirate letter forms (*kha, chha, ṭha, ḍha, tha, pha, bha*);

[1] We had written to all the concerned state departments requesting them to send us the latest publications of districts and taluks and villages but to no avail.

d) presence of conjunct consonantal letter forms (for example, *kya, khya, dhya, bhya, mya, sva, vya, hma,* yvo);

e) besides the conjunct letter forms, *anusvāra* has been used for achieving economy of space, undoubtedly a later Aśokan practice (for example, *naṁ, vaṁ, dhaṁ,* etc.).

(4) All the above features, which were developed to suit Sanskritic phonetics, and, in particular, the extensive use of conjunct letter forms, are signs of chronologically later developments. In stark contrast, none of the above five features are to be found in the earliest of the Tamil inscriptions as the ones from Māṅguḷam, Mangulam Taluk, Madurai District. On the other hand the script in these earliest Tamil inscriptions is much more rudimentary than Aśokan Brāhmī. The important features of the script of these earliest Tamiḻ inscriptions of the Pāṇḍyan country are:

(a) the basic consonants are not endowed with the inherent 'a' vowel value (for example, *k, ch, ṭ, ṇ, t, n, p, m,* and so on, instead of the Aśokan *ka, cha, ṭa, ṇa, ta, na, pa, ma,* and so on, which is in conformity with the needs of Indo-Āryan grammar);

(b) the absence of letter forms for soft sounds;

(c) the absence of aspirate letter forms;

(d) the total absence of conjunct letter forms;

(e) the absence of *anusvāra*; this and the absence of conjunct letterforms betray a lack of concern for economy of space which is certainly a later concept, starting with the appearance of Aśokan edicts.

5) In view of the unassailable and already underscored fact that the progress of Indian scripts has been, as a rule, from utter simplicity to developed forms which are chronologically datable, it is only proper to conclude that the early rudimentary scripts of a good number of the earliest Tamil inscriptions should be assigned to fourth–third centuries B.C. if not earlier.

Chronological History of Orthographical Changes in South Indian Inscriptions

In view of the fact that this dictionary is prepared on historical principles, it is necessary to take note of chronologically progressive changes which have taken place in the matter of spelling of words and phrases through the centuries. In this connection, it is important to stress that the orthography of Kannaḍa and Telugu regions, which were directly open to the influence of Prakrit and Sanskrit languages and served as buffer zones resulting in the Tamilian south (including Kēraḷa, until Malayāḷam developed into a language in course of time) retaining most of its Dravidian spellings, including the class nasals. Let me take up the case of Kannaḍa and Telugu first. The ninth–tenth centuries were important transitional periods during which class nasals gradually gave place to *anusvāra*. For instance, *teṅgu* began to be spelt as *teṁgu*, *pañcha* as *paṁcha*, *daṇḍanāyaka* as *daṁḍanāyaka*, *bandhu* as *baṁdhu*, *tamma* as *taṁma*, and so on. An even more important change was the gradual replacement of the retroflex *ṟa* by *ra* and *ḻa* by *ḷa*. Also, about the same period, in Kannaḍa and Telugu, *la* gets replaced by the liquid *ḷa*. Inexplicably, however, in copper-plate inscriptions of Hoysaḷa and Vijayanagara times, written in Nandināgarī characters, we find *ṟa* represented by the doubling of *r* as *rra*. Therefore, those who consult this dictionary for words containing these letter forms will do well to consult both forms of main entries—for example, *aḻi* (to destroy) being spelt in later centuries as *aḷi* and *keṟe* (tank) as *kere*.

In the case of Tamil, however, the alphabet has retained to this day all the class nasals (*ṅ, ñ, ṇ*) and the retroflexes *ṟa* and *ḻa* though most Tamilians these days find it difficult to pronounce *ḻa* and end up with pronouncing it as *ḷa* or even as *la*. An important development that took place in the case of Tamil is the invention of the (early strain) of *grantha* named as Pallava *grantha* from about the sixth–seventh centuries A.D., for effectively writing down words of Indo-Āryan phonetical values because the Pallavas and their contemporaries as well as all the successor royal families were avid followers of brahmanical faiths. In the subsequent centuries a popular type of *grantha* script fully adequate for Sanskritic phonetics was evolved and also came to be used in writing works on palm leaves on various subjects as the very name of the script, *grantha* implies besides being extensively used in early Choḷa, Pāṇḍya and later inscriptions. This has resulted in some common orthographical features in all the Dravidian inscriptions. A glaring instance on hand is the variant spellings of the word *dharma* in Dravidian inscriptions from tenth century onwards. Many Dravidian inscriptions, for instance, spell that word differently as *dhaṉma(-chattiram)* [Tamil], *dhanmāsanam* [Malayāḷam], *dama(-goḷaga)* [Kannada] and also as *dhama* and *dhamma* besides the more regular spellings of *dharmma* and *dharma*. One more orthographical aberration which scholars who consult this Dictionary should take note of is the different ways of spelling words involving the medial letters *m, ṁ* and *ṇ*. We frequently meet with such spellings as *daṁḍa* and *daṇḍa, daṁḍanāyaka, daṇḍanāyaka, daṁṇāyaka, daṁṇṇāyaka, daṇāyaka, daṇṇāyaka,* and other variants. Also, in all the Dravidian language inscriptions, we find confusion in spelling of words with hard, soft and aspirate letter forms as in the case of the variants *adhikāri, adikāri* and *atikāri*. To restress what has been stated earlier, these words have been retained as found written in the inscriptions and, therefore, scholars will have to search for these entry words in strictly alphabetical order.

Strictly following the system of transliteration adopted in the epigraphical publications of the Archaeological Survey of India, I have used *ch* and *chh* instead of *c* and *ch* for entry words such as *chakri* (emperor), *chhāyā* (memorial), and so on.

Entry Word and What Follows

Each entry word is followed by the language of the inscription (Kannaḍa, Malayāḷam, Tamiḻ, Telugu, Prakrit or Sanskrit, indicating the original source of the word, if any, by the mark <, its nature (such as noun, pronoun, adjective, indeclinable, and so on, given within round brackets. This is followed by the **text** (relevant extracts from the text of the inscription in question, taking care, as far as possible, in sentence form) in italics and word for word English **translation** in roman characters. These details are followed by publication references, the **dynasty,** the kingās name, and the Śaka or regnal year as given in the inscription and its Gregorian equivalent. In case no dynasty is mentioned, I have classified the inscription under miscellaneous category. If the inscription is issued by a commercial guild, it is so indicated. For undated inscriptions, I have given the century to which it can be assigned on palaeographical grounds. In cases where an entry word has the same spelling but with different import in the context of its occurrence, in each such case such word is repeated as an independent entry word with numbers 1, 2, 3, and so on, printed on top of the entry word.

I furnish now the names of the learned scholars who had prepared data cards for the dictionary before and after the interregnum. J. Sundaram, S. Swaminathan, M.D. Sampath, B.K. Pandeya, Radha D. Patel, K. Munirathnam Reddy, C. Krishnamurthy, N.K. Ramaseshan. C.S. Vasudevan had earlier arranged entries of different alphabets in separate bundles. Among the scholars mentioned above S. Swaminathan has helped on many occasions in placing undated Tamil inscriptions in their proper chronological context.

G.S. Ravishankar arranged each item in the bundles (from A to D) in alphabetical order and has, with great competence, digitized them with diacritical marks. Being himself a person of scholarly bent of mind, he has contributed enormously in giving the dictionary its present academic form. N.K. Ramaseshan, a scholar well versed in Kannaḍa literature and grammar has been working with us out of sheer love for lexicography. Over a considerably long period, the library of the Epigraphist Office at Mysore remained closed for everybody because of the shifting of the office to its own building in another part of the city. This had posed insurmountable problems for us in the compilation work because of the non-availability of many epigraphical publications. Once the library was thrown open in May 2010, T.S. Ravishankar, holding charge of the post of Director (Epigraphy) at Mysore fully cooperated with us and gave us free access to the library, besides making some academic contributions in our work. I must also record here the cooperation received from the Librarian of the Epigraphist Office, Ambica Devi. I am highly beholden to all these friends for their invaluable contributions to this project.

It is my pleasant duty to place on record my grateful thanks to the former Chairman of ICHR Sabyasachi Bhattacharya and the present Chairman Basudev Chatterji, for the keen interest they have evinced in the preparation of this volume. I am also duty bound to express my sincere thanks to B.K. Pandeya, the co-ordinator of this dictionary project. Ever since he took charge as Member Secretary of the ICHR, Ishrat Alam has shown great understanding of the problems faced by me in the compilation of the present volume of the dictionary. I cannot adequately express my thanks to these four scholars and historians.

It is matter for gratification that Oxford University Press, New Delhi, has agreed to publish the present volume as well future volumes of this dictionary.

K.V. Ramesh
Mysore

Publications

A.M.S.I.S.T. : *Ancient to Medieval South Indian Society in Transition* by Noboru Karashima, pub. Oxford University Press, Delhi (2009)

A.R.Es. : *Annual Reports on Epigraphy* prepared by the Epigraphy Branch and published by the Archaeological Survey of India, New Delhi.

A.S.I.A.R. : *Archaeological Survey of India Annual Reports*

Āvaṇam : Volumes of Tamilnadu Archaeological Society

C.K.I. : *Corpus of Koppal Inscriptions* by Hampa. Nagarajaiah, pub. Rathnatraya Prakashana, Mysore (1998)

CPIK : RD : *Copper Plate Inscriptions from Karnataka*; Recent Discoveries, Ed. M.S. Nagaraja Rao & K.V. Ramesh, pub. Directorate of Archaeology and Museums, Mysore (1985)

CPIK : RD : *Copper Plate Inscriptions from Karnataka*; Recent Discoveries, Ed. M.S. Nagaraja Rao & K.V. Ramesh, pub. Directorate of Archaeology and Museums, Mysore (1987)

Ch. Naḍ. : *Cheṅgam Naḍukaṟkaḷ*, Pub. Dept. of Archaeology, Govt. of Tamil Nadu

D.E.D. : *A Dravidian Etymological Dictionary* by T. Burrow and M.B. Emeneau, Published by Oxford University Press, Amen House, London E.C. 4, 1960

D.G.A. : *Descriptive Glossary of Administrative Terms in Ancient Karnataka*, Ed. Shrinivas Ritti, *et. al*, Published by Directorate of Archaeology & Museums, Govt. of Karnataka, Mysore (2000)

E.C. : *Epigraphia Carnatica*, Archaeological Survey of Mysore (Old editions), Vol. I (Coorg,); Vol. II (Śravaṇabeḷagoḷa); Vol. III (Mysore Dt., Gundlupet, Nanjangud and Heggadedevanakote Taluks); Vol. IV (Mysore Dt, Chamarajanagara, Yelanduru, Kollegala, Hunusuru and Periyapatna taluks); Vol. V (Mysore Dt., Krishnarajanagara, Mysore and T. Narasipura Taluks); Vol. VI (Mandya Dt., Krishnarajapete, Pandavapura and Srirangapattana Taluks) and Vols. VII to XII, Ed. B.L. Rice, Vols. XIII Index, XIV and xvi XV, Ed. M.H. Krishna; Vol. XVI Ed. K.A. Nilakanta Sastri; Vol. XVII, Ed. M. Seshadri

E.C. (R) : *Epigraphia Carnatica* (Revised/Reprinted) Published by (Kuvempu) Institute of Kannada Studies, University of Mysore, Mysore. Vol. I Coorg Dt., Ed. B.R. Gopal, (1972); Vol. II, Śravaṇabeḷagoḷa (1973); Vol III, Mysore Dt. (1974); Vol. IV, Mysore Dt. (1975); Vol. V, Mysore Dt. (1976); Vol. VI, Mandya Dt. (1977); Vol. VII, Mandya Dt. (1979); Vol. VIII, Hassan Dt. (1984); Vol. IX, Hassan Dt., Ed. B.R. Gopal & S.S. Jagirdar (1990); Vol. X, Hassan Dt. Ed. A.V. Narasimhamurthy, (1997); Vol. XI, Chikkamagalur Dt. Ed. (1998); Vol. XII, Chikkamagalur Dt. Ed. (2003); Vol. XIII.

E.I. : *Epigraphia Indica*, Pub. by the Director General, Archaeological Survey of India, New Delhi, Vol. I, Ed. Jas. Burgess, E. Hultszch and Führer (1888–92)
Vol. II, Ed. Jas. Burgess and A. Führer (1892–94)
Vols. III to VIII, Ed. E. Hultszch (1894–1906)
Vol. IX, Ed. E. Hultsch and Sten Konow (1907–08)
Vol. X, Ed. Sten Konow and V. Venkayya (1909–1910)
Vol. XI, Ed. V. Venkayya and Sten Konow (1911–12)
Vol. XII, Ed. Sten Konow (1913–14)
Vol. XIII, Ed. Sten Konow and F.W. Thomas (1915–16)
Vol. XIV-XV, Ed. F.W. Thomas (1917–20)
Vol. XVI, Ed. F.W. Thomas and H. Krishna Sastri (1921–22)
Vol. XVII, Ed. H. Krishna Sastri (1923–24)
Vol. XVIII, Ed. H. Krishna Sastri and Hirananda Sastri (1925–26),
Vols. XIX-XX, Ed. Hirananda Sastri (1927–30)
Vol. XXI, Ed. Hirananda Sastri, K.N.Dikshit and N.P. Chakravarti (1931–32)
Vols. XXII-XXVI, Ed. N.P. Chakravarti (1933–42)
Vol. XXVII, Ed. B.Ch. Chhabra and N. Lakshminarayan Rao (1948)
Vol. XXVIII, Ed. B.Ch. Chhabra and D.C. Sircar (1949–50)
Vol. XXIX, Ed. B. Ch. Chhabra, N. Lakshminaran Rao and D.C. Sircar (1951–52)
Vol. XXX, Ed. N. Lakshminarayan Rao and D.C. Sircar (1953–54)
Vol. XXXI, Ed. D.C. Sircar (1955–56)
Vol. XXXII, Ed. D.C. Sircar and B. Ch. Chhabra (1957–58)
Vols. XXXIII-XXXVI, Ed. D.C. Sircar (1959–66)
Vol. XXXVII-XXXVIII, Ed. G.S. Gai (1967–70)
Vol. XXXIX, Ed. P.R. Srinivasan (1971–73)
Vol. XL, Ed. Parts I to VI, K.G. Krishnan and Ed. Part VII, M.N. Katti (1974, 1998)
Vols. XLI-XLII, Ed. K.V. Ramesh (1975–78)

E.K.D. : *English-Kannada Dictionary* (Revised), Pub. by Prasaranga, University of Mysore, Mysore, Vol. I, A-D (1st edn., 1989, 2nd edn., 2000), Vol. II, E-L (1996), Vol. III, M-R (1999), Vol. IV, S-Z (2004)

E.T.E. : *Early Tamil Epigraphy* by Iravatham Mahadevan (Pub. by Cre–A, Chennai, India and The Department of Sanskrit and Indian Studies, Harvard University, U.S.A., 2003)

H.C.T. : *History and Culture of Tamilnadu* by Chithra Madhavan, pub. D.K. Print World, New Delhi (2005)

I.A : *Indian Antiquary* Volumes, reprinted by Swati Publications, Delhi (1994)

I.A.P. : *Inscriptions of Andhra Pradesh*, Cuddapah District Pt. I (1977) & II (1978), Ed. P.V. Parabrahmasastri, Hyderabad.

I.E. : *Indian Epemeries*, Vols. I to VI, reprinted by Agam Prakashan, Delhi (1982)

I.G.A.P. : *Inscriptional Glossary of Andhra Pradesh* (in Telugu) by Kunduri Iswara Dutt, Pub. by Andhra Pradesh Sahitya Akademi, Kalabhavan, Saifabad, Hyderabad-4 (1967)

I.K.D. : *Inscriptions from Kolhapur District* Ed. S.H. Ritti and A.B. Karveerkar, pub. Kannada University, Hampi (2000)

I.N.D. : Inscriptions from Nanded District, Ed. by Srinivasa Ritti and G.C. Shelke, pub. Srihariprakashana, Dharwar (1968)

I.P.S.	:	*Inscriptions of the Pudukkottai State* (1929)
I.V.R.	:	*Inscriptions of Vijayanagara Rulers,* Vols. I & II, pub. by ICHR, Ed. SH Ritti and B.R. Gopal
I.S.D.	:	Inscriptions from Sholapur District, Ed. By Srinivasa Ritti & Ananda Kumbhar (1988)
J.E.S.I.	:	*Journal of the Epigraphical Society of India,* pub. by E.S.I. Mysore.
Kāvēri	:	*Studies in Epigraphy, Archaeology and History,* (Y. Subbarayalu Fel. Vol. Ed. S. Rajagopal, Chennai (2001)
KGKW	:	A Kisamwār Glossary of Kannaḍa Words by U. Narasinga Rao, Mangalore, 1891
K.I.A.P.	:	*Kannada Inscriptions of Andhra Pradesh,* Ed. By P. Srinivasachar and P.B. Desi, Pub. By the Govt. of Andhra Pradesh, (1961), Hyderabad
K.I.	:	*Karnatak Inscriptions,* Pub. by Kannada Research Institute, Karnataka University, Dharwar, Vol. I (1941), Vol. II (1952) and Vol. III (1953), Ed. R.S. Panchamukhi; Vol. IV (1961) Ed. A.M. Annigeri; Vol. V (1969) and Vol. VI (1973), Ed. B.R. Gopal.
K.N.	:	*Kannaḍa Nighaṁṭu* Published by the Kannaḍa Sāhitya Parishat, Bangalore, Vols. I to VIII
K.K.E.N.	:	*Kannada-Kannada-English Nighaṁṭu,* Pub. by Kannada Sahitya Parishat, Bangalore, Vol. I, Ed. Prabhushankar *et al,* (2002)
M.A.R.	:	Mysore Archaeological Report 1931, 1932, 1933, 1936, 1938, 1942 (Ed. M.H. Krishṇa)
S.E.D.	:	*Sanskrit English Dictionary* by M. Monier Williams, New Edition Enlarged and Improved, Asian Educational Services, New Delhi,
S.I.I.	:	*South Indian Inscriptions* Series, Pub. by The Director General, Archaeological Survey of India, New Delhi. Vol. I, Ed. E. Hultzsch, Tamil and Sanskrit inscriptions chiefly collected in 1886-87 (1890, revised in 1991) 2003. Vol. II, Ed. E. Hultzsch, Tamil inscriptions of Rājarāja, Rājēndra–Chōḷa and others in the Rājarājēśvara Temple at Tanjavūr Part I: Inscriptions on the walls of the central shrine (1891, Reprinted 1991) Part II, Ed. E. Hultzsch, Inscriptions on the walls of the enclosure Part III, Ed. E. Hultzsch, Additional Inscriptions in the Tanjavūr Temple and other miscellaneous records (Reprinted in 1992 & 2001) Part IV, Ed. V. Venkayya, Other inscriptions of the Tañjāvūr Temple (Reprinted in 1992 & 2001) Part V, Ed. H. Krishna Sastri, Pallava copper-plates and Index (Reprinted in 1992 & 2001) Vol. III, Parts I & II, Ed. E. Hultzsch, Miscellaneous Inscriptions from the Tamil country (1929, reprinted 1987) Part III, Ed. H. Krishna Sastri, Inscriptions of Āditya-I, Parāntaka-I, Madiraikoṇḍa Rājakēsari–varman, Parāntaka II, Uttama-Choḷa, Pārthivēnra–varman and Āditya-Karikāla and the Tiruvālaṅ gāḍu plates of Rājēndra Choḷa (1920, Reprinted 1987) Part IV, Ed. H. Krishna Sastri, Copper-plate grants from Śinnamaṇūr, Tirukkaḷar and Tiruchcheṅgoḍu (1929, Reprinted 1987)

Vol. IV, Ed. H. Krishna Sastri, Miscellaneous Inscriptions from the Tamil, Telugu and Kannada countries and Ceylon (1923, Reprinted 1986)
Vol. V, Ed. H. Krishna Sastri, Miscellaneous Inscriptions in Tamil, Malayalam, Telugu and Kannada (1925, Reprinted 1986);
Vol. VI, Ed. K.V. Subrahmanya Aiyer, Miscellaneous Inscriptions from the Tamil, Telugu and Kannada countries (1928, Reprinted 1986)
Vol. VII, Ed. K.V. Subrahmanya Aiyer, Miscellaneous Inscriptions from the Tamil, Malayalam, Telugu and Kannada countries (1932, Reprinted 1986)
Vol. VIII, Ed. K.V. Subrahmanya Aiyer, Miscellaneous inscriptions in Tamil, Makayalam, Telugu and Kannada (1937, Reprinted 1986)
Vol. IX,
Part I, Ed. R. Shama Sastry & N. Lakshminarayan Rao, Kannada Inscriptions from the Madras Presidency (1939, Reprinted 1986)
Part II, Ed. R. Shama Sastry & N. Lakshminarayan Rao, Kannada Inscriptions from the Madras Presidency (1941, Reprinted 1986)
Vol. X, Ed. J. Ramayya Pantulu & N. Lakshminarayan Rao, Telugu Inscriptions from the Madras Presidency (1948, Reprinted 1986)
Vol. XI,
Part I, Ed. C.R. Krishnamacharlu, R.S. Panchamukhi, N. Lakshminarayan Rao, Bombay-Karnatak Inscriptions, (1940, Reprinted 1986)
Part II, Ed. N. Lakshminarayan Rao, Bombay-Karnatak Inscriptions (1952, reprinted 1986)
Vol. XII, Ed. V. Venkatasubba Ayyar, The Pallavas (1943, Reprinted 1986)
Vol. XIII, Ed. G.V. Srinivasa Rao, The Choḷas (1952, Reprinted 1986)
Vol. XIV, Ed. A.S. Ramanatha Ayyar, The Pāṇḍyas (1962, Reprinted 1986)
Vol. XV, Ed. P.B. Desai, Bombay-Karnataka Inscriptions, Vol. II (1964, reprinted 1986)
Vol. XVI, Ed. H.K. Narasimhaswami, Telugu Inscriptions of the Vijayanagara Dynasty (1972, reprinted 1988)
Vol. XVII, Ed. K.G. Krishnan, Inscriptions collected during the year 1903–04, (1964, reprinted 1988)
Vol. XVIII, Ed. N. Lakshminarayan Rao, Bombay-Karnataka Inscriptions, Vol. III (1975)
Vol. XIX, Ed. G.V. Sriṇivasa Rao, Inscriptions of Parakēsarivarman (1967, reprinted 1988)
Vol. XX, Ed. G.S. Gai, Bombay-Karnatak Inscriptions, Vol. IV(1965, reprinted 1986)
Vol. XXI (Not Printed)
Vol. XXII, part I, Ed., G.V. Srinivasa Rao, Inscriptions collected during the year 1905–06 (1983)
Vol. XXII, part III, Ed. G.V. Srinivasa Rao. Inscriptions collected during the year 1906 (1999)
Vol. XXIII, Ed. Ed. G.V. Srinivasa Rao. Inscriptions collected during the year 1906–07 (1979)
Vol. XXIV, Ed. H.K. Narasiṁhaswamy, Inscriptions of the Ranganathaswami temple, Srirangam (1982)
Vol. XXV, Not Printed
Vol. XXVI, Ed. P.R. Srinivasan, Inscriptions collected during the year 1908–09 (1990)

		Vol. XXVII, Ed. M.D. Sampath, H.K. Narasimhaswamy, Madhav N. Katti, B.R. Gopal (2001)
S.I.S.H	:	*South Indian History & Society* by Noboru Karashima, Delhi (1984)
T.A.S.	:	*Travancore Archaeological Series*, Vols. I to VI, Pub. By Department of Cultural Publications, Govt. of Kerala, Trivandrum, Kerala.
T.D.I.	:	*Tirupati Dēvasthānam Inscriptions* Vols. I to VII
T.K.C.	:	*Tamiḻk-kalveṭṭuch-chollagarādi*, Published by Santi Sadhana (Charitable Trust), Vols. I (2002) & II (2003), Ed. Y. Subbarayalu
Tulu Lex.	:	*Tulu Lexicon* Vol. I to VI, Ed.-in-Chief. U.P. Upadhyaya, Udupi (1997)

Topographical Abbreviations

Ag. Arakalagudu Tq.
Ak. Arasikere Tq.
Al. Aluru Tq.
Ank. Anekal Tq.
AP. Andhra Pradesh State
Bgp. Bāgēpalli Tq.
Bl. Beluru Tq.
Bng. Bangalore Tq.
Bow. Bowringpet Tq.
Ch. Chamarajanagara Tq.
Chik. Chikkaballapur Tq.
Chal. Challakere Tq.
Chin. Chintāmaṇi Tq.
Chp. Channapaṭṭaṇa Tq.
Chit., Chdg., Chitradurga Tq.
Chng. Channagiri Tq.
Chnk. Chikkanayakanahalli Tq.
Cm. Chikkamagalur Tq.
CP., Chnp., Channarayapattana Tq.
Db. Doddaballapur Tq.
Dev. Devanahalli Tq.
D.K. Dakshina Kannada Tq.
Dt. District
Dvg. Davanagere Tq.
Goa. Goa State
Grb. Goribidanur Tq.
Gubbi. Gubbi Tq.
Gu. Gundlupete Tq.
Hari, Harihara Tq.
Hg., H.D. Kote, Heggadadevanakote Tq.
Hir. Hiriyur Tq.
HN. Holenarasipura Tq.
Hn. Hassan Tq.
Holal, Hlkr, Holalkere Tq.
Hnl. Honnali Tq.
Hs. Hunasuru Tq.
Hsk. Hosakote Tq.
Jag. Jagalur Tq.
Karn. Karnataka State
Kd., Kdr. Kadur Tq.
Ker. Kerala St.
Kn. Krishnarajanagara Tq.
Knk. Kanakanahalli Tq.
Ko. Kollegala Tq
Kol. Kolara Tq.
Kop. Koppa Tq.
Krt. Koratagere Tq.
Kp. Koppa Tq.
Kr. Krishnarajapete Tq.
Kun. Kunigal Tq.
Mb. Muḷubāgilu Tq.
Md. Mandya Tq.
Mdg. Madhugiri Tq.
Mg. Mudagere Tq.
Mgd. Magadi Tq.
Maha. Maharashtra State
Mal. Mālūr Tq.
Ml. Malavalli Tq.
Mlk. Molakalmur Tq.
Mn. Mehaboobnagar Tq.
Mu. Madduru Tq.
My., Mys., Mysore Tq.
Ng. Nagamangala Tq.
Ngr. Nagara Tq.
Nj. Nanjanagudu Tq.
Nlm. Nelamangala Tq.
Np. Narasimharajapura Tq.
Pondy. Pondicherry State
Pp. Pandavapura Tq.
PP. Periyapattana Tq.
Pvd. Pavagada Tq.
Sh. Shimoga Tq.

Skr., Shikari., Shikaripura Tq.
Sl., Skl., Sakaleshapura Tq.
Sor. Soraba Tq.
Sdl. Sidlaghatta Tq.
Sira. Sira Tq.
Spr., Srp., Srinivasapura Tq.
Sr. Srirangapattana Tq.
Srg. Sringeri Tq.
Sg., Sgr. Sagara Tq.
Tīr. Tīrthahaḷḷi Tq.
Tk. Tarikere Tq.
T.N., T.N.pura. T. Narasipura Tq.
T. Nadu. Tamil Nadu State
Tpt. Tiptur
Tq. Taluq
Yl. Yalanduru Tq.

Dynastic Abbreviations

Ārv.	Āravīḍu
Chal. of Bād	Chalukyas of Bādāmi
Chāḷ. of Kal	Chāḷukyas of Kalyāṇa
Chāḷ. of Veṅg.	Chāḷukyas of Vēṅgi
E. Chāḷ.	Eastern Chāḷukyas of Vēṅgi
E. Gaṅga	Eastern Gaṅgas
Gut. Of Gut.	Guttas of Guttavaḷal
Hoy.	Hoysaḷas of Dvārasamudra
Kad. of Ban.	Kadaṁbas of Banavāsi
Kād. of Goa	Kādaṁbas of Goa
Kal. of Kal.	Kalachūris of Kalyaṇa
Nagire chfs.	Nagire chiefs
Nāy. of Mad.	Nāyakas of Madurai
Noḷ. Pal.	Noḷaṁba Pallava
Pall.	Pallavas
Raṭ. of Sau.	Raṭṭas of Saundatti
Rāshṭr.	Rāshṭrakūṭas of Mānyakhēṭa
Rēṇ. chfs.	Rēṇāḍu chiefs
Rule. of Trav.	Rulers of Travancore
Rule. of Vēṇ.	Rulers of Vēṇāḍu.
Śaṁb,	Śaṁbuvarāya
Sāḷ. chfs.	Sāḷuva chiefs
Sēü of Dēv.	Sēüṇas of Dēvagiri
Te. Ch.	Telugu Chōḍas
Vaid.	Vaiduṁbas
W. Gaṅga	Western Gaṅgas of Talakāḍu
Woḍ. Of Mys.	Woḍeyars of Mysore
Umm. chfs.	Ummattur Chiefs
Yad. of Dēv.	Yādavas of Dēvagiri

Miscellaneous

adj.	Adjective
advb.	Adverb
agri. Gld.	Agricultural guild
cent.	Century
chfs.	Chiefs
Ch. Vi. yr.	Chāḷukya Vikrama year
comm. gld.	Commercial guild
Cy. yr.	Cyclic year
Dy.	Dynasty
indec.	Indeclinable
K.	Kannaḍa
Kal. Yr.	Kaliyuga Year
l.	Line
ll.	Lines
M.	Malayāḷam
Misc.	Miscellaneous
Mrt.	Maraṭhi
n.	Noun
p.	Page
Pkt.	Prakrit
pp.	Pages
Pr.	Prince
pt.	Part
pron.	Pronoun
q.v.	cross reference
reg. yr.	regnal year
Ś.	Śaka
Skt.	Sanskrit
St.	State
T.	Tamiḻ
Te.	Telugu
Tq.	Taluq
vb.	Verb
tr.	Translation
<	derived from

A

ābaraṇa (K. < Skt. ābharaṇa, *n*), jewellery made of precious metals ; **text[1] :** . . . . *muṁna Ariharamahārāyaru . . . . . . Pāṁchālake hajāra siṁhāsanava māḍidalli maṁnnisidaṁtā mane kudure yettu yeṁme tottu baṁḍi . . . .* ***ābaraṇa*** *muṁtāda*. . . (text incomplete) ; **tr.** in earlier days Harihara-mahārāya had granted to the Pāṁchālas exemption from taxes on houses, horses, bullocks, buffaloes, slaves, carts, **jewellery made of precious metals** etc., as a reward for manufacturing the throne in the royal court ; *S.I.I.* IX, pt. ii, No. 439, p. 447, ll. 8–14 ; Gaunivāripalli, Hindupur Tq., Anantapur Dt., A.P. St. **Dy.** Saṅgama, Dēvarāya II, Ś. 1339 = 1418 A.D. ; **text[2] :** (badly damaged) . . . . *chiṁnada* ***ābaraṇa****gaḷu rajatādi . . . . samarpisi . . . . dēvara śrīkāryagaḷige* . . . ; **tr.** for the rituals of worship of the god **jewellery made of precious metals** such as gold and silver were presented ; *S.I.I.* IV, No. 265, p. 59, ll. 14–15 ; Hampi, Hospet Tq., Bellary Dt., Karn. St. **Dy.** Tuḷuva, Sadāśivarāya, Ś. 1467 = 1545 A.D. ; **ābaraṇam** (T. < Skt. *n*.), **text[3] :** . . . *Tirunerṟikkāraikkāvuḍaiyanāyaṉār kōyil tiruv****ābaraṇa****mum tirumuṭṭugaḷum* . . . . . ; **tr.** the **jewellery made of precious metals** and articles of worship in the temple of the god Tirunerṟikkāraikkāvuḍaiyanāyaṉār ; *S.I.I.* VIII, No. 2, p. 2, ll. 3–4 ; Kāñchīpuram, Kanchipuram Tq., Chingleput Dt., T. Nadu St. **Dy.** Chieftain of Kāḷahasti, Alluntirukkāḷattidēva, reg. year 6, in characters of 12th cent. A.D.

abbe (K. *n*.), mother/respectful suffix attached to the name of a lady ; **text[1] :** . . . *taṁma* ***abbe*** *Sōm****abbe*** *sānige puṇyamāge Ādityagrihamaṁ māḍisida* . . . . . . ; **tr.** he got constructed a temple of the Sun god for the merit of his **mother** Som-**abbe**-sāni ; *S.I.I.* IX, pt. i, No. 147, p. 130, ll. 29–30; Saṁgamēśvara, Nandikotkur Tq., Kurnool Dt., A.P. St. **Dy.** Chāḷ. of Kal., Vikramāditya VI, Ch. Vi. yr. 3 = 1079 A.D. ; **text[2] :** . . . *Benagaṁgavātma-sajjanan-enisuva Sōv* ***abbe****gaṁ dharitrītaḷadoḷu. jalanidhiya sippinoḷagaṇin anupama mauktikame puṭṭuvandadi vogedaṁ.* . . . . ; **tr.** To Benagaṅga who was by himself reputed as a good man and to Sōv-**abbe** was born (a son) on the earth comparable to the pearl found inside the sea-shell ; *S.I.I.* IX, pt. i, No. 186, p. 180, ll. 14–16 ; Guḍihaḷḷi, Harapanahalli Tq., Bellary Dt., Karn. St. **Dy.** Chāḷ. of Kal., Vikramāditya VI, Ch. Vi. yr. 36 = 1111 A.D. ; **abbi** (K. *n*.), mother ; **text[3] :** . . . . *Dēvaradāsayyana* ***abbi****gaḷ* . . . . *Chāmakabbegaḷa nisidhige* . . . . ; **tr.** the memorial of Chāmak**abbe**, the **mother** of Dēvaradāsayya ; *E.C.* VIII (R), No. 62, p. 34, ll. 5, 8–10; Aṁkanāthapura, Holenarasipura Tq., Hassan Dt., Karn. St. **Misc.**, in characters of 10th cent. A.D.

abdhi (K. < Skt. *n*.), ocean ; **text :** . . . . *suraruṁ daityarum* ***abdhi****yaṁ kaḍevutirpand-ugra-Śēshāhi bhīkara kōpāgrahi kālakūṭa vishamaṁ tuppeṁdaḍ ā dēvaruṁ asuraruṁ bhītiyin ōḍuvaṁdu.* . . . . . ; **tr.** when the gods and demons were churning the **ocean**, the fierce serpent Śēsha with extreme rage spat the *kālakūṭa* poison and the gods and the demons fled out of fear ; *S.I.I.* VII, No. 724, p. 366, ll. 54–57 ; Sēḍam, Sedam Tq., Gulbarga Dt., Karn. St. **Dy.** Chāḷ. of Kal., Bhūlōkamalla, in characters of 12th cent. A.D.

ābharaṇa (K. < Skt. *n.*), jewellery made of precious metals/ornament ; **text**[1] : . . . . *Śivasatrānurañjita bhagavatpādaik* ***ābharaṇa*** *śrīmatu Varuṇaśiva bhaṭārar*. . . . . ; **tr.** the illustrious Varuṇaśiva-bhaṭāra who was the sole **jewellery made of precious metals** set on the feet of Śivasatrānurañjita-bhagavatpāda ; *S.I.I.* IX, pt. i, No. 24, p. 13, ll. 20–23 ; Guṇimōrubāgal, Madakasira Tq., Anantapur Dt., A.P. St. **Dy.** Noḷ. Pal., Aṇṇayadēva, Ś. 858 = 936 A.D. ; **text**[2] : . . . . *Chāḷuky****ābharaṇaṁ*** *śrīmad-Āhavamalladēvara vijayarājyaṁ. . . . saluttamire* . . . . ; **tr.** when the reign of the illustrious Āhavamalladēva, who was like a **jewellery made of precious metals** in the Chāḷukya family, was in progress ; *S.I.I.* IX, pt. i, No. 73, pp. 44–45, ll. 5–7 ; Kuḍatini, Bellary Tq. and Dt., Karn. St. **Dy.** Chāḷ. of Kal., Āhavamalla, Ś. 897 = 976 A.D. ; **text**[3] : . . . *anēka śaurya guṇ****ābharaṇaṁ*** *purusha-vibhūshaṇaṁ nuḍidu tappillaṁ* . . . *Śrīmat Pallavarasa* . . . ; **tr.** the illustrious Pallavarasa, who was like a **jewellery made of precious metals,** was characterised by many good qualities such as courage and an ornament among men and one who stuck to his words ; *S.I.I.* IX, pt. i, No. 98, p. 68, ll. 8–9 ; Sirivaram, Bellary Tq. and Dt., Karn. St. **Dy.** Chāḷ. of Kal., Sōmēśvara I, Ś. 966 = 1044 A.D. ; **text**[4] : *bhuvanavanoṁde tōḷal-orbbane Kēyūrad* ***ābharaṇa****daṁte taḷedaṁ* ; **tr :** like sporting the shoulder-**ornament** on a single shoulder, he bore the entire weight of the earth on his single shoulder ; *S.I.I.* IX, pt. ii, No. 711, p. 697, ll. 3–4, Ambali, Kudligi Tq., Bellary Dt., Karn. St. **Dy.** Kādaṁba Chief, Jagadala Pāṇḍya, in characters of 12th cent. A.D. ; **text**[5] : . . . . *śrī Tiruvēṅgaḷanāthana pratishṭeyanu māḍi* . . . *navaratna khachitavāda* ***ābharaṇa****ṁgaḷanū suvarṇa rajatādyu-pakaraṇaṁgaḷa samarpisi* . . . . . *Achyutadēva mahārāyaru biṭaṁtha sīme*. . . . ; **tr.** territory granted by Achyutadēva-mahārāya to the god Tiruvēṅgaḷanātha who was installed and presented with **jewellery embedded with precious stones,** gold and silver articles ; *S.I.I.* IX, pt. ii, No. 564, p. 584, ll. 6–8, 10 ; Hampi, Hospet Tq., Bellary Dt., Karn. St. **Dy.** Tuḷuva, Achyutarāya, Ś. 1456 = 1534 A.D.

abhayahasta (K. < Skt. *n.*), a hand posture conveying divine protection ; **text :** . . . *śrī vīra-Achyutarāyaru Kaṁchi Varadarājadēvarige samarpista ratna-ghaṭita śaṅkha 1 chakraṁ 1* ***abhayahasta*** *1 tirunāma 1* . . . . ; **tr.** the illustrious Vīra-Achyutarāya presented to the god Varadarājadēva of Kaṁchi one conch shell, one discus and one ornament for the **hand** of the god

posturing divine protection studded with diamonds and one Vaishṇavite forehead mark ; *S.I.I.* IX, pt. ii, No. 547, p. 566, l. 6 ; Little Kāñchīpuram, Kanchipuram Tq., Chingleput Dt., T. Nadu St. **Dy.** Tuḷuva, Achyutarāya, Ś. 1454 = 1532 A.D.

abhayahastaṁ (Te. < Skt. *n.*), **text :** ... *śrī vīra-Achyutamahārāyalu Kaṁchi Varadarājadēvuniki samarpiṁchina ratna ghaṭita śaṅkhu 1 chakraṁ 1* ***abhayahastaṁ*** *1 tirunāmaṁ 1*; **tr.** the illustrious Vīra Achyutarāya presented to the god Varadarājadēva of Kaṁchi one conch shell, one discus and one ornament for the **hand** of the god **posturing divine protection** studded with diamonds and one Vaishṇavite forehead mark ; *S.I.I.* XVI, No. 100, p. 116, l. 1 ; Little Kāñchīpuram, Kanchipuram Tq., Chingleput Dt., T. Nadu St. **Dy.** Tuḷuva, Achyutarāya, Ś. 1454 = 1532 A.D.

abhidhāna (K. < Skt. *n.*), lexicology, discourse, vocabulary, knowledge ; **text :** .... *vyākaraṇa tarkka siddhānta kāvya nāṭaka nāṭikā vēd**ābhidhān**-āḷaṁkāra pratiśruti purāṇētihāsa mīmāṁsā nītiśāstr-ādyaneka śāstrārtha pravīṇaru .... śrī Nirvvāṇa dēvaru* ; **tr.** śrī Nirvvāṇadēva who was erudite and capable of interpreting grammar, logic, astrology, literature, drama, skits, vēdas, **lexicology**, poetics, music, lores, history, literary science, polity, etc. ; *S.I.I.* IX, pt. i, No. 235, p. 241, ll. 22–23 ; Sindigēri, Bellary Tq. and Dt., Karn. St. **Dy.** Chāḷ. of Kal., Jagadēkamalla II, reg. yr. 4 = 1141 A.D.

abhiḻeka (T. & M. < Skt. abhishēka, *n.*), anointment; **text :** ... *Amarabhujaṅgap- perumāḷukku tirumuḍiyum tiruv-ābaraṇamum paṇṇuchchu* ***abhiḻekañ****-chēvichchōm mūlaparaḍai-śēvaiyōm* ; **tr.** the members of the assembly made a sacred crown and sacred ornaments for the god Amarabhujaṅgapperumāḷ after **anointment** ; *T.A.S.* IV, No. 25, p. 119, ll. 20–22 ; Śuchīndram, Agasthishvaram Tq., Kanyakumari Dt., T. Nadu St. **Dy.** Pāṇḍya, Māṟañjaḍaiyaṉ, reg. yr. 2+3 = in characters of early 10th century A.D.

abhimāna vastu (K. < Skt. *n.*), object of reverence; **text :** .... *yī grāmagaḷige āvanobanu kāṇike kaṁdāya mēlugāṇike ārobarū apēkshisidavanu Vāraṇāsiyali mātā pitrugaḷa vadhisida pātakakke hōdavaru eṁdu abhimāna vastuvāgi dēvarige koṭadu eṁdu barsida silāśāsana* ... ; **tr.** these villages have been granted as **objects of reverence** to the god as recorded in the inscription and whoever expects to appropriate for himself the tax, revenue tax, super tax from the gifted villages would have, in effect, committed the sin of having killed his parents in Vāraṇāsi ; *S.I.I.* IX, pt. ii, No. 576, p. 593, ll. 16–21 ; Kambadūru, Kalyanadurg Tq., Anantapur Dt., A.P. St. **Dy.** Tuḷuva, Achyutarāya, Ś. 1458 = 1536 A.D.

abhishēka dakshaṇai (T. < Skt. *n.*), land gifted on the occasion of coronation ; **text :** ...... *.Tirukkuḍamukkil Mūlapaṟaḍai perumakkaḷōm Tirukkiḻkōṭṭattu .... svāmikku viṭṭu kuḍutta nilam ... nāṅgaḷ* ***abhishēka-dakshaṇai*** *peṟṟuḍaiya Arisalūr* *nilattil* . . . . . ; **tr.** the **land** in Ariśalūr which we had obtained as **gift on the occasion of coronation** by members of the local administrative body of Tirukuḍamūkku was sold to the god Tirukkīḻkōṭṭattupperumāḷ ; *S.I.I.* XIII, No. 46, p. 21, l. 1 ; Kumbhakōṇam, Kumbhakonam Tq., Tanjavur Dt, T. Nadu St. **Dy.** Chōḷa, Gaṇḍarāditya, reg. yr. 3 = 953 A.D.

abhishēka dakshiṇai (T. < Skt. *n.*), amounts gifted on the occasion of coronation ; **text :** . . *Tirukkuḍamūkkil mūlapariḍaip-perumakkaḷōm* . . . . . . *nāṅgaḷ* ***abhishēka dakshiṇai*** *peṟṟa Tirukkīḻkōṭṭattu Perumāḷukku viṟṟa Mērkāviri nilam* ; **tr.** the land located in the upper Kāvēri region received as **gift on the occasion of coronation** by members of the local administrative body of Tirukuḍamūkku was sold to the god Tirukkīḻkoṭattupperumaḷ ; *S.I.I.* XIX, No. 6, p. 3, ll. 4–6, 10–12 ; Kumbhakōṇam, Kumbhakonam Tq., Tanjavur Dt, T. Nadu St. **Dy.** Chōḷa, Āditya II, reg. yr. 2 = in characters of 11th cent. A.D.

abhishēka kaikkāṇi (Skt.+T. *n.*), tax payable on gifts made on the occasion of coronation ; **text :** . . . *Sundarapāṇḍyadēvar*. . . . *Tiruchchōpuramuḍaiya Nāyaṉārkkōyil tāṉattārkku* . . . . *Tiyāgavallipaṟṟāṉa Āṇḍāgaḷūrpaṟṟil padiṟṟuvēli nilam iṟailiy-āga kuḍuttōm*. . . . *innilattāl vaṟum* . . ***abhishēka-kaikkāṇi*** *tulābāra vari* . . . . *uḷḷiṭṭa aṉaitt-āyaṅgaḷum iṟailiyāga variyilum kaḻittōm* ; **tr.** We, Sundarapāṇḍyadēva, granted 10 *vēli* (a land measure) of land to the officials of the temple of Tiruchchōpuramuḍaiya Nāyaṉār of Tiyāgavalliparru *alias* Āṇḍāgaḷūrparru and whatever revenue incomes were to be derived from that land including the **tax payable on the gifts made on the occasion of coronation** and the tax payable in the form of *tulābhāra* (weighing a person against any chosed article) were exempted; *S.I.I.* XVII, No. 127, p. 28, ll. 5, 11–13, 20, 33–34, 37–38, 48–49 ; Tiruchchōpuram, Cuddalore Tq., S. Arcot Dt, T. Nadu St. **Dy.** Pāṇḍya, Sundarapāṇḍya, reg. yr. 13+1, in characters of 13th cent. A.D.

avishēkakkaikkāṇi (T. *n.*), ; **text :** . . . . . . *Tiruchchōpuram Uḍaiyārkkōyil Tānattārkku* ***avishēkakkaikkāṇi*** *tulābāravari uḷḷiṭṭa aṉaittu āyavaṟgamum. dēvadāna iṟaiyiliyāga . . . śelvadāga kallilum chambilum veṭṭikkoḷga* . . . . ; **tr.** have it registered on stone as well as on copper plate that all taxes including **tax payable on the gifts made on the occasion of coronation**, tax payable on the occasion of *tulābhāra* (weighing a person against any chosed article) were donated tax free to the officials of the temple of Tiruchchōpuram Uḍaiyār ; *S.I.I.* XVII, No. 128, pp. 30–31, ll. 22–23, 53–54 ; Tiruchchōpuram, Cuddallore Tq., S. Arcot Dt, T. Nadu St. **Dy.** Pāṇḍya, Vikramapāṇḍya, reg. yr. 7 = 1289-90 A.D.

abhishēka kaṭṭaḷai (Skt. + T. *n.*), endowment of money for conducting the bathing ceremony of the God ; **text :** *Vaḍagarai Vindaṉūr*

Tirumūlaṭṭāṉamuḍaiyār ***abhishēka-kaṭṭaḷai****kku Nallaperumāḷ piḷḷai ayyaṉ kuḍutta kāśu* ; **tr. money endowed** by Nallaperumāḷ piḷḷai ayyaṉ for meeting the expenses **for the ceremonial bathing** of the main deity (in the temple) at Vaḍagarai-Vindaṉūr ; *T.A.S.* V, No. 64, p. 194, ll. 3–5 ; Vindaṉūr *alias* Śambūrvaḍagarai, Shenkottai Tq., Tirunelveli Dt., T. Nadu St. **Dy.** Nāyakas of Madurai, Vīrappa Nayaka, Ś 1527 = 1605 A.D.

abhyāgata[1] (K. < Skt. *n.*), unexpected guest ; **text**[1] : . . . . *Sarppeśvaradēvar oḷagāgi samasta-dēvarge saluva nivēdya dhūpa dīpa bhōgakaṁ banda* ***abhyāgata****rgge . . . . . . Pushpagiriya naḍuve . . . . piriya kōlalu haṁneraḍu mattaru keyyumaṁ dēvara mūḍaṇa nandanavanamumaṁ . . . . koṭṭaru* . . . ; **tr.** in the midst of the village Pushpagiri, 12 *mattar* (a land measure) of land measured by *piriya-kōlu* (a longer measuring rod), the garden to the east of the temple were donated to all the gods including Sarppēśvaradēva for conducting services such as offering of food, lighting of lamp and divine enjoyments and for feeding **unexpected guests** ; *S.I.I.* IX, pt. i, No. 69, p. 42, ll. 9–14 ; Pushpagiri, Cuddappah Tq. and Dt., A.P. St. **Dy.** Rāshṭr., Kṛishṇa III, in characters of 10th cent. A.D. ; **text**[2] : . . . *Tripurāntakadēvara aṅgaraṁgabhōgakkaṁ mattam āchāryya tapōdhana adhyayana śuśrūshā brāhmara aśan-āchchhādanakkaṁ aivattunākku mānasara atithi* ***abhyāgata*** *tapōdhanara grāsakkaṁ. . . . biṭṭa 44 ūrggaḷ* . . . . ; **tr.** 44 villages granted for the services to the image and entertainment of the god Tripurāntakadēva and for the feeding and clothing of the teachers, ascetics, students, the disabled, the brāhmaṇas and for feeding of 54 male guests, **unexpected guests** and ascetics ; *S.I.I.* IX, pt. i, No. 204, pp. 203–04, ll. 26–31, 63–64 ; Tripurāntakam, Markapur Tq., Kurnool Dt., A.P. St. **Dy.** Chāḷ. of Kal., Vikramāditya VI, Ch. Vi. yr. 47 = 1122 A.D.

abhyāgata[2] (K. < Skt. *n.*), tax collected for feeding unexpected guests ; **text** : *ī gruha kshētragaḷigevu yī kshetrava māḍuva vokkalugaḷigevu siddhāya. . . āruvaṇa manevaṇa biṭṭi . . . .* ***abhyāgata*** *. . . . . . mukhyavāgi ēnu baṁdaḍam-ā mahājanaṁgaḷu ā Dēvappanavaru . . . . . yī dharmava naḍasi koḍuvaru* . . . . ; **tr.** in these houses and cultivable fields those agriculturists who cultivate these fields have to pay permanent tax at 1/6th of the produce, house tax, free labour . . . . tax collected for feeding **unexpected guests** and all such revenue income and the *mahājanas* and Dēvappa have to compensate for these payments and they will continue to conduct this charitable act ; *E.C.* V, TN. 238, p. 621, ll. 44–51 ; Taḍimālaṁgi, T. Narasipura Tq., Mysore Dt., Karn. St. **Dy.** Hoy., Narasiṁhadēva, Ś. 1212 = 1290 A.D.

abhyāgate (K. < Skt. abhyāgati, *n.*), tax levied on articles brought from outside ; **text**[1] : . .

Māvanūrali pratishṭhe māḍida Dēvēśvaradēvara Appēśvaradēvara śrīkārya amṛitapaḍi aṁgabhōga-raṁgabhōga. . . . parichāraka jīvitavarggakkevu āchaṁdrārkatāraṁbaram saluvaṁtāgi ā tavanidhi teruva sidhāya ***abhyāgate*** *. . . . koṭṭaru* . . . . ; **tr.** (a number of taxes including) permanent tax, **tax levied on articles brought from outside** were granted for the worship, feeding, etc., of the god Dēvēśvaradēva and Appēśvaradēva installed in Māvanūr and for the livelihood of the servants of those temples ; *E.C.* (R) VIII, HN. 95, p. 58, ll. 43, 44–45, 46, 49 ; Māvanūr, Holenarasipura Tq., Hassan Dt., Karn. St. **Dy.** Hoy., Narasiṁha, Ś. 1204 = 1282 A.D. ; **text**[2] **:** . . . *mahāpradhānaṁ Mādigadēva- daṁṇāyakaru kuḷava kaḍisi māṟige koṇḍu ā mahājanaṁgaḷu aramanege teṟuva* . . ***abhyāgate*** . . . . *voḷagāyidanu kuḷava kaḍisikoṁbadake ā mahājanaṁgaḷige ga 230 pa 1 1/2 varu kuḷava kaḍisi patraśāsanavanu ā mahājanaṁgaḷige koḍisidaru.* . . . ; **tr.** Mādiga-daṁṇāyaka remitted the taxes after purchasing the land from the *mahājana* and *in lieu* of the taxes including the **tax on articles brought from outside** granted to the *mahājana* 230 *gadyāṇa* (a type of gold coin) and 1 1/2 *paṇa* (a type of coin) as tax remission and recorded this agreement along with signatures on a palm leaf ; *E.C.* (R) VIII, HN. 42, p. 21, ll. 25–34 ; Hoḷēnarasīpura, Holenarasipura Tq., Hassan Dt., Karn. St. **Dy.** Hoy., Vīra Ballāḷa, Ś. 1232 = 1310 A.D.

abhyāgati (K. < Skt., *n.*), **text :** (text obscure) *śrī Goṁmaṭadēvar śrī Kamaṭha pāriśvadēvaru Bhaṁḍāryyana basadiya śrī Dēvaravallabadēvaru mukyavāda basadigaḷa dēvadānada gadde beddalu sahita khāṇa* ***abhyāgati*** *kaṭakasēse* . . . . ; **tr.** the taxes on *dēvadānas* (*q.v.*), paddy fields, rain irrigated lands, fodder, **tax collected for bringing articles from outside,** tax payable to the headquarters, etc. of the Jaina temples including those of Gommaṭadēva, Kamaṭha Pāriśvadēva and Bhaṁḍārya (were exempted) ; *E.C.* (R) II, Sb. 479, p. 293 ll 5–9 ; Śravaṇabeḷagoḷa, Channarayapattana Tq., Hassan Dt., Karn. St. **Misc.,** Ś. 1208 = 1286 A.D.

abhyaṁtarasiddhi (K. < Skt. *n.*), exemption from payment of taxes or any other dues to the government ; **text :** *Chaṭṭarasa pādapūjeyaṁ koṁḍalliya manneya samyaman**abhyantara-siddhi**yāge biṭṭa* . . . . ; **tr.** after having been worshipped Chaṭṭarasa **exempted payment of taxes or any other dues payable to the government** from his holdings ; *S.I.I.* IX, pt. i, No. 101, p. 73, l 41 ; Mōṟigēṟi, Hadagalli Tq., Bellary Dt., Karn. St. **Dy.** Chāḷ. of Kal., Sōmēśvara I, Ś. 967 = 1045 A.D.

abhyāsigaḷ (T. < Skt. *n.*), students ; **text :** *eḻubattai kaḻañju poṉkoṇḍu . . . . atithigaḷayum* ***abhyāsigaḷ****ayum muṭṭāmai ūttuvōmaṉōm* . . . . . . ; **tr.** we will feed without fail guests and ***students*** from the interest accruing from 75 *kaḻañju* of gold coins ; *S.I.I.* XIII, No. 284, p. 152, ll. 2, 3 ; Kiḻiyanūr, Tindivanam Tq., S. Arcot Dt., T. Nadu St. **Dy.** Chōḷa, Sundara Chōḷa, reg. yr. 18 = 972 A.D.

abhyavasāya (K. < Skt. *n.*), all agricultural works including irrigation, cultivation, sowing, etc. ; **text :** . . . . *śrī Chaṁnakēśavadēvara sthānika Nāganaṁbiyara makkaḷu Nallaṇṇa Sōvaṁṇṇa Kēśyaṁṇṇa mukhyavāda samasta nibandhakārarige hoṁguttageyāgi neṟevūṟugaḷa maryyādeyalu kaṁba vondakke paṇav-ondaṟa maryyādeya teṟuta baharu ā tōṭaṁgaḷa kṛishi byavsāya yēta nīradhvāna voḷagāda samast-**abhyavasāyavanū*** . . . . ; **tr.** to the lessees including Nallaṇṇa, Sōvaṁṇṇa, Kēśyaṁṇṇa, the sons of Nāganaṁbi, the permanent servant of the temple of the god Chaṁnnakēśava dēva, groves were given on the same conditions as obtaining in the neighbouring villages with the stipulation that they should pay one *paṇa* per *kaṁba* (a land measure) of land and **all the agricultural works including irrigation, cultivation, sowing, etc.** (must be looked after by them) ; *E.C.* (R) X, Ak. 233, p. 287, ll. 3–4 ; Hāranahaḷḷi, Arsikere Tq., Hassan Dt., Karn. St., Misc., Ś. 1187 = 1265 A.D.

abhyudayaṁ (K. < Skt. *n.*), prosperity ; **text :** *grāmattukku **abhyudayamā**ga dushṭarkeṭṭu viśishṭar varttipadāga* . . . . ; **tr.** so that the village may prosper, the evil minded may perish and the good ones enjoy **prosperity** ; *A.S.I. A.R.*, 1904–05, p. 145, l. 17 ; Uttiramēṟūr, Madurantakam Tq., Chingleput Dt., T. Nadu. St. **Dy.** Chōḷa, Parāntaka, reg. yr. 14 = 921 A.D.

abimānam (T. < Skt. Abhimāna, *n.*), honour ; **text :** . . . . *pūśai migudi kāṇikkai eṉṟu kēṭṭavaṉ* . . . . *taṉ **abimāṉa**ttai veṟuttavaṉukku kuḍuttavaṉum āgakkaḍavaṉ* . . . . ; **tr.** he who asks for the excess of money remaining after the performance of worship would have, in effect, forfeited his **honour** to the person whom he considers as his enemy ; *S.I.I.* VIII, No. 209, p. 106, ll. 28–29, 31, 35–37 ; Tiruppunavāśal, Arantangi Tq., Tanjavur Dt., T. Nadu St. **Dy.** Pāṇḍya, Vikramapāṇḍya, reg. yr. 2+15 = 1417 A.D.

abōha (T. < Skt. abhōga, *n.*), fallow land ; **text :** . . *dēvadānam Avanigandarva-īśvaragṛihattu Mahādēvaṟku* . . . *Ūragaṉkuḍi **abōha** kiḍanda-bhūmiyai Kallimaśeṭṭi kuḍutta nīṟnilam iraṇḍu* ; **tr.** two plots of **land** in Ūragaṉkuḍi which were lying **fallow** were reclaimed and converted into wet lands and were granted to the god Mahādēva of the *dēvadāṇa* Avanigandarvva-īśvaram by Kallimaśeṭṭi ; *S.I.I.* XIX, No. 402, p. 211, ll. 3–5, 6–9 ; Mēlappaḻuvūr, Udaiyarpalayam Tq., Tiruchirapalli Dt., T. Nadu St. **Dy.** Chōḷa, Parakēsarivarman, reg. yr. 16 = in characters of 11th cent. A.D.

achaḷa-pravṛitti (K. < Skt. *n.*), permanent administrative arrangement ; **text** : . . . . *Kontada Peggaḷayyaṁ Pandigoḷavan-**achaḷa pravṛitti**yinda* *āḷuttuṁ . . . gāvuṇḍa Nāgiyammagam-aṟuvadiṁbarggaṁ . . . koṭṭa vyavasthe. . .* ; **tr :** the order issued by Peggaḷayya of Kontur, who was ruling over Pandigoḷa as a **permanent administrative arrangement**, to Nāgiyamma-gāvuṇḍa and the association of sixty ; *S.I.I.* XI, pt. i, No. 43, p. 29, ll. 14–15, 16–17 ; Hirēhandigōḷ, Gadag Tq. and Dt, Karn. St. **Dy.** Rāshṭr., Koṭṭigadēva, Ś 893 = 970 A.D.

āchandrārkkamu (Te. < Skt. *n.*), as long as the moon and sun endure ; **text :** . . . . *Amutunūri Amṛitīśvaradēvarakun-akhaṇḍavartti dīpamunaku . . . peṭṭina gōṟiyalu eṁbhadi vīnin-āchandrārkkamu putra pautrānīkamu naḍapaṁgalavāru.* . . . ; **tr.** fifty sheep were granted for the maintenance of a perpetual lamp in the temple of Amṛitīśvaradēva at Amutunūru. This must be continued until the moon and sun last and from generation to generation ; *S.I.I.* X, No. 90, p. 40, ll. 26–28, 33–36; Amṛitalūru, Tenali Tq., Guntur Dt., A.P. St. **Dy.** Chōḍa, Rājēndra Chōḍa, Ś. 1054 = 1132 A.D.

āchandrārkkasthāyigānu (Te. < Skt. *n.*) as long as the moon and sun endure ; **text :** . . . . *Vīradēvarāyaṁgārki puṁṇyamugānu Gandhāvatī galayanu pulēṭiṁbāḍina Dēvarāyanadi āchandrārkasthāyigānu chēyiṁchiri.* . . . ; **tr.** the streams Gandhāvatī and Pulēru were connected to form the river called Dēvarāyanadi, to last as long as the moon and sun endure, for the merit of Vīradēvarāya ; *S.I.I.* XVI, No. 7, p. 7, ll. 15–20; Tripurāntakam, Markapur Tq., Kurnool Dt., A.P. St. **Dy.** Saṅgama., Harihara II, Ś. 1307 = 1385 A.D.

āchandrārkasthāyiyāgi (K. < Skt. *n.*), **text[1] :** . . . . . . *Rāmanāthadēvara pātrabhōgakke māḍida dharmmada kramaveṁtendare Nāgavve maga Hiriya-Rāmaṇṇaṁgaḷu Kētavveyanu . . pātrakke dhārāpūrvvakavāgi koṭṭarāgi ā pātrada Kētavveya jīvitakke prati grāmakke varshaṁprati baḍagigaḷu 1 akkasālegaru 1 kañchagāraru 1/2 yi prakāradalle prativarushavu koṭṭu yi dharmmavanu* ***āchaṁdrārkasthāyiyāgi*** *naḍadu* . . . . ; **tr.** Hiriya Rāmaṇṇa, son of Nāgavve, offered the services of Kētavve as a dancing girl in the temple of Rāmanātha and for her maintenance the carpenters, goldsmiths, metalsmiths from every village undertook to pay money ; in the same fashion every year this charity must be maintained **as long as the moon and the sun last** ; *E.C.* (R) III, No. 17, p. 18, l. 3 ; Guṁḍlupēṭe, Gundlupet Tq., Mysore Dt., Karn. St. Trade guild called Vīrapañchāḷas, Ś. 1294 = 1372 A.D. ; **text[2] :** . . *Vēlāpuriya śrī Chaṁnakēśavanāthadēvarige naṁma nāyakatanake saluva Gōṇibīḍa sīmeyoḷagaṇa Hāvaṇige nāḍige saluva Gaṁgāvarada grā 1* (other grants of villages and paddy follow) *Siṁgappa-nāyakaru . . .* ***āchandrārkasthāyiyāgi*** *salaluḷadu yeṁdu . . . . . silā-śāsanavanu pratishṭe māḍisidevu* . . . . ; **tr.** We, Siṁgappanāyaka got a stone inscription engraved and installed recording the allotment of grants of the village Gaṁgāvara (and many other villages and grants in kind) located in Hāvaṇige-nāḍu within the subdivision called Gōṇibīḍa-sīme which was under our *Nāyakatana*; the grant was made for **as long as the moon and the sun last** in favour of the god Chaṁna-kēśavanātha of Vēlāpuri ; *E.C. (R)* IX, Bl. 11, p. 8, ll. 8–11, 20–24 ; Bēlūr, Belur Tq., Hassan Dt., Karn. St. **Dy.** Tuḷuva, Kṛishṇadēvarāya, Ś. 1443 = 1522 A.D.

āchandrārkatāraṁbaraṁ (K. < Skt. *n.*), as long as the moon, sun, stars and the sky last ; **text :** . . . . *rājyam-uttarōttarābhivvṛiddhi pravarddhamānam- āchandrārkatāraṁbaraṁ saluttamire* . . . . ; **tr.** while the reign was flourishing progressively and with all-round growth and for as long as the moon, sun, stars and sky last ; *E.C.* (R) II, No. 176, p. 130, l. 52 ; Śravaṇabeḷagoḷa, Channarayapatna Tq., Hassan Dt., Karn. St. **Dy.** Hoy., Vishṇuvardhana, Ś. 1053 = 1131 A.D.

āchāra (K. < Skt. *n.*) code of conduct ; **text[1] :** . . . . ***āchāra**-geṭṭu pōgade moṇḍiyatanaṁ geydu naḍevaṁ śvāna-gārdabha-chaṇḍāḷan-ātaṁ sattoḍe pandi sattudu nāyi sattudu*. . . ; **tr.** if any one indulges in breach of established **code of conduct** and behaves in an adamant manner, he will be equal to a dog, donkey, an outcaste and if he dies it would be equal to the death of a pig and the death of a dog ; *S.I.I.* IX, pt. i, No. 101, p. 73, ll. 59–60 ; Mōrigēri, Hadagali Tq., Bellary Dt., Karn. St. **Dy.** Chāḷ. of Kal., Āhavamalladēva, Ś. 967 = 1045 A.D. ; **text[2] :** . . . . (inscription badly damaged) *yiṁtappadanaṁ mahājanaṁ* ***āchārava*** *. . . tāvu māḍikoṁbaru* . . . ; **tr.** the *mahājana* (an administrative body) shall without fail follow the **code of conduct** prescribed for them ; *S.I.I.* IX, pt. ii, No. 438, p. 447, ll. 21–22 ; Kadiri, Kadiri Tq., Anantapur Dt., A.P. St. **Dy.** Saṅgama, Dēvarāya, Ś. 1340 = 1418 A.D.

āchāri (K. < Skt. *n.*), artisan/engraver, a professional name suffix, goldsmith, stone mason, smiths in general, learned brāhmaṇa, spiritual guide, sculptor; **text[1] :** . . . . *yī śilā-śāsanamaṁ baredā Mahēndrapallav-**āchāri**ge mahājanaṁ ippattēḻvaruṁ nāḍanūruḷ*. . . . *keyyan-prasādaṁ geydōr* . . . ; **tr.** the twenty seven *mahājanas* granted lands in Nāḍanūru to Mahēndrapallav-āchāri who was the **engraver** of this stone inscription ; *S.I.I.* IX, pt. i, No. 46, p. 27, ll. 12–14; Peddavaḍugūru, Gooty Tq., Anantapur Dt., A.P. St. **Dy.** Chal. of Bād., Satyāśraya (Polekēśin II), 7th cent. A.D. ; **text[2] :** . . . *Nāgayyanu Gōyindayyanu Ēchayyanu Gōnayyanu Keseyammanu kaḷḷara kādi sattoḍ-Abb**āchāri**ya akkasālada bāḻa śāsanada kallu*. . . ; **tr.** the hero-stone set up in the field of the **goldsmith** Abbāchāri to commemorate the death of Nāgayya, Govindayya, Ēchayya, Gōnayya, Keseyamma in a fight with thieves ; *S.I.I.* IX, pt. i, No. 29, p. 16, ll. 4–5, 13–19 ; Honneralihaḻḻi, Madakasira Tq., Ananthapur Dt., A.P. St. **Dy.** Noḷ. Pall., Iṟiva Noḷaṁba Noḷippayya,

Ś. 885 = 963 A.D. ; **text**[3] : . . . *kalukuṭiga Māṇik-**āchāri**ge ai-guḷa ga bede gaḻdeyu beḻdele mattaru eraḍu* . . . ; **tr.** two *mattar* (a land measure) of paddy field sowable with 5 *koḷaga* (a grain measure) of seed (were given) to the **stone-mason** Māṇikāchāri ; *S.I.I.* IX, pt. i, No. 122, p. 87, ll. 26–27 ; Nandikamba (hamlet of Punabagaṭṭa), Harapanahalli Tq., Bellary Dt., Karn. St. **Dy.** Chāḷ. of Kal., Sōmēśvara I, Ś. 974 = 1053 A.D. ; **text**[4] : . . . . *Kāṭūra huṭṭida . . . Hemaḍi-**āchāri**, Hemaḍi-**āchāri**ya mamma Chāk-**āchāri**yuṁ Kamb-**āchāri** Kamb**āchāri**ya maga Hēm-**āchāri*** ; **tr.** Hemaḍi-**āchāri** born at Kāṭūru, his grandson Chāk-**āchāri** and Kamb-**āchāri** and his son Hēm-**āchāri** (text incomplete) these were obviously the stone masons and smiths involved in the construction of the temple) ; *E.C.* (R) III, Nj. 156, p. 271, ll. 13–15 ; Jōḍikāṭūru, Nanjanagud Tq., Mysore Dt., Karn. St. **Dy.** Hoy., Vīraballāḷa II, Ś. 1120 = 1198 A.D. ; **text**[5] : . . . . *teṁgina-tōṭada chatussīmeya vivara mūḍalu heddāriyiṁda paḍuvalu teṁkalu siṁkada tōḍiṁda baḍagalu mūḍalu paḍuvaṇa **āchāri**yavara tōṭadiṁda mūḍalu baḍagalu teṁka **āchāri**yara tōṭadiṁ teṁkalu yiṁtī chatussīmeya voḷaguḷa tōṭa* . . . . ; **tr.** the details of the four boundaries of the coconut grove are as follows : in the east, to the west of the main road, in the south, to the west of the canal called Siṁka, in the east, to the east of the garden of the **learned brāhmaṇa** of the west, in the north, to the south of the garden of the **learned brāhmaṇa** of the south, thus the garden located within these four boundaries . . *S.I.I.* VII, No. 342, p. 195, ll. 11–12, Chauḷikēri, Udupi Tq. and Dt. Karn. St., **Dy.** Saṅgama, Harihararāya II, Ś. 1318 = 1396 A.D. ; **text**[6] : . . . . ***āchāri** māḍida ṛishabha* ; **tr.** stone-bull made by the **sculptor** (name lost) ; *E.C.* (R) IV, Ch. 377, p. 250, l. 4 ; Mukkaḍihaḻḻi, Chamarajanagara Tq. and Dt., Karn. St., **Misc.**, in characters of 16th cent. A.D.

āchāriyaka (K. < Skt. āchāryaka, *n.*) office of a preceptor ; **text :** *shaḍudaruśana-pāraṁgatarāda Raṁganātha-bhaṭṭarige **āchariyaka**vanu vahisikoṭṭu ā dānāṅgavāgi voṁdu grāmavanu . . . . . silā-śāsanava neḍisi koṭevu* . . . . ; **tr.** having appointed Raṁganātha-bhaṭṭa who had mastered the six schools of philosophy to the **office of a preceptor**, we gave as part of the grants one village and got the same engraved on stone ; *E.C.* (R) III, Gu. 26, p. 24, ll. 10–12, 19 ; Hoṇakanahaḻḻi, Gundlupet Tq., Chamarajanagara Dt., Karn. St. **Dy.** Tuḷuva, Narasiṁharāya, Ś. 1427 = 1506 A.D.

āchāriyapūśaṉai (T. < Skt. *āchārya-pūjā, n.*), honour offered to a priest : **text** : *Tirukkōyilūr Tiruviḍai-āḻvārkku . . . . . āṟṟunīrum **āchāriya-pūśaṉai**yum puḍavai nālum snapanattukku vēṇḍuvaṉa ellām kuṟaivaṟuttu innilam-koṇḍu śeyyakaḍavōm sthānattu Vaikhānasarōm* ; **tr.** in return for taking possession of this land the *Vaikhānasas* of the temple of Tiruviḍai-Āḻvār of Tirukkōyilūr will provide for, without any lapse, all the following articles and services viz., the water from the river **for honouring the (temple) priest**, four pieces of cloth which are required for the god's bathing ceremony ; *S.I.I.* VII, No. 142, p. 62, l. 9, Tirukkōyilūr, Tiru-kkoyilur Tq., S. Arcot Dt., T.Nadu St., **Dy.** Chōḷa, Rājarāja I, reg. yr. 23 = 1008 A.D.

āchāryya pūśaṇai (T. < Skt. *āchārya pūjā, n.*), honour offered to a preceptor or priest ; **text :** .... *Saṅkirānti oṉṟiṉukku* ***āchāryapūśaṇai*** *uṭpaḍa poṉ kaḻañju kāl* .... ; **tr.** one quarter of *kaḻañju* (a gold coin) for the **honour offered to a preceptor or priest** ; *S.I.I* III, No. 128, p. 270, l. 49 ; Madras Museum, Cheṉṉai, T. Nadu St. **Dy.** Chōḷa, Uttamachōḷa, reg. yr. 16 = 987 A.D.

āchāriyar (T. < Skt. *āchāryāḥ, n.*), preceptor, (referred to in respectful plural) ; **text :** ..... *Pāṇāṭṭu Vachchaṇandi* ***āchāriyar*** *māṇākkar-ārātaṉi nōṟṟu muḍitta niśīdigai* ; **tr.** the place of salvation of the disciple of the **preceptor** Vachchaṇandi of Pāṇāḍu who had given up the mortal coils after observing penance ; *E.T.E.*, No. 115, pp. 470–71, ll. 1–3 ; Paṟaiyaṉpaṭṭu, Śenji Tq., Villuppuram Dt., T. Nadu St., **Misc.**, in characters of 6th cent. A.D.

āchāryaru (K. < Skt. *āchāryāḥ, n.*), temple priests ; **text :** .... *Sōmanāthapurada grāma madhyada śrī Prasannadēvar-oḷagāda dēvarugaḷa* ***āchāryaru*** *Vaiyishṇavaru Nambiyārugaḷu voḷagādavarugaḷige koṭṭa patra śāsana* ..... ; **tr.** the deed of charter given to the **temple priests**, *Vaishṇavas* and *Nambīs* of the temples located in the centre of the Sōmanāthapura village including that of Prasannadēva ; *E.C.* (R) V, T.N. 91, p. 484, ll. 7–10; Sōmanāthapura, Bannur Tq., Mysore Dt., Karn. St. **Dy.** Hoy., Narasiṁha, Ś. 1203 = 1281 A.D.

achārjyabhūchai (T. < Skt. *āchāryapūjā, n.*), ceremonial honour done to the temple priest ; **text :** .... *Aṟumoḻi-mūvēndavēḷān piṟandanāḷ* .... *Tiruttiṇḍīśvaramuḍaiya Mahādēvarkku* .... *snappanadravyaṅgaḷ-uttamappaḍi vēṇḍuvadukkum* ***āchārjyabhūchai****kkum* ..... *kuḍutta nilam* .... ; ***tr.*** land granted, on the birth day of Aṟumoḻi-mūvēndavēḷān, (among many other things) good articles for the ceremonial bathing of the god Tiruttiṇḍīśvaramuḍaiya mahādēva and for the **ceremonial honour to be done to the temple priest** ; *S.I.I.* VII, No. 156, p. 67, ll. 11–12, 13, 15 ; Tiṇḍivaṉam, Tindivanam Tq., S. Arcot Dt., T. Nadu St., **Dy.** Chōḷa, Rājarāja I, reg. yr. 18 = 1003 A.D.

āchārya, achāryya (K. < Skt. *n.*), learned teacher of a religious institution, temple priest, philanthropic preceptor, teacher, Jaina temple priest, Jaina ascetic, royal preceptor, professional brāhmaṇa caste surname, a brāhmaṇa temple attendant ; **text[1] :** *maṭhad-****āchāryya*** *Brahmēśvara jīyara śīgralikita*; **tr.** the writing (of the) text of the inscription is by Brahmeśvara jīyar the **learned teacher** of the *maṭha* ; *S.I.I.* IX pt. i, No. 114, p. 89, ll. 22–23 ; Kammarchōḍu, Alur Tq., Bellary Dt., Karn. St. **Dy.** Chāḷ. of Kal., Sōmēśvara I, Ś. 976 = 1054 A.D. ; **text**[2] : . . . *Kūḍala Svayambhū-Saṁgamēśvara dēvarge viśēsha puṁṇyatithigaḷiṁ paṁchāmṛita snāna gandhānulēpana dhūpa dīpa nivēdya trikāḷārchchita bhōgakke . . . Gōyindavāḍiya Saṁgamēśvaradēvara nairityadalu biṭṭa geyyalondu 1 tōṭa 2 illiy-**āchārya** Rudraśivana marma Maṁgi sthānadoḍeyan-antappudakke Gondavāḍiya Noḷamba gāvuṇḍanariva* . . . . . ; **tr.** one piece of land and two groves situated to the west of the temple of Saṅgamēśvaradēva of Gōyindavāḍi were granted to the god Kūḍala Svayaṁbhū-Saṅgamēśvaradēva for the performance of *paṁchāmṛita-snāna*, application of sandal, burning incense and lamps, offering of food and worship 3 times a day ; the **temple priest** of the place Maṁgi, the grandson of Rudraśiva and Noḷamba gāvuṇḍa of Gondavādi are witnesses to the grant ; *S.I.I.* IX, pt. i, No. 138, p. 121, ll. 14–26 ; Saṅgamēśvara, (a hamlet of Siṅgepalle), Rayadurg Tq., Bellary Dt., Karn. St. **Dy.** Chāḷ. of Kal., Vikramāditya VI, Ś. 995 = 1073 A.D. ; **text**[3] : . . . . *annadāna vinōdarityādi samasta praśasti sahitaṁ śrīmad-**āchāryar**. . .* ; **tr.** the illustrious **preceptor** (name lost) who is endowed with all epithets such as 'the one who takes pleasure in feeding [the needy]' etc., ; *K.I.* V, No. 16, p. 58, l. 17 ; Dharwar, Dharwar Tq. and Dt., Karn. St. **Dy.** Chāḷ. of Kal., Vikramāditya VI, Ch. Vi. yr. 42 = 1117 A.D. ; **text**[4] : *Kollāpurada śrī Rūpanārāyaṇa-basadiy-**āchāryar**uṁ maṇḍaḷ**āchāryar**uṁ-enippa* ; **tr.** the illustrious Rūpanārāyaṇa of Kollāpura who is the priest of the Jaina temple and was also the **preceptor** of a *maṇḍala* (i.e., territorial division); *K.I.* V, No. 21, p. 82, l. 48 ; Tērdāḷ, Jamkhandi Tq., Bijapur Dt., Karn. St. **Dy.** Chāl. of Kal., Vikramāditya VI, Ś. 1045 = 1123 A.D. ; **text**[5] : . . . . . *Yāpanīya-saṁghada Punnāgavṛiksha Mūlagaṇada śrīmad-**āchārya**ṁ Kumārakīrti- paṁḍitadēvara kālaṁ kachchi*. . . . ; **tr.** the illustrious [Jaina] **teacher** belonging to the Punnāga- vṛiksha Mūlagaṇa and Yāpanīya-saṁgha, having laved the feet of Kumārakīrtti-paṁḍitadēva ; *K.I.* V, No. 25, p. 96, ll. 32–33 ; Kolhāpur, Kolhapur Tq. and Dt., Maha. St. **Dy.** Chāḷ. of Kal., Jagadēka- malla II, reg. yr. 2 = 1139 A.D. ; **text**[6] : . . . . *Hariharamahārāyaru Yarigēri Hēmādri-**āchārya**rige Abbigēriyalli bhūmi yēkabhōgyavāgi koṭṭa tāmra śāsana* . . ; **tr.** copper plate inscription registering the grant of land in Abbigēri given to the royal **preceptor** Hēmādri of Yarigēri by the king Hariharamahārāya ; *K.I.* VI, No. 60, p. 163., ll. 4–5, 8, 9 ; Abbigēri, Ron Tq., Dharwar Dt., Karn. St. **Dy.** Saṅgama, Harihara II, Ś. 1301 = 1379 A.D. ; **text**[7] : . . . . *Vaikhānasa-sūtrada Gautama-gōtrada Ramaṇ-**āchārya**ra makaḷu Nāraṇ-**āchārya*** . . . . ; **tr.** Nāraṇ-**āchārya**, the son of Ramaṇ-**āchārya** of Gautama-gōtra and Vaikhānasa-sūtra ; *S.I.I.* IX, pt. ii, No. 564, p. 584, ll. 23–24 ; Hampi, Hospet Tq., Bellary Dt., Karn. St. **Dy.** Tuḷuva, Achyutarāya, Ś. 1456 = 1534 A.D.; **text**[8] : . . . . . *Yaju-śākheya Muḷuvāgilu Kēśavadēvara stānika Naṁdaṇ-**āchāryya**ra maga Chiṁnappayaru* ; **tr.** Chiṁnappaya, the son of Naṁdaṇ**āchārya** of Yaju śākhā, a brāhmaṇa **temple attendant** of the god Kēśavadēva of Muḷuvāgilu ; *S.I.I.* IV, No. 245, p. 40, l. 39, Hampi, Hospet Tq., Bellary Dt., Karn. St. **Dy.** Tuḷuva, Achyutarāya, Ś. 1463 = 1541 A.D.

āchāryaka (K. < Skt. *n.*), post of preceptor ; **text :** . . . . *Raṁganātha-bhaṭṭarige **āchāryaka**vanu vahisi sahiraṇyōdakavāgi koṭṭu* . . . ; **tr.** the **post of preceptor** having been bestowed on Raṁganāthabhaṭṭa with the pouring of water of libation through the gold held in hand ; *E.C.* (R) III, Gu. 26, p. 24, ll. 10–11 ; Hoṇakanahaḷḷi, Gundlupet Tq., Mysore Dt., Karn. St. **Dy.** Tuḷuva., Narasiṁha, Ś. 1428 = 1506 A.D.

achāryyabhōgam (T. < Skt. *n.*), endowment of land for the priest ; **text :** . . . . *śrī Rājarāja-īśvaramuḍaiyār kōyilil **āchāryyabhōgam** nam uḍaiyār Śarvaśiva paṇḍita Śaivācharyarkku* . . . . *iddēvar koyilil āḍavallāṉ-eṉum marakkālāl* . . . . *iṟaṇḍāyirakkala nellu āṭṭāṇḍudōrum peṟat-tiruvāymoḻindaṟuḷa* . . . . *kallil veṭṭittu* ; **tr.** having engraved on stone the royal order granting as **endowment of land for the priest** 2000 *kalams* (a grain measure) of paddy every year measured by the *marakkāl* (a grain measure) called *āḍavallāṉ* of that temple to Śarvaśiva paṇḍita śaivāchārya (a number of other donees are also mentioned in the sequel) for acting as the priest of the temple of Rājarāja Īśvaramuḍiyār ; *S.I.I.* II, No. 20, p. 107, ll. 13–14, 15, 16 ; Tañjāvūr, Tanjavur Tq. and Dt., T. Nadu St., **Dy.** Chōḷa, Rājēndra I, reg. yr. 19 = 1031 A.D.

āchāryyatva (K. < Skt. *n.*), priesthood for conducting religious functions in temple : **text :** . . *ī grāmada oḷage* . . . . *viniyōgada brāhmarugaḷige* . . . . . *koṭṭa gadeya sthaḷa vivara **āchāryyatva**kke* . . . . ; **tr.** the details of the paddy fields in the village given to the brāhmaṇas engaged in distributing the food offered to the god within these villages for their performance of **priesthood** in the temple ; *S.I.I.* IV, No. 254, p. 44, ll. 26–27, Hampi, Hospet Tq., Bellary Dt., Karn. St., **Dy.** Tuḷuva, Kṛishṇadēvarāya, Ś. 1435 = 1513 A.D.

āchchamār (T. *n.*), patrons : **text** : . . . *Tiruviḍaimarudil* . . . . *Perumānaḍigaḷ kōyilil tiruppalagaḍiyum tirukkalavum nilaiyum paḍiyum kaikkōḷapperuṁpaḍayōmināl śamaippittu eṅgaḷ **āchchamār** Tiśai āyirattaiññūṟṟuvar tampēr śattinamayil inda dharmmam Tiśai āyirattaiññūṟṟuvarum rakshai* ; **tr.** the regiment called *kaikkōḷapperumbaḍai* provided a window, a door, a doorpost and steps in the temple of Perumānaḍigaḷ and our **patrons** *Tiśai āyirattaiññūṟṟuvar* (merchantile guild) will protect these acts of piety ; *S.I.I.* XIX, No. 4, p. 2, l. 2,

3–5, Tiruviḍaimarudūr, Kumbhakonam Tq., Tanjavur Dt., T. Nadu St., **Dy.** Chōḷa, Rājēndra I, reg. yr. 7 = 1014 A.D.

āchchāri (T. < Skt. *n.*), mason : **text** : *Śeruppaḷi* ***āchchāri*** *putran Chellapparkku śilāśāsanam paṇṇikkuḍuttapaḍi* ; **tr.** as per the stone edict presented to Chellappa the son of the **mason** of Śeruppaḷi ; *S.I.I.* VII, No. 51, p. 21, l. 3, Kūram, Kanchipuram Tq., Chingleput Dt., T. Nadu St., **Dy.** Tuḷuva, Achyutarāya, Ś. 1462 = 1540 A.D.

āchchhādana (K. < Skt. *n.*), clothing ; **text** : . . *Koṭiganūra . . . . puṭṭidarthamaṁ . . . Lakulēśvara paṇḍitara maṭhada tapōdhanarkkaṁ vidyārthigaḷaśana**āchchādana**kkaṁ . . . . naḍevadu* . . . . . ; **tr.** from the revenue income collected from Koṭiganūru, the maintenance of the ascetics and the arrangements for food and **clothing**s for the students of the Lakuḷēśvarapaṇḍita-maṭha is to be arranged ; *S.I.I.* IX, pt. i, No. 135, p. 119, ll. 11, 13, 15–16, 17 ; Hūvinahaḍagalli, Hadagalli Tq., Bellary Dt., Karn. St. **Dy.** Chāḷ. of Kal., Vikramāditya VI, Ś. 993 = 1071 A.D.

āchchi (T. *n.*), Queen mother ; **text** : . . . *Uttamachōḷadēvar taṅgaḷ-**āchchi** śrī Parāntaka-mādēvaḍigaḷār-āṉa śrī Śembiyaṉ mādēviyār . . . . Kailāsamuḍaiya Mahādēvarkku kuḍutta 100 poṉ kalaśam oṉṟu* ; **tr.** a golden pinnacle of 100 *poṉ* (gold coin) donated by Parāntaka-mādēvaḍigaḷār *alias* śrī Śembiyaṉmādēviyār the **queen-mother** of Uttamachōḷadēva to the god Kailāsamuḍaiya Mahādēva ; *S.I.I.* XIII, No. 72, p. 34, ll. 8–14 ; Śembiyaṉ Mahādēvi, Nagapattinam Tq., Tanjavur Dt., T. Nadu. St., **Dy.** Chōḷa, Rājakēsarivarman, reg. yr. 3, in characters of 10th-11th cent. A.D.

āchchiyār (T. *n.*), queen-mother (plural used as a mark of respect) ; **text** : . . . *Uttamachōḷadēvar taṅgaḷ-**āchchiyār** Parāntakan-mādēviyar-āṉa śrī Śeṁbiyaṉ mādēviyār śeyda paṇigaḷ* ; **tr.** the pious deeds done by Parāntakaṉ mādēviyar *alias* śrī Śeṁbiyaṉ mādēviyār, the **queen mother** of Uttamachōḷadēva ; *S.I.I.* XIII, No. 144, p. 74, ll. 2–4 ; Tiruveṇkāḍu, Sirgali Tq., Tanjavur Dt., T. Nadu. St. **Dy.** Chōḷa, Rājakēsarivarman, regnal year 6, in characters of 10th-11th century A.D.

āchchiṉai (T. *n.*), levy on land ; **text** : . . . . *Nayiṉār Śuchīndiram uḍaiya Nayiṉār kōvilukku **āchchiṉai**-āga 1000m paṇamum pirippichchu Nayiṉāruḍaiya aḍiyēndaram ellām naḍattumbaḍikku* ; **tr.** having collected 1000 *paṇam* (a type of coin) as **levy on lands** belonging to the temple of Śuchīndiram uḍaiya Nayiṉār for the purpose of conducting all ceremonies to the god ; *T.A.S.* V, No. 53, p. 169, ll. 6–8 ; Śuchīndram, Suchindram Tq., Kanyakumari Dt., T. Nadu St., **Misc.**, Kollam 621 = 1444 A.D.

āchchiyabhōgam (T. *n.*), land earmarked for the maintenance of the queen mother ; **text** : . . . . . *Tiruvakkarai aḷuḍaiyāṟkkōytilil. . . . pūjaikkum Tiruppaṇikkum . . . . antarāyamum **āchchiyabhōgamum** . . . . dēvadānamāga viṭṭamayikku*

Kāḍuveṭṭi eḻuttu ...... ; **tr.** the signature of Kāḍuveṭṭi as witness to the *dēvadāna* grant of the internal cess and income from the endowment of **land earmarked for the maintenance of queen mother** for conducting worship and other services in the temple of the god Tiruvvakkarai Āḻuḍaiyār; *S.I.I.* XVII, No. 207, p. 74, ll. 2, 5–6 ; Tiruvakkarai, Viluppuram Tq., S. Arcot Dt., T. Nadu St., **Dy.** Chōḷa, Kulōttuṅga I, (date lost), in characters of 11th cent. A.D.

achchu (K. *n.*), (an ancient) moulded coin ; **text**[1]**:** *Svāmidēvara navil***achchin***a ponnaṁ lokkiya ponnāṇiyuṁ ā ponna tūkamumāgi poydu salisuvaru Svāmidēvarge* ; **tr.** the gold (ancient) **moulded coin** called *navilachchu* (*q.v.*) belonging to the god Svāmidēva is to be poured into the mould for the coin called *ponnāṇi* (*q.v.*) of Lokki and made over to the god Svāmidēva ; *S.I.I.* IX, pt. i, No. 164, p. 155, l. 25 ; Kuḍatini, Bellary Tq. and Dt., Karn. St. **Dy.** Chāḷ. of Kal., Vikramāditya VI, Ch. Vi. Yr. 23 = 1098 A.D. ; **text**[2] (T. *n.*) **:** ..... *Nāchchiyārkku kaḍamai koḷḷum-iḍattu* . . . *achchukkuṁ ivvilaippaḍi paṇamum* ***achchu*** *iraṇḍum koḷḷakaḍavārgaḷ- āgavum* ; **tr.** at the time of collecting revenue income for the goddess they should collect, as per the price fixed, one coin called *paṇam* (a denomination) and 2 **moulded coins** ; *S.I.I.* VIII, No. 176, p. 86, ll. 6–7 ; Kāḷaiyārkōvil, Sivaganga Tq., Ramanathapuram Dt., T. Nadu St. **Dy.** Pāṇḍya, Kulaśēkharadēva, reg. yr. 8, in characters of 11th cent. A.D. ; **text**[3] (T. *n.*) **:** .... *nāṉg-ellaikkuṭpaṭṭa iḍattil iṟuttu varum kaḍamaiyum antarāyamuṁ taruvadāṉa* ***achchum*** *poṉvariyuṁ* ... ; **tr.** revenue incomes called *kaḍamai, antarāyam,* **moulded coins**, tax in the form of gold ; *S.I.I.* VIII, No. 403, p. 213, l. 2 ; Dēvipaṭṭaṇam, Ramanathapuram Tq. and Dt., T. Nadu St. **Dy.** Pāṇḍya, Jaṭāvarman, reg. yr. 4 = 1247 A.D. **achchina-kēṇi** (K. *n.*) lease on a mould in a mint ; **text :** .... *Kēśavadēvaṁ tann***achchina-kēṇi***yalli* .... *Jīvayyana basadiya dēvarashṭavidhār chanege* ... *gadyāṇam 3ṟam* ... *koṭṭaru* .... ; **tr.** Kēśavadēva gave 3 *gadyāṇa* (gold coins) for the 8 types of worship in the *basadi* of Jīvayya from out of his **lease on a mould in a mint** ; *S.I.I.* XV, No. 119, p. 150, ll. 22–25 ; Lakkuṇḍi, Gadag Tq. and Dt., Karn. St. **Dy.** Kal. of Kal., Sōvidēva, Cy. yr. Nandana = 1173 A.D. ; **achchina kēṇikāṟa** (K. *n.*), lease holder of a mould in a mint ; **text :** .... ***achchina kēṇikāṟam*** *Kēśavadēvayyaṁgaḷu* ... *biṭṭa paṇa eṟaḍu* ... ; **tr.** 2 *paṇa* (a coin) were given by Kēśava- dēvayyaṁgaḷ a **lease holder of a mould in a mint** ; *S.I.I.* XV, No. 135, p. 178, ll. 62–63 ; Lakkuṇḍi, Gadag Tq. and Dt., Karn. St. **Dy.** Kal. of Kal., Saṅkama, Ś. 1100 = 1179 A.D. ; **achchina-moḷe** (K. *n.*), letters and design types used for striking coins ; **text :** .... *Tuṁbuṟabīḍina* . . . . *kammaṭada* ***achchina-moḷe****ya-akkasāligaḷu* . . *varishaṁ prati koḍuvaṁtāgi māḍi koṭṭa gadyāṇav-*

oṁdu. . . . ; **tr.** in the place called Tuṁbuṟabīḍu, the goldsmiths owning the unit with **letters and design types used for striking coins in the mint** undertook to grant one *gadyāṇa* (a gold coin) every year ; *S.I.I.* IX, pt. i, No. 295, p. 318, ll. 31–32 ; Bāpuram, Adavani Tq., Kurnool Dt., A.P. St. **Dy.** Kal. of Kal., Sōmēśvara, Ś. 1093 = 1172 A.D. ; **achchina-ṭaṁkasāle** (K. *n.*), mint having coin moulds ; **text :** . . . . *achchina-taṁkasāleyalu daḷakke vīsa 2* . . . ; **tr.** metal sheet costing 2 *vīsa* (a coin) used in **mint having coin moulds** ; *S.I.I.* IX, pt. i, No. 228, p. 233, l. 11 ; Pedda Tumbaḷaṁ, Adavani Tq., Kurnool Dt., A.P. St. **Dy.** Chāḷ. of Kal., Bhūlōkamalla, Ch. Vi. yr. 58 = 1133 A.D.

achchugaṭṭu (*s. a achchukaṭṭu*) (K. *n.*), partitioned areas of arable land ; **text**[1] **:** . . . . *Nēṟilakeṟeya mūḍaṇa kōḍiyiṁ teṁkaṇa hosageṟe* ***achchugaṭṭ****ādudellaṁ* . . . . ; **tr.** the lands below Hosakere which is to the south of the eastern Nēṟilēkeṟe and all the **partitioned areas of the arable land** to the south of the water course ; *E.C.* (R) II, Sb. 82, p. 65, ll. 44–45 ; Śravaṇabeḷagoḷa (Chikkabeṭṭa), Channarayapatna Tq., Hassan Dt., Karn. St. **Dy.** Hoy., Vishṇuvardhana, Ś. 1039 = 1118 A.D. ; **text**[2] **:** . . . . *yī grāmagaḷa chatuḥsīme oḷaguḷḷa gadde beddalu tōṭa tuḍike aḍumane aṇe* ***achchugaṭṭu*** *kāḍāraṁbha nīrāraṁbha* . . . *modalāda ā sakalasvāmyavu* . . . . *nimage saluvavu* ; **tr.** you will be the recipient of all these proprietories located within the boundaries of these villages such as paddy fields, rain water irrigated land, groves, place where arecanut is cured, kitchen, dam and **partitioned areas of arable land,** forest land, wet land, etc. (other such privileges are also mentioned) ; *E.C.* (R) VII, Mu. 64, p. 289, ll. 44–47, 49 ; Honnalagere, Maddur Tq., Mandya Dt., Karn. St. **Dy.** Āravīḍu, Rāmarāya, Ś. 1544 = 1623 A.D.

achchu (K. *n.*), moulded cake (of jaggery) ; **text:** (text badly damaged) . . . . *bella prati tiṁ 1 kaṁ* ***achchu*** *50* ; **tr.** jaggery at the rate of 50 **moulded cakes** per month ; *S.I.I.* VII, No. 348, p. 205, l. 14 ; Chauḷikēri, Udupi Tq. and Dt., Karn. St. **Dy.** Saṅgama, Dēvarāya, Ś. 1353 = 1431 A.D.

achchukaṭṭu (K. *n.*), area of arable land, irrigated lands under a tank ; **text**[1] **:** . . . . *Hariyasamudrada holadali huṭṭidaṁtha* ***achchukaṭṭu*** *Hariyasamudrada hola Dīkshitaru Rāmachandra dēvaru sariyāgi anubhavisaluḷavaru* . . . . . ; **tr.** Rāmachandradēva Dīkshita shall properly enjoy the yields from the lands in Hariyasamudra viz., the produce from **irrigated lands under the tank** of Hariyasamudra ; *S.I.I.* IX, pt. ii, No. 472, p. 487, ll. 4–5 ; Rāmāpura, Madakasira Tq., Anantapur Dt., A.P. St. **Dy.** Harati chiefs, Rāyapparāja, Ś. 1407 = 1485 A.D. ; **text**[2] **:** . . . . *Lakshmīsēna- bhaṭṭārakaravarige Āpinahaḷḷiyanu* . . . . *koṭṭevāgi ā grāmakke saluvanthā eṟenela kennela kāḍāraṁbha nīrāraṁbha aṇe* ***achchukaṭṭu*** . . . . *modalāgi ā grāmakke saluvantha* . . . . *sakala* *suvarṇādāya sakala bhattādāyavaru .... baresikoṭṭa dānapaṭṭi* .... ; **tr.** a charter presented to Lakshmīsēna-bhaṭṭāraka donating the village of Āpinahaḷḷi including black soil, red soil, forest land, wet land, dam, **partitioned area of arable land** .... the income in gold and income in paddy due to that village ; *E.C.* (R) VII, Ng. 96, pp. 93–94, ll. 14, 35–37, 40, 42 ; Beḷḷūru, Nagamangala Tq., Mandya Dt., Karn. St. **Dy.** Harati chiefs, Rāyapparāja, Ś. 1602 = 1680 A.D. ;

achchukkaṭṭu (T. *n.*), partitioned area of arable land ; **text** : ...... *Arappāḷadēvaṟkku kalveṭṭikuḍuttapaḍi* .... *Tāṉṟipaḷḷamum Mūlāndikkollaiyuṁ* .... *kāḍuveṭṭi kiṇaṟum kuḻittu* ... ***achchukkaṭṭākki*** *payiṟ śeyyakkaḍavarāgavum* ; **tr.** as per the stone inscription given to Arappāḷadēva, in Tāṉṟipaḷḷa and Mūlāndikkollai the forest was felled, a well was dug out and the barren land was converted into **partitioned area of arable lands** to be cultivated ; *S.I.I.* VIII, No. 72, p. 40, l. 2 ; Tiruvaṇṇāmalai, Tiruvannamalai Tq., N. Arcot Dt., T. Nadu St. **Dy.** Saṅgama, Virupaṇṇa Uḍaiyār, Ś. 1311 = 1389 A.D.

achchuttari (T. *n.*), tax levied on looms in the form of achchu coins : **text**[1] : *Śiṅgaya deṇṇāyakkar*. . . *Poṅgaḷūr Tiruvēṅgaḍam uḍaiyāṉukku kallilum śembilum veṭṭikoḷḷuvadāga kuḍutt aṟuḷina tirumugappaḍi* (after a number of grants) ***achchuttaṟi*** .. (again a number of other grants follows) *koḍuttōm* .. ; **tr.** we, Śiṅgaya–deṇṇāyakkar gave the tax called *achchuttaṟi* (**tax to be collected in the form of *achchu* coins on looms**) to the god Tiruvēṅgaḍam uḍaiyāṉ of Poṅgaḷūr, the details of the grants to be engraved both on stone and copper plate ; *S.I.I.* IV, No. 287, p. 79, ll. 2–4, 8, 10 ; Tirupati, Chandragiri Tq, Chittoor Dt., A.P. St. **Dy.** Yādava, Tiruvēṅgaḍanātha Yādvarāya, reg. yr. 8+1, in characters of 13th cent. A.D. ; **text**[2] : ... *śrī Rājarājadēvarkku yāṇḍu padiṉārāvadu uḍaiyār Tiruvattūruḍaiya-nāyaṉār pūśan-tīrttham-āga* (a number of grants of lands and revenue income are mentioned) *śāligar* ***achchuttari*** *uḷḷiṭṭa kaḍamaigaḷum uṭpaḍa dēvadānamāga viṭṭu śilālēkhai paṇṇikuḍuttēṉ Śeṅgēṇi Attimallaṉ Śambuvarāyaṉ* ... ; **tr.** during the 16th regnal year of Rājarājadēva, Attimallaṉ Śaṁbuvarāyan of Śeṅgēṇi granted as *dēvadāna* (*q.v.*) to the god Tiruvattūruḍaiya-nāyaṉār for services on the day of Pushya (among a number of other grants) the grant of **tax levied on looms in the form of achchu coins** from the weavers ; *S.I.I.* VII, No. 98, p. 42, ll. 1–3, 10, 13–15 ; Tiruvottūr, Cheyyar Tq., N. Arcot Dt., T. Nadu St. **Dy.** Chōḷa, Rājarāja III, reg. yr. 16 = 1232 A.D.

achchu pannāyada adhishṭhāyaka (K. < Skt. *n.*), revenue official in charge of collecting taxes in the form of *achchu* coins on betel leaves ; **text** : .... *śrīmad* ***achchu pannāyada adhishṭhāyakam.*** *śrīmad daṇḍnāyakaṁ Mahāvishṇuvarasaru* .... ;

tr. Mahāvishṇuvarasa, the army officer and **revenue official incharge of collecting tax on betel leaves in the form of achchu coins** ; *S.I.I.* IX, pt. i, No. 164, p. 155, ll. 39–41 ; Kuḍatini, Kudatini Tq., Bellary Dt., Karn. St. **Dy.** Chāḷ. of Kal., Vikramāditya VI, Ch. Vi. yr. 23 = 1098 A.D.

aḍa (K. *n.*), a coin ; **text**[1] **:** .... *Māragāvuṁḍaṁge nāḍa heggaḍetanavaṁ koṭṭevu 40 ūriṁge oṁdoṁdu paṇa 30 ūriṁge* ***aḍa*** *saṁtheyāya muṁtāgi koṭṭevu.* .. ; **tr.** we gave the headship of the subdivision to Māragāvuṇḍa ; we also gave him one *paṇa* each for 40 villages and one *aḍa* **coin** and the revenue from the market, etc., from 30 villages ; *E.C.* XI, Hoḷal. 137, p. 399, ll. 86–87 ; Honnakere, Hoḷalkere Tq., Chitradurga Dt., Karn. St. **Dy.** Hoy., Ballāḷa, Ś. 1229 = 1307 A.D. ; **text**[2] **:** .... *hadinālku varahanu āru haṇava****ḍa****vanu ī Basavage* .... *uṁbaḷiyāgi* ... *koṭṭidhēve* ... ; **tr.** we have given as livelihood to Basava 14 *varahas* (a type of coin) and **coin** in the form of six *aḍas* (*q.v.*); *E.C.* VII, Shikari 210, p. 295, l. 16 ; Shikaripura, Shikaripura Tq., Shimoga Dt., Karn. St. **Misc.,** Ś. 1680 = 1758 A.D.

aḍa[2] (K. *n.*), mortgage ; **text :** .... *Vidyānātha dēvarugaḷu taṁdu māṟida Kavilēśvarada bāḷanu ga. 800 ke āruvāra nirisida* ***aḍa*** *ādiyāgi baha aki mū 60 yī bāḷina hoṁnu baṁdaḍe yī dharmakke hosadāgi mūlada bāḷiṁge saluvudu* ... ; **tr.** the land earmarked for the god Kavilēśvara was sold by Vidyānāthadēva for 800 *gadyāṇa* (a gold coin) and **mortgaged** and from the **mortgaged** land the produce of 60 *mūḍe* (a grain measure) realised in the form of gold if received will be added to the value of the original lands belonging to the temple ; *S.I.I.* VII, No. 347, p. 204, ll. 42–45 ; Chauḷikēri, Udupi Tq. and Dt., Karn. St. **Dy.** Saṅgama, Harihara, Ś. 1309 = 1387 A.D. ; **aḍadavaṇa** (K. *n.*), cost paid in the form of *aḍa* coins ; **text :** *Narasiṁhadēvargge* ... *naivēdyakke* ... ***aḍadavaṇa****vāgi* ... *dhānyavaṁ koṁḍu māṟuvavaralli hoṁge sollage bhattavaṁ paḍedu koṭṭaru* ... ; **tr.** for the food offerings to the god Narasiṁhadēva one *sollage* (a grain measure) of paddy per *hoṁnu* (a gold coin) was purchased from the grain merchants by **paying cost in the form of aḍa coins** ; *S.I.I.* XVIII, No. 260, p. 343 ll. 7–11, Bijāpur, Bijapur Tq. and Dt., Karn. St. **Dy.** Sēü. of Dēv., Rāmachandra, Ś. 1205 = 1283 A.D.

āḍadeṟe (K. *n.*), tax on sheep or goats ; **text**[1] **:** . . . (text incomplete) *Tiparasayyana manusa Hulasedēvarasayyanavaru Haradurapurada sthaḷada jātre saṁtte āḍadeṟe maggadeṟe yishṭanu dēvarige sarvamānya* ..... ; **tr.** Hulasedēvarasayya the servant of Tiparasayya granted as *sarvamānya* to the god income from the **taxes** collected on the weekly fairs and **on the sheep** and loom in the village of Haradurapura ; *E.C.* (R) VIII, Ag. 17, p. 119, ll. 2–6, Haradūrapura, Arakalgud Tq., Hassan Dt., Karn. St., **Misc.,** in characters of the 15th–16th cent. A.D. ; **text**[2] **:** .... *Iṁmaḍi*

Chikarāyavoḍeyaru. . . . . ayivattu voḍeyaranu ārōgaṇa vastra kappaḍadiṁda pūje māḍi kūḍikoṁḍu yihadakāgi Ālūra Śāṁtadēvaru voḷagāgi mahāmahattige . . . . . koṭṭa dharma śāsana . . . Kuṁtūra grāmada chatusēmevoḷaguḷa gadde beddalu tōṭa . . . . kumbārade.ṟe āḍade.ṟe . . . . . . modalāda sarvvasvāmyavanu āgumāḍikonḍu . . . . ; **tr.** a grant to be respected by all given by Iṁmaḍi Chikarāya- voḍeya to Śāṁtadēva of Ālūru for feeding, clothing and worship of 50 voḍeyas in the *mahāmahattu* (a religious institution) ; the grant included revenue incomes from paddy fields, rainfed irrigated fields, groves, tax on potter and **tax on goats,** etc. ; *E.C.* (R) IV, Ko. 7, p. 401, ll. 4, 6–12 ; Kuntūru, Kollegal Tq., Chamarajanagara Dt., Karn. St. **Dy.** Umm. Chfs., Chikkarāya Voḍeya, Ś. 1434 = 1512 A.D.

aḍagu[1] (K. *n.*), flesh, meat ; **text :** . . . . . ***aḍagina*** *bāṇasigarggaṁ kaḷguḍivavarggaṁ vṛittilōpam-eṁbī nuḍiyaṁ kaḍegaṇganisade danḍaṁdettippudu* . . . . . . ; **tr.** on those who cook **meat** and on those who are addicted to alcoholic drinks, without ignoring the saying that it amounts to lapses of professional ethics, penalty should be levied ; *S.I.I.* IX pt. i, No. 117, p. 93, ll. 37–38, 39 ; Kōgaḷi, Bellary Tq. and Dt., Karn. St., **Dy.** Chāḷ. of Kal., Sōmēśvara, Ś. 977 = 1055 A.D.

aḍagu[2] (K. *n.*), pawn broker by profession ; **text :** . . ***aḍagina*** *Aṁṇiseṭṭiya makkaḷu Śāṁtaṁṇaseṭṭi* . . . . . . ; **tr.** Śāṁtaṁṇaseṭṭi son of Aṁṇaseṭṭi who was a **pawn broker by profession** ; *K.I.* I, No. 41, p. 97, l. 37 ; Kaikiṇi, Bhatkal Tq. and Dt., Karn. St. **Dy.** Saṅgama, Dēvarāya, Ś. 1340 = 1417 A.D.

aḍahu (K. *n.*), surety ; **text :** . . . . *mane ṭhāvu makki tōṭada ardha* ***aḍahā****gi koṭa ga 32* . . . . ; **tr.** a house, a site, dry land and half the grove was given as **surety** for an amount of 32 *ga.* (*gadyāṇa,* a gold coin) ; *S.I.I.* IX, pt. ii, No. 540, p. 559, l. 45 ; Basarūru, Kundapur Tq., Udupi Dt., Karn. St., **Dy.** Tuḷuva, Achyutarāya, Ś. 1453 = 1531 A.D.

aḍaikkāi (T. *n.*), arecanut ; **text :** . . . *śrīkoyil Bhaṭāra.ṟku . . . Varaguṇamahārajar ōrāṭṭaikku nel padiṉā.ṟu kalam* ***aḍaikkāi*** *nā.ṟpadu* ; **tr.** for the temple of the god Bhaṭāra 16 *kalam* (a grain measure) of paddy per year and 40 arecanuts . . . . were endowed by Varaguṇamahārāja ; *S.I.I.* XIV, No 13, p. 10, ll. 5, 64–65 ; Ambāsamudram, Ambasamudram Tq., Tirunelveli Dt., T. Nadu St. **Dy.** Pāṇḍya, Varaguṇa II, regnal year 4+12 = 875 A.D. ; **aḍaikkāy amirdu** (T. *n.*), arecanut offering ; **text :** . . . *Gaṇapatiyārkku* . . . . ***aḍaikkāy amirdu*** *pōd-eṭṭāga mūṉ.ṟu pōdaikku aḍaikkāy-amirdu iruppattunālum* . . . ; **tr. offering** of 24 **arecanuts** thrice at the rate of 8 arecanuts at a time made to the god Gaṇapati ; *S.I.I.* VIII, No. 235, p. 129, ll. 1, 9–12 ; Tiruvalañju.ḻi, Kumbhakonam Tq., Tanjavur Dt., T. Nadu St. **Misc.,** in characters of the 11th cent. A.D.

aḍaikkāi amudu (T. *n.*), arecanut offerings ;

text[1] **:** . . . . *Tirunallattu* . . . . *Gaṇapatiyārkku* . . . . . **aḍaikāi-amudu** *āṟu*. . . . *nichcharpaḍi* . . . *nibhadam śeyivōm ānōm ivvūr Tirukkōyiluḍaiyōm* ; **tr.** we, the administrators of the temple of the god Gaṇapati of Tirunallam have endowed (among other things) **offerings of** 6 **arecanuts** per day to the deity ; *S.I.I.* XIX, No. 348, p. 178, ll. 1, 6 ; Kōnērirājapuram, Tanjavur Tq. and Dt., T. Nadu St. **Dy.** Chōḷa, Parakēsari- varman I, reg. yr. 14 = 985 A.D. ; **text**[2] **:** . . . *Kariyamāṇikkapperumāḷ nagarattār maṇṭapattile eḻundaruḷgiradukku vēṇḍina* . . . . . **aḍaikkāy-amudu** *chandanakkāppu tirumālai* . . . *nāṅgaḷē nagarattār ubhayamāga naḍatta kaḍavar āgavum* ; **tr.** we, the *nagarattār* (commercial guild of a township) shall provide **arecanut offerings**, sandal garland etc., to the god Kariyamāṇikkapperumāḷ when He is brought to the hall built by the *nagarattār* ; *S.I.I.* XVII, No. 679, p. 312, ll. 27–30 ; Nāgalāpuram, Tiruvallur Tq., Chingleput Dt., T. Nadu St., **Dy.** Tuḷuva, Kṛishṇadēvarāya, Ś. 1442 = 1521 A.D.

āḍaikkāśu (T. *n.*), cost of bridal dress ; **text :** *aṇṇan vīṭṭil āḍaikkāśu eṇbadu* . . . . *Viḷakkattaraiyan vāṅgi kuḍuttu kaṇṇālañjeyyakkaḍavadāgavum* . . . . . ; **tr.** obtaining 80 *kāśu* (a coin) being the cost of bridal dress from the house of the elder brother, Viḷakkattaraiyan shall purchase the dress and have the marriage performed ; *I.P.S.*, No. 281, p. 163. ll. 21–22 ; Nārttāmalai, Kulattur Tq., Pudukkottai Dt., T. Nadu St. **Dy.** Pāṇḍya, Sundarapāṇḍya, reg. yr. 11+1 = 1227–28 A.D.

aḍaippu (T. *n.*), leased land ; **text :** . . . . *pūśikkuṁ nambimārkku aḍaippāgavum* . . . . . *śivabbirāhmaṇarkku aḍaippāgavum inda śandikaṭṭina Abimāṇatuṅga Pallavaraiyaṟkku aḍaippāgavam* ; **tr.** land leased to Nambimārs who worship the deity, land leased to the Śivabrāhmaṇas and land leased to Abimāṇatuṅga Pallavaraiyar who had instituted this service ; *S.I.I.* XVII, No. 171, p. 56, ll. 14–16 ; Tirukaṇṭhēśvaram, Cuddalore Tq., S. Arcot Dt., T. Nadu St. **Dy.** Pāṇḍya, Sundarapāṇḍya I, reg. yr. 14 = 1264 A.D. ; **aḍaippu-mudali** (T. *n.*), officer in charge of leased land ; **text :** . . . . . *Muḍigoṇḍaśōḻapurattu* . . . . *aḍaippu-mudali Vēlūruḍaiyāṇ Maṇḍalasuvami Āḻvāṇḍai perggaḍi* . . . ; **tr.** Āḻvāṇḍai-perggaḍi, the head of the subdivision Vēlūr was the **officer in charge of leased lands** in Muḍigoṇḍaśōḻapuram . . . . ; *E.C.* (R) IV, Ko. 93, p. 461, l. 1 ; Muḍigoṁḍa, Kollegal Tq., Chamarajanagara Dt., Karn. St. **Dy.** Hoy., Sōmēśvara, Cy. yr. Hēmaḷaṁbi = 1237 A.D.

aḍaittu (T. *vb.*), having constructed a barrage ; **text :** . . . . *Aṇṇāṇāṭṭu ellaiyil Tirundigai āṟṟai* **aḍaittu** *ēṟiyum veṭṭi tūmbum iṭṭu*. . . . ; **tr. having constructed a barrage** in the river Tirundigai on the border of Aṇṇāṇāḍu, having excavated a lake and having provided sluices ; *S.I.I.* VIII, No. 83, pp. 44–45, ll. 3–4 ; Tiruvaṇṇāmalai, Tiruvannamalai Tq., N. Arcot Dt., T. Nadu St. **Dy.** Chōḷa, Rājarāja III, reg. yr. 20 = 1230 A.D.

aḍaka (K. *n.*), stipulated conditions (of the grant) : **text**[1] : .... *ī **aḍaka**va tappidaḍe 1 tale 1000 hoṁnu arasiṁge daṇḍa.* **tr.** if persons fail to abide by the **stipulated conditions of the grant**, they will have to pay to the king a fine of 1000 gold coins per head. ; *S.I.I.* VII, No. 325, p. 177, l. 28, Mūḍakeri, Udupi Tq. and Dt., Karn. St. **Dy.** Saṅgama, Harihara, Ś 1302 = 1380 A.D. ; **text**[2] : *āvanōrvvanu yī **aḍaka**va tappidare ēḻu ghaṭṭadalli iḷida kapile ... brāhmaṇara .... konda dōsha . .* ; **tr.** whoever flouts this arrangement would have, in effect, committed the sin of killing tawny cows descended from the seven ghats and brāhmaṇas ; *S.I.I.* VII, No. 229, p. 116 ; l. 23 ; Kāntāvara, Karkala Tq., Udupi Dt., Karn. St. **Dy.** Saṅgama, Harihara I, Ś. 1312 = 1390 A.D.

aḍake (see also under aḍike) (K. *n.*), arecanut ; **text :** .... *gavuṇḍaru Ghaṭṭidēvargge koṭṭaḍakeya mara mūru . . .* ; **tr.** three arecanut trees were given by the *gavuṇḍa* to Ghaṭṭidēva ; *S.I.I.* IX, pt. i, No. 107, p. 82, ll. 15–17 ; Sirastahaḻḻi, Harapanahalli Tq., Bellary Dt., Karn. St. **Dy.** Chāḷ. of Kal., Traiḷōkyamalla, Ś. 970 = 1048 A.D. ; **aḍake dōṇṭa** (K. *n.*), arecanut grove ; **text :** .... *īśānyada Kaggeṟeya keḷage aḍakedōṇṭa . . .* ; **tr.** arecanut grove under the tank called Kaggeṟe in the north east ; *K.I.* IV, No. 10, p. 30, l. 64 ; Hirēhaḻḻi, Byadagi Tq., Dharwar Dt., Karn. St. **Dy.** Chāḷ. of Kal., Vikramāditya VI, Ś. 1043 = 1121 A.D. ; **aḍakeya āya** (K. *n.*), tax derived from arecanuts ; **text :** *Pāṇḍyadēvara besadim . . . śriman nūṟippadiṁbaru mūru lakshada aḍake āyamaṁ biṭṭaru* ; **tr.** on the orders of Pāṇḍyadēva, the 120 (*mahājanas*) remitted the tax income on 3 lakhs of arecanuts ; *S.I.I.* IX, pt. i, No. 118, p. 98, ll. 65–66 ; Hirēhaḍagalli, Hadagalli Tq. Bellary Dt., Karn. St. **Dy.** Chāḷ. of Kal., Vikramāditya VI, Ch. Vi. yr. 31 = 1107 A.D. ; **aḍakeya perjjuṁka** (K. *n.*), major tax levied on arecanuts ; **text :** . . . . *Pāṁḍyadēvara besadiṁ ..... daṁḍanāyakaṁ Ghaṭṭamānada Perggaḍe Attimarasaṁ mūru-lakshad **aḍakeya perjjuṅkam**aṁ biṭṭa* ..... ; **tr.** on the orders of Pāṇḍyadēva, *daṇḍanāyaka* Atti marasa the head of the village of Ghaṭṭamāna donated the **major tax levied on** 3 lakhs of **arecanuts** ; *S.I.I.* IX, pt. i, No. 118, p. 98, ll. 65–66; Hirēhaḍagalli, Hadagalli Tq. Bellary Dt., Karn. St. **Dy.** Chāḷ. of Kal., Vikramāditya VI, Ch. Vi. yr. 31 = 1107 A.D. ; **aḍakeya suṁka** (K. *n.*), tax levied on arecanuts ; **text**[1] **:** ***aḍakeya suṁka** Meysunāḍa heggaḍegāṇike ivoḷagāgi . . . apūrvvāyavellavaṁ . . . Mahālakshmidēviyara dharmakārya* ..... *salvaṁtāgi . . . koṭṭa śāsanam. . .* ; **tr.** stone edict recording the grant of future taxes such as **tax on arecanuts,** tax for the maintenance of village head in Meysunāḍu, etc. for the religious performances to the goddess Mahālakshmidēvi ; *E.C.* (R), VIII. No. 41, p. 267, ll. 11–15. ; Doḍḍagaddavaḻḻi, Hassan Tq. and Dt., Karn. St. **Dy.** Hoy., Ballāḷa, Cy. yr. Raudri = 1200 A.D. ;

text[2] **:** *paṭṭaṇadavarige saluva sthaḷa suṁka* ***aḍakeya suṁka*** *āḍadeṟege sahā suṁka ga 30* ; **tr.** 30 *gadyāṇa* (a gold coin) of tax payable to Śrīraṁgapaṭna in the form of local tax, **tax on arecanut** and tax on sheep and goats ; *E.C.* (R), VI, Pp. 134, p. 228, l. 5. ; Mēlukōṭe., Pandavapura Tq., Mandya Dt., Karn. St. **Dy.** Tuḷuva, Kṛishṇadēvarāya, Ś. 1449 = 1528 A.D. ; **aḍakeya tōṁṭa,** arecanut plantation ; **text :** .... *ūroḍeyan-Aḷiya Daṇḍiyaṇṇa tanna* ***aḍakeya tōṁṭa****doḷu naḍuvaṇa liṁgaṁ baresi biṭṭa sālomdu* ... ; **tr.** one row of arecanut trees in the **arecanut plantation** given by the headman of the village Aḷiya Daṇḍiyaṇṇa after demarking the boundary by planting a stone having the figure of a liṁga ; *S.I.I.* IX, pt. i, No. 107, p. 82, ll. 15–16 ; Sirastahaḷḷi, Harapanahalli Tq., Davanagere Dt., Karn. St. **Dy.** Chāḷ. of Kal., Trailōkyamalla, Ś. 970 = 1048 A.D. ; **aḍakeya-tōṭa** (K. *n.*), arecanut grove : **text :** ... *Nāyakara dēvadōṭadiṁ teṁkaṇa aḍakeya tōṭa* ... ; **tr.** arecanut grove to the south of the Dēvatōṭa belonging to the Nāyaka ; *S.I.I.* IV, No. 260, p. 57, l. 84, Hampi, Hospet Tq, Bellary Dt., Karn. St. **Dy.** Sāmantas of Kuṟugōḍu, Mādeya-nāyaka, Ś 1121 = 1199 A.D.

aḍakyāmudu (Te. *n.*), preparation made out of betel leaf and arecanut ; **text :** .... *Rājanārāyaṇa Viṇṇagarāruvāṟiguḍi tūrpuna mukhamaṇḍapamuna* .... *pallipīṭhamuna vijayaṁ chēsi uṁḍi* .... *nibandha sēsinapaḍi* .... ***aḍakyāmudu****naku poṁkalu 15 yākulu 30* .... ; **tr.** on the occasion when the deity of Rājanārāyaṇa Viṇṇagara visits and occupies the seat in the *mukhamaṇḍapa* as per the stipulation recorded ...... a preparation made out of 15 arecanuts and 30 betel leaves were to be provided ; *S.I.I.* V, No. 66, p. 24, ll. 4–6, 7, 30–31 ; Bhīmāvaram, Kakinada Tq., W. Godavari Dt., A.P. St. **Dy.** E. Chāḷ. of Vēṁgi, Vishṇuvardhana, reg. yr. 30, in characters of 12th cent. A.D.

aḍapa (Te. *n.*), betel bag bearer, barber ; **text**[1] **:** .... *Anavōtaya reḍḍiṁgāri* .... *aḍapa Vēmanaṁgāru* ..... ; **tr.** Vēmana the **betel bag bearer** of Anavōtayareḍḍi; *S.I.I.* X, No. 555, p. 303, l. 3 ; Tripurāntakam, Markapur Tq., Kurnool Dt., A.P. St. **Dy.** Reddi, Anavōtaya, Ś. 1278 = 1356 A.D. ; **text**[2] (K. *n.*), ... *Ādavānige saluva Mīnagoṁdiya* ***aḍapa****da Māchage saluva grāmagaḷu* ..... ; **tr.** villages belonging to the **barber** Mācha of Mīnagoṁdi in Ādavāni ; *S.I.I.* IX, pt. ii, No. 513, p. 527, ll. 14–16 ; Bolagoti, Alur Tq. Bellary Dt., Karn. St. **Dy.** Tuḷuva, Kṛishṇadēvarāya, Ś. 1443 = 1521 A.D. ; **text**[3] (Te. *n.*), ... *Anavōtayareḍḍiṁgāri ānatini* ***aḍapa*** *Vēmanaṁgāru* .... *Tripurāntaka dēvaraku baṁggārāna* ... *uṁguramunnu samarpiṁchina puṇyakāla* ..... ; **tr.** the auspicious occasion on which Vēmana, the **betel bag bearer** donated to the god Tripurāntakadēva gold ornaments including ring on the orders of his mater Anavotayareḍḍi ; *S.I.I.* X, No. 555, p. 303, ll. 3–5 ; Tripurāntakam, Markapur Tq., Kurnool

Dt., A.P. St. **Dy.** Reḍḍi, Anavōtaya, Ś. 1278 = 1356 A.D.

aḍapa hāku (K. *vb.*), mortgage ; **text** : . . . . *mumnūru varahana sālava tegedukomḍu aḍapa hāki śāsanavanu koṭṭu* . . . . ; **tr.** 300 *varaha* (a coin) were taken on loan after pledging and recording the same in inscription ; *E.C.* VIII, Tīr. 57, p. 493, l. 15 ; Tīrthahaḷḷi, Teerthahalli Tq., Shimoga Dt., Karn. St. **Dy.** Keḷadi Nāyaka, Sōmaśēkhara, Ś. 1613 = 1690 A.D.

aḍappam (T. *n.*), betel bag ; **text** : . . . . . . *Tiruppāḍivēṭṭai tirunāḷ ubaiyattukku aḍappattu Mallappanāyakkar samarppitta* . . . . *grāmam iṟaṇḍu* ; **tr.** two villages granted by Mallappanāyakkar, the **betel bag** bearer of his master for conducting the holy day of the god's hunting festival ; *S.I.I.* XVII, No. 263, p. 105, ll. 7–8 ; Ginjee, Ginjee Tq., S. Arcot Dt., T. Nadu St. **Dy.** Tuḷuva, Sadāśiva, Ś. 1472 = 1550 A.D.

aḍapu (K. *n.*), a kind of service in the temple ; **text** : . . . *Gōvimdarājadēvara naivēdya prasādavanu Tirupatiyavarige kāṇiparāgi nālku harivāṇa nambigaḷige* . . . . *mikka harivāṇagaḷanū tirumaleya samdhiya aḍapinalu* . . . . *hamchikombudu* . . . . ; **tr.** the food offerings given to the god Gōvimdarājadēva was to be shown to the persons in Tirupati and 4 plates of this *prasāda* was to be offered to those who worship the god . . . and the remaining plates of *prasāda* are to be shared among the temple servants during **service in** Tirumalai **temple** ; *S.I.I.* IX, pt. ii, No. 462, p. 474, l. 2 ; Tirupati, Chandragiri Tq., Chittoor Dt., A.P. St. **Dy.** Sāḷuva, Narasimha, Ś. 1389 = 1467 A.D.

aḍateṟe, aḍateṟige (K. *n.*), duty levied on mortgage deeds ; **text**[1] : . . . *Dēvarāyapurada grāmavanu* . . . *Namjarāyagaḷu sarvvamānyavāgi koṭṭanu* . . . *tōṭa tuḍike kaḷa koṭhāra sumka charādāya* ***aḍateṟe*** *kumbārādeṟe* . . . . *mumtāgi ēnuḷa sarvasvāmyavanu āgumāḍikomḍu Vīrabhadradēvara amgaramga-bhōgakke saludu* ; **tr.** Namjarāya granted the village of Dēvarāyapura with the stipulation that all revenue incomes from gardens, the place where the arecanuts are cured, fields, the tax on granaries, tax on moveable objects, **duty levied on mortgage deeds**, etc., as a gift to be respected by all to the god Vīrabhadradēva for services to the god's image and entertainment ; *E.C.* (R) III, Nj. 273, p. 348, ll. 7–8, 19–20, 22–24 ; Yīrēdēvanapura, Nanjanagud Tq., Mysore Dt., Karn. St. **Misc.**, Ś. 1410 = 1488 A.D. ; **text**[2] : . . . *Chikkarāyaru* . . . . *Nāgābhaṭṭarige*. . . . *koṭṭa grāmada śilāśāsanada krama* . . . *Chikkarāyasāgarada chatussīmeya gadde beddalu tōṭa tuḍike*. . . . ***aḍateṟige*** *kumbāṟa teṟige* . . . . *modalāda sakala sumka survarṇādāyavanu* . . . . *āḷikomḍu anubhavisikomḍu bahiri* ; **tr.** according to the stipulations governing the grant of the village to Nāgābhaṭṭa by Chikkarāya . . . . within the four boundaries of Chikkarāyasāgara, rain irrigated fields, garden, place where the arecanuts are cured, **duty levied on mortgage deeds** and all other such taxes and income in the form of gold have been granted ; *E.C.* (R) VII, Ml. 106, p. 408-09, ll. 7, 8, 21–22, 25–26, 29 ; Muṭṇahaḷḷi, Malavalli Tq., Mandya Dt., Karn. St. **Dy.** Tuḷuva, Narasiṁha, Ś. 1428 = 1506 A.D.

āḍavala gadyāṇa (K. *n.*), tax on uncultivated land ; **text :** *Rājavallabhaseṭṭi kerege koṭṭa gadyāṇa 40 āḍavalaṁ gadyāṇaṁ 1 . . .* ; **tr.** Rājavallabhaseṭṭi granted 40 *gadyāṇa* (a gold coin) and a **tax of one *gadyāṇa*** (*q.v.*) for the maintenance of the **uncultivated land** ; *E.C.* (R) I, Cg. No. 48, p. 34, l. 11–13 ; Hosahaḷḷi, Somavarpete Tq., Madikeri Dt., Karn. St. **Dy.** Kongāḷva chfs., Rājēndra, Ś. 993 = 1070 A.D.

āḍavallāṉ (T. *n.*), standard stone used to weigh precious metals ; grain measure ; **text[1] :** . . *Uḍaiyyār śrī Rājarājadēvar kuḍutta śrībali eḻuṇḍaruḷum poṉṉiṉ Koḷgaidēvar oruvar* ***āḍavallāṉ**-eṉṉuṁ kallāl niṟai eṉṉūṟṟi irubattombadin poṉ padiṉ kaḻañjēy mukkālēy mūṉṟu mañjāḍi. . . . .* ; **tr.** Rājarājadēva gave one gold image of Koḷgaidēvar which is to be brought during the sacred offerings weighing 829 *kaḻañju* (standard gold ingot) and 3 quarters and 3 *mañjāḍi* (unit of weight) **weighed by the standard stone** called after *āḍavallāṉ* ; *S.I.I.* II, pt. i, No. 1, p. 2, second section, ll. 3–5 ; Tañjāvūr, Tanjavur Tq. and Dt., T. Nadu St. **Dy.** Chōḷa, Rājarāja I, reg. yr. 26 = 1011 A.D. ; **text[2] :** . . . . *Uḍaiyār śrī Rājarājīśvaramuḍaiyārkku* ***āḍavallāṉ*** *eṉṉum marakkālāl peruñjeṉbaga moṭṭu tūṇippadakku . . . .* ; **tr.** to the god Rājarājīśvaram uḍaiyār was given one *tūṇi* (a grain measure) and one *padakku* (a grain measure) of cardamom seeds per year measured by the **grain measure called āḍavallāṉ** . . . . . ; *S.I.I.* II, pt. ii, No. 24, p. 122, ll. 13, 17 ; Tañjāvūr, Tanjavur Tq. and Dt., T. Nadu St., **Dy.** Chōḷa, Rājarāja I, reg. yr. 29 = 1014 A.D.

aḍavamāḍu (K. *vb.*), mortgage ; **text :** . . . . . . *Siṁgāpurada Giribhaṭṭaru . . . Doḍḍaṁṇabhaṭṭage . . . haṇa koṭṭu ī bhūmiyanna aḍavamāḍikoṁḍu anubhavisi . . . .* ; **tr.** Giribhaṭṭa of Siṁgāpura having taken on mortgage the land belonging to Doḍḍaṁṇabhaṭṭa on payment of cash was enjoying the same ; *M.A.R.* 1929, No. 18, pp. 82–83, ll. 103–105 ; Kuḍuvaḷḷi, Kadur Tq., Chickmagalur Dt., Karn. St. **Dy.** Saṅgama, Harihara, Cy. yr. Chitrabhānu = 1402 A.D.

aḍavi (Te. *n.*), forest ; **text :** . . . *saṁtesuṁkhālu . . . mī chētidhanaṁ beṭṭi aḍavin-arakiṁchi polaṁdīrpiṁchi . . .* ; **tr.** with your wealth you converted the **forest** into farm lands ; *S.I.I.* XVI, No 295, p. 300, l. 8 ; Śrīmushṇam, Chidambaram Tq., South Arcot Dt., T. Nadu St. **Dy.** Āravīḍu, Śrīraṁga I, Ś. 1505 = 1584 A.D.

ādāya (K. < Skt. *n.*) income ; **text :** . . . *hoṁna kaḷaśakke māḍida dharma alliṁda mēlaṇa ādāyavāda hoṁnanu Mahādēvara viniyōgake uḷadu matte āva vechchakkū tegeya salladu. . . . . .* ; **tr.**

for providing a golden pinnacle for the temple of Mahādēva, gold was granted and the **income** accruing from that gold should be used only for services to the god Mahādēva and should not be utilised for any other expenditure ; *S.I.I.* IX, pt. ii, No. 450, p. 460, ll. 22–24 ; Basarūru, Kundapur Tq., Udupi Dt., Karn. St. **Dy.** Saṅgama, Dēvarāya, Ś. 1366 = 1444 A.D.

ādāyam (T. < Skt. *n.*), income ; **text :** . . . . *inda ūrai nōkki varum sakala ādayattilum* . . . . . ; **tr.** from all the (revenue) incomes derived from this village ; *T.D.I.* II, No. 133, p. 306, l. 12; Tirumalai, Chittoor Tq. and Dt., A.P. St. **Dy.** Sāḷuva, Narasiṁha, Ś. 1417 = 1495 A.D.

aḍḍa (K. *n.*), a type of gold coin : **text**[1] **:** . . . . *mattariṁg* ***aḍḍa*** *chinna lekkadiṁ aṟuvaṇa* ; **tr.** 1/6th of the tax calculated as half of the **gold coin** per *mattar* (a land measure) ; *S.I.I.* V, No. 849, p. 347, l. 35, Hūli, Saundatti Tq., Belgaum Dt., Karn. St. **Dy.** Chāḷ. of Kal., Āhavamalla, Ś 966 = 1044 A.D. ; **text**[2] **:** *nityapaḍi dinavoṁdakke hāgav-eraḍaṟa lekkade adhika dinagūḍi varshavoṁdake gadyāṇaṁ hadineṁṭu haṇavēḷu* ***aḍḍa*** . . . ; **tr.** for the permanent offerings 18 *gadyāṇa* (*q.v.*) and seven *haṇa* (cash) of seven **gold coins of a type** was granted per year including the excess days for daily services ; *E.C.* (R) V, T.N. 88, p. 479, ll. 62–63; Sōmanāthapura, Bannur Tq., Mysore Dt., Karn. St. **Dy.** Hoy., Narasiṁha III, Cy. yr. Dhātri = 1276 A.D. ; **text**[3] **:** . . . . *Sōma-nāthadēvarige Bēḷūravoḷage Sōvaṁṇaseṭṭi mūlava koṭṭa bāḷina voḷage haṁneraḍu mūḍe akkige ā Chikkiseṭṭi* ***aḍḍa****vanū koṭṭanāgi ā dharmavanu mūṟukēriya halaru naḍasi pālisi baharu* ; **tr.** To the god Sōmanāthadēva a grant of 1 **coin** given by Chikkiseṭṭi for 12 *mūḍe* (a grain measure) of rice harvested from the field bought by Sōvaṁṇaseṭṭi in Bēḷūru and this grant was to be protected by the *halaru* (a group of traders) of Mūṟukēri ; *S.I.I.* VII, No. 310, p. 161 ll. 12–15, Mūḍakēri, Udupi Tq. and Dt., Karn. St. **Dy.** Saṅgama, Harihara, Ś 1334 = 1412 A.D. ; **aḍḍaderige** (K. *n.*) tax collected in the form of *aḍḍa* coins ; **text :** *ā sthaḷakke saluva gadde beddalu tōṭa* . . . . *suvarṇādāya* ***aḍḍaderige*** . . . . *sarvamānyavanu āgumāḍi anubhavisikoṁḍu baruvadu* ; **tr.** all the revenue incomes derived from that place from its paddy field, irrigated fields, gardens . . . . income in the form of gold, **tax collected in the form of gold coins**, etc., may all be collected and enjoyed ; *E.C.* (R) III, Gu. 75, p. 59, ll. 9–11 ; Sōmahaḷḷi, Gundlupet Tq., Mysore Dt., Karn. St. **Dy.** Āravīḍu, Rāmarāya, Ś. 1498 = 1576 A.D.

aḍḍadāri (K. *n.*), cross road ; **text**[1] **:** . . . *Vināyaka dēvargge Raṇadhavaḷa chamūpaṁ . . . koṭṭa keyi teṁka voladalli chikk-****aḍḍa-dāri****yiṁ baḍagal-ibbaḍḍalāgi hiriya kōla ma 2* . . . . ; **tr.** 2 *ma* (*mattars*, a land measure) measured by the bigger rod (a measuring rod) was given to the god Vināyakadēva by Raṇadhavaḷa chamūpua in the southern field which was west of the minor **cross road** ; *S.I.I.* IX, pt. i, No. 334, p. 355, ll. 12–15 ; Oruvay, Bellary Tq. and Dt., Karn. St. **Dy.** Hoy., Ballāḷa, Cy. yr. Īśvara = 1217 A.D. ; **text**[2] : . . . . . . *Basurikōḍalu Janārdanabhaṭṭaru Mūkagauḍana kaiyalu dānavaṁ paḍedu biṭṭa keyi **aḍḍa dāri**yiṁ mūḍalu akkasālegeyiṁ baḍagalu* ; **tr.** the land in Basarikōḍu granted by Janārdanabhaṭṭa after receiving it as a gift from Mūkagauḍa, located to the east of the **cross road** and to the north of the field belonging to the goldsmith ; *S.I.I.* V, No. 856, p. 351, ll. 42–43, Stone slab kept in Govt. Museum, Chennai, T. Nadu St. **Dy.** Kal. of Kal., Āhavamalla, in characters of 12th cent. A.D.

aḍḍagaḍa suṁkhaṁ (Te. *n.*), tax on embankment built across a water course ; **text** : . . . . *Vyālēśvaruniki . . . . chevali **aḍḍagaḍa-suṁkhamunu**. . . . Siddhirāju Timmarājayyavāru svāmi kalyāṇa mahōtsavānaku samarpinchinadi* . . ; **tr.** income from the **tax on the embankment built across a water course** in Chevali was granted to the god Vyālēśvara by Siddhirāju Timmarājaiah for performing the marriage festival for the deity ; *S.I.I.* XVI, No 267, p. 275, ll. 51–54 ; Chāvali, Tenali Tq., Guntur Dt., A.P. St. **Dy.** Tuḷuva, Sadaśiva, Ś. 1489 = 1568 A.D.

aḍḍagaṭṭalu (K. *n.*), embankment ; **text** : . . . . *aḍḍagaṭṭaliṁ bare teṁkaṇa mēre* . . ; **tr.** the southern border line is the **embankment** ; *S.I.I.* IX, pt. i, No 273, p. 294, ll. 96–97 ; Malayanūr, Kalyanadurga Tq., Anantapur Dt., A.P. St. **Dy.** Chāḷ. of Kal., Sōmēśvara IV, Ś. 1101 = 1179 A.D.

addika (K. *n.*), chief officer, supervision ; **text**[1] : . . .*yī sthaḷaṁgaḷige adhikāra **addika** kōlukāraru muṁtāgi ārū hōgasalladu* . . . . ; **tr.** no one including the authorised **chief officer**, staff-bearing officer, etc., should not enter these places ; *E.C.* (R) V, T. N. 91, p. 485, ll. 33–34 ; Sōmanāthapura, T. Narasipura Tq., Mysore Dt., Karn. St. **Dy.** Hoy., Narasiṁha Cy. yr. Vishu = 1281 A.D. ; **text**[2] : *Kuṁdāpura voḷagaṇa Kuṁdēśvaradēvara saṁnidhiyalū pūrvadalū vūrujagattu **addika**dalū Kūḍākūra Dēvaṁṇa-sēnabōva māḍisida dharma* . . . . ; **tr.** a grant made by Dēvaṁṇasēnabōva of Kūḍākūru in the presence of the god Kuṁdēśvaradēva located within Kundāpura under the supervision of the *ūru* (village) and *jagattu* (assembly) ; *S.I.I.* IX, pt. ii, No. 441, p. 451, ll. 12–14 ; Kundāpur, Kundapur Tq., Udupi Dt., Karn. St. **Dy.** Saṅgama, Dēvarāya II, Ś. 1348 = 1425 A.D.

aḍḍaṇekaṁḍi (K. *n.*), an outlet in a dam ; **text** : . . . *grāmakke āgnēyadalli aḍḍaṇekaṁḍi baḷiya paḍuva mukhavāgi neṭṭa kallu* ; **tr.** stone set up facing west near the **outlet in a dam** to the south east of the village ; *E.C.* XIV, Nj. 295, p. 150 ; Kaḷale, Nanjanagud Tq., Mysore Dt., Karn. St. **Dy.** Woḍ. of Mys., Chikka-Dēvarāja, Ś. 1638 = 1716. A.D.

aḍḍasārige (K. *n.*), small field that crosses the boundary of a larger one ; **text :** . . . *Nāgaṁṇṇana maga Nārasiṁhadēva koṭṭa aḍḍasārigeyoṁdu . . .* . . . ; **tr.** one piece of a small field which crosses the boundary of a larger one was donated by Nārasiṁhadēva son of Nāgaṁṇṇa ; *E.C.* (R) VIII, Hn. 71, p. 39, l. 29 ; Yaḻḻēśapura, Holenarasipur Tq., Hassan Dt., Karn. St. **Dy.** Hoy., Sōmēśvara, Ś. 1159 = 1238 A.D.

adda soḷasa (K. *n.*), half of a liquid measure called soḷasa ; **text :** *dēvara naṁdādīvige naḍevaṁtāgi . . . . . gāṇagaḷalu pratyēka nōḍikoṁbaṁtāgi biṭṭa dhāreṇṇey***adda soḷasa***. . .* ; **tr.** oil of the quantity of **half of a liquid measure called *soḷasa*** was granted from each of the oil mills so that a perpetual lamp can be burnt under supervision for the god ; *K.I.* I, No. 25, p. 50, ll. 89–90 ; Sirasangi, Saundatti Tq., Belgaum Dt., Karn. St. **Dy.** Chāḷ. of Kal., Vīra Sōmēśvara IV, Ś. 1108 = 1186 A.D.

aḍḍaderige (K. *n.*), tax imposed on carrying palanquin ; **text :** . . . *ā staḷake saluva gadde beddalu tōṭa . . . aḍumane kaḷa koṭāra suvarṇādāya aḍḍaderige . . . . . āgumāḍi anubhavisikoṁḍu baruvadu . . .* ; **tr.** you will take possession of and continue to enjoy wet lands, dry fields, gardens, . . . firewood shed, pasture, threshing floor, land revenue paid in gold, **tax imposed on carrying palanquin**, etc. ; *E.C.* (R) III, Gu. 75, p. 59, ll. 9–11 ; Sōmahaḻḻi, Gundlupet Tq., Mysore Dt., Karn. St. **Dy.** Āravīḍu, Śrīraṁgarāya, Ś. 1498 = 1576 A.D.

aḍḍavaṭṭe, aḍḍavaṭṭa (*n.*), cross road ; **text**[1] (K.) : . . . *nairityadalu aruhanakalla* ***aḍḍavaṭṭey-****āladamara* ; **tr.** the Banyan tree at the **cross road** at Aruhanakallu in the south west ; *E.C.* (R) VII, Ng. 61, p. 36, l. 46 ; Lālanakere, Nagamangala Tq., Mandya Dt., Karn. St. **Dy.** Hoy., Vishṇuvarddhana, Ś. 1059 = 1138 A.D. ; **text**[2] (Te.) : . . . *Gaṇapaya saṁsiddhasthānamaina Vēlpura aḍḍavaṭṭa* . . . . . ; **tr.** the **cross road** in the village of Vēlpūru, which was a permanent fief of Gaṇapaya . . . . . ; *S.I.I.* X, No. 314, p. 163, l. 14 ; Vēlpūru, Sattenapalli Tq., Guntur Dt., A.P. St. **Dy.** Kākatīya, Gaṇapatidēva, Ś. 1169 = 1247 A.D. ; **aḍḍavaṭṭa suṁkamu** (Te. *n.*), tax levied on goods passing through the cross roads; **text :** . . . . . *Kammanāṁṭi sthaḷamu* ***aḍḍavaṭṭa suṁkamu****lu . . . . Śaṁkaramahādēvarakun akhaṁḍa dīpamunaku . . . . ichchitimi* . . . . . ; **tr.** we have granted to the god Śaṁkaramahādēva for lighting a perpetual lamp, the **tax levied on goods passing through the cross roads** in the division of Kammanāḍu . . ; *S.I.I.* VI, No. 617, p. 222, ll. 6–10, 13 ; Konidena, Narasaraopet Tq., Guntur Dt., A.P. St. **Misc.**, Ś. 1067 = 1145 A.D. ; **aḍḍavaṭṭeya suṁka** (K. *n.*), tax levied on goods passing through the cross roads **text :** *Maṁchyarasaṁge puṇyavāgalu* ***aḍḍavaṭṭeya suṁka****vanu mānyavāgi . . . Gavarēśvaradēvarige Visvanādhadēvanu biṭṭa . . .*

. . . ; **tr.** Visvanādhadēva donated the **tax levied on goods passing through the cross roads** to the Gavarēśvaradēva for the merit of Maṁcharasa . . . ; *K.I.A.P*, pt. i, Mn. 63, p. 44, ll. 34–36 ; Vardhamānapura, Mehboobnagar Tq. and Dt., A.P. St., **Misc.,** Ś. 1150 = 1228 A.D.

addhyayana vṛitti (T. < Skt. *n.*), grant-in-aid for a student (studying vēdas) ; **text :** (damaged) . . *Vasishṭhanāyaṉār kōyilil tānattāṟōm . . . Viśvanātanukku* ***addhyayanavṛitti****yāga* . . . . . ; **tr. grant-in-aid given to the student** Viśvanāta by the officials of the temple of Vasishṭhanāyaṉār ; *S.I.I.* IV, No. 344, p. 96, ll. 4–5, Vēppūr, Gudiyattam Tq., N. Arcot Dt., T. Nadu St. **Dy.** Saṅgama, Prince Kaṁpaṇa, Cy. yr. Parābhava = 1366 A.D.

addoreya jana (K. *n.*), person bringing water from the river ; **text :** . . . . ***addoreya jana*** *eraḍakaṁ pratāpa muvvattāru* ; **tr.** thirty six *pratāpa* (coin named after the royal title pratāpa) for two persons bringing water from the river (for the bathing of the deity) ; *E.C.* XI, No 31, p. 258, l. 17 ; Rāmasāgara, Molakalmuru Tq., Chitradurga Dt., Karn. St. **Dy.** Saṅgama, Bhūpati, Ś. 1309 = 1386 A.D.

aḍeya haṇa (K. *n.*), tax in cash on the smiths' anvils ; **text :** . . . *baḍagi kaṁmāṟarige koṭārada voḷage tāne naḍasuva uvajhagaḷū teṟuva aḍeya* ***haṇa*** *ardha* ; **tr.** half haṇa (a coin denomination) to be paid by the artisans as **tax in cash on the anvils** used by the **smiths** such as carpenter, blacksmith, etc. in their own workshops ; *S.I.I.* IX, pt. ii, No. 554, p. 575, ll. 45–47 ; Kavutāḷam, Adavani Tq., Kurnool Dt., A.P. St. **Dy.** Tuḷuva, Achyutarāya, Ś. 1454 = 1533 A.D.

aḍedeṟe (K. *n.*), tax on the anvils of smiths ; **text :** . . . *Rāmanāthadēvarige naḍavaṁthā śrīkārya naḍevaṁtāgi ā grā 1 ā dēvarige saluva haḷigaḷa* ***aḍedeṟe*** *maggadeṟe* . . . . *vaḷagāgi akshatadigeya suṁka horagāgi ēnuḷa suṁkavanu dēva* (further details damaged) ; **tr.** all taxes including **tax on the anvils of smiths** such as carpenters and blacksmiths, tax on looms (many other such taxes are mentioned) with the exemption of the tax collected on the occasion of *akshaya tṛitīya* to be collected from one village is to be spent on the worship of the deity Rāmanāthadēva ; *E.C.* (R) VIII, Ag. 48, p. 147, ll. 16–18, 20 ; Rāmanāthapura, Arakalagud Tq., Hassan Dt., Karn. St. **Dy.** Saṅgama, Harihara II, Ś. 1305 = 1383 A.D. ; **āḍedere** (K. *n.*), tax on anvils used by carpenters and blacksmiths : **text** : . . . . *Iṁmaḍi Chikarāya Oḍeyaru . . . koṭṭa dharmaśāsanada kramaveṁtendeḍe nāvu āḷuva Hadināḍa āgarake saluva Kuṁtūra grāmada chatussīme voḷaguḷa* (various taxes are mentioned including) ***āḍedere*** (this word is also followed by a number of taxes) *Kuṁtūru grāmake ēnuḷa sarvasvāmyavanu āgumāḍikoṁḍu* . . . . . *koṭṭaru* ; **tr.** We, Chikarāya Voḍeya II made a gift of lands and a number taxes including the **tax levied on the anvils used by the**

carpenters and blacksmiths for providing food and clothings, within the four boundaries of the Kuṁtūru village included in Hadināḍa āgara which was under his administration; *S.I.I.* IX pt. ii, No. 701, p. 689, ll. 4–6, 8–10, 16 ; Kuṁtūru, Kollegal Tq., Chamarajanagara Dt., Karn. St. **Dy.** Umm. Chfs., Chikarāya Oḍeya II, Ś. 1434 = 1512 A.D.

aḍekaluvaṇa (K. *n.*), tax on the stone anvils of carpenters and blacksmiths collected in cash ; **text :** (text obscure) . . . . *bīravaṇa* . . . . *aḍekaluvaṇa* . . . ; **tr.** money collected as tax on the stone anvils of carpenters and blacksmiths ; *M.A.R.* 1932, No. 16, p. 172, ll. 31–32 ; Mattāvāra, Chickmagalur Tq. and Dt., Karn. St. **Dy.** Hoy., Vinayāditya, Ś. 991 = 1069 A.D. ; **aḍevaṇa** (K. *n.*), **text :** . . *Būdihāḷa sīmeyoḷage nīvu teṟuvaṁta aḍevaṇavanu naṁma taṁdegaḷu Raṁgarājayyanavarige puṁṇyavāgabēkeṁdu biṭṭevu* . . . . . . ; **tr.** we donated the tax collected on the anvils of carpenters and blacksmiths within the Būdihāḷ division for the merit of our father Raṁgarājayyanavaru . . ; *E.C.* XII, Chnk. 8, p. 201, ll. 16–18 ; Būdihāḷu, Chikkanayakanahalli Tq., Tumkur Dt., Karn. St. **Dy.** Āravīḍu, Sriraṁga, Ś. 1496 = 1573 A.D.

aḍekeya-muṟu (K. *n.*), arecanut bundle ; **text :** . . . . *Kanakagiriya śrī Vijayanāthadēvara amṛitapaḍi aṁgaraṁgabhōgakke* . . . *koṭṭa dharma śāsana* . . . . . . *Vīraṁṇana vartane ga 1 aḍekeya muṟu ga 4* . . . . . ; **tr.** grant of one *ga. gadyāṇa* (a gold coin) as regular remittance by Vīraṁṇa and a **bundle of arecanuts** valued at *ga* 4 granted (among many other taxes) for the services to the image and entertainment of the god Vijayanāthadēva of Kanakagiri . . . ; *E.C.* (R) IV, Ch. 372, p. 246, ll. 9–11, 32–33 ; Maleyūru, Chamarajanagara Tq. and Dt., Karn. St. **Dy.** Saṅgama, *Kumāra* Harihara III, Ś. 1344 = 1422 A.D.

aḍepa (K. *n.*), pouch for arecanut and betel leaves ; **text :** . . . . *aḍepad-Ayyaṁ māḍisida* . . . ; **tr.** [the inscribed slab] was prepared by Ayya, the bearer of the **pouch for arecanut and betel leaves** ; *E.C.* (R) VII, Ng. 99, p. 96, ll. 26–27 ; Āraṇi, Nagamangala Tq., Mandya Dt., Karn. St. **Dy.** W. Gaṅga, Satyavākya, reg. yr. 10 = 972 A.D.

adhigrāma (K. *n.*), main village ; **text :** . . . . *Naṁbigaṇṇiseṭṭiyaru* . . . . *Bikkigan-eḷpattaṟoḷ-* ***adhigrāma*** *Duggatiyaṁ sukhadiṁ melāḷke geyuttamire* . . . ; **tr.** while Naṁbigaṇṇaseṭṭi was happily administering Duggati the **main village** of the subdivision Bikkiga-70 . . . . . . ; *S.I.I.* IX, pt. i, No. 215, p. 218, ll. 19–21 ; Duggavatti, Harapanahalli Tq., Bellary Dt., Karn. St. **Dy.** Chāḷ. of Kal., Vikramāditya VI, Ś. 1049 = 1126 A.D.

adhikāram (T. < Skt. *n.*), administration ; **text :** . . . *Mallikārjunadēvaṟkku Māsayanāyakkar-adhikārattil peṟgaḍi Vaichchapanum Irāmaiyanum* . . . . . *kuḍuttōm* . . . ; **tr.** grant (details lost) given by the village headman Vaichchapa and Irāmaiya to the god Mallikārjunadēva during the administration of Māsayanāyakkar ; *E.C.* (R) V, TN. 84, p. 470, ll. 4–9, 12 ; Beṭṭahaḷḷi, T. Narasipura Tq., Mysore Dt., Karn. St. **Dy.** Hoy., Ballāḷa II, Cy. yr. Vikāri = 1179 A.D. ; **adhikārar** (T. < Skt. *n.*), administrator/administrators ; **text :** *Vēṇāḍu vāḻndaruḷuginṟa . . . Kōdai-Kēraḷapaṉmar tiruvaḍikkamainda adhikārar* ; **tr.** the administrator(s) assigned to Kōdai Kēraḷapaṉmar-tiruvaḍi who was gracefully residing in Vēṇāḍu ; *T.A.S.* IV, No. 6, p. 21, ll. 2–3 ; Śuchīndram, Agastheeswaram Tq., Kanyakumari Dt., T. Nadu St. **Dy.** Rulers of Vēṇāḍu, Kōdai Kēraḷavarman, Kollam 325+1 = 1151 A.D. ; **adhikārastaru** (K. < Skt. *n.*), officials serving as administrators ; **text :** . . . *aśshēsha brāhmaṇaru adhikārastaru ashṭādaśavarṇa yēkōttaraśata kulastaru mumtāda. seṭi samastara mumdiṭṭu . . . Kārēpurada maṭha Basavēśvarasvāmige vapista dharmaśāsana.* ; **tr.** a deed of donation handed over to Basavēśvarasvāmi of Kārēpura-maṭha after placing the facts before the administrative body of brāhmaṇas, **officials serving as administrators**, the 101 clans belonging to the 18 castes and the administrative body of traders ; *E.C.* (R) IV, Yl. 10, p. 279-80, ll. 34–36, 40–41 ; Yaḷandūru, Yalandur Tq., Mysore Dt., Karn. St. **Dy.** Woḍ. of Mys., Chāmarāja Woḍeya, Ś. 1697 = 1775 A.D.

adhikāri (K. < Skt. *n.*), official ; **text :** . . . *daṇḍanāyakaṁ Kāḷidāsayyaṁgaḷa samarppaṇeyiṁ* Guttiy-***adhikāri*** *perggaḍe Haṁpaṇayyaṁgaḷu . . . iṟdu Vishṇudēvarige kariya keyi mattaru nūṟu mane nivēśanamuṁ koṭṭaru* . . . . ; **tr.** the headman Haṁpaṇayya who was an official administering Gutti under the grace of *daṇḍanāyaka* Kāḷidāsayya (a few other officials are also mentioned) being present granted 100 *mattar* (a land measure) of black-soil land and a house-site to the god Vishṇu . . . ; *S.I.I.* VIII, No. 372, pp. 200–201, ll. 12–14 ; Gooty, Gooty Tq., Anantapur Dt., A.P. St. **Dy.** Chāḷ. of Kal, Vikramāditya VI, Ch. Vi. yr. 23 = 1099 A.D. ; **adhikāri** (K. < Skt. *n.*) ; used as suffix to male names ; **text :** . . . *Boṁmarasa* ***adhikāri****gaḷa madavaḷige* . . . . ; **tr.** wife of Boṁmarasa-**adhikāri** . . . . ; *K.I.* III, No. 14, p. 45, l. 39 ; Bhaṭkal, Bhatkal Tq. and Dist., Karn. St. **Dy.** Tuḷuva, Sadāśiva, Ś. 1468 = 1545 A.D. **adhikāriya-bēḍike** (K. < Skt. *n.*), requisitioned of an officer: **text**: . . . . *kōra-holadalu vakkalige baṁda meḷepāla bhattagaḷige adhikāriya-bēḍike khaṇḍuga voṁdake iṁmānada lekhadalu naḍasi bāhevu* . . . ; **tr.** we will implement the system of remitting two *māna* (a grain measure) per *khaṁḍuga* (a grain measure) being **the requisition** of the **administrator** out of the harvested paddy from the tenancy of the field called kōra ; *S.I.I.* IX, pt. ii, No. 681, p. 674 ll. 15–17, Chyabala, Gooty Tq., Ananthapur Dt., A.P. St., **Dy.** Tuḷuva, Sadāśiva, in characters of the 16th cent. A.D.

adhikari kaḍaikūṭṭu (T. *n.*), tax levied on groups of shop by the officer ; **text :** (damaged) . . .

Śevvappanāyakar ayyanukku puṉṉiyamāga Achyutappa nāyakkar . . . . . udagam paṉṉina paḍiyāle yindappaḍikku araimaṉai-śōḍi **adhikāri** ***kaḍaikkūṭṭu*** *śūḍipuṟavagai sarvamānyamāga kaṭṭaḷai iṭṭapaḍi . . .* ; **tr.** as per the order proclaimed levies such as the *śōḍi* (minor tax levied on donated land) amount payable to the palace, **tax levied on groups of shop by the officer** and *śōḍipuṟavagai* (minor tax levied on donated land and tax on traders) were granted with the pouring of the water of libation as *sarvvamānya* (to be respected by all) by Achyutappanāyaka for the merit of his father Śevvappanāyaka ; *S.I.I.* XVII, No. 581, p. 248, ll. 6–8, 16–23 ; Tiruvārūr, Nagapattinam Tq., Tanjaḍvur Dt., T. Nadu St. **Dy.** Chfs. of Niḍuṅguṉṟam, Achyutappanāyaka, Ś. 1482 = 1560 A.D.

adhikāriti (K. < Skt. *n.*), female officer ; **text :** . . . . . *Paṭṭamahādēviyaru . . . . . rājadhāni Bārahakaṁnyāpuradaramaneyalu . . . . voḍḍōlagaṁgoṭṭiralu śrīpādasaṁnidhānadalu Voḍḍamadēva Narasiṁgaheggaḍe . . . . . .* ***adhikāriti*** *Nāchivuṁ dēsipurusharu yiralu . . . .* ; **tr.** while Paṭṭamahādēvi was giving audience in the palace of the capital city Bārahakaṁnyāpura, Vaḍḍamadēva-Narasiṁga-heggaḍe . . . . . Nāchi the **female officer** and local dignitaries were present . . . ; *S.I.I.* IX, pt. i, No. 396, p. 406, ll. 2, 8–14 ; Kōṭēśvara, Kundapur Tq., Udupi Dt., Karn. St. **Dy.** Āḷupa, Paṭṭamahādēvi, Ś. 1184 = 1262 A.D.

adhikārti (K. < Skt. *n.*), wife of an officer ; **text :** . . . *Boṁmarasa adhikārigaḷa madavaḷige Nāgarasi adhikārtigaḷu* ; **tr.** Nāgarasi-**adhikārti** the wife of Bommarasa adhikāri ; *K.I.* III, No. 14, p. 45, l. 39 ; Bhaṭkal, Bhatkal Tq. and Dt., Karn. St., **Dy.** Tuḷuva, Sadāśiva, Ś. 1468 = 1545 A.D.

adhinātha (K. < Skt. *n.*), chieftain ; **text :** . . . *Ballakuṁdenāḍiṁg**adhināthaṁ*** . . . . *Irmmaḍi Bhīmaṁ* ; **tr.** Bhīma II, the **chieftain** of the territorial division called Ballakuṁde-nāḍu ; *S.I.I.* IX, pt. i, No. 249, p. 255, ll. 16–18, Kōlūru, Bellary Tq. and Dt., Karn. St. **Dy.** Chāḷ. of Kal., Jagadēkamalla, reg. yr. 10 = 1147 A.D.

adhipati (K. < Skt. *n.*), head ; **text :** . . . *svāmi Kārtikēyadēva tapōvan**ādhipati**gaḷappa . . . . Viśvarūpabrahmachārigaḷ* . . . . . . ; **tr.** Viśvarūpa-brahmachāri who was the **head** of the grove belonging to the god Kārtikēya in which the penance is performed . . . ; *S.I.I.* IX, pt. i, No. 166, p. 160, ll. 12–13 ; Kuḍatini, Bellary Tq. and Dt., Karn. St. **Dy.** Chāḷ. of Kal., Vikramāditya VI, Ch. Vi. yr. 24 = 1099 A.D. ; **adhipatitana** (K. *n.*), sovereignty ; **text :** . . . *Bhūtaḷadadhināthanāgi Kandharadēvaṁ prītiyal udayisal arinṛipar ātaṁkavanaide biṭṭar* ***adhipatitana****maṁ* . . . ; **tr.** when Kandharadēva was administering with love and affection as the lord of the earth, the worried enemy rulers gave up their **sovereignty** ; *E.C.* XI, Hari. 59, p. 136, l. 20 ; Harihara, Harihara Tq., Davanagere Dt., Karn. St. **Dy.** Sēü. of Dēv., Rāmachandra Ś. 1199 = 1277 A.D.

adhirāja (K. *n.*), emperor ; **text :** . . . . *prithvī vallabha Paramēśvara Pallav***ādhirājaṁ** . . . ; **tr.** the Pallava **emperor**, the beloved of the earth and the supreme lord . . . . ; *E.C.* XI, Chaḷ. 34, p. 277, ll. 9–10 ; Chikkamadhure, Challakere Tq., Chitradurga Dt., Karn. St. **Dy.** Rāshṭr. Jagattuṅga, in characters of 9th century A.D.

adhishṭāta (Te. < Skt. *adhishṭhātṛi, n.*), chief priest ; **text :** . . *Vuṁḍavellinṁdu Bhāskarēśvaruni guḍigaṭṭiṁchi* . . . . . *Peda liṁgayyanu* ***adhishṭātaṁ****gā chēsi* . . . . . ; **tr.** having built the temple of Bhāskarēśvara at Vuṁḍavelli Pedaliṁgayya was appointed as the **chief priest** . . . ; *S.I.I.* X, No. 737, p. 383, ll. 43–44, 59–60 ; Uṇḍavalli, Guntur Tq. and Dt., A.P. St. **Dy.** Gajapati, Pratāparudra, Ś. 1448 = 1526 A.D.

adhishṭhāna (K < Skt. *n.*), headquarters ; **text :** . . . *Kāśmīra Śrījilada śrīpravarapurada adhishṭhānada Pajjerapurada sthānadalu huṭṭida* . . . *Śāradādēvi* . . . . . ; **tr.** Śāradādēvi born in a place called Pajjerapura the headquarters of śrī Pravarapura of Śrījila in Kāśmīra . . . . ; *S.I.I.* VII, No. 376, p. 231, ll. 7–9 ; Kōṭakēri, Udupi Tq. and Dt., Karn. St. **Dy.** Āḷupa, Kavi-Āḷupēndra, Ś. 1077 = 1155 A.D.

adhiṭṭāṉam (T. influenced by M. < Skt. *adhishṭhāna, n.*), base, foundation ; **text :** . . . . . *Varkkalai Udaiyamārttāṇḍapurattu bhaṭṭārakar śirikōyil adhiṭṭāṉam tuḍaṅṅi uttarattōḷamum* . . . . *karuṅgal paṇiyum śēvichchu* . . . ; **tr.** having constructed in granite the temple of the Bhaṭṭāraka of Udaiyamārttāṇḍapura of Varkkalai from the base to the pinnacle ; *T.A.S.* IV, No. 43, p. 151, ll. 2–3 ; Varkkalai, Padmanabhapuram Tq., Tiruvanantapuram Dt., Ker. St. **Dy.** Ruler of Vēṇāḍu, Padmanābha-Mārttāṇḍavarmma, Kollam 427 = 1252 A.D.

adhishṭhāyaka (K. < Skt. *n.*), chief officer ; **text :** . . . . . *mahāpradhāna Noṇaṁbavāḍi-mūvatirchchāsirada vaḍḍarāvuḷa herjuṁkad-* ***adhisthṭhāyaka*** . . . . *Pallavarāya-daṁḍanāyakara besadiṁ* . . . . . . ; **tr.** by the order of the *mahāpradhāna* (chief minister) Pallavarāya daṁḍanāyaka, who was the **Chief Officer** administering the taxes *vaḍḍarāvuḷa* (*q.v.*) and *herjjuṁka* (major tax) in the territorial division called Noṇaṁbavāḍi-32,000 ; *S.I.I.* IX, pt. i, No. 170, p. 165, ll. 15–16 ; Ambali, Kudligi Tq., Bellary Dt., Karn. St. **Dy.** Chāḷ of Kal., Vikramāditya VI, Ch. Vi. yr. 30 = 1106 A.D. ; **adhishṭhāyakaṁ** (K. < Skt. *n.*), commander of a regiment ; **text :** . . . *Lāḷa khaṁḍeyakārar* ***adhishṭhāyakaṁ*** . . . . *Sōvaṇa daṁḍanāyaka* . . . . ; **tr.** Sōvaṇa-daṁḍanāyaka the **commander of the regiment** of soldiers from the Lāṭa country . . . ; *S.I.I.* IX, pt. i, No. 317, p. 332, ll. 10, 13 ; Kōgaḷi, Hadagalli Tq., Bellary Dt., Karn. St. **Dy.** Hoy., Narasiṁha, reg. yr. 4 = 1163 A.D.

adhivāsa (K. < Skt. *n.*), neighbourhood, village ;

text[1] : . . . . *baḍagada ke.reya* ***adhivāsa****dalu kārabayala bāḷina chatusīme* ; **tr.** the four boundaries of the gift land kārabayalu in the **neighbourhood** of the northern tank ; *S.I.I.* IX, pt. ii, No. 409, p. 416 l. 9, Kōṭēśvara, Kundapur Tq., Udupi Dt., Karn. St. **Dy.** Saṅgama, Bukka I, Ś 1287 = 1365 A.D. ; **text**[2] : . . . . *śrī Kṛishṇadēvarige kaṭṭaḷeyavaru arasige bimnaha māḍidalli Aṁṇappavoḍeyara nirūpadiṁ Siṁgarasa voḍeyaru . . . . Saguriya adhivāsadoḷage . . . koṭa bāḷu . . . . . .* ; **tr.** land in the **village** of Saguri given by Siṁgarasavoḍeya on the orders of Aṁṇappavoḍeya in response to a request made by the temple officials to the king ; *S.I.I.* VII, No. 296, p. 148 ll. 20–25, Uḍupi, Udupi Tq. and Dt., Karn. St. **Dy.** Saṅgama, Dēvarāya, Ś. 1359 = 1437 A.D. ; **text**[3] **:** . . . *Kṛishṇadēvara harivāṇa naivēdyakke Vēdavēdyatīrtha śrīpādaṁgaḷu māḍida dharmada vivara. . . . Baṁnniṁjada* ***adhivāsadoḷa****gaṇa paṁdebēṭe bayalalli Nāraṇamuke mūlada kuḷana gade mēle koṭa varaha ga. 120* ; **tr.** for carrying out the feeding service to the god Kṛishṇadēva, the pontiff Vēdavēdyatīrtha-śrīpādaṁgaḷu made the following grant : 120 *varaha* (a coin) *gadyāṇā* (a gold coin) on the land owned by Nāraṇamuke in the area called Paṁdebēṭe-bayalu in the **village** of Baṁnniṁja ; *S.I.I.* VII, No. 297, p. 149, ll. 21–24, Udupi, Udupi Tq. and Dt., Karn. St. **Dy.** Āravīḍu, Venkaṭapatirāya, Ś 1536 = 1614 A.D.

ādhiyāgi-tōru (K. *vb.*), pledge as a surety ; **text** : . . *Nārāyaṇadēvagaḷū yī śāsana-pramāṇinoḷagaṇa hoṁnanu* ***ādhiyāgi-tō.ri*** *halara kayyalu kaḍenāgi tekoṁḍa doḍava ga 300 akshāradalu munū.ru doḍavaraha. . . .* ; **tr.** a loan of 300 *doḍḍa va* (*doḍḍa varaha*, coin of higher denomination) *ga* (*gadyāṇa*, a gold coin) coins taken by Nārāyaṇadēva from the *halaru* (an administrative body) after pledging as surety the gold as has been registered in the inscription ; *S.I.I.* VII, No. 364, p. 220, ll. 22–25 ; Maṇigārakēri, Udupi Tq. and Dt., Karn. St. **Dy.** Sāḷuva, Narasiṁha II, Ś. 1421 = 1499 A.D.

adhyaksha (Te. < Skt. *n.*), head ; **text**[1] **:** . . . . . . *mahājanaṁgaḷa* ***adhyaksha****doḷ Vēdavāhana-bhaṭṭārakara kālam karchi* ; **tr.** having laved the feet of Vēdavāhanabhaṭṭāraka under the **headship** of the *mahājanas* (administrative body of brāhmaṇa settlement ; *S.I.I.* XI, pt. i, No. 22, p. 14, ll. 10–11 ; Vijayavāḍa, Vijayavada Tq., Krishna Dt., A.P. St. **Dy.** Rāshṭr., Kṛishṇa II, Ś. 818 = 897 A.D. ; **text**[2] (Te. < Skt. *n.*) **:** . . . *adhyaksha Nāgadēvaṇḍu . . . . Bejavāḍa Mallīśvara dēvarakuṁbeṭṭina akhaṁḍadīpamu . . . .* ; **tr.** . . perpetual lamp donated to the god Mallīśvara Mahādēva of Bejavāḍa . . . . by Nāgadēva, who was holding the office of **head** ; *S.I.I.* IV, No. 744, p. 243, ll. 6–7, 9–11 ; Vijayavāḍa, Vijayavada Tq., Krishna Dt., A.P. St. **Dy.** Chāḷ. of Vēṅgi, Rājarāja Narēndra, Ś. 1056 = 1134 A.D.

adhyakshadava (K. < Skt. *n.*), person holding

the office of headship ; **text :** ..... *dēvālyakkaṁ satrakkaṁ naḍava* ***adhyakshadavaṁge*** *ga. 3* ; **tr.** 3 *ga* (*gadyāṇa,* a gold coin) are to be paid to the person **holding the office of the headship** of the temple and the feeding house ; *E.C.* (R) VII, Md. 30, p. 215, l. 19 ; Basarāḷu, Mandya Tq. and Dt., Karn. St. **Dy.** Hoy., Sōmēśvara, Cy. yr. Hēviḷaṁbi = 1237 A.D.

adhyāpana (K. < Skt. *n.*), teaching ; **text :** ... *Ṛig-Yajus-Sām-Atharvaṇa-vēdapāragar yajana yājanādhyayana* ***adhyāpana*** *dāna pratigraha shaṭkarma niratar ... sarvvanamasyad agrahāraṁ Tuṁbuḷadaśēsha mahājanaṁgaḷ* ; **tr.** the brāhmaṇa administrative body of the great brāhmaṇa settlement Tuṁbuḷa who were experts in the four vēdas viz., Ṛig, Yajus, Sāma and Atharvaṇa and devoted to the six duties of performing sacrifices, conducting sacrifices, learning, **teaching**, munificence, accepting grants ... ; *S.I.I.* IX, pt. i, No. 295, p. 317, ll. 15–17 ; Bāpuram, Adavāni Tq., Kurnool Dt., A.P. St. **Dy.** Chāḷ. of Kal., Sōmēśvara, Ś. 1093 = 1172 A.D.

adhyayana (K. < Skt. *n.*), studying (especially the Vēdās) ; **text :** ... *Tripurāntakadēvara aṁgaraṁgabhōgakkaṁ mattam āchāryya tapōdhana* ***adhyayana*** *śuśrūshā brāhmar aśan-āchchhādanakkaṁ aivattunākku mānasara atithi abhyāgata tapōdhanara grāsakkaṁ ... biṭṭa 44 ūrggaḷ* .... ; **tr.** 44 villages granted for the services to the image and entertainment of the god Tripurāntakadēva and for the feeding and clothing of the teachers, ascetics, **for studying (especially the Vēdas)**, the disabled, the brāhmaṇas and for feeding of 54 male guests, unexpected visitors and ascetics ; *S.I.I.* IX, pt. i, No. 204, pp. 203–04, ll. 26–31, 63-64 ; Tripurāntakam, Markapur Tq., Kurnool Dt., A.P. St. ; **Dy.** Chāḷ. of Kal., Vikramāditya VI, Ch. Vi. yr. 47 = 1122 A.D. ; **adhyayanam** (T. < Skt. *n.*), ; **text :** ... *Irāyavibhāṭan śandiyile nāḷtōrum oru pēr adhyayanam paṉṉumpaḍikku. ... iṟailiyāga ... śellakaḍavadāga kalveṭṭikuḍuttōm.* ; **tr.** this stone inscription is engraved with the stipulation that tax free gift of land is made for enabling one person to undertake (Vēdic) studies every day during the service called *Rāyavibhāṭa*. ... ; *S.I.I.* VIII, No. 163, p. 74, ll. 6–7 ; Tiruvaṇṇāmalai, Tiruvannamalai Tq., N. Arcot Dt., T. Nadu St. **Dy.** Saṅgama., Virūpāksha, Ś. 1310 = 1389 A.D.

aḍi (K. *n.*), foot length ; **text :** (text obscure) .. *Chottamman biṭṭudu ondaḍi* ; **tr.** one foot length given by Chottamma ; *E.C.* (R) V, Mys. 183, p. 299, ll. 6–8 ; Varuṇa, Mysore Tq. and Dt., Karn. St. **Dy.** W. Gaṅga, Śrīpurusha, in characters of the 8th cent. A.D.

adichchi (T. *n.*), maid servant ; **text :** ... *Rājēndraśōḻavinṉagar Āḻvārkku .... Chēralaṉ-mādēviyār* ***adichchi*** *vaichcha viḷakku arai* ; **tr.** half the expense towards burning a lamp was donated by the maid servant of Chēralaṉ Mādēviyār in the temple of Rājēndraśōḻavinṉagar Āḻvār ;

S.I.I. XIV, No 150, p. 80, ll. 2–3 ; Maṉṉārkōyil, Ambasamudram Tq., Tirunelveli Dt., T. Nadu St. **Dy.** Chōḷa-Pāṇḍya, Sundarachōḷapāṇḍya, reg. yr. 14, in characters of 10th cent. A.D.

aḍichchu-taḷi (T. influenced by M. *n.*), service of temple cleaning; **text :** ... *peṇvaḻikkāṇiyāyuḷḷa kārāṇmai Tiruchchāraṇattu Bhagavati kōyilil aḍichchu-taḷi mudalāy=uḷḷa piravartti eppērppaṭṭadum. . . . kōvilil pādamūlattavarē kaimāṟichchu* ; **tr.** the right of cultivation (*kārāṇmai*) of the lands belonging to the female line, earmarked for the **service of cleaning** the premises of **the temple** of Bhagavatī at Tiruchchāraṇam was transferred to the *Pādamūlam* (temple servants) ; *T.A.S.* IV, No 42, pp. 149–150, ll. 12–22 ; Chitaral, Viplavangod Tq., Padmanabhapuram Dt., Ker. St. **Misc.**, Kollam 540 = 1365 A.D.

Ādidāsachaṇḍēśvarar (T. < Skt. *n.*), devine accountant of Śiva temples in whose name all temple transactions take place ; **text :** .. *āga taḍi mūṉṟiṉāṟ kuḻi iraṇḍāyiramum tirunāmattukkāṇiyāga Ādidāsachaṇḍēśvaraṟku viṟṟukkuḍukka. . . . Vīrapperumāḷ nāchchi pakkal nāṅgaḷ kaikkoṇḍa kāśu 2000 . . . ,* **tr.** in order to give two thousand *kuḻi* (land measure) of land measured by 3 *taḍi* (measuring rod) as a gift to Ādichaṇḍēśvarar after purchasing the same from Vīrapperumāḷ Nāchchi by paying an amount of 2000 *kāśu* (a coin), *S.I.I.* VII, No. 104, p. 44, ll. 5–7, Tiruvottūr, Cheyyar Tq., N. Arcot Dt., T. Nadu St. **Dy.** Kāḍava, Kōpperuñjiṅga, reg. yr. 22, in characters of 13th cent. A.D.

aḍigabu (K. *n.*), firewood (used for cooking) : **text :** . . . . *Viṭhaladēvaru naṁma tōṭada voḷagaṇa parāṁkuśa maṁṭapake chittaisida dinagaḷu. . . 142 kaṁ . . . eṇṇe, tuppa, sakhare ga 1/2 aḍigabu aḍugūli ga 1/2* ; **tr.** provision was made for the supply of oil, ghee and sugar at a payment 1/2 *ga* (*gadyāṇa*, a gold coin) for fire wood and for payment to the cook, 1/2 *ga* for services to the god Viṭhaladēva on 142 days in a year, when He visits the Parāṁkuśa *maṁṭapa* within our garden ; *S.I.I.* IX pt. ii, No. 668, p. 661, l. 4, Hampi, Hospet Tq., Bellary Dt., Karn. St., **Dy.** Tuḷuva, Sadāśiva, Ś 1480 = 1559 A.D.

aḍigaḷ (K. *n.*), temple priest, family name ; **text :** . . . *Mahādēvara . . . . pūjeya māḍuva **aḍigaḷige** naḍasikoḍuva bhatta nālvaṁḍeyalu muḍi 27 . . .* ; **tr.** to the **temple priest** performing worship of the deity Mahādēva is earmarked 27 *muḍi* (a grain measure) measured by *nālvaṁḍe* (four units of the measuring vessel haṁde) of paddy . . ; *S.I.I.* IX pt. ii, No. 449, p. 459, l. 26–27 ; Basarūru, Kundapur Tq., Udupi Dt, Karn. St. **Dy.** Saṅgama, Dēvarāya, Ś. 1366 = 1444 A.D.

aḍigaḷmār (T. *n.*), priests who sing sacred Tamil songs in the presence of the deity ; **text :** . . . *Tiruppaḻuvūr Paramēśvararkku Tiruppadiyam mūṉṟu sandhiyum pāḍuvār iruvar **aḍigalmārkku** . . .* . Parāntakanēṉ kuḍutta nilan ; **tr.** land donated by Parāntaka to two **priests who sing Tiruppadiyam** three times a day daily in the presence of the god Paramēśvara of Tiruppaḻuvūr; *S.I.I.* XIII, No 141, p. 72, ll. 2–4 ; Paḻūr, Tiruchi- rappaḷḷi Tq. and Dt., T. Nadu St. **Dy.** Chōḷa, Gaṇḍarāditya, reg. yr. 6, in characters of the 10th cent. A.D. ; **aḍigaḷmār** (T. *n.*), devotee (in respectful plural) ; **text :** . . . . *Tirumalaippaḷḷiyil niśadam oru* ***aḍigaḷmār****kku śōṟu vaittār . . . Ēraṉ-puttugaṉ* . . . ; **tr.** Ēraṉputtugaṉ provided food daily for one Jaina **devotee** at Tirumalai ; *S.I.I.* III, No. 97, p. 230, ll. 3–5 ; Tirumalai, Polur Tq., N. Arcot Dt., T. Nadu St. **Dy.** Chōḷa, Parakēsari-varman, reg. yr. 4 = 911 A.D.

adikāram (T. < Skt. adhikāra, *n.*), administration; **text :** . . . *Vēlūr Bommu-Nāyakkar adikārattil* ; **tr.** under the **administration** of the Bommu-nāyakka of Vēlūr ; *S.I.I.* XXII, No. 127, p. 105, ll. 34–35 ; Jambai, Tirukkoyilur Tq., Villupuram Dt., T. Nadu St., **Dy.** Tuḷuva, Achyutadēva, Ś 1452 = 1530 A.D.

adigeya māḍu (K. *vb.*), to cook ; **text :** . . . *maṭhadalu . . . brāhmaru pratidina 1 kaṁ jana 12* ***aḍigeya māḍu****va jana 2 ubhayaṁ jana 14* ; **tr.** *brāhamaṇas* being fed in the *maṭha* every day are 12 in number ; the persons engaged **to cook** are 2 in number, the total being 14 ; *S.I.I.* VII, No. 332, p. 183, ll. 7-8 ; Mūḍakēri, Udupi Tq. and Dt., Karn. St., **Dy.** Saṅgama, Bukka I, Ś 1287 = 1365 A.D.

aḍikaḍamai (M. *n.*), taxes to be paid : **text**: *inda nilam irukalaṉē ēḻukuṟuṇiyum Biramattuvam āga Tiruviḍaikkōṭṭam Kaṉiñāṅgōḍu girāmattār vaśam kaiyyāḷikkeyil śī bhaṇḍārarkkum* ***aḍikaḍamai****yum iṟuttu* . . . . ; **tr.** land of the extent of being sown with 2 *kalam* (a grain measure) and 7 *kuṟuṇi* (a grain measure) of seeds given as *brahmatva* and entrusted to the villagers of Kaṉiñāṅgōḍu in Tiruviḍaikkōṭṭam with the stipulation that the **taxes to be paid** should be paid into the trust of the temple treasurers ; *T.A.S.* V, No. 43, p. 150, ll. 66–73, Tiruviḍaikkōḍu, Padmanabhapura Tq., Tiruvananthapuram Dt., Ker. St. **Dy.** Misc., Kollam 902, Ś 1649 = 1727 A.D.

adikāri (T. < Skt. *n.*), administrative officer ; temple official ; **text**[1] **:** . . . . *Nīlagaṅgaraiyaṉ Aṉṉāvaṇāṭṭaḍigaḷukku ivar* ***adikāri*** *Kēśavaṉambi Viṉṉappattiṉāl Tiruppaṉṟikuṉṟil Āḻvārkku* . . . *Śrīkaraṇapperuñjēriyeṉṟu kuḍiyēṭri ichchēri irukkum kuḍigaḷ śeyyum kuḍimai.* . . . . ; **tr.** Nīlagaṅgaraiyaṉ Aṉṉāvaṇāṭṭaḍigaḷ founded at the request of his administrative officer Kēśavanambi, the village of Śrīkaraṇapperuñjēri with the stipulation that those who were made the inhabitants of that village should assign the levies from that village for services to the god Āḻvār at Tiruppaṉṟikuṉṟu; *S.I.I.* XVII, No. 260, p. 103, ll. 1–8 ; Śiṅgavaram, Ginjee Tq., S. Arcot Dt., T. Nadu St. **Misc.**, in characters of 10th century A.D. ; **text**[2] **:** . . . *Tiruvallikkēṇi Teḷḷiyaśiṅgapperumāḷukku*

. . . . . *Śēṉamudaliyārum kōyil tāṉattārum* ***adikāri*** *Koppūri Obarāśayyaṉ . . . . śilāśādaṉum paṉṉikuḍuttōm* ; **tr.** we Śēṉamudaliyār, temple officials, and Koppūri Ōbarasayya the temple official dedicated this stone edict to the god Teḷḷiyaśiṅgapperumāḷ of Tiruvallikkēṉi . . . . ; *S.I.I.* VIII, No. 534, p. 271, ll. 2–3 ; Chennai, Chennai Tq. and Dt., T. Nadu St. **Dy.** Āravīḍu., Veṅkaṭapatirāya, Ś. 1521 = 1599 A.D.

adikārigaḷ[1] (T. < Skt. *n.*), an honorific surname ; **text :** . . . *Pūvaṇavaṉ Tirumāl* ***adikārigaḷ*** *pērāl Tiruvēṅgaḍadēvarkku kuḍukka ivvūr māsabai . . . kuḍutta nilam* ; **tr.** the *mahāsabhā* (administrative body of brāhmaṇa) of the place granted land to be donated to the god Tiruvēṅgaḍadēva in the name of Pūvaṇavaṉ Tirumāl-**adikārigaḷ** ; *S.I.I.* XIV, No 67, p. 45, ll. 6–7, 9 ; Vijayanārāyaṇam, Nanguneri Tq., Tirunelveli Dt., T. Nadu St. **Dy.** Pāṇḍya, Śaḍaiya- Māṟaṉ, reg. yr. 2+17, in characters of 8th cent. A.D.

adikārigaḷ[2] (T. < Skt. *n.*), officer (plural used as a mark of respect) : . . . . *Kūram . . . . āḷum sabhaiyōm Kachchipēṭṭ* ***adikārigaḷ*** *Mīṉavaṉ-mūvēndavēḷār viṭṭa vīṭṭin mēlpakkattu Īśvarālayattu tirumuṟṟatte mahāsabhai kuṟaivaṟakkūḍi irundu* ; **tr.** the village administrative body of brāhmaṇas Kūram having met in full quoram in the hall of the Īśvara temple to the west of the house donated by Mīnavaṉ-mūvēndavēḷār, the **respectful officer** of Kachchippēḍu : *S.I.I.* VII, No. 34, p. 14, l. 1, Kūram, Kanchipuram Tq., Chingleput Dt., T. Nadu. St. **Dy.** Chōḷa, Rājarāja I, reg. yr. 10 = 906 A.D.

adikārijōḍi (T. < Skt. + T. *n.*), tax payable (in cash or kind) to the officials ; **text :** . . . *inda ūṟku . . . . adikārijōḍi karaṇikkarjōḍi . . . . maṟṟum eppērpaṭṭa pala viṉiyōgaṅgaḷum . . . karpitta aḷavukku . . . . anubhavittukoḷḷavum* ; **tr.** whatever tax in cash or kind payable to the officials and to the accountant of the village (many other such incomes are mentioned) is to be enjoyed as per the quantum fixed ; *S.I.I.* VIII, No. 293, p. 161, ll. 13, 16–19, 21 ; Tiṭṭaguḍi, Vriddhachalam Tq., S. Arcot Dt., T. Nadu St. **Dy.** Saṅgama, Dēvarāya, Cy. yr. Prabhava, in characters of 15th cent. A.D.

adikāripēṟu, (T. < Skt. + T. *n.*), tax to be paid to the revenue officer ; **text :** (fragmentary) . . . . *Dēvarāyamūvarāyar śaṟuvamāṉiyam paṇṇi kuḍuttapaḍi . . . . .* ***adikāripēṟ*** *āṇa kōṟṟilakkai . . . . śaṟvamānyamāga naḍakka kaḍavadu* ; **tr.** as per the *sarvamānya* (to be respected by all) arrangements made by Dēvarāyamūvarāyar, the proceeds from (a number of levies including) **tax to be paid to the revenue officer** (also termed *koṟṟilakkai*) is to be respected by all ; *S.I.I.* XVII, No. 532, p. 218, ll. 5, 7, 9 ; Vēdāraṇyam, Tirutturaipundi Tq., Tanjavūr Dt., T. Nadu St. **Dy.** Saṅgama, Pratāpadēvarāya, Cy. yr. Vyaya = 1466 A.D.

adikāriyaḷ (T. < Skt. *n.*), temple official ; **text :**

. . . . *śrī mūlasthānattu* . . . . *Mādēvarkku vēṇḍum nivandaṅgaḷakku vuḍalāga ivvūril pārkkiṟa* ***adikāriyaḷ*** *Maṉṉaikoṇḍa-Chōḷapallavarayar tiruttiṉa nilam*. . . . . ; **tr.** land reassessed by Maṉṉaikoṇḍa-Chōḷapallavarayar, the temple official looking after the gift lands in that place belonging to the main deity Mādēva . . . ; *S.I.I.* VII, No. 467, p. 290, ll. 45–48 ; Madhurāntakam, Madhurantakam Tq., Chingleput Dt., T. Nadu St. **Dy.** Chōḷa, Vīrarājēndra, reg. yr. 5 = 1068 A.D.

adikāriyār (T. < Skt. *n.*), official referred to in respectful plural ; **text :** . . . *Śeḻiyarkōṉ nāyaṉ piḷḷai Āṇḍi adikāriyār pārupattiyattil kaṭṭaḷai iṭṭapaḍi* ; **tr.** as per the order proclaimed during his administration by Śeḻiyarkōṉnāyaṉpiḷḷai Āṇḍi, the temple **official referred to in respectful plural** . . . . . ; *S.I.I.* VIII, No. 424, p. 223, ll. 14–18 ; Tiruvādavūr, Melur Tq., Madurai Dt., T. Nadu St. **Dy.** Nāyakas of Madurai, Vīśvanāthanāyaka, Cy. yr. Rākshasa, in characters of 16th cent. A.D.

āḍikārttigai pachchai (T. *n.*), tax levied on crops harvested in the months of Āḍi and Kārttigai ; **text :** *āyamum āḷamañjiyum* ***āḍikārattigai-pachchaiyum*** *ivvāṇḍu mudal Aiyyaṉ viṭṭa paḍiye* . . . . . *viṭṭēṉ* ; **tr.** taxes such as revenued income, those derived from forced labour, **tax levied on crops harvested in the months of Āḍi and Kārttigai** were waived as per the orders of Aiyyan from the ongoing year onwards ; *S.I.I.* VII, No. 1011, p. 480, ll. 2–3 ; Tirunaṟuṅgoṇḍai, Tiṇḍivanam Tq., S. Arcot Dt., T. Nadu St. **Dy.** Chōḷa, Kulōttuṅga I, reg. yr. 9 = 1079 A.D.

aḍikāsu (K. *n.*), tax levied on shop-sites ; **text :** . . . . . *Bhairavadēvara saṁnadhiya saṁte kilavāgiralāgi pratihuṭṭisi aḷḷu aḍi-kāsu saha dravya-mukhadiṁ dēvara dīpārādhanege*. . . . . *kaṭṭaḷeyan-ikki*. . . . *biṭṭa dēvadāya* ; **tr.** the **taxes levied on shop-sites** for restoring the shandy of the god Bhairavadēva which had fallen into disuse have been made over to the god as a grant to the temple ; *S.I.I.* IX, pt. ii, No. 532, p. 547, ll. 8–10, 13-14 ; Adhamaṉkōṭṭai, Dharmapuri Tq., Salem Dt., T. Nadu. St. **Dy.** Tuḷuva, Achyutarāya, Ś. 1452 = 1530 A.D.

aḍikeya hēru (K. *n.*), head load of arecanuts ; **text :** . . . *Mallināthadēvarige koṭṭa*. . . . . *dharma aḍikeya hēru hattu* . . . ; **tr.** ten **head loads of arecanuts** were granted to the deity Mallināthadēva; *E.C.* (R) IV, Ko. 57, p. 436, ll. 14, 18 ; Kāmagere, Kollegal Tq., Chamarajanagara Dt., Karn. St. **Dy.** Saṅgama, Kaṁpaṇṇa-Voḍeya, Ś. 1288 = 1366 A.D.

aḍikkiṉṟa vāriyaṉmār (T. influenced by M. *n.*), supervisors of the cleaning of temples ; **text :** ***aḍikkiṉṟa vāriyaṉmār*** *śīvitaṁ Palelmuṭṭattu ñāḻāla-maṇiyāl koḷḷum nel muppattu muppaṟa* ; **tr.** thirty three *paṟas* (a grain measure) of paddy measured by *ñāḻāla maṇi* (name of a grain measure) in Pālelmuṭṭam for the livelihood of the **supervisors of the cleaning of the temple** ;

T.A.S. IV, No. 7, p. 51, ll. 78–79 ; Kollūrmaḍam, Suchindram Tq., Tirunelveli Dt., T. Nadu St. **Dy.** Rulers of Vēṇāḍu, Vīra-Udaiya-Mārttāṇḍavarman, Kollam 364 = 1188 A.D.

aḍikkōl (T. *n.*), measuring rod ; **text :** . . . . *Tirumalai nāyakkarum Tiruvakkarai uḍaiya-nayiṉār śrī bhaṇḍārattārum śilālekai paṇṇikkuḍuttapaḍi . . . . Śaivamaṭattukku Māyēśvara pūjeykku 24* ***aḍikkōl**āl nañjay kuḻi 500 . . . naḍakka kaḍavadāguvam* ; **tr.** grant of fertile land of the extent of 24 **measuring rods** given by Tirumalainâyakkar and the treasurers of the temple of Tiruvakkarai Uḍaiyaṉayiṉār for the Māhēśvarapūjā in the Śaiva maṭha at Tiruvakkarai as per the stone edict ; *S.I.I.* XVII, No. 211, p. 76, ll. 1–4 ; Tiruvakkarai, Villupuram Tq., S. Arcot Dt., T. Nadu St. **Dy.** Tuḷuva, Kṛishṇadēvarāya, Ś. 1437 = 1515 A.D.

ādi kraya (K. *n.*), original value ; **text :** . . . *yī brahma kshētravanu* ***ādi kraya*** *dāna parivartanake salladu. . . .* ; **tr.** this *brāhmaṇa* settlement should not be assessed on its **original value** and converted (at any later time) . . . ; *S.I.I.* IX, pt. ii, No. 421, p. 429, ll. 168, 171 ; Mōdaḷḷi, Kollegal Tq., Chamarajanagar Dt., Karn. St. **Dy.** Saṅgama., Harihara, Ś. 1313 = 1392 A.D.

aḍimai (T. *n.*), slave : **text**: *Śuchīndiram-uḍaiya-nayiṉār tiru mūṅgilaḍiyil aṉugraham āṉa kālattil-uganda* ***aḍimai****gaḷ yōgipparadēśigaḷ eṉṟu chembilum śilayilum kāṇumbaḍik . . . keykkoṇḍu* ; **tr.** the god Śuchīndiramuḍaiya Nayiṉār was pleased while seated at the foot of the sacred bamboo, to order the appointment of 23 *yōgi-paradēśigaḷ* (migrant ascetics) as **slaves** of the temple as has been engraved on copper plates and on stone ; *T.A.S.* V, No. 53, p. 169, ll. 4–6, Śuchīndram, Agasteesvaram Tq., Kanyakumari Dt. T. Nadu St. **Misc.**, Kollam 621, Ś 1367 = 1444 A.D.

aḍime (K. *n.*), slave : **text**: *Sambhunāthadēvara . . . . sthānakke Mūlibhaktanu* ***aḍime****yāgihanu* ; **tr.** Mūlibhakta is a **slave** to the temple of the god Sambhunāthadēva ; *E.C.* (R) IV, Ch. 282, p. 173, ll. 2, 6-7, Haradanahalli, Chamarajanagar Tq. and Dt., Karn. St. **Misc.**, in characters of 16th cent. A.D.

Āḍipūrappachchai (T. *n.*), perquisite payable in grain in the month of Āḍi probably on harvest : **text**: . . . . *iṉṉilaṅgaḷāl varum nelkaḍamai kāśu . . . . kāttigaippachchai* ***āḍippūrappachchai*** *Piḷḷaiyār nōṉputtevai . . . . uḷpaṭṭa ivaiyum variyilār kaṇakkilum kaḻikkumpaḍi śollivittōm* . . . . ; **tr.** we have ordered that from the lands granted the levy of paddy . . . . perquisite payable in grain in the month of Kārttigai, **perquisite payable in grain in the month of Āḍi** should be made over for the worship of the god Piḷḷaiyār ; *S.I.I.* VII, No. 22, p. 8, ll. 3–4 ; Tāramaṅgalam, Omalur Tq., Salem Dt., T. Nadu St. **Dy.** Chōḷa, Kōnērinmaikoṇḍāṉ, in characters of 11th cent. A.D.

aditāṇam (T. < Skt. *adhishṭhāna, n.*), stone bed ; **text :** . . . *Mōchi śeyida* ***aditāṇam*** *3* ; **tr.** 3 **stone**

beds made by Mōchi ; *E.T.E.*, No. 23, p. 427, l. 2 ; Toṇḍūr, Gingee Tq. Villupuram Dt., T. Nadu St. **Misc.**, in characters of 3rd cent. A.D.

āḍita (K. *n.*), lubrication an oil mill ; **text :** . . . *eṇṇeya gāṇakke . . . . ardha solligeyanu āḍitakke eṟevaru* ; **tr.** half *sollige* (liquid measure) of oil had to be poured into the oil mill (*gāṇa*) for its operation . . . . . ; *S.I.I.* IX, pt. i, No. 336, p. 357, l. 27 ; Kuḍatini, Bellary Tq. and Dt., Karn. St. **Dy.** Hoy., Ballāḷa II, Ś. 1140 = 1219 A.D.

aḍiyāṉ (T. *n.*), servant ; **text :** . . . . *Mayēndira ppotareśaru* ***aḍiyāṉ*** *Kandaśēṉaṉ* ; **tr.** Kandasēna the **servant** of Mayēndirappotareśar ; *S.I.I.* II, No. 141, p. 117, ll. 10–11, 23–24 ; Elvānāśūr, Tirukkoyilur Tq., S. Arcot Dt., T. Nadu St. **Dy.** Chōḷa, Rājēndrachōḷa I, reg. yr. 5 = 1016-17 A.D.

adiyāḷ (T. *n.*), maid servant ; **text :** . . . . . . *Iṟaiyāṉaraiyūr . . . Astradēvarkku . . . . tirunandavanan-tiruttavum pūpparikkavum Tiruvaraṅgaṉ ittēvarkku* ***aḍiyāḷ****āga kuḍutta Veḷḷāḷan tāi* ; **tr.** for the maintenance of the temple garden and for plucking flowers therein in the temple of the god Astradēva, the lord of Iṟaiyāṉaraiyūr Tiruvaraṅgaṉ donated the mother of Veḷḷāḷan as a **maid servant** ; *S.I.I.* XXII, No. 141, p. 117, ll. 10–11, 23–24 ; Elvanāśūr, Tirukkoyilur Tq., S. Arcot Dt., T. Nadu St. **Dy.** Chōḷa, Rājēndra I, reg. yr. 5 = 1016-17 A.D.

aḍiyār (T. *n.*), devotees ; **text :** . . . . *Tiruvaṇṇāmalaiyuḍayāraich-chēvikka vanda śivayōgigaḷ uḷḷiṭṭa* ***aḍiyār****ai ūṭṭuga. . . .* ; **tr.** the **devotees** including the Śivayōgis who come to offer worship to the god Tiruvaṇṇāmalaiyuḍaiyār have to be fed ; *S.I.I.* VIII, No. 68, p. 38, l. 3 ; Tiruvaṇṇāmalai, Tiruvannamalai Tq., N. Arcot Dt., T. Nadu St. **Dy.** Chōḷa, Rājēndra I , reg. yr. 27 = 1039 A.D.

aḍiyār (T. *n.*), female devotee ; **text :** . . . . *emberumāṉ* ***aḍiyār****il Cheṇḍikādēvi* ; **tr.** Cheṇḍikādēvi, a **female devotee** of the god ; *E.C.* X, Māl. 21, p. 98, l. 1 ; Tēkallu, Malur Tq., Kolar Dt., Karn. St. ; **Misc.**, Ś. 1278 = 1356 A.D.

āḍlapaṭṭu (Te. *n.*), land for sowing a particular quantity of paddy seeds ; **text :** . . . . *Bhīmaraṭṭāḍikin ichchina . . . tommidi puṭṭul-****āḍlapaṭṭu****. . .* ; **tr.** . . . **land** of the extent of **being sown with a particular quantity of paddy seeds** given to Bhīmaraṭṭāḍi . ; *S.I.I.* VI, No. 115, p. 55, l. 10 ; Chēbrōlu, Bapatla Tq., Guntur Dt., A.P. St. **Misc.**, in characters of 10th century A.D.

āḍlu (Te. *n.*), a variety of paddy ; **text :** *ēṇḍu puṭlu āḍlu* ; **tr.** a variety of paddy measuring 7 *puṭṭi* (a grain measure.) ; *I.A.P.* Cuddapah I, No. 104, p. 133, l. 21 ; Vēlpucherla, Jammalamadugu Tq., Cuddapah Dt., A.P. St. **Misc.**, in characters of 10th cent. A.D.

āḍu (T. *n.*), sheep ; **text :** (damaged) . . . . *Kūṟṟamaṅgalaṅkiḻāṉ Mādēvan . . . . vaitta* ***āḍu*** *viḷakku oṉṟu* ; **tr.** Mādēvan the headman of Kūṟṟamaṅgalam donated one **sheep** for burning a lamp ; *S.I.I.* XXII, pt. i, No. 184, p. 150, ll. 2, 4 ;

Grāmam, Tirukkoyilur Tq., S. Arcot Dt., T. Nadu St. **Dy.** Chōḷa, Parāntaka I, reg. yr. 41 = 947–48 A.D.

āḍuder̤e (K. *n.*), tax on goat ; **text :** . . . *Rāmanāthadēvara nandādīvigege* . . . . *amṛitapaḍi vīḷayakke naḍavaṁtāgi Dēvarahaḷi Kōtehaḷa maggader̤e* ***āḍuder̤e*** . . . . . *akhaṁḍanandādīvigeya* . . . . *pūjākāri naḍusuvanu* . . . ; **tr.** . . . the temple priest will arrange for the burning of the perpetual lamp and for offering services like food and betel offerings in the temple of the god Rāmanāthadēva from income from tax on looms, **tax on goat** (some more taxes are mentioned) to be collected from the villages of Dēvarahaḷi and Kōṭehaḷa ; *E.C.* (R) VIII, Ag. 45, p. 143, ll. 9–12, 17–18. ; Rāmanāthapura, Arakalagud Tq., Hassan Dt., Karn. St. ; **Dy.** Hoy., Narasiṁha III, Ś. 1197 = 1275 A.D.

aḍugabu (K. *n.*), (see also *aḍigabu* above), fire-wood used for cooking : **text:** . . . . . *Viṭhaladēvarige*. . . *nayivēdyakke* . . . . ***aḍugabu*** *aḍugari aḍugarisuva kūli saha ga 12* . . . ; **tr.** 12 gadyāṇa (a gold coin) for meeting the expenses on **firewood used for cooking**, coal including the payment for collecting coal for the purpose of offering the food to the deity Viṭhaladēva ; *S.I.I.* IX, pt. ii, p. 648, ll. 2, 5 ; Hampi, Hospet Tq., Bellary Dt., Karn. St. **Dy.** Tuḷuva, Sadāśivarāya, Ś 1476 = 1554 A.D. **; aḍugarbu** (K. *n.*), ; **text :** . . . . *Svayaṁbhū Kalidēvara sthaḷakke naḍeyisuva dharmma*. . . . . . . ***aḍugarbu*** *tiṁgaḷiṁge baṁḍi 1* . . . . . ; **tr.** one cart load of **fire-wood used for cooking** (many other donated objects are mentioned) given as a pious donation to the temple of the god Svayaṁbhū Kalidēva . ; *S.I.I.* IX, pt. i, No. 258, p. 275, ll. 24, 27 ; Bāgaḷi, Harapanahalli Tq., Bellary Dt., Karn. St. **Dy.** Chāl. of Kal., Jagadēkamalla II, reg. yr. 16 = 1153 A.D.

aḍugari (K. *n.*), cooking coal ; **text:** . . . *Viṭhaladēvarige* . . . . *nayivēdyakke* . . . . *aḍugabu* ***aḍugari*** *aḍugarisuva kūli saha ga 12* . . ; **tr.** 12 gadyāṇa (a gold coin) for meeting the expenses on fire-wood for **cooking coal** including the payment for collecting coal for the purpose of offering food to the deity Viṭhaladēva ; *S.I.I.* IX, pt. ii, p. 648, ll. 2, 5, Hampi, Hospet Tq., Bellary Dt. Karn. St. **Dy.** Tuḷuva, Sadāśiva, Ś. 1476 = 1554 A.D.

aḍugarisu (K. *vb.*), preparing coal for cooking : **text** :. . . . *Viṭhaladēvarige*. . . . *nayivēdyakke* . . . *aḍugabu, aḍugari,* ***aḍugarisu****va kūli saha ga 12* . . . ; **tr.** 12 gadyāṇa (a gold coin) for meeting the expenses on fire wood, preparing the coal for cooking including the payment for collecting coal for the purpose of offering food to the deity Viṭhaladēva ; *S.I.I.* IX, pt. ii, p. 648, ll. 2, 5, Hampi, Hospet Tq., Bellary Dt. Karn. St. **Dy.** Tuḷuva, Sadāśivarāya, Ś. 1476 = 1554 A.D.

āḍugōbhūmi (K. *n.*), grazing land for goats and cows ; **text :** . . . . *Chikkarāyasāgarada* *chatussīmeya* . . . . ***āḍugōbhūmi*** . . . . *Chikkarāyaru Ālikoṁḍa Nāgābhaṭṭarige agrahāravāgi dhāreyaneredu koṭṭubiṭṭa Chikkarāyasāgara* ; **tr.** the village of Chikkarāyasāgara (along with many other revenue incomes) including the **grazing land for goats and cows** was given as *agrahāra* (*q.v.*) to Nāgabhaṭṭa of Ālikoṁḍa by Chikkarāya; *E.C.* (R) . VII, Ml. 106, p. 409, ll. 20, 21, 29–31 ; Mutṇahaḷḷi, Malavalli Tq. Mandya Dt., Karn. St. ; **Dy.** Umm. Chfs., Mallarāja, Ś. 1428 = 1506 A.D.

aḍugūli (K. *n.***),** wages paid for cooking food ; **text :** . . . *Viṭhaladēvaru naṁma tōṭada voḷagaṇa parāṁkuśamaṁṭapake chittaisida dinagaḷu* . . . . . *142 kaṁ . . . eṇṇe tuppa, sakhare ga 1/2 aḍigabu* ***aḍugūli*** *ga 1/2* ; **tr.** provision was made for the supply of oil, ghee and sugar at a payment 1/2 *ga* (*gadyāṇa,* a gold coin) for fire wood and for payment to the cook 1/2 gold coin for services to the god Viṭhaladēva on 142 days in a year, when He visits the Parāṁkuśamaṁṭapa within our garden ; *S.I.I.* IX, pt. ii, No. 668, p. 661, l. 4, Hampi, Hospet Tq., Bellary Dt., Karn. St. **Dy.** Tuḷuva, Sadāśivarāya, Ś 1480 = 1559 A.D.

aḍugukōlu (Te. *n.*), measuring rod of one foot ; **text :** *ChitalūriYalayya Moyiḻḻakāluva gramakaṭnaṁ* ***aḍugukōlu*** *sahagānu Tiruvēṁganāṁtaniki* . . . *samarpiṁchhanu* ; **tr.** Yalayya of Chitaluru donated to the god Tiruveṁganāṁta the pasture land measured by the **measuring rod of one foot** in Moyiḻḻakāluva ; *I.A.P.* Cuddapah II, No. 124, p. 158, ll. 35–38 ; Moyiḻḻkāluva, Cuddappah Tq. and Dt., A.P. St. **Dy.** Tuḷuva, Achyutarāya, Ś. 1458 = 1536 A.D.

aḍukkaḷaikāṇī (M. *n.*), land granted for maintaining kitchen (of the temple) ; **text :** ***aḍukkaḷaikāṇi****yāga* . . . . *Mattiyūr* . . . *araikkaṇiyum* ; **tr.** 1/2 *kāṇi* (a land measure) of **land** at Mattiyūr was **granted for maintaining the kitchen** (of the temple) ; *T.A.S.* IV, No. 44, p. 154, ll. 6–7 ; Āṟṟūr, Padmanabhapuram Tq., Tiruvananthapura Dt., Ker. St. **Misc.**, Kollam 821 = 1646 A.D.

aḍumane (K. *n.*), lumber room for storing fire wood ; **text :** . . . . *śrī Naṁjuṁḍēśvaradēvarige* . . . *Kalukaṇiya grāmake saluva* . . . . ***aḍumane*** *muṁtāda sarvasvāmyasahavāgi* (further text damaged) ; **tr.** for the god Naṁjuṁḍēśvaradēva (were given) a number of grants to be respected by all including the **lumber room for storing firewood**. . . . . ; *E.C.* (R) VII, Ml. 146, p. 444, ll. 11–13 ; Kalkuṇi, Malavalli Tq., Mandya Dt., Karn. St. ; **Dy.** Umm. Chfs., Naṁjarāya-oḍeya, Ś. 1433 = 1511 A.D.

āḍusuṁka (K. *n.*), tax on sheep ; **text :** *yī mūṟu grāmada chatussīmeyoḷaguḷa gade bedalu tōṭa* ***āḍusuṁka*** *enuṁṭāda sakala ādāyavanu anubhavisikoṁḍu* ; **tr.** enjoying all incomes from the wet land, dry land, garden, **tax on sheep** from within the four boundaries of the 3 villages ; *E.C.* (R) III, Gu. No. 23, p. 22, ll. 10–11 ; Masahaḷḷi, Gundlupet Tq., Mysore Dt., Karn.

St. **Dy.** Tuḷuva, Sadāśiva, Ś. 1468 = 1546 A.D.

āḍutiṟai (T. *n.*), tax on sheep ; **text :** . . . . . . *Jommaṇṇa Uḍaiyār kāṇikkai sārigai magamai* . . . . ***āḍutiṟai***. . . . *maṟṟum ivvūr nāyaṉārkku dhārāpūrvvamāga* . . . ; **tr.** Jommaṇṇa Uḍaiyār waived taxes such as tributes, transporation tax, *magamai* (a kind of tax), **tax on sheep** etc., as gift to the god with the pouring of water of libation . . ; *E.C.* X, Chin. 99, l. 14 ; Kaivāra, Chintamani Tq., Kolar Dt., Karn. St. **Dy.** Saṅgama, Jommaṇṇa Uḍaiyār, Ś. 1296 = 1374 A.D.

aḍuva brāhmaṇa (K. *n.*), brāhmaṇa cook ; **text :** . . . . *maṭhadalu uṁba brāhmaṇa ja 5 ā chatrada* ***aḍuva brāhmaṇa****ru jana 1 ubhayaṁ jana 6* . . . ; **tr.** five brāhmaṇas taking food in the maṭha and one brāhmaṇa cook of the choultry comprising in all six persons ; *S.I.I.* VII, No. 346, p. 201, ll. 11–12 ; Chauḷikēri, Udupi Tq. and Dt., Karn. St. **Dy.** Saṅgama, Virūpāksha, Ś. 1397 = 1475 A.D.

aḍuvala (K. *n.*), pasturage ; **text :** . . . *agrahārada* . . . ***aḍuvala****da bhūmiya chatussīme* . . . . ; **tr.** the four boundaries of pasturage of the brāhmaṇa settlement ; *M.A.R.* 1931 , No. 58, p. 163, ll. 58–59 ; Mūḍala agrahāra, Chamarajanagara Tq. and Dt., Karn. St. **Dy.** Tāyūrnāḍ. Chfs, Perumāḷadēva, Ś. 1335 = 1413 A.D.

aḍuvāṉ (T. *n.*), cook ; **text**[1] **:** . . . ***aḍuvāṉ*** *oruvaṉukku niśadi nel aññāḻi* . . . . ; **tr.** for one **cook** a daily allotment of 5 *nāḻi* (a grain measure) of paddy ; *S.I.I.* III, pt. iii, No. 106, p. 240, l. 15 ; Āṉaimalai, Madurai Tq. and Dt., T. Nadu St. **Dy.** Chōḷa, Parāntaka I, reg. yr. 33 = 1040 A.D. ; **text**[2] **:** . . . *uppu miḷagukkum pākkukkum veṟṟilaikkum* ***aḍuvāṉ****ukkum ariśi aripaṉukkum-āga muṉṉāḻiyāga niśadaṁ kuṟuṇi nel* . . . . ; **tr.** one *kuṟuṇi* (a grain measure) of paddy daily measured by *muṉṉāḻi* (3 units of a grain measure called *naḻi*) for expenses on salt, pepper, arecanuts, betel leaves, **cook** and the rice-winnower . . . . ; *S.I.I.* VIII, No. 677, p. 340, ll. 14–15 ; Allūr, Tiruchirapalli Tq. and Dt., T. Nadu St. **Dy.** Chōḷa, Rājēndra I, reg. yr. 4 = 1016 A.D. ; **aḍuvār** (T. *n.*), cooks ; **text :** . . . . ***aḍuvār****kku nellu kuṟuṇiyum* . . ; **tr.** one *kuṟuṇi* (a grain measure) of paddy for the **cooks** . . . ; *S.I.I.* VIII, No. 66, p. 34, l. 10 ; Tiruvaṇṇāmalai, Tiruvannamalai Tq., N. Arcot Dt., T. Nadu St. **Dy.** Chōḷa, Rājēndra I, reg. yr. 19 = 1031 A.D.

āḍuvaṇa (K. *n.*), tax on sheep ; **text :** . . . *Rāmanāthadēvara śrīkāryakke ā Narasiṁha-maṁgalavanu siddhāya* . . . . ***āḍuvaṇa*** *magga kāṇike muṁtāda ellā kiṟukuḷavanu biṭṭu* ; **tr.** having granted all the minor taxes such as the permanent tax, **tax on sheep**, tax on looms, tributes etc., from Narasiṁhamaṁgala for the performance of religious activities in the temple of the god Rāmanāthadēva ; *E.C.* (R) IV, Ch. 295, p. 191, ll. 28–31, 33–35 ; Narasamaṅgala, Chamarajanagara Tq. and Dt., Karn. St. **Dy.** Hoy., Ballāḷa III, Ś. 1258 = 1337 A.D.

aḍuvava (K. *n.*), cook ; **text :** . . . *Chōḷiyakēriya*

Kellaṁgereya taṁma tōṭada maṭhada chchatradalli vuṁba brāhamaru 12 ***aḍuvavan*** *obba aṁtu 13 kaṁ māḍida dharmmada bāḷina vivara* . . . . . ; **tr.** the details of land granted for the feeding of 12 brāhmaṇas and one **cook** totalling 13 persons at the choultry of the *maṭha* in the grove of Kellaṁgere of Chōḷiyakēṟi . . . . ; *S.I.I.* VII, No. 387, p. 243, ll. 8–9 ; Kōṭakēri, Udupi Tq. and Dt., Karn. St. **Dy.** Saṅgama, Bukkarāya, Ś. 1294 = 1372 A.D.

aḍuvina maṇṇu (K. *n.*), clay soil ; **text :** . . *Būveyanāyaka* . . . *haḍuvaṇa tūbina modalēriyalu 1 1/2 khaṁḍuga bayalmaṁ 2 khaṇḍuga* ***aḍuvina maṇṇu****maṁ Padmaṇaṁdidēvarige* . . . *biṭṭu koṭṭa* . . . . ; **tr.** Būveyanāyaka granted 1 1/2 *khaṁḍuga* (a grain measure) of open field and two *khaṁḍuga* of land with **clay soil** under the western sluice of the first lake to Padmaṇaṁdidēva . . ; *E.C.* (R) VIII, Hn. 135, p. 96, ll. 7–15 ; Gubbi, Holenarasipura Tq., Hassan Dt., Karn. St. ; **Dy.** Koṅgāḷvas., Tribhuvanamalla Chōḷakoṅgāḷva, in characters of 11th–12th cent. A.D.

aḍuvu (K. *n.*), grazing ground ; **text**[1] **:** . . . *Nandigundarge dānaṁgoṭṭudu Kesugoḷada mājanaṁ onda****ḍuvu*** *Mardūroḷ* . . . ; **tr.** one **grazing ground** in Mardūr was given to Nandigundar by the *mahājana* (an administrative body of brāhmaṇas) of Kesugoḷa. ; *E.C.* (R) III, HD Kote 90, p. 498, ll. 36–37 ; Saragūru, Heggadadevanakote Tq., Mysore Dt., Karn. St. **Dy.** W. Gaṅga, Śrīpurusha, in characters of the 8th cent. A.D. ; **text**[2] **:** . . . *Kaṁmaravaḷḷiya Vaḷagere tōṭa beddalu* ***aḍuvu*** *sahā kaṁ gu 84 haṇavina bhūmi* . . . . ; **tr.** land worth *kaṁ* (*kaṁba*, a land measure) gu (*guṁṭe*, a land measure) 84 *haṇa* (a coin) which include garden, dry land and grazing ground in the tank-bed of Kaṁmaravaḷḷi. ; *E.C.* (R) V, Mys. 213, p. 315, ll. 22–23 ; Māṇikyapura, Mysore Tq. and Dt., Karn. St. **Dy.** Woḍ. of Mys., Chikkadēvamahārāya, Ś. 1607 = 1685 A.D.

aḍvobbe (K. *n.*), cross-wise fence ; **text :** . . . *Haḷimuḷūra* ***aḍvobbe****yiṁ kālveyiṁ teṁkaṇa* . . . . *haḷḷa.* . . . ; **tr.** the stream running southwards from the **cross-wise fence** and the canal of Haḷimuḷūru ; *E.C.* (R) V, T.N. No. 225, p. 605, ll. 12–13 ; Kaliyūru, T. Narasipura Tq., Mysore Dt., Karn. St. **Dy.** Tuḷuva., Kṛishṇadēvarāya, Ś. 1445 = 1521 A.D.

agaḷa (K. *n.*), breadth ; **text :** . . . . *Rēvagāvuṁḍaṁ māḍisida Śivālayaṁgaḷge pūje punaskāra nivēdya jīrṇṇōddhārakkameṁdu biṭṭa bhūmi 56 gēṇu ghaḷeyim nīḷada bhujeyaṁ dviguṇisiy-****agaḷa****doḷ-oṁdaṁ kūḍi guṇisuv-ī kramad-aḷateyalu.* . . . . *koṭṭaru.* . . . ; **tr.** for the conduct of worship, other services, offering of food and repair works in the Śiva temples built by Rēvagāvuṁḍa, land measured by the measuring rod of the length of 56 *gēṇu* (a span's length) in arm's length and double of that in **breadth**, thus being the method of calculating area of gift land ; *S.I.I.* IX, pt. i,

No. 249, p. 257-58, ll. 75–77 ; Kōlūr, Bellary Tq. and Dt., Karn. St. **Dy.** Chāḷ. of Kal., Jagadēkamalla II, reg. yr. 10 = 1147 A.D.

agaḷi (K. *n.*), ditch ; **text :** . . . *ā bāḷina chatusīme teṁkalu hoḷeyiṁdaṁ baḍagalu* ***agaḷiṁdaṁ*** *teṁkalu mūḍalu hosa māḍida gaddeyiṁdaṁ paḍuvalu Hāykana . . bāḷa gaḍiyindaṁ mūḍalu* . . . . ; **tr.** the four boundaries of the gift land are ; in the south to the north of the stream, to the south of the **ditch**, to the east of the newly cultivated paddy field, to the east of the boundary of the field belonging to Hāyka ; *S.I.I.* VII, No. 319, p. 169, ll. 15–18 ; Hampi, Hospet Tq., Bellary Dt., Karn. St. **Dy.** Saṅgama, Bukka I, Ś. 1293 = 1371 A.D.

agaḷisu (K. *vb.*), dig up ; **text :** . . . . *keṟeyoḷage bāviyan**agaḷisi** Sōmatīrthameṁdu pesaraniṭṭu pūdōṁṭaṁ nandanavanamumam iṭṭu Noḷaṁbēśvaradēvarige koṭṭar* . . . ; **tr.** having **dug up** the well within the tank and renaming it as Sōmatīrtha, it was donated to the god Noḷaṁbēśvaradēva along with a flower garden and a garden ; *S.I.I.* IX, pt. i, No. 104, p. 79, ll. 32–33 ; Mōrigēri, Bellary Tq. and Dt., Karn. St. **Dy.** Chāḷ. of Kal., Sōmēśvara I, Ś. 967 = 1046 A.D.

agaḷu (K. *n.*), ditch : **text :** . . . *hanneraḍu kōlagalada pramāṇinalu* ***agaḷu*** . . . . ; **tr.** a **ditch** dug out to the width of 12 measures of the measuring rod ; *S.I.I.* IX, pt. ii, No. 457, p. 469, l. 37 ; Basarūru, Kundapur Tq., Udupi Dt., Karn. St. **Dy.** Saṅgama, Mallikārjuna, Ś. 1377 = 1455 A.D.

agampaḍikuḍi (M. *n.*), the inhabitants of the temple waiting for offering service ; **text :** *tirunāḷil* ***agampaḍikuḍi*** *varunna āḷ parichārakāṟarkku ariśippaḍi paṇam padineṭṭu* ; **tr.** for the temple **inhabitants waiting for offerings services** to the god, one measure of rice and 18 *paṇam* (coin) are earmarked ; *T.A.S.* IV, pts. i and ii, No. 15, p. 87, l. 14 ; Āṟṟūr, Padmanabhapuram Tq., Tiruvanantapuram Dt., Ker. St. **Dy.** Chieftains of Kīḻappērūr, Vīra-Ravi-Udayamārttāṇḍavarman, Ś. 1173 and Kollam 426 = 1251 A.D.

agampaḍimudaligaḷ (T. *n.*), male and female domestic officers of the palace : **text :** *tiruvāśalil* ***agaṁpaḍimudaligaḷil*** *peṇḍugaḷukkum vidvāṉukkuṁ* (text incomplete) . . ; **tr.** among the male and female domestic officers of the palace, the female officers and the learned persons . . . ; *S.I.I.* IV, No. 319, p. 88, l. 2 ; Tiruvallam, Gudiyattam Tq., N. Arcot Dt., T. Nadu St. **Dy.** Śambuvarāya, Veṉṟumaṇkoṇḍa Śambuvarāyar, reg. yr. 16, in characters of 12th cent. A.D.

agampaḍipeṇḍugaḷ (T. *n.*), maids-in-waiting ; **text:** . . . *Aṉuppattūr-**agampaḍipeṇḍugaḷiṟ**-Kaḷappāḷa Nāchchi* ; **tr.** Kaḷappāḷa Nāchchi among the **maids-in-waiting** in Aṉuppattūr ; *S.I.I.* VII, No. 104, p. 44, l. 4, Tiruvottūr, Cheyyar Tq., N. Arcot Dt., T. Nadu St. **Dy.** Kāḍava, Kōpperuñjiṅga, reg. yr. 22 = 1264 A.D.

agaṁḍḍadīpamu (Te. < Skt. *akhaṇḍadīpa, n.*), perpetual lamp ; **text :** . . . . . . *Nāgireḍiki annalu*

Mallayyareḍiki Mēḍayareḍikini dharmamugānu beṭṭina śilākaṁbamunu ***agaṁḍḍadī pamunu*** ... ; **tr.** a stone pillar and a **perpetual lamp** dedicated for the merit of Nāgireḍḍi, his elder brothers Mallayyareḍḍi and Mēḍayareḍḍi ; *S.I.I.* X, No. 511, p. 278, ll. 6–8 ; Mōgallu, Bhimavaram Tq., West Godavari Dt., A.P. St. **Misc.**, Ś. 1237 = 1315 A.D.

āgāmi (K. < Skt. *n.*), prospective (land yet to be brought under cultivation in future) ; **text :** ... *Māyaṁṇagaḷa makkaḷu Gaṁgaṁṇagaḷige keṟeya keḷagaṇa hiriya haḷḷadalu kīḻērige biṭṭa sthaḷa* ***āgāmi*** *saha ..... gadde bījavari 10 koḷaga* ... . . ; **tr.** to Gaṁgaṁṇa son of Māyaṁṇa was granted **land yet to be brought under cultivation in future** of the extent of being sown with 10 koḷaga (a grain measure) of seed under the tank in the major stream below the lake ; *S.I.I.* IX, pt. ii, No. 440, p. 449, ll. 33–34 ; Rajabavanahaḷḷi, Harapanahalli Tq., Bellary Dt., Karn. St. **Dy.** Saṅgama, Dēvarāya, Ś. 1341 = 1419 A.D.

agampaḍiyār (T. *n.*), person belonging to agambadi community : **text**: ***agampaḍiyāril*** *Tandirapālaṉ Periyuḍayān ēn* ... ; **tr.** I, Tandirapālan Periyuḍa-yānēṉ **belonging to the agaṁpaḍiyār community**; *E.C.* X, Mb. 53, p. 56, l. 2, Muḷubāgilu, Muḷubagilu Tq., Kolar Dt., Karn. St. **Dy.** Pallalva, Dantivikrama, reg. yr. 21 = 1225 A.D.

agampaḍimaṟamudali (T. *n.*), leader of the agampaḍimaṟavar community : **text**: ***agampaḍi maṟamudali****gaḷil Nāṟṟaṉ periyaṉāṇa Vīramaḻagiya Pallavarayyaṉ* .... ; **tr.** Nāṟṟaṉ *alias* Vīramaḻagiya Pallavarayyaṉ, **leader of the agampadimaṟavar community** ; *I.P.S.* 1929, No. 181, p. 104, ll. 4–5, Kuḍumiyāmalai, Kulattur Tq., Pudukkottai Dt., T. Nadu St. **Dy.** Chōḷa, Rājādhirāja III, reg. yr. 5 = 1221 A.D.

agamuḍaiyāḷ (T. *n.*), wife ; **text**[1] **:** .... *Tiruvēṅgaḍattiṉ* ***agamuḍaiyāḷ*** *Kāṟaikkālammaiyēṉ inNāyanāṟkku Tai-māsam mudal nittam-oṟu tiruviḷakku .... Tirumalai mēle eriyakkaḍavadāga .... kuḍutta kāśu 15* ; **tr.** 15 *kāśu* (a coin) endowed by Kāṟaikkālammai the **wife** of Tiruvēngaḍam for burning a lamp every day for the god Nāyaṉār on the hill-top from the commencement of the month of Tai ; *S.I.I.* XXII, pt. i, No. 145, p. 122, ll. 3–6 ; Eḷavānāśūr, Tirukkoyilur Tq., S. Arcot Dt., T. Nadu St. **Dy.** Chōḷa, Kulōttuṅga I, reg. yr. 2 = 1072 A.D. ; **text**[2] **:** .... *Pērāyūrkkuṉṟaṁ kiḻān Ādināthaṉ Uḍaiyāṉ* ***agamuḍaiyāḷ*** *Udaiyañcheydāḷ Uḍaiyār Tirukkāḷatti Uḍaiyārku vaitta śandiviḷakku iraṇḍu* .... ; **tr.** two twilight lamps donated to the temple of the god Tirukkāḷatti Uḍaiyār by Udaiyañcheydāḷ the wife of Ādināthaṉ Uḍaiyāṉ, the headman of the village Pērāyūrkuṉṟam ; *S.I.I.* VIII, No. 477, pp. 250–51, ll. 2–5 ; Kāḷahasti, Kalahasti Tq., Chittoor Dt., A.P. St. **Dy.** Chōḷa, Kulōttuṅga I, reg. yr. 19 = 1089 A.D.

aganāḻigai (T. *n.*), *sanctum sanctorum* of the temple ; **text :** *Kaḍigaipaṭṭinattu uḍaiyār Kaṟai-*

kkaṇḍīśvaramuḍaiya Mahādēvaṟku ***aganāḻigai*** *śelavu kaṟpichcha ariśi irunāḻi* ; **tr.** two *nāḻi* (a grain measure) of rice earmarked for food offerings within the ***sanctum sanctorum*** **of the temple** of the god Kaṟaikkaṇḍīśvaramuḍaiya Mahādēva of Kaḍigaipaṭṭinam ; *T.A.S.* IV, No. 13, p. 82, ll. 1–2; Tirunayinārkuṟichchi, Eraniel Tq., Padmanabhapuram Dt., Ker. St. **Dy.** Rulers of Vēṇāḍu, Ravi Kēraḷavarmaṉ, Kollam 395 = 1217 A.D. ; **aganāḻigaiyār** (T. *n.*), committee in charge of *sanctum sanctorum* of the temple ; **text :** .. *Tiruppōttuḍaiyāḻvār* ***aganāḻigaiyār*** *Munnūṟruvaṉ-Chēndaṉum āṉa Nakkaṉ* ..... *sakalaśivaṉum* ... .. *Tiruppōttuḍaiy-āḻvārkku vaitta Tirunondāviḷakku oṉṟukku niśadi uḻakku ney* ; **tr.** one *uḻakku* (a liquid measure) of ghee donated to the temple of the god Tiruppottuḍaiy-āḻvār by Munnūṟṟuvaṉ Śēndan *alias* Nakkaṉ Sakalaśivaṉ a member of the **committee in charge of the *sanctum sanctorum*** of the temple for burning a perpetual lamp ; *S.I.I.* XIV, No. 36, p. 28, ll. 15–30 ; Ambāsamudram, Ambasamudram Tq., Tirunelveli Dt., T. Nadu St. **Dy.** Pāṇḍya, Māṟañjaḍaiyaṉ, reg. yr. 35, in characters of 9th cent. A.D.

āgāntuka (K. *n.*), a kind of tax ; **text :** .... *Ballāḷamahīkāṁtana* ... *maṁtrivallabhaṁ Ballayaṁ santata Jina pūjaneg-**āgāntuka**maṁ Bhōgavadiya basadige biṭṭa* .... ; **tr.** Ballaya the minister of king Ballāḷa, gave the income from **the tax called *āgāntuka*** for conducting constant worship of the Jina at Bhōgavadi ; *E.C.* VII, Ng. 184, p. 184, l. 3 ; Bōgādi, Nagamangala Tq., Mandya Dt., Karn. St. **Dy.** Hoy., Ballāḷa II, Ś. 1095 = 1173 A.D.

agapparivāram (T. *n.*), group of temple attendants; **text :** .... *Piḷḷaiyār Aḻagapperumāḷ* ***agapparivāra****ttu Ulagaḷandāṉ Aḻagapperumāḷāṉa Avaṉi-Nārāyaṇadēvaṉ* ; **tr.** Avaṉi-Nārāyaṇadēva *alias* Ulagaḷandāṉ Aḻagapperumāḷ belonging to the **group of temple attendants** of the god Piḷḷaiyār Aḻagapperumāḷ ; *S.I.I.* VIII, No. 431, p. 225, l. 5 ; Pirāṉmalai, Tiruppattur Tq., Ramnad Dt., T. Nadu St. **Dy.** Pāṇḍya, Kulaśēkhara, reg. yr. 13+14 = 1295 A.D.

agappiṇavar (T. *n.*), the name of a community ; **text :** *Śekkār uḻukkaikku mēṟkkum* ***agappiṇavar*** *teṟuvukku vaḍakkum* ... ; **tr.** to the south of the street of the Śekkār community and to the north of the street of **agappiṇavar community** ; *S.I.I.* XVII, No. 588, p. 255, ll. 7–8 ; Tiruvārūr, Nagapattinam Tq., Tanjavur Dt., T. Nadu St. **Dy.** Chōḷa, Rājādhirāja II, reg. yr. 5 = 1167 A.D.

agappoduvāḷ (T. influenced by M. *n.*), manager of temple affairs ; **text :** *Peruṅṅaṉmalaiyil mēṟpaḍiyūr viruttikku* ***agappoduvāḷ*** ..... *Māmbaḷḷi* .... *koḷḷun nel irupadu paṟa* .... ; **tr.** for the development of the village Peruṅṅaṉmalai, the **manager of temple affairs** took possession of 20 *paṟa* (a grain measure) of paddy from Māmbaḷḷi ; *T.A.S.* IV, No. 7, p. 52, ll. 96–98 ; Kollūrmaḍam, Padmanabhapuram Tq.,

Tiruvanantapuram Dt., Ker. St. **Dy.** Rulers of Vēṇāḍu, Udaiya Mārttāṇḍavarman, Kollam 364 = 1188 A.D.

āgara (K. *n.*), a salt pan, land, territorial division, a grove, temple, ; **text**[1] : . . . . *dēvara* ***āgara****da kaṟukeya teṁkakaḍeya hosamaṁṭapada uppin-* ***āgara****da gēṇiyiṁ varusha 1 kaṁ baha rokka ga* (*gadyāṇa*, a gold coin) *6* . . . . ; **tr.** the annual lease income realised from the **salt pan** of the new *maṁṭapa* on the southern side of the lawn of the temple is 6 gold coins ; *S.I.I.* IX, pt. ii, No. 409, p. 416, ll. 21–22 ; Kōṭēśvara, Kundapur Tq., Udupi Dt., Karn. St. **Dy.** Saṅgama, Bukka I, Ś. 1287 = 1365 A.D. ; **text**[2] : . . . . *Paḍuvakēriya halaru Rudrāksha Oḍeyarige mūlava koṭṭa* ***āgara****da mēle ayivara dharma naḍavadu* . . . . . ; **tr.** the charity for the 5 donors will be effected from the **land** given to Rudrāksha Oḍeya by the *halaru* (an administrative body) of Paḍuvakēri ; *S.I.I.* IX, pt. ii, No. 473, p. 488, ll. 15–17 ; Basarūru, Kundapur Tq., Udupi Dt., Karn. St. **Dy.** Saṅgama, Virūpāksha, Ś. 1408 = 1487 A.D. ; **text**[3] : *Iṁmaḍi Chikarāya Oḍeyaru* . . . . . *nāvu āḷuva Hadināḍa* ***āgara****ke saluva Kuṁtūra grāmake ēnu uḷḷa sarvasvāmyavanu āgumāḍikoṁḍu* . . . . *koṭṭaru* ; **tr.** Chikarāya Voḍeya II made a gift of all the privileges enjoyed by the Kuṁtūru village which belonged to the **territorial division** called hadināḍu which was under his administration ; *S.I.I.* IX, pt. ii, No. 701, p. 689, ll. 4, 8, 12, 16 ; Kuntūru, Kollegal Tq., Chamarajanagara Dt., Karn. St. **Dy.** Umm. Chfs., Iṁmaḍi Chikarāya Oḍeya, Ś. 1434 = 1512 A.D.

agarabrahmadēyam (T. < Skt. *agrahāra-brahmadēya*, *n.*), a brāhmaṇa settlement ; **text** : . . . . *Kēraḷaśiṅgavaḷanāṭṭu* ***agarabrahmadēyam*** . . . . . *Ambalattāḍichatupēdimaṅgalameṉṉum pērāl iruvadu brāhmaṇarkku Tōrāpati-vēḷāṉ śeyda dhammam* ; **tr.** Tōrāpati-vēḷāṉ created a **brāhmaṇa settlement** called Ambalattāḍichatupēdimaṅgalam in Kēraḷaśiṅga-vaḷanāḍu for 20 brāhmaṇas ; *S.I.I.* XIV, No. 243, p. 149, ll. 3, 8 ; Śivapuri, Tiruppattur Tq., Ramanathapuram Dt., T. Nadu St. **Dy.** Pāṇḍya, Jaṭāvarman Śrīvallabha, reg. yr. 18, in characters of 12th cent. A.D. ; **agarachchīmai** (T. < Skt. *agrahārasīmā*, *n.*), defined area of brāhmaṇa settlement ; **text** : *Udaiya Mārttāṇḍavarmmar* . . . . *Śōḻakulavallipurattu Vīramārttāṇḍachaturvvēdi maṅgalameṉṟu nam pērāl vaiytta* ***agarachchīmai****yil pudiya vīṭṭil nām vīḍāyirundu* **tr.** We, Udaiya Mārttāṇḍavarmman having taken up residence in the new house in the **defined area of the brāhmaṇa settlement** created and named after us as Vīramārttāṇḍachaturvēdimaṅgalam in Śōḻakula- vallipuram ; *T.A.S.* IV, No. 19, p. 100, ll. 9–11, Tōvāḷai, Suchindram Tq., Kanyakumari Dt., T. Nadu St. **Dy.** Rulers of Vēṇāḍu, Vīramārttāṇḍa- varmma, Kollam 708 = 1533 A.D.

agara iṟaiyili (T. *n.*), tax free brāhmaṇa settlement; **text** : (text obscure) . . . . *paṅgu aimbattāṟum* *agara iṟaiyiliyāga* ; **tr.** 56 shares (of land) granted **tax free to brāhmaṇa settlement** ; *S.I.I.* VII, No. 57, p. 25, ll. 20–21 ; Viḷāppākkam, Walajapet Tq., N. Arcot Dt., T. Nadu St. **Dy.** Śambuvarāya, Śaṁbuvarāyaṉ, in characters of the 11th cent. A.D.

agaram (T. < Skt. *agrahāra, n.*), brāhmaṇa settlement ; **text**[1] : .... *Mudaliyār Tiruvaiyāṟuḍaiyār Tillaināyakacharupēdimaṅgalam eṉṉum tirunāmattāl vaitta agarattu brāhmaṇar* ; **tr.** the brāhmaṇas of the **brāhmaṇa settlement** created by Mudaliyār Tiruvaiyāṟuḍaiyār and given the name of Tillaināyaka-charupēdimaṅgalam ; *S.I.I.* VIII, No. 43, p. 21, ll. 2–3 ; Chidambaram, Chidambaram Tq., S. Arcot Dt., T. Nadu St. **Dy.** Kāḍava, Kōpperuñjiṅga, reg. yr. 36, in characters of 13th cent. A.D. ; **text**[2] : ... *Vāṇagōppāḍināṭṭu Maṟuvūr* ***agara****ttu mahāsabhaiyār pakkal vilaikoṇḍa-nilamāvadu* .... ; **tr.** land purchased from the members of the *mahāsabhā* (an administrative body of brāhmaṇas.) of the **brāhmaṇa settlement** Maṟuvūr in Vāṇagōppāḍināḍu ; *S.I.I.* VII, No. 128, p. 54, l. 11, Tirukkōyilūr, Tirukkoyilur Tq., S. Arcot Dt., T. Nadu St. **Dy.** Pāṇḍya, Vikrama Pāṇḍya, reg. yr. 8 = 1257 A.D. ; **text**[3] (M. *n.*) : *Bhūtappāṇḍi* ***agara****ttu Mādēvaṉ puttiraṉ Śūriya-nārāyaṇapaṭṭar uḷḷiṭṭārukku kalpichchukkoḍutta tuliyam* ; **tr.** a convention given in favour of Mādēvaṉ's son Suryanārāyaṇapaṭṭar and others of the **brāhmaṇa settlement** Bhūtappāṇḍi ; *T.A.S.* V, No. 32, p. 124, ll. 69–71, Vaḍaśēri, Keralapuram Tq., Tiruvanantapuram Dt., Ker. St. **Misc.**, Kollam 945 = 1769 A.D.

agara oṭṭu (T. *n.*), payment of taxes in brāhmaṇa settlements as per agreement ; **text :** (text obscure) .... *Vīrapperumāḷmaṅgalam nilam oṟu māvināl nellu muppattiēḻu kalam* ***agara oṭṭu****paḍi nellu padinaiṅkalam ēḻu kuṟuṇi* ; **tr.** as per the **agreement on payment of taxes in brāhmaṇa settlement** on 37 *kalam* (a grain measure) of paddy from one *mā* (a land measure) of land at Vīrapperumāḷmaṅgalam 15 *kalam* of paddy is to be paid as levy ; *S.I.I.* VIII, No. 56, p. 30, l. 14 ; Chidambaram, Chidambaram Tq., S. Arcot Dt., T. Nadu St. **Dy.** Kāḍava, Kōpperuñjiṅga, reg. yr. 16, in characters of the 12th cent. A.D.

agarappaṟṟu (T. *n.*), land attached to brāhmaṇa settlement ; **text :** .... *Jayaṅgoṇḍachōḻamaṇḍalattu nāṭṭavar.... kaḍamai iṟukkum iḍattu dēvadāṇamum tiruviḍaiyāṭṭamum paḷḷichchandamum* ***agara-ppaṟṟum*** *vaṉṉiya paṟṟum jīvita paṟṟum paḍai-paṟṟum uṭpaḍa daṇḍavariśey-aḍiyil .... aṟukala tuṇḍamum viṭṭōm* ..... ; **tr.** the *Nāṭṭavar* (administrative body of nāḍu) of Jayaṅgoṇḍa-chōḻamaṇḍalam remitted 6 *kalam* (a grain measure) of revenue income from land donated to temples, for temple festivals, to Jaina temples, **lands attached to brāhmaṇa settlements**, lands donated to the agriculturists, for livelihood and for the maintenance of the army, in whichever case such taxation is permissible ; *S.I.I.* XVII, No. 714, p. 341, ll. 3–14 ; Rāmagiri, Tiruvaḷḷūr Tq., Chingleput Dt., T. Nadu St. **Dy.** Pottappi-Chōḷa, Madhurāntaka, reg. yr. 2, in characters of 11th-12th cent. A.D.

agasa (K. *n.*), washerman ; **text :** .... *baḍagalū* ***agasa****ra-bāviya baḷiya baṁḍe mēre* .... ; **tr.** on the north, the boundary is the boulder near the well of the **washerman** ; *S.I.I.* IX, pt. ii, No. 668, p. 661, l. 2, Hampi, Hospet Tq., Bellary Dt., Karn. St. **Dy.** Tuḷuva, Sadāśiva, Ś. 1480 = 1559 A.D.

agasālyayaru (K. *s.a. akkasāleyaru, n.*), goldsmiths; **text :** .... *koṭṭa guttige jāga ā guttigeyāgiruva sandakke teruvudu bidageyaṟu gadya* 5 ***agasālyayaru*** *ga 8 kammāraru ga 8 nāyindaru ga 8* ..... ; **tr.** on the land leased out, the bamboo workers will pay a rental of 5 *gadyā*, (*gadyāṇa*, a gold coin) **goldsmiths** will pay a rental of 8 *ga*, the blacksmiths will pay a rental of 8 *ga* and the barbers will pay a rental of 8 *ga* ; *E.C.* (R) IV, Yl. No. 134, p. 348, ll. 9–11 ; Agara, Yelanduru Tq., Chamarajanagara Dt., Karn. St. **Misc.**, in characters of the 14th cent. A.D.

agasara bāvi (K. *n.*), well used by washermen ; **text :** .... *baḍagalu* ***agasara bāvi****ya baḷiya baṁḍe* .... ; **tr.** on the north, the boulder near the **well used by washermen** .... ; *S.I.I.* IX, pt. ii, No. 11, p. 661, l. 2 ; Hampi, Hospet Tq., Bellary Dt., Karn. St. **Dy.** Tuḷuva, Sadāśivarāya, Ś. 1480 = 1559 A.D.

agasara kāluve (K. *n.*), canal used by washermen; **text :** *teṁkalu* ***agasara kāluve*** *mēle* ; **tr.** the **canal used by the washermen** is the boundary in the south ; *S.I.I.* IX, pt. ii, No. 11, p. 661, l. 2; Hampi, Hospet Tq., Bellary Dt., Karn. St. **Dy.** Tuḷuva, Sadāśiva, Ś. 1480 = 1559 A.D.

agattār (T. *n.*), persons attached to the palace ; **text :** (text obscure) .... *Viṇṇakōvarayyar* ***agattār*** ; **tr.** **persons attached to the palace** of Viṇṇakōvarayyar ; *S.I.I.* XII, No. 42, p. 17, l. 7 ; Toṇḍūr, Ginjee Tq., S. Arcot Dt., T. Nadu St. **Dy.** Pallava, Dantivikrama, reg. yr. 6, in characters of 8th cent. A.D.

agavāṟu (T. *n.*), inner bank of a river ; **text :** .... *mēlellai* .... ***agavāṟ****ṟaṭṭagattukku kiḻakku* ; **tr.** the western boundary is to the east of a land portion adjoining the **inner bank of the river** ; *S.I.I.* XIV, No. 19, p. 19, ll. 24–26 ; Tirukkuṟuṅguḍi, Nanguneri Tq., Tirunelveli Dt., T. Nadu St. **Dy.** Pāṇḍya, Māraňjaḍaiyaṉ, reg. yr. 4, in characters of the 8th cent. A.D.

agavāy (T. *n.*), inner canal ; **text :** .... *ivvūr* ***agavāy****in Veṅgūr nālāṅkaṇṇāru* ; **tr.** the fourth branch of the **inner canal** at Veṅgūr ; *S.I.I.* XIII, No. 287, p. 154, ll. 5–6 ; Tiruverumbūr, Tiruchira- palli Tq. and Dt., T. Nadu St. **Dy.** Chōḷa, Āditya I, reg. yr. 19 = 890 A.D.

agaviṉai (T. *n.*), free labour ; **text :** .... *śennīrkk****agaviṉai*** *śeyyādadāgavum* ; **tr.** getting the canal excavated through **free labour** is proscribed ; *S.I.I.* V, No. 518, p. 206, l. 9 ; Tiruvaiyyār, Tanjavur Tq. and Dt., T. Nadu St. **Dy.** Chōḷa, Rājarāja I, reg. yr. 21 = 1006 A.D.

agayāṟu (T. *s.a. agavāṟu above, n.*), inner bank of a river ; **text :** . . . . *Kaḍuvāyāṟraṅgaraiyil vaḍapakkattilum tenpakkattilum kamuguniṉṟa nilattilum* ***agayāṟ****ṟupaḍugaiyilum* ; **tr.** in the arecanut groves on the northern and southern banks of the river Kaḍuvāy and in the land on the **inner bank of the river** ; *S.I.I.* XVII, No. 604, p. 272, l. 5 ; Tiruvārūr, Nagapattinam Tq., Tanajavur Dt., T. Nadu St. **Dy.** Chōḷa, Kulōttuṅga III, reg. yr. 39 = 1217 A.D.

aggaḷa (K. *n.*), army ; **text :** *Bidirūra* ***aggaḷa****miḷivalli . . . . kādida Bidayitta sattan* ; **tr.** when the army invaded Bidirūru Bidayitta fought and died ; *E.C.* X, Srp. 27, p. 348, l. 23 ; Hebbaṭa, Srinivasapura Tq., Kolar Dt., Karn. St. **Dy.** Noḷ. Pal., Noḷaṁbādhirāja, in characters of 9th cent A.D.

agghavaṇi (K. < Skt. *arghyapāni, n.*), sacred water for anointing the god's image ; **text :** *aysāvantaru dēvar****agghavaṇi****ya bindigege āvagegalana koṭṭaru;* **tr.** the *aysāvantas* (a group of 5 subordinate chiefs) donated a pot burnt on the potter's kiln for collecting the **sacred water for anointing the god's image** ; *K.I.* VI, No. 73, p. 212, l. 75 ; Saundatti, Saundatti Tq. Belgaum Dt., Karn. St. **Dy.** Raṭṭas of Saundatti, Lakshmidēva, Ś. 1151 = 1228 A.D.

aggishṭige (K. < Skt. *agnishṭhikā, n.*), traditional religious portable fire-pan ; **text :** . . . . *mahājana Saṁjamaṭhake* ***aggishṭige****ge koṭṭa gadyāṇa mūru;* **tr.** for the maintenance of a **traditional religious portable fire-pan** in the Saṁjamaṭha, the *mahājana* (an administrative body of brāhmaṇas) gave 3 *gadyāṇa* (gold coin) ; *E.C.* (R) V, TN. 69, p. 460, l. 2 ; Bannūru, T. Narasipura Tq., Mysore Dt., Karn. St. **Dy.** Hoy., Vishṇuvardhana, Ś. 1058 = 1135 A.D.

agi (K. *vb.*), to sink (a well), to dig ; **text :** . . . *Periyāḷuvaseṭṭi Heṁjeṟa paṭṭaṇadalu udakadāna nimittavāgi* ***agi****dappa bāviyan agaḷisi tat-samīpadalu samasta dēsiy-anumatadiṁ Dēsīśvaradēvara pratishṭheyaṁ māḍi. . . . .* ; **tr.** Periyāḷuvaseṭṭi having deepened the already **dug** well for purposes of supply of water and having installed, in the vicinity of the well, the image of the god Dēsīśvara with the permission of the commercial guild called Dēsi in the town of Heṁjeṟa ; *S.I.I.* IX, pt. i, No. 268, p. 286, ll. 40–48 ; Hēmāvati, Madakasira Tq., Anantapur Dt., A.P. St. **Dy.** Chāḷ. of Kal., Taila III, Ś. 1084 = 1162 A.D.

agisu (K. *vb.*), to dig ; to sink (a well) ; **text :** . . *Narasarājanu . . . . Virupākshadēvara guḍi garbhagṛiha sukhanāsi raṁgamaṁṭapavanu kaṭisi bāviyanū* ***agisi*** *māvina tōpanu ikkistanu . . .* ; **tr.** Narasarāja got the temple of Virūpākshadēva along with the *sanctum sanctorum, sukanāsi* (porch in front of the *sanctum* of a temple) and the entertainment hall built, **got a well sunk** and planted a mango grove ; *S.I.I.* IX, pt. ii, No. 477, p. 492, ll. 19–24 ; Gulya, Alur Tq., Bellary Dt., Karn. St. **Dy.** Tuḷuva, Kṛishṇadēvarāya, Ś. 1430 = 1509 A.D.

agitam (T. < Skt. *ahitaṁ, adj.*), hindrance ; **text:** .... *idukku* ***agitam*** *paṇṇiṉavaṉ tāyai koṉṟa pāvam koḷvāṉ* ; **tr.** whoever creates **hindrance** to the implementation of the grant would have, in effect, committed the sin of having killed his own mother ; *S.I.I.* XXII, No. 88, p. 83, ll. 18-20 ; Jambai, Tirukkoyilur Tq., S. Arcot Dt., T. Nadu St. **Dy.** Tuḷuva, Sadāśiva, Ś. 1477 = 1555 A.D. ; **agutam** ; **text** : *idukku agutam paṇṇiṉavaṉ Gaṅgaikkaraiyil kārāmpaśuvaiyum taṉṉiḍa tāyi tagappaṉaiyum guruvaiyum koṉṟavan pāvattile pōgakkaḍavāṉāgavum*; **tr.** whoever creates **hindrance** to the implementation of this grant would have, in effect, committed the sin of having killed tawny cows, his own parents and teacher on the banks of the river Ganges ; *S.I.I.* XXII, No. 103, p. 93, l. 6 ; Jambai, Tirukkoyilur Tq., S. Arcot Dt., T. Nadu St. **Dy.** Tuḷuva, Achyutarāya, Ś. 1454 = 1532 A.D.

āgñāparipālaka (K. < Skt. *ājñāparipālaka, n.*), one who carries out his master's orders ; **text :** *Hoysaḷanāḍa Piriyarasakaḷa āgñāparipālakarāda Sōvarasaru* .... ; **tr.** Sōvarasa **who carries out the orders of his master** Piriyarasa of Hoysaḷa-nāḍu ; *E.C.* (R) V, T.N. 143, p. 553, ll. 6–7 ; Vijayapura, T. Narasipura Tq., Mysore Dt., Karn. St. **Dy.** Saṅgama, Dēvarāya, Ś. 1348 = 1426 A.D.

agnishṭage (K. < Skt. *n.*), traditional religious portable fire-pan ; **text :** ..... *agrahāraṁ Tuṁbuḷada mahājanaṁ nūranālvadiṁbargaṁ* .... *biṭṭa dharma ūralu dharmavattaḷeyāgi tiṟuva siddhāyada ponnoḷage* ..... *agnishṭageya brāhmaṇaṅge gadyāṇav-eṟaḍu* .... ; **tr.** as per the grant handed over to the care of the 140 *mahājana* (an administrative body of brāhmaṇas) of the *agrahāra* (brāhmaṇa settlement) Tuṁbuḷa, from the permanent tax in the form of gold earmarked for charitable purposes, two *gadyāṇa* (gold coin) are to be paid to the brāhmaṇa who maintains the **traditional religious portable fire-pan** ; *S.I.I.* IX, pt. i, No. 175, p. 169, ll. 18–20, 24-25 ; Chinnatuṁbaḷam, Adavani Tq., Kurnool Dt., A. P. St. **Dy.** Chāḷ. of Kal., Vikramāditya VI, Ch. Vi. yr. 32 = 1107 A.D.

agrabhōjanam (T. < Skt. *n.*), first offering of temple food to brāhmaṇas : **text** : . . . *iddēvar kōyililē Karuṇākaraṉ śālai* ***agrabhōjaṇattukku*** *kalam aiñjukku ariśi kuṟuṇi iruṇāḻikkum nel mukkuṟuṇi oṟu nāḻi* .... ; **tr.** in the Karuṇākaraṉ dining hall of the temple, for the first feeding of caste brāhmaṇas were alloted 1 *kuṟuṇi* (a grain measure) and 2 *nāḻi* (a grain measure) of rice measuring 5 *kalam* (a grain measure) and derived from paddy measuring 3 *kuṟuṇi* and 1 *nāḻi* ; *S.I.I.* VII, No. 409, p. 260, l. 9, Teṉṉēri, Kanchipuram Tq., Chingleput Dt., T. Nadu St. **Dy.** Chōḷa,

Kulōttuṅga I, reg. yr. 41 = 1111 A.D.

agrahāra (Skt. *n.*), brāhmaṇa settlement ; **text**[1] : ..... *mantrī sa eva matimān Pāṇḍyasya Parāntakābhidhānasya amitarddhiṁ agrajēbhyaḥ prādādimam-agrahāram* ... ; **tr.** the intelligent minister of Pāṇḍya Parāntaka gave a very rich *agrahāra* to the brāhmaṇas ; *S.I.I.* XIV, No. 1, p. 1, ll. 3–6 ; *Ep. Ind.* VIII, p. 320 ; Āṉaimalai, Madurai Tq. and Dt., T. Nadu St. **Dy.** Pāṇḍya, Parāntaka, Kali 3871 = 770 A.D. ; **text**[2] (K. < Skt.) : ...... *piriyagrahāraṁ Bāguḷiya aivadiṁbaru* .... *Kalidēvaroḷagaṇa Narasiṁhadēvara amṛitapaḍige Kaṭṭaḷakeṟeya keḷage koṭa kaṁba 10*..... ; **tr.** 10 *kaṁba* (a land measure) of land under the tank called Kaṭṭaḷakeṟe was donated by the Fifty (*mahajana*, an administrative body of brāhmaṇas) for providing food service to the god Narasiṁhadēva of the temple of Kalidēva in the major **brāhmaṇa settlement** ; *S.I.I.* XVII, No. 93, p. 22, ll. 1–3, 5–7 ; Bāgaḷi, Harapanahalli Tq., Bellary Dt., Karn. St. **Misc.**, Cy. yr. Plava = 1031 A.D. ; **text**[3] : ..... *Kōgaḷināḍoḷesevudu nānāvidvajjana sthāna Nīrggundavenip agrahāravatyānandakāri jagakellaṁ*. ... ; **tr.** within the territorial division called Kōgaḷināḍu, there flourished a **brāhmaṇa settlement** called Nīrggunda where a number of learned residents lived and thereby was a source of pleasure to the entire world ; *S.I.I.* IX, pt. i, No. 141, p. 124, ll. 10–12 ; Nīlagunda, Harapanahalli Tq., Bellary Dt., Karn. St. **Dy.** Chāḷ of Kal., Vikramāditya VI, Ch. Vi. yr. 4 = 1079 A.D. ; **text**[4] (Skt. *n.*), : ... *Kāvērī Kapilā nadīpravilasat kshētrē* ... *prakhyāta śriyam**agrahāram** akarochchhrī Kṛishnarājājñayā* ... ; **tr.** in the excellent area of the region of Kāvērī and Kapilā, on the orders of Kṛishṇarāja, a blissful **brāhmaṇa settlement** was created ; *E.C.* (R) IV, Ch. 291, p. 180, ll. 49–50 ; Haradanahaḷḷi, Chamarajanagar Tq. and Dt., Karn. St. **Dy.** Woḍ. of Mys., Kṛishṇarāja II, Ś. 1666 = 1744 A.D. ; **agrahāraṁ** (Te. < Skt. *n.*), brāhmaṇa settlement; **text**[5] : (text damaged) . ..... *Chilumakūru Śirigirirājupalle **agrahāram*** ; **tr.** the **brāhmaṇa settlement** called Śirigirirājupalle in Chilumakūru ... ; *S.I.I.* XVI, No. 148, p. 158, ll. 61–62 ; Chilama- kūru, Kamalapuram Tq., Cuddapah Dt., A.P. St. **Dy.** Tuḷuva, Sadāśiva, Ś. 1469 = 1546 A.D. ; **text**[6] : ***agrāhārada** mahājanaṁgaḷu viśēsha pūjegāgi* .... *samarpisida vṛitti 1*.... ; **tr.** 1 share of land granted by the *mahājana* of the **brāhmaṇa settlement** for conducting special worship ; *S.I.I.* IX, pt. ii, No. 514, p. 529, ll. 17–18; Kurikuppe, Hospet Tq., Bellary Dt., Karn. St. **Dy.** Tuḷuva, Kṛishṇadēvarāya, Ś. 1445 = 1523 A.D.

agrahāraṁbulu (Te. < Skt. *n.*), brāhmaṇa settlements ; **text** : .... *iruvādinālgu **agrahārambulu*** ..... ; **tr.** 24 **brāhmaṇa settlements** ; *I.A.P.* Cuddappah I, No 100, Second Side ll. 3–4, p. 126, Arakaṭavēmula, Proddatur Tq., Cuddapah Dt., A.P. St. **Dy.** Tel. Chōḍa, Chidyaṇa, in characters of

10th cent. A.D. ; **anādi agrahāra** (K. < Skt. *n.*), brāhmaṇa settlement in existence from time immemorial ; **text :** .... *śrīmad* ***anādi agrahāram.*** *Taḷilūra aśēshamahājanaṁgaḷa samakshamadalli . . . . Madhusūdanadēvara saṁje soḍariṁge... aydu haṇa.* . ; **tr.** five *haṇa* (a coin denomination) granted for the lighting of evening lamp for the god Madhusūdana made in the presence of all the *mahajanas* (an administrative body of brāhmaṇas) of Taḷilūru, the **brāhmaṇa settlement in existence from time immemorial** ; *E.C.* (R) X, No. 166, p. 220, ll. 1–3 ; Taḻalūru, Arasikere Tq., Hassan Dt., Karn. St. **Misc.**, Ś. 1142 = 1220 A.D.

agrajāḥ (Skt. *n.*), brāhmaṇas ; **text :** . . . . *mantrī sa eva matimān Pāṇḍyasya Parāntakābhidhānasya amitarddhiṁ* ***agrajēbhyaḥ*** *-prādād-imam-agrahāram.* .... ; **tr.** the intelligent minister of Pāṇḍya Parāntaka gave a very rich *agrahāra* to the **brāhmaṇas** ; *S.I.I.* XIV, No. 1, p. 1, ll. 3–6 ; *Ep. Ind.* VIII, p. 320 ; Āṉaimalai, Madurai Tq. and Dt., T. Nadu St. **Dy.** Pāṇḍya, Parāntaka, Kali 3871 = 770 A.D.

agrajaṁ (K. < Skt. *n.*), first born son ; **text :** . . . . *Chāḷuky-ābharaṇaṁ śrī Jayasiṁhavallabh-* ***āgrajaṁ*** . . . . *Āhavamalladēva* . . . . ; **tr.** Āhavamalladēva, the **first born son** of Jayasiṁhavallabha, the ornament of the Chāḷukya dynasty ; *S.I.I.* IX, pt. i, No. 101, p. 71, ll. 2–3, Mōrigēri, Hadagalli Tq., Bellary Dt., Karn. St. **Dy.** Chāḷ. of Kal., Āhavamalla, Ś. 967 = 1045 A.D.

agraje (K. < Skt. *n.*), eldest daughter ; **text :** . . . . *Kṛishṇarājana sati saṁtānite Padmaladēvi mahīnutan****agraje*** *Mahēśa daṁḍādipana* ; **tr.** Padmaladēvi the wife of Kṛishṇarāja bestowed with progeny was the **first born daughter** of Mahēśa *daṇḍādhipa* ; *S.I.I.* IX, pt. i, No. 213, p. 215, ll. 54–55, Tripurāntakam, Markapuram Tq., Kurnool Dt., A.P. St. **Dy.** Chāḷ. of Kal., Vikramāditya VI, Ch. Vi. yr. 51 = 1126 A.D.

agramahishī (Skt. *n.*), crowned queen ; **text :** . . *śrīmad Buddha mahīśvar****āgramahishī*** *Guṁḍāṁbikā suvratā* ..... ; **tr.** Guṁḍāṁbikā of good character who was the **crowned queen** of the illustrious Buddha-mahīśvara; *S.I.I.* IV, No. 680, p. 211, ll. 6–7, Nādeṇḍla, Narasaraopet Tq., Guntur Dt., A.P. St. **Misc.**, Ś. 1093 = 1171 A.D.

agrapūje (K. < Skt. *n.*), first honour ; **text :** *ā viprōttamaroḷage kaḷāvidaratyamaḷakīrtti-kāntādhiparurvīvandyar****agra pūjege*** *tāvadhipar-Pemmagēriy ayvattayvaru* ; **tr.** the fifty five (*mahājana*) of Pemmagēri who were the best among the brāhmaṇas, skilled in the arts, the lords of the lady of fame, revered in the world were entitled for the first honours ; *K.I.* V, No. 24, p. 92, ll. 33–34 ; Naragund, Naragund Tq., Dharwar Dt., Karn. St. **Dy.** Chāḷ. of Kal., Sōmēśvara III, reg. yr. 13 = 1138 A.D.

agraputraṁ (K. < Skt. *n.*), eldest son ; **text :** . . . *Iṟiva Noḷambādhirājaṁ pṛithvī rājyaṁ geyyuttire tatpāda padmōpajīviy* ***agraputraṁ*** *Chhaladaṁka-*

kār̤aṁ . . . ; **tr.** Chhaladaṁkakār̤a, the **eldest son** and the worshipper at the feet of his father Ir̤iva Nol̤ambādhirāja who was ruling the earth ; *S.I.I.* IX, pt. i, No. 30, p. 17, ll. 9–13, Kambadūru, Kalyanadurga Tq., Anantapur Dt., A.P. St. **Dy.** Noḷ. Pal., Ir̤iva Nol̤ambādhirāja, Ś. 887 = 965 A.D.

agrāsana (K. < Skt. *n.*), first seat of honour earmarked for brāhmaṇas ; **text** : . . . *ayvadiṁbara sannidhānadoḷ Svayaṁbhu-Kalidēvasvāmiy-agrāsanada brāhmaṇara satrakke vīsamam biṭṭar* . . . . . . ; **tr.** one *vīsa* of money was gifted in the august presence of 50 (*mahājana*) for the **first seats of honour earmarked for the brāhmaṇa** in the dining hall of the temple of the self born god Kalidēvasvami ; *S.I.I.* IX, pt. i, No. 168, p. 162, ll. 30–31, Bāgaḷi, Harapanahalli Tq., Bellary Dt., Karn. St. **Dy.** Chāḷ. of Kal., Vikramāditya VI, Ch. Vi. yr. 28 = 1103 A.D.

agrasutaṁ (Skt. *n.*), eldest son ; **text** : . . *Noḷaṁba Ghaṭeyaṁkakār̤adēvaṁ tasya* ***agrasutaṁ*** . . . *Jagadēkamalla Noḷamba-Udayādityadēvaṁ* . . . . ; **tr.** Jagadēkamalla Noḷaṁba Udayādityadēva, the **eldest son** of Noḷaṁba Ghaṭeyaṁkakār̤adēva ; *S.I.I.* IX, pt. i, No. 101, p. 71, ll. 6–7, Mōrigēri, Hadagalli Tq., Bellary Dt., Karn. St. **Dy.** Chāḷ. of Kal., Āhavamalla, Ś. 967 = 1045 A.D.

agratanaya (Skt. *n.*), eldest son ; **text** : . . . . *Jagadēkamalla Noḷamban-Udayādityadēvaṁ tasya* ***agratanayam*** *Jagadēkamalla Noḷaṁbaṁ* . . . ; **tr.** Jagadēkamalla Noḷaṁba, the **eldest son** of Jagadēkamalla Noḷaṁban-Udayādityadēva ; *S.I.I.* IX, pt. i, No. 101, p. 71, ll. 6–7, Mōrigēri, Hadagalli Tq., Bellary Dt., Karn. St. **Dy.** Chāḷ. of Kal., Āhavamalla, Ś. 967 = 1045 A.D.

agratanūja (K. < Skt. *n.*), eldest son ; **text** : . . *Chhaladaṅkakār̤an-ātana* ***agratanūjaṁ*** . . . . *śrīmat Pol̤alchōradēvam* . . . . . ; **tr.** the illustrious Pol̤alchōradēva, the **eldest son** of Chhaladaṅkakār̤a; *S.I.I.* IX, pt. i, No. 30, p. 17, ll. 13–14, 33–34, Kambadūru, Kalyanadurga Tq., Anantapur Dt., A.P. St. **Dy.** Noḷ. Pal., Ir̤iva Nol̤ambādhirāja, Ś. 887 = 965 A.D.

agrātmaja (K. < Skt. *n.*), eldest son ; **text** : . . *Kauṁḍilya gōtrōdbhavanenisida Mārttāṇḍa dēvaṁge* . . . . *Chākāṁbikeg-udayisida* ***agrātmajaṁ*** *Sāyidēvaṁ* . . . . ; **tr.** Sāyidēva, the **eldest son** born to Mārttāṇḍadēva of Kauṇḍilya gōtra and Chākāṁbikā ; *S.I.I.* IX, pt. i, No. 297, p. 325, l. 57, Kurugōḍu, Bellary Tq. and Dt., Karn. St. **Dy.** Kal. of Kal., Śaṅkhavarmadēva, Ś. 1099 = 1177 A.D.

āhaḷa (K. *n.*), community of smiths ; **text** : . . . . . *yī dharmavanu āvanobba aḷipidavanu* . . . . . . ***āhaḷ****akke horagu* . . . ; **tr.** he who destroys (the provisions of) this grant will be ostracised from the **community of smiths**; *E.C.* (R) III, Gu. 17, p. 18, l. 4 ; Guṇḍlupēṭe, Gundlupet Tq., Mysore Dt., Karn. St. Commercial guild, Ś. 1294 = 1372 A.D.

āhaḷader̤ige (K. *n.*), tax on the community of smiths ; **text** : . . . . *ōjugaḷa ter̤ige dāsugaḷa ter̤ige* ***āhaḷader̤ige*** *asagara ter̤ige* . . . . *muṁtāda sarvva* *teṟige* . . . ; **tr.** all taxes including those on sculptors, slaves, the **community of smiths** and washermen, etc. ; *E.C.* (R) III, Gu. 134, p. 97, ll. 16–17 ; Triyaṁbakapura, Gundlupet Tq., Mysore Dt., Karn. St. **Dy.** Tuḷuva, Krishṇadēvarāya, Ś. 1444 = 1521 A.D.

āhāradāna (K. < Skt. *n.*), free feeding ; **text**[1] : . . . . *Noḷaṁbēśvaradēvar aṁgabhōga pūje punaskāra snāna nivēdyakkam ondu bhāgaṁ illiya divya tapōdhanar-**āhāradāna**kkam ondu bhāga vidyādānakkakam ondu bhāga* . . . . . . ; **tr.** one share of the grant was earmarked for the services to the image and for the entertainment of the god Noḷaṁbēśvara and also for the god's worship, bathing, offering of food etc., one share of the grant was earmarked for the **free feeding** of asectics and one share of the grant was earmarked for free education ; *S.I.I.* IX, pt. i, p. 111, ll. 37–39 ; Guḍihaḷḷi, Harapanahalli Tq., Bellary Dt., Karn. St. **Dy.** Chāḷ of Kal., Trailōkyamalla, Ś. 987 = 1065 A.D. ; **text**[2] : . . . . *Daṁḍanāyaka Dāsimarasaru* . . . . . . *Basadiya khaṁḍasphuṭita jīrṇṇōddhārakkaṁ dēvatā pūjegaṁ munijan-āhāradānakkaṁ* . . . . . *biṭṭa ī dharmma* . . . . . ; **tr.** Daṁḍanāyaka Dāsimarasa gave this grant to the Jaina temple for repairs and renovation, for worship of the deity and for **free feeding** of the ascetics ; *K.I.* V, No. 25, pp. 96-97, ll. 21, 33–35 ; Kolhāpur, Kolhapur Tq. and Dt., Maha. St. **Dy.** Chāḷ. of Kal., Jagadēka malla II, reg. yr. 2 = 1139 A.D. ; **text**[3] : . . . . ***ahāradāna**ke biṭṭa bastiya muṁdaṇa gadde*. . . ; **tr.** donation of wet land in front of the Jaina temple for **free feeding** ; *K.I.* III, No. 9, l. 14 ; Bastimakki, Bhatkal Tq. and Dt., Karn. St. **Dy.** Tuḷuva, Krishṇadēvarāya, Ś. 1461 = 1538 A.D.

ahitam (T. < Skt. *n.*), hindrance ; **text** : . . . . *inda dharmattukku ahitam śeydavaṉ* . . *guruvum mātāpitāvaiyum vadai śeydavaṉ* . . . ; **tr.** whoever creates hindrance to this grant would have, in effect, killed his preceptor and parents ; *S.I.I.* VIII, No. 439, p. 230, l. 21 ; Pirāṉmalai, Tirupattur Tq., Ramnathapuram Dt., T. Nadu St. **Dy.** Tuḷuva, Achyutarāya, Ś. 1422 = 1500 A.D.

āhava (K. < Skt. *n.*), war ; **text** : . . . . *Ballāḷaṁ Vishṇunṛipāḷakan-Udayādityaneṁba mūvarum-udārar-**āhava** dhīrar* ; **tr.** all the three viz., Ballāḷa, Vishṇunṛipāḷaka and Udayāditya were munificent and brave in **war** ; *E.C.* (R) X, Ak. 162, pp. 215–16, ll. 11–13 ; Taḷalūr, Arasikere Tq., Hassan Dt., Karn St. **Dy.** Hoy., Vīraballāla, in characters of 12th cent. A.D.

aikamatya (K. *n.*), unanimity ; **text** : . . . . *mahāgrahāraṁ Māṁgoḷad ūroḍeya pramukha-mahājanav innūrvaruṁ aikamatyadiṁ* . . . *anubhavisuttamire* . . . ; **tr.** when the 200 *mahājana* (an administrative body of brāhmaṇas) lead by the village-head were enjoying the rights over the village Māṁgoḷa with **unanimity** ; *S.I.I.* IX, pt. i, No. 195, p. 190, ll. 18–20 ; Raṅgapuram, Hadagalli

Tq., Bellary Dt., Karn. St. **Dy.** Chāḷ. of Kal., Vikramāditya VI, Ch. Vi. yr. 41 = 1116 A.D.

aindalai maṇi (T. *n.*), a hand bell with five heads ; **text :** . . . . . *Tiruvaṇṇāmalai uḍaiya Nāyaṉār Tirukkōvilil* . . . . ***aindalai maṇi** iḍugaiyāl* . . . ; **tr.** the grant of a **hand bell with five heads** to the holy temple of the god Tiruvaṇṇāmalai uḍaiya Nāyanār ; *S.I.I.* VIII, No. 151, p. 68, ll. 3-4 ; Tiruvaṇṇāmalai, Tiruvannamalai Tq. and Dt., T. Nadu St. **Dy.** Chōḷa, Kulōttuṅga III, Ś. 1124 = 1202 A.D.

aindram (T. < Skt. *n.*), vehicle on which the deity is taken in procession ; **text :** . . . . *ittēvaṉ ēṟi valam śeiyya aindram* ; **tr. vehicle on which the deity is taken in procession** with the image of the deity mounted on it ; *S.I.I.* XXII, No. 135, p. 110, ll. 9-10 ; Eḷavānāśūr, Tirukkoyilur Tq., S. Arcot Dt., T. Nadu St. **Dy.** Chōḷa, Rājēndra I, reg. yr. 13 = 1024-25 A.D.

aiñjiraṇḍu vaṇṇam (T. *n.*), 2 X 5 units of a grain measure ; **text :** . . . . *mūnṟusandhikkuṁ kuttalariśi paṉṉir ṉāḻi kuttalarisiyāl **aiñjiraṇḍu vaṇṇam** oru nāḻikku vanda nellu eḻutūmbiruṉāḻi* ; **tr.** for the three services in the temple, **2X5 units of grain measure** of de-husked rice was donated to the tune of 7 *tūmbu* (a grain measure) and 2 *nāḻi* (a grain measure) of paddy ; *S.I.I.* VIII, No. 521, p. 267, ll. 33-37 ; Guḍimallam, Gudiyattam Tq., N. Arcot Dt., T. Nadu St. **Dy.** Chōḷa, Rājarāja I, reg. yr. 4 = 989 A.D.

aiññūṟṟuvar (T. *n.*), a body of five hundred members ; **text :** . . . *Pramōda saṁvatsarattu Vaikāsi māsam inda nānādēśikaiyiṟ ponnaṟakkoṇḍu aiññuṟṟvarum maṉṉaṟakkuḍuttu* (incomplete) . . . ; **tr.** in the month of Vaikāśi in the cyclic year Pramōda, **the body of five hundred** purchased land from *nānādēśi* (trade guild doing business in different countries) by paying gold and made the same tax free grant ; *E.C.* (R) IV, Yl. 158, p. 361, ll. 12-15 ; Māmbaḷḷi, Yelandur Tq., Chamarajanagar Dt., Karn. St. **Dy.** Hoy., Vīranarasiṁha, Cy. yr. Pramōda = 1330 A.D.

ainūrbbar (K. *n.*), a merchant guild of five hundred (known as five hundred *svāmis* of Ayyāvoḷe) ; **text :** . . . . *Saraṭapurada ayvadiṁbarge* . . . *ōleya Chandiganuṁ Gāḷiganuṁ modalāge ainūrbbaruṁ tuppavanuḷidōr* . . ; **tr.** the **merchant guild of five hundred** including Chandiga the messenger and Gāḷiga donated ghee to the body known as *ayvadiṁbar* (*q.v.*) of Saraṭūr ; *S.I.I.* XI, pt. i, No. 12, p. 8, ll. 12-15, Soraṭūr, Gadag Tq. and Dt., Karn. St. **Dy.** Rāshṭr., Amōghavarsha I, Ś. 788 = 867-68 A.D. **ainūrvaru** (K. *n.*), a body of five hundred members : **text :** (text damaged) . . . . . *dīpāvaḷigeyalu śrī Sōmēśvara dēvarige iṁnūrvvaruṁ aynūrvvaruṁ neredirdu* . . ; **tr.** (perhaps records the grant) made to the god Sōmēśvara by the two bodies known as the two hundred and five hundred who had gathered for the purpose on the occasion of dīpāvaḷi ; *S.I.I.* IX, pt. i, No. 194, p. 189, ll. 36–37, Māgoḷa, Hadagalli Tq., Bellary Dt., Karn. St. **Dy.** Chāḷ. of Kal., Vikramāditya VI, Ch. Vi. yr. 41 = 1116 A.D.

aiśvarya (K. < Skt. *n.*), wealth ; **text :** .... *idanāvaṁ pratipāḷipaṁ ... ātaṁge .... **aiśvaryamuṁ** śauryyamuṁ mudamuṁ .. śāśvatamāgi nilke ...* ; **tr.** whoever protects (this grant) he will enjoy **wealth,** bravery and happiness permanently ; *S.I.I.* IX, pt. i, No. 277, p. 299, ll. 42–44 ; Malkāpuram, Adavani Tq., Kurnool Dt., A.P. St. **Dy.** Chāḷ. of Kal., Sōmēśvara III, Ś. 1106 = 1184 A.D.

aivaru samasta halaru (K. *n.*), five members of a body called *samasta halaru* ; **text :** ...... *Chōḷikēriya aivaru samasta halaru koṁḍāḍuvaṁthā Kellaṁgeṟeya Vināyaka dēvara saṁnidhi* ..... ; **tr.** in the holy presence of the god Vināyaka of Kellaṁgeṟe, Who is celebrated by the **five members of the body called *samasta halaru*** ..... ; *S.I.I.* VII, No. 347, p. 203, l. 9 ; Chauḷikēri, Udupi Tq. and Dt., Karn. St. **Dy.** Saṁgama, Harihara, Ś. 1309 = 1387 A.D.

aivadimbaru (K. *n.*), a body consisting of fifty members ; **text** : .. *ī dharmavan **aivadiṁbaruṁ.** ... pratipāḷisuvar* .... ; **tr.** the **body consisting of fifty members** shall protect this gift ; *S.I.I.* IX, pt. i, No. 89, p. 60, ll. 22–23, Bāgaḷi, Harapanahalli Tq., Bellary Dt., Karn. St. **Dy.** Chāḷ. of Kal., Jayasiṁha II ; Ś. 957 = 1035 A.D.

aiyyanavar (K. *n.*), a suffix added to male names ; **text :** .... *Dēvaṁṇa **aiyyanavar**ige nāku vṛitti.* ..... ; **tr.** four shares (of the land grant) given to Dēvaṁṇa **aiyyanavar** ; *E.C.* (R) XIII, Tīr. 212, p. 570, l. 41 ; Mēgaravaḷḷi, Tirthahalli Tq., Shimoga Dt., Karn. St. **Dy.** Saṅgama, Dēvarāya I, Ś. 1339 = 1417 A.D.

ājiraṁga (K. *n.*), battle-field ; **text[1] :** (damaged). . . . ***ājiraṁga**doḷ* ....; **tr.** in the **battle-field** ; *S.I.I.* IX, pt. i, No. 247, p. 251, l. 19, Śrīnivāsapuram, Harapanahalli Tq., Bellary Dt., Karn. St. **Dy.** Chāḷ of Kal., Jayasiṁha II., Cy. yr. Prabhava = 1147 A.D. ; **text[2] :** ...... *Vikramāṁkana Kahaḷāravaṁ nuḍiyutirpudu **ājiraṁga**dalu* .... ; **tr.** the sound of the bugle of Vikramāṁka is resounding in the **battle-field** ; *S.I.I.* IX, pt. i, No. 276, p. 297, l. 36, Mannera-Mosaḷevāḍa, Harapanahalli Tq. Bellary Dt., Karn. St. **Dy.** Kal. of Kal., Rāya- nārāyaṇa Āhavamalla, reg. yr. 4 = 1183 A.D.

ajja (K. *n.*), an elder ; **text :** .... *Chōḷikēriya halara gaḍiyiṁdaṁ paḍuvalu ajjara Vishṇumayyara gaḍiyiṁdaṁ mūḍalu yiṁtī gaḍiy-oḷage gadde mū 1/2* ... ; **tr.** 1/2 *mū* (a grain measure) of paddy field within the boundaries having the field of *halaru* (a group of traders) of Chōḷikēri in the west and the boundary of the field belonging to the **elder** Vishṇumayya in the east ; *S.I.I.* VII, No. 389, p. 246, ll. 26–27, Hosakēri, Udupi Tq. and Dt., Karn. St. **Dy.** Tuḷuva, Sadāśiva, Ś. 1491 = 1569 A.D.

ājñādhāraka (K. < Skt. *n.*), an officer who

carries out the royal order ; **text**[1] : . . . . *Veṁkaṭapatimahārāyaru . . . . . sakalarājyavanu pratipālisutta yidda kāladali avara* ***ājñādhāraka****rāda Keḷadi Veṅkaṭappanāyakarū Tuḷurājaya Malerājyavanu . . āḷuva kāladali* . . ; **tr.** when Veṁkaṭapatimahārāya was ruling over the entire empire, the **officer who carries out his royal order** Keḷadi Veṁṭappanāyaka was administrating Tuḷurājya and Malerājya ; *S.I.I.* VII, No. 297, pp. 148-149, ll. 4–6, Uḍupi, Udupi Tq. and Dt., Karn. St. **Dy.** Āravīḍu, Veṁkaṭapatirāya, Ś. 1536 = 1614 A.D. ; **text**[2] : . . . *Vīrapratāpa-Prauḍhadēvarāyamahārāyaru . . . . pratipālisuttiha kāladalu ā rāyara* ***ājñādhāraka****rumappa . . . Siṁgarasa Daṁṇāyakkoḍeyara nirūpadiṁ Viṭhṭharasa Oḍeyaru Bārakkūra Tuḷurājyavanu pratipālisuttiha kāladalū* . . . . ; **tr.** when Vīrapratāpa Prauḍhadēvarāyamahārāya was reigning, on the orders of Siṁgarasa, the **officer who carries out the royal orders,** Viṭhṭharasavoḍeya was administering Bārakūra-Tuḷurājya ; *S.I.I.* VII, No. 355, p. 213, ll. 5–9, Maṇigārakēri, Udupi Tq. and Dt., Karn. St. **Dy.** Saṅgama, Prauḍha Dēvarāya II, Ś. 1393 = 1471 A.D.

ājñeyanu irisu (K. *vb.*), promulgate the royal order ; **text** : . . . *Achyutarāyamahārāyaru prithvīrājyaṁ geyiyuttam iralu . . . . Sāḷuvanāyakanu* ***ājñeyanū yirisi*** . . . ; **tr.** during the reign of the emperor Achyutarāyamahārāya, Sāḷuvanāyaka has **promulgated the royal order** (details follow) ; *S.I.I.* IX, pt. ii, No. 547, p. 566, ll. 1–2, Little-Kāñchīpuram, Kanchipuram Tq., Chingleput Dt., T. Nadu St. **Dy.** Tuḷuva, Achyutarāya, Ś. 1454 = 1532 A.D.

akālavṛishṭi (K. < Skt. *n.*) unseasonal rains ; **text** : . . . . *Attiyabbege pathaśrama māдoḍ****akālavṛishṭi*** *yāytinnavu dēvabhaktigadu chōdyamē* . . . ; **tr.** is it not a surprise that when Attiyabbe suffered from travel weariness there was a refreshing **unseasonal rainfall** as a mark of her great devotion ? ; *S.I.I.* XI, pt. i, No. 52, p. 40, ll. 19–20 ; Lakkuṁḍi, Gadag Tq. and Dt., Karn. St. **Dy.** Chāḷ. of Kal., Āhavamalla, Ś. 929 = 1007-08 A.D.

akara (K. < Skt. *n.*), tax-free ; **text**[1] : . . . . . *bhaṭṭarggī gaḷde voḍḍali ā pattondi viṭṭār* ***akara*** . . . . ; **tr.** may this paddy field go to the bhaṭṭar and in that connection 1/10th of the tax was declared **tax-free** ; *M.A.R.* 1936, No. 16, p. 73, l. 16 ; Halmiḍi, Belur Tq., Hassan Dt., Karn. St. **Dy.** Kadambas of Banavāsi, Mṛigēśavarma, C. 450 A.D. ; **text**[2] : . . . *ā dēvasvake vosage* ***akara****villa* . . . . ; **tr.** donations to the temple are declared **tax-free** ; *K.I.* III, pt. i, No. 2, p. 3, l. 8 ; Śirāḷi, Bhatkal Tq., N. K. Dt., Karn. St. **Dy.** Āḷupā., Basavaśaṅkara Ajaidēarasa, Ś. 1225 = 1304 A.D.

akarakhaṁḍike (K. < Skt. *aksharakhaṇḍikā, n.*) school teaching alphabets ; **text :** ***akara khaṇḍike****ge mattaru ippattu* . . . . ; **tr.** twenty *mattar* (a land measure) of land to the **school teaching**

alphabets ; *K.I.* II, No. 16, p. 70, l. 44; Akkalkōṭ, Akkalkot Tq., Solapur Dt., Maha. St. **Dy.** Chāḷ. of Kal., Vikramāditya VI, Ch. Vi. yr. 48 = 1122 A.D.

akaramu (Te. < Skt. *n.*), tax-free ; **text**[1] **:** *Arshavelli-grāmamunaṁdu padipuṭla bhūmi tāṁbraśāsanamu **akaramu**gāṁbaḍasi dīnilō nēnupuṭla bhūmi Gaṁganārāyaṇa brahmadēyamuna . . . brāhmaṇulaku . . . ichchi* . . . ; **tr.** having given to the brāhmaṇas of Gaṁganārāyaṇa-brahmadēya 7 *puṭlu* (extant of the land being sown with seven putlu of seeds.) of land from out of the 10 *puṭlu* of land which was donated **tax-free** through a copper plate charter in the village Arshavalli ; *S.I.I.* V, No. 1342, p. 487, ll. 9–13 ; Arasavelli, Srikakulam Tq. and Dt., A.P. St. **Dy.** E. Gaṅga, Anantavarmadēva, reg. yr. 58, in characters of 12th cent. A.D.

akhaṁḍadīpa hastapratimā (Te. < Skt. *n.*), a statue with a perpetual lamp held in its hand ; **text : ** *Vīranarasiṁhadēvamahārājulakunnu dīrghāyushmat suputrāvāptyarthamu . . . . . Kūrmmanāthuni sannidhini **akhaṁḍadīpa-hastapratimannu** . . . . . samarpichidi. . . .* ; **tr.** a **statue with a perpetual lamp in its hand** was donated to the temple of the god Kūrmmanātha so that Narasiṁhadēvamahārāja be blessed with a son with a long life ; *S.I.I.* V, No. 1189, p. 434, ll. 13–18 ; Śrīkūrmmam, Srikakulam Tq. and Dt., A.P. St. **Dy.** E. Gaṅga, Vīranarasiṁha, Ś. 1264 = 1342 A.D.

akhaṁḍadīpamu (Te. *n.*), perpetual lamp ; **text :** (text damaged) . . . . ***akhaṁḍadīpamu*** *naḍichē . . . . . Vīrēswaruniki . . . . .* ; **tr.** for burning a **perpetual lamp** for the god Vīrēśvara ; *S.I.I.* XVI, No. 108, p. 123, ll. 4–5 ; Rāyachōti, Rayachoti Tq., Cuddapah Dt., A.P. St. **Dy.** Tuḷuva, Achyutarāya, Ś. 1456 = 1534 A.D.

akhaṁḍadīpārādhana (Te. < Skt. *n.*), offering worship with perpetual lamp ; **text :** . . *taḷasuṁkaṁ Cheṁnakēśvaradēvuniki pratishṭhākālamaṁdu **akhaṁḍadīpārādhana**ku . . . . . samarpistimi . . .* . . . ; **tr.** we grant the revenue income of the place for **offering worship with a perpetual lamp** at the time of the installation of the deity Chaṁnakēśavadēva ; *S.I.I.* XVI, No. 70, p. 82, ll. 6–8 ; Dommara-Nandyāla, Jammalamadagu Tq., Cuddapah Dt., A.P. St. **Dy.** Tuḷuva, Kṛishṇadēvarāya, Ś. 1443 = 1521 A.D.

akasāle (K. *n.*), goldsmith ; **text**[1] **:** . . . *Āḷugōḍa akasāle Baḷachāri Doḍayāchāriya maga Kētachāri Bōgāchāri māḍisikoṭṭa dēvālaya* . . . ; **tr.** the temple constructed by Kētachāri Bōgāchāri son of the **goldsmith** Baḷachāri Doḍayāchari of Āḷugōdu; *E.C.* (R) V, T. N. 301, p. 663, ll. 5–8 ; Algōḍu, T. Narasipura Tq., Mysore Dt., Karn. St. **Dy.** Hoy., Narasiṁha III, Cy. yr. Bahudhānya = 1278 A.D. ; **text**[2] **:** . . . . *maṭhada chatusīme vivara **akasāle**ya maṭhada gaḍiyiṁdaṁ paḍuvalu. Malayāḷa Voḍeyara maṭhada gaḍiyiṁ baḍagalu dēvālyada madiliṁdaṁ mūḍalu mūḍa upparige saritadiṁda* *teṁkalu* . . ; **tr.** the details of the four boundaries of the religious institution are as follows : on the west the boundary of the **goldsmith**'s *maṭha*, on the north the boundary of the residence of Malayāḷa Voḍeya, on the east the outer wall of the temple and on the south the slope of higher elevation ; *S.I.I.* IX, pt. ii, No. 673, p. 665, ll. 9–12, ; Kōṭēśvara, Kundapur Tq., Udupi Dt., Karn. St. **Dy.** Tuḷuva, Sadāśiva, Ś. 1484 = 1562 A.D. ; **akasālevāḷu** (K. *n.*), land granted to goldsmith for his livelihood ; **text :** . . . *baḍḍagivāḷa Biṇṇōjage koṭṭa matta 5 akasālevāḷu bāḷige matta 5*. . . . ; **tr.** 5 *matta* (a land measure) of land given to the carpenter Biṇṇōja for his livelihood and 5 *matta* of **land granted to the goldsmith for his livelihood** ; *S.I.I* IX, pt. i, No. 123, p. 105, l. 26 ; Dōnekallu, Gooty Tq., Anantapur Dt., A.P. St. **Dy.** Chāḷ. of Kal., Trailōkyamalla, Ś. 981 = 1059 A.D.

akka[1] (K. *n.*), term of respectful address to women, elder sister ; **text**[1] : . . . *teṁkalu Gauriy**akka**na bāḷiṁdaṁ baḍagalu* ; **tr.** the southern boundary is to the north of the land belonging to the **respectful lady** Gauri ; *S.I.I.* VII, No. 322, p. 172, ll. 11–12, Mūḍakēri, Udupi Tq. and Dt., Karn. St. **Dy.** Saṅgama, Bukkarāya, Ś. 1282 = 1360 A.D. ; **text**[2] : . . . *paḍuvalu nālvattu hāne akkana gadde* . . . . ; **tr.** on the west a field of the extent of being sown with forty *hāne* (a grain measure) of seed belonging to the **elder sister** ; *S.I.I.* VII, No. 372, p. 227, l. 17, Maṇigārakēri, Udupi Tq. and Dt., Karn. St. **Dy.** Saṅgama, Dēvarāya, Ś. 1359 = 1437 A.D.

akka[2] (K. *n.*), suffix added at the end of masculine name ; **text** : . . . *Mār**akka** arasar Banavāsināḍāḷe* . . . . ; **tr.** while Mār**akka** arasar was governing Banavāsināḍu ; *S.I.I.* XX, No. 10, p. 10, ll. 1–2, Siḍēnūr, Hirekerur Tq., Dharwar Dt., Karn. St. **Dy.** Rāshṭr., Dhruva, in characters of 8th cent. A.D.

akkaḷmaga (K. *n.*), elder sister's son ; **text :** . . . . *Tribuvanabhujagan* ***akkaḷmagan*** ; **tr.** Tribhuvanabhujagan's **elder sister's son** ; *E.C.* X, Ko. 23, p. 6, l. 5 ; Suḷidēnahaḻḻi, Kolar Tq. and Dt., Karn. St. **Misc.**, in characters of 10th century A.D.

ākkal vāṇiyar (T. influenced by M. *n.*), smiths-cum-traders ; **text :** ***ākkal-vāṇiyar****kku koḻḻun-nel-irupadu paṟa* ; **tr.** twenty *paṟa* (a grain measure) of paddy bought for the **smiths-cum-traders** ; *T.A.S.* IV, pts. i & ii, No. 7, p. 55, ll. 148–49 ; Kollūrmaḍam, Padmanabhapuram Tq., Tiruvanantapuram Dt., Ker. St. **Dy.** Rulers of Vēṇāḍu, Vīra-Udaya-Mārttāṇḍavarma-Tiruvaḍi, Kollam 364 = 1188 A.D.

akkam (T. *n.*), fraction of the coin *kāśu* ; **text :** . . . *Tirumaṟaikkāḍuḍaiyārkku . . . Kīḻkāṟaivēḷāṉ vaitta kāśu 7 . . . . idaṉ paliśaiyāl niśadam . . . irupala-śarkkaraiku tiṅgaḷ ōr **akkam**āga āṇḍuvarai paṉṉiraṇḍ-**akkam** iḍuvōm-āṉōm* ; **tr.** Kīḻkkāṟaivēḷāṉ endowed 7 *kāśu* (coin) for the service of the god

Tirumaṟaikkāḍuḍaiyār with the stipulation that the annual interest of 12 ***akkam*** (**fraction of a coin called *kāśu***) accruing from that amount shall be used for purchasing 2 *palam* (a grain measure) of sugar for daily offering to the deity ; *S.I.I.* XVII, No. 472, p. 195, ll. 3–4, 8–15 ; Vēdāraṇyam, Tirutturaipundi Tq., Tanjavur Dt., T. Nadu St. **Dy.** Chōḷa, Rājarāja I, reg. yr. 9 = 994 A.D.

akkaṉ (T. *n.*), elder sister ; **text :** . . . . . *Rājarājīśvaramuḍaiyārkku nāṅkuḍuttanavum* ***akkaṉ*** *kuḍuttaṉavum* . . . . . . *vimānattilkkallile veṭṭuga* ; **tr.** may this donation given by me and my **elder sister** to the god Rājarājīśvaramuḍaiyār be recorded on the stone of the *vimāna* (tower over central shrine) of the temple; *S.I.I.* II, No. 1, p. 2, first section l. 7, second section l. 1 ; Tañjāvūr, Tanjavur Tq. and Dt., T. Nadu St. **Dy.** Chōḷa, Rājarāja I, reg. yr. 26 = 1011 A.D.

akkaṉ-kāṇikkai (T. *n.*), tax levied for maintenance of the elder sister of the king ; **text :** . . . . . *vaḻinaḍai-kāṇikkai* ***akkaṉ-kāṇikkai*** *Kārtigai kāṇikkai*; **tr.** road tax, **tax levied for maintenance of the elder sister of the king** and tax collected in the month of Kārttigai ; *T.D.I.* I, No. 101, p. 130, l. 3 ; Tirumala, Tirupati Tq., Chittoor Dt., A.P. St. **Dy.** Yādavarāya, Tiruveṅkaṭanātha, reg. yr. 12 = 1330 A.D.

akkaraṁboy (K. *vb.*), incise letters on stone or copper plates ; **text[1] :** . . . . . *akkaraṁboyda* . . . *Māṇikāchārige kaṇḍuga gaḷde koḍaṁge koṭṭar* . ; **tr.** paddy field with a sowable capacity of 1 *kaṇḍuga* (a grain measure) of seed was given to Maṇikāchāri who had incised the letters on copper plate ; *E.C.* IX, No. 111, p. 224, ll. 9–10 ; Kammasandra, Hsk Tq., Bangalore Dt., Karn. St. **Dy.** Chōḷa, Rājarāja I, Ś. 923 = 1001 A.D. ; **text[2]:** . . . *Muḍigan**akkaraṁboy**da* ; **tr.** Muḍigan **incised the letters** ; *M.A.R.* 1942, No. 61, p. 190, l. 13 ; Kāsaravaḷḷi, Shikaripur Tq., Shimoga Dt., Karn. St. **Dy.** Chāḷ. of Kal., Āhavamalla, Ś. 923 = 1001-1002 A.D.

akkaraṁgaḷ (K. < Skt. *aksharāṇi*, *n.*), alphabets ; **text :** . . . . . *baredan-ādaradiṁ* . . . . *Tilu-Tivuḷa-Kaṁnaḍa Nāgarad**akkaraṅgaḷa*** ; **tr.** . . . . he wrote with great attention the alphabets of Telugu, Tamil, Kannaḍa and Nāgari ; *S.I.I.* IX, pt. i, No. 118, p. 96, l. 42 ; Hirēhaḍagaḷḷi, Hadagalli Tq., Bellary Dt., Karn. St. **Dy.** Chāḷ. of Kal., Sōmēśvara, Ś. 978 = 1057 A.D.

akkariga (K. < Skt. *n.*), literate person ; **text :** . . . . . *akkariga Mallapana gaḍiṁdaṁ. teṁkalu* . ; **tr.** to the south of the boundary of the land of Mallapa the literate person ; *S.I.I.* VII, No. 333, p. 184, l. 10 ; Mūḍakēri, Udupi Tq. and Dt., Karn. St. **Dy.** Ajila chieftains, Ajilaseṭṭi, Ś. 1470 = 1548 A.D.

akkarigavṛitti (K. *n.*), land gifted to a literate person ; **text :** *Nāgadēsigarge* . . . *poḷutal āhāramum varshakkoṁḍu kappaḍavuvan ikki ōdisi guṇaśāsana din āḷv**akkarigavṛitti*** *mattar irppattaidu maneyoṁdu*

tr. 1 house and 25 *mattar* (land measure) of **land gifted to** Nāgadēsiga **a literate person** for his livelihood who was given food at proper intervals and one clothing per year for having taught competently; *Ep. Ind.* XX, No. 6, p. 68, ll. 26–28. ; Kōṭavumachagi, Gadag Tq. and Dt., Karn. St. **Dy.** Chāḷ. of Kal., Vikramāditya, Ś. 934 = 1012 A.D.

akkasāla (K. *n.*), goldsmith ; **text :** . . . . *Abbāchāriya akkasālada bāḻa sāsanada kallu* ; **tr.** the inscribed slab set up in the field of the **goldsmith** Abbāchāri ; *S.I.I.* IX, pt. i, No. 29, p. 16, ll. 14–19 ; Honnēralihaḷḷi, Madakasira Tq. Anantapur Dt., A.P. St. **Dy.** Noḻaṁba, Iṟiva- Noḷ. Pal., Noḷaṁba Noḻipayya, Ś. 885 = 963 A.D.

akkasāladacchina kammaṭa (K. < Skt. *n.*), mint producing coins with the seal of the goldsmith ; **text :** . . . . *Nannēśvara dēvara aṁgabhōga* . . . *naḍavantāgi* . . . ***akkasāladachchina kammaṭa****dalu* . . . *Śaṁkarasеṭṭiyaru biṭṭa paṇa aydu* ; **tr.** five *paṇa* (a coin) granted by Śaṁkarasеṭṭi from the **mint producing coins with the seal of the goldsmith** for services to the image of the god Nannēśvara . . . ; *S.I.I.* XV, No. 70, p. 96, ll. 3–5 ; Lakkuṁḍi, Gadag Tq. and Dt., Karn. St. **Dy.** Chāḷ. of Kal., Sōmēśvara IV, Ś. 1108 = 1186 A.D.

akkasālada kēṇi (K. *n.*) leased land given to goldsmith ; **text :** . . . . *hiriya kēṇikāṟa Vinayasiṁhanappa Yēchiseṭṭi taṁnn****akkasālada kēṇi****yalu dīpāvaḷiya parvvadalu dēvara vīḷayakke aḍake nānūru* ; **tr.** Vinayasiṁha *alias* Yēchiseṭṭi the senior lease holder granted four hundred arecanuts for the betel services to the god during the dīpāvaḷi festival from the **land leased to him as goldsmith** ; *S.I.I.* XV, No. 559, p. 375, l. 2 ; Lakkuṁḍi, Gadag Tq. and Dt., Karn. St. **Misc.**, in characters of 12th cent A.D.

akkasāle (K. *n.*), goldsmith ; **text**[1] **:** *Janārddana Bhaṭṭaru Mūkagavuḍana kaiyalu dānavaṁ paḍedu biṭṭa keyi aḍḍa-dāriyiṁ mūḍalu* ***akkasāle*** *geyyiṁ-baḍagalu hiriyakōla mattaru* . . . ; **tr.** the land measuring one *mattar* (a land measure) measured by the *hiriya-kōlu* (measuring rod) donated by Janārddana Bhaṭṭa after obtaining it as grant from Mūka-gavuḍa lay to the east of cross-road and to the north of the **goldsmith's** land ; *S.I.I.* V, No. 856, p. 351, ll. 42–43, stone kept in the Madras Museum, Chennai Tq. & Dt., T. Nadu St. **Dy.** Chāḷ. of Kal., Sōmeśvara I, date lost., in characters of 10th cent. A.D. ; **text**[2] **:** ***akkasāle*** *Mallōjana maga Sōmayya Rājayyaṁge vṛitti 1* ; **tr.** one share (of the land granted) to Sōmayya and Rājaiah, the sons of the **goldsmith** Mallōja ; *E.C.* (R) VII, Md. 34, p. 218, l. 37 ; Rāyaseṭṭipura, Mandya Tq. and Dt., Karn. St. **Dy.** Hoy., Sōmēśvara, Ś. 1173 = 1251 A.D. ; **text**[3] **:** *Dēvarahaḷḷi* ***akkasāle*** *Chikkāchāri māḍida śēvārta* ; **tr.** the pious service rendered by the **goldsmith** Chikkāchāri of Dēvarahaḷḷi ; *E.C.* (R) VII, Ng. 146, p. 143, ll. 3–5; Dēvarahaḷḷi, Nagamanagala Tq., Mandya Dt., Karn. St. **Misc.**, in characters of 19th cent. A.D.

akkaśālai (T. *n.*), goldsmith's profession ; **text :** . . . . . . *yāvarun toḻun toḻiladāna* ***akkaśālai*** . . . ; **tr.** the **goldsmith's profession** which is adored by all ; *S.I.I.* VI, No. 439, p. 178, l. 4 ; Āląṅguḍi, Nannilam Tq., Tanjavur Dt., T. Nadu St. Comm. gld., Ś. 1186 = 1264 A.D. ; **akkasāli** (K. *n.*), goldsmith ; **text :** . . . *Bāḻguḷi. ayvadimbarum* . . . . . . *Kalidēva svāmiya dēvālayadoḷ neredu*. . . . . . ***akkasāli****ya- āya uppu-oḷagāgi dhānyaṁgaḷoḷ-ellaṁ poṁgeraḍu baḷḷavaṁ koḷvaṁtāgi* . . . . . *koṭṭu koṇḍa poṁgadyāṇa 103* . . . . ; **tr.** the 50 mahājanas of Baḻguḷi having assembled in the temple of Kalidēvasvāmi settled to collect the tax on the goldsmith and sale at the rate of *baḷḷa* (a grain measure) out of the quantity worth a *poṁnu* (gold coin) in each kind and invest 103 *poṁ-gadyāṇa* (a gold coin) realised from the sale of the collection ; *S.I.I.* IX, pt. i, No. 89, p. 60, ll. 17–18 ; Bāgaḷi, Harapanahalli Tq., Bellary Dt., Karn. St. **Dy.** Chāḷ. of Kal., Jayasiṁha II, Ś. 957 = 1035 A.D.

akkasālegaru (K. *n.*), goldsmiths ; **text :** *Rāma-nāthadēvara pātrabhōgakke māḍida dharmmada kramaveṁteṁdare Nāgavve maga Hiriya-Rāmaṇṇaṁgaḷu Kētavveyanu* . . *pātrakke* . . . . . *koṭṭarāgi ā pātrada Kētavveya jīvitakke prati grāmakke varshaṁprati baḍagigaḷu 1* ***akkasālegaru*** *1 kañchagāraru 1/2 yi prakāradalle prativarushavu koṭṭu yi dharmmavanu āchaṁdrārka sthāyiyāgi naḍadu* . . . ; **tr.** Hiriya Rāmaṇṇa son of Nāgavve offered the services of Kētavve as a dancing girl in the temple of Rāmanātha and for her maintenance the carpenters, **goldsmiths**, metalsmiths from every village undertook to pay money at specific rates; in the same fashion every year this charity must be maintained as long as the moon and the sun last ; *E.C.* (R) III, No. 17, p. 18, l. 3 ; Guṁḍlupēṭe, Gundlupet Tq., Mysore Dt., Karn. St. **Dy.** Trade guild called Vīrapañchāḷas, Ś. 1294 = 1372 A.D.

akki (K. *n.*), rice ; **text**[1] **:** . . . . ***akki*** *mā 5 hesaru mā 1 tuppa soḷasige 2* . . . *Vēdapāragarappa padināru* . . . *brāhmaṇarige chhatrakke biṭṭaru* ; **tr.** 5 *mā* (a grain measure) of **rice**, one *mā* of green gram, 2 *soḷasige* (a liquid measure) of ghee . . . . were given to the choultry for the feeding of 16 brāhmaṇas who were well versed in the vēdic lore ; *S.I.I.* IX, pt. i, No. 245, p. 250, l. 34; Chaṭnahaḷḷi, Harapanahalli Tq., Bellary Dt., Karn. St. **Dy.** Chāḷ. of Kal., Jagadēkamalla, reg. yr. 9 = 1146 A.D. ; **text**[2] : . . . *sāmaṁta Lakhkheyanāyaka Mādayanāyakana kaiyal uttarāyaṇa saṁkramaṇa nimittavāgi maiduna Chauḍayyaṁ dhārāpūrvvakaṁ māḍikoṁḍu sarvabādhā parihārārthavāgi biṭṭa dattiyeṁtene Virūpāksha dēvara nivēdyakke* ***akki*** *baḷḷa 1 Haṁpādēviya nivēdyakke* ***akki*** *ba 1 Bhairavadēvara nivēdyakke* ***akki*** *ba 2* . . . . ; **tr.** the details of the grant made by *maiduna* (brother-in-law) Chauḍayya after pouring ablutionary water and entrusting the same to sāmaṁta Lakhkheya Nāyaka and Mādaya Nāyaka made on the occasion of Uttarāyaṇa- saṁkrāṁti with all the lets and hindrances removed are as follows: for the food offering of god Virūpākshadēva one *baḷḷa* (a grain measure) of **rice** ; for the food offerings of Haṁpādēvi one *ba.* (*balla*) of **rice** ; for the food offerings of Bhairavadēva 2 ba of **rice** ; *S.I.I.* IV, No. 260, p. 57, ll. 72–75, Hampi, Hospet Tq., Bellary Dt., Karn. St. **Misc.**, Ś 1121 = 1199 A.D. ; **text**[3] : . . . . *Gōpināthadēvariṁge upārada 23* ***akki*** *Śrīdharana maga Mādhavaṁge upārada 13* ***akki*** *Subhadreya maga Hariharaṁge mūla āśraṁṇaṁge nāḍa iṁmāna* ***akki*** *viśēśada 40* ***akki*** *haṁ* ‖ *āśraṁṇnaṁge iṁttī* ***akki*** *ālatara dēvasvadiṁda* ***akki*** *mū 40* ‖ *nū tāvu taṁdu koṁbaṟu.* . . ; **tr.** 23 (measurement not mentioned) **rice** for the offering of the god Gōpināthadēva ; to Mādhava son of Śrīdhara 13 (measures not mentioned) **rice** for performing offerings to the god ; to Harihara the son of Subhadrā, the original **āśraṁṇa** a special **rice** of 40 *hāne* (a grain measure) measured by the local *immāna* (a grain measure), thus *āśraṁṇa* is to be given from the temple 40 *mūḍe* (a grain measure) of **rice** to be taken by him ; *S.I.I.* VII, No. 326, p. 178, ll. 11–14, Mūḍakēri, Udupi Tq. and Dt., Karn. St. **Misc.**, in characters of 14th century A.D. ; **akki mūḍe** (K. *n.*), rice preserved in a bundle formed of twisted hay containing a fixed quantity of rice ; **text**[1] : . . . . . *bāhiri tānu tettu Nāyaru mūlavāgi hiḍidu kālakālakke nashṭa tushṭi ennade naḍasi bahanāda hāne 40 ṟalu* ***akki mūḍe*** *14* ; **tr.** whatever lease land is under *bāhiri* for his cultivation, he should remit whatever tax imposed through the official called *Nāyaru*, he should cultivate the land by sowing 14 ***akki-mūḍes*** of paddy measured by the *hāne* (a grain measure) of the capacity of 40 *mūḍe* (a grain measure) without complaining about loss, fertility etc. occuring from time to time ; *S.I.I.* VII, No. 344, p. 197, ll. 20–23 ; Chauḷikēri, Udupi Tq., and Dt., Karn. St., **Dy.** Saṅgama, Harihara II, Ś. 1314 = 1392 A.D. ; **text**[2] : . . . *ī aivattoṁdu mūḍe akkiyalli Chaṁndranāthana abhishēka 3 kke* ***akkimūḍe*** *6* ; **tr.** from out of this 51 muḍes of rice, 6 *akkimūḍes* are meant for 3 *abhishēkas* (ritualistic bathing) of Chaṁdranātha ; *S.I.I.* VII, No. 244, p. 122, ll. 12-14, Hiriyaṁgaḍi, Karkala Tq., S. Kanara Dt., Karn. St. **Misc.**, Ś. 1514 = 1592 A.D. ; **akki pēṭhe** (K. *n.*), rice market ; **text** : . . . *Vijayanāgarada paṭṭaṇadoḷage . . . . kuṁbāṟa-gērige paḍuvalu* ***akki pēṭhe****ge baḍagalu . . . Kuṁmaraguṁṭeya sthaḷa* ; **tr.** the place known as Kuṁmaraguṁṭe to the west of the potter's street and to the north of the **rice market** in the city of Vijayanāgara ; *S.I.I.* IX, pt. ii, No. 510, p. 522, ll. 10–12, Kamalāpura, Hospet Tq., Bellary Dt., Karn. St. **Dy.** Tuḷuva, Kṛishṇadēvarāya, Ś. 1439 = 1518 A.D.

akkiram (T. < Skt. *agram, n.*), first preferential feeding ; **text** : . . ***akkiram****iraṇḍukku arināṉāḻi* ; **tr.** *nāṉāḻi* (a grain measure) of rice for the **first**

preferential feeding of two (brāhmaṇas); *T.A.S.* IV, pts. i and ii, No. 4, p. 19, l. 4, Śuchīndram, Agastheeshvaram Tq., Kanyakumari Dt., T. Nadu St. Rulers of Vēṇāḍu, Kōdai Kēraḷavarman, Kollam 320 = 1145 A.D.

akkiṟāram (T. < Skt. *agrahāram, n.*), brāhmaṇa settlement ; **text** : . . *Vaṇaṁgāmuḍi Mudaliyār*. . . . *Vaṇaṁgāmuḍisamuttiram-eṉṉum nāmadēyam paṇṇi* ***akkiṟāraṁ*** *viṭṭēṉ*. . . . ; **tr.** I, Vaṇaṁgāmuḍi Mudaliyār, created and donated a **brāhmaṇa settlement** after naming it as Vaṇaṁgāmuḍi-samuddiram ; *S.I.I.* VII, No. 27, p. 11, ll. 7, 10–11 ; Tāramaṅgalam, Omalur Tq., Salem Dt., T. Nadu St. **Dy.** Tuḷuva, Sadāśiva, Kali year 4646 = 1545 A.D.

akkiraśālai (T. < Skt. *agraśālā, n.*), feeding hall for the brāhmaṇas ; **text** : . . . *Tiruchchivīndirattu mahāsabhaiyōm* . . . . . *tiru****akkiraśālai****yiṟ kūḍam niṟamba kūḍi irukka* ; **tr.** the members of the body called *mahāsabhā* (an administrative body) of Tiruchchivīndiram having assembled in full quorum in the **feeding hall for the brāhmaṇas**; *T.A.S.* II, No. 1, p. 7, ll. 8–10 ; Śuchīndiram, Agastheeshvaram Tq., Kanyakumari Dt., T. Nadu St. **Dy.** Chōla, Rājarāja I, reg. yr. 14 = 999 A.D.

akki teru (K. *n.*) levy in the form of rice ; **text:** . . . . . *Mūrukēṟiya halara munḍiṭṭu* . . . *Nāraṇaseṭṭiyaru kaṭṭiśida maṭakke biṭṭa 3 gadde yidake gēṇi* ***akki teru*** *dēvasva kaḷedu kālaṁprati* . . . *nāgaṁḍugadalu akki mū 14 hadinālku mūḍe* . . . . ; **tr.** with the consent of the *halaru* (an administrative body) of Mūrukēṟi Nāraṇaseṭṭi caused to be constructed a *maṭa* (monastry) . . . . . to which were granted 3 paddy fields with the exemption of lease money, **levy in the form of rice** and temple tax, 14 *mū* (*mūḍe*, a grain measure) of rice had to be given at fixed intervals ; *S.I.I.* VII, No. 321, pp. 170–71, ll. 7–9, 21–22, Mūḍakēri, Udupi Tq. and Dt., Karn. St. **Dy.** Tuḷuva, Sadāśiva, Ś. 1507 = 1585 A.D.

akrutya (K. < Skt. *akṛitya, adj.*), improper act ; **text** : . . . *Vishṇustānadalli durjanaru māḍida* ***akrutya****gaḷanu biḍisi girimlaṇa Vēdagiriperumāḷige tirunāḷanu sāgisi pūjeyanu māḍisūdu* ; **tr.** after purifying the holy temple-site of Vishṇu from the effects of **improper acts** of evil persons, worship should be conducted on holy days to the god Vēdagiriperumāḷ on top of the hill ; *S.I.I.* IX, pt. ii, No. 527, p. 543, l. 6–7, Nāgalāpuram, Ponneri Tq., Chingleput Dt., T. Nadu St. **Dy.** Tuḷuva, Kṛishṇadēvarāya, Ś. 1451 = 1529 A.D.

akshapaṭaḷādhipati (K. < Skt.), officer in charge of the store where records are kept ; **text :** . . . . *akhiḷarājyabharaṇirūpita mahāmantr-****āksha paṭaḷādhipati*** . . . . *Dhalla* . . . . . . ; **tr.** Dhalla who bore the burden of the entire kingdom and was the great minister who was the **officer in charge of the store in which the records were kept** ; *S.I.I.* IX, pt. i, No. 52, p. 39, ll. 7–8, Lakkuṁḍi, Gadag Tq. and Dt.,

Karn. St. Chāḷ. of Kal., Āhavamalla, Ś. 929 = 1007 A.D.

akshāra (K. < Skt. *akshara, n.*), word form ; **text** : . . *Penugoṁḍeya bāgila baḷiyalli Raghunāthadēvaranu pratishṭeyanu māḍi ī dēvarige amṛitapaḍige samarpista kshētragaḷa vivara* . . . . . *sthaḷa 4kke gadde kha 1* ***akshāradalū*** *khaṁḍugada gadde 1* . . . . ; **tr.** for the food offerings of the god Raghunāthadēva installed near the gateway of Penugoṁḍe, the details of grants are : . . . . for 4 pieces of land, 1 *kha* (land of the extent of being sown with 1 khaṁḍuga of seeds), **in word form** one *khaṁḍuga* of paddy field . . . ; *S.I.I.* IV, No. 245, p. 39, ll. 7–9, 15–16, Hampi, Hospet Tq., Bellary Dt., Karn. St. Tuḷuva, Achyutarāya, Ś. 1463 = 1541 A.D.

aksharakal (K. < Skt. *n.*), inscribed stone or rock ; **text** : . . . *Taṭṭaggeṟeya kīḻkeṟe pōgi* ***aksharakal*** . . . . ; **tr.** proceeding from the lower tank in Taṭṭaggeṟe is the **inscribed stone or rock** . . . . ; *E.C.* (R) II, Sb. 38, p. 14, l. 5, Chikkabeṭṭa, Channarayapatna Tq., Hassan Dt., Karn. St. **Dy.** Rāshṭr., Raṇāvalōka Kamabayya, in characters of 8th cent. A.D.

akshara khaṁḍika (K. < Skt. *n.*) ; school for teaching alphabets ; **text :** *vēda khaṁḍika śāstra khaṁḍika tarkav****akshara khaṁḍika*** . . . . *inituvaṁ naḍasuvaṁtāgi* . . . . ; **tr.** so that the school for teaching the *vēdas*, the *śāstras, tarka* and **the school for teaching alphabets** can be run ; *E.C.* (R) XII, Kd. 150, p. 164, ll. 64–65 ; Brahmasamudra, Kadur Tq., Chikmagalur Dt., Karn. St. **Dy.** Hoy., Narasiṁha I, Cy. yr. Virōdhi = 1169 A.D.

akaramu (Te. < Skt. *n.*), tax-free ; **text :** *Arshavelli-grāmamunudu padipuṭtla bhūmi tāṁbraśāsanamu* ***akaramu****ga baḍasi dīnilō ēnupuṭla bhūmi Gaṁganārāyaṇabrahmadēyamuna* . . . *nēvūru brāhmaṇalaku* . . . *ichchi* . . . . ; **tr.** having given to the 7 brāhmaṇas of Gaṁganārāyaṇa brahmadēya 7 *puṭlu* (a land measure) of land from out of the 10 *puṭlu* of land which was donated tax free through a copper plate charter in the village Arshavelli ; *S.I.I.* V, No. 1342, p. 487, ll. 9–13 ; Arasavilli, Srikakulam Tq. and Dt., A.P. St. **Dy.** E. Gaṅga, Anantavarmadēva, reg. yr. 58, in characters of 12th cent. A.D.

akshaya (K. < Skt. *adj.*), irreducible ; **text :** . . *Kōgiḷiya tīrthada Channapārśvadēvarige* . . . *Tippaṇana kumāri Chokaladēvi* ***akshaya bhaṁḍāravāgi*** *nityābhiśēkakke koṭṭa ga 1* . . . . ; **tr.** for the daily sacred bath of the god Chaṁnapārśvadēva of the holy place Kōgiḷi Chokaladēvi the daughter of Tippaṇa made an **irreducible** grant of 1 *ga* (*gadyāṇa*, a coin) ; *S.I.I.* IX, pt. i, No. 346, p. 369, ll. 4, 34, Kōgaḷi, Hadagalli Tq., Bellary Dt., Karn. St. **Dy.** Sēü. of Dēv., Rāmanātha, Ś. 1197 = 1275 A.D.

akshaya bhaṁḍāra (K. < Skt. *n.*), permanent endowment ; **text :** . . . . *Tippaṇana kumāri Chokaladēvi* ***akshaya bhaṁḍāra****vāgi nitya-*

abhishēkakke koṭṭa ga. 1 . . . . . ; **tr.** Chokaladēvi, the daughter of Tippaṇa instituted a permanent endowment of 1 ga (gadyāṇa, gold coin) for the daily ritualistic bath of the deity ; *S.I.I.* IX, pt. i, No. 346, p. 369, l. 34 ; Kōgaḷi, Hadagalli Tq., Bellary Dt., Karn. St. **Dy.** Hoy., Rāmanātha, Cy. yr. Yuva = 1275 A.D.

akshiṇi (K. < Skt. *n.*), undiminished (one of the eight conditions or privileges attached to the landed property which stands for **undiminished** yield) ; **text :** . . . . *Āchayyanu . . . ikkeyi mane* ***akshiṇi*** *āgāmi sahita samasta baḷi sahita . . . . Chandrabhūshaṇadēvara kaiyallu Lokkiya . . . . gadyāṇa 52 maṁ koṁḍu . . Grāmēśvaradēvarige krayadānavāgi koṭṭaru* ; **tr.** Āchayya took 52 *Lokki-gadhyāṇa* (gold coin minted at Lokkiguṁḍi) from Chaṁdrabhūshaṇadēva for the piece of land and house along with the **undiminished** privileges and *āgāmi* (*q.v.*) ; *K.I.* V, No. 32, p. 132, ll. 69, 71–72 ; Dhārwar, Dharwar Tq and Dt., Karn. St. **Dy.** Chāḷ. of Kal., Sōmēśvara, reg. yr. 28 = 1215 A.D.

akshiṇi (T. < Skt. *n.*), **text :** . . . . *paḷavari puduvari nidhinikshēpam jalapāshāṇam* ***akshiṇi*** *āgāmi tējasvāmyam uṭpaṭṭa sakala svarṇādāyām bhaktādāyam uṭpaṭṭa śuṅgam* ; **tr.** taxes including old revenue incomes, newly imposed taxes, wealth, underground valuables, water, stones and priveleges like **undiminished** privileges and *āgāmi* (*q.v.*) and *tējasvāmya* (ownership of the land along with conventional 8 previleges) ; *S.I.I.* VIII, No. 276, p. 151, ll. 13–14 ; Tiṭṭaguḍi, Vriddhachalam Tq., S. Arcot Dt., T. Nadu St. **Dy.** Saṅgama, Prince Vīrabhūpati, Ś. 1341 = 1419 A.D.

ākulamantrāyaṁ (Te. *n.*), tax income from betel-leaves ; **text :** . . . . *Channapaku ākuṁdōtelu sēsēvāriki śēśi aṁdul* ***ākulamaṁtrāyamuṇṇu*** *mīku trikālamugā yistimi . . . . .* ; **tr.** I give to Chennapa who maintains the betel leaf garden the **tax income from betel leaves** for all times to come ; *S.I.I.* XVI, No. 183, p. 190, ll. 18–21 ; Mārkāpur, Markapur Tq., Kurnool Dt., A.P. St. **Dy.** Tuḷuva, Sadāśiva, Ś. 1474 = 1552 A.D.

ākulu (Te. *n.*), betel leaves ; **text :** . . *Parvata Nāyaniṁgāru . . . . Nelaṁdalūri Chokkanāthadēvuniki ichchina . . . . padi* ***ākulu*** . . . ; **tr.** a grant of 10 **betel leaves** (among many other grants) made do the god Chokkanāthadēva of Nelaṁdalūru by Parvata Nāyaniṁgāru ; *S.I.I.* XVI, No. 40, p. 43, ll. 18, 24–25, 46 ; Nandalūru, Rajampet Tq., Cuddapah Dt., A.P. St. **Dy.** Sāḷuva, Immaḍi Narasimha, Ś. 1423 = 1501 A.D.

ākuṁdōṭa (Te.), betel leaf garden ; **text :** . . . . . *Mārakāpuraṁ* ***ākuṁdōṭalu*** *sēsēvāriki yichina . . śāsanaṁ* . . ; **tr.** grant given to the person maintaining the **betel leaf garden** at Mārakāpura; *S.I.I.* XVI, No. 183, p. 190, ll. 15–18. ; Mārkāpur, Markapur Tq., Kurnool Dt., A.P. St. **Dy.** Tuḷuva, Sadāśiva, Ś. 1475 = 1552 A.D.

ākutōṭavāru (Te. *n.*), owner of betel leaf garden; **text :** . . . . . . *Vīranārāyaṇadēvuni raṁgabhōgamu*

. . . *chellanu* . . . ***ākutōtavāru*** . . . ; **tr.** for the entertainment of the god Vīranārāyaṇadēva (many other such gifts) a gift was collected from the **owner of betel leaf garden** ; *S.I.I.* X, No. 528, p. 286, ll. 8–10 ; Pāṇem, Nandyal Tq., Kurnool Dt., A.P. St. **Dy.** Kākatīya, Pratāpa-rudradēva, Ś. 1241 = 1319 A.D.

āḷ (K. *n.*), personal servant ; **text :** . . *Vijayādityar* . . . *āḷvandu avar**āḷ** Chennavūroḷe Eramma Āsandiyāḷe* . . . . ; **tr.** while Vijayāditya was ruling, his **personal servant** Eramma was administering Āsandi from Chennavūru ; *E.C.* VI, Kdr. 145, p. 128, ll. 4–5 ; Āsandi, Kadur Tq., Chickmagalur Dt., Karn. St. **Dy.** W. Gaṅga, Śrīpurusha, in characters of 8th cent. A.D. ;

āḷ (T. *n.*), (temple) servant ; **text[1] :** . . . *chittiramēḻip-periyanāṭṭōm* . . . . *muṉbu veiyttukkuḍuttapaḍiye āṭṭaikku ēṟukku padakku nellum **āḷ**ukku kuṟuṇi nellum* . . . *vaittuk kuḍuttōm* . . . . ; **tr.** we the agricultural guild called Chittaramēḻip-periyanāṭṭōm granted as we had done earlier, one *padakku* (a grain measure) of paddy per plough and one *kuṟuṇi* (a grain measure) of paddy for the **(temple) servant** ; *S.I.I.* VII, No. 129, p. 55, ll. 7, 10 ; Tirukkōyilūr, Tirukkoyilur Tq., S. Arcot Dt., T. Nadu St. **Misc.**, in characters of 11th cent. A.D. ; **text[2]** :. . . . . *Tiruttēru ūḻiyamum periya tirunāḷ koḍi kuḍai eḍukkira **āḷ**um.* . . ; **tr.** the service of drawing the holy temple car and the **temple servant** bearing the holy umbrella on major festival days ; *S.I.I.* VIII, No. 158, p. 71, ll. 8–9, Tiruvaṇṇāmalai, Tiruvannamalai Tq., N. Arcot Dt., T Nadu St. **Dy.** Tuḷuva, Sadāśiva, Ś. 1489 = 1567 A.D. ; **āḷina-jana** (K. *n.*), persons serving in the temple ; **text :** (damaged). . . . . ***āḷina jana*** *5 kaṁ harivāṇa 2* . . . . ; **tr.** 2 plates of (offerings to the god) earmarked for 5 **persons serving in the temple** ; *S.I.I.* IX, pt. ii, No. 489, p. 504, l. 54 ; Kāḷahasti, Chandragiri Tq., Chittoor Dt., A.P. St. **Dy.** Tuḷuva, Kṛishṇadēvarāya, Ś. 1435 = 1513 A.D.

aḷa (K. *vb.*), to measure (the gifted land) ; **text :** . . *Kuṁdāpuradoḷagaṇa grāma jagattu mukkālaṭṭigaḷanu karasi vichārisi purōhita sthaḷavan-**aḷad** ā kuḷava kaṭṭi aramanege sidddhāya nashṭavillade* . . . *naḍeva dharmada bhūmi* . . . . ; **tr.** donated land which was confirmed as belonging to the priest of the place after due enquiry conducted by the village administrative bodies called *grāmajagattu* after summoning the *mukkālaṭṭi* (temple servants) within Kuṁdāpura was once again **measured** and granted without any loss of revenue to the palace ; *S.I.I.* IX, pt. ii, No. 441, p. 451, ll. 15–18 ; Kundāpur, Kundapur Tq., Udupi Dt., Karn. St. **Dy.** Saṅgama, Dēvarāya II, Ś. 1348 = 1425 A.D.

āḷaḍiyaṟa (M. *n.*), a succession fee in Travancore equal to one fourth of the value of the property left by a person of the matriarchal system of inheritance, when a person dies intestate leaving only distant kindred to succeed to the property ; **text :** . . . . . . *uḷppatti . . . muṉbumuṟa muṟama . . . dānamāna sambandaṅgaḷ ūrāma pāśivalai* ***āḷaḍiyaṟa*** *maṟṟum. eppērpaṭṭadiṉu mērppaḍi ammāvaṉmār kalpichchu paḍuttum* . . ; **tr.** having given all rights such as source of income, the ancient customary payments, customary payments, grants and gifts, marital relationship, **a succession fee in Travancore equal to one fourth of the value of the property left by a person of the matriarchal system of inheritance, when a person dies intestate leaving only distant kindred to succeed to the property**, fishing rights etc. shall be held in succession ; *T.A.S.* IV, pts. i and ii, No. 44, p. 158, ll. 34–36 ; Āṟṟūr, Padmanabhapuram Tq., Tiruvanantapuram Dt., Ker. St. **Dy.** Chiefs of Kīḻappērūr, Ravivarmaṉ, Kollam 821 = 1646 A.D.

aḻagerudu (T. *n.*), quality bull ; **text[1] :** . . . *Rājēndraśōḻa- viṇṇagardēvarkku vēṇḍum nivandangaḷukku . . . . dēvadānamāy . . .* ***aḻag erudu*** *. . . . ūrkaḷaiñju koḷḷāde iddēvarkkē . . . śurukki koḷḷavum* . . . . ; **tr.** without taking to the royal treasury taxes on the **quality bull** and the coins levied as tax in gold coins from the town were assigned as a temple gift for the services of the god installed in Rājēndraśōḻaviṇṇagar ; *S.I.I.* XIV, No. 145, p. 76, l. 3 ; Maṉṉārkōyil, Ambasamudram Tq., Tirunelveli Dt., T. Nadu St. **Dy.** Chōḷa-Pāṇḍya, Jaṭāvarman Sundara Chōḷa-Pāṇḍya, reg. yr. 13, in characters of 9th cent. A.D. ; **text[2] :** *dēvadānaṅgaḷaikkoṇḍu vaṟumbaḍi* ***aḻagerudu*** *kāṭchikāśum kāṭchierudu kāśum ūrkaḷaiñjum koḷḷadēy iddēvarkēy dēvadāna iṟayiliyāga variyil iṭṭadu.* . . . ; **tr.** the income from the *dēvadāna* (land grants to temple), tax income on **quality bulls,** tax income on bulls and the gold coin collected as tax from the village are not to be appropriated but given to the deity as tax free *dēvadāna* ; *S.I.I.* XIV, No. 145, p. 77, l. 7 ; Maṉṉārkōyil, Ambasamudram.Tq., Tirunelveli Dt., T. Nadu St. **Dy.** Chōḷa-Pāṇḍya, Sundara, reg. yr. 13 = 1038 A.D. ; **text[3]** (M. *n.*) **:** *iddēśattu . . . . . . oṭṭiṟ-kaḍamaiyum . . . vey nellum* ***aḻagerudum*** *. . . taṟitaḷai viṭṭukoḍuttār amainda adikārar.* . . . ; **tr.** belonging to this *dēśam*, the balance of the incomes of the fee paid by the brick-layer, fee paid for collecting bamboo grain from the forest, **quality bull** from this territory were given to the temple by the authorised offical ; *T.A.S.* IV, pts. i and ii, No. 16, p. 91, ll. 2–3 ; Kēraḷāpuram, Padmanabhapuram Tq., Tiruvanantapuram Dt., Ker. St. **Dy.** Rulers of Vēṇāḍu, Udaiya Mārttāṇḍavarmaṉ, Kollam 491 = 1317 A.D.

alagu (K. *n.*), edge, border, milled edge of coin ; **text** : . . . *Telligēśvaradēvaraṁ . . . . pratishṭhe māḍi . . . . telligaru eḷḷa māṟa koṁḍavaru horage kaṭṭid**alagina** chikka tārava teṟuvaru* . . . . . . ; **tr.** having installed the god Telligēśvaradēva, the oil mongers gifted to the temple one copper coin with its milled edge per load of the gingili purchased ; *S.I.I.* IX, pt. i, No. 336, p. 357, ll. 20, 25–26, Kuḍatini, Bellary Tq. and Dt., Karn. St. **Dy.** Hoy., Ballāḷa II, Ś. 1140 = 1219 A.D.

alagunilai (T. *n.*), total weight ; **text :** . . . . . *veḷḷiyiṉ kalaśappāṉai 1 alagunilai 3 kaḻañju* (expressed by symbol) ; **tr.** the total weight of one silver vessel was 3 *kaḻañju* (weight in gold) . . . ; *S.I.I.* XIII, No. 1, p. 1, l. 3 ; Tiruvārūr, Nagapattinam Tq., Thanjavur Dt., T. Nadu St. **Dy.** Chōḷa, Rājarāja I, reg. yr. 2 = 987 A.D.

alaiēṟu (T. *n.*), raising tidal wave ; **text :** . . . *āṟukutti* ***alaiēṟum*** *śarindu puṉattalai āy irukkayil*; **tr.** because of the level of the river having raised and the wall having collapsed as a result of the **raising tidal wave**, the temple precincts had been covered by sand ; *S.I.I.* XXII, No. 93, p. 86, l. 6 ; Jambai, Tirukkoyilur Tq., S. Arcot Dt., T. Nadu St. **Dy.** Saṅgama, Virūpāksha, Ś. 1393 = 1471 A.D.

āḻākku (T. *n.*), liquid/grain measure ; **text[1] :** . . . . *oru tirunandāviaḻakku erippadaṟkku niśadam uḻakkā****ḻākke****ṉṉai* . . . ; **tr.** one ***āḻākku*** and *uḻakku* (liquid measure) of oil to be provided daily for burning one perpetual lamp . . ; *S.I.I.* III, pts. i & ii, No. 44, p. 95, ll. 9–10 ; Tiruvallam, Chittoor Tq. and Dt., A.P. St. **Dy.** Bāṇa, Mahāvalivāṇarāja, Ś. 810 = 888 A.D. ; **text[2] :** . . . . *iddēvarkku* . . . *niśada ney āḻākkāga iddēvar paṇḍārattil* . . . *veitta aṉṟāḍu naṟkāśu oṉbadu* ; **tr.** an amount of nine valid current *kāśu* (coin) was kept in the treasury of the god for (among other things) a daily provision of one **āḻākku** of ghee ; *S.I.I.* XVII, No. 319, p. 144, ll. 35–37 ; Kāḷahasti, Kalahasti Tq., Chittor Dt., A.P. St. **Dy.** Chōḷa, Rājēndrachōḷa I, reg. yr. 12 = 1023–24 A.D. ; **text[3] :** . . . . *Tirukkaṉṉīśvaram uḍaiya nāyaṉārkku amudupaḍikku ariśi kuṟuṇiyum kaṟi-amudu eḍai iruvattunāṟpalamum uppamudu* ***āḻākkum*** ; **tr.** for offering food services to the god Tirukkaṉṉīśvara, one *kuṟuṇi* (grain measure) of rice, vegetable weighing 24 *palams* (measure of weight) and one ***āḻākku*** (grain measure) of salt ; *S.I.I.* XVII, No. 171, p. 56, l. 12, Tirukaṇṭhēśvaram, Cuddalore Tq., S. Arcot Dt., T. Nadu St. **Dy.** Pāṇḍya, Sundarapāṇḍya I, reg. yr. 14 = 1264 A.D.; **text[4] :** . . . *akkāḷi prasādam* ***aḻākku*** ; **tr.** an offering of one ***aḻākku*** of a preparation called *akkāḷi* ; *S.I.I.* XVII, No. 275, p. 113, l. 8 ; Tirumalai, Chandragiri Tq., Chittor Dt., A.P. St. **Dy.** Sāḷuva, Narasiṁha, Ś. 1389 = 1468 A.D.

aḷam (T. *n.*), (salt-) pan ; **text :** . . . . *ivvūr uppupaḍukkum* ***aḷam*** . . . . ; **tr.** the **pan** in the village on which **salt** settles down ; *S.I.I.* VIII, No. 31, p. 15, l. 2 ; Śeyyūr, Madurantakam Tq., Chingleput Dt., T. Nadu St. **Dy.** Chōḷa, Kulōttuṅga I, reg. yr. 4 = 1074 A.D.

āḷ amañji (T. *n.*), forced labour ; **text[1] :** . . . *kāś-āyamum* ***āḷ amañji*** *tēvaigaḷum* . . . . *Aṅgada-vallavarkku jīvitamāga viṭṭu kalveṭṭi kuḍuttēṉ* ; **tr.** I gave as livelihood to Aṅgadavallavar land made free of taxes such as tax in cash, requirements of **forced labour**, etc. ; *S.I.I.* XVII, No. 755, p. 360, ll. 2–3 ; Tiruppāṟkaḍal, Walajapet Tq., N. Arcot Dt., T. Nadu St. **Dy.** Chōḷa, Kulōttuṅga III, reg. yr. 30 = 1207-08 A.D. ; **text**[2] : . . . . *tari iṟai taṭṭārpāṭṭam* . . . . ***āḷ amañji*** . . *uḷḷiṭṭa aṉaitt-āyavarggaṅgaḷ* ; **tr.** all varieties of taxes including tax on looms, tax on metal smith . . . . tax on **forced labour**, etc. ; *S.I.I.* VIII, No. 143, p. 40, ll. 13–15 ; Tīrthanagari, Cuddalore Tq., S. Arcot Dt., T. Nadu St. **Dy.** Pāṇḍya, Sundarapāṇḍya I, reg. yr. 13 + 3 = 1265 A.D. ; **text**[3] : . . . . *iṟaivari echchōṟu* ***āḷ amañji*** *nīrkūli yippaḍikkotta chil iṟaiyaḷum vēṇḍām eṉṟu kaṭṭaḷayiṭṭōm* ; **tr.** we ordered that the land be granted after exempting it from taxes such as *iṟaivari echchōru* **forced labour**, water cess and such other minor taxes ; *S.I.I.* XVII, No. 762, p. 364, ll. 16–18 ; Neḍuṅguḷam, Wandiwash Tq., N. Arcot Dt., T. Nadu St. **Dy.** Nāyakas of Tañjāvūr, Raghunātha-nāyakar, Cy. yr. Ānanda = 1614 A.D.

aḷaṁkāra (K. < Skt. *alaṁkāra*, *n.*), rhetoric ; **text:** . . . . *gaṇitaṁ vātsyāyanaṁ jyōtiśaṁ. . . . aḷaṁkāraṁ mahākāvya nāṭakaṁ eṁba . . . . kaḷāvidyeg-Anantavīryyamunipar sarvagñyar ī dhātriyoḷ* . . . . . ; **tr.** the ascetic Anantavvīryya was well versed in this world on arts and other subjects such as mathematics, erotics, astrology, **rhetoric**, the epics, drama, etc. ; *S.I.I.* XI, No. 61, p. 51, ll. 23–27 ; Marōḷ, Hungund Tq., Bijapur Dt., Karn. St. **Dy.** Chāḷ. of Kal., Jagadēkamalla I, Ś. 946 = 1024 A.D.

alaṁkāra satraṁ (Te. *n.*), school teaching rhetorics ; **text :** . . . *Ādivarāhasvāmi* ***alaṁkāra satrānaku*** *yichchina Bhūdāna dharma śāsanamu* ; **tr.** a pious edict recording the grant of land for the maintenance of the **school teaching rhetorics** in the temple of Ādivarāhasvāmi ; *S.I.I.* XVI, No. 298, p. 305, l. 5 ; Śrīmushṇaṁ, Chidambaram Tq., S. Arcot Dt., T. Nadu St. **Dy.** Āraviḍu, Veṅkaṭapati, Ś. 1503 = 1581 A.D.

āḷāniṉṟa kālam (T. *n.*), reign period ; **text :** . . . . *Kāviriyin vaḍakarai ellām* ***āḷāniṉṟa****-kālattu* . . . . ; **tr.** during his **reign period** when he was administering the entire area on the northern bank of the river Kāviri ; *Ch. naḍ.* 1971, No. 47, l. 5 ; Vīrāṇam, Chengam Tq., N. Arcot Dt., T. Nadu St. **Dy.** Pallava, Kampavarmaṉ, reg. yr. 14 = 860 A.D.

āḷa panṭuvake (K. *n.*), persons assigned to serve as a mark of honour ; **text :** . . . *Pallavāditya Noḷaṁbaseṭṭiendu pesaraṁ dayageydu paṭṭaṁgaṭṭi.* . . . . *kudure koḍe* ***āḷa panṭuvake*** . . . . *rāja chihnava koṭṭu* . . . . . ; **tr.** having conferred on him the title Pallavāditya Noḷaṁbaseṭṭi, he was given as symbols of dignity . . . horse, parasol, **persons assinged to serve as a mark of honour** and other honours of royal insignia ; *S.I.I.* IX, pt. i, No. 41, p. 24, ll. 14–15 ; Nelapalli, Punganur Tq. and Dt., A.P. St. **Dy.** Noḷ-Pal, Iṟiva Noḷaṁba II, in characters of 10th cent. A.D.

aḷappaṉa (T. *prn.*), commodities to be weighed ;

text[1] **:** .... *nellum ariśiyum maṟṟum* ***aḷappaṇa*** *koḍu vandu* ... ; **tr.** having brought in paddy, rice and other commodities to be weighed .. ; *S.I.I.* III, pts. iii & iv, No. 90, p. 222, ll. 4–5 ; Tirumeyjñānam, Nannilam Tq., Tanjavur Dt., T. Nadu St. **Dy.** Chōḷa, Āditya I, reg. yr. 2 = 873 A.D. ; **text**[2] **:** ..... *tuṟaiyilēṟuvaṇa iṟakkuvaṇa* .... ***aḷappaṇa*** .... *utpaṭṭa pāṭṭaṅgaḷ* ; **tr.** items including those to be loaded, unloaded, **weighed** in the harbour ; *S.I.I.* VIII, No. 403, p. 214, l. 3 ; Tiruppaḷani, Ramnad Tq. and Dt., T. Nadu St. **Dy.** Pāṇḍya, Vikramapāṇḍya, reg. yr. 4 = 1247 A.D.

aḷate (K. *prn.*), measure ; **text**[1] **:** .... *Nīḷada bhujeyaṁ dviguṇisi agaladoḷ oṁda kūḍi guṇisuvī kramad****aḷate****yalu śrī Sōmēśvaradēvarggūra mūḍa kaggurukkeyim teṁka mattaru mūru*.... ; **tr.** three *mattar* (a land measure) of land located to the east of the town and south of the Kagguṟu field, **measure**d according to the method of doubling of the length of the shoulders and adding one more shoulder length, donated to the god Sōmēśvaradēva; *S.I.I.* IX, pt. i, No. 249, p. 258, ll. 76–78 ; Kōlur, Bellary Tq. and Dt., Karn. St. **Dy.** Chāḷ. of Kal., Jagadēkamalla II, reg. yr. 10 = 1147 A.D. ; **text**[2] **:** .... *Naṛasiṁgarāya mahārāyara hesaralu Narasāṁbudhi eṁba hesaralu keṟeya kaṭṭikoṁḍu ā keṟeya gaddegaḷa* ***aḷate****yalu nāṟ-khaṁḍuga gadeyanu ... anubhavisaluḷavaru* ....; **tr.** having excavated a tank called Narasāṁbudhi after the king Narasiṁgarāya-mahārāya, a **measure** of 4 *khanḍugas* (land of the extent of being sown with 4 khaṁduga of seeds) of land under the tank was to be enjoyed (by the donor) ; *S.I.I.* IX, pt. ii, No. 472, p. 487, l. 3 ; Rāmāpuram, Madakasira Tq., Anantapur Dt., A.P. St. **Dy.** Sāḷuva, Narasiṁha, Ś. 1407 = 1485 A.D.

aḷavar (T. *n.*), agricultural community ; **text :** .. .. *uṅgal brahmakshētramāgil nīṅgaḷ uḻudu iṟukkai iṉṟiyē veḷḷāḷaṟ* ***aḷavar*** *paḷḷigaḷ paṟambar utpaḍa uḻudu iruttu* ..... ; **tr.** when you were asked to produce documents to prove that this is a land belonging to the brāhmaṇas which they were not cultivating and instead the **agirucultural communities** such as veḷḷāḷar, aḷavar, paḷḷigaḷ, paṟambar and others had been cultivating this land ; *S.I.I.* VII, No. 759, p. 385, l. 2 ; Tiruppā-ppuliyūr, Cuddalore Tq., S. Arcot Dt., T. Nadu. St. **Dy.** Pāṇḍya, Vikramapāṇḍya, in characters of the 13th cent. A.D.

aḷavu (K. *vb.*), weigh ; **text**[1] **:** .... *paradēśigaḷu* ***aḷava*** *tūguvay sambaraṁgaḷaluṁ eṇisuva davasaṁ māṟidalli koṭṭa hoṁge hāga 1* ... ; **tr.** the outside traders shall pay 1 *hāga* (a coin) for one *hoṁnu* (gold coin) for selling spices and grains **weighed** in a balance ; *S.I.I.* IX, pt. i, No. 297, p. 324, ll. 44–45 ; Kurugōḍu, Bellary Tq. and Dt., Karn. St. **Dy.** Kal. of Kal., Śaṅkhavarmadēva, Ś. 1099 = 1177 A.D. ; **text**[2] **:** .... *tāvu āḷutta irdda Ballaseya nālku gaḍiyiṁda voḷagaṇa samasta vṛittige kaṭṭida* *gēṇiya oḷage aramanege* ***aḷava*** *gēṇiya hāneyalu mūḍe 1 kkaṁ hāne 30 lekkadalu bhattada mūḍe 1000* ..... ; **tr.** from within the four boundaries of all the gift lands which were within the village of Ballase, which you were administering, 1000 *mūḍe* (a grain measure) of paddy measured by 30 *hāṇe* (a grain measure) for each *mūḍe* measured with the *hāṇe* **weighed** as per the royal balance of the palace had to be paid as tax ; *S.I.I.* VII, No. 203, p. 99, l. 6 ; Mūḍabidure, Mudabidure Tq., Udupi Dt., Karn. St. **Dy.** Chiefs of Nagire, Bhairavadēva, Ś. 1384 = 1462 A.D.

aḷavu varggam (T. *n.*), (tax on) a set of measures ; **text :** .... *innilattukku* ... *puṉpayir kuḷavaḍai* ***aḷavu varggam*** ...... *uḷḷiṭṭa aṉaittuvarggam* .... *utpaḍa iṟaiyiliyāga kallilum śembilum veṭṭikoḷḷachchoṉṉōm* ... ; **tr.** we have ordered it to be engraved on stone and copper that this land shall be free from taxes including those on dry crops and tank and taxes on **set of measures** ; *S.I.I.* II, pt. ii, No. 61, p. 247, ll. 8–11 ; Tañjāvūr, Tanjavur Tq. and Dt., T. Nadu St. **Dy.** Chōḷa, Kōṉēriṉmaikoṇḍāṉ, in characters of the 10th-11th cent. A.D.

āḻdana (K. *n.*), master ; **text :** .... *Ballahana besad āḷu Gajāṁkuśa Chōḷana mēge daṇḍu vōgalu Dilīpa Noḷaṁba daṇḍinalu kūḍi ibīḻida kāḷegadalu* ***āḻdana*** *besavēḍi sattam Ponnayya* ...... ; **tr.** when the soldiers of Ballaha waged a war against Gajāṁkuśa Chōḷa, Dilīpa Noḷaṁba joined his forces and in the battle of Ibīḻi, Ponnayya begged his **master** for permission to fight and laid down his life ; *S.I.I.* IX, pt. i, No. 25, p. 13, ll. 7–9 ; Maḍakasira, Madakasira Tq., Anantapur Dt., A.P. St. **Dy.** Rāshṭr., Kṛishṇa III (Ballaha), Ś. 870 = 948 A.D.

āḷe (K. *indec.*), while ruling ; **text :** .... *Gaṇḍatriṇētra Vaiduṁba mahārājar pṛithivi rājyaṁ geye Bālūchchoraṇi Sūramāṟaveḷi* ***āḷe*** ... ; **tr.** Gaṇḍatriṇētra Vaiduṁba Mahārāja was ruling over the earth **while** Bālūchchoraṇi was **ruling** over Sūramāṟaveḷi ; *S.I.I.* IX, pt. i, No. 13, p. 5, ll. 2–3 ; Basinikoṇḍa, Madanapalle Tq., Chittoor Dt., A.P. St. **Dy.** Vaid., Gaṇḍaṭriṇētra, in characters of 9th cent. A.D.

aḷe (K. *vb.*), to measure (the gifted land) ; **text :** ... *Beḷivaḷḷada mūḍana disābhāgadoḷu* ***aḷedu*** *koṭṭa keyi mattar 24* .... ; **tr.** 24 *mattar* (a land measure) of land on the eastern side of Beḷivaḷḷa was **measured** and granted ; *S.I.I.* IX, pt. i, No. 102, p. 75, ll. 25–26 ; Mailāra, Hadagalli Tq., Bellary Dt., Karn. St. **Dy.** Chāḷ. of Kal., Trailōkyamalla, Ś. 968 = 1046 A.D.

āle (K. *n.*), sugarcane crushing mill ; **text :** *Vaidyanāthadēvara aṁgaraṁga bhōgakke* ... *koṭṭaddu* .... *Kiṟugusūra grāmadiṁda aramanege Beḷakavāḍiya ṭhāṇeyakke* .... *saluvanta magga* ... *gāṇa* ... ***āle*** *muṁtāgi* ... *suṁka varaha ga 6 aksharadalu āṟu hoṁnu* .... ; **tr.** grant of tax incomes made to the god Vaidyanāthadēva from the taxes including those from handlooms, oil mills . . . **sugarcane crushing mill,** etc., which were normally payable from the village Kiṟugusūru to the palace and military establishment at Beḷakavāḍi ; *E.C.* (R) VII, Ml. 102, p. 405, ll. 10–12 ; Kiragasūru, Malavalli Tq., Mandya Dt., Karn. St. **Dy.** Saṅgama, Dēvarāya II, Ś. 1362 = 1440 A.D.

āledeṟe (K. *n.*), tax on sugar cane crushing mill ; **text[1]** : . . . *nall-ettu nall-eṁme* ***āledeṟe*** *maggadeṟe . . . inti oḷagāda ella hadikeyanū . . . pariharisikoṭṭu* . . . . ; **tr.** remmitting such taxes and hindrances as those on quality bullocks, quality buffaloes, **tax on sugarcane crushing mill,** tax on handlooms, etc. ; *E.C.* (R) VII, Ng. 73, p. 63, ll. 49–50, Beḻḻūru, Nagamangala Tq., Mandya Dt., Karn. St. **Dy.** Hoy., Vīranarasiṁha, Ś. 1206 = 1284 A.D. ; **text[2]** : (damaged). *Śrīnāḍa āledeṟe. . .* ; **tr. tax on the sugarcane crushing mills** of Śrīnāḍu ; *E.C.* (R) VII, Ml. 44, p. 373, l. 20 ; Naḍagalpura, Malavalli Tq., Mandya Dt., Karn. St. **Misc.**, Cy. yr. Pramādi = 1510 A.D.

ālemane (K. *n.*), place where sugarcane juice is extracted and jaggery prepared ; **text :** (damaged) *Koraṭahaḷiya pura teṟuva sidāya . . . ālemaneyali hōda ā pūrvvāya salipa haṇa* . . . ; **tr.** in the village of Koraṭahaḷi revenue collected in the form of permanent tax . . the arrears of money from the **place where sugarcane juice is extracted and jaggery prepared** ; *E.C.* (R) VII, Ml. 43, p. 372, ll. 9, 13–15 ; Basavanapura, Malavalli Tq., Mandya Dt., Karn. St. **Misc.**, Cy. yr. Śrīmukha = 1513 A.D.

ālesuṁka (K. *n.*), tax on sugarcane curshing mill; **text :** *Tuggilūra keṟe keḷagaṇa gadde tōṭa* . . . . . *maravaḷiya suṁka* ***ālesuṁka*** *samasta baḷi saha* . . . . . ; **tr.** all incomes including taxes on the wet land under the tank of Tuggilūru, the groves . . . . tax on yield from trees, **tax on sugarcane crushing mill** ; *E.C.* (R) VII, Ml. 139, p. 434, ll. 168–71 ; Sujjalūru, Malavalli Tq., Mandya Dt., Karn. St. **Dy.** Saṅgama, Virūpāksha, Ś. 1396 = 1473 A.D. ; **āleya-suṁka** ; **text :** *jāti terige samaya terige* ***āleya suṁka*** . . . *modalāda* . . . *sakala suṁka suvarṇādāya* ; **tr.** all tax and gold incomes such as tax on caste, tax on customs, tax on **sugarcane crushing mill,** etc., ; *E.C.* (R) VII, Ml. 106, p. 409, ll. 23–25 ; Muṭṉahaḻḻi, Malavalli. Tq., Mandya Dt., Karn. St. **Dy.** Tuḷuva, Narasiṁha, Ś. 1428 = 1506 A.D.

āḷgaḷ (T. *n.*), labourers, ; **text :** *tirunanda-vanañcheygiṟa* ***āḷgaḷ****ukku śōṟṟukkum irukkaikkum . . . viṭṭēn Vīranārasiṅgadēvaṉ* ; **tr.** I, Vīranāraśiṅga-dēva made an endowment for the feeding and residence of the **labourers** who were maintaining the temple garden ; *S.I.I.* VIII, No. 482, p. 252, l. 4 ; Kāḷahasti, Kalahasti Tq., Chittoor Dt., A.P. St. **Dy.** Chōḷa., Rājarāja III, reg. yr. 8 = 1224 A.D.

āḷi (K. *n.*), collection ; **text :** *sāsirvvaruv ayinūṟa nāluvaru nāluku paṭṭaṇada seṭigutaru mukhyavāgi ā mahājanaṁgaḷa saṁnnidhānadalu Dēviya* *chaitrada paruvakeṁdu eleya bojaṁgaru āḷinalu hā 1 daṁ biṭṭaru* .; **tr.** in the presence of the 1504 *mahājana* (an administrative body), seṭigutas of 4 towns, 1 *hā* (*hāga,* 1/4th portion) out of a **collection** of betel leaves were donated by the betel merchants for the festivities to the Goddess in the month of Chaitra ; *K.I.* V, No. 66, p. 248, ll. 22–25 ; Dhārwāḍa, Dharwar Tq. and Dt., Karn. St. **Dy.** Kād. of Goa, Jayakēśi III, reg. yr. 20 = 1206 A.D.

aḷi (K, *vb.*), to destroy ; **text :** *Chārukīrti-paṁḍitadēva ayyagaḷige .... biṭṭa .... haravariya dharmma-sthaḷavanu suṭṭu brāhmaṇanu aḷida saṁmaṁda ....* ; **tr.** a brāhmaṇa having burnt and **destroyed** the land gifted to Chārukīrti-paṁḍitadēva ayyagaḷ ; *S.I.I.* VII, No. 368, p. 224, ll. 9–10 ; Maṇigārakēri, Udupi Tq. and Dt., Karn. St. **Dy.** Saṅgama, Mallikārjuna, Ś. 1375 = 1453 A.D.

aḷidava (K. *n.*) violator of the provisions of a grant ; **text :** ..... *yī dharmavanu aṁnyāya* ***aḷidavaru*** *Vāraṇāsiyali sāvira kavileya vadhisida pāpadalu hōharu* ; **tr.** those who illegal **violaters of the provisions of this grant** would have, in effect, committed the sin of having killed one thousand tawny cows in Vāraṇāsi ; *S.I.I.* VIII, No. 379, p. 235, ll. 27–28 ; Kōṭakēṟi, Udupi Tq. and Dt., Karn. St. **Dy.** Saṅgama, Harihara II, Ś. 1304 = 1382 A.D. ; **aḷidāta** (K. *n.*) one who has destroyed ; **text :** *idan-**aḷidāta** Vāraṇāsiyuma kavileyuman-aḷida pātakanakku* ; **tr. he who has destroyed** the provisions of this grant would have, in effect, committed the sin of having **destroyed** Vāraṇāsi and tawny cows ; *S.I.I.* IX, pt. i, No. 54, p. 31, ll. 16–18 ; Rāmadurga, Bellary Tq. and Dt., Karn. St. **Dy.** Rāshṭr. Amōghavarsha, in characters of the 9th cent. A.D.

āḷina jana (K. *n.*), servants (in a temple) ; **text :** (damaged) .... ***āḷina jana*** *5 kaṁ harivāṇa 2* ; **tr.** five plates of food offerings earmarked for the **servants** (in the temple) ; *S.I.I.* IX, pt. ii, No. 489, p. 504, l. 54 ; Kāḷahasti, Kalahasti Tq., Chittoor Dt., A.P. St. **Dy.** Tuḷuva, Kṛishṇadēvarāya, Ś. 1435 = 1514 A.D.

aḷipu (K. *vb.*), destroy ; **text:** .... *yī dharmavanu āvanobba aḷipidavanu paṁchāḷakke hoṟagu āhaḷakke hoṟagu samayakkeū nāḍigū horagu* ; **tr.** whoever **destroys** the provisions of this grant will be ostracised from the community of five artisans, community of smiths, from his religion and from the district ; *E.C.* (R) III, Gu. 17, p. 18, l. 4 ; Guṁḍlupēṭe, Gundlupet Tq., Mysore Dt., Karn. St. Comm. gld, Ś. 1294 = 1372 A.D.

āḷiti virāḷālu (Te. *n.*), a kind of tax ; **text :** (obscure) ..... *mī pēṭalō pannuparāyalu* ***āḷiti virāḷālu,*** *suṅkha surākāralu vēttivēmulu yivi sakala munnu yivi ārabhyaṁgānu mūḍeṁḍlu paryantaṁ mānitini* .... ; **tr.** we exempt from collecting all taxes from your market town such as *pannuparāya* (*q.v.*), **aḷitivirāḷa,** suṅkha surākāra, veṭṭivēmu upto three years from now ; *S.I.I.* XVI, No. 334, p.

340, ll. 8–9 ; Amṛitalūru, Tenali Tq., Guntur Dt., A.P. St. **Dy.** Āravīḍu, Srīraṁga IV, Cy. yr. Dhātu = 1576 A.D.

aḷivam bage (K. *vb.*), intend to destroy (provisions of a grant) ; **text :** . . . . *yī dharmakk-***aḷivam-bage***dāta Vāraṇāsi-Kurukshētradoḷu kavileyma brāhmaṇarumaṁ koṁda mahāpātaka* . . . ; **tr.** he who **intends to destroy** the provisions of this grant would have, in effect, incurred the sin of having destroyed tawny cows and brāhmaṇas in Vāraṇāsi and Kurukshētra ; *S.I.I.* IX, pt. i, No. 206, p. 208, ll. 43–44 ; Rāmaghaṭṭa, Harapanahalli Tq., Bellary Dt., Karn. St. **Dy.** Chāḷ. of Kal., Vikramāditya VI, Ch. Vi. yr. 47 = 1122 A.D.

aḷivu (K. *n.*), depreciation tax ; **text :** . . . *mānyada mane 8 kaḷadu uḷida manegaḷige māḍida dinaṁmodalāgi mūru varusha mānya nākaneya varusha haṁneraḍu kaiyagalada mūvattu kai uddada mane 1 kke aḷivu anyāyagūḍi kaṭṭu guttageyāgi manevaṇa paṇa* . . . ; **tr.** with the exception of the 8 houses granted, for the rest of the houses from the date of their construction for 3 years there will not be levied any tax, after which from the 4th year onwards for houses measuring in width 12 cubics and 30 cubics in length for each such house a tax of 5 *paṇa* (a coin denomination) as house tax will have to be paid for such taxes as **depreciation tax** and *anyāya* (punitive tax) in accordance with the lease agreement ; *E.C.* (R) IV, Yl. 62, p. 306, ll. 32–38 ; Maddūru, Maddur Tq., Mandya Dt., Karn. St. **Dy.** Hoy., Ballāḷa III, Ś. 1250 = 1328 A.D.

aḻivu niṉai (T. *vb.*), think of violating (the provisions of the grant) ; **text :** . . . . *yi dharmmattukk aḻivu niṉaippār Gaṅgai iḍaik Kumari iḍai śeydār śeyda pāpam paḍuvār* ; **tr.** whoever **thinks of violating** the provisions of the grant would have, in effect, committed the sin in the area lying between the Ganges and Kanyākumari; *S.I.I.* VII, No. 443, p. 279, l. 5 ; Kalavai, Walajapet Tq., N. Arcot Dt., T. Nadu. St. **Dy.** Chōḷa., Vikramachōḷa, reg. yr. 7 = 1125 A.D.

aḻivu (T. *vb.*), expenditure ; **text :** . . . . *kōyilil* . . . . *eṇṇai eripadaṟkku* . . . **aḻivu** *śolla vaitta poṉ kaḻañju* ; **tr.** one gold *kaḻañju* (a coin) deposited for **expenditure** on oil for burning a lamp in the temple ; *S.I.I.* XXII, pt. i, No. 125, p. 103, ll. 2–4 ; Jambai, Tirukkoyilur Tq., S. Arcot Dt., T. Nadu St. **Dy.** Rāshṭr., Krishṇa III, reg. yr. 28 = 964–65 A.D.

aḻivu piḻai (T. *n.*), fine imposed on defaulter ; **text :** . . . . *iddēśattu* . . . . *uvviyum vey nellum aḻagerudum* . . . . **aḻivu piḻai***yum* . . . *viṭṭukoḍuttār amainda adikārar* . . . . ; **tr.** the concerned officer exempted payment of taxes such as *uvvi*, *vēy nel*, quality ox, **fine imposed on defaulter** in that area ; *T.A.S.* IV, No. 16, p. 91, ll. 2–3 ; Kēraḷāpuram, Padmanabhapuram Tq., Tiruvanantapuram Dt., Ker. St. **Dy.** Rulers of Vēṇāḍu, Udaiya Mārttāṇḍavarma, Kollam 491 = 1317 A.D.

aḷiya (K. *n.*), son-in-law / nephew ; **text**[1] : .... *daṇḍanāyaka Mārttaṇḍayyan-**aḷiya** Sattiyūra oḍeya Sōvimayya.... Sattiyūra Mahādēvargge .... eraḍu khaṇḍuga vedegaḻde .. viṭṭar* ; **tr.** Sōvimayya, the ***son-in-law / nephew*** *of daṇḍanāyaka* (commander of the army) Mārttaṇḍayya and administrator of Sattiyūru granted to the god Mahādēva of Sattiyūru 2 *khaṇḍugas* (a grain measure) of sowable wet land ; *S.I.I.* IX, pt. i, No. 99, p. 69, ll. 15–16, 19, 21, 24 ; Satturu, Bellary Tq. and Dt., Karn. St. **Dy.** Chāḷ. of Kal., Sōmēśvara I, Ś. 966 = 1044 A.D. ; **text**[2] : .... *Kāntārada baḍagaṇa maṭhada Rājarājēśvaratīrtha śrīpādaṁgaḷa bhikshā svāsthege ...... Kāṁtārada nāḍoḷage sāliya baḷiya Suḷakāṁtuvina **aḷiya** Pīlumaṭha-Dēvaraseṭṭiya braṁhadāya mūlada bhūmi vuḻḻiraḍiy-eṁba beṭṭina gaddegaḷu..... sarvamānyavāgi koṭṭevu* ; **tr.** for the proper conduct of the *bhikshe* ritual of Rājarājēśvaratīrtha śrīpādaṁgaḷu of the northern *maṭha* (religious institution) of Kāntāra, arable lands located at a higher level in an area called Vuḻḻiraḍi belonging to the *brahmdāya* given by Dēvaruseṭṭi of Pīlumaṭha, the **son-in-law/newphew** of Suḷakāntu, residing in Kāntāranāḍu ; *S.I.I.* VII, No. 230, pp. 116–17, ll. 7–8, 9–12, 17–18, Kāntāvara, Karkala Tq., Udupi Dt., Karn. St. **Dy.** Saṅgama, Dēvarāya, Ś. 1355 = 1433 A.D.

aḻiyāmē (T. *indec.*), without the principal amount being reduced ; **text** : ...... *iddharmam chandrādityavaṟ niṟkkumvaṇṇam ippoṉ mudal aḻiyāmēy idiṉāl vanda bhōgam uṇṇapperuvārāga vaittadu.....* ; **tr.** this endowment of gold has been granted to endure until the moon and sun last with the stipulation that, without reducing the principal, only the interest out of endowment is to be enjoyed : *S.I.I.* XIX, No. 458, p. 235, l. 5 ; Śembiyanmahādēvi, Nagapattinam Tq., Tanjavur Dt., T. Nadu St. **Dy.** Chōḷa, Uttama Chōḷa, in characters of 10th cent. A.D.

aḷiya saṁtāna (K. *n.*), matriarchal lineage of succession by son-in-law/nephew ; **text** : .... *Cheṁnaṁnaṇapaṇṇaṁg**aḷiya saṁtānaṁ**... Yelapa-bhūpālan* ; **tr.** the Lord Yalapa, the matriarchal successor of Chaṁnaṇapaṇṇa : *E.C.* VIII, Hn. 1, p. 214, ll. 10–12; Hassan, Hassan Tq. and Dt., Karn. St. **Dy.** Tuḷuva, Achyutarāya, Ś. 1454 = 1531 A.D.

āḷke (K. *n.*), administration ; **text** : .... *Piriyarasi Tribhuvanamalla Paṭṭamahādēvi Malayamatīdēviyaru Śrīdharayya daṁḍanāyakana binnapadim Siṁdavāḍināḍoḷage tamm-**āḷke**y-agrahāraṁ Tuṁbaḷada mahājanaṁ nūra-nālvadiṁbargaṁ .... biṭṭa dharma ...* ; **tr.** the senior crowned queen of the emperor Tribhuvanamalla viz., Malayamatīdēvi, at the request of Śrīdharayya daṇḍnāyaka who was administering Siṁdavāḍināḍu, made a grant to the 104 *mahājana* (an administrative body) of the *agrahāra* (brāhmaṇa settlement) Tumbuḷa which was within the area of the daṁḍanāyaka's **administration** ; *S.I.I.* IX, pt. i, No. 175, p. 169, ll. 14–15, 17–20 ; Chinnatuṁbaḷaṁ, Adavani Tq., Kurnool Dt., A.P. St. **Dy.** Chāḷ. of Kal., Tribhuvanamalla, Ch. Vi. yr. 32 = 1107 A.D.

āḷ kūli (T. *n.*), labourer's wages ; **text :** (damaged) . . . . *pattu mā nilam ivan-tāṉum tann uṟavu muṟaiyārum taṅgaḷ* . . . . ***āḷkūli****y-aṭṭi pasānamudal tiruttalnilam tirutti*. . . . . ; **tr.** having corrected the demarcation before cultivation with the help of **labourers** by paying the **wages**, the person (name not given) and his relatives who owned the land of the extent of 10 *mā* (land measure) ; *S.I.I.* VIII, No. 685, p. 345, l. 4 ; Allūr, Tiruchirapalli Tq. and Dt., T. Nadu St. **Dy.** Chōḷa, Kulōttuṅga III, reg. yr. 37 = 1215 A.D.

aḷḷu (K. *n.*), wages paid for measuring grains etc., in a shandy ; **text :** . . . *Bhairavadēvara saṁnidhiya saṁte kilavāgiralāgi prati huṭṭisi* ***aḷḷu*** *aḍikāsu saha dravya-mukhadiṁ dēvara dīpārādhanege*. . . . *kaṭṭaḷeyanikki* . . . . ; **tr.** the shandy of the temple of Bhairavadēva had become disfunctional. It was resumed and the income from that shandy including tax on **wages paid for measuring grains** etc. in a shandy and ground tax in the form of articles of kind were donated for providing a lamp for the god Bhairavadēva : *S.I.I.* IX, pt. ii, No. 532, p. 547, ll. 8–10, 13 ; Adamankōṭṭai, Dharmapuri Tq., Salem Dt., T. Nadu St. **Dy.** Tuḷuva, Achyutarāya, Ś. 1452 = 1530 A.D.

āḷ pōkku (M. *n.*), foot paths ; **text** : . . *śōlayum* ***āḷ pōkkum*** *vaḻiyum nīṟpōkkum* ; **tr.** the grove, the **foot paths**, the streets and the canals; *T.A.S.* Vol. V, No. 50, p. 165, ll. 8–10, Tiruvananta puram, Tiruvanantapuram Tq. and Dt., Ker. St. **Misc.**, Kollam 925 = 1749–50 A.D.

āḷ tēvai (T. *n.*), tax on servants ; **text :** . . . . *aṅgavaidyan* . . . *vaidyapurandararkku Vāṉavaṉmādēvi nāṉgellai uṭpaṭṭa* . . . . *veṭṭi* ***āḷ-tēvai*** *tachchuttēvai* . . . *maṟṟum eppērpaṭṭa iṟaigaḷum* . . . . . *tandōm* ; **tr.** we granted to the surgeon Vaidyapurandara all taxes (a number of taxes are mentioned) including free labour, **tax on servants**, tax on carpenter, etc. ; *S.I.I.* XXII, pt. i, No. 13, p. 9, ll. 1–2, 10–11, 13 ; Nāmakkal, Namakkal Tq., Salem Dt., T. Nadu St. **Dy.** Pāṇḍya, Sundarapāṇḍya, reg. yr. 8, in characters of 10th cent. A.D.

āḷu (K. *n.*), servant, agricultural labourer ; **text[1] :** . . . . *Vijayittanā****ḷu*** *Bāṇataṭṭaran tanna* ***āḷu*** . . . . *Kuṁtiāladali kudure ēṟi barutire Gaṇamūrti echchoḍe* . . . *idire naḍadu* . . . . . *taḷtu satta* . . . . . ; **tr.** the **servant** of Bāṇa-taṭṭara, a **servant** of Vijayitta was confronted at Kuṁtiāla by a mounted enemy Gaṇamūrti with whom he fought and killed and himself died ; *S.I.I.* IX, pt. i, No. 6, p. 3, ll. 7–11 ; Karshaṇapalle, Punganur Tq., Chittoor Dt., A.P. St. **Dy.** Bāṇa, Mahāvali, in characters of 9th cent. A.D. ; **text[2]** : (damaged) . . . ***āḷ****ige mū hēṟu* . . . . ; **tr.** 3 head loads are earmarked for the **agricultural labourer** ; *S.I.I.* IX, pt. ii, No. 411, p. 418, l. 20, Modalli, Kollegal Tq., Chamarajanagara

Dist., Karn. St. **Dy.** Saṅgama, Bukka I, Ś. 1288 = 1366 A.D.

āḷu (K. *vb.*), to administer, to rule ; **text**[1] : .... *Śrīmat Bijja Kōgaḻiyaynūṟu Māsiyavāḍi nūṟa-nālvattum-**āḷu**ttire* ..... ; **tr.** when the illustrious Bijja was **administer**ing Kōgaḻi-500 and Māsiyavāḍi-140 ; *S.I.I.* IX, pt. i, No. 57, p. 32, ll. 6–7 ; Kaḍabagere, Harapanahalli Tq., Bellary Dt., Karn. St. **Dy.** Rāshṭr., Indra III, Ś. 844 = 922 A.D. ; **text**[2] : ..... *Chirapi panneraḍu Mallaṇa Sivari **āḷe** Oḷageṟeya kaṭṭi paḍeda sāsana*..... ; **tr.** this inscription was commissioned when the Oḷageṟe tank was constructed by Mallaṇa Sivari while he was **administer**ing Chirapi-12 ; *S.I.I.* IX, pt. i, No. 26, p. 14, ll. 7–9 ; Maḍakaśira, Madakasira Tq., Anantapur Dt., A.P. St. **Dy.** Noḷ-Pal, Iṟiva Noḷaṁba, Ś. 872 = 950 A.D. ; **text**[3] : ..... *Sadāśivarāya-mahārāyaru Vijayanagariya siṁhāsanavan-**āḷu**va kāladalu* . . . *Ellapa Voḍeyaru Bārakūra siṁhāsanadalu kuḷitu rājyavan **āḷu**va kāladalu* ; ***tr.*** when the emperor Sadāśivarāya was **ruling** from the throne at Vijayanagari and when Ellappa Voḍeya was **administer**ing while seated on the throne at Bārakūra ; *S.I.I.* VII, No. 366, p. 222-23, ll. 7, 9–10 ; Maṇigārakēri, Udupi Tq. and Dt., Karn. St. **Dy.** Tuḷuva, Sadāśiva, Ś. 1486 = 1564 A.D.

āḷuḍaiyār (T. *n.*), deity, God ; **text**[1] : . . . *vēṭṭaikāraṉ. . . Śīyamuttarayaṉum. . . vēṭṭaikāran Pandalum vēṭṭai ponaviḍattu inda Śīyamuttaraiyaṉ kaiyil ambālē indap Pandal paṭṭameyil inda kuṟṟam nīṅga **Āḷuḍaiyār*** (text incomplete) . . . . ; **tr.** when the hunters Śīyamuttaraiyan and Pandal had gone on a hunting expedition Pandal was accidentally killed by the arrow from Śīyamuttaraiyan who in order to get himself cleared of the crime (gave to the) **god** (rest of the text is lost) ; *S.I.I.* VII, No. 105, p. 44, ll. 2–3, Tiruvottūr, Cheyyar Tq., N. Arcot Dt., T. Nadu St. **Dy.** Chōḻa, Rājādhirāja II, reg. yr. 4 = 1150 A.D. ; **text**[2] : . . . ***Āḷuḍaiyār** Tiruvirāmēśvaramuḍaiya nāyaṉāṟkku* ...... *amudupaḍi* (text incomplete). . . . ; **tr.** to the **god** Tiruvirāmēśvaramuḍaiyanāyaṉār (grants were made) for offering services such as *amudupaḍi* (*q.v.*) ; *E.C.* X, Muḷ. 73, p. 59, l. 3, Āvani, Mulbagal Tq., Kolar Dt., Karn. St. **Misc.**, Ś. 1249 = 1327 A.D.

alugu (Te. *n.*), weir ; **text** : . . . . . *Komāra Tiṁmānāyaniki puṇyaṁ gānu Kulūrichervu tūrpu palugu kaṭṭiṁchumani sabhavāru āṇatichchēganaka cheruvuku **alugu** muppadi mūḍu śilāsthaṁbhālu nilipi* .... *sōpānālu kalugu kaṭṭaṁgānu* ... *Rudrappa nāyiṁḍu kaṭṭiṁchinadi* .... ; **tr.** Rudrappa nāyiḍu, on the orders of the assembly of Kullūru, constructed for the merit of his father Komāra Timmanāyaḍu the eastern **weir** of Kullūru tank and fixed 33 stone slabs and built side walls and flight of steps in stone ; *N.D.I.* No. 35, p. 248–49, ll. 16–19, Kullūr, Atmakūr Tq., Nellore Dt., A.P. St. **Dy.** Āravīḍu, Veṅkaṭapatirāya, Ś. 1534 = 1612 A.D.

alugu rūkalu (Te. *n.*), tax levied on sluice ; **text:** . . . *Sōṁpalle kōṭa Chauṁḍēśvarammaku . . . . Sōṁpalle agrahāraṁ chatuśīmalōnu Mahārāja-tēvalaku vachhē* ***alugu-rūkalu*** *. . . . pūjaku . . . . istimi* ; **tr.** we grant the income from the **tax levied on the sluice** for the needs of the king collected within the four boundaries of Sōṁpalle agrahāra for offering worship to the goddess Chauṁḍēśvaramma ; *S.I.I.* XVI, No. 237, p. 243, ll. 4–5, 6–7, Sōṁpāḷem, Madanapalle Tq., Chittoor Dt., A.P. St. **Dy.** Tuḷuva, Sadāśiva, Ś. 1480 = 1559 A.D.

aḻugal śarakku (T. *n.*), tax levied on perishable items ; **text :** . . . . . . *innilattāl varum neṟkaḍamai kāśu kaḍamai . . . . . . payiṟ kaḍamai . . . .* ***aḻugal śarakku*** *. . . maṟṟum uḷḷa samasta prāptigaḷum . . . . . iṟaiyiliyāga kuḍuttōm . . . .* ; **tr.** we gave as tax free grant the revenues from paddy fields, tax in cash, tax on agricultural products, **tax levied on perishable items** and all such taxes raised on these lands ; *S.I.I.* VIII, No. 753, p. 384, ll. 8, 13–15, Paṇayavaram, ViluppuramTq., S. Arcot Dt., T. Nadu St. **Dy.** Chōḷa, Kulōttuṅga I, in characters of 11th cent. A.D. ; **aḻugaṟ śarakku, text :** . . . *tuṟaiyil ēṟuvaṉa iṟakkuvaṉa . . . . aḷappaṉa . . .* ***aḻugaṟ śarakku*** *. . . maṟṟum eppēṟppaṭṭaṉavum . . . . . .* ; **tr.** items including those to be loaded, unloaded, measured and the **tax levied on perishable items** in the harbour ; *S.I.I.* VIII, No. 403, p. 214, l. 3 ; Tiruppaḻani, Ramanatapuram Tq. and Dt., T. Nadu St. **Dy.** Pāṇḍya, Vikrama-pāṇḍya, reg. yr. 4 = 1247 A.D.

aḷuhu (K. *n.*), punitive tax on intentional damge ; **text :** . . . . . *aḷuhu anyāya aḍadeṟe . . . .* ; **tr.** taxes including punitive **tax on intentional damage,** *anyāya* (*q.v.*), *aḍadeṟe* (*q.v.*) etc. : *E.C.* (R) VII, Ml. 105, p. 407, l. 39 ; Tigaḍahaḷḷi, Malavalli Tq., Mandya Dt., Karn. St. **Dy.** Hoy., Ballāḷa III, Ś. 1260 = 1337 A.D.

āḷuṅgaṇam (T. *n.*), administrative body of brāhmaṇa settlements ; **text :** *Kāṇa-chchaturvēdimaṅgalattu* ***āḷuṅgaṇattu*** *kandāḍai . . Vāsudēva bhaṭṭaṉuṁ . . . . uḷḷiṭṭa sabhaiyōm . . . .* ; **tr.** the *sabhā* (committee) which included among others Kandāḍai Vasudēvabhaṭṭa a member of the **administrative body** of the brāhmaṇa settlement Kāṇachchaturvēdimaṅgalam ; *S.I.I.* VII, No. 415, p. 263, ll. 1–2 ; Kavantaṇḍalam, Kanchipuram Tq., Chingleput Dt., T. Nadu St. **Dy.** Chōḷa, Kulōttuṅga I, reg. yr. 26 = 1196 A.D. ; **āḷuṅgaṇattār** ; **text**[1]**:** . . . . . *Rājamalla-chchaturvēdimaṅgalam* ***āḷuṅgaṇattāru****ḷ maṇaṟpākkattu Kumāraḍibhaṭṭa vājapēyiyār* ; **tr.** Kumāraḍibhaṭṭa Vājapēyi of Maṇaṟpākkam who is a member of the **admnistrative body of the brāhmaṇa settlement** Rājamalla chaturvvēdimaṅgalam ; *S.I.I.* XIII, No. 292, p. 156, ll. 3–6 ; Brahmadēśam, Cheyyar Tq., N. Arcot Dt., T. Nadu St. **Dy.** Chōḷa, Rājakēsarivarman, reg. yr. 20 = 891 A.D. ; **text**[2] **:** *Śōḻaṉāṭṭu vaḍagarai Nallāṟṟūrnāṭṭu brahmadēyam*

Viḍēlviḍuguchaturvēdimaṅgalamāgiya Valliyanallūr ***āḷuṅgaṇattāruḷ*** *Aviśāgai Mahādēvabhaṭṭar magaṉ Gōvardhana-kramavittaṉ*. . . . . . (text damaged) ; **tr.** Gōvardhana kramavittaṉ, the son of Aviśāgai Mahādēvabhaṭṭar, a member of the **administrative body of the brāhmaṇa settlement** of the brahmadēya Viḍēlviḍugu chaturvēdimaṅgalam *alias* Valliyanallūr in Nallāṟṟūrnāḍu on the north bank (of the river) of Śōḻanāḍu ; *S.I.I.* VIII, No. 748, pp. 380–81, ll. 2–3 ; Tiruvāṉattūr, Viluppuram Tq., S. Arcot Dt., T. Nadu St. **Dy.** Chōḷa, Rājarāja I, reg. yr. 13 = 998 A.D.

aḷupu (K. *vb.*), to destroy ; **text**[1] : *ī dharma śāsana grāmavanu muṁde ārobbarū naḍesade aḷupidavaruge Gaṁgeya taḍiyalli . . . . brāṁṇaranū kapileyanū vadhisida pāpa* ; **tr.** whoever in future dares to destroy this village granted through a meritorious edict would have committed the sin of having killed brāhmaṇas and tawny cows on the banks of the river Ganges ; *E.C.* (R) III, Nj. 285, p. 361, ll. 24–28 ; Raṅgūpura, Nanjanagud Tq., Mysore Dt., Karn. St. **Dy.** Sāḷuva, Narasiṁha , Ś. 1435 = 1513 A.D. ; **text**[2] : *ī biṭṭanta patrasālavanu āvanādarū* ***aḷupi****dare Kāśi Rāmēśvaradalli sahasra kapileyanu brāhmaṇaranu koṁda pāpa* ; **tr.** whoever dares to destroy this letter of mortgage-release would have committed the sin of having killed tawny cows and brāhmaṇas in Kāśi and Rāmēśvara ; *E.C.* (R) II, Sb. 352, p. 204, ll. 26–30; Śravaṇabeḷagoḷa, Channarayapatna Tq., Hassan Dt., Karn. St. **Dy.** Woḍ. of Mys., Chāmarāja Woḍeya, Ś. 1556 = 1634 A.D.

āḷutanam (K. *n.*), service ; **text :** (damaged) . . . . *bhaṭārar rājyaṁ geye okkalan* ***āḷutanam*** *geye āneya . . . kondu kādi . . . . biddan* ; **tr.** while . . . . . *bhaṭāra* was ruling and a certain person (name lost) was in **service** as a tenant, he fought with an elephant, killed it and himself died ; *S.I.I.* IX, pt. i, No. 12, p. 5, ll. 2–3 ; Karshaṇapalle, Punganoor Tq., Chittoor Dt., A.P. St. **Dy.** Bāṇa, in characters of the 9th cent. A.D.

āḻvāṉ (T. *n.*), deity ; **text :** . . . . *ivvāḻvāṉukku nittappaḍikku irunāḻi tayiramudu śeygaikku* . . . . ; **tr.** for providing two *nāḻi* (liquid measure) of curd for the daily requirements of services to this deity ; *S.I.I.* III, No. 74, p. 164, l. 4 ; Kāñchīpuram, Kanchipuram Tq., Chengleput Dt., T. Nadu St. **Dy.** Chōḷa, Kulōttuṅga I, reg. yr. 39 = 1109 A.D.

aḻvār, āḻvār (T. *n.*), deity ; **text :** . . . . *Tiruvāmāttūr* ***āḻvār****kku śiṟukālaisandhiyilāḍi aruḷa . . . sabhaiyōmum ūrōmum . . . koṇḍa poṉ mukkaḻañju*; **tr.** for performing the devotional services to the **deity** of Tiruvāmāttūr , the *sabhā* (an administrative body) and the inhabitants of the village took charge of 3 gold *kaḻañjus* (coin) ; *S.I.I.* VIII, No. 748, p. 381, ll. 3–4; Tiruvāmāttūr, Viluppuram Tq., S. Arcot Dt., T. Nadu St. **Dy.** Chōḷa, Rājarāja I, reg. yr. 15 = 998 A.D. ; **āḻvār kaṉvigaḷ** (T. *n.*), servants of the deity ; **text :** . . . . *ippaḍi iśaindu śammadittu kuḍuttōm* ***āḻvārkaṉvigaḷ****ōm* ; **tr.** having agreed, we the **servants of the deity** gave our undertaking in writing ; *S.I.I.* III, pts. i & ii, No. 70, p. 150, l. 16 ; Śrīraṅgam, Tiruchirapalli Tq. and Dt., T. Nadu St. **Dy.** Chōḷa, Kulōttuṅga I, reg. yr. 18 = 1088 A.D.

āḷvari (T. *n.*), tax on persons employing servants ; **text:** . . . . *antarāyamum kammāḷa-magaḷmaiyum taṟi iṟaiyum* ***āḷvari****yum . . . . uḷḷiṭṭa kaḍamaigaḷellām Tiruvachchiṟupākkattu . . . . . Mādēvarkku. . . . kuḍuttōm . . . . . sabhaiyōm* ; **tr.** the members of the *sabhā* (committee) donated to the god Mādēva of Tiruvachchiṟupākkam, all incomes on taxes such as *antarāya* (*q.v.*), tax on smiths, tax on looms and **tax on persons employing servants** ; *S.I.I.* VII, No. 467, p. 290, ll. 41–42, 44–45, 50 ; Achcharapākkam, Madurantakam Tq., Chingleput Dt., T. Nadu St. **Dy.** Chōḷa, Vīrarājēndra, reg. yr. 5 = 1068 A.D.

āḷva prabhu (K. *n.*), ruling chieftain ; **text :** . . . . *Kōgiḷiyatīrthada Cheṁna Pārśvadēvarige* ***āḷva prabhu*** *Dēviseṭṭiyaru akshaya- bhaṁḍāravāgi nityābhishēkakke koṭṭa ga 1* . . . ; **tr.** the **ruling chieftain** Dēviseṭṭi donated to the god Cheṁna Pārśvadēva of the holy place Kōgiḷi 1 *ga* (*gadyāṇa,* a gold coin) as a permanent endowment for the daily anointment of the deity ; *S.I.I.* IX, pt. i, No. 346, p. 369, ll. 4–5 ; Kōgaḷi, Hadagalli Tq., Bellary Dt., Karn. St. **Dy.** Yādava, Rāmanātha, Cy. yr. Yuva = 1276 A.D.

āḷvār-bhaṇḍāram (T. *n.*), temple treasury ; **text :** . . . . *nilaṉ mūvēli . . . . kollayāga āḷvār bhaṇḍārattu idiṉukku tiruttuvīśam illāmayil tiruttuvīśamāga koṇḍa poṉ 300 kaḻañju. . . .* ; **tr.** 3 *vēli* (a land measure) of land having fallen fallow for want of money 300 gold coins of the denomination of *kaḻañju* (a gold coin) were given for reclaiming the fallow land ; *S.I.I.* XIX, No. 400, p. 210, ll. 7, 8 ; Uḍaiyārguḍi, Chidambaram Tq., S. Arcot Dt., T. Nadu St. **Dy.** Chōḷa, Uttamachōḷa, reg. yr. 16 = 987 A.D.

aḷuve (K. *n.*), river delta ; **text :** (damaged) . . . . *Basarūra . . . . aḷuveya . . . .* ; **tr.** river delta of Basarūru ; *S.I.I.* IX, pt. ii, No. 459, p. 471, l. 22 ; Basarūru, Kundapur Tq., Udupi Dt., Karn. St. **Dy.** Saṅgama, Mallikārjuna, Ś. 1387 = 1465 A.D.

āḷ vilai pramāṇa iśaivutīṭṭu (T. *n.*), deed of agreement for fixing the price on sale of slaves; **text :** . . . *Ediriliśōḷa-Gaṅgaināḍāḷvāṉēṉ* ***āḷ vilai pramāṇa iśaivutīṭṭu****kkuḍutta pariśu* ; **tr.** the price paid by Ediriliśōḷa Gaṅgaināḍāḷvāṉ as per the **deed of agreement for fixing the price on sale of slaves** ; *S.I.I.* XVII, No. 541, p. 224, ll. 2–4 ; Vēdāraṇyam, Tirutturaipundi Tq., Tanjavur Dt., T. Nadu St. **Dy.** Chōḷa, Rājarāja III, reg. yr. 3 = 1218-19 A.D.

ama (T. *n.*), to lie down ; **text :** . . . . *Gaṇi Nāgaṉ Gaṇi Nadaṉ iruvar* ***ama*** *kal* . . . . ; **tr.** the stone (beds) on which two Jaina priests Gaṇi Nāgaṉ and Gaṇi Nadaṉ *lie down* (to fast unto death) ; *E.T.E*, No. 48, p. 383, l. 1 ; Aḻagarmalai,

Melur Tq., Madurai Dt., T. Nadu St. **Misc.**, about 100 B. C.

amadaṭṭu (K. *n.*), flat land ; **text :** . . . . *Bēḍarahaḷi grāmakke . . . . saluva chatusīmege neṭṭa vāmana mudre kallige voḷagāda gadde beddalu tōṭa . . . amadaṭṭu kāḍāraṁbādi sakala suvarṇādāya . . . . ashṭabhōgatēja svāmyaṁgaḷanu . . . . anubhavisi . . . yeṁdu koṭa grāmada śilāśāsana . . . .* ; **tr.** the village edict at Bēḍarahaḷḷi registering the grant of all revenues in gold derived from paddy fields, dry land, garden, **flat land,** cultivated forest land etc., lying within the four boundaries of the village Bēḍarahaḷi for the enjoyment of all the 8 privileges ; *E.C.* (R) VIII, Hn. 55, p. 31, ll. 18–26; Kallubyāḍarahaḷḷi, Holenarasipur Tq., Hassan Dt., Karn. St. **Dy.** Āravīḍu, Śrīraṁgarāya, Ś. 1579 = 1658 A.D.

amaichchu (T. influenced by M., *n.*), ministry ; **text :** . . . . *ippariś oṭṭiṉa kālattu muṭṭāde cheluttād-oḻivarāgil* ***amaichchuḷḷu**ṟutta kōyil-adhikārikku mūṟṟukkaḻaññum . . . . poṉ daṇḍap-paḍakkaḍavar* . . . . ; **tr.** in case of failure to abide by the payment of stipulated expenses the defaulter shall be liable to pay a fine of 100 *kaḻañju* (coin) of gold to the officer of the temple in the presence of the **ministry** ; *T.A.S.* V, No. 11, p. 35, l. 4, Peruneyil (suburb of Cheṅganachery), Chenganachery Tq., Ker. St. **Misc.**, in characters of 10th-11th cent. A.D.

amainda adikārar (T. influenced by M. *n.*), designated officer ; **text :** *Muttalaikkuṟichchi vīra Kēraḷa Īchchuvarattu Mādēvarkku chelaviṉṉum tirunandāviḷakkiṉṉum eḻudi viṭṭu koḍuttār* ***amainda adikārar*** ; **tr.** to meet the expenses of lighting a perpetual lamp to the god Mādēva in the temple of Vīra Kēraḷa Īśvaram in Muttalai-kkuṟichchi the **designated officer** wrote this edict making necessary grants ; *T.A.S.* IV, No. 16, p. 91, l. 2 ; Kēraḷāpuram, Padmanabhapuram Tq., Tiruvananthapuram Dt., Ker. St. **Dy.** Rulers of Vēṇāḍu, Udaiya-Mārttāṇḍavarmaṉ, Kollam 491, reg. yr. 4 = 1317 A.D.

amaiñja adikārar (T. influenced by M. *n.*), designated officer ; **text**[2] **:** *śiri vīra Pattaṉābha-Māttāṇḍavarmma Tiruvaḍikk* ***amaiñja adikārar*** ; **tr.** the **designated officer** under śrī Vīra Padmanābha Mārttaṇḍavarmman-tiruvaḍi ; *T.A.S.* IV, No. 43, p. 152, l. 4 ; Varkalai, Padmanabhapuram.Tq. and Dt., Ker. St. **Dy.** Rulers of Vēṇāḍu, Udaiya-Padmanābha-Mārttāṇḍavarmaṉ, Kollam 427 = 1252 A.D.

amaiñji (T. *n.*), forced labour ; **text :** . . . . *inniḻam uḻudār kalichcheṅgālakku vēṇḍum* ***amaiñji*** *śeyvārgaḷāgavum. . . .* ; **tr.** those who cultivate the land below the excess water flowing from the dam shall engage required **forced labour** ; *S.I.I.* VIII, No. 1, p. 2, l. 9 ; Vēppaṅguḷam, Kanchipuram Tq., Chingleput Dt., T. Nadu St. **Dy.** Chōḷa, Rājēndra II, reg. yr. 6 = 1060 A.D. ; **amañji** (T. *n.*) ; **text:** *ibhūmiyāl vanda . . .* ***amañji*** *veṭṭi . . . . eppēṟpaṭṭa* *iṟaiyum kāṭṭa peṟādomānōm* ..... ; **tr.** we shall not show all revenue income derived from **forced labour**, free labour and all such incomes .. ; *S.I.I.* III, pts. iii and iv, No. 116, p. 252, ll. 12–14 ; Vēḷachchēri, Saidapet Tq., Chinglept Dt., T. Nadu. St. **Dy.** Chōḷa, Parāntaka II Sundara Chōḷa, reg. yr. 7 = 964 A.D.

amaladāra (K. < Mrt. *n.*), revenue officer ; **text:** *Prasaṁna Naṁjuṁḍēśvaradēvarige* ..... *varshaṁpratiyallū munnūra toṁbhatta mūru varahāvu aydu haṇa tastīku naḍaśikoṁḍu baruvaṁte yī Mysūru tālōku* ***amaladāra****nige sahā namma āḷida mahāsvāmiyavara buddhi saṁnadu arpaṇe māḍiśi koṭṭu idhe* ..... ; **tr.** the king has issued orders to the **revenue officer** of Mysore taluk that a sum of three hundred and ninety three *varaha* (a coin) and five *haṇa* (a coin denomination) should be paid each year to the god Prasaṁna Naṁjuṁḍēśvaradēva ; *E.C.* (R) V, Mys. 1, p. 145, ll. 19–22 ; Mysore, Mysore Tq. and Dt., Karn. St. **Dy.** Woḍ. of Mys., Kṛishṇarāja III, Ś. 1743 = 1821 A.D. ; **amaludār** (K. *n.*), revenue officer ; **text :** ... *Heggaḍadēvanakōṭe* ***amaludāra*** *Śāṁtayyana maga Dēvachandrayyage yināmāgi appaṇe koḍisiddu* ... *Narasiṁhapura grāmadali bedalu kaṁḍu 12* .... ; **tr.** a gift of 12 *kaṁḍu* (khaṁḍuga, land to the extent of being sown with 12 khaṁḍuga of seeds) of dry land in the village of Narasiṁhapura in Heggaḍadēvanakōṭe was ordered to be given to Dēvachaṁdrayya the son of the **revenue officer** Śāṁtayya ; *E.C.* (R) III, Hg. 118, p. 512, ll. 9–11 ; Narasīpura, H.D. Kote Tq., Mysore Dt., Karn. St. **Dy.** Woḍ. of Mys., Kṛishṇarāja III, Ś. 1751 = 1829 A.D.

amaṇan (T. < Skt. *śramaṇa, n.*), Jaina monk ; **text** : .... ***amaṇaṉ*** *Madirai Attiraṉ uṟai* ; **tr.** the abode of Attiraṉ, the **Jaina monk** from Madirai ; *E.T.E.*, No. 24, p. 351, l. 1, Mēṭṭupaṭṭi, Nilakottai Tq., Dindigal Dt., T.Nadu St. **Misc.** in characters of about 2nd cent. B.C. ; **amaṇṇaṉ** ; **text** : ... *amaṇṇaṉ Yāṟṟūr Śeṅkāyapaṉ uṟaiy* ; **tr.** the abode of the **Jaina monk** Śeṅkāyapaṉ of Yāṟṟūr ; *E.T.E.*, No. 61, p. 405, l. 1, Pugaḷūr, Karur Tq. and Dt., T. Nadu St. **Misc.**, in characters of about 2nd cent. A.D.

amara (K. < Skt. *n.*), permanent fiefdom ; **text** : ... Suṁkaṇanāyakarige *Kṛishṇadēva mahārāyaru namage* ***amara****ke pālisida Ādavāniya durggadoḷagaṇa keṟe* ; **tr.** the tank located inside the fort of Ādavāni which was granted to us, Suṁkaṇanāyaka, made as a **permanent fiefdom** by Kṛishṇadēvarāya ; S.I.I. IX, pt. ii, No. 521, p. 537, ll. 5–6, 10–13, Cheruvu Beḷagallu, Kurnool Tq. and Dt., A.P. St. **Dy.** Tuḷuva, Kṛishṇadēvarāya, Cy. yr. Sarvajit = 1527 A.D. ; **amara daṁṇāyakatana** (K. < Skt. *n.*), permanent Army Commandership ; **text :** .. *Achutarāya mahārāyaru Keṟeya Timmarasayanavarige* ***amara daṁṇāyakatana****ke pālisida Śāntigrāma* ; **tr.** the village of Śāntigrāma given as a gift for the post of **permanent Army**

commandership to Timmarasaya of Keṟe by Achyutadēvamahārāya ; *E.C.* (R) VIII, Hn. 166, p. 400, ll. 11–12, Śāntigrāma, Hassan Tq. and Dt., Karn. St. **Dy.** Tuḷuva, Achyuta, Ś. 1454 = 1532 A.D.

amara grāma (K < Skt. *n.*), village gifted permanently ; **text** : . . . *Huligeṟeyanāḍa* . . . ***amara grāma*** *bhaṇḍāragrāmagaḷa heṇṇu gaṁḍina maduveya suṁkavanu biṭṭevu* ; ***tr.*** we granted the tax amount levied on brides and grooms in the **village gifted permanently** and in the villages belonging to the royal treasury ; *S.I.I.* XX, No. 238, p. 289, ll. 17–19, 22 ; Lakshmēśvara, Shirahatti Tq., Dharwar Dt., Karn. St. **Dy.** Tuḷuva, Sadāśiva, Ś. 1469 = 1547 A.D.

amaram (T. < Skt. *n.*), permanent fiefdom ; **text:** . . . . . . *iṟaiyilippaṟṟu paṇḍāravāḍai* ***amaram*** *likitachchīvitam uḷḷiṭṭa nāḍu nāṭṭavarkku nirūpam* ; **tr.** order issued in regard to tax free holdings, villages belonging to the royal treasury, **permanent fiefdom** and land leased in writing for subsistence; *S.I.I.* XVII, No. 562, p. 237, ll. 6–8 ; Tēvūr, Nagapattinam Tq., Tanjavur Dt., T. Nadu St. **Dy.** Saṅgama, Dēvarāya II, Ś. 1347 = 1426 A.D. ; **amara māgaṇe** (Skt. + K., *n.*), permanent fiefdom; **text** : (damaged) . . . *Rāma* . . . . *namage* ***amara māgaṇe****ge naḍeva Vijayanagarada mūḍalu Udagiriya bāgila muṁdaṇa Anaṁtapurada grāma*; **tr.** the village of Anaṁtapura situated to the east of Vijayanagara facing the gateway of Udagiri being enjoyed as a **permanent fiefdom** by Rāma . . . . ; *S.I.I.* IX, pt. ii, No. 654, p. 649, l. 2, 5, Hampi, Hospet Tq., Bellary Dt., Karn. St. **Dy.** Tuḷuva, Sadāśiva, Ś. 1476 = 1554 A.D.

amara māgaṇi (Skt. + K. *n.*), permanent fiefdom; **text** : . . . *Sadāśiva- dēvamahārāyarugaḷu* . . . . *Veṁkaṭādrirāja ayinavarige* ***amara magaṇi****ge pālisida Ādavāni sīme*. . . . ; **tr.** permanent **fiefdom** of Ādavāni territory bestowed upon Veṁkaṭādrirāja-ayinavaru by Sadāśivarāya mahārāyaru ; *S.I.I.* IX, pt. ii, No. 671, p. 663, ll. 10–11, 15–17 ; Būdūru, Adavani Tq., Kurnool Dt., A.P. St. **Dy.** Tuḷuva, Sadāśiva, Ś. 1482 = 1560 A.D. ; **amara māgaṇi** (Skt. + Te. *n.*) ; **text** : . . . . *Raṁgājeṭṭigāru* . . . . . *māku* ***amara magaṇi*** *pāliṁchina guttisīma*. . . . ; **tr.** the territory of Gutti given to me as **permanent fiefdom** by Raṁgājeṭṭi ; *S.I.I.* XVI, No. 284, p. 289, ll. 8, 10–11 ; Chitrachēḍu, Gooty Tq., Anantapur Dt., A.P. St. **Dy.** Āravīḍu, Śrīraṁga I, Cy. yr. Śrīmukha = 1573 A.D. : **amara māgaḷe** (Skt. + K. *n.*), permanent fiefdom ; **text** : . . . *Kṛishṇapa-nāyakanavara* ***amara māgaḷe****ge salluva Morabada sīmeyoḷagaṇa Paṁnula-Nuṁkanahaḷḷiyanu Dēvalāpurada Vasanta Mallikārjuna dēvarige* . . . *koṭṭa grāma* ; **tr.** village of Paṁnula-Nuṁkanahaḷḷi situated within the Moraba district which was a **permanent fiefdom** enjoyed by Kṛishṇapanāyaka was granted to the god Vasanta-Mallikārjunadēva of Dēvalāpura ; *S.I.I.* IX, pt. ii, No. 647, p. 643, ll. 11–13, 17 ; Dēvalāpura, Kudligi Tq., Bellary Dt., Karn. St. **Dy.**

Tuḷuva, Sadāśiva, Ś 1474 = 1552 A.D.

amara nāyakatana (Skt. + Kan. *n.*), headship of permanent fiefdom ; **text :** . . . . *Aṁṇamarsaru Tiruvadiya Vīraṭadēvarige koṭṭa dharmaśāsana. . . . . . namma amara-nāyakatana Vaḷidilaṁbaṭina-chāvaḍiya . . . . . Satyābharaṇa-nallūra grāma* ; **tr.** the pious edict of the Satyābharaṇa-nallūru given to the god Vīraṭadēva of Tiruvadi by Aṁṇamarasa during his **headship of the permanent fiefdom**; *S.I.I.* IX, pt. ii, No. 463, p. 475, ll. 2, 5–6 ; Tiruvadi, Cuddalore Tq., S. Arcot Dt., T. Nadu St. **Dy.** Sāḷuva, Narasiṁha, Cy. yr. Vikṛiti = 1470 A.D.

amara perggaḍe (K. *n.*), person holding permanent position of headmanship ; **text :** . . . ***amara perggaḍe*** *Cheṇṇanayyanuṁ avara kōlgāra Gaṇapatiyuṁ . . . Bāḍada Svayaṁbhū dēvargge . . . aydu . . naṁdādīvige biṭṭaru* ; **tr.** Cheṇṇanayya, **holding permanent position of headmanship** and his staff-bearer Gaṇapati granted five perpetual lamps to the god Svayaṁbhūdēva of Bāḍa ; *E.C.* XI, Dg. 141, p. 197, ll. 29, 34–36 ; Bāḍagrāma, Davanagere Tq. and Dt., Karn. St. **Dy.** Chāḷ. of Kal., Trailōkyamalla, Ś. 986 = 1065 A.D.

amara pradhāni (K. *n.*), minister holding permanent fief ; **text :** . . . *Ajilara ilada* ***amara pradhāni*** *Biṁṇāṇiṁbaḷiya Ādyadēvarasaru Yēnūra Śāṁtīśvara chaityālayadalū chaturviṁśati tīrthakara pratimeyanu . . . . māḍi . . . . barasta śilāśāsana* ; **tr.** stone edict registering the installation of the images of the 24 Tīrthakaras in the temple of Śāṁtīśvara at Yēnūru by Ādyadēvarasa of the lineage of Biṁṇāṇi, who was **holding permanent fiefdom** as **minister** in the palace of the Ajila ruler ; *S.I.I.* VII, No. 256, p. 130, ll. 7–10, 12 ; Vēṇūr, Karkala Tq., Udupi Dt., Karn. St. **Dy.** Ajila, Pāṇḍyadēva, Ś. 1459 = 1537 A.D.

amātya (K. < Skt. *n.*), minister ; **text[1] :** . . . *śrī Poḻalchōradēvanisht**āmātyaṁ*** *Śrīvatsagōtrajaṁ Chāvuṇḍayya* ; **tr.** Chāvuṇḍayya of Śrīvatsagōtra the favourite **minister** of Poḻalchōradēva ; *S.I.I.* IX, pt. i, No. 30, p. 17, ll. 65–67, Kambadūru, Kalyanadurga Tq., Anantapur Dt., A.P. St. **Dy.** Noḷ-Pal., Iṟiva-Noḻambādhirāja, Ś 887 = 965 A.D. ; **text[2] :** *mahāmaṁḍaḷēśvaraṁ Tailahadēvaru . . . āḷuttamire avar-****amātya*** *mahāpradhānaṁ daṁṇḍanāyaka Tīkimayyaṁ Tiḷivaḷiyanāḷuttamire*; **tr.** when *mahāpradhāna* (chief minister) *daṁṇḍanāyaka* (commander of the army) Tīkimayya the **minister** was administering Tiḷivaḷi during the reign of *Mahāmaṇḍaḷēśvara* (a great divisional administrator) Tailahadēva ; *K.I.* V, No. 23, p. 86, ll. 9–11 ; Tiḷivaḷḷi, Hangal Tq., Dharwar Dt., Karn. St. **Dy.** Chāḷ. of Kal., Sōmēśvara III, reg. yr. 3 = 1129 A.D. ; **text[3]** (Skt. *n.*) **:** . . . . . *asti śrī Rāyas-āṁko dvijakulatilakas Sōma****yāmātya****sūnuḥ* ; **tr.** there flourishes the illustrious Rāyasa who is a forehead mark in the community of brāhmaṇas and who is the son of the **minister** Sōmaya ; *S.I.I.* VII, No. 572, p. 341, ll. 10–12 ; Penukoṇḍa, Penukonda Tq., Anantapur Dt., A.P. St. **Dy.** Tuḷuva, Achyutarāya,

Ś. 1454 = 1532 A.D.

amāvāśipuram (T. *n.*), endowment made for the occasion of *amāvāsyā* ; **text :** . . . . *nāṅgaḷ* ***amāvāśi ppuṟamāga*** *uṉgaikku ivvuḷḷūr brāhmaṇar pattu kalamum apūrvigaḷ pattu brāhmaṇar pattu kalamum āga kalam iruvudum uṉgaikku . . . . iṟaiyili nilam kuḍutta pariśu* ; **tr.** we granted a tax-free land yielding 20 *kalam* (a grain measure) of grain out of which 10 *kalam* was **endowed for** feeding local *brāhmaṇas* and 10 *kalam* for feeding unexpected guests **on the day of *amāvāsyā*** ; *S.I.I.* XVII, No. 607, p. 275, l. 4 ; Tiruvārūr, Nagapattinam Tq., Tanjavur Dt., T. Nadu St. **Dy.** Chōḷa, Vikramachōḷa, reg. yr. 3 = 1120–21 A.D.

ambala (K. *n.*), public hall ; pavilion ; **text[1] :** . . *Kaṁbaḷiyada mahājanaṁ grāmasamudāya māḍi paḍeda dāna Koṅgaḷkeya Pudigeṟeya Koṇavūra tammūra paḍeda dhanamuṁ keṟegaṁ dēgulakkaṁ basadigaṁ* ***ambala****kkaṁ atithigaṁ koṭṭar* . . . . ; **tr.** money-grant received by the *mahājanas* (an administrative body) of Kaṁbaḷi who had met together and had received as grant the villages of Koṅgaḷke, Pudigeṟe, Koṇavūru and their own village for the tank, temple, Jain temple and **public hall** and guests ; *E.C.* (R) III, Gu. 92, p. 70, ll. 1–4 ; Saṁpigepura, Gundlupet Tq., Mysore Dt., Karn. St. **Misc.,** in characters of 9th cent. A.D. ; **text[2] :** . . . *Baṭakaḷada* ***aṁbala****da aṁgaḍiyalli Yekapanāyakana hesaralu yikkida vīragalinalli kālampratiyalu eṟeva aravaṭṭige dharma* . . . . ; **tr.** a charitable road side shed where water, buttermilk, etc., are offered free to travelers was established permanently by the side of the hero stone set up in the name of Yekapanāyaka in the stall adjoining the **public hall** of Baṭakaḷa ; *K.I.* III, pt. i, No. 14, p. 47, ll. 64–65 ; Bhaṭkaḷ, Bhatkal Tq., Karwar Dt., Karn. St. **Dy.** Tuḷuva, Sadāśiva, Ś. 1467 = 1545 A.D. **aṁbalagoṭṭage** (K. *n.*), outhouse of a public hall; **text :** . . . . *araḷiya kaṭṭeyali kuḍinīran eṟeva brāhmaṇage biṭṭa mūlada bāḷina vivara . . . . idaṟoḷagaṇa ādāyavū maṭhake* ***aṁbalagoṭṭagege*** *bāvige* . . . . ; **tr.** the details of the land given to the brāhmaṇa who was engaged in supplying drinking water at the platform of the peepal tree is as follows . . . the revenue income coming from that land is remitted to the maṭha, to the **outhouse of the public hall** and the well ; *S.I.I.* IX, pt. ii, No. 446, p. 456, ll. 51–52, 60 ; Basarūru, Kundapur Tq., Udupi Dt., Karn. St. **Dy.** Saṅgama, Dēvarāya, Ś. 1358 = 1436 A.D. ;

ambalam (T. *n.*); **text[1] :** *Sundaraśōḷacheruppēdi-maṅgalattu sabhaiyōm ivāṇḍu mithuna nāyiṟṟu 26 āntiyadi nāḷkuṟichāṟṟi maṇiy-****ambala****ttukkūṭṭam kuṟaivaṟak-kūḍiyirundu* ; **tr.** the *sabhā* (committee) of the brāhamaṇa settlement Sundara-chōḷacheruppēdimaṅgaḷam having met in full quorum in the **pavilion** called maṇiambalam on the previously fixed 26th day which was a Sunday in the month of Mithuna in that year ;

T.A.S. IV, No. 34, p. 138, ll. 3–6 ; Śuchīndram, Agastheeswaram Tq., Kanyakumari Dt., T. Nadu St. **Dy.** Chōḷa-Pāṇḍya, Jaṭāvarmaṉ, reg. yr. 24 = 1042 A.D. ; **text**[2] : . . . . *Kuḻutturai-dēśattu Mañjaviḷāgattu vīṭṭil Pichchapiḷḷai Kaṉṉampiḷḷai paḻaya-sandayil* . . . . ***ambala****vum keṭṭi kiṇaṟum veṭṭi toṭṭiyum adichchiṭṭu* . . . . . ; Pichchappiḷḷai Kannampiḷḷai having built a **public hall**, dug a well and made a water-cistern in the old market of the house of Mañjaviḷāgam in Kuḻutturai-dēśam ; *T.A.S.* V, No. 37, pp. 134–35, ll. 7–10, 13–16, Slab in the Govt Museum at Tiruvanantapuram, Tiruvanantapuram Tq. and Dt., Ker. St. **Misc.**, Kollam 957 = 1782 A.D. ; **ambalam meḻuguvāḷ** (T. *n.*), lady who mops the public hall ; **text :** (text damaged) . . . ***ambalam meḻuguvāḷ****ukku niśadi nel* ; **tr.** daily paddy for the **lady who mops the the public hall** ; *S.I.I.* VIII, No. 612, p. 313, l. 61 ; Tiruchchenduṟai, Tiruchirapalli Tq. and Dt., T. Nadu St. **Dy.** Chōḷa, Rājakēsarivarman, reg. yr. 8, in characters of 10th–11th cent. A.D.

ambalappaṭṭi (T. *n.*), land endowed for the maintenance of the public hall ; **text :** . . . . *Rājēndraśōḷa Īśvaramuḍaiya Mahādēvar tirunandavāṉattukkum* ***ambalapaṭṭi****kkum* . . . . . *mērkku* ; **tr.** to the west of the garden of the temple of Rājēndrachōḷa Īśvaramahādēva lies the **land endowed for the maintenance of the public hall** ; *S.I.I.* VIII, No. 67, p. 36, l. 4 ; Tiruvaṇṇāmalai, Tiruvannamalai Tq., N. Arcot Dt., T. Nadu St. **Dy.** Chōḷa, Rājēndra I, reg. yr. 18 = 1030 A.D. ; **ambalappuram** (T. *n.*), land enodwed for the maintenance of a public hall ; **text :** . *brahmadēyam. Viḍēlviḍugu-maṅgalattu nāṉ eḍupitta ambalattukku* ***ambalappuṟam*** ; **tr. land endowed for the maintenance of the public hall** built by me in Viḍēlviḍugumaṅgalam; *S.I.I.* VIII, No. 612, p. 313, ll. 52–54 ; Tiruchchenduṟai, Tiruchirapalli Tq. and Dt., T. Nadu St. **Dy.** Chōḷa, Rājakēsarivarman, reg. yr. 6, in characters of the 10th-11th cent. A.D.

ambalimaṉ (K. *n.*), land granted to a person for his livelihood for services rendered; **text :** . . . *Taḷavananagara Śrīvijaya jinālayakke* . . . . *pannirkkaṇḍuga* ***aṁbalimaṇ****ṇuṁ* . . . *pririkeṟeyoḷaṁ rājamānaṁ* . . . . *pannirkkaṇḍugaṁ dattaṁ* ; **tr.** twelve *khaṇḍuga* (land to the extent of being sown with 12 khaṁḍuga of seeds) of **land granted to a person for his livelihood for services rendered** and 12 *khaṇḍuga* of land measured by the royal measuring rod in Pirikeṟe were given to Śrīvijaya Jinālaya of Taḷavananagara ; *E.C.* (R). I, Cg. 1, p. 2, ll. 18, 20–21 ; Maḍikēri, Madikeri Tq., Kodagu Dt., Karn. St. **Dy.** W. Gaṅga, Avinīta, Ś. 388 = 466 A.D.

aṁbara (K. < Skt. *n.*), firmament ; **text :** . . *Yādavakul-****āṁbara****-dyumaṇi sarvajña-chūḍāmaṇi* ; **tr.** the ornament in the **firmament** of the Yādava family and the pearl on the forehead indicative of omniscience ; *E.C.* (R) X, Ak. 232, p. 285,

l. 29–30 ; Hāranahaḷḷi, Arasikere Tq., Hassan Dt., Karn. St. **Dy.** Hoy., Narasiṁha II, Ś. 1156 = 1234 A.D.

aṁbaṭṭan (T. *n.*), barber ; **text :** ... ***ambaṭṭa****nukku karaṇikku piṟandān rathakāranāṉa kammāraṉ* . . . . . ; **tr.** a person born to the **barber** and a woman of mixed caste is designated as a blacksmith and also as a *rathakāra* (chariot-maker) . . ; *S.I.I.* XVII, No. 603, p. 271, l. 13 ; Tiruvārūr, Nagapattinam Tq., Tanjavur Dt., T. Nadu St. **Misc.**, in characters of 12th cent. A.D.

aṁbaṭṭakamma (K. *n.*), barbers' profession ; **text :** (damaged) . . . . . . ***ambaṭṭakamma*** . . . ; **tr. barbers' profession** ; *E.C.* VII, Sh. 115, p. 116, ll. 13–14 ; Kuṁsi, Shimoga Tq. and Dt., Karn. St. **Misc.**, undated, in characters of 10th cent. A.D.

aṁbigadeṟe (K. *n.*), professional tax levied on ferrymen ; **text :** . . . . *Ānūra* ***aṁbigadeṟe****ya Rāmanāthadēvara naṁdādīvige naivēdyakke biṭṭa dhanu* ; **tr.** the **professional tax levied on ferry men** collected at that village was granted as charity for the perpetual lamp and food service to the deity Rāmanāthadēva ; *E.C.* VII, Hnl. 8, p. 370, ll. 62–64, Honnāḷi, Honnali Tq., Shimoga Dt., Karn. St. **Dy.** Hoy., Narasiṁha, Ś. 1150 = 1228 A.D.

aṁbigageyi (K. *n.*), land granted to a ferry man in recognition of services rendered ; **text :** . . . . *Perggaḍegeyi matta 8* ***aṁbigageyi*** *matta 8 taḷāṟageyi matta 12* ; **tr.** 8 *matta* (a land measure.) of land granted to the village headman, 8 *matta* of **land granted to ferry man in recognition of his services rendered** and 12 *matta* of land given to the town watchman ; *S.I.I.* IX, pt. i, No. 74, p. 45 , ll. 8–9, Kañchagāra-Beḷagallu, Alur Tq., Bellary Dt., Karn. St. **Dy.** Chāḷ. of Kal., Sōmēśvara I, Ś 903 = 981 A.D.

aṁbōdhi (K. < Skt.), ocean ; **text :** . . . . *ā narapatig-****aṁbōdhi****ganūnagabhīrateye samanisirpaṁtire sanmānini Yēchaladēvi* . . . *samanisidaḷ* . . . . ; **tr.** just as flawless majesty adorns the **ocean,** so also the respected Yēchaladēvi adorned the ruler as his queen ; *E.C.* (R) X, Ak. 162, p. 215, ll. 8–10, Taḷalūru, Arsikere Tq., Hassan Dt., Karn. St. **Dy.** Hoy., Ballāḷa. in characters of 12th cent. A.D.

aṁbu[1], arrow ; **text**[1] (K. *n.*) **:** (obscure) . . . . *uṟakkīlichchidava****aṁbu*** . . ; **tr.** the **arrow** which has pierced the chest (of the enemy) ; *S.I.I.* IX, pt. i, No. 392, p. 403, l. 3 ; Kariyaṅgaḷa, Mangalore Tq. and Dist., Karn. St. **Dy.** Āḷupa, Raṇasāgara, in characters of 8th cent. A.D. ; **text**[2] (T. *n.*) **:** . . . *vēṭṭaikāraṉ* . . . . *Śīyamuttarayaṉum* . . . . *vēṭṭaikāraṉ Pandalum vēṭṭai pōnaviḍattu inda Śīyamuttaraiyaṉ kaiyil-****ambālē*** *indap-Pandal paṭṭaṉayil inda kuṟṟam nīṅga āḷuḍaiyār* (the text is incomplete) . . . ; **tr.** when the hunters Śīyamuttaraiyaṉ and Pandal had gone on a hunting expedition Pandal was accidentally killed by the **arrow** from Śīyamuttaraiyaṉ who, in order to get himself cleared of the crime (gave to the god) Āḷuḍaiyār (rest of the text is lost) ;

S.I.I. VII, No. 105, p. 44, ll. 2–3, Tiruvottūr, Cheyyar Tq., N. Arcot Dt., T. Nadu St. **Dy.** Chōḷa, Rājādhirāja II, reg. yr. 4 = 1150 A.D. ; **text**[3] (T. *n.*) : . . . .*vēṭṭai pōnda iḍattu . . . eyda* ***ambu*** *. . . tappi dēvanai . . . paṭṭadukku pi.r.āyachittamāga nāyanārkku vaitta tirunandāviḷakku* . ; **tr.** a perpetual lamp dedicated to the god for the atonement of having killed Dēvan by mistake when he shot the **arrow** ; *S.I.I.* VIII, No. 115, pp. 57–58, ll. 2–4 ; Tiruvaṇṇāmalai, Tiruvannamalai Tq., N. Arcot Dt., T. Nadu St. **Dy.** Chōḷa, Rājadhirāja II, reg. yr. 4 = 1150 A.D.

ambu[2] (T. *n.*), seasonal crop ; **text** : (text obscure) . . . . . . *kaḍaippūvum* ***ambum*** *. . . uḷḷiṭṭa aṉaittu payi.r.um* ; **tr.** all crops including flowers for sale, **seasonal crops**, etc. ; *S.I.I.* II, pt. i, No. 22, p. 114, l. 8; Tañjāvur, Tanjavur Tq. and Dt., T. Nadu St. **Dy.** Pāṇḍya, Kōnēriṉmaikoṇḍāṉ, in characters of 12th cent. A.D.

aṁbudhi (K. < Skt. *n.*), irrigation tank ; **text** : *. . . ā sthaḷadalu Narasiṅgarāyamahārāyara hesaralu Naras**āṁbudhi** eṁba hesaralu ke.r.eya kaṭṭikoṁḍu ā ke.r.eya gaddegaḷa aḷateyalu nākhaṁḍuga gaderu dhāreneradu koṭṭa* . . . ; **tr.** gave with the ablution of water 4 *khaṁḍuga* (land to the extent of being sown with 12 khaṁḍuga of seeds) of wet fields under the **irrigation tank** built in the name of Narasiṁha mahārāya in that place ; *S.I.I.* IX, pt. ii, No. 472, p. 487, ll. 2–3, Rāmāpuram, Madakasira Tq., Anantapur Dt., A.P. St. **Dy.** Sāḷuva, Narasiṁha, Ś. 1407 = 1485 A.D.

ambumudu (K. *n.*), a kind pearl ; **text** : . . . *ku.r.umuttum nimboḷamum payiṭṭamum* ***ambumudum*** *ka.r.aḍum* . . . . ; **tr.** small pearls, nimboḷa, payiṭṭa, **a kind of pearl**, crude pearls, etc. ; *S.I.I.* II, pt. i, No. 3, p. 26, 16th section, ll. 1–4 ; Tañjāvūr, Tanjavur Tq. and Dt., T. Nadu St. **Dy.** Chōḷa, Rājarāja I, reg. yr. 29 = 1015 A.D.

aṁchu ōṇi (K. *n.*), boundary lane ; **text** : . . . . *Chōḷikēriya halara gaḍiyiṁda baḷaga Chōḷikēriya halara paḍuva mane Hatvārara gaḍiyiṁda mūḍa heddāri* ***aṁchu vōṇi*** *iṁdaṁ teṅka yī gaḍiyoḷage bittuva gadde muḍi 13*. . . . ; **tr.** the paddy field of the extent of being sown with 13 *muḍi* (a grain measure) of seeds situated to the north of the boundary of *halaru* (an administrative body) of Chōḷikēri, to the east of the western house of Hatvār a member of the *halaru* of Chōḷikēri and to the south of the **boundary lane** of the high way ; *S.I.I.* VII, No. 375, p. 231, ll. 34–37, Maṇigārakēri, Udupi Tq. and Dt., Karn. St. **Dy.** Āravīḍu, Śrīraṁga, Ś. 1502 = 1580 A.D.

aṁdalaṁ (Te. *n.*), a palanquin, an insignia of a subordinate chief ; **text** : . . . . *ātani bhaktiki śaktiki mechchi* ***aṁdalaṁ***. . . . . *ātapatra nicheyaṁbunuṁ* . . . . *Kaṁṭanikichche* ; **tr.** appreciating the devotion and strength of Kaṁṭa, he was rewarded with a **palanquin**, an parasol and other insignia ; *S.I.I.* IV, No. 675, p. 207, ll. 30–33, Nādeṇḍla, Narasaraopet Tq., Guntur Dt.,

A.P. St. **Dy.** Nādeṇḍla Chfs., Goṁka, Ś. 1062 = 1140 A.D.

āṁdupannu (K. *n*), a kind of tax ; **text** : . . . . *Kuṟukuṁdiya grāmada nāyiṁdarige* . . . ***āṁdupannu*** *biṭi* . . . *biḍisidāta Kaṁdanavōḷa*. . . . *Koṁḍōja* . . . . . ; **tr.** the barbers of the village Kurukuṁdi were exempted from payment of taxes such as **aṁdupannu**, forced labour etc., through the good offices of Koṁḍōja of Kaṁdanavōḷu ; *S.I.I.* IX, pt. ii, No. 615, p. 621, ll. 8–13 ; Kuṟukundi, Ālūr Tq., Bellary Dt., Karn. St. **Dy.** Tuḷuva, Sadāśiva, Ś. 1466 = 1545 A.D.

aṁga (K. *n*.), corporeal remains ; **text :** . . . . . . *śrīman Noḷaṁba mahādēviyar**aṁga**vaṁ Gaṁgeyoḷ-ikki baṁda brāhmaṇa Mādhava śaḍaṁgi* . . . ; **tr.** the brāhmaṇa Mādhava śadaṁgi who had returned after consigning the corporeal remains of the illustrious Noḷaṁba-mahādēvi in the river Gaṁgā; *S.I.I.* IX, pt. i, No. 91, p. 62, ll. 32–36 ; Oruvayi, Bellary Tq. and Dt., Karn. St. **Dy.** Chāḷ. of Kal, Jayasiṁha II, Ś. 958 = 1036 A.D.

aṁgabhōga (K. < Skt. *n*.), services to the deity's image : **text**[1] : . . . . *dēvara **aṁgabhōga**kke mattaru 10* . . . . . ; **tr.** 10 *mattar* (a land measure) land granted for the **services to the deity's image** ; *S.I.I.* IX, pt. i, No. 133, p. 116, l. 27, Chinnatumbaḷam, Adavani Tq., Kurnool Dt., A.P. St. **Dy.** Chāḷ. of Kal., Sōmēśvara II, Ś. 990 = 1068 A.D. ; **text**[2] : . . . . *Sāvaṁtēśvaradēvaraṁ pratishṭheyaṁ māḍi ā dēvara śrīkāryakkaṁ **aṁgabhōga** raṅga bhōgakkaṁ biṭṭa dharmma* . . ; **tr.** grant made for the general services, **services to the deity's image** and entertainment of the deity Sāvaṁtēśvara after installing the image ; *K.I.* V, No. 42, p. 173, l. 77, Tiḷivaḷḷi, Hangal Tq., Dharwar Dt., Karn. St. **Dy.** Sēü. of Dēv., Siṁghaṇa II, Ś. 1160 = 1238 A.D.

aṁgabhōgamu (Te. < Skt. *n*.), ; **text** : . . . *iṁtavaṭṭu dēvaraku aṁgabhōgamu* . . . ; **tr.** in this way the **services to the deity's image** is to be performed ; *S.I.I.* X, No. 334, p. 174, l. 92 ; Durgi, Palnad Tq., Guntur Dt., A.P. St. **Dy.** Kākatīya, Gaṇapatidēva, Ś. 1173 = 1251 A.D.

aṁgachitta (K. < Skt. *n*.), ornament offered as gift to a person : (in verse) . . . . *Kuntaḷa chakravartiyoḷu* . . . . *paḍedaṁ dhare baṁṇisal**aṁgachitta**maṁ sadamaḷa rājachihnavan* . . . . ; **tr.** he obtained from the emperor of Kuntaḷa the world famous ornament, the pure royal insignia ; *K.I.* IV, No. 10, p. 27, ll. 18–19, Hirehaḷḷi, Byadagi Tq., Dharwar Dt., Karn. St. **Dy.** Chāḷ. of Kal., Vikramāditya VI, Ś. 1043 = 1121 A.D.

aṁgadaṭṭā (K. < Skt. *n*.), a cloth to cover the upper part of male body or the image of a male deity ; **text :** *teresīre **aṁgadaṭṭā** sīguri chāmara ālavaṭṭakkevuṁ ga* 3 *pa* 5. . . . ; **tr.** (donation of) 3 *ga* (*gadyāṇa*, a coin) and 5 *pa* (*paṇa*, a coin) for the provision of a curtain, **a cloth for covering the upper part of the image**, an umbrella, a fly-whisk and a hand fan ; *E.C.* (R) V, T. N. 96, p. 495, ll. 78–79 ; Sōmanāthapura, Bannur Tq., Mysore Dt., Karn. St. **Dy.** Hoy., Narasiṁha III, Ś. 1192 = 1270 A.D.

aṁgadhāra (K. *n.*), bodyguard ; **text** : . . . . *sakalaguṇa saṁpannarappa Sāṁtayya-dēvavaḍeyara* ***aṁgadhāranu*** . . . . . *Vīrapanu Śrī giri Mallikārjuna dēvarige . . . . biṭṭa Mallināthapurada maṭhadeṟe* . . . . . ; **tr.** the tax on the religious institution in Mallināthapura gifted to the god Mallikārjunadēva of Śrīgiri by Vīrapa, the **bodyguard** of Saṁtayyadēva-vaḍeya who was endowed with all good qualities ; *E.C.* (R) IV, Pp. 89, p. 551, ll. 2–7 ; Mallināthapura, Piriyapatna Tq., Mysore Dt., Karn. St. **Misc.**, Cy. yr. Subhānu = 1403 A.D.

aṁgaḍi (K. *n.*), shop ; **text**[1] : . . . . *Āhavamalladēvar . . . . koṭṭa vyavasthe eṁtendaḍe . . . . . . seṭṭiyargge mattar eṇchhāsiram avargge mānyaṁ mattar eṁṭu nūṟu tōṁṭaveṁṭu* ***aṁgaḍi*** *eṁṭu* . . . . ; **tr.** as per the arrangment made by the Āhavamalladēva, the seṭṭis (traders) were given eight thousand *mattar* (a land measure) of land, another eight hundred *mattar* of land, eight groves and eight **shops** ; *S.I.I.* IX, pt. i, No. 77, p. 48, ll. 2, 19, Kōgaḷi, Hadagalli Tq., Bellary Dt., Karn. St. **Dy.** Chāḷ. of Kal., Sōmēśvara I, Ś. 914 = 992 A.D. ; **text**[2] : . . . . *satrakke biṭṭa dhammaveṁteṁdaḍe hoṟagaṇiṁ bandettu* . . . . *dēvar****aṁgaḍi*** . . . . ; **tr.** tax incomes from bull brought from outside, (a number of shops including) the shop in which articles of worship are sold are granted to the choultry . . ; *K.I.* II, No. 21, p. 82, ll. 21–24 ; Telsang, Athani Tq., Belgaum Dt., Karn. St. **Dy.** Chāḷ. of Kal., Jagadēkamalla, Ś 1069 = 1147 A.D. ; **text**[3] : . . . . *sīmeya vivara* . . . . *beṁṇeya Bhaṁḍāriyavar-****aṁgaḍi****ya* . . . *gaḍiyiṁdaṁ* . . . . *paḍuvalu* . . . . ; **tr.** as per the details of the boundaries, the land lay to the west of the boundary of the shop of Bhaṁḍāri a butter merchant ; *S.I.I.* VII, No. 349, p. 207, ll. 15–16, Chauḷikēri, Udupi Tq. and Dt., Karn. St. **Dy.** Saṅgama, Bukkarāya, Ś. 1328 = 1406 A.D.

aṁgaḍi āya (K. *n.*), revenue from shops ; **text** : . . . . . *mahāmaṇḍalēśvara* . . . *Raṁggarāja rāmarāja-ayanavaru biṭu koṭa Chikadēvarabasti dēva Śāṁtināthasvāmige koṭa dīvaṭigege* ***aṁgaḍi āya*** . . . . . ; **tr.** the **revenue from shops** granted to Śāṁtināthasvāmi of Chikadēvarabasti by Raṁggarājarāmarāja-ayanavaru for lighting a torch; *S.I.I.* IV, No. 247, p. 40, ll. 13–17, Hampi, Hospet Tq., Bellary Dt., Karn. St. **Dy.** Tuḷuva, Sadāśiva, Ś. 1479 = 1557 A.D. ; **aṁgaḍidappade** (K. *indec.*), all shops without exemption ; **text** : . . . *dēvargge* ***aṁgaḍidappad****ondu māna lekka* . . . . *jōḷamaṁ koṭṭar.* . . . . ; **tr.** one *māna* (a grain measure) of millet was donated to the god from **all the shops without exception** ; *S.I.I.* XI, pt. i, No. 116, p. 116, l. 39, Kop, Bagalakote Tq. and Dt., Karn. St. **Dy.** Chāḷ of Kal., Sōmēśvara II, Ś. 997 = 1075 A.D.

aṁgaḍider̤e (K. *n.*), tax on shop ; **text** : . . . . *Beḷḷūroḷagaṇa dēvara **aṁgaḍider̤e**yiṁda ā dēvarugaḷa amṛitapaḍigeyuṁ ā nibaṁdhada parivārada jīvitavarggavoḷagāyitakke eṁdeṁdigevū naḍeva maryyāde śrīmanu mahāpradhānaṁ Perumāḷedēva daṁṇāyakaru parichayisida paḍi* . . . . . ; **tr.** the arrangment made by the illustrious chief minister Perumāḷedēva-daṁṇāyaka for performing the services such as food offerings to the deities and for the livelihood of the concerned temple staff from the taxes levied on the shops; *E.C.* (R)VII, Ng. 73, p. 63, ll. 51–53, Beḷḷūr, Nagamangala Tq., Mandya Dt., Karn. St. **Dy.** Hoy., Narasiṁha III, Ś. 1206 = 1284 A.D.

aṁgaḍi horigeya baḷḷa (K. *n.*), licensed grain measure to be used in shops ; **text** :. . . . . ***aṁgaḍi horigeya baḷḷa*** *aivattara lekkada akki mūḍe 24* . . . ; **tr.** 24 *mūḍe* (a grain measure) of rice at the rate of 50 licensed grain measure to be used in shops ; *Ep. Ind.* XX, No. 8, p. 94, ll. 44–45, Kāpu, Udupi Tq. and Dt., Karn. St. Nāyakas Keḷadi, Sadāśivanāyaka, Ś. 1479 = 1557 A.D.

aṁgaḍi mane (K. *n.*), shop-cum-residence ; **text** :. . . . . . *Svayambhū Rāmēśvaradēvara hālumaṇḍagege hiriyakōla eṁṭu mattarkeyyumaṁ. . . . aṁgaḍimane yumaṁ*. . . . ; **tr.** for the offering of a sweet dish called *hālumaṁḍege* to the god Svayambhū āmēśvaradēva eight *mattar* of land measured by he bigger rod and one shop-cum-residence were given ; I *K.I.* II, No. 24, p. 91, ll. 33–34, Rāmatīrtha, Athaṇi Tq., Belgaum Dt., Karn. St. Kal. of Kal., Bijjaḷa, Ś. 1089 = 1166 A.D.

aṁgaḍi nāyakuḍu (Te. *n.*), Superintendent of market ; **text** : . . . *Oḍḍavāḍi Chiṁgamaśeṭṭi manumaṁḍu Bhīmuśeṭṭi koḍuku **aṁgaḍi-nāyakuṁḍa**ina Arjamaśeṭṭi . . . Śrīkūrmanāthuniki . . . dīpamu chelluṭakunu peṭṭinā . . . kaṁchu dīpa*; **tr.** the bronze lamp gifted to the temple of the god Śrīkūrmanātha by Arjamaśeṭṭi, the **Superintendent of market** who was the son of Bhīmuśeṭṭi and grandson of Chiṁgamaśetti of Oḍḍavāḍi ; *S.I.I.* V, No. 1163, p. 423, ll. 5–8 ; Śrīkūrmam, Srikakakulam Tq., Ganjam Dt., A.P. St. **Misc.**, Ś. 1206 = 1284 A.D.

aṁgaḍi suṁkamu (Te. *n.*), tax on shops ; **text :** . . . . *Dēvēśvara śrī Mahādēvaranu pratishṭha śēsi nivēdyapaḍulakūnu aṁgaraṁgabhōgālakūnu Naṁdamūrupalliya* . . . . ***aṁgaḍi suṁkamu****nu* . . . . . *istimi* . . . . . ; **tr.** we donate the **tax on shops** collected from Nandamūrupalli for the offering of food and services to the image of the god Dēvēśvara śrī Mahādēva after installing the image of the deity ; *S.I.I.* V, No. 116, p. 43, l. 8 ; Rājamahēndravaram, Rajamahendravaram Tq., E. Godavari Dt., A.P. St. **Dy.** Kākatīya, Gaṇapatidēva, Ś. 1170 = 1248 A.D.

aṁgaḍiya suṁka (K. *n.*), **tax on shops** ; **text** : *Hāsanada sahasraliṁgada śrī Rāmanāthadēvarige Koṁganāḍa suṁkada Haṁpaṁṇa Guṁmaṁṇa Basavaṁṇanavaru dēvara amṛitapaḍi vīḷayakkevū* *naḍavaṁtāgi . . . . maggadere āḍude..re bālavaṇa kabbu ūroḷagṇa paṁchakārakaru . . ā . . . dēvara maṭha eraḍ**aṁgaḍiya suṁka** . . . dēvarige . . . māḍikoṭṭa datti. . . . . ;* **tr.** grant given by Haṁpaṁṇa, Guṁmaṁṇa and Basavaṁṇa the revenue officials of Koṁganāḍu to the god śrī Rāmanāthadēva, for the offering of food and betel leaves, including tax incomes such as on looms, sheep, cattle, sugarcane, marriage and the artisans as well as **tax on two shops** ; *E.C.* (R) VIII, Ag. 45, p. 143, ll. 6–8, 9–14, 23–24, Rāmanāthapura, Arakalagud Tq., Hassan Dt., Karn. St. **Dy.** Hoy., Narasiṁha III, Ś. 1197 = 1275 A.D.

aṁgajāvige (K. *n.*), bodyguards doing duty by turns ; **text** : *mahājanaṁgaḷige koṭṭa Śrōtriya-agrahāra dānaśilāśāsanada kramaveṁteṁdare . . . . . **aṁgajāvige** . . . adhikāriya uḍugo..re sēnabōyike . . . muṁtāgi ēnuḷa sarvvasvāmyavanu nīvu . . . āgumāḍikoṁḍu bhōgisibahudu . . .* ; **tr.** as per the grant of the brāhamaṇa settlement Śrōtriya-agrahāra given to the *mahājana* (an administrative body), they were to enjoy all revenue incomes such as those imposed on **bodyguards doing duty by turns**, gifts given to the officials and tax on the office of the village head, etc. ; *S.I.I.* IX, pt. ii, No. 440, pp. 448–49, ll. 12–13, 26–30, Rājabāvanahaḷḷi, Harapanahalli Tq., Bellary Dt., Karn. St. **Dy.** Saṅgama, Dēvarāya, Ś. 1341 = 1419 A.D.

aṁgaṇa (K. *n.*), land in front of a building ; **text :** (damaged) . . . ***aṁgaṇa**da mu. 20* ; **tr.** 20 *mu* (*muḍi*, land measurement) from the **land in front of the building** ; *S.I.I.* VII, No. 274, p. 142, l. 14, Kāpu, Udupi Tq. and Dt., Karn. St. **Dy.** Āḷupa, Sōyidēva, Ś. 1247 = 1325 A.D.

aṁgaḷa (K. *n.*), sa. aṁgaṇa ;**text :** *Uḍupin**aṁgaḷa**d iṁda baḍaga . . . Kṛshṇadēvara bāḷina chatusīmeya vivara. . . .* ; **tr.** details of the four boundaries of the land belonging to the god Kṛishṇadēva located to the north of the open **land in front of the temple** at Udupi ; *S.I.I.* VII, No. 299, p. 152, ll. 36–37, Udupi, Udupi Tq. and Dt., Karn. St. **Dy.** Saṅgama, Harihararāya, Ś. 1317 = 1395 A.D.

aṁgarakka nāyaka (K. *n.*), chief bodyguard ; **text :** ***aṁgarakka nāyaka**ṁge gadyāṇaṁ hattu . . . .* ; **tr.** ten *gadyāṇa* (gold coin) for the **chief bodyguard** ; *E.C.* (R) V, T. N. 88, p. 480, l. 85 ; Sōmanāthapura, Bannur Tq., Mysore Dt., Karn. St. **Dy.** Hoy., Narasiṁha III, Cy. yr. Dhātri = 1276 A.D.

aṁgarakshe (K. *n.*), providing protection ; **text :** *samastarājyada bhavyajanaṁgaḷa anumatadiṁda Beḷuguḷada tīrthadalli vaishṇava **aṁgarakshe**gōsuga. . . . Jainaru bāgilugaṭṭaḷeyāgi mane manege varshakke 1 haṇa koṭṭu ā ettida hoṁniṁge dēvara **aṁgarakshe**ge ippattāḷanu saṁtaviṭṭu mikka hoṁniṁge jīrṇa jinālayaṁgaḷige sōdayanikkuvudu . . .* ; **tr.** with the permission of the entire Jaina laity in the kingdom, in the holy place of Beḷuguḷa, for **providing protection** to the image of the Vaishṇava deity, one *haṇa* (a coin denomination) of money per year was collected from each house as individual house contribution and from the amount thus collected for the protection of the deity's image 20 persons were appointed and the rest of the gold was spent on the white washing of the dilapidated Jaina temples ; *E.C.* (R) II, Sb. 475, p. 286, ll. 22–26 ; Śravaṇabeḷagoḷa, Channarayapatna Tq., Hassan Dt., Karn. St. **Dy.** Saṅgama, Bukka I, Ś. 1290 = 1368 A.D.

aṁgaraṁga (K. *n.*), offering of services to the god such as application of perfume etc. to the deity's image and arranging for cultural events such as dances in the *raṁgamaṁṭapa* of the temple ; **text :** *Kalpajoisaru Bhaṭakaḷadoḷage Yīśvara dēvālyavanu kaṭisi, ā dēvariṁge naḍava aṁgaraṁga naivēdya muṁtāda dharmaṁgaḷige biḍu dēvasvavāgi kshētraṁgaḷa biṭṭtu . . .* ; **tr.** Kalpa-jōyisaru having built a temple for the god Yīśvara in Bhaṭakaḷa, he donated as exclusive *dēvasva,* lands for the **offering of services to the deity such as the application of perfume etc., on the image, arrangement of cultural programmes such as dances, offering of food and such other acts of piety** ; *K.I.* III, pt. i, No. 7, pp. 14–15, ll. 12–13, Mūḍa-Bhaṭkaḷa, Bhatkal Tq. and Dt., Karn. St. **Dy.** Tuḷuva, Kṛishṇadēvarāya, Ś. 1449 = 1527 A.D.

aṁgaraṁgabhōga (K. < Skt. *n.*), anointing with fragrant substances after sacred bath of the image of the deity and arranging for dancing, singing and other entertainments before the deity; **text**[1] **:** *Pāriśva tīrthēśvarara pratishṭheyaṁ māḍisi ā dēvarige **aṁgaraṁgabhōga** naivēdyakke . . . . biṭṭa dharmma kshētrada sīmāsaṁbaṁdha meṁteṁdoḍe* ; **tr.** the details of the boundary of the land gifted for the **anointing with fragrant substances after sacred bath of the image of the deity and arranging for dancing, singing and other entertainments before the deity** for the image of Parīśvatīrtha after installation in the temple ; *K.I.* I, No. 41, p. 97, ll. 27–28, Kaikiṇi, Bhatkal Tq. and Dt., Karn. St. **Dy.** Saṅgama, Dēvarāya I, Ś. 1340 = 1417 A.D. ; **text**[2] **:** . . . . *sarvasvāṁmyavanu āgumāḍikoṁḍu Vīrabhadra dēvara **aṁgaraṁgabhōga**ke saludu. . . .* ; **tr.** after taking over all the endowed properties it is to be utilised for **anointing with fragrant substances after sacred bath of the image of the deity and arranging for dancing, singing and other entertainments before the deity** Vīrabhadradēva; *MAR.* 1946, No. 18, p. 45, ll. 22–24 ; Yīredēvanapura, Nanjanagud Tq., Mysore Dt., Karn. St. **Misc.**, Ś. 1410 = 1488 A.D. ; **text**[3] (T. < Skt. *n.*): . . . . *Tiṭṭaikuḍi āṉa Vidyāraṇyapurattu Uḍaiyār Ūruḍaiyārkku **aṁgaraṁgabhōga** amṛitapaḍi tiruppaṇikku kuḍutta paṭṭayam. . . .* ; **tr.** the deed given to the deity registering the grant for the **anointing the image of the deity and arranging for dancing, singing and other entertainments**

before the deity Ūruḍaiyār in Vidyāraṇyapura *alias* Tiṭṭaikuḍi ; *S.I.I.* VIII, No. 276, p. 150, ll. 5–6 ; Tiṭṭaguḍi, Vriddhachalam Tq., S. Arcot Dt., T. Nadu St. **Dy.** Saṅgama, Vīrabhūpati Uḍaiyār, Ś. 1341 = 1419 A.D.

aṁgaraṅgabhōgālu (Te. < Skt. *n.*) anointing the image of the deity and arranging for dancing, singing and other entertainments before the deity; **text**[1] : . . *Kākatīya Rudradēva mahārājaru . . . Kumāragiri Tripurāntakadēvara* ***aṁgaraṁgabhōgāla****ku Koṇḍapalli nāṁṭilōni Kṛishṇavēṇī nadītīramaṁdu Rēvūrunu ichchiri. . . .* . . ; **tr.** Rudradēva, the Kākatīya king granted the village of Rēvūru in Koṇḍapallināḍu situated on the banks of the river Kṛishṇavēṇi, for the services of attending to the image of the deity and **for the anointing the image of the deity and arranging for dancing, singing and other entertainments before the deity** Tripurāntakadēva of Kumāragiri ; *S.I.I.* X, No. 241, p. 122, ll. 6–7, 8–11 ; Tripurāntakam, Markapur Tq., Kurnool Dt., A.P. St. **Dy.** Kākatīya, Rudradēva I, Ś. 1107 = 1185 A.D. ; ; **text**[2] : *Sōveṁṇavoḍeyalu Mōṁpuri Bhairavadēvara aṁgaraṁgabhōgālaku Puliviṁndala bhūmilōnu Nāgūruṁnnu . . . . ichchēnu* . . . ; **tr.** I, Sōveṁṇavoḍeya granted the village of Nāgūru in Puliviṁdala territory for the performance of the **anointment of the god's image and for dancing and singing in the temple** ; *S.I.I.* XVI, No. 1, p. 1, ll. 6, 7–9, 11. ; Mōpūr, Pulivendla Tq., Cuddapah Dt., A.P. St. **Dy.** Saṅgama, Sōveṁṇa Oḍeya, Ś. 1273 = 1351 A.D.

aṁgaraṁgapātrabhōgalu (Te. < Skt. *n*), anointing with fragrant substances after sacred bath of the image of the deity and arranging for dancing through dancing girls, singing and other entertainments before the deity ; **text :** . . . *Pānēna dēvunikī* ***aṁgaraṁgapātrabhōgā****laku peṭṭina yāṁbai varālu* . . . . ; **tr.** fifty *varāhas* (a coin) endowed for **anointing with fragrant substances after sacred bath of the image of the deity and arranging for dancing through dancing girls, singing and other entertainments before the deity** of Pānēm ; *S.I.I.* XVI, No. 82, p. 98, ll. 16–17 ; Pānēm, Nandyal Tq., Kurnool Dt., A.P. St. **Dy.** Tuḷuva, Kṛishṇadēvarāya, Ś. 1451 = 1529 A.D. ;

aṁgaraṁga vaibhōgam (T. *n.*), for the enjoyment and pleasures of the deity ; **text :** . . . . *aṁga-raṁgavaibhōgaṅgaḷukku* ; **tr.** worship to include all kinds of enjoyments and pleasures of the deity ; *S.I.I.* XXII, No. 174, p. 143, l. 11 ; Eḷavānāśūr, Tirukkoyilur Tq., S. Arcot Dt., T. Nadu St. **Dy.** Tuḷuva, Achyutarāya, Ś. 1457 = 1535 A.D.

aṁgarika (K. *n.*), security guard ; **text :** . . . . *hūdōṭada tōṭigarige ga 3 mālegāraṁge ga 3 davasigarige ga 6* ***aṁgarika****ṁge ga 3 kuṁbāraṁge ga 1* ; **tr.** for the gardner of the flower garden 3 *ga* (*gadyāṇa*, gold coin), for the garland maker 3 *ga*, for the store keeper 6 *ga*, for the **security**

guard 3 *ga*, for the potter 1 *ga* ; *E.C.* (R) VII, Md. 30, p. 215, ll. 16–17 ; Basarāḷu, Mandya Tq. and Dt., Karn. St. **Dy.** Hoy., Sōmēśvara, Cy. yr. Hēmaḷaṁbi = 1237 A.D.

aṁgasasi (K. *n.*), saplings grown as ancilliary crop ; **text :** .... *mane maneṭhāvu* ... *aṁgasasi* .... *sahitavāgi* .... *Maḍakēsvaradēvara stānadali nitya purāṇa naḍavaṁtāgi* ... *dharmavāgi* .... *koṭṭaru* ; **tr.** including house, house site, **saplings grown as ancilliary crop,** etc. were given for the daily exposition of the purāṇas in the temple of the god Maḍakēsvara ; *K.I.* I, No. 53, p. 128, ll. 19–20 ; Bailūr, Bhatkal Tq. and Dt., Karn. St. **Dy.** Saṅgama, Dēvarāya, Ś. 1355 = 1433 A.D.

aṁgavaidyar (T. < Skt. *n.*), surgical doctor ; **text :** ***aṁgavaidyar****il Ādittadēvaṉ* ... *Vaidyapurandaraṟkku* .... *nañjai puñjaiyum ṉattamum* .... *iraiyiliyāga tandōm* .... ; **tr.** we made a tax free grant of wet and dry lands and house site to the **surgical doctor** Ādittadēvaṉ .. .. Vaidyapurandarar ; *S.I.I.* XXII, pt. i, No. 13, p. 9, ll. 1–4, 7–8 ; Namakkal, Namakkal Tq., Salem Dt., T. Nadu St. **Dy.** Pāṇḍya, Sundarapāṇḍya, reg. yr. 8, in characters of 11th century A.D.

aṁgavastra (K. *n.*), a cloth to cover the upper part of male body or the image of a male deity; **text :** .. *Kāḷahasti Īśvaradēvarige* .... *samarpista* .... *hachchaḍa 25 paṭṭe sīre 31 aṁgavastra 5* .... ; **tr.** 25 covering cloths, 31 silk cloths and 5 **cloths for covering the upper part of the image** were granted to the deity Kāḷahasti Īśvara; *S.I.I.* IX, pt. ii, No. 551, p. 571, ll. 2–4 ; Kāḷahasti, Chandragiri Tq., Chittoor Dt., A.P. St. **Dy.** Tuḷuva, Achyutarāya, Ś. 1484 = 1562 A.D.

aṁgōḍu (K. *n.*), land for brick kiln ; **text :** .... *tōṭa mane nela hola aṁgōḍu sahita* ; **tr.** including the grove, house, ground, field and **land for brick kiln** ; *K.I.* III, No. 6, p. 11, ll. 19–20 ; Iḍaguṁji, Honnavar Tq., Uttar Kannada Dt., Karn. St. **Dy.** Āḷupa, Sōmidēva, Cy. yr. Sarvajitu = 1348 A.D.

aṁgulīyaka (Skt. *n.*), finger rings ; **text :** .... *vastrayugmam cha sōshṇīśam kauśēyam ratna-kuṁḍale* ***aṁgulīyaka*** *mukhyāni kalpayitvā* ; **tr.** a pair of garments with turban, silken cloth, ear rings studded with gems and **finger rings** ; *E.C.* V, T.N. No. 16, p. 354, ll. 98–99 ; T. Narasīpura, T. Narasipur Tq., Mysore Dt., Karn. St. **Dy.** Woḍ. of Mys., Krishṇarāja, Ś. 1671 = 1749.

amīla (K. < Arabic, *n.*), bailiff ; lowest executive official of a civil court ; **text :** .... ***amīla****na rajā talabinalli yiddukoṁḍu sarakārada Ahaṁmadi davalattige śrēyassu apēkshisikoṁḍu* .... *yirōdu* .. ... ; **tr.** when the **bailiff** was drawing his leave salary, he was to be praying for the welfare of the fortunes of the Ahamadi government ; *E.C.* IX, Db. 12, p. 137, ll. 2–7 ; Tūbagere, Doddaballapur Tq., Bangalore Dt., Karn. St. **Misc.**, in characters of 18th cent. A.D.

aṁka (K. < Skt. *n.*), numerical figure ; **text :** ..

. . *Chaṭṭa Jinālayada dēvaraṁgabhōgakke . . Kariyūra baṭṭeyiṁ paḍuva biṭṭa kariyanelaṁ mattar irpattanālku* ***aṁka****doḷaṁ matta 24* ; **tr.** for the anointment and entertainment of the god of Chaṭṭa Jinālaya twenty four *matta* (a land measure) 24 *matta* in **numerical figures** of black soil land to the west of the lane leading to Kariyūr ; *S.I.I.* IX, pt. i, No. 150, p. 132, ll. 27–32 ; Kōṇakoṇḍla, Gooty Tq., Anantapur Dt., A.P. St. **Dy.** Chāḷ. of Kal., Vikramāditya VI, Ch. Vi. yr. 6 = 1081 A.D.

aṁkachēya (K. *n.*), a warrior ; **text :** . . . . *morevō gad****aṁkachēyar*** *iḷidōḍada durgada gaṁḍar* ; **tr.** warriors who will not surrender and war heroes who will not run away from the fort ; *E.C.* VII, Skr. 118, p. 218, l. 11 ; Śikāripura, Shikaripura Tq., Shimoga Dt., Karn. St. **Dy.** Chāḷ. of Kal., Traiḷōkyamalla, Ś. 976 = 1054 A.D.

aṁkagadyāṇa (K. *n.*), a type of marked coin ; **text :** . . . *Chāmuṁḍarasar Poḷalguṁdeyumaṁ saptārdhalaksheyoḷellav****aṁka gadyāṇamuṁ*** . . . . . . *āḷuttalire* . . . . ; **tr.** when Chāmuṁḍarasar was administering the village Poḷalguṁde and the minting of the **marked coin**s within the territory of seven and a half lakhs ; *S.I.I.* IX, pt. i, No. 163, p. 152, ll. 18–19 ; Halagondi, Hadagalli Tq., Bellary Dt., Karn. St. **Dy.** Chāḷ. of Kal., Vikramāditya VI, Ch. Vi. yr. 17 = 1093 A.D.

aṁkakāṟa (Te. < Skt. *n.*), warrior, servant, devotee; **text¹ :** . . . . *Vipravaṁśāḷaṁkāra Sattigan****aṁkakāṟa*** *sāhityavidyānidhi.* . . . ; **tr.** he who was an ornament to his brāhmaṇa lineage, a **warrior/servant** of Sattiga who was a treasure-house of literary knowledge ; *S.I.I.* VI, No. 102, p. 49, ll. 5–6 ; Chēbrōlu, Bapatla Tq., Guntur Dt., A.P. St. **Dy.** Chāḷ. of Kal., Āhavamalla, Ś. 920 = 998 A.D.; **text² :** . . . *mahāmaṇḍalēśvaraṁ* . . . . *Bhīmadēvarāṇeyaṁ* . . . . *mahāmaṁḍalēśvaraṁ* . . . . *Bhagavati* ***aṁkakāṟa*** *Nāgarasana kumāra Vīraboṁmarasaṁge Basurukōḍanu* . . . *koṭṭanu* ; **tr.** *mahāmaṇḍalēśvara* (a great divisional administrator) Bhīmadēvarāṇeya granted the village of Basurukōḍu to Vīraboṁmarasa son of *mahāmaṁḍalēśvara* Nāgarasa who was a **devotee** of the goddess Bhagavati ; *S.I.I.* IX, pt. i, No. 377, p. 393, l. 12 ; Basarakōḍu, Adavani Tq., Kurnool Dt., A.P. St. **Dy.** Yād. of Dēv., Rāmachandradēva, Ś. 1200 = 1278 A.D.

aṁkamāle (K. < Skt. *n.*), panegyric, a song describing the heroic deeds of a warrior ; **text :** . . . *āhavadoḷ nalidāḍi pāḍidar sūḷamaṟuḷgaḷ ugghaḍisi heggaḍe Bāḷegan* ***aṁkamāle****yaṁ* . . . ; **tr.** on the battle field the courtesans danced and **sang** with great enthusiasm **the heroic deeds** of heggaḍe Bāḷega ; *E.C.* VIII, Sg. 15, p. 254, ll 52–53 ; Sāgara, Sagara Tq., Shimoga Dt., Karn. St. **Dy.** Hoy., Ballāḷa, Ś. 1140 = 1218 A.D.

aṁkaṇa (K. *n.*), space between any two beams or pillars in a house, a land measure ; **text¹ :** . . . *Paṭṭaṇōjana maga Chikabācheyana* ***aṁkaṇa*** . . . . ; **tr.** space between any two beams or pillars in a house belonging to Chikabācheya son of Paṭṭaṇōja; *E.C.* XIV, K. R. Pet 86, p. 53, ll. 3–4, Krishṇa- rājapete, K. R. Pete Tq., Mandya Dt., Karn. St. **Misc.**, in characters of 14th cent. A.D. ; **text**[2] : . . . . *Naṁjarāya-oḍeyaru ī Haraveyalli haṁneraḍu hoṁnanu kuḷava kaḍidu sāviradamunūṟu beddalanū ā basadiya muṁde eṁṭ-**aṁkaṇa** maneyanū* . . . . . *koṭṭaru* . . . ; **tr.** in the village of Harave Naṁjarāya-oḍeya granted 1300 rainfed lands after deducting 12 *hoṁnu* (gold coin) of tax and also granted a **house measuring eight aṁkaṇa** in front of that temple ; *E.C.* (R) IV, Ch. 390, p. 258, ll. 5–6 ; Harave, Chamarajanagar Tq. and Dt., Karn. St. **Dy.** Umm. Chfs., Vīrasōmarāya, Ś. 1404 = 1482 A.D. ; **text**[3] : . . . . . . *ayidu aṁkaṇa maneyanu* . . . . *krayavāgi koṭṭadu ga 10*. . . . ; **tr.** house measuring 5 **aṁkaṇa** was sold and bought for 10 *ga* (*gadyāṇa*, a gold coin.) ; *E.C.* (R) IV, Yl. 162, p. 364, ll. 11–12 ; Māṁbaḷḷi, Yelandur Tq., Chamarajanagara Dt., Karn. St. **Misc.**, Cy. yr. Raudri = 1560 A.D. ; **text**[4] : *Arkēśvara svāmiyavarige* . . . . . *karaṇika* . . . . *Liṁgaṁṇa beḷasida doḍḍa Aśvathada baḷi **aṁkaṇa** 12 māḍida sēvā* ; **tr.** a donation of 12 ***aṁkaṇa*** of land lying by the side of huge Pipal tree grown by the accountant Liṁgaṁṇa was granted to the god Arkēśvarasvāmi; *E.C.* (R) V, Kn. 5, p. 5, ll. 1, 7–9. ; Kṛishṇarājanagara, K. R. Nagara Tq., Mysore Dt., Karn. St. **Misc.**, Ś. 1637 = 1715 A.D.

aṁkaṇamu (Te. < Skt. *n.*), land ; **text** : . . . ***aṁkaṇā**nanu khilamai pōtēnu* . . . . *Mahamandu khulli Padashaha* . . . *ājñākramānanu* . . . . . *Rāmaliṁgamununnu pratishṭha chēsi ī dēvaguḍlu gaṭiṁchi*. . . . ; **tr.** under the orders of Mohammad Quli Badshah a number of persons (names given) built a temple and installed the deity Ramaliṁga on the fallow **land** measuring 8 sq. yards ; *S.I.I.* X, No. 749, p. 391, ll. 7, 10, 15–16 ; Juttiga, Tanuku Tq., W. Godavari Dt., A.P. St. **Dy.** Ādil Shahi, Muhammad Quli Bādshāh, Ś. 1505 = 1583 A.D.

aṁkaṇiyokku (K. *vb.*), overwhelm ; **text** : . . . *dhāḷiyaniṭṭu Koṁkaṇaman **aṁkaṇiyokki**dapaṁ*. . . . . . ; **tr.** having attacked Koṁkaṇa he completely routed that kingdom ; *E.C.* VII, Skr. 136, p. 247, l. 25 ; Baḷḷigāme, Shikaripura Tq., Shimoga Dt., Karn. St. **Dy.** Chāḷ. of Kal., Traiḷōkyamalla, Ś. 990 = 1068 A.D.

aṁkasuṁka (K. *n.*), war cess ; **text** : . . . . *besavokkalu **aṁkasuṁka** ṭaṁkasāle taḷavārike nidhi nikshēpa* . . . . . . *sarvādāya prāpti sahitavāgi Padmaṇamātyanu anubhavisuvudeṁdu* . . . *koṭṭa* . . . . . *dharma śāsana* . . . . ; **tr.** according to the charitable deed recorded, all revenue incomes collected from agricultural labour, **war cess**, mint, village servant, treasure troves etc. are to be enjoyed by Padmaṇ-āmātya ; *E.C.* VIII, Sgr. 163, p. 335, ll. 20–25, Sāgara, Shimoga Tq. and Dt., Karn. St. **Dy.** Sāḷuva, Sāḷuvēndra, Ś 1410 = 1488 A.D.

aṁkaṭaṁka (K. *n.*), privilege to have coins

minted with one's insignia ; **text :** . . . *paṁchāṁga pasāya chhatra sukhāsana balaragaddige* ***aṁkaṭaṁka*** *daṁḍa kaṁḍana aṭṭabhōga tējasvāmya* . . . . ; **tr.** eight privileges such as having one's own almanac, receiving gifts, having a parasol, a comfortable seat, a strong seat, **privilege to have coins minted with one's own insignia,** a staff of honour, receiving tributes in kind ; *E.C.* VII, Skr. 12, p. 128, l. 12, Śikāripura, Shikaripura Tq., Shimoga Dt., Karn. St. **Misc.,** Ś 1114 = 1192 A.D.

aṁkaṭeṁke (K. *n.*), ; **text :** . . . *koḍe haḍapa dīpamāleya kaṁbha* ***aṁkaṭeṁke*** *muṁtāda tējamānyavanuḷḷa Haivaṇṇanāyakaru* **; tr.** Haivaṇṇanāyaka who enjoyed the privileges of a parasol, small bag for keeping betel leaves and acrecanuts, a pillar with provision for lighting series of lamps and privilege of having **coins minted with one's own insignia,** etc. ; *E.C.* VIII, Sgr. 60, p. 277, ll. 8–9, Yiḍuvaṇi, Sagara Tq., Shimoga Dt., Karn. St. **Dy.** Saṅgama, Virūpāksha, Ś. 1395 = 1472 A.D.

aṁkavaṇa (K. *n.*), a kind of tax ; **text :** . . . *prāyaśchitta dakashiṇay* ***aṁkavaṇaṁ*** *pasuṁbevaṇam- emb-initaroḷ mārdd-utpattiyaṁ* . . . . ; **tr.** the revenue income generated from such taxes as emancipatory tax, ***aṁkavaṇa,*** *pasumbevaṇa* etc. ; *E.I.* XIII, No. 29, p. 333, l. 70, Kaḷasa, Bankapur Tq., Dharwar Dt., Karn. St. **Dy.** Rāshṭra, Govinda IV, Ś 851 = 929 A.D.

aṁkemāḍikoḷḷu (K. *vb.*), to subjugate ; **text :** . . . . . . *upadrapaḍisi grāmagaḷaṁnu* . ***aṁkemāḍikoṁḍu*** *mattu nānābage kirukuḷa updragaḷa naḍesuvadāgi kēḷapaṭṭu idhītu* ; **tr.** having troubled the villages **to subjugate** them and having heard that they were being harrassed and troubled ; *M.A.R.* 1938, No. 16, p. 116, ll. 10–11 ; Mysore, Mysore Tq. and Dt., Karn. St. **Dy.** Woḍ. of Mys., Kṛishṇarāja Woḍeyar II, Ś. 1684 = 1762 A.D.

aṁkisu (K. *vb.*), to subjugate ; **text :** (damaged). . . . . ***aṁkusu****vaṁge siḍil* . . . . *Chaṭṭamaneṁba jaṭṭigaṁ* ; **tr.** the wrestler Chaṭṭama was like a thunder to one who tried **to subjugate** him ; *E.C.* XI, Dvg. 43, p. 126, l. 43 ; Harihar, Davanagere Tq. and Dt., Karn. St. **Dy.** Chāḷ. of Kal., Jagadēkamalla, Ś. 1086 = 1164 A.D.

aṁkusa (K. < Skt. *aṁkuśa n.*), goad ; **text[1] :** . . . . *pagevar-aṁkusam* . . . . *śrīmatu Dhōrapayyaṁ* . . . . ; **tr.** the illustrious Dhōrapayya who was like a **goad** to his enemies ; *S.I.I.* IX, pt. i, No. 66, p. 38, ll. 16–17, 19 ; Bāgaḷi, Bellary Tq. and Dt., Karn. St. **Dy.** Rāshṭr., Krishṇa III, Ś. 878 = 956 A.D ; **text[2] :** . . . . . . *Māḷavarāya Madanatriṇētra Gūrjjararāyavāraṇ-****āṁkusaṁ*** . . . . ; **tr.** who was like Śiva to Manmatha i.e., the Ruler of Māḷava and who was like a **goad** to the elephant i.e., the ruler of Gūrjjara ; *S.I.I.* IX, pt. i, No. 380, p. 395, l. 7-8, Haluvagalu, Harapanahalli Tq., Bellary Dt., Karn. St. **Dy.** Yād. of Dēv., Rāmachandra, Ś 1204 = 1282 A.D.

aṁma, ama[1] (K. *n.*), a suffix at the end of men's

name ; **text**[1] : . . . *Chandiyammarasar dēvargge maṇṇaṁ koṭṭar* . . . . ; **tr.** Chandiya**ṁma**rasa donated land to the god ; *E.C.* XI, Chdg. 24, p. 17, l. 1, Gaṁjigaṭṭi, Chitradurga Tq. and Dt., Karn. St. **Misc.,** in characters of 6th century A.D. ; **text**[2] : . . . *Kaḍakoḷada Sāvaṁta Siriy**ama**-gauṁḍana heṁḍati* Chaṁḍigauḍi sarvanivṛittiyaṁ kaikoṇḍu . . . muḍipi svarggaprapteyāda niśidiya staṁbhaṁ. . . . ; **tr.** memorial pillar of Chaṁḍigauḍi wife of Sāvaṁta Siriy**ama** gauṁḍa of Kaḍkoḷa who ended her life after having adopted the method of final salvation ; *I.A.* XII, No. 2, p. 101, ll. 4–7, Kaḍakoḷ, Karjagi Tq., Dharwar Dt., Karn. St. **Misc.,** Ś 1201 = 1279 A.D.

aṁma[2] (K. *n.*), an honorific suffix to the proper names of females ; **text :** . . . *Timmarājaru koṭṭa dharma . . . . kuḷa-pālanu kaḷadu rāja-pālige baṁda phalavanu naṁma taṁdegaḷu Chikatimmarāja-voḍeyarigu naṁma tāyigaḷu Kōnāji-**aṁma**navarigū puṁṇyavāga bēku yeṁdu . . . . śrī Rāmachandra dēvarige koṭṭa dharmaśāsana . . .* ; **tr.** the pious edict recording grants of the incomes accuring to the king and deducting the share of the family to the god Rāmachandradēva given by Timmarāja for the merit of his father Chikatimmarājavoḍeya and his mother Kōnāji **amma** ; *S.I.I.* IV, No. 250, p. 42, ll. 2, 5, 9, Hampi, Hospet Tq., Bellary Dt., Karn. St. **Dy.** Tuḷuva, Kṛishṇadēvarāya, Ś 1443 = 1521 A.D.

aṁmai (T. *n.*), mother ; **text :** . . . *idu mīṟuvāṉ taṅgaḷ **ammai**kku tāmne miṉāḷan āvāṉ* ; **tr.** he who flouts the provisions of this grand would have in effect molested his own mother . . . . ; *S.I.I.* VIII, No. 136, p. 64, ll. 4–5, Tiruvaṇṇāmalai, Tiruvannamalai Tq., N. Arcot Dt., T. Nadu St. **Misc.,** in characters of 11th cent. A.D.

aṁmaldāru (K. *n.*), Revenue Officer ; **text :** . . . *chhowkhi maṭada svāmigaḷu . . . . brāhamaṇaṟu Pāḷyēgāṟa Sivōjināyakarige **aṁmaldāru** Paṭelaṟige piṟyāde hēḷidaṟu* . . . . ; **tr.** the svāmi of chowki maṭha and the brāhmaṇas lodged a complaint with the Pāḷegār Śivōjināyaka, the Revenue Officer and the Head of the village ; *E.C.*(R) VII, Md. No. 63, p. 241, ll. 9–12 ; Guttalu, Mandya Tq. and Dt., Karn. St. **Misc.,** Ś. 1576 = 1654 A.D

ammāṉ (T. *n.*), maternal uncle ; **text :** . . . . . . *Śundarachōḷa Pāṇḍyadēvar . . . eḻundaruḷi . . . . . Tiruvālīśvaramuḍaiya mahādēvarkku . . . vēṇḍum nivandagaḷukku iṟuppadāga Rājarājachcharu ppēdi-maṅgalattu piḍāgai Kākkalūrile nilaṅkuḍukkaveṉṟu **ammāṉ** aruḷichchēydamayil* ; **tr.** the **maternal uncle** of the king in royal presence made a gift of land in Kākalūr a hamlet of Rājarājachcheruppēdi maṅgalam for offering services to the deity Tiruvālīśvaramuḍaiya Mahādēva ; *S.I.I.* XIV, No. 161, p. 89, ll. 11–12, 14 ; Tiruvālīśvaram, Ambasamudram Tq., Tirunelveli Dt., T. Nadu St. **Dy.** Chōḷa Pāṇḍya, Sundarachōḷa Pāṇḍya, reg. yr. 17, in characters of 11th–12th cent. A.D.

aṁmegadde (K. *n.*), name of a paddy field ; **text :** . . . . . *mane teṁgina hittilu adakke baṁda gadde* ***aṁmegadde*** *kāṇigadde saha* . . . . ; **tr.** the **paddy fields** called aṁmegadde and kāṇigadde etc., within the coconut grove behind the house ; *K.I.* III, No. 11, p. 34, l. 65 ; Kaikaṇi, Bhatkala Tq., N. Kanara Dt., Karn. St. **Dy.** Haive chfs., Kṛishṇa dēvarasa, Ś. 1465 = 1542 A.D.

aṁminā (Te. *indec.*), selling ; **text :** . . . *yeddula* ***aṁminā*** *koṁnā suṁkhaṁ lēdu* . . . . ; **tr.** no tax will be levied for **selling** and buying bulls ; *S.I.I.* XVI, No. 333, p. 339, l. 14 ; Gaṅgāvaram, Kalyanadurga Tq., Anantapur Dt., A.P. St. **Dy.** Āravīḍu, Śrīraṅga III, Ś. 1578 = 1656 A.D.

aṁṇa (K. *n.*), elder brother ; **text :** . . . . ***aṁṇana*** *gaḍiyiṁdaṁ paḍuvalu* . . . . . ; **tr.** to the west of boundary of the **elder brother**'s land ; *S.I.I.* VII, No. 356, p. 214, l. 23 ; Maṇigārakēri, Udupi Tq. and Dt., Karn. St. **Dy.** Saṅgama, Harihara II, Ś. 1316 = 1394 A.D. ; **aṁṇṇana gaṁdhavāraṇa** (K. *n.*) fighter in support of his elder brother like an elephant in rut, a title ; **text :** . . . . *mahāpradhānaṁ sarvvādhikāri Chauḍiśeṭṭiyara* ***aṁṇṇana gaṁdhavāraṇa*** *śrīmat sarvvādhikāri Mārisetṭiyaru* . . ; **tr.** Mārisetṭi, an officer with absolute power, and a valiant hero **fighting like an elephant in rut in support of his elder brother** Chowḍisetṭi chief minister and officer with absolute power ; *S.I.I.* IX, pt. i, No. 264, p. 281, ll. 46–48 ; Halyam, Kudligi Tq., Bellary Dt., Karn. St. **Dy.** Chāḷ. of Kal., Vikramāditya VI, Ś. 1085 (wrong for 1075) = 1154 A.D. (since the ruler had ended his reign 1126 A.D., it is likely that the grant was recorded on stone later in 1154 A.D.).

aṁnachhatra (K. < *Skt. n.*), feeding house ; **text:** . . . . *Haradanahaḷiyalu naṁma dharmavāgi brāhmarige* ***aṁnachhatra*** *naḍeva mariyādige* . . . . *koṭṭadu* . . . . . *Bommanahaḷḷi grāma* . . . . . ; **tr.** the village of Bommanahaḷḷi granted for the customary feeding of brāhmaṇas in the **feeding house** as a charity in the village of Haradanahaḷi; *E.C.* (R) IV, Ch. 249, p. 153, ll. 6–9 ; Veṅkaṭayyanachhatra, Chamarajanagara Tq. and Dt., Karn. St. **Dy.** Woḍ. of Mys., Dēvarāja Woḍeya, Ś. 1598 = 1676 A.D. ; **aṁnadāna** (Skt. *n.*), free feeding ; **text :** . . . *Sudhīṁdrayatīṁdrāya* . . . . *maṭhē nity-āṁnadān-ārtham* . . . . *Rāma-chaṁdrārchanāya cha grāmapaṁchakaṁ* . . . *dattaṁ* . . . ; **tr.** five villages (names given) were granted to the saint Sudhīṁdratīrtha for the daily free feeding in his religious institution and for the worship of the god Rāmchandra ; *E.C.* III, Nj. No. 112, p. 201, ll. 17–18, 25, 33 ; Naṁjanagūḍu, Nanjanagud Tq., Mysore Dt., Karn. St. **Dy.** Āravīḍu, Śrīraṁgarāya I, Ś. 1497 = 1576 A.D. ; **aṁnadānaṁ** (Te. < Skt. *n.*), free feeding ; **text :** . . . . *alaṁkāra satram yiṁṭōnu brāhmalaku nitya krityamuṁnu* ***aṁnadānaṁ*** *śēśēṭaṭlu kaṭaḍa śēśi ichchina* . . . *dharma śāsanamu* . . ; **tr.** an edict of charity recording construction of a building for the alaṁkārasatra for the performance of daily rituals by the brāhamaṇas and for their **free feeding** ; *S.I.I.* XVI, No. 298, p. 305, ll. 10–12. ; Śrīmushṇam, Chidambaram Tq., S. Arcot Dt., T. Nadu St. **Dy.** Āravīḍu, Veṅkaṭapati, Ś. 1603 (wrong for 1503) = 1581 A.D. ; **aṁnasatra** (K. *n.*), feeding house ; **text :** *Mysūra....... Dēvarā-jayanavaru ..... brāhmarige **aṁnasatra**ke iṭṭa grāma Rāgibommenahaḷi ....* ; **tr.** the village of Rāgibommenahaḷi donated by Dēvarājaya of Mysore for a feeding house for the brāhmaṇas ; *E.C.* (R) II, Sb. 551, p. 337, ll. 8–9, 12–17 ; Rāgibommanahaḷḷi, Channarayapatna Tq., Hassan Dt., Karn. St. **Dy.** Woḍ. of Mys., Doḍḍadēvarāja, Ś. 1595 = 1672 A.D. ; **aṁnnasatturu** (Te. *n.*), choultry for free feeding ; **text :** . . *Hālaharivi Cheṁnnakēśavadēvuniki .... vacchē paradēśi brāṁhmalaku sūdrulaku aṁnnasatturuvu* ; **tr.** choultry for feeding for the itinerant brāhmaṇas and śūdras visiting on pilgrimage the temple of Cheṁnnakēśava of Hālaharivi ; *S.I.I.* XVI, No. 273, p. 279, ll. 2–6 ; Hālaharivi, Ālūru Tq., Bellary Dt., Karn. St. **Dy.** Tuḷuva, Sadāśiva, in characters of 16th cent. A.D.

aṁna śuddhi (K. *n.*), purifying the cooked rice (with ghee) ; **text:** .. *Sadānaṁdaseṭi .. koṭa doḍa varaha ga 70 ke maṭhadalli nitya ja 1 kke dharmake .... **aṁna-śuddhi** tupa ....* ; **tr.** a grant of doḍa varaha ga (*q.v.*) 70 made by Sadānaṁdaseṭi for feeding of one person daily in the religious institution and for **purifying of cooked rice with ghee** ; *S.I.I.* IX, pt. ii No. 540, p. 560, ll. 52–55 ; Basarūru, Kundapur Tq., Udupi Dt., Karn. St. **Dy.** Tuḷuva, Achyutarāya, Cy. yr. Khara = 1531 A.D.

ammāvaṉ (T. *n.*), maternal uncle ; **text :** *Kulaśēkara- pperumāḷ **ammāvaṉ** kalpichchu Mmuttaḷaikuṟichiyāna śrī Vīrakēraḷapurattu kōyilil marappaṇi korichchu kalpaṇi mugittu tērum tirunāḷum vaikakyil* ; **tr.** at the time when the **maternal uncle** of Kulaśekarapperumāḷ removed the wodden parts and replaced the same with stone work, donated a chariot and established a festival day in the temple in Muttaḷaikuṟichi *alias* śrī Vīrakēraḷapura ; *T.A.S.* IV, pts. i and ii, No. 44, p. 156, ll. 24–25 ; Āṟṟūr, Padmanabhapuram Tq., Tiruvanantapuram Dt., Kēr. St. **Dy.** Kīḻappērūr chfs., Ravivarmaṉ, Kollam 821 = 1646 A.D.

aṁpanaṁ (Te. *n.*), a kind of tax ; **text :** . . . . *siddhyāyaṁ kaṭṭiga talārika magama **aṁpanaṁ** grāmavraya sahitaṁgānu . . . Śiryādēvi aṁmaṁ-gārikinni . . . puṇyaṁgānu . . . chellaṁgaladi. . .* ; **tr.** all **tax**es such as *Siddhāya, kaṭṭiga, talārika, magama, **aṁpanam**, grāmavraya* etc., were donated to the goddess Śiryādēviaṁmaṅgāru ; *S.I.I.* XVI, No. 34, pp. 36–37, ll. 15–19 ; Guṇḍlūru, Rajampet Tq., Cuddapah Dt., A.P. St. **Dy.** Saṅgama, Dēvarāya (II), in characters of 15th cent. A.D.

amritadāna (K. < Skt. *n.*), perpetual gift : . . . . *mahāgrahāraṁ Naṟugundada paḍuvagēṟiya* *vipraru . . . . Chāḷukya Vīranoḷaṁbarājana Kaiyōḷ paḍedant-**amritadāna*** ; **tr.** a **perpetual gift** obtained at the hands of Chāḷukya Vīranoḷaṁbarāja by the brāhmaṇas of the western part of the great brāhmaṇa settlement Naṟugunda; *K.I.* V, No. 11, pp. 36–37, ll. 35–37 , Naragund, Naragund Tq., Dharwar Dt., Karn. St. Chāḷ. of Kal. Vikramāditya VI, Cy. yr. Kāḷayukta = 1078 A.D.

amritagaṇa (T. < Skt. *n.*), village administrative body : . . *Tiruvoṟṟiyūr Mahādēvarkkoru nandā viḷakkeripadaṟku vaitta poṉ . . . . muppadiṉ kaḻañju ippoṉ koṇḍu kaḍavōṉ Tiruvoṟṟiyūrpuṟattu Ādambākattu sabhaiyōmum **amritagaṇa**ttōrum* ; **tr.** registers an agreement made by *sabha* (*q.v.*) and the administrative body called ***amritagaṇa*** of Ādambākkam, a suburb of Tiruvoṟṟiyūr to burn a perpetual lamp in the temple of the god Mahādēva at Tiruvaṟṟiyūr in lieu of the interest on thirty *kaḻañju* (*q.v.*) of gold ; *S.I.I.* XII, No. 87, p. 37, ll. 5–11, Tiruvoṟṟiyūr, Saidapet Tq., Chingleput Dt., T. Nadu St. **Dy.** Pallava, Aparājita, reg. yr. 4 = 874 A.D.

amṛitapaḍi, amrutapaḍi, amritapaḍi (K. < Skt. *n.*), perpetual offerings of food made to the god : **text**[1] : . . . *Lakshmīnarasiṁhadēvara pratishṭheyaṁ māḍi upakaraṇaṁgaḷaṁ ābharaṇaṁgaḷaṁ māḍisikoṭṭu dēvar-**amṛitapaḍi**ge . . . . tāvu chakravartti Nārasiṁhadēvana kayyalū dhāreya haḍada vṛitti oṁdu* ; **tr.** one share of land obtained with the pouring of water of ablution from the hands of Chakravartti Narasiṁhadēva for **perpetual food offerings to the deity** Lakhsmīnarasiṁhadēva after installing the deity's image and after preparing the necessary sacred vessels and ornaments ; *E.C.* (R) X, No. 232, p. 285, ll. 35–36, Hāranahaḷḷi, Arasikere Tq., Hassan Dt., Karn. St. **Dy.** Hoy., Narasiṁha II, Ś. 1156 = 1234 A.D. ; **text**[2] : . . . *Nakharajinālayda Ādidēvara . . . ashṭavidhārchane **amṛitapaḍi** sahita śrikāryavanu nakaraṁgaḷu niyāmisikoṭṭa paḍiyanu kuṁdade naḍesuvevu* ; **tr.** we will conduct without any lapse the arrangment made by the *Nakara* (*q.v.*) for perfoming the eight types of worship, the **perpetual food offerings** and other services to the god Ādidēva of Nakhara Jinālaya; *E.C.* (R) II, No. 458, p. 280, ll. 8–9, 11–14, Śravaṇa-beḷagoḷa, Channarayapatna Tq., Hassan Dt., Karn. St. Comm. gld. **Misc.,** Ś. 1203 = 1279 A.D. ; **text**[3] : . . . *Taṁbulageṟeya śrī Sōmanāthadēvara **amrutapaḍige** prati dina 1 kke akki nāḍahāne 1 ṟa lekkadi varusha 1 kke bhatta mū 23 . . . .* ; **tr.** a grant of 23 *mūḍe* (a grain measure) of paddy dehusked into rice measured by one *nāḍa-hāṉe* (a grain measure) **for the perpetual offering of food** service daily **to the god** Sōmanāthadēva of Taṁbulageṟe ; *S.I.I.* VII, No. 330, p. 180, ll. 9, 23–24 Mūḍakēri, Udupi Tq. and Dt., Karn. St. **Dy.** Saṅgama, Bukkarāya, Ś. 1281 = 1359 A.D. ; **text**[4] : . . . . *Paṁchaliṁgadēvara bhaṁṇḍāradiṁda* *mūḍe 1 kkaṁ nāgaṁḍugada lekkadali . . . . . **amrutapaḍi**ge akki mūḍe* (*q.v.*) *12. . . prativarushavū naḍadu bahudu* ; **tr.** every year there shall be a grant of 12 *mūḍe* (a grain measure) for the **perpetual food offering** to the deity Paṁcha-lingadēva, the rice being measure by the *nāgaṁḍuga* (a grain measure), per *mūḍe* in vogue in the temple treasury ; *S.I.I.* VII, No. 384, p. 239, ll. 11–13, Kōṭakēri, Udupi Tq. and Dt, Karn. St. Saṅgama, Dēvarāya II, Ś. 1347 = 1425 A.D. ; **text**[5] : . . . *Pāriśvadēvara **amritapaḍi**ge bhatta mu 90* ; **tr.** for the **perpetual food offering** to the deity Pāriśvadēva 90 *mu* (*q.v.*) were granted ; *K.I.* III, Pt. i, No. 9, p. 22, l. 24, Bastimakki, Bhatkal Tq., N. Kanara Dt, Karn. St. **Dy.** Tuḷuva, Krishṇadēvarāya, Ś. 1460 = 1538 A.D.

aṁśa (K. < Skt. *n.*), share, portion ; **text** : . . . *Nagadēva tann-**aṁśada** . . . . tōṁṭa . . . dēvara nivēdyakke koṭṭu gaṁdha dhūpakke 1 gadyāṇa ponnaṁ biṭṭan* . . . . ; **tr.** Nāgadēva donated his **share** of the grove for the food offerings to the god and also granted 1 gold coin for offering of incense to the deity ; *S.I.I.* IX, pt. i, No. 165, p. 159, l. 70, Kuruvatti, Harapanahalli Tq., Bellary Dt., Karn. St. **Dy.** Chāḷ. of Kal., Vikramāditya VI, Ch. Vi. yr. 24 = 1099 A.D. **aṁtaḥpasāyita** (K. *n.*), Officer in charge of royal of herem ; **text** : . . . . *aṁtaḥpasāyitanu ātmarakshapāḷakanu enisida Beḷḷappayyanāyaka* . . . . . . ; **tr.** Beḷḷappayyanāyaka who was the Officer in charge of royal harem and was the body guard of the king ; *E.C.* (R) V, Chnp. 76, p. 507, ll. 35–36, Bidare, Channarayapatna Tq., Hassan Dt., Karn. St. **Dy.** Hoy., Narasiṁha I, Ś 1087 = 1165 A.D.

aṁtaḥpura (K. < Skt. *n.*), royal harem ; **text** : . . . . . . *samastāvanipā**ṁtaḥpura** viśadavirājamāna rūpavidyādhari . . . . piriyarasi Padmala paṭṭamahādēviyar* ; **tr.** Padmaladēvi the senior crowned queen who was of exemplary beauty and well versed was the occupant of the **royal herem** of the king who was ruling over the entire earth ; *S.I.I.* IX, pt. i, No. 330, p. 348, ll. 19–20, 22-23 ; Hirehaḍagalli, Hadagalli Tq., Bellary Dt., Karn. St. **Dy.** Hoy., Ballāḷa II, Ś. 1133 = 1212 A.D.

aṁtaḥpuraverggaḍe (K. *n.*), officer in charge of the royal harem ; **text** : . . . . *Śrīmadaṁtaḥ puraverggaḍe daṁḍanāyakaṁ Vāmadēvayyaṅgaḷ* . . . . ; **tr.** the illustrious Vāmadēvayya who was the **officer in charge of the royal harem** and was an army general ; *K.I.* VI, No. 15, p. 40, ll. 7–8 ; Malghāṇ, Sindgi Tq., Bijapur Dt., Karn. St. **Dy.** Chāḷ. of Kal., Vikramāditya VI, Ch. Vi. yr. 25 = 1100 A.D.

aṁtarāḷike (K. *n.*), administration of local area ; **text** : . . . . *heggaḍe Siriyaṁṇaṁ taṁn**aṁtarāḷike**ya Mūlevarta mukhyavāgi* . . . . ; **tr.** with Mūlevarta as the main village, the village officer Siriyaṁṇa was **administering the local area** ; *M.A.R.* 1929, No. 62, p. 128, ll. 10–11 ; Beḷgāme, Shikaripur Tq.,

Shimoga Dt., Karn. St. **Dy.** Hoy., Ballāḷa III, reg. yr. 29 = 1319 A.D.

aṁtarāruvāra (K. < Skt. *n.*), sub-lease ; **text :** . . . . *aṁtarāruvāravāgi koṭa va ga 20* . . . ; **tr.** 20 *va ga* (*varaha gadyāṇa,* coin) to be paid as a **sub-lease** amount ; *S.I.I.* IX, pt. ii, No. 540, p. 558, l. 7; Basarūru, Kundapur Tq., Udupi Dt., Karn. St. **Dy.** Tuḷuva, Achyutarāya, Ś. 1453 = 1531 A.D.

aṁttu (K. *indec.*), thus ; **text :** . . . *aṁttu sthaḷa 4 kke gadde kha 1* . . . . ; **tr.** **thus** for 4 fields 1 paddy field with sowing capacity of 1 *kha.* (*q.v.*) of seeds ; *S.I.I.* IV, No. 245, p. 39, l. 15 ; Hampi, Hospet Tq., Bellary Dt., Karn. St. **Dy.** Tuḷuva, Achyutarāya, Ś. 1463 = 1541 A.D.

amudālu (Te. *n.*), oil seeds ; **text :** *bīyam āmudāluṁnmu ī modalaina* . . . . ; **tr.** grains such as paddy, oil seeds etc. ; *N.D.I.*, pt. iii, Udayagiri 25, p. 1369, l. 1 ; Udayagiri, Udayagiri Tq., Nellore Dt., A.P. St. **Misc.,** in characters of 16th century A.D.

amudāṭṭupāṭṭam (T. *n.*), a kind of tax ; **text :** *vaṉṉāṟappāṟaiyum* ***amudāṭṭuppāṭṭam****um iḍaṅgai-valaṅgai-magaḻ maiyum* ; **tr.** taxes such as *vaṉṉāṟappāṟai, amudāṭṭupāṭṭam, iḍaṅgai-valaṅgai-magaḻmai* ; *S.I.I.* XVII, No. 301-B , p. 127, ll. 2–4 ; Yōgimallavaram, Puttur Tq., Chittoor Dt., A.P. St. **Dy.** Chōḷa, Vīrarājēndra, Ś. 991 = 1069 A.D.

amudupaḍi (T. < Skt. amṛitapaḍi), food offerings to god ; **text :** . . *in-Ṉāchchiyāṟku* ***amudu paḍi****kku* . . . . *viṭṭa nellu* ; **tr.** paddy earmarked for the food offerings to the goddess ; *S.I.I.* VIII, No. 280, p. 152, ll. 6–7, 12 ; Tiṭṭaguḍi, Vriddhachalam Tq., S. Arcot Dt., T. Nadu St. **Dy.** Chōḷa, Vīrarājēndra, reg. yr. 7 = 1014 A.D. ; **text**[2] : . . *Nayiṉār Tiruvāḻumārba nayiṉārkku.* . . . . *pāl-pāyiśattukku* ***amudupaḍi*** *iru-ṉāḻi,* **tr.** two *nāḻi* (*q.v.*) of sweet milk parridge **for the feeding of the god** Tiruvaḻumārban ; *T.A.S.* V, pts. i, ii and iii, No. 46, p. 158, ll. 2–3, 5 ; Tiruppatīśāram, Tovala Tq., Padmanabhapuraṁ Dt., Ker. St. **Misc.,** Kollam 789 = 1613 A.D.

aṇa (T. *s.a. aṇai, n.*) dam ; **text :** . . . . *Māśakōḍu nīr-aṇa vāy* ; **tr.** mouth of the dam across the water course at Māśakōḍu ; *E.T.E.,* No. 120., p. 479, ll. 1–2 ; Eḻuttukallu, Nilambur Tq., Malapuram Dt., Ker. St. **Misc.,** in characters of about 6th cent. A.D.

aṉādēśam (T. < Skt. *anyadēśa, n.*), foreign land; **text :** . . . . *śattarkkum* ***aṉādēśam*** *pōṉārkkun talaimāṟu avvavarkku aḍutta muṟai kaḍavār* . . ; **tr.** (the benefits) will go the next generation of those who have respectively passed away or have gone to foreign lands . . ; *S.I.I.* II, No. 65, p. 254, l. 3 ; Tañjāvūr, Tanjavur Tq. and Dt., T. Nadu St. **Dy.** Chōḷa, Rājarāja I, reg. yr. 29 = 1014 A.D.

anādi (T. < Skt., *adj.*), from time immemorial : . . . . *Muṉṉiyūr tiruvagattīśvaramuḍaiya mahādēvarkkuṁ kshētrapāladēvarkkum muṉbu ānadiyāy iṟaiyili śeydu kuḍuttu nilam* . . . . ; **tr.** land made tax free and granted **from time**

immemorial to the gods Agattīśvaramuḍaiya Mahādēva and Kshētrapāladēva of Muṉṉiyūr ; *S.I.I.* VIII, No. 207, p. 105, ll. 45–50 ; Muṉiyūr, Kumbhakonam Tq., Thanjavur Dt., T. Nadu St. **Dy.** Chōḷa, Rājarāja III, reg. yr. 4 = 1220 A.D.

anādi kāla (K. < Skt. *n.*), from time immemorial; **text :** . . . . *Kaṁnēśvaradēvarggam Rāmanāthadēvarggam haraḷa-beṁcheyiṁ mūḍal**anādi kāla**diṁ naḍavutirda mattaru 2 ka 450* . . . . ; **tr.** 2 *mattar* (*q.v.*) and 450 *ka* (*q.v.*) of land, situated to the east of the white boulder which had been granted **from time immemorial** to the gods Kaṁnēśvaradēva and Rāmanāthadēva ; *S.I.I.* IX, pt. i, No. 298., p. 327, ll. 58–62 ; Nāgēnahaḷḷi, Rayadurga Tq., Bellary Dt., Karn. St. **Dy.** Kal. of Kal., Saṅkama, Ś. 1118 = 1196 A.D.

anādi agrahāra (K. < Skt. *n.*), brāhmaṇa settlement in existence from time immemorial ; **text :** . . *śrīmad**anādi agrahāra**m. Taḷilūra aśēsha mahājanaṁgaḷa samakshamadalli . . . . Madhusūdanadēvara saṁje soḍariṁge. . . aydu haṇa.* . ; **tr.** five *haṇa* (coin) granted for the lighting of evening lamp for the god Madhusūdana made in the presence of all the mahajanas of Taḷilūru, the ancient **brāhmaṇa settlement in existence from time immemorial** ; *E.C.* (R) X, No. 166, p. 220, ll. 1–3 ; Taḻalūru, Arsikere Tq., Hassan Dt., Karn. St. **Misc.**, Ś. 1142 = 1220 A.D.

aṇagu (K. *vb.*), discontinue ; **text :** . . . . *Chandra giriya Mallikārjuna dēvarige . . . . . amṛitapaḍige . . . chaṁdu bahaṁta. . . . Śivarātri modalāgi bahadaṁta kāṇikeyanu yīga pūrvvamaṟiyāde **aṇagi** . . . . muṁdake Tāraṇa samvatsara . . . . ārabhyavāgi ā Sivarātri kāṇike ippata aidu varahana hoṁna pūrvamaryāde tappada hāṁge* (further text obscure) . . ; **tr.** the earlier custom of perpetual food offerings to the god Mallikārjunadēva of Chaṁdragiri having been **discontinued**, the same was restored from the day of Śivarātri in the Cyclic year Tāraṇa with the endowment of 25 gold *varaha* (*q.v.*) and was to be continued without fail ; *S.I.I.* IX, pt. ii, No. 429, p. 437, ll. 9–16, 27–29, 33 ; Tamballapalle, Madanapalle Tq., Chittoor Dt., A.P. St. **Dy.** Saṅgama, Dēvarāya II, Ś. 1327 = 1405 A.D.

āṇai (T. *n.*), elephant ; **text :** . . . . *kudirai oṉṟukku achchu kālum **āṇai** oṉṟukku achchu araiyum maṟṟum eppērppaṭṭa śarakkugaḷukkum . . . śamaiya piḍipāḍu paṇṇikuḍuttōm.* . . . ; **tr.** we fixed by convention tax to be collected at the rate of quarter of *achchu* (*q.v.*) on each horse and half *achchu* for each **elephant** as well as taxes for any and all types of goods ; *S.I.I.* VIII, No. 442, p. 233, l. 22; Pirāṉmalai, Tirupattur Tq., Ramnad Dt., T. Nadu St. Comm. gld., in characters of 11th-12th cent. A.D.

āṇai achchu (T. *n.*), coin with the figure of an elephant ; **text :** . . . . *śrībhaṇḍārattu Āḻvār kaṇmigaḷōḍum kūḍa uḍukkina **āṇai achchu** āṟu* . . . . ; **tr.** six **coins with the figure of an**

elephant was set apart along with the servants of the Āḻvār of the temple treasury ; *S.I.I.* XIV, No. 212, p. 121, l. 4 ; Śērmādēvi, Ambasamudram Tq., Tirunelveli Dt., T. Nadu St. **Dy.** Pāṇḍya, Śrīvallabha, reg. yr. 6, in characters of 12th cent. A.D.

āṇaiāḷ (T. *n.*), messenger who conveys royal orders ; **text :** .... *Rājarājan̲-āṇa Pāṇḍyarājan̲ **āṇaiāḷ*** ; **tr.** the **messenger who conveys the orders** of Rājarāja *alias* Pāṇḍyarāja ; *S.I.I.* XVII, No. 301 B, p. 128, l. 24 ; Yōgimallavaram, Puttur Tq., Chittoor Dt., A.P. St. **Dy.** Chōḻa, Vīrarājēndra, Ś. 991 = 1069 A.D.

āṇaichchālai (T. *n.*), elephant stable ; **text :** .. .... *Tribhuvanachakravartti Kōn̲ērin̲koṇḍān̲ Ādittadēvan̲ ... Vaidya purandararkku ... Vāṇavan̲mādēvi .... samastaprāptigaḷum iṟaiyiliyāga tandōm ittālvarum .... āṇaichchālai kudiraippandi maṟṟum eppērpaṭṭa iṟaigaḷum ...... tandōm* ; **tr.** the king Kōn̲ērmaikoṇḍān donated to Ādittadēvan who had the title of *Vaidyapurandara* the village of Vāṇavan̲mādēvi including all taxes derived therefrom such as on elephant stables, horse stables etc., after declaring the same as tax free ; *S.I.I.* XXII, pt. i, No. 13, pp. 9–10, ll. 1–2, 3, 11–12 ; Nāmakkal, Namakkal Tq., Salem Dt., T. Nadu St. **Dy.** Pāṇḍya, Sundara Pāṇḍya, reg. yr. 8, in characters of the 12th-13th cent. A.D.

aṇaikuṟi (T. *n.*), demarcation of a tank bund ; **text :** .... *Madurantakan̲-āṇa Karunilakkuḍināḍāḻvān iṭṭa **aṇaikuṟi*** .... ; **tr.** Madurāntakan *alias* Karunilakkuḍināḍāḻvān̲ set up the slab of **demarcation of the tank bund** ; *S.I.I.* XIV, No. 203, p. 115, ll. 2–3 ; Vēppilaippaṭṭi, Sattur Tq., Ramanathapuram Dt., T. Nadu St. **Dy.** Pāṇḍya, Śrīvallabha, reg. yr. 3, in characters of 13th cent. A.D.

āṇaippāgar (T. *n.*), elephant drivers ; **text :** ... . *Mummaḍiśōḻaterinda **āṇaippāgaril** Śūṟṟi nādanukku paṅgu on̲ṟu* .... ; **tr.** one share for Śūṟṟinādan̲ who belongs to the elephant corps of the **elephant drivers** of Mummaḍichōḻa. ... ; *S.I.I.* II, No. 66, section iii, p. 275, l. 11 ; Tañjāvūr, Tanjavur Tq. and Dt., T. Nadu St. **Dy.** Chōḻa, Rājarāja I, reg. yr. 29 = 1014 A.D.

aṇaittēvai (T. *n.*), tax collected for maintenance of the dam ; **text :** .... *Maḻavarāyar vaitta agaraṁ Kulaśēkara chchaturvvēdimaṅgalattu bhaṭṭargaḷukku .... **aṇaittēvai** uḷḷiṭṭa aṇaittu upādhigaḷuṁ. uṭpaḍa nam. variyilār kaṇakkiḻuṅ kaḻittu .... bhūdāṇamāga.... iṟailiyāga tandōm.*; **tr.** we gave as tax free grant, land-tax collected from **tax**es such as the one levied **for the maintenance of the dam** etc. to the *brāhmaṇas* of the *agrahāra* called Kulaśēkara chchaturvēdi-maṁgalam founded by Maḻavarāyar ; *S.I.I.* VII, No. 145, p. 63, l. 3, 12–13 ; Vṛiddhāchalam, Vriddhachalam Tq., S. Arcot Dt., T. Nadu St. **Dy.** Chōḻa, Kōn̲ērin̲maikoṇḍān, reg. yr. 4+1, in characters of about 12th cent. A.D.

āṇaivāḷ (T. *n.*), personal attendant ; **text** : . . *Nāyiṉār Śuchīndramuḍaiya Nayiṉār kōvilukku yōgipparadēśigaḷ pēr 23 m . . . **āṇaivāḷ**-āga naḍakkuṁbaḍikku śembiluñchilaiyilum veṭṭipichchu-kkuḍuttōm* ; **tr.** we gave to the temple of the god Śuchīndramuḍaiya Nayiṉār 23 *yōgipparadēśis* (*q.v.*) as **personal attendants** by getting this grant engraved on copper as well as stone ; *T.A.S.* V, No. 53, p. 168–70, ll. 10–12, Śuchīndram, Agasteeswaram Tq., Kanyakumari Dt., T. Nadu St. **Misc.**, Kollam 621 = 1444 A.D.

āṉaiyāḷ (T. *n.*), mahout, elephant rider ; **text :** . . . . *Rājēndrachōḷadēvar perundanattu **āṉaiyāḷ**gaḷ* . . . . ; **tr.** . . . the **elephant riders** of the royal treasury of the king Rājēndrachōḷadēva . . . . ; *S.I.I.* II, pt. i, No. 54, p. 221, l. 2 ; Tañjāvūr, Tanjavur Tq. and Dt., T. Nadu St. **Dy.** Chōḷa, Rājēndra I, reg. yr. 10 = 1022 A.D.

anāpu (K. *s. a. anupu, n.*), entry tax ; **text** : . . . *mahāmaṁḍaḷēśvara Dēvarājavoḍeyaru . . . namma śrī Guru śrī Rudrākshivoḍeyarige . . . Goṁdi-ganahaḷḷige saluva gadde beddalu tōṭa . . . **anāpu** . . . . muṁtāda . . . . sarvasvāmyavanu anubhavisuviri eṁdu koṭṭa liṅgamudre śilāśāsana* . . ; **tr.** tax incomes such as on paddy fields, dry lands, groves, **entry tax** were granted to our preceptor Rudrākshivoḍeya by *mahāmaṁḍaḷēśvara* (*q.v.*) Dēvarājavoḍeya as recorded in the stone slab with the insignia of the liṁga . . . ; *E.C.* (R) III, Gu. 176, p. 138, ll. 4–7, 13, 16–17 ; Śivapura, Gundlupet Tq., Mysore Dt., Karn. St. **Dy.** Umm. Chfs., Dēvarāja Woḍeya, Ś. 1391 = 1469 A.D.

aṉaśaṉam (T. *n.*), abstinence from food ; **text :** . . . . *aiṁbattēḻ **aṉaśaṉa**n-nōṟṟa Chandiranandi āśirigar niśidigai* . . . . ; **tr.** the death-bed of Chandiranandi āśirigaru who attained salvation throuhg **abstinence from food** for 57 days ; *E.T.E.*, No. 116, p. 473, ll. 1–4 ; Tirunātharkuṉṟu, Senji Tq., Villuppuram Dt., T. Nadu St. **Misc.**, in characters of about 6th cent. A.D.

anātha (K. < Skt. *n.*), destitute ; **text :** . . . . . . *dīnānāth-āśrita-jana- kalpa-vṛikshaṛ* . . . . ; **tr.** he who was like the wish-fulfilling tree to the weak, **destitute** and dependant persons ; *S.I.I.* IX, pt. i, No. 187, p. 182, ll. 18–19, Kottūru, Kudligi Tq., Bellary Dt., Karn. St. **Dy.** Chāḷ. of Kal., Vikramāditya VI, Ch. Vi. yr. 36 = 1112 A.D.

āṇatti (T. < Skt. *ājñapti, n.*), officer carrying out the orders of his master ; **text**[1] **:** . . . . *Nambaṉ **āṇatti**yāga Tirukkāṭṭuppaḷḷi . . . . . Yajñabhaṭṭar eḍuppitta Yajñēśvarattu Mahādēvar*. . . . ; **tr.** the temple of Yajñēśvara Mahādēva caused to be constructed by Yajña-bhaṭṭar of Tirukkāṭṭappaḷḷi when Nambaṉ was the **Officer carrying out orders of his master** . . ; *S.I.I.* II, pt. iii, iv and v, No. 98, p. 509, ll. 49–50 ; Vēlūrpāḷaiyam, Arakonam Tq. and Dt., T. Nadu St. **Dy.** Pallava, Nandivarman II, reg. yr. 6 = 716 A.D. ; **text**[2] **:** . . . . *Nakkaṉ kaṉichchaṉāṉa Śōḻa Mūvēndavēḷārum **āṇatti**yum vāykkēḻviyumāykkēṭṭu* . . . . ; **tr.** Śōḻa-

Mūvēndavēḷār *alias* Nakkaṉkaṇichchan and the **officer carrying out the orders of his master** having heard the oral royal orders ; *S.I.I.* XXII, No. 286 section ii, p. 229, ll. 26–27, Tirumālpuram, Walajapet Tq., N. Arcot Dt., T. Nadu St. **Dy.** Chōḷa, Uttamachōḷa, reg. yr. 14, in characters of 11th cent. A.D.

anāya (K. < Skt. *anyāya, n.*), punitive tax levied in the form of fine ; **text** : . . . . *ā bāḷina mēle baṁdanthā samudāya* ***anāya*** *ēnuḷadanū arsina kayallu . . . . koḍisikoṁḍu Kāḷimarsaru dharmavanu naḍasibaharu. . .* ; **tr.** the collective **punitive tax levied in the form of fine** on that land and whatever else comes as income is to be taken from the king as gift and with that money Kāḷimarsa should perform acts of charities ; *S.I.I.* VII, No. 330, p. 180, ll. 38–40, Mūḍakēri, Udupi Tq. and Dt., Karn. St. **Dy.** Saṅgama, Bukkarāya I, Ś. 1281 = 1359 A.D.

andaṇaṉ (T. *n.*), brāhmaṇa ; **text** : . . . *aṇaittuch-chātigaḷuṁ* ***andaṇaṉ*** *talaiyāga arippaṉ kaḍaiyāga.* . . . . ; **tr.** all the castes with the **brāhmaṇa** in the lead and lower caste in the rear ; *S.I.I.* VII, No. 118, p. 49, l. 4, Chengaṁ, Tiruvannamalai Tq., N. Arcot Dt., T. Nadu St. **Misc.**, Ś. 1180 = 1258 A.D.

āṇḍār (T. *n.*), temple priest ; **text** : . . . . *Kāyvāṉtaṇḍalamāgiyachaturvvēdimaṅgalattu . . . Uḍaiyārkku . . . Tiruppaṇi seigiṟa* ***āṇḍār*** . . . . . *vilai-iṭṭu koṇḍa bhūmi* . . . ; **tr.** land purchased after payment of money by the **temple priest** performing the service of worship in the temple of Uḍaiyār in the brāhmaṇa settlement of Kāyvāntaṇḍalam ; *S.I.I.* VII, No. 418, p. 264, l. 2, Kāvantaṇḍalam, Kanchipuram Tq., Chingleput Dt., T. Nadu. St. **Dy.** Chōḷa, Vikramachōḷa I, reg. yr. 6 = 1124 A.D.

āṇḍārgaḷ (T. *n.*), temple priests ; **text**[1] : . . . *Tiruvottūruḍaiyāṟku tiruvīdi-paṇi-śeyyuṁ tiruvīdi* ***āṇḍārgaḷ****ukku amudu śeigaikku . . . . aṉṟāḍu naṟkāśu iruvadum. kuḍuttōm.* . . . . ; **tr.** we gave 20 valid current coins for the preparation of food for the **temple priests** working on the temple street of the god Tiruvattūruḍaiyār ; *S.I.I.* VII, No. 97, p. 41, ll. 21–22, Tiruvottūr, Cheyyar Tq., N. Arcot Dt., T. Nadu St. **Dy.** Choḷa, Vikramachōḷa, reg. yr. 8 = 1126 A.D. ; **text**[2] : . . . *Kaṇḍi ūril kāṇi uḍaiya* ***āṇḍārgaḷ****il Maṉṉagamuḍaiyāṉ* . . . . ; **tr.** Maṉṉagamuḍaiyāṉ one among the **temple priests** owning land in Kaṇḍi ūr ; *S.I.I.* VIII, No. 254, p. 142, ll. 8–9, Tirukkaḷar, Mannargudi Tq., Tanjavur Dt., T. Nadu St. **Dy.** Saṅgama, Virūpāksha, Ś. 1315 = 1393 A.D.

āne (K. *n.*), elephant ; **text** : . . . . . *Āhavamalladēvar . . . nūrā-aivatt-****āne****yuman Roddada bīḍinoḷ-koṇḍu* . . . ; **tr.** Āhavamalladēva having captured 150 **elephants** in the camp at Rodda ; *S.I.I.* IX, pt. i, No. 77, pp. 47–48, ll. 2, 4 ; Kōgaḷi, Hadagalli Tq. and Dt., Karn. St. **Dy.** Chāḷ. of Kal., Sōmēśvara I, Ś. 914 = 992 A.D. ; **āneya pon** (K. *n.*), gold coin with the figure of an elephant ; **text** : . . . *Āditya dēvargge . . . koṭṭa tōṁṭada kamma aṟuvattu ā* *tōṁṭava . . . Kaṁnayya taṁna makkaḷ makkaḷbara salahid uṇba varsham-prativarsha* ***āneya*** *ponn-āṟu gadyāṇa. . .* ; **tr.** Ādityadēva was granted 60 *kamma* (*q.v.*) of garden, and for the maintenance of the same Kaṁnayya and his progeny were given for their subsistence every year 6 **gold coins having the figure of elephant** ; *S.I.I.* IX, pt. i, No. 75, p. 46, ll. 8–10, Bāgaḷi, Harapanahalli Tq., Bellary Dt., Karn. St. **Dy.** Chāḷ. of Kal, Sōmēśvara I, Ś. 909 = 987 A.D.

āṇe (K. *n.*), oath ; **text** : . . . *poydaṁge-eṁṭu paṇam* ***āṇe****yam mikkaṁge panneraḍu paṇam mīṟidaṁge panneraḍu gadyāṇam daṇḍam. . . .* ; **tr.** for the person breaking the **oath** a fine of 8 paṇas (coin), for the person who exceeds the stipulation of the **oath** a fine of 12 *paṇas* and for the person who transgresses the **oath** a fine of 12 *gadyāṇa* (a coin) ; *S.I.I.* IX, pt. i, No. 77, p. 49, ll. 33–34, Kōgaḷi, Hadagalli Tq., Bellary Dt., Karn. St. **Dy.** Chāḷ. of Kal, Sōmēśvara I, Ś. 914 = 992 A.D.

aṇe (K. *n.*), embankment, dam ; **text**[1] : . . . . . *Nārāyaṇa dēvargge vidyādānakkaṁ biṭṭa bhūmi mattaru 30 . . . . sarvanamasyaṁ māḍi koṭṭa datti beṭṭad-****aṇe****ya keṟe oṁdu mane 50 . . .* ; **tr.** to the temple of god Nārāyaṇadēva was granted, for the promotion of education, land to the extent of 30 *mattar* (*q.v.*) . . . . and one tank with *embankment* and 50 housed were granted to be respected by all ; *S.I.I.* IX, pt. i, No. 133, p. 116, ll. 24–27, Chinnatumbaḷam, Adavani Tq., Kurnool Dt., A.P. St. **Dy.** Chāḷ. of Kal, Sōmēśvara II, Ś. 990 = 1068 A.D. ; **text**[2] : . . . . *Kaṁchēnahaḷḷi yeṁbī grāmavanu nāvu nimage . . . koṭevāda kāraṇa ā grāmake saluva chatussīmege voḷagāda gadde beddalu tōṭa tuḍike* ***aṇe*** *achchukaṭṭu kāḍāraṁbha nīrāraṁbhagaḷemba ashṭabōgaṁgaḷanu . . . . nīvu sukhadalli anubhavisikoṁḍu iral uḷḷavaru . . . .* ; **tr.** we have granted to you the village of Kaṁchēnahaḷḷi including the eight *bhōga (q.v.)* within the village boundary viz., paddy field, dry field, a portion of a grove, an **embankment**, irrigated land, forest land and marshy land for your enjoyment ; *E.C.* (R) VIII, Ag. 20, p. 124–25, ll. 121–25, 146–47 ; Kaṁchēnahaḷḷi, Arakalagud Tq., Hassan Dt., Karn. St. **Dy.** Hoḷenarasīpura Chiefs, Narasiṁhanāyaka, Ś. 1587 = 1665 A.D.

āṇe ājñe (K. *n.*), order ; **text :** . . . *Achyutadēva mahārāyaru . . . . Cheluviṁḍla . . . grāmada gauḍuprajegaḷige nirūpa nimma grāmavanu Lēpākshi Pāpavināśanadēvarige . . . . Virūpaṁṇage Gaṇapatihaḷiyanū Cheluviṁḍla grāmavanw dāna koṭevu Vijinagarada paṭṭaṇada taḷavāṟa Virūpaṁṇage śāsanastavāgi pālisidevu Virupaṁṇana* ***āṇe ājñe****goḷagāgi naḍavudāda kāraṇa. ā stitiyanu nirūpadi chittaisidevu . . .* ; **tr.** Achyutadēvarāya mahārāya gave an **order** to the *gauḍu praje* (*q.v.*) of Cheluviṁḍla grāma statiang that, that village was donated to Pāpavināśanadēva of Lēpākshi and that the village of Gaṇapatihaḷi as well as

Cheluviṁḍla grāma was given to the *taḷavāṟa* (watchman) Virūpaṁṇa in the form of a recorded inscription and we have given charge of this grant to Virūpaṁṇa because he will be obeying our **orders** ; *S.I.I.* IX, pt. ii, No. 537, p. 556, ll. 1–2, Lēpākshi, Hindupur Tq., Anantapur Dt., A.P. St. **Dy.** Tuḷuva, Achyutarāya, Cy. yr. Khara = 1531 A.D.

ānedeṟe (K. *n.*), tax for maintenance of elephants; **text :** . . . *Rāmanāthadēvarige naḍevaṁta Rāmanāthapurada grā 1 ā dēvarige saluva haḷigaḷa āḍadeṟe maggadeṟe* .... ***ānedeṟe*** .... *dēvarige upahāra sahitavāgi tappade naḍesuta bahiri* . . . ; **tr.** the village named Rāmanāthapura was granted to the god Rāmanāthadēva ; from the villages belonging to that god tax incomes such as on sheep, handlooms, **tax for maintenance of elephants** etc., were to be used without fail for the services of the god ; *E.C.* (R) VIII, Ag. 48, p. 146, ll. 16–19, 24–25; Rāmanāthapura, Arakalagud Tq., Hassan Dt., Karn. St. **Dy.** Saṅgama, Harihara II, Ś. 1305 = 1383 A.D.

āṇe patra (K. *n.*), written affidavit ; **text :** . . *Chakravarti besasal-anibarumiḻdu Boppanaṁ karedu nīnuṁ ninna vaṁśadavaruṁ Hoḻaḷa manneyama māṇbudendu māṇisal ātanuvaṁte-geyvenendu āṇe-patramam koṭṭu* ; **tr.** Boppa, on being ordered by the emperer in the presence of all and being told that he and his descendants will not have any claim over the principality of Hoḻaḷu agreed to the condition and gave a **written affidavit** ; *S.I.I.* IX, pt. i, No. 169, pp. 163–64, ll. 22–25, Kuruvatti, Harapanahalli Tq., Bellary Dt., Karn. St. **Dy.** Chāḷ. of Kal., Vikramāditya VI, Ch. Vi. yr. 29 = 1104 A.D.

ānedoṟe (K. *n.*), river bank used to be frequented by elephants for drinking water ; **text :** . . *Nīrgguṁdada bhaṇḍi-vaṭṭeyiṁd-**ānedoṟe** viḍidaṁte Nāraṇōjhara keṟeya mūḍaṇa kōḍiyaṁ kūḍittu* ; **tr.** the eastern corner of the tank belonging to Nāraṇōjha had joined the cart road of Nīrguṁda adjoining the **river bank used to be frequented by elephants for drinking water** ; *S.I.I.* IX, pt. i, No. 80, p. 51, ll. 29–31, Bāgaḷi, Harapanahalli Tq., Bellary Dt., Karn. St. **Dy.** Chāḷ. of Kal., Jayasiṁha II, Ś. 940 = 1018 A.D.

āne-tūbu (K. *n.*), elephantine sluice ; **text :** . . *Bhaṁḍārada Timmarasara nirūpadiṁda Koṇḍapanu **āne-tūbi**nalu hākisida śilā-sāsana* . . . . ; **tr.** stone inscription set up at the **elephantine sluice** by Koṁḍapa on the orders of Timmarasa of the treasury ; *S.I.I.* IX, pt. ii, No.561, p. 581, l. 33–35, Bukkāpaṭṇam, Penukonda Tq., Anantapur Dt., A.P. St. **Dy.** Tuḷuva, Achyutarāya, Ś. 1455 = 1534 A.D.

āneya haṇa (K. *n.*), coin bearing the figure of an elephant ; **text :** (damaged) . . . *Gaṇāchāra maṭhada āneyahaṇa* .... *Mallikārjunadēvarige biṭṭavu*. . . . ; **tr. coin bearing the figure of an elephant** belonging to the Gaṇāchāra maṭha was donated to the god Mallikārjunadēva ; *E.C.* (R) IV, Ko. No. 34, p. 421, ll. 17–18, 20–21 ; Saragūru, Kollegal Tq., Chamarajanagar Dt., Karn. St. **Misc.,** in characters of 15th–16th cent. A.D.

āneya kallu (K. *n.*), boundary stone with the figure of an elephant ; **text :** (damaged) . . . . *alliṁ haḍuva basadiya* ***āneya kallu*** ; **tr.** from there to the west the **boundary stone with the figure of an elephant** in the jaina temple ; *S.I.I.* IX, pt. i, No. 251, p. 263, l. 62, Beṇṇehaḷḷi, Harapanahalli Tq., Bellary Dt., Karn. St. **Dy.** Chāḷ. of Kal., Jagadēkamalla II, reg. yr. 11 = 1149 A.D.

āneya khēḍe (K. *n.*), act of capturing wild elephants ; **text :** . . . . *Naṁjalugūḍu Śrīkaṇṭhadēvara amrutapaḍi aṁgaraṁga bhōgake* . . . . *Dēvarāyapurada grāmavanū* ***āneya-khēḍeya*** *Naṁjarāyagaḷu sarvamānyavāgi koṭṭaru* . . . . . ; **tr.** for the food offering, anointment and entertainment of the deity, Śrīkaṇṭhadēva of Naṁjalugūḍu, expert in **capturing wild elephants** Naṁjarāya granted the village of Dēvarāyapura ; *E.C.* (R) III, Nj. 273, p. 348, ll. 4–5, 7–8 ; Yīrēdēvanapura, Nanjanagudu Tq., Mysore Dt., Karn. St. **Misc.,** Ś. 1410 = 1488 A.D.

āneya māvanta (K. *n.*), elephant driver ; **text :** . . . . . . *Vīraballāḷadēvara. . . pādapadmōpa jīvigaḷapp****āneya māvaṁt****ara kulada* . . . . *chāgameṁtene* . . ; **tr.** the munificense of the family of the **elephant drivers** who were devoted to the feet of Vīraballāḷadēva . . . . ; *E.C.* (R) X, No. 214, p. 263, ll. 27, 29–30 ; Muduḍi, Arasikere Tq., Hassan Dt., Karn. St. **Dy.** Hoy., Ballāḷa II, Ś. 1117 = 1195 A.D.

āneya sāhaṇi (K. < Skt. *n.*), commander of elephant corps ; **text :** . . *mahāmaṁḍalēśvaraṁ Tribhuvanamalla Rāyapāṇḍyadēvargge* ***āneya-sāhaṇi*** *pasāyta Keṁgaṇa binnapaṁ geydu śrī Rāmēśvaradēvargge biḍisida gadde mattar ondu kammaṁ nūṟu* . . . . . ; **tr.** one *mattar* (a land measure.) and 100 *kamma* (a land measure.) were released in favour of the god Rāmēśvaradēva by *mahāmaṁḍalēśvara* (a great divisional administrator) Tribhuvanamalla Rāyapāṇḍyadēva at the request of the royal favourite Keṁgaṇa who was the **commander of the elephant corps** ; *S.I.I.* IX, pt. i, No. 206, p. 207, ll. 30–32, Rāmaghaṭṭa, Harapanahalli Tq., Bellary Dt., Karn. St. **Dy.** Chaḷ. of Kal., Vikramāditya VI, Ch. Vi. yr. 48 = 1122 A.D.

āneya sēse (K. *n.*), tax levied for the maintenance of elephants ; **text**[1] **:** . . . . *Būtanāthadēvara* . . . *siddhāyav-****āneya sese*** *kudureya sese* . . . . . *kumāra-gāṇike aḍakeya suṅka* . . . . *iv-voḷagāgi muṁde huṭṭuva apūrvvāyavellavaṁ māṇisi* . . *Mahālakshmī dēviyara dharmakārya* . . . *salvaṁtāgi Jāgaravaḷḷiyaṁ* . . . *biṭṭu* . . . *koṭṭa śāsanaṁ* . . . ; **tr.** an edict through which the village of Jāgaravaḷḷi was granted for the religious services of the goddess Mahālakshmīdēvi after exempting taxes granted in favour of the god Bhūtanāthadēva such as the permanent tax, the **tax for the maintenance of elephants,** tax for the maintenance of horses, tributes to be paid to the prince and all new taxes which may be levied in future ; *E.C.* (R) VIII, Hn. 41, p. 267, ll. 9–10, 11–15, Doḍḍagaddavaḷḷi, Hassan Tq. and Dt., Karn. St. **Dy.** Hoy., Ballāḷa II, Cy. yr. Raudri = 1200 A.D. ; **text[2] :** . . *Nīrahaḷḷige pūrbbāya apūrbbāya . . . . kaṭaka sēse* ***āneya sēse*** *. . . . . voḷagāda . . . . hadinemṭu virpaṇadalu . . . barasi ā dēvaru ā damṇṇāyakarige saluvamtāgi śrī Vīraballāḷa dēvarasaru . . . . patra śāsanavanu koṭṭa stiti* . . ; **tr.** king Ballāḷadēva gave a written order to the effect that the payment of certain taxes such as the current taxes as well the taxes to be levied in future, tax on the capital, **tax for the maintenance of elephants** etc. to the *damṇṇāyaka* (*q.v.*) ; *E.C.* (R) VIII, HN. 42, pp. 21–22, ll. 34–43, Hoḷenarasīpura, Holenarasipura Tq., Hassan Dt., Karn. St. **Dy.** Hoy., Ballāḷa, Ś. 1232 = 1310 A.D.

aṅgāḍi (K. *n.*), shop ; **text[1] :** . . . . . . ***aṅgāḍi****yuḷ-irumānam eṇṇeyumuṁ arisinamuṁ* . . . . . . ; **tr.** two *māna* (*q.v.*) of oil and turmeric within the shop ; *K.I.* I, No. 2, p. 3, l. 11–12 ; Bādāmi, Badami Tq., Bagalakote Dt., Karn. St. **Dy.** Chal. of Bādāmi, Vijayāditya, Ś. 621 = 699 A.D.

aṅgāḍi kūli (T. *n.*), wages paid to the porters of a shop ; **text :** . . . . . *Mahādēvarkku nāṅgaḷ viṭṭu-kkuḍutta eṅgaḷūrkkaḍaitteruvil* ***aṅgāḍikūli****yāvadu* . . . . . ; **tr.** the **wages paid to the porters of the shop** in the commercial street of our village as donated by us to the god Mahādēva ; *S.I.I.* III, pts. iii and iv, No. 90, p. 222, ll. 3–4 ; Tirumeyjñānam, Tanjavur Tq. and Dt., T. Nadu St. **Dy.** Chōḷa, Āditya I, reg. yr. 2 = 873 A.D.

aṅgāḍippāṭṭam (T. *n.*), tax income from group of shops; **text[1] :** *Rājēndraśōḷadēvaraṇukki Nakkaṇpāvaiuḍaiyār Tiruch-Chiṟṟambalam Uḍaiyār . . . . . eḻundaruḷum aṟṟaiku . . . . .* ***aṅgāḍi-ppāṭṭa****ttukku vaikkakkaḍava kāśu nāṟpadi nālum uḷpaḍa kuṟitta nivandangaḷ . . . śellak kalveṭṭiyadu . . . .* ; **tr.** Nakkanpāvaiuḍaiyār, the courtesan of Rājēndraśōḷadēva got this stone inscription engraved recording the grant (a number of grants in cash and kind are mentioned in great detail) of State revenue **income from group of shops** on the day of the ceremonial procession of god Tiruchchiṟṟambalam Uḍaiyār ; *S.I.I.* IV, No. 223, p. 30, ll. 15, 23, 33 ; Chidambaram, Chidambaram Tq., S. Arcot Dt., T. Nadu St. **Dy.** Chōḷa, Rājēndra, reg. yr. 24 = 1038 A.D. ; **text[2] :** (damaged) *inNāyanāṟ tirumaḍaiviḷāgattu kaḍaippāṭṭamum* ***aṅgāḍippāṭṭam****um* . . . . ; **tr. the tax income fr om** shops and **groups of sh**ops were donated to the kitchen of the temple of the god ; *S.I.I.* VIII, No. 252, p. 141, l. 7 ; Tirukkaḷar, Mannargudi Tq., Tanjavur Dt., T. Nadu St. **Dy.** Chōḷa, Kulōttuṅga III, reg. yr. 10 = 1189 A.D.

aṇi[1] (K. *n.*), infantry ; **text[1] :** . . . . ***aṇi****yoḷ dāvaṇaṁ* *voḍḍuvōn* . . . . ; **tr.** he who pierces through the lines of the **infantry** ; *Ep. Ind.* IX, No. . ., pp. 17–18, ll. 10–11 ; Udyāvara, Udupi Tq. and Dt., Karn. St. **Dy.** Āḷupa, Raṇasāgara, in characters of 8th cent. A.D. ; **text**[2] : . . . . *Ūṇukalla kōṭeyoḷagiḻda**ṇi*** . . . . *sandaṇiyāge* . . . . ; **tr.** the **infantry** deployed within the fort of Ūṇakallu having fallen into disarray ; *S.I.I.* XI, pt. i, No. 51, p. 39, l. 5 ; Yali-Sirūr, Gadag Tq. and Dt., Karn. St. **Dy.** Chāḷ. of Kal., Iṟivabeḍeṅga, Ś. 937 = 1006 A.D.

aṇichelva (K. *n.*), valorous soldier (a title) ; **text:** . . . ***aṇichelvan*** *aṇumaparākraman vīramahāmēru* . . . . ; **tr.** he who was a valourous soldier, of unequalled prowess like the Mēru mountain in bravery ; *E.C.* X, Sr. No. 6, p. 342, l. 4 ; Śrinivāsapur, Srinivasapur Tq.,Kolar Dt., Karn. St. **Dy.** Bāṇa, Mahābali, in characters of 8th cent. A.D.

aṇiyaṁkakāṟa (K. *n.*), one who confronts enemy fource single handedly (a title) ; **text** : . . . . Banavāsipuravarēśvaraṁ ***aṇiyaṁkakāṟa*** . . . . *śrīmadadityavarmarasar Kōgaḷi aiynūṟuvaṁ sundavatti panneraḍuvannāḷuttamire* . . . ; **tr.** when the illustricous Ādityavarmarasa, lord of Banavāsipura, **one who confronts enemy army single handedly** was ruling over Kōgaḷi-500 and Sundavatti-12 ; *S.I.I.* IX, pt. i, No. 77, p. 48, l. 9–10 ; Kōgaḷi, Hadagalli Tq., Bellary Dt., Karn. St. **Dy.** Chāḷ. of Kal., Āhavamalla, Ś. 914 = 993 A.D.

aṇiyōḍegaṁḍa (K. *n.*), on sighting whom the enemy army runs helter-skelter ; **text** : . . . . ***aṇiyōḍegaṁḍa****num raṇararaṁganīṟanum yiṁtī nāmāvaḷi praśasti sahitarappa śrī maṁnu mahāmaṇḍaḷika Bammarasadēvaru* . . . *Āsaṁdi nelevīḍinoḷu rājyaṁ* . . . *saluttamire* . . ; **tr.** while mahāmaṇḍlika Bammarasadēva, **on sighting whom the enemy army runs helter-skelter**, who had passion for battle fields, was ruling from his headquarters at Āsaṁdi ; *E.C.* (R) XII, Tk. 3, p. 337, ll. 34, 39–41 ; Attimogge, Tarikere Tq., Chikkamagalur Dt., Karn. St. **Dy.** Hoy., Nārasiṁha I, in characters of the 12th cent. A.D. ;

aṇiviṇigey (K. *vb.*), behave rashly ; **text** : . . . . ***aṇiviṇigeydī*** *dharmaman* . . . . *aḷidaṁge teṟatu gatiyilla* . . . . ; **tr.** there is no salvation for any one who **behaves rashly** and destroys this act of charity ; *E.C.* VII, Skr. 153, p. 260, l. 35 ; Kiṭṭadahaḷḷi, Shikaripura Tq., Shimoga Dt., Karn. St. **Dy.** Chāḷ. of Kal., King's name lost, Ś. 960 = 1038 A.D.

āṇi[2] (T. *n.*), sharp metal piece ; **text** : . . . . *śeṁbiṉ* ***āṇi****gaḷum śaraḍum nīkki niṟai irubattiru kaḻañju* . . . . ; **tr.** twenty two *kaḻañju* (*q.v.*) refined by removing the **sharp metal pieces** and threads ; *S.I.I.* II, pt. ii, No. 51, p. 208, ll. 220–23 ; Tañjāvūr, Tanjavur Tq. and Dt., T. Nadu St. **Dy.** Chōḷa, Rājarāja I, reg. yr. 29 = 1014 A.D.

āṇi[3] (K. *n.*), equal in value ; **text** : . . . *Svāmidēvara navilachchina poṁnaṁ lokkiya ponn****āṇi****yum ā poṁna tūkamumāgi poydu salisuvaru*. . . . ; **tr.** the gold coin bearing the figure of peacok minted on behalf of Swāmidēva shall be **equal in value** and weight of the gold coin of the mint of Lokki when the molten liquid metal is poured into the grue ; *S.I.I.* IX, pt. i, No. 164, p. 155, ll. 25–26 ; Kuḍatini, Bellary Tq. and Dt., Karn. St. **Dy.** Chāḷ. of Kal., Vikramāditya VI, Ch. Vi. yr. 23 = 1098 A.D.

aṇi[4] (K. *s.a.* *aṇe*, *n.*), embankment ; **text :** . . . *Iṁmaḍi-Kāchāpura eṁba grāmake saluva chatussīmeyoḷagāda keṟe kuṁṭe ēta guyyalu gade beddalu* ***aṇi*** *achchukaṭṭu sahavāgi ā Śaṁkaradēvara nivēdya sahā dēvatā vaibhava naḍeyabēkendu samarpisidevu.* . . . ; **tr.** we granted within the four boundaries of the village Immaḍi-Kāchāpura, tank, pond, mechanism of lifting water, irrigated land, paddy field, dry land, **embankment**, partitioned irrigated land for the offering of food and other services to the god Śaṁkaradēva ; *S.I.I.* IX, pt. ii, No. 474, p. 489, ll. 16–18 ; Agaḷi, Madakasira Tq., Anantapur Dt., A.P. St. **Dy.** Sāḷuva, Narasiṁha, Ś. 1420 = 1498 A.D.

anīka (K. *n.*), group ; **text :** . . . . *aśōkāmra-punnāga-tāḷ-ōrvij-**anīka**ṅgaḷiṁ* . . . . *kaṇgoḷisuva Ballakuṁde* . . . . ; **tr.** the village of Ballakuṁde which was attractive because of the **group** of trees born out of the earth such as *aśōka, āmra, punnāga* and *tāḷa* ; *S.I.I.* IX, pt. i, No. 297, p. 323, ll. 8, 10 ; Kurugōḍu, Bellary Tq. and Dt., Karn. St. **Dy.** Kal. of Kal., Śaṁkhavarma, Ś. 1099 = 1177 A.D.

āṇikkal (T. *n.*), weighing stone ; **text :** . . . . . . Kachchippēṭṭ**āṇikkal**lāl niṟai irubadiṉ kaḻañju . . . . ; **tr.** twenty *kaḻañju* (coin) of gold weighed by the **weighing stone** of Kachchippēḍu ; *S.I.I.* I, No. 85, first part, p. 117, First part ; Kāñchīpuram, Kanchipuram Tq., Chingleput Dt., T. Nadu St. **Dy.** Chōḷa, Parakēsarivarman, reg. yr. 4 = 911 A.D.

anīnu (K. *n.*), bridle ; **text :** . . . . *aśvaratnada ābharaṇada lekhkhā* . . . . . . *anīnu 2* . . . . ; **tr.** the account of the jewellery of the quality horse include 2 **bridles** ; *E.C.* (R) III, No. 105, p. 185 ; Naṁjanagūḍu, Nanjanagud Tq., Mysore Dt., Karn. St. **Dy.** Woḍ. of Mys., Kṛishṇarāja Woḍeyar III, Ś. 1769 = 1847 A.D.

ānīta-birāḍa (K. *n.*), tax on imports ; **text :** . . . . . *Viṭhalarājayyanavaru* . . . . *krayavāgi koṁḍa tōṭadoḷagaṇa teṁgu halasu māvu hēruḷe niṁbe ēnuṁṭāda phalagaḷa tōṭavanu Hihiriya-Anantapurada Mallikārjuna dēvara amṛutapaḍige* . . . . *ānīta-birāḍa sahavāgi.* . . . . . *koṭṭaru* . . . ; **tr.** Viṭhalarājayya granted after purchase, for the perpetual offering of food to the god Mallikārjunadēva of Hiriya-Anantapura, a grove along with all the fruit yielding trees such as jackfruit, mango, citrus and lemon as well as all incomes including **tax on imports** ; *S.I.I.* IX, pt. ii, No. 642, p. 640, ll. 10, 12–19, 21 ; Antapuram, Hospet Tq., Bellary Dt., Karn. St. **Dy.** Tuḷuva, Sadāśivarāya, Ś. 1473 = 1551 A.D.

añjāli (T. *n.*), tax levied on paddy fields in South Kerala ; **text :** *849 varsham paśāṇam mudal 869* *varsham paśāṉam varai* ***añjāli*** *aḍaichchu* ; **tr.** having paid the tax on **paddy fields** over the agricultural products between the years 849 and 869 ; *T.A.S.* V, No. 71, pp. 210–11, ll. 6–7, Vaḍaśēri, Kerala St. **Misc.,** Kollam 873 = 1635 A.D.

añjiṉāṉpugaliḍam (M. *n.*), place of refuge for the frightened, (a title) **: text:** *padiṉeṉ viśayattārkku mēṟppaḍiyār irukkiṟaviḍam . . . . Śeṇbaga Irāmaṉteruveṉṟun* ***añ jiṉāṉ-pugal-iḍam*** *eṉṟum nālu ellaikkum kal veṭṭi nāṭṭi-kkuḍuttadu,* ; **tr.** an inscription on stone was engraved to the effect that the place where those of the eighteen territorial divisions resided is to be called Śeṇbaga Irāmaṉteru and **añjiṉāṉpugaliḍam** ; *T.A.S.* IV, No. 18, pp. 98–99, ll. 11–29, Kollam, Kollam Tq and Dt., Ker. St. **Dy.** Rulers of Travancore, Vīra-Rāma-Rāma-Varman, Kollam 653 = 1478 A.D.

añjiraṇḍu vaṇṇam (T. *n.*), 2 units of dehusked paddy against 5 units of paddy with husk; **text:** *Tiruvaṇṇāmalaiyil eḻundaruḷuvitta Pichchadēvarkku . . . . nāḷ oṉṟiṉukku tiruvamudu ariśi kuṟiṉiyināl añjiraṇḍu vaṇṇattāl nellu padakku nānāḻi* ; **tr.** for the feeding services to the god Pichchadēvar installed in Tiruvaṇṇāmalai **2 units of dehusked paddy as against 5 units of paddy with husk** were granted ; *S.I.I.* VIII, No. 66, p. 33, l. 4, Tiruvaṇṇāmalai, Tiruvannamalai Tq., N. Arcot Dt., T. Nadu St., **Dy.** Chōḷa, Rājēndrachōḷa I, reg. yr. 19 = 1031 A.D.

añjuvaṇṇam (T. *n.*), five classes of artisans : ***añ juvaṇṇam*** *uḍaiya Īssūppu Iṟappāṉukkum . . . . ivan . . . . santati pirakiriti.* ***añ juvaṇṇam*** *santati pirakiriti. . . .* ; **tr.** to *Īssuppu Iṟappāṉ* of **five classes of artisans,** (we have) given rights of heriditary belonging to **five classes of artisans** ; *Ep. Ind.,* III, No. 11, p. 68, ll. 15, 19, 20 ; Cochin, Cochin Tq. and Dt., Ker. St. **Dy.** Tiruvaḍis of Cochin, Bhāskara Ravivarman, reg. yr. 36 + 2., in characters of 10th century A.D.

aṅka[1] (K. < Skt.), battle, ; **text**[1] **:** . . . *Bidirūra aggaḷam iḷivaḷḷi* ***aṅka****ke kādida Bidayita sattan . . .* ; **tr :** Bidayita died in the **battle** when Bidirūru was attacked by the army ; *E.C.* X, Spr. 27, p. 348, ll. 22–25 ; Śrīnivāsapura, Srinivasapura Tq., Kolar Dt., Karn. St. **Dy.** Noḷ. Pal., Noḷaṁbādhirāja, in characters of 9th cent. A.D.

aṅka[2] (K. < Skt.), professional fighter ; **text :**. . . . *Bīra- chūḍāmaṇi eḷdu paḍayāṅgelvandu avarā munde palabar nāyakarā kōlāhalamāge surigeyindiṟidu sattōn . . . .* ***aṅkan*** *Tējamāni eṁbōn*; **tr.** when Bīra Chūḍamaṇi was winning a battle a number of army leaders were involved in hue and cry and in the sequel **the professional fighter** Tējamāni was killed on being pierced with a sword while fighting ; *S.I.I.* IX, pt. i, No. 20, p. 10, ll. 8–11 ; Kaḷakāṭūr, Punganoor Tq., Chittoor Dt., A.P. St. **Dy.** Noḷ. Pal., Noḷaṁbadiyarasa, in characters of 9th century A.D.

aṅka[3] (K. *n.*), wrestler ; **text :**. . . . *Pallavādityaṁ pṛithvīrājyaṁgeyyuttaṁ . . . Pallavāditya Noḷaṁba-*

seṭṭi-endu pesaram daya-geydu . . . . . ***aṅka****van-nōḍal-paḍedu Pulināḍa Koḷatūraṁ Pallavādityapuravāge nakaram māḍi vaiśyadattiyāge māḍi NoḷaṁbaseṭṭIge* . . . *koṭṭam* . . . ; **tr :** when Pallavāditya was ruling over the earth, he gave the honourable name of Pallavāditya Noḷaṁbaseṭṭi and after watching his prowess as a **wrestler** granted to him as *vaiśyadatti,* the town of Koḷattūru in Pulināḍu after renaming it as Pallavādityapura ; *S.I.I.* IX, pt. i, No. 41, p. 24, ll. 10–11, 13, 15–17 ; Nelapalli, Puṅganūru Tq., Chittoor Dt., A.P., **Dy.** Noḷ. Pal., Iṟiva Noḷaṁba Pallavāditya, in characters of 10th cent. A.D.

aṅkakāṟa (K. *n.*), warrior ; **text** . . . . *Bhūtugan-**aṅkakāṟa** Śrīmat Maṇelēṟaṅge anuvaradoḷ mechchi bēḍikoḷḷendoḍe*. . . . *Kāḷiyaṁ dayegeyaṁdu koṇḍanānāya*. . . . ; **tr.** Būtuga having appreciated his follower Maṇalēra's bravery on the battle filed bade him to ask for a favour ; Maṇalēra in his turn requested that he be given the dog named Kāḷi ; *E.C.* (R) VII, Mu. 42, p. 277, l. 9 ; Ātakūru, Maddur Tq., Mandya Dt., Karn. St. **Dy.** Rāshṭr, Krishṇa III, Ś. 872 = 950 A.D.

āṇma (K. *n.*), hero ; **text :** . . . . *mahāsāmanta*. . . . *sanmanad-āṇmaṁ* . . . . . *śrīmat Ṟoṭṭayyaṁ* . *Māsivāḍi nūṟanālvattuvaṁ* . . . . . *āḷuttamire* . . . . . . ; **tr.** when the illustrious *mahāsāmanta* (*q.v.*) Ṟoṭṭayya, a hero with pure mind, was administering Māsivāḍi one hundred and forty etc. ; *S.I.I.* IX, pt. i, No. 66, p. 38, ll. 5–8 ; Bāgaḷi, Harapanahalli Tq., Bellary Dt., Karn. St. **Dy.** Rāshṭr., Krishṇa III, Ś. 878 = 956 A.D.

āṉmatyāgam (T. *n.*), self-immolation ; **text :** . . . . *Kaṇavadinaṁbi Ārūraṉ dēvaruḍaiya śrī kāriyattukkāga taṉṉai* ***āṉmatyāgam*** *śeiya ivaṉukkāga dēvarkku* . . . *oṟu nandā-viḷakkerippadarkku* . . . *iṟaiyiliyāga śeydu kuḍutta nilam* . . ; **tr.** tax free land granted for lighting one perpetual lamp for the god as a tribute to the **self-immolation** committed by Kaṇavadinaṁbi Ārūraṉ as part of his service to the god ; *S.I.I.* XIII, No. 131, p. 67, ll. 2–3 ; Pēraṅgiyūr, Tirukkoyilur Tq., S. Arcot Dt., T. Nadu St. **Dy.** Chōḷa, Rājarāja I, reg. yr. 6 = 992 A.D.

aṇṇanaṁkakāra (K. *n.*), who who assists his elder brother in battles (a title) ; **text :** . . . . *parabaḷa Bhīma sāhasōttuṅga* ***aṇṇan-aṁkakāṟa*** . . . *pusidu nuḍivara gaṁḍa* . . ; **tr.** a very Bhīma to the enemy army, who was at the height of his valour and who **assists his elder brother in battle** ; *K.I.* IV, No. 48, p. 101, ll. 23–24 ; Maḍalūr, Hirekerur Tq., Dharwar Dt., Karn. St. **Dy.** Chāḷ. of Kal., Tribhuvanamalla, in characters of 11th cent. A.D. ; **aṇṇanabaṁṭa** (K. *n.*), elder brother's follower, (a title) ; **text :** . . . . *Bōgaya mārpaḍe goṟaṁṭan aṇṇanabaṁṭa* . . ; **tr.** Bōgaya who was a terror to the enemy army and who was his **elder brother's follower** ; *E.C.* (R) II, Sb. 171, p. 115, ll. 2–3 ; Chikkabeṭṭa, Channarayapatna Tq., Hassan Dt., Karn. St. **Misc.**, in characters of 10th cent. A.D.

aṇṇanadaṇḍa (K < Skt. *n.*) a fighting arm of his elder brother, a title ; **text :** . . . . *Kaliyaṇṇa turugoḷ-tānu kādi Tamaḷēśvara bhaktaṁ aṇṇanadaṇḍa* . . ; **tr.** Kaliyaṇṇa who was fighting a battle for protecting cattle, who was a devotee of the god Tamaḷēśvara and who was like the **fighting arm of his elder brother**; *Mysore Archaeological Report*, 1915–19, 171, Karn. St. **Misc.**, Ś. 819 = 897 A.D.

aṇṇanasiṅga (K. *n.*), fighting in support of his elder brother like a lion ; **text :** . . . . *rājavidyā bhujaṅgaṁ aṁṇanasiṅgaṁ* . . ; **tr.** . . . . **fighting in support of his elder brother like a lion** ; *Ep.Ind.* IV, No. 30, p. 215, l. 5 ; Jatiṅgarāmēśvara, Jagalur, Chitradurga Dt., Karn. St. **Dy.** Chāḷ. of Kal., Jayasiṁha III, Ś. 993 = 1072 A.D.

aṇṇanavatiga (K, *n.*) obedient to his elder brother ; **text :** (obscure). *aṇṇnanavatigan Antakaṅgaṁjadōn* . . . *Bhānudāsan.* . . . . ; **tr.** Bhānudāsa who is **obedient to his elder brother** and one who does not fear the god of death ; *M.A.R.* 1939, No. 22 pp. 117–18, ll. 7–8, 16–19 ; Hiremadhure, Challakere Tq., Chitradurga Dt, Karn. St. **Dy.** W. Gaṅga, Koṅguṇi arasar, in characters of 8th century A.D.

annagṛiha (K. *n.*), feeding house ; **text :** . . . *Beḷvoladadhikāradoḷ naḍedum anyataṭākadoḷ eyde dēvatā niḷaya mahādvi**jānnagṛiha** satranikētana divya dīrghikāvaḷi-gaḷanoppe māḍisida Mādhavan*; **tr.** Mādhava who had migrated from Beḷvoḷa to Anyataṭāka built in that place a temple, a **feeding house** for great brāhmaṇas, a choultry and tanks; *K.I.* V, No. 14, p. 49, ll. 18–20 ; Chikkahandigōḷ, Gadag Tq. and Dt., Karn. St. **Dy.** Chāḷ. of Kal., Vikramāditya VI, Ch. Vi. yr. 24 = 1100 A.D.

aṇṇale (K. *adj.*), pretentious ; **text :** . . . . . *uravaṇiyiṁde baṁda Magadhāṁdhra. Kaḷiṅga Chaḷukya Pāṁḍya Gūrjjarenipa aggad**aṇṇalegaḷ**ennoḷe bhaṁgamanāṁtu. pōdar*. . . ; **tr.** the **pretentious** rulers of Magadha, Āndhra, Kaḷiṁṅga, Chaḷukya, Pāṁḍya and Gūrjjara who had invaded recklessly had to flee ; *S.I.I.* IX, pt. i, No. 297, p. 323, ll. 18–19 ; Kurugōḍu, Bellary Tq. and Dt, Karn. St. **Dy.** Kal. of Kal, Śaṅkhavarma, Ś. 1099 = 1177 A.D.

anneya (K. *s.a.* Skt. *anyāya, n.*), punitive tax ; **text :** . . . *dēvarige* . . . . *śaraṇeṁdu* . . . *kai mugiyu-vudallade* . . . *kāṇike sēse tapp**anneya**vāyadāyamivu sallavu* . . . ; **tr.** having surrendered with folded hands exemptions were granted for taxes such as *kāṇike* (*q.v.*), *sēse* (*q.v.*), *tappu* (*q.v.*), punitive tax, āya-dāya ; *S.I.I.* IX, pt. i, No.251, p. 262, ll. 45–46 ; Beṇṇehaḷḷi, Harapanahalli Tq., Bellary Dt., Karn. St. **Dy.** Chāḷ of Kal., Jayasiṁha II, Cy. yr. Śukla = 1149 A.D.

anniyāyam (T. *n.*), injustice ; **text :** . . . . . *mahā sabhaiyyōm* . . . . *Tiruvālanduṟaiuḍaiyanāyaṉār* . . . *tirunāmattukkāṇiyāy* . . . *iṟukkum nilam muṉṉāḷ iruvattoṉṟāvadu mudal iṟuvattārāvadu vaṟaiyum ūrōḍe kūḍi kaḍamai iṟuttupōgayil* . . . . ***aṇṇiyāyam***

śeidōm eṉṟu ivūrku paḻiyāga ... innāyaṉār innālgaḷil iṟuttu uḍaimai tāṉattār kanakka paḍaiye kuḍuppadāga nāṅgaḷ ... eḻudi kuḍuttu .... ; **tr.** we, the members of the *mahāsabhā* (an administrative body) having confessed that earlier from the year 21 till the year 26 the temple's land having been appropriated by the villagers, it was decided that **injustice** had been done to the temple of the god Tiruvālanduṟai Uḍaiyaṉāyaṉār and that the lands will be restored with all its past revenues to the temple as calculated by the temple officials ; *S.I.I.* VIII, No. 193, p. 95, ll. 1–4 ; Anbil, Tiruchirapalli Tq. and Dt., T. Nadu St. **Dy.** Chōḷa, Rājēndra III, reg. yr. 4 = 1249 A.D.

anṟāḍu (T. *adj.*), daily ; **text** : .... ***anṟāḍu*** *kōvilukku aṟu kaḻañju poṉ paḍuvadāga ..... kuḍuttōm* ; **tr.** we gave to the temple a **daily** fine of six kaḻañju (coin) of gold ; *T.A.S.* V, No. 7B, p. 30, ll. 3–4 ; Chēramaṅgalam, Eraniel Tq., Padmanabhapuram Dt., Ker St. **Dy.** Chōḷa-Pāṇḍya, Sundaraśōḻapāṇḍyadēva, reg. yr. 6, in characters of the 10th cent. A.D. ; **anṟāḍu nalkāśu** (T. *n.*), coin in day to day currency ; **text** : .... *śrī kōyilil Āḍavalārkku ... vaitta ... tirunundāviḷakku oṉṟukku ... tanda* ***anṟāḍu nalkāśu*** *20* ; **tr.** 20 **coins** valid **in day to day currency** were granted for the purpose of lighting one perpetual lamp before the deity Āḍavallār in the temple ; *S.I.I.* XXII, pt. i, No. 81, p. 77, l. 27 ; Jambai, Tirukkoyilur Tq., S. Arcot Dt., T. Nadu St. **Dy.** Chōḷa, Rājādhirāja I, reg. yr. 32 = 1049–50 A.D. ; **anṟāḍu-naṟkāśu** (T. *n.*), coin in day to day currency ; **text**[1] : .... *kuḍiyiruppāga viṭṭa kollai nilam ... innilattuku vilaiyāga emmil iśeynda* ***anṟāḍu-naṟkāśu*** *irubadum vilaiyāgakkoṇḍu viṟṟu vilaiāvaṇam śeydu koḍuttōm* ; **tr.** we gave a sale deed for the sale of hinterland meant for habitation for twenty **coins in day to day currency** which we had agreed to pay ; *S.I.I.* XXII, pt. i, No. 287, p. 233, ll. 34, 36–37 ; Tirumālpuram, Wallajapet Tq., N. Arcot Dt., T. Nadu St. **Dy.** Chōḷa, Kulōttuṅga I, reg. yr. 41 = 1110–11 A.D. ; **text**[2] : .. *viḷai nilam oṉṟē āṟumāvum maṉai kuḻi nārpadum .... emmil iśainda ....* ***anṟāḍu naṟkāśiṉāl*** *... paṇam nūṟṟu muppattu nālum ... kaikkoṇḍu .... vilaippiramāṇam paṇṇikuḍuttēṉ .. Dēvaru kaṇḍaṉēṉ* ; **tr.** Dēvarkaṇḍaṉ granted to the god Bhuvanēkvīra Akaḷaṅkanāḍāḻvār through a sale deed fertile lands of six *mā* (a land measure.) one house measuring forty *kuḻi* (a land measure.) which he agreed to pay for a price of one hundred and thirty four *paṇam* (coin) ; *S.I.I.* VIII, No. 243, p. 135, l. 9, Tirumiyachchūr, Nannilam Tq., Tanjavur., T. Nadu St. **Dy.** Pāṇḍya, Kulaśēkhara, reg. yr. 21 = 1337 A.D.

anṟāḍunaṟpaḻaṅkāśu (T. *n.*), old valid coin still in circulation ; **text** : ... *vilaipporuḷ* ***anṟāḍu naṟpaḻaṅkāśu*** *80* ... ; **tr.** a price of 80 **old valid coins still in circulation** ; *S.I.I.* VII, No. 430, p. 271, l. 2, Māgaral, Kanchipuram Tq., Chingleput Dt., T. Nadu St. **Dy.** Chōḷa, Rājarāja III,

reg. yr. 5 = 1220 A.D.

aṉṟāḍu naṟpaṇam (T. *n.*), coins in valid currency; **text :** .... *vilaiporuḷ* ***aṉṟāḍu naṟpaṇam*** *1500* ; **tr.** a price of 1500 **coins in valid currency** ; *S.I.I.* VII, No. 25, p. 10, l. 5, Tāramaṅgalam, Omalur Tq., Salem Dt., T. Nadu St. **Dy.** Pāṇḍya, Sundara Pāṇḍya, reg. yr. 6 = 1281 A.D.

antaḥpurādhyaksha (K. *n.*), presiding officer of the royal harem ; **text :** . . . *śrī-manmahā-pradhān**āntaḥpurādhyaksha** karituragasāhaṇi* . . . . *Barmadēvayyaṁgaḷ*. . . . . ; **tr.** Barmadēvayya, the illustrious chief minister and the presiding officer of the **royal harem** who was the head of the elephant corps and cavalry ; *S.I.I.* IX, pt. i, No. 232, p. 236, ll. 7–8, 10–11 ; Ubacherla, Gooty Tq., Anantapur Dt., A. P. St. **Dy.** Chāḷ. of Kal., Bhūlōkamalla, reg. yr. 10 = 1135 A.D.

antai (T. *n.*), an honorifix suffix for an elderly man ; **text :** . ... ***antai*** *Asutaṉ piṇaü koḍupitōṉ* .... ; **tr.** *Asutaṉ with an honorific suffix for an elderly man caused to be given the lattice* ; *J.L.I.T.* No. 3, pp. 141–42, ll. 3–4 ; Māṅguḷam, Mangulam Tq., Madurai Dt., T. Nadu St. **Misc.**, in characters of the 2nd century B.C.

antarāyam (T. *n.*), internal revenue ; **text**[1] **:** . . . *i bhūmiyāl vanda iṟaiyum* . . . . *veṭṭi* . . . . ***antarāyamum*** *eppērpaṭṭa iṟaiyum kāṭṭa peṟādōm āṉōm* . . ; **tr.** all the taxes such as land tax, forced labour, **internal revenue** and all other such revenue income is not to be shown .. ; *S.I.I.* III, pts. iii & iv, No. 116, p. 252, ll. 12–14 ; Vēḷachēri, Saidapet Tq., Chingleput Dt., T. Nadu. St. **Dy.** Chōḷa, Sundarachōḷa, reg. yr. 7 = 964 A.D.; **text**[2] **:** .... *Vīrarājēndrapurattu* ... *Mahādēvarkku* ... *nāṟpadāvudu modal* ***antarāyam*** *uṭpaḍa dēvadāṉa iṟaiyili iṭṭamaikku chandrādittavaṟ śelvadāga* ; **tr.** from the fortieth regnar year onwards the **internal revenue** including tax free *dēvadāṉa* (*q.v.*) was donated permanently to the god Mahādēva of Vīrarājēndrapura ; *S.I.I.* XXII, No. 68, pp. 66–67 ; Jambai, Tirukkoyilūr Tq., S. Arcot Dt., T. Nadu St. **Dy.** Chōḷa, Kulōttuṅga I, reg. yr. 40 = 1109–10 A.D. ; **text**[3] **:** .... *Maṟudaṉguḍiyāṉa Perumāḷ Tiruchōḷacheruppēdimaṅgaḷattukku kaḍamai* ***antarāyam*** .... *maṟṟum eppērpaṭṭa variyum uḷpaḍa piḍipāḍu paṉṉikuḍuttōṉ Śēṟṟūr ūrkkuchamainda nāṭṭōmum* . . . *ūrōmum* ; **tr.** inhabitants of the territorial division and the inhabitants of the village of Śēṟṟūr remitted to the brāhmaṇa settlement of Maṟudaṉguḍi *alias* Perumāḷ Tiruchōḷacheruppēdimaṅgaḷam the taxes such as *kaḍamai* (*q.v.*), internal taxes etc. ; *S.I.I.* VIII, No. 171, pp. 80–81, ll. 14–16 ; Kāḷaiyārkōyil, Sivagangai Tq., Ramanathapuram Dt., T. Nadu St. **Dy.** Pāṇḍya, Kulaśēkhara, reg. yr. 37+1 = 1365 A.D. ; **text**[4] (Skt.) **:** .... *Bhīmēśa kramukavanāli pālikairyō dēyaḥ syāt pratisamama**ṁtarāya** saṁjñah saṁ karaṁ samadiśadarka chaṁdra tāraṁ Lakshmīvān akhila jagatprasiddha kīrtiḥ* .... ; **tr.** the world famous Lakshmīvān ordered that until the sun, moon and stars last, the **internal tax** has to be paid every year by the guardians of arecanut grove belonging to Bhīmēśa ; *S.I.I.* IV, No. 1214, p. 420, ll. 7–8 ; Drākshārāma, Ramachandrapuram Tq., Godavari Dt., A.P. St. **Misc.**, Ś. 1038 = 1116 A.D.

antarisu (K. *vb.*), fall into disuse ; **text :** . . . . . . *muṁnaṁ śrī Svāmidēvargge Kṛishṇarājaṁ koṭṭa antā dharmam bahukālāntaradoḷ-**antarisal**-adane Ballāḷa mahīkāntāmātyam sthiramappantu punar-dattamāgi vinayadim ittam* . . . . ; **tr.** the pious grant which Kṛishṇarāja had earlier made to śrī Svāmidēva having **fallen into disuse** over a long time, it was re-granted on a permanent footing by the the minister of the ruler Ballāḷa ; *S.I.I.* IX, pt. i, No. 326, p. 342, ll. 84–88 ; Saṁḍūru, Sanduru Tq., Bellary Dt., Karn. St. **Dy.** Hoy., Ballāḷa II, Ś. 1128 = 1206 A.D.

aṉubandham (M. < Skt. *adj.*), support ; **text :** *vilakkum avagaḷkk-**aṉubandham** paṟaiyum avagaḷum iddaṇḍamē paḍuvadu* ; **tr.** those who set aside the provisions of this grant and those who **support** the violators of this grant also will pay the same fine ; *T.A.S.* V, No. 2, p. 6, l. 2, Kaviyūr, Tiruvallam Tq., Kollam Dt., Ker. St. **Misc.**, Kali 4052 = 951–52 A.D.

anubhava avakāśam (M. < Skt. *adj.*), opportunity to enjoy ; **text :** *Poduvāḷku īvaṉṉam kalppichcha dāna **anubhava avakāśam** koḍutttu* . . . . ; **tr.** in this manner an **opportunity** was created for the Poduvāl **to enjoy** the gift ; *T.A.S.* V, No. 21, p. 59, ll. 13–14, Tiruvelunnaṉṉūr, Trivandrum Tq. and Dt., Ker. St. **Misc.**, Kollam 878 = 1703 A.D.

anubhavaṇe. (K < Skt. *n.*), arrangemet ; **text :** *Sōmēśvaradēvargge* . . . . *khaṇḍasphuṭitakkendu* . . . . *biṭṭa uppina hēṟu ayvattu yī **anubhavaṇe**ya arorbba naḍevaravarade dharma* . . . . ; **tr.** for effecting repairs to the temple of the god Sōmēśvara . . . . 50 loads of salt were given. Whoever implements this **arrangment**, he would have earned the merit for the same ; *S.I.I.* XX, No. 34, pp. 37–38, ll. 18–21, Kalkēri, Hangal Tq., Dharwar Dt., Karn. St. **Dy.** Chāḷ. of Kal., Sōmēśvara I, Ś. 975 = 1053 A.D. ; **anubhavaṇi.** (K < Skt. *n.*), administration ; **text :** *mahāsēnādhipati Śiraśśēkhara neraḍarunūṟaṟ**anubhavaṇi**yoḷam* . . . ; **tr.** under the **administration** of the two Six-hundred divisions by the great commander Śiraśśēkhara ; *S.I.I.* XI, pt. i, No. 147, p. 179, l. 12, Chikkahandigōḷ, Gadag Tq. and Dt., Karn. St. **Dy.** Chāḷ. of Kal., Vikramāditya VI, Ch. Vi. yr. 24 = 1099 A.D.

anubhaviṁchi (Te. < Skt. *indec.*), enjoying ; **text :** . . . . . *vṛitti velisēnu nīrunēla dēvadāyamu* . . . . ***anubhaviṁchi** stānāpatulu* . . . . ; **tr.** the head of the temple will be **enjoying** the share of water and land as well as the donation made to the god etc. ; *S.I.I.* XVI, No. 6, p. 5, ll. 22–24 ; Chilamakūru, Kamalapuram Tq., Cuddapah Dt., A.P. St. **Dy.** Saṅgama, Harihara II, Ś. 1304 = 1382 A.D.

anubhavisūdu (K. < Skt. *vb.*), to enjoy ; **text :**

. . . . *eraḍu hoṁnnu ī paṇavanū . . . . dēvarāyamahārāyara hesaralū tirunāḷu voṁdu avasaravanū naḍasikoṁḍu . . . . . sukhadalu* ***anubhavisūdu*** *eṁdu koṭa dharṁma śāsana* . . . . ; **tr.** this pious grant of two *paṇa* (coin) was given stipulating that this money is **to be enjoyed** after an auspicious day in the name of Dēvarāya mahārāya ; *S.I.I.* VII, No. 789, p. 401, l. 4 ; Tirumaṇikuḻi, Cuddalore Tq., S. Arcot Dt., T. Nadu St. **Dy.** Saṅgama, Dēvarāya II, in characters of 15th cent. A.D.

aṇuchaṇagey (K. *vb.*), serve as a subordinate official ; **text :** *Tailapadēvaru Banavāse pannichchā siramum āḷuttire Nāgarakhaṇḍakkeppatake . . . . Tikkimeyyanu anuchaṇageyyuttamiralu* ; **tr.** when Tailapadēvarasa was ruling over Banavāse - 12,000 Tikkimeyya was serving as a **subordinate official** in Nāgarakhaṇḍa-70 ; *K.I.* IV, No. 48, p. 100, ll. 17–19, Maḍalūr, Hirekerur Tq., Dharwar Dt., Dy. Chāḷ. of Kal., Vikramāditya VI, in characters of 11th cent. A.D.

aṇuga (K. < Skt. *n.*), follower ; **text :** (damaged) . . . . *Rāchana magan-**aṇugan** Chiḷabarasu māḍisidōn* . . . . ; **tr.** (the memorial stone) was got made by the **follower** of the son of Rācha ; *S.I.I.* IX, pt. i, No. 22, p. 11, l. 14 ; Hēmāvati, Madakasira Tq., Anantapur Dt., A.P. St. **Dy.** Noḷ. Pal., king's name lost, Ś. 845 = 923-24 A.D.

aṇuga jīvita (K. < Skt. *n.*), livelihood provided for one's follower ; **text :** *Śrī Koṭṭigadēvara . . pādapadmōpajīvi . . . . Śrīmat Mārasiṅgha Permāḍi Purigeṟe mūnūṟu Beḷvola mūnūrumana**aṇuga jīvita** māgāḷuttire* ; **tr.** when the illustrious Mārasiṅgha Permāḍi was administering Purigeṟe-300 and Beḷvola-300 granted to him for his **livelihood provided** by Koṭṭigadēva whose **follower** he was ; *K.I.* V, No. 4, p. 12, l. 10, Hirehandigōḷ, Gadag Tq. and Dt., St. **Dy.** Rāshṭr., Nityavarsha Koṭṭiga, Ś. 893 = 970 A.D.

aṇugi (K. *n.*), female follower ; **text :** . . . . . *Jagadēkamalladēvara viśālōrasthaḷa jayāṁgane . . . . Noḷaṁbana **aṇugi*** . . . . Dēvaḷadēvi . . . ; **tr.** Dēvaḷadēvi, the **female follower** of Noḷaṁba, who was like the victorious damsel on the expansive chest of Jagadēkamalla ; *S.I.I.* IX, pt. i, No. 91, p. 62, ll. 15–17, 21 ; Oruvayi, Bellary Tq. and Dt., Karn. St. **Dy.** Chāḷ. of Kal., Jayasiṁha II, Ś. 958 = 1036 A.D.

aṇugina taneyam (K. < Skt. *n.*), beloved son ; **text :** . . . . . *Padmanābhaṁ**aṇugina taneyam*** . . . . . *Kṛishṇarāja* . . . . ; **tr.** Kṛishṇarāja the **beloved son** of the famous Padmanābha ; *S.I.I.* IX, pt. i, No. 213, p. 215, ll. 29–30, 33 ; Tripurāntakam, Markapuram Tq., Kurnool Dt., A.P. St. **Dy.** Chāḷ. of Kal., Vikramāditya VI, Ch. Vi. yr. 51 = 1126 A.D.

anugrāma (K. < Skt. *n.*), hamlet attached to a village ; **text :** *Hagariṭṭage 300 ṟa grām**ānugrāma**dalu . . . . salvaṁtāgi pratyēka oṁdoṁdu hoṁnnaṁ koṭṭaru* ; **tr.** from each village and its hamlet in the subdivision Hagariṭṭage 300 one *hoṁnnu* (*q.v.*) was given as was the custom ; *S.I.I.* XV, No. 143, p. 187, ll. 25–28, Tāḷikōṭi, Muddebihāḷ Tq., Bijapur Dt., Karn. St. **Dy.** Chāḷ. of Kal., Āhavamalla, Cy. yr. Plava = 1181 A.D.

anuja (K. < Skt. *n.*), younger brother ; **text :** . . . . . *Kāḷidāsana**nuja**ṁ* . . . . . *Mēchikaṁge sadākālaṁ varadanakke Dēvaradēvaṁ*. . . ; **tr.** may the god of gods always shower His boons on Mēchika the **younger brother** of Kāḷidāsa ; *S.I.I.* IX, pt. i, No. 102, p. 76, ll. 38–39 ; Mailāra, Bellary Tq. and Dt., Karn. St. **Dy.** Chāḷ. of Kal., Sōmēśvara, Ś. 968 = 1046 A.D. ; **anujāta** (K. < Skt. *n.*) ; **text :** . . . . ***anujāta**nādan ātaṅganimisha guruvenipa Niṁbadaṁḍādhipan* . . ; **tr.** his **younger brother** who was of divine qualities named Niṁbadaṁḍādhipa ; *K.I.A.P.* No. 2, p. 3, l. 65–66 ; Nāgai, Chincholi Tq., Gulbarga Dt., Karn. St., **Dy.** Chāḷ. of Kal., Traiḷōkyamalla, Ś. 980 = 1058 A.D.

anujeyar (K. < Skt. *n.*), younger sisters ; **text :** . . . . *Saṁkaragauḍaṁ Manunibhanāyaka-Gauḍaṅga**nujeyar**oppavaru Mailamaṁ Hālamanuṁ* . . . . . ; **tr.** Mailam and Hālama are the worthy **younger sisters** of Sankaragauḍa who was equal to Manu and was leader among gauḍas ; *S.I.I.* IX, pt. i, No. 249, p. 256, l. 34 ; Koḷūr, Bellary Tq. and Dt., Karn. St. **Dy.** Chāḷ. of Kal., Jagadēkamalla II, Cy. yr. Prabhava = 1147 A.D.

anujñe (K. < Skt. *n.*), (royal) order, consent ; **text**[1] **:** . . . . . *mahāmaṁḍaḷēśvaraṁ Vijaya-pāṁṇḍyarasara**nujñe**yiṁ* . . . . *70 mattar bhūmiyaṁ Śrīmadāhavamallēśvaradēvargge* . . . . *Bācharasa* . . . . *paḍeda* . . ; **tr.** Bācharasa received 70 *mattar* (*q.v.*) of land for the temple of Āhavamallēśvaradēva granted on the **order** of *mahāmaṁḍaḷēśvara* (*q.v.*) Vīrapāṇḍyadēvarasa ; *S.I.I.* IX, pt. i, No. 389, p. 401, ll. 5, 7–9 ; Kuruvatti, Harapanahalli Tq. and Dt., Karn. St. **Dy.** Guttas, Vikramāditya II, Ś. 1104 = 1181 A.D. ; **text**[2] **:** . . . . . *gāṇada aṟuvattu okkalugaḷ ellaruṁ neradu yajamānaralu dharmava māḍal**anujñe**yaṁ paḍedu Telligēśvaradēvaraṁ* . . . *pratishṭheya māḍi* . . . *koṭṭāya* . . . ; **tr.** having installed the god Telligēśvara, all the 60 tenants of oil mills granted to the god with the **consent** of their leader ; *S.I.I.* IX, pt. i, No. 336, p. 357, ll. 18–20, 25 ; Kuḍatini, Bellary Tq. and Dt., Karn. St. **Dy.** Hoy., Ballāḷa II, Ś. 1140 = 1218 A.D.

aṇukkaṉ (T. *n.*), close confidant ; **text :** . . . . *Kulōttuṅgachōḷa aṇukkaṉ Udaiyāṇḍai magaṉ Nuḷamba dēvarkku* ; **tr.** Nuḷambadēvar son of Udaiyāṇḍai, the **close confidant** of Kulōttuṅgachōḷa; *E.C.* X, Mul. 79 B. p. 166, ll. 2–3 ; Avani, Mulbagal Tq., Kolar Dt., Karn. St. **Dy.** Chōḷa, Kulōttuṅga, Cy. yr. Saumya = 1249 A.D. ; **aṇukkar** (T. *n.*), close confidants ; **text :** . . . . *araiyaṉ **aṇukkar**il Pūvaṉ Paṟaiyaṉēṉ* ; **tr.** Pūvaṉ Paṟaiyaṉ one of the **close confidants** of the king ; *S.I.I.* XIV, No. 56. p. 41, l. 6 ; Ambāsamudram, Ambasamudram Tq., Tirunelveli Dt., T. Nadu St. **Dy.** Pāṇḍya, reg. yr. 2+9 = in characters of 8th cent. A.D.

aṇukki (T. *n.*), mistress/lady-in-waiting at the royal court ; **text[1]** : . . . . *Irāśagambira-chchēdirāyar* ***aṇukki*** *Kāñchipurattu Uḍaiyyār Tiruvēkampamuḍayyanāyaṉār koyiliṟ dēvaraḍiyāḷ Puṇṇyañcheydāḷ* ; **tr.** Puṇṇyañcheydāḷ, lady dedicated to the god Tiruvēkampamuḍayya Nāyaṉār of Kañchipuram who was also the **mistress** of Irāśagambirachchēdirāyar ; *S.I.I.* XXII, No. 87, p. 82, ll. 5–7 ; Jambai, Tirukkoyilur Tq., S. Arcot Dt., T. Nadu St. **Dy.** Chōḷa, Kulōttuṅga I, reg. yr. 24 = 1094 A.D. ; **text[2]** : . . . *Tirukkōṭṭiyūr periyakōyil bhaṭārarkku Kīḻiraṇiyamuṭṭattu kaṇṇikkuḍi . . . pirāṭṭiyāṇa* ***aṇukki*** *Sundaravalli vaitta tirunondāviḷakkoṉṟu* ; **tr.** one perpetual lamp donated by Sundarvalli of Kaṇṇikkuḍi in Kīḻiraṇiyamuṭṭam, who was a **lady-in-waiting at the royal cour**t to the big temple of the god of Tirukkōṭṭiyūr ; *S.I.I.* XIV, No. 49, p. 37, ll. 3–9 ; Tirukkōṭṭiyūr, Tiruppattur Tq., Ramanathapuram Dt., T. Nadu St. **Dy.** Pāṇḍya, Śaḍaiyya Māṟaṉ, reg. yr. 2+1, in characters of 12th cent. A.D.

aṇuṁgi (K. *n.*), daughter ; **text** : . . . . *Sattigana****ṇuṁgi*** . . . *atyudāraśāḷini* . . . . *śrīman mahādēviyar.* . . . . ; **tr.** the illustrious Mahādēvi who was very munificent by nature and who was the **daughter** of Sattiga ; *S.I.I.* XI, pt. i, No. 61, p. 51, ll. 38–41 ; Marōḷ, Hungund Tq., Bijapur Dt., Karn. St. **Dy.** Chāḷ. of Kal., Jagadēkamalla I, Ś. 946 = 1324 A.D.

aṇuṁgu (K. *n.*), benevolence, dear female companion ; **text[1]** : . . . . . *śrīmat Kannayya Āḍanūran abhyaṁtarasiddhiyāge* . . . . ***anuṁgi****noḷ āḷuttire* . . . . ; **tr.** when the illustrious Kannayya was administering with **benevolence** Āḍanūru as a permanent fief ; *E.C.* XI, Hlkr 30, p. 339, l. 6; Āḍanūru, Hoḷalkere Tq., Chitradurga Dt., Karn. St., **Misc.,** Ś. 886 = 964 A.D. ; **text[2]** (Te. *n.*) : . . . . *Keṁdūri Chōḍamahārājaina Permmāḍidēvani* ***anuṁgu*** *Rekamadēvi* . . . ; **tr.** Rēkamadēvī **the dear female companion** of Permmāḍidēva the Keṁdūri Chōḷa king ; *S.I.I.* X, No. 88, p. 37, ll. 4–5 ; Kommūru, Bapatla Tq., Tenali Dt., A.P. St. **Dy.** Keṁdūri Chōḍa, Permmāḍidēva, Ś. 1051 = 1129 A.D.

anupu (K. *n.*), entry tax ; **text[1]** : . . . . . *samasta halaru koṭṭa vritti* ***anupu*** *ettu 10 kke ippaṇava koṭṭaru* . . . ; **tr.** the *samasta halaru* (*q.v.*) paid two paṇa (*q.v.*) as **entry tax** on 10 oxen ; *S.I.I.* IX, pt. i, No. 384, p. 398, ll. 23–24, Neraniki, Alur Tq., Bellary Dt., Karn. St. **Dy.** Yād. of Dēv., Rāmachandra dēva, Ś. 1209 = 1287 A.D. ; **text[2]** : . . . . . . *Prasannavirūpākshadēvarige* . . . . . . *Nāgalāpurada grāmake saluva* . . . . . *sakala bhatta ādāya sthaḷada suṁka* . . . . *grāmagaḷa* . . . . . ***anupu*** . . *modalāda ēnuṁṭādaru* . *samarpisidevu* . . . . ; **tr.** we granted to the god Prasanna Virūpākshadēva, revenue incomes on all paddy yields, local taxes, **entry tax** and all such taxes ; *S.I.I.* IX, pt. ii, No. 491, p. 506, ll. 4, 15–17, 20 ; Hampi, Hospet Tq., Bellary Dt., Karn. St. **Dy.**

Tuḷuva, Kṛishṇadēvarāya, Ś. 1435 = 1513 A.D.

anupina kallu (K. *n.*), a barrier stone indicating the place where the entry tax is to be paid ; **text :** . . . . . . *Kaḍavūra gaḍiya* ***anupina kallu*** ; **tr.** a **barrier stone** set up on the border of Kaḍavūru **indicating the place where the tax called entry tax is to be paid** ; *E. C.* (R) XIII, No. 81, p. 124, ll. 244–45 ; Mattūra agrahāra, Shimoga Tq. and Dt., Karn. St. **Dy.** Tuḷuva, Kṛishṇadēvarāya, Ś. 1444 = 1523 A.D.

anupu kaṭige (K. *n.*), entry tax on fire wood ; **text :** . . . . *hoḷe-yāche anupu-kaṭige* . . . . *ha*ṟ*ugōlavaru koḍuva te*ṟ*ige* . . . . . ; **tr.** the **entry tax on fire wood** paid by the ferry men coming from across the river ; *S.I.I.* IV, No. 255, p. 47, l. 11, Hampi, Hospet Tq., Bellary Dt. Karn. St. **Dy.** Tuḷuva, Kṛishṇadēvarāya, Ś. 1435 = 1513 A.D.

anupu mānya (K. *n.*), exemption from paying entry tax ; **text :** (damaged) . . . . *anupu mānyavāgi* . . . . . *vokkaliddaru.* . . . . ; **tr.** they were living as tenants enjoying **exemption from entry tax** ; *E.C.* XII, Śira 76, p. 289, l. 17, Eliyūru, Sira Tq., Tumkur Dt., Karn. St. **Dy.** Saṅgama, Harihara, Cy. yr. Siddhārthi = 1379 A.D.

anupu suṁka. (K. *n.*) entry tax ; **text :** (damaged) . . . . *Gaṁga maṇḍaliya rājyada Sūgūra* ***anupu suṁka****da oḷage* . . . . ; **tr.** from within the **entry tax** collected at Sūgūru included in Gaṁgamaṇḍaliya rājya ; *E.C.* (R) XIII, Kūḍli 40, p. 38, ll. 22–23, Kūḍli, Shimoga Tq. and Dt., Karn. St. **Dy.** Hoy., Narasiṁha III, Ś. 1214 = 1291 A.D.

anuvartigaḷ (K. < Skt.), those who conform ; **text:** . . . . *ī dharmakk****anuvartigaḷ*** . . . *sukhigaḷ mattī dharmavidēkeṁbarivar* . . . *pāpishṭaru.* . . . ; **tr. those who conform** to the provisions of this grant will be happy and those who question the provisions of this grant will be the sinners ; *S.I.I.* IX, pt. ii, No. 711, p. 697, l. 7, Aṁbali, Kudligi Tq., Bellary Dt., Karn. St. **Dy.** Kādaṁba, Jagadaḷapāṁḍya, in characters of 13th cent. A.D.

anusari (K. < Skt. *n.*), follower(s) ; **text :** . . . . *Adittanahaḷige ne*ṟ*enāḍu paranāḍu arasu anusari inda ādaṁthā bādheyanū Bārakūra hattukē*ṟ*iya halarū arasū* . . . . . . *pariharisi ā dhārmava pālisuvaru* ; **tr.** the *halaru* (*q.v.*) of ten quarters of Bārakūru and the king will set right the harm caused to the grant of Adittanahaḷi by the rulers and **followers** of the neighbouring and other principalities ; *S.I.I.* VII, No. 351, p. 210, ll. 43–45 ; Chauḷikēri, Udupi Tq. and Dt., Karn. St. **Dy.** Saṅgama, Harihararāya, Ś. 1308 = 1386 A.D.

anvaya (K. < Skt. *n.*), lineage ; **text[1] :** . . . *Kṛishṇarājadēvapādapadmōpajīvi Gaṅg****ānvaya*** *kulatiḷakaṁ Būtayyaperumāḍi* . . . ; **tr.** Būtayya-perumāḍi who was like the forehead mark of the Gaṅga **lineage** was the servant at the feet of the illustrious Kṛishnārājadēva ; *S.I.I.* XI, pt. i, No. 38, p. 24, ll. 2–3, Narēgal, Ron Tq., Dharwar Dt., Karn. St. **Dy.** Rāshṭr., Kṛishṇa III, Ś. 873 = 950 A.D. ; **text[2] :** . . . . *Vīra Bukkaṁṇavoḍeyaru*

Hoysaḷānvaya Mahīpālara mēdini-maṇḍalavanu nijabhuja- maṁḍanavāgi pālisuta Hosapaṭṭaṇadali . . . rājyam geyyutta . . . . . ; **tr.** when Vīra Bukkaṇṇavoḍeya was ruling over the kingdom of the rulers belonging to the Hoysaḷa **lineage** by the strength of his own arm from the capital city of Hosapaṭṭaṇa ; *S.I.I.* VII, No. 566, p. 336, ll. 4–5, Penukoṇḍa, Penukonda Tq., Anantapur Dt., A.P. St. **Dy.** Saṅgama, Bukka I, Ś. 1276 = 1354 A.D.

anvayam (T. < Skt. *n.*), lineage ; **text :** . . . . *Sōmanāthadēvarkku śiṟunilai viḷakku . . . erikaikku vaitta āḍu aimbadu . . . ivvāḍu aimbadum ivvāṇḍu mudal . . . kaikkoṇḍu en makkaḷ makkaḷ* ***anvayam****uḷḷadaṇayum nittam uḻakku ṉey . . . śeluttuvār* . . . . ; **tr.** fifty sheep were donated for burning a small lamp in the temple of Sōmanāthadēva and these fifty sheep were to be taken charge of by my sons and their sons as long as my family **lineage** continues by contributing one uḻakku of ghee every day ; *S.I.I.* XIV, No. 230, p. 134, ll. 8, 17–19, Āttūr, Tiruchchendur Tq., Tirunelveli Dt., T. Nadu St. **Dy.** Pāṇḍya, Śrīvallabha, in characters of 12th cent. A.D.

anvayattār (T. < Skt. *n.*), linege ; **text :** . . *Sundarśōḷa Mūvēndavēḷāṉum ivaṉ* ***anvayattār****um Śrīvaishṇavarum . . . . . daṇḍamiḍavum peruvārāgavum* ; **tr.** Sundarachōḷa Mūvēndavēḷāṉ and the members of his **lineage** and the Śrīvaishṇavas are liable to pay fines ; *S.I.I.* XIII, No. 151, p. 80, l. 6 ; Kōyil-Tēvarāyaṉpēṭṭai, Papanasam Tq., Tanjavur Dt., T. Nadu St. **Dy.** Chōḷa, Sundarachōḷa, in characters of 10th cent. A.D.

anyāya[1] (K. < Skt. *n.*), punitive tax, sinful act ; **text**[1] **:** . . . *Agaḷiya mahājanaṁ yippadiṁbarum yī bhūmiyoḷāda* ***anyāya****maṁ kāvudu . . . . . .* ; **tr.** the twenty *mahājana* (*q.v.*) of Agaḷi will collect the **punitive tax** on this land ; *S.I.I.* IX, pt. i, No. 33, p. 19, ll. 39–43, Agaḷi, Madakasira Tq., Anantapur Dt., A.P. St. **Dy.** Noḷaṁba, Noḷaṁbādhirāja, in characters of 10th cent. A.D. ; **text**[2] **:** . . . . . . (damaged) *ā mahājanaṁgaḷige . . . . ā Nīrahaḷḷige . . . . . .* ***anyāya****villendu dēvara hadineṁṭu virpaṇadalu . . barasi . . . . dhāreyaneredu koṭṭu . . .* ; **tr.** getting it written in the eighteen registers of the temple that there will be no taxes for natural losses and **punitive tax** for **sinful act**s and granted the charter to the *mahājana* (*q.v.*) of Nīrahaḷḷi ; *E.C.* (R) VIII, Hn. 42, p. 21, ll. 34–35, 37–39, Hoḷenarasīpura, Holenarasipur Tq., Hassan Dt., Karn. St. **Dy.** Hoy., Vīraballāḷa III, Ś. 1237 = 1310 A.D. ; **text**[3] **:** . . . . . *chatusīmeyoḷagāda gadde beddalu kaṭṭe kāluve aṇe achchukaṭṭu holamēre nīruvaḷi ivellavu voḷagāgi kāṇike kappa . . . . . .* ***anyāya*** *. . . . . yivu modalu Hāsanada śrī Virūpāksha dēvarige . . . . . . dānaśāsana pratishṭheyanu māḍidaru* ; **tr.** a donative edict was set up granting to the god Virūpākshadēva of Hāsana all the paddy field, dry field, embankment, canal, dam, irrigated land, land boundaries, water channels exempting these from **punitive tax** ; *E.C.* (R) VIII, Hn. 2, p. 215, ll. 16–19, 23–24, Hassan, Hassan Tq. and Dt., Karn. St. **Dy.** Tuḷuva, Sadāśiva, Ś. 1485 = 1563 A.D.

anyāya[2] (K. < Skt. *n.*), injustice ; **text**[2] **:** (damaged) .... *mummuri-daṇḍaṁgaḷu neṟedu māḍida ajñeya śāsana eṁteṁdaḍe ūrige* ***anyāya*** *avāntara bandaḍam* ..... ; **tr.** according to the order issued by the *mummuridaṇḍa* (*q.v.*) in case any **injustice** or havoc occurs in the village .... ; *S.I.I.* IX, pt. i, No. 327, p. 343, ll. 8–11, Kuḍatini, Bellary Tq. and Dt., Karn. St. **Dy.** Hoy., Ballāḷa II, Cy. yr. Prabhava = 1207 A.D.

aparādha (K. < Skt. *n.*), penalty ; **text :** .... *Maiṁda kaṭṭida hosa maneyiṁda mūḍalāgi ārobbaru manegaḷa .... kaṭṭidare Puttigeya Sōmanāthadēvarigū Parśvanāthasvāmigū tappidavarū chavuṭarige 1200 varahana* ***aparādha****vanu .... koḍuvaru* .... ; **tr.** if any one builds houses on either side of the road leading to the house built by Maiṁda would have offended the gods Sōmanāthadēva and Pārśvanāthasvāmi of Puttige; they will have to pay a **penalty** of 1200 *varaha* (*q.v.*) to the Chavuṭa ; *S.I.I.* VII, 226, p. 114, ll. 12–17 ; Mūḍabidure, Karkala Tq., Udupi Dt., Karn. St. **Dy.** Chauṭa, Chikkarājarasa, Ś 1500 = 1578 A.D.

aparādhaṁ (Te. < Skt. *n.*), penalty ; **text :** .... *Yellappanāyinigāru ...* ***aparādhaṁ*** *panḍranḍu rūkale kāsanimariyokuḍu konarādu* ; **tr.** Yellappa nāyinigāru assures that he would take only the dues specified in the agreement would not collect any **penalty** ; *I.A.P.* Cuddapah I, pt. ii, No. 120, p. 152, ll. 10, 26–27 ; Pulivēndala, Pulivendla Tq., Cuddaph Dt., A.P. St. **Dy.** Tuḷuva, Achyutaraya, Ś. 1457 = 1535 A.D.

aparādakāṇikkai, (T. < Skt. *n.*), tribute paid as penalty ; **text :** .. *Aṇṇāmalaināthaṉ ... sēvāparādhastānattukku aparādakāṇikkai varushaṁ oṉṟukku nūṟṟuirubadu poṉ araimaṉaippaṇḍārattukku kuḍukka-kaḍavārgaḷ āgavuṁ* ... ; **tr.** a tribute of penalty at the rate of 120 *poṉ* (*q.v.*) per year has to be paid to the treasury of the palace for not having paid dues to the god Aṇṇāmalainathaṉ ; *S.I.I.* VIII, No. 157, p. 71, ll. 12–13 ; Tiruvaṇṇāmalai, Tiruvannamalai Tq., N. Arcot Dt., T. Nadu St. **Dy.** Saṅgama, Dēvarāya, in characters of 14th cent. A.D.

apasubāḷu (K. *n.*), irrigated land ; **text :** ... *Kētayyana ...* ***apasubāḷa*** *hola mēre* ... ; **tr.** the field boundary of the irrigated land belonging to Kētaya ; *S.I.I.* IX, pt. i, No. 284, p. 305, ll. 8–9 ; Dēvaguḍi, Jammalamadagu Tq., Cuddappah Dt., A.P. St. **Dy.** Chāḷ. of Kal., Traiḷōkyamalla, Cy. yr. Śukla, in characters of 12th cent. A.D.

apōhanam (T. < Skt. *n.*), fallow land ; **text :** ... ***apōhanaṅ****kiḍanda bhūmi* .... ; **tr. land** which is lying **fallow** ; *S.I.I.* XIII, No. 227, p. 123, ll. 4–5 ; Mēlappaḻuvūr, Udayarpalayam Tq., Tiruchira-palli Dt., T. Nadu St. **Dy.** Chōḷa., Rājakēsari, in characters of 10th–11th cent. A.D.

apōvanam (T. < Skt. *n.*), fallow land ; **text :** . . . ***apōvanam****ēi kiḍanda nilam.* . . . . ; **tr. land** which is lying **fallow** ; *S.I.I.* VIII, No. 694, p. 350, ll. 5–6 ; Allūr, Tiruchirapalli Tq. and Dt., T. Nadu St. **Dy.** Chōḷa, Rājakēsari, reg. yr. 3, in characters of 10th-11th cent. A.D.

appaṇe (K. *n.*), order ; **text :** . . . . *Rāmarājayyana* ***appaṇe*** *pālisi taṁma kelasa-nāyiṁda Koṇḍōjage taṁma sīmeya mēlaṇa nāyaṁdarige sidhāya kaṭṭaḷeya . . . . pālista silāsāsana. . .* ; **tr.** the royal **order** of Rāmārājayya conveyed to his personal barber Koṇḍōja granting exemption of permanent tax and customary privileges to the barbers within the territory under his control ; *S.I.I.* IX, pt. ii, No. 611, p. 619, ll. 4–7 ; Muradi, Rayadurga Tq., Bellary Dt., Karn. St. **Dy.** Tuḷuva, Sadāśiva, Ś. 1467 = 1544 A.D. ; **appaṇekāṟa** (K. *n.*), one who conveys royal/official orders ; **text :** . . . . *adhikārigaḷu nālvaru ballāḷugaḷayvaru horahinavaru sthaḷada sēnabōvanu* ***appaṇekāṟ****anembivaru kūḍi . . . Chaṁḍōgrapārśvadēvara śrīkāryakke . . . . koṭṭa kshētra* . . . ; **tr.** land donated for the services of the god Chaṁḍōgrapārśvadēva jointly by four officers, five Ballāḷus, outsiders, head of the village and one who **conveys official orders** ; *S.I.I.* VII, No. 211, p. 107, l. 6–7 ; Mūḍabidure, Karkala Tq., Udupi Dt., Karn. St. **Dy.** Saṅgama, Bukkarāya, Ś. 1329 = 1407 A.D.

appayaṇada kuppa (K. *n.*), halting station where a journey is broken ; **text :** . . . . *Tribhuvana malladēvaru Bhōjana mēle paśchima diśāvarakkettidalli Bhīmaratiya tīrad****appayṇada kuppa****dalu . . . rājyaṁ geyyuttaviralu* . . . ; **tr.** when the Tribhuvanamalladēva was proceeding on an expedition against Bhōja in the western direction, he **broke his journey** at the **halting station** on the banks of the river Bhīmarati and was administering the empire from there ; *K.I.* VI, No. 15, p. 40, ll. 2–4 ; Malghāṇ, Sindagi Tq., Bijapur Dt., Karn. St. **Dy.** Chāḷ. of Kal., Vikramāditya VI, Ch. Vi. yr. 25 = 1100 A.D.

appayaṇa vīḍu (K. *n.*), halting station where a journey is broken ; **text :** . . . . *Sindavāḍi nāḍa baḷiya grāmam Puli****appayaṇavīḍ****inoḷ* . . . . .; **tr.** in the **halting station** called Hūli within the Sindavāḍināḍu **where the journey was broken**; *Ep. Ind.* XV, No. 6, p. 88, l. 28 ; Sūḍi, Ron Tq., Dharwar Dt., Karn. St. **Dy.** Chāḷ. of Kal., Sōmēśvara I, Ś. 981 = 1059-60. A.D.

apūrvāya (K. < Skt.), taxes which may be levied in future. ; **text :** . . . . *aḍekeya suṁka . . . . heggaḍekāṇike ivoḷagāgi muṁde huṭṭuva* ***apūrvāya****vellavaṁ māṇisi* . . . . *Mahālakshmī dēviyara dharmakārya . . . salvaṁtāgi Chāgaravaḷḷiyaṁ biṭṭu. . . koṭṭa śāsanaṁ* . . . ; **tr.** stone edict recording the grant of the village of Chāgaravaḷḷi in order that all the religious activities may be conducted for the goddess Mahālakshmīdēvi with the income from the tax on betel nuts, tributes to be paid to the village head and all such other **taxes which may be levied in future**. ; *E.C.* (R) VIII, Hn. 41, p. 267, ll. 11–15 ; Doḍḍagaddavaḷḷi, Hassan Tq. and Dt., Karn. St. **Dy.** Hoy., Vīra Ballāḷa II, Cy. yr. Raudri, 1200 A.D. ; **apūrbāya** (K. *n.*), ; **text :** .....*pūrbāya* ***apūrbāya*** *modalāda samastanu* ... . *saluvantāgi* .... *Gōpināthadēvarige koṭṭadakke pramāṇavāgi baresikoṭṭa śilāśāsana* ; **tr.** a stone edict written as proof for the grant of all incomes such as existing taxes and **taxes which may be levied in future** to the god Gōpināthadēva ; *E.C.* (R) IV, Ch. 306, p. 200, ll. 49–50, 53–54 ; Kilagere, Chamarajanagara Tq. and Dt., Karn. St. **Dy.** Hoy., Ballāḷa III, Ś. 1240 = 1318 A.D.

apūrvāyam (T. *n.*), ; **text :** .... *pūrvāyam* ***apūrvāyam*** *uḷḷaduvum uḷḷaduvum maṟṟum eppēṟpaṭṭa palavaṟiyum* .... *vāḻavanda perumāḷukkum villiyārkkum* .... *viṭṭōm* ... ; **tr.** we donated to the god Vāḻavandaperumāḷ and the goddess Villiyār, the existing taxes and the **taxes which may be levied in future** and all other revenue incomes ; *E.C.* X, Kol. 101, p. 15, ll. 7–10 ; Beḷḷūr, Kolar Tq. and Dt., Karn. St. **Dy.** Saṅgama, prince Kampaṇṇa Uḍaiyār, Ś. 1284 = 1362 A.D.

apūrvi (T. < Skt. *n.*), newly arrived (with special reference to vēdic brāhmṇas) ; **text :** .... *Tirukkarapurattu perumāṉaḍigaḷ amuduśeyyum-poḻudu tāme eḍupitta śālai maṇḍagatte vēdam valla* ***apūrvi****gaḷe niśadi nālvar brāhmaṇarkku nālu kaṟiyum* ... *āḻākkuneyyum* .... *nāḻitayirum aṭṭi* ... *muṭṭāme ipparíśu* .... *ūṭṭuvippōm* ...... ; **tr.** at the time when offerings are made to the lord of our village Tirukkarapuram ... in the feeding hall constructed by him without any break four **newly arrived vēdic brāhmaṇas** versed in the vēdas are to be supplied with four vegetables, one *āḻākku* (*q.v.*) of ghee and one *nāḻi* (liquid measure) of curd for each individual ; *S.I.I.* III, pts. iii and iv, No. 99, p. 232, l. 4 ; Tiruppāṟkkaḍal, Walajapet Tq., N. Arcot Dt., T. Nadu. St. **Dy.** Chōḷa, Parāntaka I, reg. yr. 12 = 907 A.D.

apūrvigaḷ (T. < Skt. *n.*), itenerant vēdic brahmaṇas; **text[1] :** (fragmentary) ... *mūṉṟu samvatsarattil* ***apūrvigaḷ****ukke paṇippadāguvum* ... ; **tr.** in the course of three years service should be provided only for the **intenerant vedic brāhmaṇas** ; *S.I.I.* VI, No. 322, p. 154, l. 5 ; Uttaramallūr, Maduran takam Tq., Chingleput Dt., T. Nadu St. **Dy.** Chōḷa, in characters of 10th cent. A.D. ; **text[2] :** . . . *Śivabaktarālayattu* ***apūrvigaḷ*** *vanduṉṉum mahāṉgaḷukku āhārārthamāgavum adukku vēṇḍum nibandaṅgaḷum* .... *Śivārthamāga* .... *koṇḍār Rājarājaṉ. Jayaṅgoṇḍaśōḻaṉ* .. ; **tr.** Rājarāja Jayaṅgoṇḍaśōḻan accepted as a gift in the name of the god Śiva for meeting expenses for feeding the great **itenarant vedic brāhmaṇas** ; *S.I.I.* VIII, No. 754, p. 385, l. 3 ; Panāyavaram, Viluppuram Tq., S. Arcot Dt., T. Nadu St. **Dy.** Chōḷa,

Adhirājēndra, reg. yr. 3 = 1072 A.D.

aputrakaporuḷ (Skt+K. *n.*), property belonging to one without male issue ; **text :** (obscure) . . . *Vinayāditya . . . . pṛithivīrājayaṁ keye . . .* ***aputraka poruḷ****umān viṭṭār* . . . ; **tr.** while Vinayāditya was ruling the empire, **property belonging to one without male issue** was donated ; *E.C.* VII, Skr. 154, p. 261, ll. 1, 3, 6 ; Shikāripura, Shikaripur Tq., Shimoga Dt., Karn. St. **Dy.** Chal. of Bād., Vinayāditya, in characters of 7th century A.D.

aputrika dhana (K. < Skt *n.*), wealth belonging to a father whose daughter had no male issues ; **text :** . . . *āru illadiddaḍe* ***aputrikadhana*** *kaṟa dēvālyakkikkuvudu* . . . ; **tr.** the **wealth belonging to the father whose daughter had no male issues** will be dedicated to the temple ; *E.C.* IX, Chp. 73, p. 325, ll. 35–36 ; Bēvūru, Channapatna Tq., Ramanagara Dt., Karn. St. **Dy.** Hoy., Ballāḷa, Ś. 1240 = 1318 A.D.

ārāchchi (T. *n.*), investigation ; **text :** . . . *Pirāntaka Mūvēndavēḷār* ***ārāchchi****yil Tiraimūr sabhyaiyōmum ūrōmum Tiruviḍaimarudil nagarattōmum . . . . malligai Nandavānattukku kāl-śeyyum Paṇmāhēśvarattoṇḍaṉ śeyda Malligai Nandavānattukku kālśeyyum nibandhamāga śeydu kuḍuttōm* ; **tr.** subsequent to the **investigation** of Pirāntaka Mūvēndavēḷār, the *sabhā* (*q.v.*) and the *ūrār* (*q.v.*) of Tiraimūr and the *nagarattār* of Tiruviḍaimarudu and the officials of the temple gave a quarter *śey* (*q.v.*) of the land each to two individuals for raising Jasmine gardens for the temple ; *S.I.I.* XIII, No. 270, p. 143, ll. 3–18 ; Tiruviḍaimarudūr, Kumbhakonam Tq., Tanjavur Dt., T. Nadu St. **Dy.** Chōḷa, Parāntaka II Sundara-chōḷa, reg. yr. 17 = 972 A.D. ; **ārāchchināyagam** (T. *n.*), Chief Investigator ; **text :** . . *Rāja rājadēvar sēnāpati Mummaḍiśōḻabrahmamārāyaṉ* ***ārāchchināyaga****ttu mūttavar* ; **tr.** Mummaḍi śōḻabrahmamārāya, the commander under Rājarājadēva and the senior **Chief Investigator**; *S.I.I.* V, No. 652, p. 275, l. 81 ; Tirumaḻavāḍi, Uḍaiyarpalaiyam Tq., Tiruchirappalli Dt, T. Nadu St. **Dy.** Chōḷa, Rājarāja I, reg. yr. 28 = 1014 A.D.

ārādhya (K. *n.*), priestly class ; worshipful priest; **text**[1] **:** . . . . *Baṁmidēvarasaru . . . . tamm****ārādhyar*** *Arasiyabīḍina Sōmayāji Hiriyaṇṇaṁgaḷa saṁnidhiyalu . . . . Bāḷguḷiya Svayaṁbhū-Kalidēvara aṁgabhōga raṁga bhōgakkaṁ . . . . biṭṭa dharma* . . . . . . ; **tr.** the grant made for the service to the image and entertainment of the deity Svayaṁbhū-Kalidēva of Bāḷguḷi by Baṁmidēvarasa in the august presence of his **worshipful priest** Hiriyaṁṇa Sōmayāji of Arasiyabīḍu ; *S.I.I.* IX, pt. i, No. 331, pp. 350–51, ll. 5–8, 11 ; Bāgaḷi, Harapanahalli Tq., Bellary Dt., Karn. St. **Dy.** Kottūr Chiefs, Baṁmidēvarasa, Cy. yr. Āṅgīrasa = 1212 A.D. ; **text**[2] **:** . . . . . *rāyarājaguru Sāmavēdī yajanādishaṭkarmma nirataraha* ***ārādhya****rugaḷa oppa* . . . ; **tr.** the signature of the royal preceptor belonging to

Sāmavēda and devoted performer of six duties including vedic ritual belonging to the **priestly class** ; *S.I.I.* VII, No. 357, p. 215, ll. 22–24 ; Maṇigārakēri, Udupi Tq. and Dt., Karn. St. **Dy.** Saṅgama, Dēvarāya, Ś. 1343 = 1421 A.D.

ārādhyulu (Te. *n.*), worshipful Śaivite priest ; **text :** .... *mā* ***ārādhyulu*** .... *Liṁgamanāyakuniki nitya prasāda* ...... ; **tr.** one plate of daily offering given to my **worshipful Śaivite priest** Liṁgamanāyaka ; *S.I.I.* VI, No. 1118, p. 450, ll. 23, 25–26 ; Siṁhāchalam, Vishakhapatnam Tq. and Dt, A.P. St. **Dy.** Chōḍa-Gaṁga, Anantavarma, Ś. 1203 = 1281 A.D.

ārādiṉai (T. < Skt. *ārādhane, n.*), worship ; **text :** .... *id dēvarkku vēṇḍum* ***ārādiṉai****gaḷ. eppēr-ppaṭṭaṉa aṉaichchukkum uttamāgramāga nāṉ kuḍutta ūr*..... ; **tr.** the village given by me as *uttamāgra* (*q.v.*) for providing all the articles needed for the **worship** of the god ; *S.I.I.* XIX, No. 357, p. 184, ll. 20–21 ; Gōvindaputtūr, Udaiyar-palayam Tq., Tiruchirapalli Dt., T. Nadu St. **Dy.** Chōḷa, Uttamachōḷa, reg. yr. 14 = 985 A.D.

aradiviya (Te. *n.*), half a perpetual lamp ; **text :** .... *Bhāvanārāyaṇadēvaraku .... akahaṁḍavartti dīpamunakuṁ beṭṭina birudumāḍalu paṁḍreṁḍu vīniṁ jēkōni .... Permmāḍi* ***aradiviya****yuṁ ... Nāgadēvaṇḍu* ***aradiviya****yunumgān iddaṟum gūḍi . ... imānēṁḍu nēyi vōyaṅgalavāru*...... ; **tr.** for lighting **half a perpetual lamp** for the god Bhāvanārāyaṇadēva twelve *birudumāḍa* (*q.v.*) were granted. With this amount Permmāḍi and Nāgadēva each gave two *māna* (*q.v.*) of ghee for **half a perpetual lamp** ; *S.I.I.* VI, No. 151, p. 76, ll. 8–12; Bāpaṭla, Bapatla Tq., Guntur Dt, A.P. St. **Dy.** Chōḷa, Rājarāja, Ś. 1076 = 1154 A.D.

aragaṇḍuga (K. *n.*), half *khaṁḍuga* (a grain measure) ; **text :** (damaged) .... *Niravadya jinālayake ... Ujjaniyoḷa ...* ***aragaṇḍuga****. ... ittar* ... ; **tr.** land of the extent of being sown with **half *khaṁduga*** (*q.v.*) of seeds was given to the Niravadya jinālaya ; *E.C.* (R) XI, No. 177, p. 108, ll. 6, 10, 13 ; Kaḍavanti, Chikmagalur Tq. and Dt, Karn. St. **Dy.** Sēnāvara, Khachara Kandarpa, in characters of 11th cent. A.D.

aragaṭṭa (K. < Skt. *araghaṭṭa, n.*), wheel to draw water ; **text :** .... *Chāgi .* ***aragaṭṭa****ṁ kaṭṭisidaṁdu Kaṁṇamaṁgalada Rāmēśvaradēvage īrmattar maṁṇa biṭṭaṁ* ... ; **tr.** on the day on which Chāgi had set up the **wheel for drawing water** he granted 2 mattar (*q.v.*) of land to god Rāmēśvara of Kaṁṇamaṁgala ; *E.C.* (R) XII, Trk. 73, p. 411, ll. 4–7 ; Bukkāṁbudhi, Tarikere Tq., Chikmagalur Dt, Karn. St. **Misc.**, Ś. 811 = 889 A.D. ;

arakaṭṭa (K. < Skt. *araghaṭṭa, n.*), wheel for drawing water ; **text :** .... *tataḥ prāg gatvā Nēṟelgeṟe* .... *tataḥ dakshiṇa diśam āvṛitya arakaṭṭaṁ*....... ; **tr.** thence moving eastward is the tank Nēṟelgeṟe, then moving south wards the land mark is the **wheel for drawing water**; *E.C.* XI, Dvg. 66, p. 145, ll. 33–34 ; Harihara, Harihara Tq., Davanagere Dt, Karn. St. **Dy.** Chal. of Bād., Vinayāditya, reg. yr. 14 = 694 A.D.

āṟai (M. *n.*), temple treasury ; **text :** ***āṟai****yāl padiṉāḻikkoḷḷum paṟaiyāl niyadam ōrō paṟai chcheydu* ; **tr.** by the **temple treasury** daily one *paṟai* (grain measure of ten *nāḻi* capacity) of paddy was collected ; *T.A.S. V*, No. 13, p. 40–46, Kollam, Kollam Tq. and Dt., Ker. St. **Dy.** Chēra; ; Kulaśēkhara-chakravartti, Ś. 1025 = 1103 A.D.

āraike (K. *n.*), look after ; **text :** . . . *yī dharmada* ***āraike*** *Chauḷikēṟiyalli mūvaru seṭṭikāraru samasta halaru pratipālisuvaru*. . . . ; **tr.** the three *seṭṭikāra* (*q.v.*) and *samasta halaru* (*q.v.*) will **look after** and maintain this grant ; *S.I.I.* VII, No. 387, p. 245, l. 73 ; Kōṭakēri, Udupi Tq. and Dt., Karn. St. **Dy.** Saṅgama, Bukkarāya, Ś. 1294 = 1372 A.D.

araikkāṇi (T. *n.*), half of a hereditary right ; **text:** *nilaṉ ēḻē iraṇḍu mā* ***araikkāṇi***. . . . ; **tr.** land to the extent of 7 and 2 *mā* (*q.v.*) which was held as **half of a hereditary right** ; *T.A.S.* IV, No. 223, p. 30, l. 20 ; Chidambaram, Chidambaram Tq., S. Arcot Dt., T. Nadu St. **Dy.** Chōḷa, Rājēndra, reg. year 24 = 1038.

araimaṉai (T. *n.*), palace ; **text :** . . . . *Śivasthānam Vishṇusthānaṅgaḷile pūrvvam mudalāga* ***araimaṉai****kku iṟuttuvarugira jōḍi poṉ padināyiramum anda anda dēvasthānaṅgaḷakku* . . . . . . *viṭṭa dharmaśāsana rāyasam* ; **tr.** the ten thousand *jōḍi poṉ* (*q.v.*) being paid to the palace from earlier times from the revenues collected from the Śaiva and Vaishṇava temples. were remitted back to those respective temples through this royal order ; *S.I.I.* VIII, No. 352, pp. 189–90, ll. 4–5 ; Śēndamaṅgalam, Tindivanam Tq., S. Arcot Dt., T. Nadu St. **Dy.** Tuḷuva, Kṛishṇadēvarāya, Ś. 1439 = 1518 A.D. ; **araimaṉai mahāpradhāni** (T. *n.*), the great minister of the palace ; **text :** . . . . *Kampaṇa Uḍaiyaru Muḷamayil paṭṭaṇattil rājiyampaṇṇiṉa kālattil avar* ***araimaṉai mahāapradhāni*** *Sōmappa Uḍaiyavar* ; **tr.** while Kaṁpaṇṇa Uḍaiyavar was ruling the kingdom from the town of Muḷamayil his **great minister of the palace** was Somappa Voḍeyavar ; *E.C.* X, Kol. 203, p. 41, ll. 12–15 ; Kōlār, Kolar Tq. and Dt., Karn. St. **Dy.** Saṅgama, prince Kaṁpaṇa, Ś. 1283 = 1361 A.D. ; **araimaṉaippaṇḍāram** (T. *n.*), palace treasury ; **text :** . . . . *sēvaparādha sthānattukku aparādha kāṇikkai varusham oṉṟukku nūṟṟu yirubadu poṉ* ***araimaṉaippaṇḍā****rattukku kuḍukka kaḍavārgaḷ āguvam* ; **tr.** for failing to fulfill the duties in the temple, a fine of 120 poṉ (*q.v.*) as punitive tax shall be paid into the **palace treasury** ; *S.I.I.* VIII, No. 157, p. 71, ll. 12–13 ; Tiruvaṇṇāmalai, Tiruvannamalai Tq., N. Arcot Dt., T. Nadu St. **Dy.** Saṅgama, Dēvarāya, in characters of 14th cent. A.D. ; **araimaṉai śōḍi** (T. *n.*), minimum tax payable to the palace ; **text :** (damaged) . . . . . *Śevvappanāyakar ayyanukku puṇṇiyamāga Achyutappa nāyakkar* . . . . . *udagam* *paṇṇina paḍiyāle yindappaḍikku* ***araimaṇai-śōḍi*** *adhikāri kaḍaikkūṭṭu śūḍipuṟavagai sarvamānya māga kaṭṭaḷai iṭṭapaḍi* . . . ; **tr.** as per the order proclaimed, levies such as the **minimum tax amount payable to the palace**, *adhikāri kaḍaikūṭṭu* (*q.v.*) and *śōḍipuṟavagai* (*q.v.*) were granted with the pouring of the water of libation as *sarvvamānya* (*q.v.*) by Achyutappanāyaka for the merit of his father Śevvappanāyaka ; *S.I.I.* XVII, No. 581, p. 248, ll. 6–8, 16–23 ; Tiruvārūr, Nagapattinam Tq., Thanjavur Dt., T. Nadu St. **Dy.** Chiefs of Niduṅguṉṟam, Achyutappa, Ś. 1482 = 1560 A.D.

araiśaru (T. *n.*), ruler ; **text :** *Vāṇa perumāṉ* ***araiśaru*** ; **tr.** the **ruler** Vāṇaperumāṉ ; *Ep. Ind.* XXXIX, p. 213, l. 2 ; Pāpāmbāḍi, Karur Tq., Dharmapuri Dt., T. Nadu St. **Dy.** Gaṅga, Vāṇaperumāṉ, in characters of 5th cent. A.D.

araiyaṉ (T. *n.*), ruler ; **text :** *Pāṇḍi amirtta maṅgalav**araiyaṉ** āyiṉa Śāttaṅgaṇapati tiruttuvittadu tirukkoyilum śrītaṭākamum* ; **tr.** the temple and the tank renovated by the **ruler** Paṇḍi Amirttamangalavaraiyaṉ *alias* Śattaṉ-Gaṇapati ; *S.I.I.* XIV, No. 3, p. 2, ll. 5–9 ; Tirupparaṅkuṉṟan, Madurai Tq. and Dt., T. Nadu St. **Dy.** Pāṇḍya, Māṟañjaḍaiyaṉ, reg. yr. 6 = 767 A.D.

aṟaiyōlai (T. *n.*), document registering religious grants ; **text**[1] **:** . . . . *kallum kaḷḷiyuṁ nāṭṭi* ***aṟaiyōlai*** *śeydu viḍudaga veṉṟu nāṭṭārkku tirumugam viḍa* . . . . *nāṭṭār viḍutta* ***aṟaiyōlai*** *paḍi nilattukkellai* . . . . ; **tr.** the donor having planted along the boundary stones milkhedges and having prepared the **document registering the religious grants** ordered the *nāṭṭār* (*q.v.*) who in obedience granted the village with its boundary in accordance with the document ; *S.I.I.* II, No. 98, p. 516, (Tamil portion) ; Vēlūrpāḷayam, Arakonam Tq., N. Arcot Dt., T. Nadu St. **Dy.** Pallava, Vijayanandi- varman III, reg. yr. 8 = 845 A.D. ; **text**[2] **:** (damaged) . . . . . *ippariśu* ***aṟaiyōlai*** *śeidu kuḍuttōm Allūr ūrōm*; **tr.** this **document registering regiligious grants** was was given by the inhabitants of the village Allūr ; *S.I.I.* VIII, No. 686, p. 345, ll. 11–12; Allūr, Tiruchirapalli Tq. and Dt., T. Nadu St. **Dy.** Chōḷa, Parāntaka I, reg. yr. 41 = 948 A.D. ; **text**[3] **:** . . . *ippaḍipaṭṭa viyavasthayōḍu* . . . . *kuḍinīkkā dēvadāna iṟaiyilayāga* ***aṟaiyōḷai*** *eḻudi* . . . (text incomplete); **tr.** having **written the document confirming the tax free** ***dēvadāna*** (*q.v.*) stipulating the condition that the tenants should not be evicted ; *S.I.I.* XIX, No. 344, p. 176 (sec. iii), l. 4 ; Tiruviḍai-marudūr, Kumbhakonam Tq., Tanjavur Dt., T. Nadu St. **Misc.**, in characters of the 11th cent. A.D.

aṟaivān (T. *n.*), public proclaimer ; **text :** . . . *tiruviḻāv**aṟaivān**ukkuppuḍavai oṉṟukkukkāśu nālukku nel yirutūṇi irunāḻi* ; **tr.** two *tūṇi* (*q.v.*) and two *nāḻi* (*q.v.*) of paddy worth four *kāśu* (*q.v.*) for providing one clothing for the **public proclaimer** on the festival day ; *E.C.* X, Kol. 112 a, p. 26, l. 12; Kōlār, Kolar Tq. and Dt., Karn. St. **Dy.** Chōḷa, Kulōttuṅga I, reg. yr. 3 = 1073 A.D.

arakāṇike (K. *n.*), tribute to be paid to the king; **text :** . . . . . *bhaṇḍiya battada suṁka uppara nelavaḷi anupu āḷu* ***arakāṇike*** *kaḍḍāyavu*. . . . . ; **tr.** payment of tax on paddy brought in carts, produce from elevated lands, entry tax and tax on labour as well as **payment of tribute to the king** are compulsory ; *S.I.I.* IX, pt. ii, No. 438, p. 446, ll. 15–17 ; Kadiri, Kadiri Tq., Anantapur Dt., A.P. St. **Dy.** Saṅgama, Dēvarāya, Cy. yr. Hēviḷaṁbi = 1418 A.D.

āṟa kuṁṭe (K. *n.*), dried up tank ; **text :** (damaged) . . . . ***āṟa kuṁṭe*** *mēre*. . . . .; **tr. dried up tank** is the boundary ; *S.I.I.* IX, pt. i, No. 119, p. 101, ll. 57–58 ; Kottapalle, Nandikotkur Tq., Kurnool Dt., A.P. St. **Dy.** Chāḷ. of Kal., Sōmēśvara, Ś. 980 = 1057 A.D.

arakku (T. *n.*), lac ; **text :** ***arakku*** *niṟai eṉkaḻañjē ēḻmañjāḍiyum* . . . ; **tr. lac** weighing eight *kaḻañju* (gold coin.) and seven *mañjāḍi* (coin) ; *S.I.I.* II, No. 3, p. 22, ll. 4–6 ; Tañjāvūr, Tanjavur Tq. and Dt., T. Nadu St. **Dy.** Chōḻa, Rājarāja I, reg. yr. 29 = 1014 A.D.

aṟakkuḷam (T. *n.*), charity tank ; **text :** *teṉṉellai Chēndasvāmikramavitta Sōmāśiyār kalluvichcha* ***aṟakkuḷa****ttukkaraikku vaḍakkum*. . . . ; **tr.** the southern boundary was to the north of the bank of the **charity tank** built of stone by Chēnda svāmikramavitta Sōmaśiyār ; *S.I.I.* XIV, No. 19, p. 19, ll. 16–21 ; Tirukkuṟuṅguḍi, Nanguneri Tq., Tirunelveli Dt., T. Nadu St. **Dy.** Pāṇḍya, Māṟañjaḍaiyaṉ, reg. yr. 4 = 772 A.D.

aṟam (T. *n.*), religious act, righteousness ; **text**[1] **:** . . . . *Iḷaṅkāyipaṉ ēva Agaḻūr* ***aṟam*** . . . . ; **tr.** the **religious act** made at the instance of Iḷaṅkāyipaṉ at Agaḻūr . . . . , *E.T.E.* No. xxxiii, p. 427, l. 1, Toṇḍūr, Senji Tq., Villuppuram Dt., T. Nadu St. **Misc.**, in characters of C. 3rd cent. A.D. ; **text**[2] **:** . . . ***aṟam*** *vaḷara kali meliya* . . . ; **tr. righteousness** may grow and the evil may decline ; *S.I.I.* VII, No. 129, p. 54, l. 5, Cheṅgam, Tirukkoyilur Tq., S. Arcot Dt., T. Nadu St. Agricultural guild, in characters of 11th cent. A.D. ; **text**[3] **:** . . . . *inda daṉmam yādāmoruvaṉ paripālanam paṇṇiṉavargaḷ* ***aṟam*** *śeiydāṉ* ***aṟam*** *kāttāṉ* ; **tr.** whoever protects this grant would have in effect done a **righteous** act, would have protected a **righteous** act ; *S.I.I.* VIII, No. 441, p. 231, l. 14 ; Pirāṉmalai, Tiruppattur Tq., Ramnathapuram Dt., T. Nadu St. **Misc.**, Ś. 1500 = 1578 A.D.

ārāma (K. < Skt. *n.*), garden ; **text :** . . . . ***ārāma*** *kūpa oḷagāda ashṭabhōga tējasvāmya ēnuḷḷadanu Baṁgaru Hariyaṁṇaṁgaḷige* . . . . *dhāreyaneradu koṭṭaru* . . . . . ; **tr.** the Baṁga chieftain gave to Hariyaṁṇa with the libation of water all the eight traditional privileges connected with land including the **garden**, well and their ownership ; *S.I.I.* VII, No. 261, p. 133, ll. 19–21, Pāvaṁje, Suratkal Tq., D. K. Dt., Karn. St. **Dy.** Saṅgama, Dēvarāya, Ś 1340 = 1418 A.D. ; **ārāmakshētra** (K. < Skt. *n.*), garden land ; **text:** . . . . *40 vṛittiyaṁnu 33 maṁdi* *brāhmarugaḷige . . . Chāmarājasamudravemba . . . . . agrahāravanu ī grāmakke uṁṭāda . . . ashṭabhōgatējasvāmyagaḷu gṛi**hārāmakshētra** . . . ēnuṁṭāda sakalāya svāmyavanū sukhadiṁda anubhavisikoṁḍu . . . . . . śēruviri eṁdu koṭṭa tāmra śāsana* . . . . ; **tr.** the brāhmaṇa settlement Chāmarājasamudra was divided into 40 shares, was recorded on a copper plate and was given to 33 brāhmaṇas with the traditional eight privileges and ownership rights which included houses, **garden land** etc. ; *E.C.* (R) V, T. N. 15, p. 344, ll. 156, 159–160, 169, 177 ; T. Narasīpura, T. Narasipur Tq., Mysore Dt., Karn. St. **Dy.** Āravīḍu, Aḷiya Rāmarāya, Ś. 1544 = 1622 A.D.

aramāna (K. *n.*), half of a liquid/solid measure ; **text :** . . . . . . *Kaṇṇaṁ Siṁdavāḍi sāyiramuman āḷuttu . . . . koṭṭa sthiti āvudeṁdoḍe . . . . Sivenāya kaṁge **aramāna** tuppa kūḻge ōrbaḷḷa aramānaṁ koṭṭa sthiti* . . . . ; **tr.** when Kaṇṇa was administering Siṁdavāḍi 1000 he gave a grant to Sivenāyaka as follows: for one baḷḷa and **half a measure** of cooked rice **half a measure** of ghee was given; *S.I.I.* IX, pt. i, No. 55, p. 31, ll. 8–12, Maṁchāḷa, Adavani Tq., Kurnool Dt., A.P. St. **Dy.** Rāshṭr., Kṛishṇa III, Ś. 815 = 893 A.D. ; **aravāna** (K. s.a. *aramāna*), ; **text :** *Kalināthadēvarige . . . koṭṭa mānya . . . ōrbaḷa akki mosarōgara . . . **aravāna** tuppa* . . . . ; **tr.** to the god Kalināthadēva was given as *mānya* one baḷḷa of rice, a curd rice, **half measure** of ghee, etc. ; *S.I.I.* IX, pt. i, No. 376, pp. 392–93, ll. 6–7, 9–11, Neraniki, Ālūr Tq., Bellary Dt., Karn. St. **Dy.** Sēü. of Dēv., Rāmachandra, Ś 1198 = 1276 A.D.

aramane (K. *n.*), palace ; **text**[1] **:** (damaged) . . . . . *Bhāraṇāsiyalu . . . . pārvaru keṟeyu polamu **aramane**yanaḻida. pañchamahāpātakanakku* . . . . ; **tr.** (he who flouts the provisions of this grant) would have committed in effect the five great sins of having destroyed brāhmaṇas, tank, cultivable field and the **palace** in Vāraṇāsi ; *S.I.I.* IX, pt. i, No. 18, p. 8, ll. 37–41, Kambadūru, Kalyandurga Tq., Anantapur Dt., A.P. St. **Dy.** Noḷ. Pal., Mahēndra, Ś. 805 = 883 A.D. ; **text**[2] **:** . . . . . *Kaviyāḷpēndradēvaru Bārakānyāpurad-**aramane**yali sukasankathā vinōdadiṁ rājyaṁ geyyuttire*. . . . . ; **tr.** when Kaviyāḷpēndradēva was ruling with happiness and peace, his kingdom from the **palace** in the city of Bārakanyāpur; *S.I.I.* VII, No. 376, p. 231, ll. 3–5, Kōṭakēri, Udupi Tq. and Dt., Karn. St. **Dy.** Āḷupa, Kaviyāḷpēndra, Ś. 1077 = 1155 A.D. ; **text**[3] **:** . . . . *Nārāyaṇa dēvagaḷige koṭṭa bhūdāna dharmaśāsanada kramaveṁteṁdare . . . . **aramane**ge teṟuva siddhāyada hoṁninoḷage . . . . doḍavaraha nālvattanālku varahaṁnu . . . anubhavisi bahiri* . . . . . ; **tr.** as per the details recorded about the land grant in the inscription, the donee Nārāyaṇadēva is to enjoy the permanent levy of forty four doḍḍa *varaha* (*q.v.*) payable to the **palace** ; *S.I.I.* VII, No. 364, p. 220, ll. 9–10, 14–17, Maṇigārakēri,

Udupi Tq. and Dt., Karn. St. **Dy.** Sāḷuva, Narasiṁha, Ś. 1421 = 1499 A.D. ; **aramanege naḍeva ga** (K. *n.*), tax in the form of gadyāṇa to be paid to palace : . . . . *mūṟu grāmadali baradu naṭṭa śāsanadallidda* ***aramanege naḍeva ga*** *36* . . . ; **tr.** 36 *ga* (*q.v.*) paid as **tax in the form of gadyāṇa to be paid to the palace** as per the stone inscription set up in the three villages ; *S.I.I.* VII, No. 349, p. 192, ll. 10–11, Chauḷikēri, Udupi Tq. and Dt., Karn. St. **Dy.** Saṅgama, Dēvarāya, Ś. 1338 = 1416 A.D. ; **aramaneya aṁkagaḷu** (K. *n.*), professional wrestlers attached to a palace ; **text** : . . . *mahāsāmanta Chāmuṇḍarasar Poḷalgundeyumam* . . . ***aramaneyaṁkaṁgaḷa*** *jīvitadoḷu daśavandhamumam* . . . . *āḷuttamire*. . . . ; **tr.** when the great subordinate was administering the village Poḷalgunde and was incharge of 1/10th of the livelihood expenses of the professional **wrestlers attached to a palace**; *S.I.I.* IX, pt. i, No. 163, p. 152, ll. 18–19, Halagondi, Hadagalli Tq., Bellary Dt., Karn. St. **Dy.** Chāḷ. of Kal., Vikramāditya VI, Ch.Vi. yr. 17 = 1093 A.D.

aramaneya āya (K. *n.*), palace revenue ; **text :** (damaged) . . . . ***aramaneya āya*** . . . ; **tr. palace revenue** ; *S.I.I.* IX, pt. ii, No. 681, p. 674, l. 11, Chyabala, Gooty Tq., Ananthapur Dt., A.P. St. **Dy.** Tuḷuva, Sadāśiva, in characters of 16th cent. A.D.

aramaneya suṁka (K. *n.*), tax to be paid to palace ; **text :** . . . . *Tirumaḍavaḷanū* . . . . *Bemmaseṭṭiyanū Dharmmapaṭṭaṇada nakharadaluḷavaru koṁdadake paḍuva kēriya halaru seṭṭikāṟaru ā eraḍu kuṭuṁbadavaru nakharadavara kayyalū māḍisida prāyaśchitta Basaṟūralū* ***aramaneya-suṁka*** *kāṭi-ga 10 honnu* ; **tr.** Tirumahaḍavaḷa and Bemmaseṭṭi having committed a crime of murder, the halaru *seṭṭikāraru* (*q.v.*) of Paḍuvakēri gave judgement that the two families of the murderers should, as expiation, pay to the *nakhara* (*q.v.*) of Dharmmapaṭṭaṇa 10 quality gold coins as **tax to the palace** at Basaṟūru ; *S.I.I.* IX, pt. ii, No. 450, p. 459, l. 12–17, Basarūru, Kundapur Tq., Udupi Dt., Karn. St. **Dy.** Saṅgama, Dēvarāya, Ś. 1366 = 1444 A.D.

aramaneyavaru (K. *n.*), members of the royal house hold ; **text** : . . . *Kavatāḷada sīmeya samastagauḍuprajegaḷige koṭa silāsasana* . . . . *niṁma Kavatāḷada sīmeyalu* ***aramaneyavaru*** *avanāyava māḍalāgi avanāyake aṁji nīvu samasta prajegaḷū sīmeyanu biṭṭu* . . . . *hōgi iralāgi* . . . . ; **tr.** the details of the edict given to all the *gauḍa* inhabitants of the Kavatāḷa territory . . . . in your Kavatāḷa territory the **members of the royal household** having harassed you, all of you had, out of fear, fled from the region ; *S.I.I.* IX, pt. ii, No. 554, p. 574, ll. 9–15, Kavutāḷam, Adavani Tq, Kurnool Dt., Karn. St. **Dy.** Tuḷuva, Achyutarāya, Ś. 1454 = 1533 A.D.

araman̤ (K. *n.*), excellent soil ; **text** : . . . *Chōrayyanu Eraḍumura gāmuṇḍugaḷu pannasigaru Ayyappadēvanalli kerege bittuvāṭava paḍeda* *aramaṇ* . . . . ; **tr.** a land of **excellent soil** obtained from Ayyappadēva for the purpose of the maintenance of the tank by Chōrayya and the *gāmuṇḍu* (*q.v.*) and donees of Eraḍumura ; *S.I.I.* IX, pt. i, No. 21, p. 10, ll. 5–8 ; Manepalle, Hindupur Tq., Anantapur Dt., A.P. St. **Dy.** Noḷ. Pal., Ayyapadēva, in characters of about 9th cent. A.D.

āraṁbhamu (Te. *n.*), cultivation ; **text :** . . . *Birudarāju Lakkayyadēvamahārājulu Allāḷadēva mahārāju* . . . . *māviḍlu chiṁtalu nārikēḷālu yīṁdulu sahitamaina phalavṛikshālu taḍlu yēṁni peṭṭinānu aṁdula phalamuṁnnu ā nēlanu peṭina atuvaṁṭi* ***āraṁbhamu****ṁnnu* . . . *sahitaṁgānu Bhairava dēvaraku vṛitti yistimi*. . . . . . ; **tr.** Birudarāju, Lakkayyadēva mahārāju and Allāḷadēvamahārāju gave as *vṛitti* (*q.v.*) to the god Bhairavadēva, the land which contained fruit yielding trees such as Mango, Tamarind, Coconut etc., along with all the rights of **cultivation** and enjoyment of the fruits from the trees ; *S.I.I.* XVI, No. 16, p. 17, ll. 17–21 ; Palagūrāḷḷapalle, Badvel Tq., Cuddapah Dt., A.P. St. **Dy.** Saṅgama, Dēvarāya, Ś. 1318 = 1396 A.D.

ārame (K. < Skt. *n.*), garden ; **text**[1] **:** (fragmentary) . . . . . *keṟe* ***ārame*** *sahita*. . . . .; **tr.** along with the tank and the **garden** ; *S.I.I.* XI, pt. i, No. 15, p. 11, l. 4, Chiñchli, Gadag Tq. and Dt., Karn. St. **Dy.** Rāshṭr., Amōghavarsha I, Ś. 793 = 871 A.D. ; **text**[2] **:** (damaged) . . . . *keṟeyiṁ bāviyiṁ śatradiṁ pūgoḷaniṁ tōṁṭaṅgaḷid****ārame****yineseva dēvālya* . . ; **tr.** the temple was resplendant with a tank, a well, a choultry, flower pond, a grove and a **garden** ; *S.I.I.* IX, pt. i, No. 163, p. 152, l. 4 ; Halagondi, Hadagalli Tq., Bellary Dt., Karn. St. **Dy.** Chāḷ. of Kal., Vikramāditya VI, Ch. Vi. yr. 17 = 1093 A.D.

araṇamu (Te. *n.*), wedding gift ; **text :** (damaged) . . . . . . *Vijayādityadēvachakravartti tama kūṁtuṟu Mailāradēvini asaṁṭṭi Sūraparājunakichchi* . . . *Pōṅkatōṁṭa ēnūru* . . . ***araṇa****michchenu* . . . . . . ; **tr.** I, the emperor Vijayādityadēva gave my daughter Mailāradēvi in marriage to Asaṁṭṭi Sūraparāja and gave as **wedding gift** a grove consisting of 500 arecanut trees ; *S.I.I.* X, No. 349, p. 182, ll. 7–9 ; Achanta, Narasapuram Tq., W. Godavari Dt., A.P. St. **Dy.** E. Chāḷ., Vishṇuvardhana Vijayāditya, Ś. 1177 = 1255 A.D.

ārāñji (T. *vb.*), to supervise ; **text :** . . *nandā viḷakku erippadāgavum mañjāḍikku padiṉpalam pōgiyanūl iḷai iṭṭu erippadāga innilam kuḍuttēṉ Nakkaṅkaṇḍaṉēṉ idi* ***ārāñji*** *erippippar Viśayāṅkunaracharuppēdimaṁgalattu sabhaiyār*. . . . . ; **tr.** Nakkaṉ Kaṇḍaṉ gave for the burning of one perpetual lamp ten *palam* (*q.v.*) of thread for one *mañjāḍi* (*q.v.*) for preparaing wicks for the lamp and the *Sabhaiyār* (*q.v.*) of Viśayāṁkunara-charuppēdimaṅgalam will **supervise** the burning of the lamp ; *S.I.I.* VIII, No. 566, p. 290, ll. 4–6; Tiruppālatturai, Tiruchirapalli Tq. and Dt. T. Nadu

St. **Dy.** Chōḷa, Parāntaka I, reg. yr. 28 = 935 A.D.

araṁṇya (K. < Skt. *araṇya, n.*), ; forest ; **text :** .... *Arasiyakereyiṁda mūḍalu* .... ***araṁṇya**vāgi ida bhūmiyanū* .... *mahājanaṁgaḷu kaṁḍu yī bhūmiya voḷage nāvu sāvira saṁkhyeya hoṁnanu* . .... *kereya kaṭṭisi Hariyasamudraveṁba nāmadalu* ... *puravanu māḍireṁdu nimage hēḷida nāvu ā grāmavanu māḍuvadakke koḍisidavaru* .... ; **tr.** the *mahājana* (*q.v.*) saw the **forest** land to the east of Arasiyakere and after excavating a tank by spending 1000 *hoṁnu* (*q.v.*) renamed that township as Hariyasamudrapura and we gave that township to the persons who had done the work ; *S.I.I.* IX, pt. ii, No. 440, p. 448, ll. 13–15, Rājabavanahaḻḻi, Harapanahalli Tq., Bellary Dt., Karn. St. **Dy.** Saṅgama, Dēvarāya, Ś. 1341 = 1419 A.D.

aṟappuṟam (T. *n.*), land earmarked for the maintenance of charities ; **text :** .... *mukkoḍeyavar ttam **aṟappuṟam**āna tiṟappaḍanīki* ... ; **tr.** having excluded the **land earmarked for the maintenance of** Jaina **charities** ; *S.I.I.* VII, No. 863, p. 435, l. 5, Kīḻūr, Tirukkoyilur Tq., S. Arcot Dt., T. Nadu St. **Dy.** Chōḷa, Rājarāja I, in characters of 10th cent. A.D.

arasa (K. *n.*), king ; suffix to proper names ; **text**[1] **:** .... *Mahāvalikulōdbhava śrī Mahāvali Vāṇ**arasar** Vijayādityan* ... *Vaḍugavaḻi pannichāsiramuṁ Maṇṇeyuṁ mūḍāyum pruthuvi rājyaṁgeye* .... ; **tr.** while the Bāṇa **king** Mahāvali Vijayāditya was ruling over Vaḍugavaḻi 12000 and eastern Maṇṇe ; *S.I.I.* IX, pt. i, No. 5, p. 3, ll. 3–6, Puṅganūr, Chittoor Tq. and Dt., A.P. St. **Dy.** Bāṇa, Vijayāditya II, in characters of 9th cent. A.D. ; **text**[2] **:** .... *maṇḍaḷika Bij**jarasa**na Perggaḍe Kāḷidāsayya baredaṁ* .... ; **tr.** Kāḷidāsayya, the Officer under Bij**jarasa**, wrote (the text of the inscription) ; *S.I.I.* IX, pt. i, No. 89, p. 60, ll. 29–30, Bāgaḷi, Harapanahalli Tq., Bellary Dt., Karn. St. Chāḷ. of Kal., Jayasiṁha II, Ś. 957 = 1035 A.D. ; **text**[3] **:** .... *Penugoṁḍeya* .... *App**arasa**navara Basav**arasa**ra maga Tiṁmayanu Sēnabōva Tiṁm**arasa**ra maga Lakkayanu* .... ; **tr.** Tiṁmaya son of Basav**arasa** who was a subordinate of App**arasa** of Penugoṁḍe and Lakkaya the son of the village accountant Timm**arasa** ; *S.I.I.* VIII, No. 362, p. 193, ll. 2–3, Gooty, Gooty Tq., Anantapur Dt., A.P. St. **Misc.**, Ś. 1429 = 1507 A.D.

arasādhikāri (K. *n.*), officer working under the king ; **text :** ***arasādhikāri**gaḷu suṅkavaṁ maṁnisuvaru*.... ; **tr.** the **officer working under the king** will order exemption from tax ; *K.I.* I, No. 30, p. 70., l. 49, Munavaḻḻi, Saundatti. Tq., Belgaum Dt., Karn. St. **Dy.** Sēü. of Dēv. ; Siṅghaṇa-dēva, Ś. 1144 = 1222 A.D.

araśar (T. *n.*), king ; **text :** ...... *Hoysaḷa bhujabala śrī Vīra Rāmanāthadēvar**araśar**ukku yāṇḍu 3ṟāvadu* .... ; **tr.** in the 3rd regnal year of the **king** Vīra Rāmanāthadēva, who belongs to the Hoysaḷa dynasty was known for the power of his shoulders ; *E.C.* X, Kol. 27, p. 3, ll. 11–13, Kolar, Kolar Tq. and Dt., Karn. St. **Dy.** Hoy., Vīra Rāmanātha, reg. yr. 3 = 1285 A.D.

arasaṁka Bhīmaṁ (K. *n.*), a royal wrestler veritable Bhīma to the enemies ; **text** *: parabaḷa sūṟekāṟaṁ* .... ***arasaṁka Bhīmaṁ*** ; **tr.** royal wrestler who is a looter of the enemy forces and who is **a veritable Bhīma to the enemies** ; *S.I.I.* XX, No. 18, p. 16, ll. 8–9, Saundatti, Saundatti Tq., Belgaum Dist., Karn St. **Dy.** Chāḷ. of Kal., Taila II, Ś. 902 = 980 A.D. ; **arasaṁka karagasa ;** a royal wrestler who is a veritable saw to the enemy ; **text :** . . . ***arasaṁka karagasaṁ*** . . *Bīradēvarasaru*; **tr.** Bīradēvarasa **a royal wrestler who was a veritable saw to the enemies** ; *M.A.R.* 1929, 72, l. 4 ; 1253 A.D. ; **arasaṁka gāḷa,** royal wrestler who is a veritable goad to the enemies ; **text :** ***arasaṁkagāḷan*** ..... *parabaḷake Gajēṁdravairi* ; **tr. a royal wrestler who is a veritable goad to the** army of the **enemies** and who was the very Vishṇu to the elephant corpus of the enemy forces ; *E.C.* XI, Dvg 43, p. 127, ll. 88–89, ; Dāvaṇagere, Davanagere Tq. and Dt., Karn. St. **Dy.** Kal. of Kal., Bhujabaḷamalla, reg. yr. 8 = 1172 A.D. ; **arasaṁka monegāṟa,** one who grapples with other wrestlers ; **text:** ; *śrīman mahāmaṁḍaḷēśvara* ....*pesāḷi Hanuma* ***arasaṁka monegāṟa*** ; **tr.** *mahāmaṁḍaḷēśvara* (*q.v.*) pesāḷi Hanuma **who grapples with other wrestlers** and defeats them in duels ; *M.A.R.* 1946, 25, l. 2 ; 1495 A.D. ; **arasaṁka rakkasa,** a veritable demon of a wrestler ; **Text** *:* ***arasaṁka rakkasan*** *anēka nāmāvaḷī mukhyanappa Duddarasaṁ* ; **tr.** Duddarasa who has a number of titles and who is **a veritable demon of a wrestlers** to the enemies ; *E.C.* (R) I, No. 62, p. 41, ll. 19–21 ; Yeḍūr, Somawarpet Tq., Coorg Dt., Karn. St. **Dy.** Kadamba of Manjarabād, Duddarasa, Ś. 1017 = 1095 A .D. ; **arasaṁka sūnegāṟa,** a royal wrestler who is a veritable butcher to the enemies ; **text** : ***arasaṁka sūnegāṟa*** *gajabēṭegāṟa śrīman mahāvīra Naṁjarāja Voḍeyara kumāraru śrīman mahāvīra immaḍi Chikarāya Voḍeyaru* ; **tr.** the great warrior Chikarāya Woḍeya II was the son of the great warrior Naṁjarāja Voḍeyar, **a royal wrestler who was a veritable butcher** to the enemies ; *S.I.I.* IX, pt. ii, No. 701, p. 689, ll. 3–4 ; Kuntūr, Kollegal Tq., Chamarajanagar Dt., Karn. St. **Dy.** Umm. Chfs., Chikarāya II, Ś 1434 = 1512 A.D. ; ***arasaṁka sūregāṟa,*** *a royal wrestler plundering enemies ;* **text** *:* ***arasaṁka sūregāṟa*** *sakala dharma pratipāḷakaṁ . . . Ummattūru śrī Naṁjarāja Voḍeyaru* ; **tr.** the illustrious Naṁjarāja Voḍeya of Uṁmattūru who was the protector of all religions and was **a royal wrestler plundering enemies** ; *E.C.* (R) III, Gu. 115, p. 87, ll. 10–13 ; Terakaṇāṁbi, Gundlupete Tq., Mysore Dt., Karn. St. **Dy.** Umm. Chfs., Naṁjarāja Voḍeya, Ś. 1426 = 1504 A.D.

arasara kāṇike (K. *n.*), tribute payable to the

king ; **text :** .... *ī dharmmadoḷ* ***arasara kāṇike*** ..... *kiṟusunkaṁ* ..... *koṁḍavaṁ chāṁḍāḷaṁ* ; **tr.** he who misappropriates (among other things) the **tribute payable to the king** and the minor taxes will be declared an outcaste ; *K.I.* II, No. 12, p. 44, ll. 58–60 ; Akkalkōṭ, Solapur Tq. and Dt., Maha. St. **Dy.** Chāḷ. of Kal., Vikramāditya VI, Ch. Vi. yr. 39 = 1114 A.D.

arasi (K. *n.*), queen, a suffix to female proper names ; **text[1] :** .... *akhiḷabhuvanataḷaratna bhūteyarappa Jāyabb**arasi**yarggaṁ puṭṭidaṁ śrī Mahēndrādhirājaṁ* .... *Ayyappadēvaṁgaṁgara magaḷ Pollabb**arasi**gaṁ puṭṭidōn Aṇṇigan* ... ; **tr.** Mahēndrādhirāja was born to Jāyabb**arasi** who was like a diamond ornament to entire world .. ... Aṇṇigan was born to Ayyappadēva and Pollabb**arasi** the daughter of the Gaṅga rulers ; *S.I.I.* IX, pt. i, No. 23, p. 12, ll. 18–23, 27–31, Dharmapuri, Dharmapuri Tq., Salem Dt., T. Nadu. St. **Dy.** Noḷ. Pal., Iruḷachōra, Ś. 851 = 929 A. D. ; **text[2] :** .... *ūroḍeyapramukhamahājanavinnūrvaru* ... *Padmaladēviyargge binnapaṁ geyyal ā biṁnapakk**arasi**yaru kāruṇyaṁ geydu* .. *Nārasiṁghadēvargge* ..... *bhūmiyaṁ* ... *biṭṭar* ... ; **tr.** at the request of the 200 *mahājana* (*q.v.*) lead by the village head made to Padmaladēvi, the **queen** condescended and granted land to the god Nārasiṁghadēva ; *S.I.I.* IX, pt. i, No. 195, p. 190, ll. 22–25, Raṁgapura, Hadagalli Tq., Bellary Dt., Karn. St. **Dy.** Chāḷ. of Kal., Vikramāditya VI, Ch. Vi. yr. 41 = 1116 A.D.

araśikāṇam (T. *n.*), tribute to be paid to the queen ; **text :** .... *poṉvari* .... ***araśikāṇam*** . .... *maṟṟum ippaṟṟil palavarigaḷum* ... *Chōḷēndrasiṁha Uḍaiyanāyanāṟkku* .. *kuḍuttōm* ; **tr.** we gave to the god Chōḷēndrasiṁha Uḍaiya nāyaṉār many tax incomes including tax collected in gold, **tribute to be paid to the queen**, etc. ; *S.I.I.* IV, No. 318, p. 88, ll. 11–14, 16–17 ; Mēlpāḍi, Chittoor Tq. and Dt., AP. St. **Dy.** Saṅgama, Prince Kaṁpaṇa, Cy. yr. Plava, in characters of 14th cent. A.D.

arasiya perggaḍe (K. *n.*), officer of the queen's establishment ; **text :** .... *maṭakam dēgulakaṁ samane paṁnneraḍu maneya nivēśana* ... *māḍisidaṁ arasiya perggaḍe Kannayyan* ; **tr.** to the religious institution and the temple equally were given twelve house sites by Kannayya, **an officer of the queen's establishment** ; *Ep. Ind.* IV, No. 50, p. 353, ll. 24–26 ; Hebbāḷ, Dharwar Tq. and Dt., Karn. St. **Dy.** Rāshṭr., Kṛishṇa, Ś. 896 = 975 A.D.

arasollage (K. *n.*), half of a liquid measure ; **text:** .... *Billēśvaradēvarge* ... *naṁdādīvige naḍevaṁtāgi gāṇadali **arasollage**ya* ...... *yeṁṇeyam biṭṭaru* ; **tr. oil measuring half of a liquid measure** was granted from the oil mill for burning a perpetual lamp for the god Billēśvara ; *S.I.I.* XV, No. 210, p. 253, ll. 12, 16–17, Mēvuṇḍi, Mundargi Tq., Dharwar Dt., Karn. St. **Dy.** Hoy., Ballāḷa II, reg. yr. 5 = 1196 A.D.

arasu (K. *n.*), king ; **text :** .... *iṁtī dharmamaṁ sāsirvvaruṁ* ***arasuṁ*** *pratipālisuvaru* ; **tr.** thus this donation shall be protected by the Thousland (an administrative body) and the **king** ; *K.I.* V, No. 17, p. 61, ll. 22–23, Tiḷivaḷḷi, Hangal Tq., Dharwar Dt., Karn. St. **Dy.** Chāḷ. of Kal., Vikramāditya VI , Ch. Vi. yr. 42 = 1118 A.D. ; **arasugaḷ** (K. *n.*), rulers ; **text :** .... *yī śāsana maryādeya tappalīyade taṁtaṁma putra-pautrādigaḷuṁ* ***arasugaḷum*** *pratipālisuvaṁtāgi* ..... *śāsanamaṁ māḍi* .... *nilisidaru* ... ; **tr.** the inscribed slab was set up stipulating that the provisions of this grant should be continuously protected by their sons and grandsons etc. and by successive **rulers** ; *S.I.I.* VII, No. 723, p. 365, ll. 48–52, Sēḍam, Chitapur Tq., Gulbarga Dt., Karn. St. **Dy.** Chāḷ. of Kal., Vikramāditya VI, Ch. Vi. yr. 48 = 1123 A.D.

arasugaḷu (K. *n.*), rulers ; **text :** .... *Virūpāksha dēvarige bhōganaivēdyakke māḍidanthā puṁṇyagaḷige Hāsanada sīmeya* ***arasugaḷu*** *prabhugaḷa sēnabōvaru gauḍaprajegaḷu adhikāri-gaḷu yivaroḷagāgi āvanānobbanu tappi anyāyava māḍidare .. naraka yātaneyanu anubhavisuvaru* ; **tr.** whoever among the rulers, nobles, village accountants, village heads and officers flout the pious grant made to the god Virūpākshadēva for His enjoyment and food offerings would suffer hellish misery ; *E.C.* (R) VIII, Hn. 2, p. 215, ll. 31–34, 38 ; Hāsana, Hassan Tq. and Dt., Karn. St. **Dy.** Tuḷuva, Sadāśivarāya, Cy. yr. Plava = 1563 A.D. ; **arasumakkaḷ** (T. *n.*), community of royal dependants ; **text :** .... ***arasumakkaḷum*** *maṟamudaligaḷum piramāṇam paṇṇikuḍutta pariśu* ; **tr.** dispensation given under authentication by the **community of royal dependants** and by the people belonging to the caste *maṟamodali* ; *I.P.S.* No. 393, p. 268, l. 5, Virāchchilai, Tirumaiyam Tq., Pudukkottai Dt., T. Nadu St. **Dy.** Pāṇḍya, Kulaśēkhara, reg. yr. 15 = 1293 A.D.

arasu anusari (K. *n.*), king's followers ; **text :** ..... *yī dharmavanū arasu-anusari ottidare pariharisi koḍuvaru Kōṭiyakēriya halaru seṭṭikāṟaru eṁdu baradu naṭa śilāsāsana* .... ; **tr.** this stone inscription has been set up stipulating that in case the king's followers harm the provisions of thc grant, the same will be compensated by the halaru seṭṭikāḷaru of Kōṭiyakēri ; *S.I.I.* VII, No. 385, p. 241, ll. 43–45 ; Koṭakēri, Udupi Tq. and Dt., Karn. St. **Dy.** Saṅgama, Dēvarāya, Ś. 1347 = 1425 A.D.

arasu bhaṁḍāri (K. *n.*), officer in-charge of royal treasury ; **text :** (damaged) .... *Koṭīśvara dēvarige* .... *arasu-bhaṁḍāriyū* ... *Śivarātriya pūjege māḍida dharmma* .. ; **tr. officer in-charge of the royal treasury** made a grant for conducting the worship of the god Kūṭīśvaradēva on the occasion of Śivarātri ; *S.I.I.* IX, pt. ii, No. 407, p. 413, ll. 7–8, 10–11 ; Kōṭēśvara, Kundapur Tq. Udupi Dt., Karn. St. **Dy.** Saṅgama, Bukka,

Ś. 1287 = 1364 A.D.

arasugey (K. *vb.*), to rule over ; **text :** ...... *mahāmaṇḍalēśvaraṁ Jōyimayyarasars Siṁdavāḍi-sāsiramaṁ* ... *sukhadin**arasugey**yuttamire*.... ; **tr.** while *mahāmaṁḍaḷēśvara* (*q.v.*) Jōyimayyarasa was happily **ruling over** Siṅdavāḍi-1000 ; *S.I.I.* IX, pt. i, No. 142, p. 125, ll. 10–11, Chinnatumbaḷam, Advani Tq., Kurnool Dt., A.P. St. **Dy.** Chāḷ. of Kal., Vikramāditya VI, Ch. Vi. yr. 4 = 1079 A.D.

arasugeyye (K. *indec.*), while ruling ; **text :** ... *mahāmaṇḍaḷēśvaraṁ* (*q.v.*) *Chiddaṇṇa Chōḷa mahārājar Siṁdavāḍi sāsiramumaṁ* .... *arasugeyye* .... ; **tr. while** *mahāmaṁḍalēśvara* (*q.v.*) Chiddaṇṇa Chōḷa mahārāja was **ruling** over Siṁdavāḍi-1000 ; *S.I.I.* IX, pt. i, No. 123, p. 105, ll. 10–12 ; Dōṇekallu, Gooty Tq., Anantapur Dt., A.P. St. **Dy.** Chāḷ. of Kal., Trailōkyamalla, Ś. 981 = 1079–80 A.D.

araśukaṭṭu (T. *n.*), a kind of tax ; **text :** ... . *pāḍikāval **araśukaṭṭu** maṟṟum eppērpaṭṭa śuvandiraṅgaḷum* .... ; **tr.** all taxes including the tax for seeking the chieftain's protection and the **tax called araśukaṭṭu** ; *I.P.S.*, No. 453, p. 324, l. 14 ; Ādaṉūr, Tirumaiyam Tq., Pudukottai Dt., T. Nadu St. **Dy.** Pāṇḍya, Vīrapāṇḍya, 1426 A.D.

araśupēṟu (T. *n.*), levy collected for the king ; **text[1] :** .... *Veḷḷiyiḍunagarattu ūravarōm* .... *Tiruveḷḷiyaṅkuṉṟamuḍayāṟukku tirunandāviḷakkeṉṉai* .... ***araśupēṟāga** kuḍuppitta* .... *nilam oru mā* ; **tr.** the inhabitants of Veḷḷiyiḍunagaram made over to the god Tiruveḷḷiyaṅkuṉṟamuḍaiyār, **the levy collected for the king** for providing oil for burning one perpetual lamp in the temple ; *S.I.I.* XVII, No. 577, p. 244, ll. 8–15 ; Tirutteṅgūr, Tirutturaippundi Tq., Tanjavur Dt., T. Nadu St. **Dy.** Chōḷa, Rājarāja III, reg. yr. 24+1 = 1241 A.D. ; **text[2] :** .... *Vishṇusthānam Śivasthānam mudalāna daivasthānaṅgaḷakku* ..... *nilavaṟi **araśupēṟu** maṟṟum pala piṟavarigaḷum* ... *viṭṭa dhanmasādhana rāyasam* ; **tr.** royal edict recording the grant of a number of taxes including tax on land and **tax levied for the king** for all the Vaishṇava, Śaiva and other temples ; *S.I.I.* VIII, No. 597, p. 305, ll. 7–9 ; Tiruppalātturai, Tiruchirapalli Tq. and Dt., T. Nadu St. **Dy.** Tuḷuva, Kṛishṇadēvarāya, Ś. 1439 = 1517 A.D.

arasuvēru (K. *n.*) ; king size load ; **text :** ... . . *piriya kereya kelasakke naḍevaṁ-tāgiy**arasuvēriṁ**ge munnannaḍeva pāgamallade mattoṁdu pāgam* ; **tr.** for every king-size load an additional *pāga* (*q.v.*) over the already payable single *pāga* was granted. ; *S.I.I.* IX, pt. i, No. 192, p. 187, ll. 27–29 ; Bāgaḷi, Harapanahalli Tq., Bellary Dt., Karn. St. **Dy.** Chāḷ. of Kal., Vikramāditya VI, Ch. Vi. yr. 39 = 1115 A.D.

arateṟe (K. *n.*), tax paid to the king ; **text :** .. ... *Ganahūralondu haḷḷige haṇavaidu **arateṟe*** .. ... ; **tr.** for each village in Ganahūru five *haṇa* (*q.v.*) were paid as **tax paid to the king** ; *E.C.* (R) I, No. 87, p. 55, ll. 11–12; Nadigunda,

Somavarpet Tq., Coorg Dt., Karn. St. **Dy.** Koṅgāḷva, Vīrachōḷakoṅgāḷva, Cy. yr. Manmatha = 1175 A.D.

aratal̤āra (K. *n.*), chief village official in charge of watch and ward duty ; **text :** *Poḷaloḷage aratal̤āram keṭṭudarke koṭṭu kāvaṁ* . . . . ; **tr.** within the town, in cases where any thing is lost, the **chief village official in charge of watch and ward duty** of the town has to make it good ; *Ep. Ind.* Vol. XV, No. 6 D, p. 79, l. 24 ; Sūḍi, Ron Tq., Dharwar Dt., Karn. St. **Dy.** Chāḷ. of Kal., Sōmēśvara, Ś 973 = 1050 A.D.

arāti (K. < Skt. *n.*), enemy ; **text :** *kadanadoḷ-āṁt-**arāti**gaḷa daṁtiya daṁtamanotti kīl̤tu* . . . . *Narasiṁhabhūpa* ; **tr.** the king Narasiṁhabhūpa used to forcibly pull out the tusks of the elphants of the enemy who confronted him in war ; *E.C.* (R) X, Ak. 44, p. 58, ll. 9–10 ; Arasīkere, Arasikere Tq., Hassan Dt., Karn. St. **Dy.** Hoy., Ballāḷa II, Ś. 1111 = 1189 A.D.

ar̤avaṁṭe (K. *n.*), road side shed where water, buttermilk, etc., are offered free to travellers ; **text :** . . . . *Beḷugoḷada . Chchārukīrti paṁḍitadēvayyagaḷige* . . . . *biṭa **ar̤avaṁṭe**ya haravariya dharmmasthaḷavanu suṭṭu brāhmaṇanu aḷida saṁmaṁdadiṁda Dēvaṇṇavoḍeyaru Sōmanāthadēvara pātrabhōgakke Ādipara-mēśvarara hāladhārege biṭṭadu* . . . ; **tr.** Dēvaṇṇa Voḍeya made a grant for the entertainment of the god Sōmanāthadēva and for the ritual pouring of the milk on the image of Ādiparamēśvara as compensation for killing a *brāhmaṇa* and for having burnt down the sacred place in which the **road side shed** belonging to Chārukīrti Paṁḍitadēvayya in which **water, buttermilk, etc., were offered free to travellers** ; *S.I.I.* VII, No. 368, p. 224, ll. 9–11, Maṇigārakēri, Udupi Tq. and Dt., Karn. St. **Dy.** Saṅgama, Mallikārjuna, Ś 1375 = 1453 A.D.

ar̤avaṁtage (K. *n.*), road side shed where water, buttermilk, etc., are offered free to travellers ; **text :** *Hariyaṁṇanu Muttageya* . . . . *prabhu* . . . . *Bappayya-Bammayyana kaiyyalu* . . . *bhūmiyanu haḍadu **ar̤avaṁtageya** udaka-dānakkaṁ* . . . . *biṭṭa* . . . . ; **tr.** Hariyaṁṇa obtained land from the hands of Boppayya-Bommaya, the head of Muttage and granted the same to the **road side shed where water, buttermilk, etc., are offered free to travellers** for providing the required quantity of water ; *S.I.I.* IX, pt. i, No. 332, p. 352, ll. 28–30, 32 ; Muttagi, Harapanahalli Tq., Bellary Dt., Karn. St. **Dy.** Hoy., Ballāḷa, Ś. 1136 = 1213 A.D. ;

ar̤avaṁṭige (K. *n.*), **text**[1] **:** . . . . . *agrahāraṁ Tuṁbuḷadaśēsha mahā-janaṁgaḷa kayyalu **ar̤avaṁṭige**ge Chakra-seṭṭi biḍisida mattaru 1* . . ; **tr.** one *mattar* (*q.v.*) of land released by Chakraseṭṭi on behalf of the entire body of *mahajana* (*q.v.*) of Tuṁbuḷa, a brāhmaṇa settlement for establishing a **road side shed where water, buttermilk, etc., are offered free to travellers** ; *S.I.I.* IX, pt. i, No. 175, p. 170, ll. 31–32 ; Chinnatuṁbuḷam,

Adavani Tq., Kurnool Dt., A.P. St. **Dy.** Chāḷ. of Kal., Vikramāditya VI, Ch. Vi. yr. 32 = 1107 A.D.; **text**[2] **:** *ubhaya nānādēsi Kumāra Nāraṇanāyakaru Gadduṁbaḷḷiya aśēshamahājanaṁgaḷige hoṁge tiṁgaḷige hāga vṛiddhiyaṁ koṭṭa gadyāṇavār̤u ivar̤a vṛidhiyalu Dōrasamudrada heddāriyalu bēsageya nālku tiṁgaḷu* ***aravaṁṭige*** *naḍesuvaru* . . . ; **tr.** Kumāra Nāraṇanāyaka, an *ubhaya nānādēsi* (*q.v.*) gave per month one hāga of interest per hoṁnnu (*q.v.*) to the *aśeshamahājanas* (*q.v.*) of Gadduṁbaḷḷi with the stipulation that the interest amount should be spent on maintaining **road side shed where water, buttermilk, etc., are offered free to travellers** on the highway of Dōrasamudra during the four summer months ; *E.C.* (R) VIII, Hn. 33, pp. 261–62, ll. 3–12 ; Doḍḍagaddavaḷḷi, Hassan Tq. and Dt., Karn. St. Mercantile guild, Cy. yr. Sarvvajit = 1168 A.D.

aravāna (K. *n.*), half measure ; **text :** *Lokkiguṁḍiya jōḷadangaḍiya davaṇiga ...... Mar̤uḷēśvaradēvarige aṁgaḍiyal* ***aravāna****ṁgoḷva saṁtuga bhattamaṁ koṭṭaru.* . . . . ; **tr.** the owner of the shop selling jowar at Lokkiguṁḍi gave half of ladle's measure of paddy to the god Maruḷēśvaradēva ; *K.I.* II, No. 10, p. 31, l. 15, Lakkunḍi, Gadag Tq. and Dt arn. St. **Dy.** Chāḷ. of Kal., Vikramāditya VI, Ś 1103 = 1181 A.D. ; **aravana** (K. *s.a.* as *aramāna, n.*), half measure ; **text :** *baḷḷavondu hēriṅge bhattav****aravana*** ; **tr.** for one load of balla (a grain measure) **half measure** of paddy ; *K.I.* I, No. 25, p. 50, l. 89, Sirasangi, Saundatti Tq., Dharwar Dt., Karn. St. **Dy.** Chaḷ. of Kal., Vīra Sōmēśvara IV, Ś 1108 = 1186 A.D.

ar̤avaṭige (K. *n.*), road side shed where water, buttermilk, etc., are offered free to travellers ; **text :** *mūr̤u vṛitti dharma ā ar̤avaṭigeya dharmakke saluvavu.* . . ; **tr.** three shares of the grant are earmarked for the **road side shed where water, buttermilk, etc., are offered free to travellers** ; *S.I.I.* IX, pt. ii, No. 436, p. 446, ll. 32–33 ; Malapanaguḍi, Hospet Tq., Bellary Dt., Karn. St. **Dy.** Saṅgama, Dēvarāya, Ś. 1333 = 1412 A.D. ; **ar̤avaṭṭige** (K. *n.*), **text :** *Sōmanapurada ūra muṁdaṇa ōṇiyum* ***ar̤avaṭṭige*** . ; **tr. road side shed where water, buttermilk, etc., are offered free to travellers** at the lane leading to the village Sōmanapura ; *E.C.* (R) V, T.N. 225, p. 605, ll. 14–15 ; Kaliyūru, T. Narasipura Tq., Mysore Dt., Karn. St. **Dy.** Tuḷuva, Kṛishṇadēvarāya, Ś. 1445 = 1521 A.D.

aravattokkalu (K. *n.*), an agricultural body of sixty tenants ; **text :** . . . *Goṁkajinālayakke* . . . . *pannīr gāvuṇḍugaḷuṁ aravatt****okkaluṁ*** *hannirdhānyakkaṁ rāsigoḷagavaṁ biṭaru* ; **tr.** the twelve *gāvuṇḍu* (*q.v.*) and the agricultural body of 60 tenants gave to the Goṁkajinālaya, a huge quantity of twelve varieties of grains ; *K.I.* V, No. 21, p. 83, ll. 52–53, Tērdāḷ, Jamkhandi Tq., Bijapur Dt., Karn. St. **Dy.** Chā. of Kal., Vikramāditya VI, Ś. 1045 = 1123 A.D.

ārave (K. < Skt. *n.*), garden ; **text**[1] **:** . . . . . *kaṭṭisida keṟe* . . . . . *iṭṭ**ārave*** . . . . . *satra* . . . . . *aṟavaṭṭige* . . . . . *Kalidēvaseṭṭi māḍida dharmaṁ* ; **tr.** the charitable acts done by Kalidēvaseṭṭi include the excavation of a tank, laying a **garden**, building a choultry, a **road side shed where water and butter milk are supplied free to the travellers** etc. . . . ; *S.I.I.* IX, pt. i, No. 296, p. 321, ll. 48–49; Kuṟugōḍu, Bellary Tq. and Dt., Karn. St. **Dy.** Kal. of Kal., Sōvidēva, Ś. 1097 = 1176 A.D. ; **text**[2] **:** (damaged) . . . . . . *naḍava hittiliha sthaḷa ārave āṟaveya sthaḷa* . . . . ; **tr.** the backyard meant for walking, garden and the land in which the garden is laid . . . ; *K.I.* VI, No. 69, p. 189, ll. 29–30; Dharwāḍa, Dharwar Tq. and Dt., Karn. St. **Dy.** Tuḷuva, Kṛishṇadēvarāya, Ś. 1449 = 1526 A.D.

aṟavōlai (T. *n.*), gift-deed ; **text :** . . . . . *nāṅgellaikkum uṭpaṭṭa nilamum āga innilaṅgaḷ kalveṭṭi **aṟavōlai** śeidu kuḍuttōm.* . . . . *sabhaiyyōm* . . . ; **tr.** we the members of the *sabhā* (*q.v.*) got an inscription on stone engraved and a **gift-deed** written for the grant given including land situated within the four boundaries and other pieces of land . . . . ; *S.I.I.* VII, No. 137, p. 58, l. 17, Tirukkōyilūr, Tirukkoyilur Tq., S. Arcot Dt., T. Nadu St. **Dy.** Chōḷa, Kulōttuṅga I, reg. yr. 6 = 1076 A.D.

archaka (K. *n.*), temple priest ; **text**[1] **:** . . . *Daṇḍanāyakan ī Vishṇugṛihamanettisi Vishṇu bhaṭārage koṭṭa maṇṇu āvudendaḍe kereya keḷage pannirkhaṁḍuga archakarge pola key eraḍu* . . . ; **tr.** The daṇḍanāyaka having built the temple of Vishṇu gave to the god land under the tank to the extent of being sown with 12 *khaṁḍugas* (*q.v.*) of seeds and gave to the **temple priest** land of the extent of being sown with 2 *key* (*q.v.*) of seeds ; *S.I.I.* IX, pt. i, No. 33, p. 19, ll. 6–13 ; Agaḷi, Madakasira Tq., Anantapur Dt., A.P. St. **Dy.** Noḷ. Pal., Noḷaṁbādhirāja, in characters of 10th cent. A.D. ; **text**[2] **:** . . *Chāmarāja Voḍeyaravaru* . . . *paṁchaliṁga pratishṭeyanu māḍisi dēvatāpūje neyvēdyakke Satyagālada* . . . . *Kṛishṇaṁbaṭana svāstiyaṁnu krayake koṁḍu archaka* . . . . *Sītayyage koṭu.* . . . ; **tr.** Chāmarāja Voḍeya installed five liṁgas and for the conduct of divine worship and offerings of food to the deity, purchased land from Kṛishṇaṁbhaṭṭa of Satyagāla and handed it over to the temple priest Sītayya ; *E.C.* (R) IV, Ko. 31, p. 420, ll. 15–19 ; Satyagāla, Kollegala Tq., Chamarajanagara Dt., Karn. St. **Dy.** Woḍ. of Mys., Kṛishṇarāja Voḍeya II, Ś. 1641 = 1720 A.D.

archchanābhōga iṟaiyili (T. *adj.*), land exempted from taxes, set apart for meeting the expenses of offerings and worship to the deity ; **text :** . . . *Tiruvārūr uḍaiyār śrīmūlattāṉamuḍaiyār kōyilil eḻundaruḷi irukkum Āḷuḍaiyanambikkum Paravai nāchchiyarkkum **archchanābhōga iṟaiyiliyāga*** . . . . . *iṭṭa innāṭṭu dēvadānamāna Gaṅgaikoṇḍa-śōḻanallūr* . . . . ; **tr.** Gaṅgaikoṇḍaśōḻanallūr which was a dēvadāna village **exempted from taxes, set apart for meeting the expenses of offerings and worship to the deities** Āḷuḍaiyanambi and Paravaināchchiyār installed in the temple of Mūlattānamuḍaiyār at Tiruvārūr .....; *S.I.I.* VII, No. 485, p. 298, l. 4 ; Tiruvārūr, Nagapattinam Tq., Tanjavur Dt., T. Nadu St. **Dy.** Chōḷa, Kulōttuṅga II, reg. yr. 7 = 1140 A.D.

archanābhōgam (T. < Skt.), offerings and worship to the deity ; **text** : . . . *Kaḻaniyūr Rāmīśvaramuḍaiya Mahādēvarkku . . . avibali* ***archanābhōgattukku*** *. . . viṭṭa nilam kuḻi āyiram* . . . ; **tr.** one thousand *kuḻi* (*q.v.*) for conducting rituals and for offerings and worships of the god Rāmīśvaramuḍaiya Mahādēva of Kaḻaniyūr ; *E.C.* X, Kol. 149a, p. 38, ll. 18–20, 27–28, 33–34, Kōlār, Kolar Tq. and Dt., Karn. St. **Dy.** Chōḷa, Kulōttuṅga I, reg. yr. 20 = 1090 A.D.

archchanakhaṁḍika (Te. < Skt. *n.*), a piece of land endowed for the worship of the deity ; **text** : . ... *Koṁḍavītiśimalōni Nādiṁḍla gramānanu grāmānaku nirṛiti bhāgānanu* ***archanakhaṁḍḍikeku*** ...... *kha* 1 ; **tr.** 1 *kha* (*q.v*) of **land** situated to the south west of the village Nadiṁḍlagrāma within Koṇḍavīṭi sīmā was **endowed for worship** ....; *S.I.I.* IV, No. 686, p. 214, ll. 12–14 ; Nādeṇḍla, Narasaraopet Tq., Guntur Dt., A.P. St. **Dy.** Āravīḍu, Śrīraṁgarāya, Ś. 1502 = 1580 A.D.

archchanā śēsham (T. < Skt. *n.*), land apportioned for meeting the expenses of worship ; **text** : . . . . . . *Rājarāja Cheṁbuvarāyaṉēṉ. . . . . Tiruttāntōṉṟi-Aḷuḍaiyārkku* ***archchanā śēsham****-āga nāṉ viṭṭa nilam* ; **tr.** I, Rājarāja Cheṁbuvarāyaṉ, apportioned the land for meeting the expenses of worship of the deity Tiruttāntōṉṟi-Āḷuḍaiyār ; *S.I.I.* XVII, No. 244, p. 95, ll. 3–4 ; Mēlśēvūr, Senji Tq., S. Arcot Dt., T. Nadu St. **Dy.** Chōḷa, Rājādhirāja II, reg. yr. 13 = 1175 A.D.

archanā virutti (T. < Skt. °*vṛitti, n.*), land endowed for conducting worship ; **text** : .... ***archchaṉā virutti*** *mahāsabhaiyōm iṭṭa nilam arai mā araikkāṇi* ....; **tr.** half *mā* (*q.v.*) and half *kāṇi* (*q.v.*) of **land was endowed** by the *mahāsabhā* (*q.v.*) for **offerings and worship** ; *S.I.I.* VIII, No. 452, p. 240, l. 5, Māṟamaṅgalam, Srivaikuntam Tq., Tirunelveli Dt., T. Nadu St. **Dy.** Pāṇḍya, Vīrapāṇḍya, reg. yr. 11 = in characters of 12th cent. A.D.

archanā vṛitti (K. < Skt. *n.*), village/land endowed for conducting worship of the deity ; **text**[1] : . . . . . *Hiriya-Ballāḷadēvarasaru Sivālayavanu māḍisi ā Ballāḷēsvaradēvarige* ***archanāvṛitti****yāgi . . . Chaṁgavāḍiyanu biṭṭaru* ....; **tr.** the senior Ballāḷadēvarasa having built a temple for Śiva called as Ballāḷēśvaradēva, **endowed the village** of Chaṁgavāḍi **for conducting worship of the deity** and other services ; *E.C.* (R) VII, Ml. 93, p. 399, ll. 7–10, Chaṁgavāḍi, Malavalli Tq., Mandya Dt., Karn. St. **Dy.** Hoy., Ballāḷa III, Cy. yr. Krōdhi

= 1305 A.D. ; **text**[2] (Te. < Skt. *n.*), ... *Tiruveṅgaḷanāthuni* . . . . . *Anantayyagāriki* ***archanāvṛitti****kigānu Bharasamudraṁ* . . . . . *istimi* ; **tr.** the **village** of Bairasamudraṁ was **endowed** in favour of Anantayyagāru for **conducting worship of the deity** Tiruveṅgaḍanātha ; *S.I.I.* XVI, No. 74, p. 80, ll. 8–9, 31–32, 35. ; Bhairasamudraṁ, Kalyanadurga Tq., Anantapur Dt., A.P. St. **Dy.** Tuḷuva, Kṛishṇadēvarāya, Ś. 1444 = 1522 A.D. ; **text**[3] (Te. *n.*), **:** . . . *Kōnapagāriki icchina* ***archanavṛitti*** *Bhūdāna patra kramamu*. . . . . . ; **tr.** the **land endowed** through gift deed given to Kōnapagāru for conducting worship of the deity; *S.I.I.* XVI, No. 238, p. 244, ll. 12–13 ; Kūrmāyi, Palmaner Tq., Chittoor Dt., A.P. St. **Dy.** Tuḷuva, Sadāśiva, Ś. 1482 = 1559 A.D. ; **text**[4] (K. *n.*) **:** *Mysūra* . . . . *Rāju vaḍēyaru Raghupatisvāmiya archanāvṛitti* . . . . *saluvāgi* . . . . . . *Bēvinahaḷḷiya grāmavanu* . . . . *samarpisidevu* . . . . ; **tr.** We, Rāju Vaḍēyar, the ruler of Mysore **endowed the village** of Bēvinahaḷḷi **for conducting worship of the deity** Raghupatisvāmi ; *E.C.* (R) V, T.N. 50, p. 449, ll. 11–13, 21–23 ; Bannūru, T. Narasipura Tq., Mysore Dt., Karn. St. **Dy.** Woḍ. of Mys., Rāja Woḍeyar, Ś. 1537 = 1615 A.D.

ardhabhāgi (K. < Skt. *n.*), entitled for half share ; **text :** . . . . *ā sthaḷadoḷage namage* . . . ***ardhabhāgi*** *ā stānagadeya mēlaṇa tōṭadoḷage namage*. . . ***ardhabhāgi*** . . . . ; **tr.** we get **half a share** in that locality and **half share** in the grove above that locality ; *S.I.I.* VII, No. 345, p. 200, l. 21, Chauḷikēri, Udupi Tq. and Dt., Karn. St. **Dy.** Sāḷuva, Narasiṁha, Ś. 1424 = 1502 A.D.

aṟevāna (K. *n.*), half of a measure ; **text :** (damaged) . . . *Narasiṁhadēva* . . . . *nakharaṁgaḷu kūḍi koṭṭa dharmma* . . . . . *aravāna koṭṭalli* ***are-vāna*** *hēṟinalu yele* . . . . ; **tr.** to the god Narasiṁhadēva was given jointly by all the Nakhara (*q.v.*) half of a measure of load of betel leaves ; *S.I.I.* IX, pt. i, No. 367, p. 385, ll. 35–37 ; Chinna-Tumbaḷam, Adoni Tq., Kurnul Dt., A.P. St. **Dy.** Yād. of Dēv., Jaitugi, Ś. 1151 = 1229 A.D.

arevattalu (K. *n.*), half of a mattar of land measure ; **text :** . . . . *Hariharagavuṁḍan****arevattalu*** *gaddeyaṁ biṭṭaru*. . . . . ; **tr.** Hariharagavuṁḍa granted **half of a mattar of land measure** ; *S.I.I.* XX, No. 142, p. 181, l. 41 ; Bāḷaṁbīḍ, Hangal Tq., Dharwar Dt., Karn. St. **Dy.** Kal. of Kal., Bijjaḷa, Cy. yr. Pārthiva = 1165 A.D.

arevattar (K. *n.*), half of a mattar of land measure ; **text :** . . . . *Haraḷakaṭada hiṁde gade* ***arevattaru*** . . . *ā teṁkaṇa kōḍiyalu arevattaru eṟe*. . . . ; **tr.** at the back of Haraḷakaṭa paddy field of the extent of **half a matter of a land measure** and at the southern corner fertile soil of the extent of half a mattar of land measure ; *E.C.* XI, Dg. 171, p. 217, ll. 15–16 ; Hemmanabētūr, Davanagere Tq. and Dt., Karn. St. **Dy.** Sēü. of Dēv., Mahadēva, Ś. 1080 = 1258 A.D.

are vīsa (K. *n.*), half a vīsa coin ; **text :** . . . .

Kalidēvasvāmi agrāsanada brāhmaṇara satrakke yeleya pē̤ṟiṁgey-oṁdu vīsam talevo̤ṟegey arevīsamaṁ biṭṭar . . . . ; **tr.** one *vīsa* for one load of plantain leaf and **half vīsa of coin** for one head load was granted, for the choultry, for first feeding of brāhmaṇas of the temple of Kalidēvasvāmi ; *S.I.I.* IX, pt. i, No. 168, p. 162, ll. 31–33 ; Bāgaḷi, Harapanahalli Tq., Bellary Dt., Karn. St. **Dy.** Chāḷ. of Kal, Vikramāditya VI, Ch. Vi. yr. 28 = 1103 A.D.

ari[1] (K. < Skt. *n.*), enemy ; **text :** ***ari****rāyavibhāḍa bhāshege tappuva rāyara gaṁḍa* ; **tr.** one who destroys **enemy** kings and one who is a terror to rulers who break their own words ; *I.V.R.* I, pt. i, No. 5, p. 8, l. 5 ; Śriṅgēri, Sringeri Tq., Chickmagalur Dt., Karn. St. **Dy.** Saṅgama, Harihara I, Ś. 1268 = .1346 A.D.

ari[2] (T. *n.*), rice ; **text :** *tiruvamudukku* ***ari*** *nāṉāḻiyum*. . . *akkiramiraṇḍukku ari nāṉāḻiyum* ; **tr.** for food offerings to the deity four *nāḻi* (*q.v.*) of **rice** and for the first feeding of brāhmaṇas 4 *nāḻi* of rice ; *T.A.S.* IV, No. 4, pp. 18–20, ll. 3–4; Suchīndrum, Agasteeshvaram Tq., Kanyakumari Dt., T. Nadu St. **Dy.** Rulers of Vēṇāḍu, Kēraḷavaṉmar, Kollam 320 = 1145 A.D.

āṟiḍupaḍugai (T. *n.*), flat land on the banks of a river ; **text :** . . . *āṟum* ***āṟiḍupaḍugai****yum* ; **tr.** the river and the **flat lands on its bank** ; *S.I.I.* VIII, No. 336, p. 180, l. 8 ; Jaṁbukēśvaram, Tiruchirappalli Tq. and Dt., T. Nadu St. **Dy.** Chōḷa, Rājarāja III, reg. yr. 20 = 1236 A.D.

arihadabojagar (K. *n.*), skilful cutters (of arecanuts); **text :** . . . . . *Harabhavanaman* ***arihadabo jagaru*** . . . . *māḍisidar* ; **tr.** the temple of Śiva was constructed by those **skilful cutters (of arecanuts)**; *E.C.* (R) X, Ak. 33, p. 45, ll. 61–62 ; Arasikere, Arasikere Tq., Hassan Dt., Karn. St. **Dy.** Hoy., Ballāḷa II, Ś. 1105 = 1184 A.D.

arikoḻi (T. *n.*), sifting of paddy ; **text :** (obscure) . . . . *ivvūr peṟṟa* . . . . *viśakkāṇamum kuśakkāṇamum* ***arikoḻi****yum* . . . *ivar tāmē uṇṇapeṟuvārāguvum* . . ; **tr.** they themselves shall enjoy the exemptions including the share of the headman, the share of the potter, the **sifting of paddy** etc. . ; *S.I.I.* II, pts. iii-v, No. 73, p. 352, l. 124 ; Kaśākkuḍi, Pondicherry Tq. and Dt., T. Nadu St. **Dy.** Pallava, Nandivarman II, reg. yr. 22 = 753 A.D.

arimukkai (T. *n.*), tax levied on rice produce ; **text :** . . . . *Tiruvattūrum Vayalūrum* . . . . *uḷḷiṭṭa* . . . . *arimukkai uḷḷiṭṭa. nellāyamum kāśāyamum* . . . . . *Tiruvattūr Uḍayaṇāyaṉārkku viṭṭēṉ Śeṅgēṇi Ammayappaṉ* . . . . ; **tr.** I, Śeṅgēṇi Ammayappan made a grant of taxes levied on paddy produce including **tax levied on rice produce**, revenue income in cash etc., to the god Tiruvattūr Uḍayanāyaṉār from the villages of Tiruvattūr, Vayalūr etc. ; *S.I.I.* VII, No. 103, p. 43, ll. 7–9, 13–14 ; Tiruvottūr, Cheyyar Tq., N. Arcot Dt., T. Nadu. St. **Dy.** Chōḷa, Kulōttuṅga II, reg. yr. 33, in characters of 13th cent. A.D.

arinīr (T. *n.*), water made available for irrigation during drought ; **text :** .... *innilattukku* ***arinīr*** ... *iṟaittukkoḷḷavum* ; **tr. water made available for irrigation during drought** be used for irrigating this land ; *I.P.S.*, No. 476, p. 343, l. 15; Vaittikōyil, Kulattur Tq., Pudukkottai Dt., T. Nadu St. **Dy.** Pāṇḍya, Sundarapāṇḍya, in characters of 13th cent. A.D.

arippāḷ (T. *n.*), woman employed for cleaning rice ; **text :** .... *ariśi* ***arippāḷukku*** .... *uṇṇa iṭṭa veṇkalam 1* ; **tr.** 1 bronze vessel was earmarked for feeding the **woman employed for cleaning rice** . . ; *S.I.I.* VIII, No. 679, p. 341, l. 4 ; Allūr, Tiruchirappalli Tq. and Dt., T. Nadu St. **Dy.** Chōḷa, Rājarāja I, reg. yr. 22 = 1007 A.D.

arippaṉ (T. *n.*), of lower caste ; **text :** . . . *aṉaittuch-chātigaḷuṁ andaṇaṉ talaiyāga* ***arippaṉ*** *kaḍaiyāga* . . . ; **tr.** all the castes with the *brāhmaṇa* in the lead and **lower caste** in the rear ; *S.I.I.* VII, No. 118, p. 49, l. 4, Chengaṁ, Tiruvannamalai Tq., N. Arcot Dt., T. Nadu St., **Misc.**, Ś. 1180 = 1258 A.D.

ariśi (T. *n.*), rice ; **text :** .... *Tirukkārīśvara-muḍaiyārku* .. *amurdupaḍikku* ***ariśi*** *nānāḻikku nellu-kkuṟuṇi irunāḻi* ; **tr.** two *nāḻi* (grain measure.) and one *kuṟuṇi* (grain mesure) of paddy yielding 4 nāḻi of rice for offering food to Tirukkārīśvaram-uḍaiyār ; *S.I.I.* VII, No. 445, p. 279, l. 2 ; Kalavai, Walajapet Tq., N. Arcot Dt., T. Nadu St. **Dy.** Chōḷa, Vikramachōḷa, reg. yr 4 = 1122 A.D.

ariśikāṇam (T. *n.*), tax on dehusking ; **text :** .... *Irāśanārāyaṇaṉ Śambuvarāyaṉ Kalavaipaṟṟu nāṭṭārkku taṅgaḷ paṟṟil* .... *payirchcheyvār illādapaḍiyāle* .... *paṇa vaṟgamum* ***ariśikāṇamum*** ..... *koḷḷādapaḍi śollivitta aḷavukku* .... *kalveṭṭuvittukoṇḍu* .... *naḍattipōdavum* ; **tr.** Rājanārāyaṇa Śambuvarāyaṉ having instructed that, since there were no persons to cultivate the lands the *nāṭār* (*q.v.*) of Kalavināḍu need not pay taxes in cash and **tax on dehusking** and they were asked to have this engraved on an inscription . .; *S.I.I.* VII, No. 444, p. 279, ll. 1–3, 5 ; Kalavai, Walajapet Tq., N. Arcot Dt., T. Nadu St. **Dy.** Śambuvarāya, Rājanārāyaṇa, reg. yr. 7 = in characters of 11th cent. A.D. ; **ariśikkāśu** (T. *n.*), cash realised from the sale of rice ; **text :** .... *ikkōyilil* ***ariśikkāśum*** *śrīkāryyappēṟum* .... *kalveṭṭi kuḍuttōm* ; **tr.** we donated the **cash realised from the sale of rice** and materials for performance of rituals in the temple after getting the details engraved on stone . . . ; *I.P.S.*, No. 335, p. 205, ll. 5–6 ; Kaṇṇaṉūr, Tirumayyam Tq., Pudukkottai Dt., T. Nadu St. **Dy.** Pāṇḍya, Kulaśēkhara, reg. yr. 13 + 13, in characters of 13th cent. A.D.

arivāṇamu (Te. *n.*), yield from land ; **text :** . . . *Bhikirāju nilpina datti Apimana Goravalakichchina nēla nūṭayiruvadi maṟutuḍlu rājamānaṁbu dīni* ***arivāṇaṁbu*** *paṇḍreṇḍu puṭlu* ..... ; **tr.** Bhikirāju gave this grant of one hundred and twenty *maṟutu* (land measure.) measured by *rājamāna* (royal measuring rod) of land fetching 12 *puṭṭi* (a grain measure) of paddy to the preceptor Apimana Gorava ; *S.I.I.* X, No. 594, p. 327, ll. 6–12 ; Mutukūru, Pulivendla Tq., Cuddappah Dt., A.P. St. **Dy.** Rēnāṇḍu Chōḍa, Chōḍamahārāja, in characters of 9th cent. A.D.

arivāṭpadakku (T. *n.*), tax levied on each measure of grain while reaping ; **text :** .... *vaṇṇārapāṟai* ***arivāṭpadakku*** *uḷḷiṭṭa* ... *iṟaiyum* ; **tr.** taxes including those imposed on the washermanās boulder and **tax levied on each measure of grain while reaping** ..... ; *I.P.S.*, No. 90, p. 38, l. 4 ; Tiruviḷāṅguḍi, Kulattur Tq., Pudukkottai Dt., T. Nadu St. **Dy.** Chōḷa, Rājarāja I, reg. yr. 28 = 1013 A.D.

āriyakkūttu (T. *n.*), a kind of folk dance ; **text :** .... *Perumāṉaḍigaḷakku* ***āriyakūttāḍa*** ... *nivandamśeydu kuḍutta* .... *nilam* ; **tr.** land endowed for the performance of **a kind of folk dance** in the presence of the temple deity ... ; *S.I.I.* V, No. 718, p. 302, l. 2 ; Tiruviḍaimarudūr, Kumbhakonam Tq., Tanjavur Dt., T. Nadu St. **Dy.** Chōḷa, Āditya II, reg. yr. 4 = 962 A.D.

āriya kshatriya kula (K. *n.*), the lineage of the āriya-kshatriya ; **text :** .... *Chaṭanahaḷiya grāmavanu āriyakshatriya kulada* .... *Visaṇarāvuttaru* .. *Nārāyaṇabhaṭṭarige* .. *koṭevu* ; **tr.** We, Visaṇarāvutta belonging to the **lineage of āriyakshatriya** donated to Narāyaṇabhaṭṭa, the village of Chaṭaṇahaḷḷi ; *S.I.I.* IX, pt. ii, No. 515, p. 529, ll. 18–19, 20–21, 25–26, 32 ; Chaṭṇahaḷḷi, Harapanahalli Tq., Bellary Dt., Karn. St. **Dy.** Tuḷuva, Kṛishṇadēvarāya, Ś. 1446 = 1524 A.D.

āriyam pāḍuvār (T. *n.*), those who recite Sanskrit hymns in the temple ; **text :** .... ***āriyam pāḍuvār*** *mūvarkku Araiyaṉ Ambalanātaṉ* ... *nāl-araiyuṁ* ; **tr.** 4 1/2 shares (of gift land) handed over to Araiyaṉ Ambalanātaṉ for 3 persons who recite Sanskrit hymns in the temple .... ; *S.I.I.* II, pts. iii-v, No. 66, p. 275, l. 11 ; Tañjāvūr, Tanjavur Tq. and Dt., T. Nadu St. **Dy.** Chōḷa, Rājarāja I, reg. yr. 29 = 1014 A.D.

āriyar (T. influenced by M., *n.*), upper caste ; **text :** ***āriyar****ōḍu vanna virodhattiṉu prāyachchitta- ttiṉu* ... *paḍiṉāḷikkoḷḷum paṟaiyāl niyadam ōrōpaṟaichcheydu nel Irāmēchuvarattu.* ; **tr.** as as atonement for incurring enmity with the **upper caste**, paddy of one *paṟai* (grain measure) measured by *paṟai* holding ten *nāḷi* (grain measure) was granted to the temple of Rāmēśvaram ; *T.A.S.* Vol. V, pts. i-iii, No. 13, p. 44, ll. 21–30, Kollam, Kollam Tq. and Dt., Ker. St. **Dy.** Chēra, Kulaśēkhara, Ś. 1025 = 1103 A.D.

ārōgaṇe (K. *n.*), providing free food ; **text**[1] **:** .. *Kōṭēśvaradēvara saṁnidhiyalu kaṭiya habbadalu ubhaya jaṁgamarige* ***ārōgaṇe****ya dharmake koṇḍa bāḷu* ; **tr.** land purchased for **providing free food** to two *jaṁgama* (*q.v.*) during the festival of lights in the temple of the god Kōṭēśvara ; *S.I.I.*

IX, pt. ii, No. 415, p. 420, ll. 9–11, Kōṭēśvara, Kundapur Tq., Udupi Dt., Karn. St. **Dy.** Saṅgama, Bukka I, Ś. 1295 = 1373 A.D. ; **text**[2] : . . . . *ārōgaṇegege naivēdyada harivāṇa 3* . . . ; **tr.** food offered to the god and kept in 3 plates **for providing free food** ; *S.I.I.* IX, pt. ii, No. 489, p. 503, l. 40, Kāḷahasti, Chandragiri Tq., Chittoor Dt., A.P. St. **Dy.** Tuḷuva, Kṛishṇadēvarāya, Ś. 1434 = 1513 A.D.

āṟṟaṅkāl (T. *n.*), canal ; **text** : aṁgavaidyaril *Ādittadēvaṉ . . . Vaidyapurandaraṟkku . . . . nañjai puñjaiyum ṉattamum . . . .* ***āṟṟaṅkālum*** *. . . . maṟṟum eppērpaṭṭa samasta prāptigaḷum . . . iraiyiliyāga tandōm . . . .* ; **tr.** we made a tax free grant of wet and dry lands and house site, a **canal** and all other privileges to the surgical doctor Ādittadēvan . . . . Vaidyapurandarar ; *S.I.I.* XXII, pt. i, No. 13, p. 9, ll. 1–5, 7–8 ; Namakkal, Namakkal Tq., Salem Dt., T. Nadu St. **Dy.** Pāṇḍya, Sundarapāṇḍya, reg. yr. 8, in characters of 11th century A.D.

āṟṟaṅkarai (T. *n.*), river bank ; **text** : (obscure) . . . . *ivvūr teṟkil* ***āṟṟaṅkarai*** ; **tr.** the **river bank** to the south of the village ; *S.I.I.* No. VII, p. 18, l. 18 ; Śevallimēḍu, Kanchipuram Tq., Chingleput Dt., T. Nadu St., **Dy.** Śamb., Rājanārāyaṇa, Ś. 1268 = 1346 A.D.

āṟṟaṅkarai paḍugai (T. *n.*), land situated adjacent to the river bank ; **text** : *vaḍakīḷ mūlayil* ***āṟṟaṅkaṟai paḍugaiyile*** *innāyaṉārkku nīrvārttu koḍuttōm.* ; **tr.** we gave to the deity with the pouring of the water of libation, **land situated** in the north east corner **adjacent to the river bank** ; *JMTS* No. XIV, p. 209, l. 5 ; Pērāvūr, Tiruvaduturai Tq., Tanjavur Dt., T. Nadu St. **Dy.** Chōaḷa, Kulōttuṅga III, reg. yr. 25 = 1095 A.D.

āṟṟukkāl (T. *n.*), river channel ; **text** : *Śēyāṟṟālum Veṅkāviṉālum TIraiyaṉēriyālum . . . . . nīrinda vaḻi* ***āṟṟukkālum*** *veḷḷakkālum tōṇḍikkoṇḍuṉṉa-ppeṟuvārāguvam* . . . ; **tr.** (the donee) shall be permitted to dig **river channel** and inundation channels for conducting water from Śeyāru, the Veṅka and the tank Tiraiyaṉ ; *S.I.I.* II, No. 73, p. 352, ll. 115–17 ; Kaśākkuḍi, Pondicherry Tq., Puducherry U.T. **Dy.** Pallava, Nandivarman II, reg. yr. 22 = 753 A.D.

artha[1] (K. < Skt. *n.*), wealth (part of a title) ; **text** : (damaged) . . . *nyāyōpārit**ārtharum**. . . .* ; **tr.** who had earned **wealth** lawfully ; *S.I.I.* IX, pt. i, No. 95, p. 66, l. 38, Śivapada, Harapanahaḷḷi Tq, Bellary Dt., Karn. St. **Dy.** Chāḷ. of Kal., Jagadēkamalla, Ś. 963 = 1041–42 A.D.

artha[2] (K. < Skt. *n.*), revenue ; **text** : . . . *sarvanamasyavāgi biṭṭukoṭṭarāyūra puṭṭid**arthamaṁ** dēvarupabhōgakkaṁ khaṁḍasphuṭita jīrṇōddhārakkam . . . .* ; **tr.** the **revenue** income from the village was granted, to be respected by all, for the services to the deity, for repairing the damaged parts of the temple etc. ; *S.I.I.* IX, pt. i, No. 135, p. 119, ll. 13–14, Hūvinahaḍagalli, Hadagalli

Tq, Bellary Dt., Karn. St. **Dy.** Chāḷ. of Kal., Vikramāditya VI, Ś. 993 = 1071 A.D.

artha[3] (K. < Skt. *n.*), money ; **text :** .... *tāvu kaṭṭisida maṭhada dharmake* .... *Dugganaseṭṭiyaru koṭṭa* ***artha*** *kāṭi ga 650* .... ; **tr.** money 650 *kāṭi ga* (kāṭi gadyāṇa, superior quality of gold coin)) were given by Dugganaseṭṭi for the maṭha built by him ; *S.I.I.* IX, pt. ii, No. 465, p. 478–79, ll. 6, 45–46, Basarūru, Kundapur Tq., Udupi Dt., Karn. St. **Dy.** Saṅgama, Virūpāksha, Ś. 1395 = 1472 A.D.

arthaparichchhēda (K. < Skt. *n.*), price decided upon ; **text :** ... *Sarvappa daṁṇṇāyakaru Bārakūra* .... *Pārśvadēvarige* ... *yī bāḷanu* ***artha-parichchhēda****vāgi koṁḍu mūlaparichchhēdavāgi* .... *koṭṭenu* ... ; **tr.** Sarvappa daṁṇṇāyaka purchased this land at the **price decided upon** and gave it away on ownership basis to the god Pārśvadēva of Bārakūru ; *S.I.I.* VII, No. 391, p. 250, ll. 7, 16–17, Maṇigārakēri, Udupi Tq. and Dt., Karn. St. **Dy.** Saṅgama, Harihara II, Ś 1312 = 1390 A.D. ; **arthaparichchhēdya** ; **text :** .... *Māhaḷappasēnabōvaru*.... *Raghunāthadēvara maṭha dēvālyava kaṭṭisuvadake* .. ***artha parichchhēdyavāgi*** ... *koṁḍu mūla parichchhēdyavāgi koṭṭa* .... *sthaḷa* ..... ; **tr.** the land purchased at the **price decided upon** and given on ownership basis for building a *maṭha* (*q.v.*) and the temple of the god Raghunātha by Māhaḷappa sēnabōva ; *K.I.* VI, No. 69, p. 188, ll. 13–14 ; Mirjān, Kumta Tq., Karwar Dt., Karn. St. **Dy.** Tuḷuva, Kṛishṇadēvarāya, Ś. 1449 = 1526 A.D. ; **arthaparitsēda** ; **text :** ...... *Hubbaḷḷiya* ..... *Kāḷimarasaru* ... *Sōmanāthadēvarige* ***arthaparitsēdavāgi*** *koṭṭu mūlaparitsēdhavāgi* .... *eṟesikoṁḍu kaṭṭisida maṭhadalli naḍeva dharmma* .... ; **tr.** religious charity being conducted in the *maṭha* built by Kāḷimarasa in the temple of Sōmanāthadēva by purchasing land at the **price fixed upon** and donating the same on ownership basis by Kāḷimarasa of Hubbaḷḷi ; *S.I.I.* VII, No. 330, p. 180, ll. 17–19, Mūḍakēri, Udipi Tq. and Dt., Karn. St. **Dy.** Saṅgama, Bukkarāya, Ś. 1281 = 1359 A.D.

arthasādana pramāṇa (K. *n.*), certified coin denomination ; **text :** (obscure)...... ***arthsādana pramāṇ****ina varaha gadyāṇa* ; **tr.** *varaha gadyāṇa* (gold coin.) a **certified coin denomination** ; *K.I.* III, pt. i, No. 11, p. 33, l. 42 ; Kaikani, Bhatkal Tq. and Dt., Karn. St. **Dy.** Nagire Chfs., Kṛishṇadēvarasavoḍeya, Ś. 1465 = 1542 A.D.

arthaśāstra (Skt. *n.*), the science of polity ; **text :** .... *Mādhava mahādhirājasya* .... ***artha-śāstra****jñānāhita samskārōpa bṛiṁhit ātmaśakti samutpāṭitāśēsha ripumaṇḍalēna* ... ; **tr.** Mādhava mahādhirāja .... uprooter of all the hosts of enemies, by his own energy strengthned by his skill too deep even for those versed in the **science of polity** ; *E.C.* (R) VIII, Hn. 10, p. 237, ll. 7–9, Hāsana, Hassan Tq. and Dt., Karn. St. **Dy.** W. Gaṅga, Mādhava III, in characters of about 7th century A.D.

arthijana (K. < Skt. *n.*), supplicants ; **text :** . . . . ***arthijana*** *chiṁtāmaṇi* . . . . ; **tr.** a sympathiser of the cause of the **supplicants** ; *S.I.I.* IX, pt. i, No. 195, p. 190, ll. 8–9, Raṁgapuraṁ, Hadagalli Tq., Bellary Dt., Karn. St. **Dy.** Chāḷ. of Kal., Vikramāditya VI, Ch. Vi. yr. 41 = 1116 A.D.

āṟu (T. *n.*), river ; **text :** . . . . ***āṟum*** *āṟiḍu-paḍugaiyum* ; **tr.** the **river** and the flat land on its bank ; *S.I.I.* VIII, No. 336, p. 180, l. 8 ; Jaṁbukēśvaram, Tiruchirappalli Tq. and Dt., T. Nadu St. **Dy.** Chōḷa, Rājarāja III, reg. yr. 20 = 1236 A.D.

arttam (T. < Skt. *artha, n.*), wealth ; **text :** . . *balattālum* ***arttattālum*** *urśāgattālum Pāṇḍināḍu kaikkoṇḍu* ; **tr.** having conquered the Pāṇḍya kingdom with the help of strength, power of **wealth** and enthusiasm ; *Ep. Ind.* XXI, No. 31, p. 190, l. 18, Pallavarāyaṉpēṭai, Mayavaram Tq., Tanjavur Dt., T. Nadu St. **Dy.** Chōḷa, Rājādhirāja II, reg. 8 = 1154 A.D.

aṟtta pattu śīṭṭu (T. *n.*), document relating to monetary transactions ; **text :** . . .*paṇam 500kku eḻudivāṅgiṉa* ***aṟtta-pattu-śīṭṭu*** *1* . . . *śirībanḍārattil kaiyyāḷikkuvum śeydōm* ; **tr.** we got written the **document relating to monetary transactions** for 500 *paṇam* (coin) and had the same deposited in the temple treasury ; *T.A.S.* V, No. 32, p. 124, l. 75–77, Napier Museum, Tiruvanantapura, Tiruvanantapuram Tq. and Dt., Ker. St. **Misc.**, Kollam 945, Ś 1691 = 1769 A.D.

aṟu (K. *n.*), a kind of tax ; **text :** . . . . . . *ā grāmakke saluva chatuśīmege neṭṭa Vāmana mudre kallige voḷagāda gadde* . . . . *tōṭa* . . . ***aṟu*** . . . *anubhavisi* . . . . *yeṁdu koṭa grāmada śilśāsana* ; **tr.** the stone inscription in the village stipulating that paddy field, groves, and income from **a kind of tax** derived from the village within the boundary demarked by the stone having the portrait of Vāmana ; *E.C.* (R) VIII, HN. 55, p. 31, ll. 18–20, 24–26, Kallubyāḍarahaḷḷi, Holenarasipura Tq., Hassan Dt., Karn. St. **Dy.** Āravīḍu, Śrīraṁgarāya, Ś. 1579 = 1658 A.D.

arugaḍi (K. *n.*), tax collected at the tollgate ; **text :** . . . *Nārāyaṇabhaṭṭaru eṟada sthalaṁgaḷiṁge teṟu* . . . ***arugaḍi*** *manehaṇa nogahaṇa* . . . . *modalāgi āvudū salla* ; **tr.** for those places which Nārāyaṇa bhaṭṭa has donated with the pouring of the water of libation all taxes including **tax collected at the toll gate**, tax on houses, tax on yokes are exempted ; *K.I.* I, No. 54, p. 131, l. 3, Bailūr, Bhatkal Tq. and Dt., Karn. St. **Dy.** Saṅgama, Dēvarāya II, Ś. 1356 = 1433 A.D.

aṟugai vāṇigar (T. *n.*), cloth merchants ; **text :** . . . . *Sirikaṇṭapurattu* ***aṟugai vāṇigar*** ; **tr. cloth merchants** of Sirikaṇṭapuram . . . . .; *S.I.I.* VII, No. 525, p. 319, ll. 29–31 ; Tiruchchennampūṇḍi, Tanjavur Tq. and Dt., T. Nadu St., **Dy.** Pallava, Nandivarman II, in characters of 9th cent. A.D.

aṟugai vaṇiyaṉ (T. *n.*), cloth merchant ; **text :** . . . . *Puṟattāyanāttīḷḷakkantuṟai* ***aṟugai vaṇiyaṉ***

kaṉṉi Paḻañji vaichcha tirunondāviḷakkoṉṟu ; **tr.** the cloth merchant Kaṉṉipaḻañji of Īḻakkanturai of Puṟattāyanāḍu gave one perpetual lamp ; *T.A.S.* IV, No. 27, p. 123, ll. 5–8 ; Suchīndram, Agastheeswaram Tq., Kanyakumari Dt., T. Nadu St. **Dy.** Pāṇḍya, Śaḍaiya Māṟan, in characters of 10th cent. A.D.

aṟukāḍu (T. *n.*), deforested area ; **text :** (obscure) . . . ***aṟukā ḍu*** ; **tr. deforested area** ; *Ep. Ind.* V, No. 8, p. 51, l. 15 ; Rāyakōṭe, Krishnagiri Tq., Salem Dt., T. Nadu St. **Dy.** Pallava, Kandaśishya, in characters of 6th–7th cent. A.D.

āṟukuttal (T. *n.*), erosion by river's tidel wave ; **text :** . . . ***āṟukutti*** *alaiēṟum śarindu puṉattalai āy irukkayil* ; **tr.** because of the level of the river having raised and the wall having collapsed as a result of the **erosion by the river's tidal wave,** the temple precincts had been covered by sand ; *S.I.I.* XXII, No. 93, p. 86, l. 6 ; Jambai, Tirukkoyilur Tq., S. Arcot Dt., T. Nadu St. **Dy.** Saṅgama, Virūpākshadēva, Ś. 1393 = 1471 A.D.

āṟuṁbāḍa (K. *n.*), a sub-division consisting of 6 villages ; **text :** . . . . . *Hastināvatiya vaḷitada svāmi* ***āṟuṁbāḍa****vāda Dōravadiya vēṁṭheyakke saluva* . . . . *Kuṟiyakuppeyeṁba* . . . . *agrahāradalu* . . . . *Virūpākshadēvara pratishṭheyanu māḍi*. . . *pūje* . . . *nitya sēvegaḷige* . . *mahājanaṁgaḷa kayyalli krayadānavāgi koṁḍu* . . . . *samarpisida vṛitti 1* ; **tr.** the image of the deity Virūpākshadēva having been installeld in the brāhamaṇa settlement Kuṟiyakuppe falling within the Dōravadiya vēṁṭhe, **a sub-division consisting of six villages** in Hastināvati division, one *vṛitti* (share.) of land was purchased from the *mahājana (q.v.)* and granted to that deity ; *S.I.I.* IX, pt. ii, No. 514, pp. 528–29, ll. 5–8, 11–14, Kurikuppe, Hospet Tq., Bellary Dt., Karn. St. **Dy.** Tuḷuva, Kṛishṇadēvarāya, Ś. 1445 = 1523 A.D.

āṟumāṟiḍupaḍugai (T. *n.*), land exposed on river changing its course ; **text :** *ōḍayum uḍaippum* ***āṟumāṟiḍupaḍugai****yum* . . . ; **tr.** the stream, the breach and **the land exposed by the river changing its course** ; *S.I.I.* III, No. 151, p. 305, l. 101, Kōṉēripuram, Kumbhakonam Tq., Tanjavur Dt., T. Nadu St. **Dy.** Chōḷa, Uttamachōḷa, in characters of 10th cent. A.D.

aṟumoḻidēvaṉ (T. *n.*), grain measure named after the title of Chōḷa king Rājarāja I ; **text :** (damaged) . . . . . ***aṟumōḻidēvaṉ****āl aḷakka kaḍavad-āgavum* . . . ; **tr.** to be measured by the **grain measure** called aṟumoḻidēvan **named after the title of Chōḷa king Rājarāja I** ; *S.I.I.* XVII, No. 300, p. 126, ll. 2–3, Yōgimallavaram, Puttur Tq., Chittoor Dt., A.P. St. **Dy.** Chōḷa, Rājarāja I, reg. yr. 23 = 1008 A.D.

arumoḻidēvaṉ marakkāl (T. *n.*), a grain measure named after the Chōḷa king Rājarāja I ; **text :** *Rājarājadēvaṉ kiṇaṟṟilttoṭṭikku nīriṟaippārkku* ***arumoḻidēvaṉ marakkāl****āl niśadam nel 2 kuṟuṇi āga tiṅgaḷ 6 ikku nel muppadu kalam* ; **tr.**

30 *kalam* (grain measure) of paddy for 6 months at the rate of 2 *kuṛuṇi* (grain measure) of paddy per day measured by aṛumoḻidēvan marakkāḷ **named after the title of Chōḷa king Rājarāja I** was earmarked for those who draw water for the cistern from the well named after Rājarāja ; *S.I.I.* III, pts. i and ii, No. 4, p. 7, ll. 6–7 ; Ukkal, Wandiwash Tq., N. Arcot Dt., T. Nadu St. **Dy.** Chōḷa, Rājarāja I, reg. yr. 29 = 1014 A.D.

aṛunīr (T. *n.*), water made available for irrigation during drought ; *inda nilattukku* ***aṛunīr*** *. . . . . . iṛaittukkoḷḷavum* **tr.** let **water made available for irrigation during drought** be used for irrigating this land ; *S.I.I.* XVII, No. 732, p. 350, l. 7, Tirumullaivāyal, Saidapet Tq., Chingleput Dt., T. Nadu St. **Dy.** Saṅgama, Harihara II, Cy. yr. Prabhava = 1388 A.D.

aṛupitta (T. *vb.*), caused to be carved ; **text :** . . . . . *Kuṛṛaṉ* ***arupitta*** *adiṭṭāṇam* . . . ; **tr.** the basement was caused to be carved by Kuṛṛan ; *E.T.E.* No. 63, p. 409, ll. 2–3, Pugaḻūr, Karur Tq., and Dt., T. Nadu St. **Misc.,** in characters of 2nd cent. A.D.

aṛuppu (T. *n.*), harvesting ; **text :** (damaged) . . . . *kuṛuṇi nellu* ***aruppile*** *peṛṛu* . . . . *aṇubhavippāṇāga* . . . ; **tr.** obtaining one *kuṛuṇi* (grain measure) of paddy on **harvesting** to be enjoyed ; *I.P.S.* No. 380, p. 257, l. 8 ; Iḍaiyāttūr, Tirumaiyam Tq., Pudukkōṭṭai Dt., T. Nadu St. **Dy.** Pāṇḍya, Vīrapāṇḍya, reg. yr. 21, in characters of 13th cent. A.D.

aṛuvadiṁbar (T. *n.*), agricultural guild of 60 members ; **text :** *Pandigoḷavan achaḷapravṛitti-yindāḷutta . . . . gāvuṇḍa Nāṇiyammam-* ***aruvadiṁbargge*** *koṭṭa vyavasthe ;* **tr.** arrangements made for the **agricultural guild of 60 members** by *gāvuṇḍa* (village headman) Nāṇiyamma who was permanently administering the village called Pandigoḷa ; *K.I.* V, No. 4, p. 12, ll. 15–17, Hirē Handigōḷ, Gadag Tq. and Dt., Karn. St. **Dy.** Rāshṭr., Khoṭṭiga, Ś. 893 = 970 A.D.

aṛuvai vaṇigaṉ (T. *n.*), cloth merchant ; **text :** . . . . . *Veṇpaḷḷi* ***aṛuvai vaṇigaṉ*** *Eḷa Aṭṭan* ; **tr.** Eḷa Aṭṭṉ the **cloth merchant** from Veṇpaḷḷi ; *E.T.E.* No. 46, p. 381, l. 1, Aḻagarmalai, Melur Tq., Madurai Dt., T. Nadu St. **Misc.,** in characters of the 1st cent. B.C.

aruvaṇa (K. *n.*), tax levied on plough ; **text[1] :** . . . *basadige dānaśālege . . . . Mārasiṁghaiyyaṁ . . . . keṛeyaṁ biṭṭaṁ kiṛudeṛege ondu gadyāṇavaruvaṇa* . . . ; **tr.** Mārasiṁghayya donated to the charity house of the basadi a tank and a minor **tax levied on plough** aruvaṇa in gold ; *S.I.I.* XI, pt. i, No. 38, p. 24, ll. 7, 11, 13–14, Narēgal, Ron Tq., Dharwar Dt., Karn. St. **Dy.** Rāshṭr., Kṛishṇa III, Ś 872 = 950 A.D. ; **text[2] :** . . . . *Nēṛilakeṛeya naḍustaḷakaṁ pūrvvada tōṭakkaṁ hiriyarasaru koṁḍa maryyādeya* ***ṛuvaṇa*** *gadyāṇaṁ nālku* ; **tr.** the senior ruler **levied** the customary **tax on plough** from the land situation to the east of the garden from the centre of the Nēr̤ila tank; *K.I.* IV, No. 48, p. 101, l. 45, Maḍalūr, Hirekerur Tq., Dharwar Dt. Karn. St. **Dy.** Sēü of Dēv. Siṁghaṇa, Ś. 1169 = 1247 A.D.

aruvaṇamu (Te. *n.*), tax levied on plough ; **text:** (obscure) . . . . ***aruvanamu*** . . . . . . ; **tr.** tax levied on plough ; *S.I.I.* X, No. 211, p. 110, l. 18 ; Viśākhapaṭṇam, Vishakhapatnam Tq. and Dt., A.P. St. **Dy.** Chōḷa, Kulōttuṅga, in characters of 12th cent. A.D.

ar̤uvaṇapaṇa (K. *n.*), tax levied on plough in cash ; **text :** . . . . *ā mūr̤u mattargam ar̤uvaṇapaṇa voṁdu vīsam* ; **tr.** for these three mattars of land, a **tax** of one *vīsa* was **levied in cash on ploughs** ; *S.I.I.* V, No. 848, p. 345, ll. 36–37, Hūli, Saundatti Tq., Belgaum Dt., Karn. St. **Dy.** Chāḷ. of Kal., Vikramāditya VI, Ch. Vi. yr. 7 = 1083 A.D.

āruvāra (K. *n.*), mortgaged land ; **text**[1] **:** *bāḷiṁda biṭṭuva gēṇige* ***āruvāra****da akki mūḍe 13* . . . . . ; **tr.** 13 *mūḍes* (a grain measure) of rice realised by the mortgagee from the mortgager out of the seed sown on **mortgaged land** ; *S.I.I.* VII, No. 387, p. 244, ll. 52–53; Chauḷikēri, Udupi Tq. and Dt., Karn. St. **Dy.** Saṅgama, Bukka I, Ś. 1294 = 1372 A.D. ; **text**[2] **:** *kōṭeyoḷage Hammu-bēhāriya keyya* ***ār̤uvāra****va māḍikoṇḍa* . . . . *seṭṭikāra* . . ; **tr.** the seṭṭikāra who had taken on lease the **mortgaged land** within the fort belonging to Hammu-bēhāri on condition of sharing the produce between land lord and tenant ; *S.I.I.* VII, No. 389, p. 247, ll. 40–42 ; Hosakēri, Udupi Tq. and Dt., Karn. St. **Dy.** Tuḷuva, Sadāśivarāya, Ś. 1491 = 1569 A.D.

aṁtarāruvāra (K. < Skt. *n.*), sub-lease ; **text :** . . . . ***aṁtarāruvāra****vāgi koṭa va ga 20* . . . ; **tr.** 20 *va ga* (varaha gadyāṇa) to be paid as a **sub-lease** amount ; *S.I.I.* IX, pt. ii, No. 540, p. 558, l. 7 ; Basarūru, Kundapur Tq., Udupi Dt., Karn. St. **Dy.** Tuḷuva, Achyutarāya, Ś. 1453 = 1531 A.D.

āruvara-patra (K. *n.*), lease-deed ; **text :** . . . . *Kaṁdāürada adhivāsada mūlada sarvasvavū yī maṭhake koṭa* ***āruvāra****-patra* . . . . ; **tr.** the **lease-deed** pertaining to the full ownership of the land given to this maṭha located in the village of Kaṁdāüra ; *S.I.I.* IX, pt. ii, No. 446, p. 456, ll. 47–48 ; Basarūr, Kundapur Tq., Udupi Dt., Karn. St. **Dy.** Saṅgama, Dēvarāya, Ś. 1358 = 1436 A.D.

āruāravahiḍidabāḷu (K. *n.*), land taken on lease ; **text :** . . . . *Nāraṇa-hebbārana kayyali* ***ār̤uvārava hiḍida bāḷu*** *kabbayala oḷage bayalu gade* . . . ; **tr.** the open field and wet **land** situated in Kabbayalu **taken on lease** from the hands of Nāraṇahebbāra; *S.I.I.* IX, pt. ii, No. 452, p. 462, l. 20 ; Basarūru, Kundapur Tq., Udupi Dt., Karn. St. **Dy.** Saṅgama, Mallikārjuna, Ś. 1373 = 1450 A.D.

aruvaṭṭigaru (K. *n.*), persons in-charge of alms-shed ; **text :** . . . . *nagaraṁgaḷu tāvu tegeda yeleya hēriṁgaṁ adarind****aruvaṭṭigaru*** *tegeda hērige nūrele* . . . . *biṭṭaru* ; **tr.** the *nagara* (an administrative body) gave one hundred leaves per bundle to the **persons in charge of the alms shed** out of the bundles of leaves collected by them ; *K.I.* V, No. 21, p. 83, ll. 53–54 ; Tērdāḷ, Jamkhandi Tq., Bijapur Dt., Karn. St. **Dy.** Chaḷ. of Kal., Vikramāditya VI, Ś. 1045 = 1123 A.D.

aruvi (T. *n.*), water fall ; ***aruvi****vaḻikku mēṟkkunōkki pōnda peruvaḻikku vaḍakku* ; **tr.** to the north of the main street proceeding to the west of the road leading to the **water fall** ; *S.I.I.* XIX, No. 91, p. 98, l. 13, Tiruviḷakkuḍi, Mayavaram Tq., Tanjavur Dt., T. Nadu St. **Dy.** Chōḷa, Parakēsarivarman, in characters of 10th cent. A.D.

asādhya (K. *n.*), income generated from land that is to be cultivated in future. ; **text :** . . *Mallapa Voḍeyaru paḍuva kēriya halaru seṭikārara kayyalu . . . . Mahādēvarige Belatūra . . . . ūralu aramanege saluva . . . .* ***asādhya*** *. . . . sahavāgi . . . . bāḷuvaṁtāgi . . . bāḷiyendu baresikoṭṭa śilāśāsana . . . .* ; **tr.** a stone edict engraved to the effect that Malapa Voḍeya handed over to the *halaru seṭikāraru* on behalf of the god Mahādēva, the village of Belatūru with the stipulation registered in stone edict that the receipients will continue to enjoy all incomes including **income generated from land that is to be cultivated in future** ; *S.I.I.* IX, pt. ii, No. 479, p. 494, ll. 7–9, 13–14 ; Basarūru, Kunadapur Tq., Udupi Dt., Karn. St. **Dy.** Sāḷuva., Narasiṁha, Ś. 1433 = 1510 A.D.

asaga (K. *s.a. agasa, n.*), washerman ; **text[1] :** . . . . *daṁḍanāyakaṁ Kēsimayyaṁ Mattūra tuṟuvaṁ koḷuvalli* ***asaga****ra Kāḷeya tuṟuvaṁ magurchchi . . . suralōka prāptanāda. . .* ; **tr.** when the general Kēsimayya was rustling the cattle of Mattūra the **washerman** Kāḷeya died after successfully recovering the cattle ; *K.I.* VI, No. 36, p. 89, ll. 3–6 ; Mattūru, Hirekerur Tq., Haveri Dt., Karn. St. **Dy.** Kal. of Kal., Sōvidēva, reg. yr. 6 = 1172 A.D.; **text[2] :** ***asaga****ra hoḷeya kālveyiṁ baḍagalu Kāvēridēviyiṁ mūḍalu . . . . .* ; **tr.** (land situated to) the north of the **washermen's** canal issuing from the stream and to the east of the goddess Kāvēri (river) ; *E.C.* (R) V, Kn., 112, p. 110, l. 7 ; Hampāpura, Krishnarajanagara Tq., Mysore Dt., Karn. St. **Misc.,** Ś. 1344 = 1422 A.D. ; **asagadeṟe** (K. *n.*), tax on the washermen's profession **; text:** . . *Dharṁmāpurada . . Kēśava dēvariṁge ā vūra . . . . . kuṁbāradeṟe asagadeṟe . . . . . nāvidadeṟe intinisaṟa teṟeyaru. . . . . biṭṭaru . . .* ; **tr.** incomes such as **taxes on the professions** of potters, **washermen**, barbers etc., were donated to the god Kēśava of the village Dharṁmāpura ; *E.C.* (R) IV, Hs. 24, p. 499, ll. 39–41 ; Dharmāpura, Hunasur Tq., Mysore Dt., Karn. St. **Dy.** Hoy., Narasiṁha I, Ś. 1084 = 1162 A.D. ; **asaga-poḻe** (K. *n.*), streamlet used by washermen ; **text :** (obscure) . . . . . . ***asaga poḻeya*** *kiṟubīḍim baḻiya puṇuse* ; **tr.** the tamarind tree near the smallhouse by the side of **streamlet used by washermen** ; *E.C.* (R) V, My. 102, p. 237, ll. 19–20 ; Mysore, Mysore Tq. and Dt., Karn. St. **Dy.** W. Gaṅga, Chāgipermmāḍi, in charathers of 8th cent. A.D.

asagara gadde (K. *n.*), land belonging to a washerman ; **text :** . . . . *ā kaṁṭhada mēlaṇa teṁginamara* ***asagara gadde*** *asagara hittilu* . . . ; **tr.** the Coconut tree grown above the raising ground, the paddy **field belonging to washerman** and the backyard of the house of washer man ; *K.I.* III, pt. I, No. 14, p. 45, l. 38 ; Bhaṭkaḷ, Bhatkal Tq. and Dt., Karn. St. **Dy.** Tuḷuva, Sadāśiva, Ś. 1467 = 1545 A.D. ; **asagara hittilu** (K. *n.*), backyard of the house of washerman ; **text :** . . *ā kaṁṭhada mēlaṇa teṁgina mara asagara gade asagara hittilu* . . . ; **tr.** the Coconut tree grown above the raising ground, the paddy field belonging to washerman and the **backyard of the house washer man** ; *K.I.* III, pt. I, No. 14, p. 45, l. 38 ; Bhaṭkaḷ, Bhatkal Tq., N. Kanara Dt., Karn. St. **Dy.** Tuḷuva, Sadāśiva, Ś. 1467 = 1545 A.D. ; **asagara ter̤ige** (K. *n.*), tax on washerman ; **text :** *Terakaṇāṁbeya bhaṁḍārakke saṁdu baruttida* ***asagara ter̤ige*** *nāyindara ter̤ige kuṁbāra ter̤ige gāṇada suṁka* . . . . *ēnuṁṭāda sarvva ter̤igeyanu Gōviṁdarājayagaḷu Triyaṁbaka dēvarige koṭṭa dharma śilāśāsana* ; **tr.** the edict of donation recording the grant of all revenue incomes from the treasury of Terakaṇāṁbe such as **taxes on washermen**, barbers, potters, oil mill, etc., by Gōvindarājaya to the god Triyaṁbakadēva ; *E.C.* (R) III, Gu. 136, p. 100, ll. 16, 18–19, 24–25, 27 ; Triyaṁbakapura, Gundlupet Tq. Mysore Dt., Karn. St. **Dy.** Tuḷuva, Kṛishṇadēvarāya, Ś. 1435 = 1513 A.D.

asagrayālu (Te. *n.*), a kind of tax ; **text :** . . . . *Pottapināṁṭi bhūmimīdanu* . . . . *kānika* . . . . *veṭṭi* . . . *asagrayālu modalayina pannulu* . . . . *Chokkanātha Perumāḷla sannidhini* . . . *istimi* ; **tr.** we granted to the god Chokkanāthaperumāḷ taxes such as tributes, free labour, **a kind of tax** called *asgrayālu* etc., levied on the lands in Pottapināḍu ; *I.A.P.* Cuddapah II, No. 38, p. 44, ll. 18–27 ; Nandalūru, Rajampet Tq., Cuddapah Dt., A.P. St. **Dy.** Saṅgama, Dēvarāya, Ś. 1355 = 1433 A.D.

asaṁtāya (K. *n.*), income from a tax called '*asatu*' ; **text**[1] **:** *Mahābalabhaṭṭaru* . . . . *Mādaṁṇagaḷa magaḷu Virupāyigaḷige ter̤uva* . . . . ***asaṁtāya*** . . . *koṭaru* . . . ; **tr.** Mahābalabhaṭṭa gave to Virupāyi the daughter of Mādaṁṇa, the revenue **incomes** such as those collected from **a tax called** ***asatu*** etc. ; *K.I.* VI, No. 62, p. 169, ll. 18–20 ; Babbarawāḍa, Ankola Tq., Karwar Dt., Karn. St. **Dy.** Saṅgama, Harihara II, Ś. 1324 = 1401 A.D.; **text**[2] **:** *Mahābalēśvaradēvara saṁnidhiyalli* . . . . . *ā sthaḷaṅgaḷa mēle terage mānyavāgi matāva* . . . . . ***asaṁtāya*** . . . *anyāya kāṇike* . . . . *muṁtāgi* . . . *biṭukoṭevu* . . . . ; **tr.** we granted to the god Mahābalēśvaradēva, revenue incomes such as income from a **tax called** ***asatu,*** punitive tax and tributes etc. ; *K.I.* VI, No. 70, p. 194, l. 38–40 ; Uḷavari, Ankola Tq., Karwar Dt., Karn. St. **Dy.** Tuḷuva., Sadāśivarāya, Ś 1473 = 1550 A.D.

asana (K. < Skt. *aśana, n.*), food ; **text :** . . . . .

*Koṭiganūra .... puṭṭidarthamaṁ ... Lakulēśvara paṇḍitara maṭhada tapōdhanarkkaṁ vidyārthigaḷ**asana**āchchādanakkaṁ .... naḍevadu .....* ; **tr.** from the revenue income collected from Koṭiganūru, the maintenance of the ascetics and the arrangements for the **food** and clothings for the students of the Lakuḷēśvarapaṇḍita maṭha is to be made ; *S.I.I.* IX, pt. i, No. 135, p. 119, ll. 11, 13, 15–17 ; Hūvinahaḍagalli, Hadagalli Tq., Bellary Dt., Karn. St. **Dy.** Chāḷ. of Kal., Vikramāditya VI, Ś. 993 = 1071 A.D.

aśana (K. < Skt. *n.*), food ; **text :** . . *Rudrapūjeya mūvaru brāhmaṇa bhōjanakke nitya stiti* ***aśana*** *tōya tuppa śāka majjige vīḷaya aḍike .....* ; **tr.** a permanent endowment for providing **food** for 3 brāhmaṇas after Rudrapūje along with water, ghee, vegetables, butter milk, betel leaves and arecanuts ; *S.I.I.* IX, pt. i, No. 377, p. 232, ll. 12–13; Kōṭakēri, Udupi Tq. and Dt., Karn. St. **Dy.** Saṅgama, Dēvarāya, Ś. 1338 = 1416 A.D.

aśaṅgādagaṇḍaṉ kōl (T. *n.*), measuring rod named after the title *aśaṅgādagaṇḍan* ; **text :** *Nallaperumāḷāna Oṟṟiaraśar tammoḍeya kāṇiāṭchiyāna Veḷḷānūrile* ***aśaṅgādagaṇḍaṉ****kōlālkkuḻi. Eṇṇūr* ; **tr.** eight hundred *kuḻi* (land measure) of land measured by the **measuring rod named after the title 'the unshakable hero'** was donated by Nallaperumāḷ *alias* Oṟṟiaraśar in Veḷḷānūr heriditarily owned by him ; *S.I.I.* XVII, No. 725, p. 346, ll. 5–7 ; Tirumullaivāyal, Saidapet Tq., Chingleput Dt., T. Nadu St. **Dy.** Saṅgama, Bukka II, Cy. yr. Pārthiva = 1406 A.D.

asatu (K. *n.*), a kind of tax ; **text**[1] **:** . . . . *Attimabbarasiyaru .... Lokkigoṁḍiyūra basadige pūjānimittadiṁ bēḍi paḍeda .... tōṁṭakke ....* ***asatu*** *modalāge sarva bādhā parihāraṁ.....* ; **tr.** all let and hindrances including the tax called ***asatu*** are exempted for the grove in Lokkigoṇḍi obtained by Attimabbarasi for performing worship etc. in the *basadi* ; *S.I.I.* XI, pt. i, No. 52, p. 42, ll. 66, 72, 74 ; Lakkuṁḍi, Gadag Tq. and Dt., Karn. St. **Dy.** Chāḷ. of Kal., Āhavamalla, Ś. 929 = 1007 A.D.

asavrayālu (Te. *n.*), a kind of tax ; **text :** . . *Pottapināṁṭi bhūmivāru ichchina dharmaśāsanaṁ. ....* ***asavrayālu*** *mōdalaina pannulu ... Chokkanātha Perumāḷḷa sannidhini ....* ; **tr.** the land owners of Pottapināḍu granted in the august presence of the god Chokkanātha Perumāḷ some **tax** incomes including ***asavrayālu***, etc. ; *S.I.I.* XVI, No. 31, p. 33, ll. 17–18, 20–21, 22–23 ; Nandalūru, Rājampet Tq., Cuddapah Dt., A.P. St. **Dy.** Saṅgama, Dēvarāya II, Ś. 1355 = 1433 A.D.

aśēsha mahājanaṁgaḷu (K. < Skt. *n.*), full quorum of the administrative body of a brāhamaṇa village ; **text :** *agrahāraṁ Nīrguṁdad aśēshamahājanaṁgaḷu mūnūrbbaru. ...* ; **tr. full quorum of the administrative body of the brāhmaṇa village** of Nīrgunda consisting of 300 members ; *S.I.I.* IX, pt. i, No. 141, p. 124, l. 21 ; Nīlagunda,

Harapanahalli Tq., Bellary Dt., Karn. St. **Dy.** Chāḷ. of Kal., Vikramāditya VI, Ch. Vi. yr. 4 = 1079 A.D.

ashṭabhōgatējasvāmya (K. < Skt. *n.*), eight types of privileges to be enjoyed by the owner of the granted land ; **text**[1] **:** *Kaṁtarikeyeṁba grāmamaṁ pūrvaprasiddhasīmasamanvitamāgi* ***ashṭabhōgatēja svāmya*** *sahitamāgi . . . koṭṭar. . . . .* ; **tr.** the village of Kaṁtarike with all its well recognised boundaries was granted along with the **eight types privileges to be enjoyed by the donee** ; *S.I.I.* IX, pt. i, No. 277, p. 299, ll. 35–38 ; Malkāpuram, Adavani Tq., Kurnool Dt., A.P. St. **Dy.** Chāḷ. of Kal., Sōmēśvara IV, Ś. 1106 = 1184 A.D. ; **text**[2] (Te. *n.*): *Jarivūṭi grāmānaku . . ashṭabhōga tēja svāmyatalumnu . . . Rāmayadēvuniki samarpistimi* ; **tr.** the village of Jarivūṭi was granted along with the **eight types privileges** to the god Rāma ; *S.I.I.* XVI, No. 38, p. 41, ll. 21, 27–29 ; Rāmāpuram, Gooty Tq., Anantapur Dt., A.P. St. **Dy.** Sāḷuva, Narasiṁha II, Ś. 1419 = 1497 A.D. ; **ashṭabhōga dēśa (tēja) svāmyaṅgaḷ ; text** (T. *n.*) **:** . . . . *Kākkūr . . . .* ***ashṭabhōga dēśa svāmyaṅgaḷ****akku dānādi vinimayaṅgaḷakku yōgymāga . . . .* **tr.** in keeping with the conditions governing the grants of lands, the eight privileges within Kākkūr were granted along with the village ; *T.A.S.* V, No. 4, p. 15, ll. 46–50 ; Tiruvanantapuram, Tiruvananta puram Tq. and Dt., Ker. St. **Dy.** Sētupati Rulers of Rāmnāḍ, Mutturāmaliṅga Vijaya Raṁganātha Sētupati, Ś. 1691, Kollam 945 = 1769 A.D.

ashṭamāṁśa (K. < Skt. *n.*), one eighth share ; **text :** . . . . *Nāgaladēviya aramanaeya pura dēvastānakkeū* ***ashṭamāṁśa****danitakkeū taṁma rāyasa prakāradale hākida śāsana ellekaṭṭu* ; **tr.** the boundary stone set up as per the royal order for **one eighth share** of land for the temple in front of the palace of Nāgaladēvi ; *S.I.I.* IX, pt. ii, No. 527, p. 543, ll. 2–3 ; Nāgalāpuram, Ponneri Tq., Chingleput Dt., T. Nadu St. **Dy.** Tuḷuva, Kṛishṇadēvarāya, Cy. yr. Sarvvadhāri = 1529 A.D.

āśirigar (T. < Skt., *n.*), Jaina ascetic ; **text :** *Chandiranandi* ***āśirigar*** *niśīdigai . . . . .* ; **tr.** the death bed of the **Jaina ascetic** Chandiranandi ; *E.T.E.*, No. 38, p. 473, ll. 3–4 ; Tirunātharkuṉṟu, Senji Tq., Villupuram Dt., T. Nadu St. **Misc.**, in characters of the 6th cent. A.D. ; **āśiriyaṉ** (T. < Skt. *āchārya*, *n.*), (a Jaina) preceptor ; **text :** *vaḷaṅgeḻutirunagar Madirai* ***āśiriyaṉ*** *. . . . .* ; **tr.** the Jain preceptor of Madirai, the sacred and prosperous city . . ; *S.I.I.* XIV, No. 45, p. 35, l. 2; Śittaṉṉavāśal, Kulattur Tq., Tiruchirapalli Dt., T. Nadu St. **Dy.** Pāṇḍya, Śrīvallavaṉ, in characters of 10th cent. A.D.

āśiriyam (T. < Skt. āśraya), refuge ; **text :** *viśaiyēndirarkku* ***āśiriyam*** *. . . . .* ; **tr.** the **refuge** for Viśaiyēndira . . . ; *I.P.S.* No. 582, p. 413, ll. 11–12 ; Pēyal, Kuḷattur Tq., Pudukkottai Dt., T. Nadu St., **Dy.** Pāṇḍya, Kulaśēkhara, reg. yr. 33 = 1301 A.D.

asivechchaṁ (Te. *n.*), tax on barber's razor ; **text:** ..... *Koṁḍōjunna Tiṁmōjunna manavi vinnapaṁ chēsukōni* ...... ***aśivechchaṁ*** *āṭapannu* .... *sarvamānyaṁ sēstimi* ... ; **tr.** we have exempted on the request of Koṁḍōja and Tiṁmōja, **taxes** such as the one levied **on the barber's razor**, āṭapannu, etc. ; *S.I.I.* XVI, No. 178, p. 184, ll. 13-14, 18-20 ; Taṁgēḍa, Palnad Tq., Guntur Dt., A.P. St. **Dy.** Tuḷuva, Sadāśivarāya, Ś. 1473 = 1551 A.D.

asti kaḍai (T. *n.*), fierce battle ; **text :** ..... *Pāṇḍiyaṉum Īḻattaraiyaṉum vandu Perumāṉ aḍigaḷōḍu vēḷūr* ***astikaḍai*** *śeyda ñāṉṟu* ; **tr.** on the day when the rulers of Pāṇḍya country and Īḻam came and waged **fierce battle** against the Perumāṉaḍigaḷ at Vēḷūr ; *S.I.I.* III, pts. iii and iv, No. 99, p. 232, l. 3 ; Tiruppāṟkaḍal, Walajapet Tq., N. Arcot Dt., T. Nadu St. **Dy.** Chōḷa, Parāntaka, reg. yr. 12 = 919 A.D.

āśupodumakkaḷ (T. *n.*), town guards ; **text :** .... ***āśupodumakkaḷ****aikkoḷḷumvari eṉṉaippandam uḷḷiṭṭa iṟaigaḷ* .... ; **tr.** taxes levied for the maintenance of **town guards** granted and oil for torch carried by them at night ; *S.I.I.* VII, No. 936, p. 458, ll. 8-9 ; Tirukkoyilūr, Tirukkoyilur Tq., N. Arcot Dt., T. Nadu St. **Misc.**, in characters of about 14th cent. A.D.

āśuvakkaḍamai (T. *n.*), a tax levied on weavers ; **text :** ... *Ulaguyyavandaperumāḷukku* .... *ivv-ūril* .... *taṟi-iṟai taṭṭārppāṭṭam* ***āśuvakkaḍamai*** *śakkirai kaḍai iṟai maṟṟum uḷḷaṉa* ... *nandāviḷakkukku* . . . *śelvadāga viṭṭēṉ* ... ; **tr.** I granted income from taxes such as on looms, goldsmiths, **tax levied on yarn merchants**, etc. for burning a perpetual lamp in the temple of the god Ulaguyyavandaperumāḷ of this village ; *E.C.* X, Kol. 28, p. 4, ll. 4-5, 7, 10-11, 13-14 ; Maḍivāḷa, Kolar Tq. and Dt., Karn. St. **Misc.**, in characters of about 12th cent. A.D.

āśuvatipērkkaḍamai (T. *n.*), tax on the community of weavers ; **text :** . . *Tiruppaṉṟikuṉṟil Nāyaṉār Paṉṟi āḷvārkku* .... *kōyiṟtēvaigaḷakkum Tiruppaṉikkum* ... *Śiṅgapura mudalaḍaṅga iṟailiyāga māvaḍai kuḷavaḍai* ***āśuvatipērkkaḍamai*** ... *maṟṟum iv-ellai uṭpaṭṭa samasta prāptigaḷum* . . *viṭṭōm* ... ; **tr.** We granted in favour of the god Paṉṟi Āḻvār of Tiruppaṉṟikuṉṟu the village of Śiṅgapura including the tax free grants therefrom such as *māvaḍai* (income from wild animals) *kuḷavaḍai* (tax on land.), **tax on community of the weavers**, etc. ; *S.I.I.* XVII, No. 253, p. 100, ll. 3, 4-5, 6-9 ; Śiṅgavaram, Gingee Tq., S. Arcot Dt., T. Nadu St. **Dy.** Pāṇḍya, Kulaśēkhara I, reg. yr. 30 = 1298 A.D.

āśuvikkaḍamai (T. *n.*), tax levied on weavers ; **text :** (damaged) . . . ***āśuvi-kkaḍamai*** *uḷḷitta kāśāyamum āḷamañji tēvaigaḷum* .... *Aṅgada-vallavarkku jīvitamāga viṭṭu kalveṭṭi kuḍuttēṉ* ; **tr.** I granted through this stone edict for the livelihood of Aṅgadavallavar, tax incomes in cash including the **tax on weavers** and forced labour. ; *S.I.I.*

XVII, No. 755, p. 360, ll. 2–3 ; Tiruppāṟkaḍal, Walajpet Tq., N. Arcot Dt., T. Nadu St. **Dy.** Chōḷa, Kulōttuṅga III, reg. yr. 30 = 1207–08 A.D. ;

āsuvigaḷ pērkaḍamai (T. *n.*), tax levied on community of weavers ; **text :** . . . *Tiruvattūrum Vayalūrum . . . . uḷḷiṭṭa ūrgaḷil veṭṭi . . . . arimukkai uḷḷiṭṭa. nellāyamum kāśāyamum* . . **āsuvigaḷ pērkaḍamai** *peṟiyiṟai uḷḷiṭṭaṉa eppērpataṉavum Tiruvattūr Uḍayaṉāyaṉārkku . . . viṭṭēṉ Śeṅgēṉi Ammayappan . . .* ; **tr.** I Śeṅgēṉi Amayyappan gave a grant of revenue income including the tax on paddy, tax in cash, **tax on the community of weavers**, tax on handlooms, etc. from the villages of Tiruvattūr, Vayalūr etc., to the god Tiruvattūr Uḍayaṉāyaṉār; *S.I.I.* VII, No. 103, p. 43, ll. 7–9, 10, 13–14 ; Tiruvottūr, Cheyyar Tq., N. Arcot Dt., T. Nadu St. **Dy.** Chōḷa, Kulōttuṅga III, reg. yr. 33, in characters of 13th cent. A.D.

āśuvi kāśu (T. *n.*), tax levied in cash on weavers; **text :** . . . . *Vaṇakōvareyaṉēṉ taṟi iṟai kāśum kaḍai iṟaiyum . . . .* ***aśuvi kāśum*** *. . . . uḍaiyārkku viṭṭu kalveṭṭiṉēṉ* ; **tr.** I Vaṇakōvareya donated taxes on handlooms, shops and **tax levied in cash on weavers,** etc., to the deity. . . .; *S.I.I.* VII, No. 912, p. 451, ll. 7, 8–10 ; Kīḻūr, Tirukkoyilur Tq., S. Arcot Dt., T. Nadu St. **Dy.** Chōḷa, Kulōttuṅga I, reg. yr. 33 = 1103 A.D.

aśvādhyaksha (K. < Skt. *n.*), Head of the cavalry; **text :** . . . . . . *mahāpradhānaṁ sarvādhikāri Hiriyabhaṁḍāri Huḷḷayaṁgaḷa maiduna* ***aśvādhyaksha****da heggaḍe Hariyaṇṇaṁ Kuṁbeyanahaḷḷiya dēvara māḍisi koṭṭa* ; **tr.** Hariyaṇṇa the **head of the cavalry** and brother-in-law of *mahāpradhāna* (*q.v.*) *sarvādhikāri* (*q.v.*) *hiriyabhaṇḍāri* (*q.v.*) Huḷḷayya got the image of the god made for the village Kuṁbeyanahaḷḷi ; *E.C.* II, Sb. 572, p. 358, ll. 30–32 ; Kuṁbēnahaḷḷi, Channarayaptna Tq., Hassan Dt., Karn. St. **Dy.** Hoy., Ballāḷa I, in characters of 12th cent. A.D.

āṭa kūṭa (K. *n.*), team of performers ; **text :** . . . *Kuruvattiyūroḍeyapramukhamahājanaṁ innūrvaru parama prēmadiṁdabhinava Sōmēśvara dēvaraṁga bhōgakkaṁ tapōdhanararāhāradānakkāmm* ***āṭa-kūṭa****kkaṁ . . . . koṭṭa . . . . mattar 15 . . . .* ; **tr.** the two hundred *mahājana* (an administrative body) an administrative body lead by the head of the town Kuruvatti donated with great affection 15 *mattar* (land measure) of land for the worship and services to the god Abhinava Sōmēśvara, for the feeding of the ascetics and for expenses for the **team of performers** ; *S.I.I.* IX, pt. i, No. 165, p. 158, ll. 41–43 ; Kuṟuvatti, Harapanahalli Tq. Bellary Dt., Karn. St. **Dy.** Chāḷ. of Kal., Vikramāditya VI, Ch. Vi. yr. 24 = 1099 A.D.

āṭapannu (Te. *n.*), a tax levied on performers ; **text :** . . *Koṇḍōjunna Timmōjunna manavi vinnapaṁ chēsukōni . . . . . .* ***āṭapannu*** *. . . . sarvamānyaṁ sēstimi . . .* ; **tr.** we have exempted on the request of Koṇḍōja and Timmōja, taxes such as the one levied on the barber's razor and

tax levied on performers, etc. ; *S.I.I.* XVI, No. 178, p. 184, ll. 13–14, 18–20 ; Taṁgēḍa, Palnad Tq., Guntur Dt., A.P. St. **Dy.** Tuḷuva, Sadāśiva, Ś. 1473 = 1551 A.D.

aṭhavaṇe (K. *n.*), department maintaining land revenue records ; **text :** . . . *śilāśāsana* . . . . . ***aṭhavaṇe****ya Nāgarasa na baraha* . . . . . ; **tr.** the stone inscription written by Nāgarasa of the **department maintaining land revenue records**; *S.I.I.* VII, No. 340, p. 194, ll. 58, 59 ; Chauḷikēri, Udipi Tq. and Dt., Karn. St. **Dy.** Saṅgama, Dēvarāya, Ś. 1353 = 1431 A.D.

aṭhavaṇe bhūmi (K. *n.*), revenue land ; **text :** . . . *dēvasthānada hōbaḷige badalu bhūmiyannu* ***aṭhavaṇe bhūmi****yalli viṁgaḍisi koṭṭu* . . . . . ; **tr.** as an alternative to the land belonging to the temple a portion of the **revenue land** was given ; *M.A.R.* 1938, No. 79, p. 199, ll. 13–14 ; Venkatayyachhatra, Chamarajanagar Tq. and Dt., Karn. St. **Dy.** Woḍ. of Mys., Kṛishṇarāja, Cy. yr. Saumya = 1849 A.D.

aṭhavaṇe hōbaḷi (K. *n.*), revenue division ; **text :** . . . ***aṭhavaṇe hōbaḷige*** *pārupatyegāra* . . . . ; **tr.** overseer of a **revenue division** ; *M.A.R.* 1933, No. 31, p. 201, l. 34 ; Śṛiṁgēri, Sringeri Tq., Chickmagalur Dt., Karn. St. **Dy.** Woḍ. of Mys., Kṛishṇarāja II, Ś. 1659 = 1737 A.D.

aṭika (Te. *n.*), a small earthen vessel with a wide mouth ; **text :** . . . . *Pratāpārjuna Dēvarājulu tamaku abhīshṭārthasiddhigānu śrī Narasimha nāthuniki* . . . . ***aṭika****lu 2* . . . *istimi* . . . ; **tr.** for the sake of the realisation of his desire Pratāpārjuna Dēvarāju granted to the god Narasiṁhanātha (among many other items) 2 **small earthen vessels with wide mouth** ; *S.I.I.* VI, No. 829, p. 318, ll. 7, 9, 11; Siṁhāchalam, Vishakhapatnam Tq. and Dt., A. P. St. **Misc.,** Ś. 1334 = 1412 A.D.

atiṭaṉam (T. < Skt. *adhishṭhāna, n.*), stone bed ; **text :** . . . *Teṉku Śiṟuppōśil Iḷayar śeyda* ***atiṭaṉam*** . . . . ; **tr.** the **stone bed** made by Iḷayar of Teṉku Śiruppōśil ; *E.T.E.* No. 13, p. 385, ll. 2–3 ; Śittannavāśal, Pudukkottai Tq. and Dt., T. Nadu St. **Misc.,** C. 1st century B.C.

atithi (K. < Skt. *n.*), unexpected guest ; **text :** . . . *Tripurāṁtakadēvara aṁgaraṁgabhōgakkaṁ mattam-āchāryya-tapōdhana adhyayana śuśrūshā-brāhmara aśana āchchhādanakkaṁ aivattunākku mānasara* ***atithi*** *abhyāgata tapōdhanara grāsakkaṁ* . . . *biṭṭa 44 ūrggaḷ* . . . . ; **tr.** 44 villages granted for the services to the image and entertainment of the god Tripurāṁtakadēva and for the feeding and clothing of the teachers, ascetics, students, the disabled, the brāhmaṇas and for feeding of 54 male guests, **unexpected guests** and ascetics ; *S.I.I.* IX, pt. i, No. 204, p. 203-04, ll. 26–31, 63–64 ; Tripurāntakam, Markapur Tq., Kurnool Dt., A.P. St. ; **Dy.** Chāḷ. of Kal., Vikramāditya VI, Ch. Vi. yr. 47 = 1122 A.D.

atithi mahattu (K. < Skt. *n.*), unexpected mendicant priests ; **text :** . . . . . *ī biḍāravu* ***atithi mahattu****gaḷige salūvudu* . . . ; **tr.** this residence is earmarked for

unexpected mendicant priests ; *E.C.* III, Nj. 380, p. 420, l. 11 ; Hura, Nanjanagud Tq., Mysore Dt., Karn. St. **Misc.**, in characters of 17th cent. A.D.

ātithya (K. < Skt. *n.*), hospitality ; **text :** *brāhmaṇi Māchiyabbeyaru tamma . . . . dēvālyakke Kottaḷi ainūra nālvaru . . . koṭṭa Lokkiya dravyadoḷage . . . . . dēvara nandadīvigege biṭṭa gadyāṇa 50 mattavar**ātithya**kke biṭṭa gadyāṇa 50* ; **tr.** from the money given to the brāhamaṇa lady Māchiyabbe by *Kottaḷi* (an administrative body) 504 she granted 50 *gadyāṇa* (gold coin) for a perpetual lamp to the god in the temple built by her husband and 50 *gadyāṇa* for **hospitality** expenses ; *K.I.* V, No. 17, p. 61, ll. 12–17 ; Tiḷivaḷḷi, Hangal Tq., Dharwar Dt., Karn. St. **Dy.** Chāḷ. of Kal., Vikramāditya VI, Ch. Vi. yr. 42 = 1118 A.D.

āṭśumai (T. *n.*), a load carried by a person ; **text :** . . . . . *palamaṇḍalaśarakkukku . . . oru **āṭśumai**kku oru māppaṇam . . . .* ; **tr.** for goods coming from different divisions one *mā* (land measure) of money was to be paid as wages for **a load carried by a person** ; *S.I.I.* VIII, No. 405, p. 215, l. 7 ; Dēvipaṭṭaṇam, Ramnad Tq. and Dt., T. Nadu St. **Dy.** Pāṇḍya, Kulaśēkhara, reg. yr. 2+1 = 1317 A.D.

ātta (K. *adj.*), acceptable ; **text :** . . . . . *ī bāḷimge āruvārake koṭa ātta kāṭi ga 450* ; **tr.** *450* **acceptable** *kāṭi ga* (*kāṭi gadyāṇa*, a purer gold coin) which was due as lease amount for this land was exempted ; *S.I.I.* IX, pt. ii, No. 424, p. 432, l. 40 ; Basarūru, Kundapur Tq. Udupi Dt., Karn. St. **Dy.** Saṅgama, Harihara, Ś. 1323 = 1401 A.D.

aṭṭadeṟe (K. *n.*), major tax ; **text :** . . . . . *Maṇeleyaraṁ Kanakagiriya tīrthada mēge basadiyaṁ māḍisi arasaradhyakshadoḷ Kanakasēna bhaṭarargge Tippe ūroḷāda **aṭṭadeṟe**yuṁ kuṟudeṟeyuṁ . . . . biṭṭan* ; **tr.** Maṇaleyara got constructed a Jaina temple on top of Kanakagiri and in the presence of the king made a gift of income from **major tax** and minor tax, etc. to Kanakasēna bhaṭarar ; *E.C.* (R) VII, Mu. 100, p. 313, ll. 8–11 ; Kuḷigeṟe, Maddur Tq., Mandya Dt., Karn. St. **Dy.** W. Gaṅga, Nītimārga, Ś. 838 = 916-17 A.D.

āṭṭai (T. *n.*), per year ; **text :** . . . *emperumāṉukku . . . . tiruppaṇigaḷukku . . . nam kīḻ paṇimakkaḷ **āṭṭai**kku iraṇḍu kāśu iḍakkaḍavargaḷāgavum* ; **tr.** (among many other annual grants) for the service of the god the servants working under us will remit 2 *kāśu* (coin) **per year** ; *S.I.I.* VIII, No. 291, p. 160, l. 7 ; Tiṭṭaguḍi, Vriddhachalam Tq., S. Arcot Dt., T. Nadu St. **Dy.** Chōḷa, Rājadhirāja II, reg. yr. 4 = 1168 A.D.

āṭṭaikaḍaṉ (T. *n.*), annual cess ; **text :** . . . *innilattil ellā payirgaḷ śeydukoṇḍum **āṭṭaikaḍaṉ** ūrkkālāl innellu irunūṟṟukalame koḷḷakkaḍavadāguvam* ; **tr.** all kinds of crops are to be produced on this land and two hundred *kalam* (a grain measure) measured by the town's standard measure is to be collected as **annual**

cess ; *S.I.I.* VII, No. 772, p. 391, l. 6 ; Tirumāṇikuḻi, Cuddalore Tq., S. Arcot Dt., T. Nadu St. **Dy.** Chōḷa, Vikramachōḷa, reg. yr. 11 = 1129 A.D.

āṭṭaikkōl (T. *n.*), annual cess ; **text :** . . . *Peruneydal āṭṭaikkoḷāl nālppadiṉ kalam nel* ; **tr.** 40 *kalam* (***a grain measure***) of paddy to be collected as **annual cess** from Peruneydal ; *T.A.S.* V, No. 12, p. 38, ll. 15–18, Peruneyil, (suburb of Cheṅganachery), Ker. St. **Dy.** Chēra, Kulaśēkhara kōyiladhikāri, in characters of 11th–12th cent. A.D.

āṭṭaikkoḷvār (T. *n.*), collector of annual cess ; **text :** . . . . *Iḍaiyīḍaṉ. . . . **āṭṭaikkoḷ**vārkku poṉṉumkūḍa daṇḍam paḍakkaḍaviyaṉ* ; **tr.** Iḍaiyīḍaṉ shall pay a fine of one *poṉ* (a gold coin) to the **collector of annual cess** ; *T.A.S.* V, No. 56, p. 178, ll. 2–4, Tirukkaḍittāṉam, Ker. St. **Dy.** Rulers of Travancore, Bhāskara Ravivarmantiruvaḍi, reg. yr 2+12, in characters of 11th-12th cent. A.D.

attāndira kkaṇakku (T. *n.*), accountant keeping track of the transfers of property ; **text :** . . . . ***attāndira-kkaṇakku*** *kaṉṉāyiram eḻuttu* ; **tr.** the signature of the Kaṉṉāyiram the **accountant keeping track of the transfer of property** : *T.A.S.* V, No. 66, p. 197, ll. 94–95, Kanyākumari, Kanyakumari Tq. and Dt., T. Nadu St. **Dy.** Nāyakas of Madurai, Viśvanātha Nāyaka, Kollam 782, Ś. 1529 = 1607 A.D.

āṭṭaipāḻ (T. *n.*), land lying fallow during any particular year ; **text :** (damaged) . . . *paṟampaṟaipāḻ āṭṭaipāḻ* . . . . ; **tr.** land lying fallow for generations and **land lying fallow during any particular year** ; *S.I.I.* IV, No. 525, p. 155, l. 21 ; Gaṅgaikoṇḍa chōḷapuram, Udaiyarpalayam Tq., Tiruchirapalli Dt., T. Nadu St. **Dy.** Pāṇḍya, Kulaśēkhara, reg. yr. 5 = in characters of 10–11th cent. A.D.

āṭṭaivāriyar (T. *n.*), annually constituted committee; **text :** . . . . *iññagarattu nagaramāḷvāṉum* ***āṭṭai vāriyarum*** . . . . *āṇḍudōṟum tiruviḻāchcheyda vaḷave kaṇakku kāṇbadāguvum* ; **tr.** the administrator of the town and the **annually constituted committee** of the town shall audit the accounts in connection with the celebration of annual festival . . . . ; *S.I.I.* III, pts. iii and iv, No. 128, p. 271, ll. 110–12 ; Madras Museum, Chennai Tq. and Dt., T. Nadu St. **Dy.** Chōḷa, Uttamachōḷa, reg. yr. 16 = 987 A.D.

āṭṭaivaṭṭam (T. *n.*), annual interest ; **text :** . . *Gōkarṇamahādēvarkku* . . . *Vāmaṉaṉ vaitta tuḷaippoṉ 1 ippoṉṉukku* . . . ***āṭṭaivaṭṭam*** *aṭṭakaḍavadu* . . . ; **tr.** an amount of 1 *tuḷaippoṉ* (a gold coin with a whole in centre) was endowed by Vāmaṉaṉ in the temple of Gōkarṇamahādēva on which an amount of **annual interest** was to be used for temple services ; *S.I.I.* XIX, No. 435, p. 225, ll. 3–9 ; Tirugōkarṇam, Pudukkottai Tq., Tiruchirapalli Dt., T. Nadu St. **Dy.** Chōḷa, Parāntaka I, reg. yr. 31 = 938 A.D.

attaiyār (T. *n.*), aunt/mother-in-law ; **text :** . . . *eṅgaḷ* ***attaiyār****kku naṉṟāga eḻundaruḷuvitta piḷḷai* ;

tr. the image of the deity which was installed for the well being of our **aunt/mother-in-law** ; *E.C.* X, Kol. 234, p. 42, l. 11–13 ; Kōlār, Kolar Tq. and Dt., Karn. St. **Dy.** Hoy., Vīra Rāmanātha, reg. yr. 37 = 1293 A.D.

atte (K. *n.*), aunt/mother-in-law ; **text :** .... *Vikramādityarasargge brāhmaṇa bhōjanadoḷage āṟu manushyara bhōjanada phalaṁ Vikramāditya-arasar**atte**gaḷu Kētabbarasiyargge* ... ; **tr.** out of the feeding of the brāhmaṇas from a grant made by Vikramādityarasa, the merit for feeding six brāhmaṇas will go to his **aunt/mother-in-law** Kētabbarasi ; *S.I.I.* IX, pt. i, No. 258, p. 275, ll. 32–34 ; Bāgaḷi, Harapanahalli Tq., Bellary Dt., Karn. St. **Dy.** Chāḷ. of Kal., Jayasiṁha II, reg. yr. 16 = 1153. A.D.

āṭṭēvai (T. < āḷ-tēvai, *n.*), tax on labourers ; **text :** .... *ivvūrkku .... āṭ-tēvai veṭṭi maṟṟum ēppērpaṭṭa viṉiyōgaṅgaḷum kaḻittu* ... ; **tr.** having exempted such **tax**es as the ones levied **on labourers** and free labour and all other taxes levied in that village ; *S.I.I.* VIII, No. 438, p. 229, ll. 18–19 ; Pirāṉmalai, Tirupattur Tq., Ramnad Dt., T. Nadu St. **Dy.** Pāṇḍya, Parākrama Pāṇḍya, reg. yr. 10, in characters of 11th cent. A.D.

āṭṭeṇḍam (T. < *āḷ-daṇḍam, n.*), punitive tax levied on servants ; **text :** .... *śīpādam tāṅgavārāda **āṭṭeṇḍam**um* ... ; **tr. punitive tax levied on servants** who do not present themselves for carrying the deity ; *S.I.I.* VII, No. 912, p. 451, ll. 8–9 ; Tirukkōyilūr, Tirukkoyilur Tq., S. Arcot Dt., T. Nadu St. **Dy.** Chōḷa, Kulōttuṅga I, reg. yr. 33 = 1103 A.D.

aṭṭilpēṟu (T. *n.*), privilege given under a gift deed ; **text :** .... *Peruneydal āṭṭaikkōlāl nālppadiṉ kalam nellum Peruneydal aramaiyum **aṭṭilpēṟ**āi tirukkai nanaichaṟuḷiyār* ; **tr.** 40 *kalam* (a grain measure) of paddy to be collected as annual cess from Peruneydal as a **privilege given under a gift deed** ; *T.A.S.* V, No. 12, p. 38, ll. 15–19, Peruneyil (suburb of Cheṅganachery), Ker. St. **Dy.** Chēra, Kulashēkhara kōyiladhikāri, in characters of 11th–12th cent. A.D.

aṭṭippeṟu (M. *n.*), privileges given under a gift deed ; **text :** ...... *Tiruvēṅgaḍa-nilaiy-āḻvārkku kaṟpitta ariśi nāṉāḻiyilum iruṉāḻi ariśichchōṟu Paḻḻiyāṇḍikku **aṭṭippēṟāga** ..... vaittukkoṇḍu varumāṟu kalveṭṭikkoḷga* ; **tr.** four *ṉāḻi* (a grain measure) of rice to be given towards the expenses of Tiruvēṅgaḍanilay-Āḻwār and that Paḻḻiyāṇḍi should received the same as gifts and **privileges given under a gift deed** ; *T.A.S.* IV, No. 5, p. 20, ll. 3–6 ; Śuchīndiram, Agasteesvaram Tq., Kanya-kumari Dt., T. Nadu St. **Dy.** Rulers of Vēṇāḍu, Kōdai-Kēraḷavarman, Kollam 320 = 1145 A.D.

ātulaśālai (T. < Skt. *n.*), hospital ; **text :** ***ātulaśalai**kku vēṇḍum kalamiḍukuśavaṉ* ; **tr.** the potter who makes pots for the **hospital** ; *Ep. Ind.* XXI, No. 38, p. 240, l. 46, Tirumukkūḍal, Madurantakam Tq., Chingleput Dt., T. Nadu St.

Dy. Chōḷa, Vīrarājendra, reg. yr. 5 = 1068.

āṭṭukāṇam (T. *n.*), tax on sheep ; **text :** *ivvūr peṟṟa parihāram* ***āṭṭukāṇam****um nāvidakkāṇamum vaṇṇārkāṇamum* ; **tr.** the exemptions enjoyed by this village include **tax on sheep**, tax on barbers, tax on washermen, etc. ; *Ep. Ind.* XXXVI, No. 20, p. 158, l. 118, Kuḻḻūr, Tanjavur Tq. and Dt., T. Nadu St. **Dy.** Pallava, Nandivarman II, in characters of 8th cent. A.D.

āvagegala (K. *n.*), earthen pot made by burning on the potter's kiln ; **text[1] :** *kumbhāṟaru .... āhāradāna naḍavaṁtāgi dānaśālege* ***āvagegala****na biṭṭaru* .. ; **tr.** the potters donated the **earthen pots made by burning on the potter's kilns** for feeding in the choultry ; *K.I.* V, No. 21, p. 83, l. 55 ; Tērdāḷ, Jamkhandi Tq., Bijapur Dt., Karn. St. **Dy.** Chāḷ. of Kal., Vikramāditya VI, Ś. 1045 = 1123 A.D. ; **text[2] :** *ā sthaḷadalaysāvaṁtaru* dēvaragghavaṇiya biṁdigege **āvagegala**na koṭṭaru ..... ; **tr.** the five *sāmantas* gave **earthen pot made from burning on the potter's kiln** for offering oblations to the god ; *K.I.* VI, No. 73, p. 212, l. 75 ; Saundatti, Saundatti Tq., Belgaum Dt., Karn. St. **Dy.** Raṭṭas of Saundatti, Lakshmidēva II, Ś. 1151 = 1228 A.D.

āvaṇam (T. *n.*), document ; **text :** ... *svāmibhōgam Tirumañjina nīraṭṭuvāṇukku innilaṅkālum* ***āvaṇam*** *śeydu .... kuḍuttōm* .... ; **tr.** we gave through a **document** a piece of land for the person who was supplying water for the ceremonial bathing of the god ; *S.I.I.* XIX, No. 131, p. 66, l. 3 ; Kumbhakōṇam, Kumbhakonam Tq., Tanjavur Dt., T. Nadu St. **Dy.** Chōḷa, Parakēsarivarman, reg. yr. 5, in characters of 10th cent. A.D.

āvaṇakkaḷam (T. *n.*), Registrar's Office ; **text :** (damaged) .... *emmiliśainda vilaiporuḷ aṉṟāḍu vaḷaṅguṅguḷigai 150 indappaṇam nūṟṟaimbadukkum vilaikuṟavara viṟṟa vilai* ***āvaṇakkaḷa****ttē kaipporuḷarakoṇḍu viṟṟu vilaipramāṇam paṇṇikuḍuttōm* ..... ; **tr.** as agreed upon between us 150 paṇam which was validly current as *guḷigai* (a type of coin) was fixed as the price for the land and the same was registered in the **registrar's office** to be handed over to the temple ; *S.I.I.* VIII, No. 438, p. 229, ll. 13–14 ; Pirāṉmalai, Tiruppattur Tq., Ramanathapuram Dt., T. Nadu St. **Dy.** Pāṇḍya, Jaṭāvarmaṉ Parākrama Pāṇḍya, reg. yr. 14, in characters of the 10th–11th cent. A.D.

āvaṇakkaḷari (T. *n.*), ; **text :** .... *inNāyaṉāṟkku viṟṟukuḍutta koḷvadāna emmilaiśainda vilaipporuḷ aṉṟāḍu naṟkkāśu 12000 ik-kāśu paṉṉīrāyiramum* ***āvaṇakkaḷari****yē ... kaichelavaṟakkoṇḍamayil* ..... ; **tr.** having got registered in the **registrar's office** the purchase of land by paying 12000 current **kāśu** (coin.) which was exempted from tax, as agreed upon between us, the said land was made over to the temple ; *S.I.I.* VIII, No. 289, p. 158, ll. 31–33 ; Tiṭṭaguḍi, Vriddhachalam Tq., S. Arcot Dt., T. Nadu St. **Dy.** Chōḷa, Rājarāja III,

reg. yr. 2 = 1242 A.D.

āvaṇakkaḷi (T. *n.*), **text :** .... *Tiurukkurakkuttuṟai Perumāṉaḍigaḷakku iṟaiyili dēvadānamāga viṟṟukuḍuttu ivvilaipoṟul nūṟṟaimbattaṟu kaḷañjēy eṭṭumañjāḍi poṉṉum* ***āvaṇakkaḷi****yey arakkoṇḍu innilam ... viṟṟu nilay āvaṇañjeydu kuḍuttōm...* ; **tr.** having donated to the god of Tiurukkura kkuttuṟai tax free land as *dēvadāna* (*q.v.*) after purchasing the same for 156 *kaḷañju* (a type of gold coin) and 8 *mañjāḍi* (a type of gold coin) of *poṉ* (gold.), the same was got registered in the **registrar's office** ; *S.I.I.* XVII, No. 636, p. 293, ll. 19–20 Śrīnivāsanallūr, Musiri Tq., Tiruchira- palli Dt., T. Nadu St. **Dy.** Chōḷa, Parāntaka I, reg. yr. 29 = 935–36 A.D. ; **āvaṇakkāṟaṉ** (T. *n.*), Registration Officer ; **text:** .. ***āvaṇakkāṟaṉum*** *Toḻilvāriyanum*; **tr.** the **Registration Officer**, Labour Superviser ; *Āvaṇam*, Vol. II, No. 3, p. 7, ll. 15–17 ; Samuddirapaṭṭi, Nattam Tq., Dindigal Dt., T. Nadu St. **Dy.** Chōḷa-Pāṇḍya, Vikrama, reg. yr. 26 = 1050 A.D.

āvaṇaōlai (T. *n.*), palm leaf document ; **text :** . ... *nilaṉ kālēkāṇiyum ... viṟṟu .... vilai* ***āvaṇa ōlai*** *eḻudi...* ; **tr.** having registered on **palm leaf** the sale of quarter *kāṇi* (a land measure) of land ; *S.I.I.* XIV, No. 19, p. 20, ll. 79–80, 83–84 ; Tiruppuna-vāśal, Arantangi Tq., Tanjavur Dt., T. Nadu St. **Dy.** Pāṇḍya, Jaṭāvarmaṉ Sundarapāṇḍya, reg. yr. 14, in characters of 8th century A.D.

avanāya (K. *n.*), excessive taxation ; **text :** ... *Kavatāḷada sīmeyalu aramaneyavarū* ***avanāya****va māḍalāgi* ***avanāya****ke aṁji nīvu samasta prajegaḷū sīmeyanu biṭṭu haṭa māḍi Māsaveya sīmege biṭṭu hōgi* ..... ; **tr.** all of you who were the inhabitants of the territorial division of Kavatāḷa, protesting the **excessive taxation** imposed upon you by the palace authorities migrated to the territorial division of Māsave ; *S.I.I.* IX, pt. ii, No. 554, p. 574, ll. 11–15 ; Kavutāḷam, Adavani Tq., Kurnool Dt., A.P. St. **Dy.** Tuḷuva, Achyutarāya, Ś. 1454 = 1533 A.D.

avaṉisurar (T. < Skt. *n.*), brāhmaṇas ; **text :** . ... *Kalikalushamaṟaṉīki aṟpamallā dravyam koḍutt****avanisurar*** *iḍarnīki* .... ; **tr.** having freed the Kali age from contamination and having given munificent wealth to the **brāhmaṇas** thus ridding them of their misery ; *S.I.I.* III, pts. iii and iv, No. 206 b, p. 463, ll. 25–27 ; Chennai, Chennai Tq. and Dt., T. Nadu St. **Dy.** Pāṇḍya, Śaḍaiyaṉ, in characters of 9th cent. A.D.

avasara (K. *n.*), palace official ; **text :** .... *Sāḷva Narasiṅgayyadēva mahā-arasugaḷa* ***avasara****da Aṁṇamarsaru Tiruvadiya Vīraṭa dēvarige koṭṭa dharmaśāsana*..... ; **tr.** the religious edict given to the god Vīraṭadēva by Tiruvadi Aṁṇamarsa, the **palace official** of Sāḷva Narasiṅgayyadēva mahā arasu ; *S.I.I.* IX, pt.ii, No. 463, p. 475, l. 2; Tiruvadi, Cuddalore Tq., S. Arcot Dt., T. Nadu St. **Dy.** Sāḷuva, Narasiṁha, Cy. yr. Vikṛiti = 1470 A.D. ; **avasaram** (T. *n.*), **text :** .... *Gavurādēvi avvaigaḷ* ***avasarattukku*** *irāyar* ....

Dēvarāya mahārāyar Tiruvaṇṇāmalai tānikarkku nirūpam ; **tr.** the order issued to the temple officials of Tiruvaṇṇāmalai by Dēvarāya Mahārāya to the **palace official** of Gavurādēvi avvai ; *S.I.I.* VIII, No. 160, p. 72, ll. 4–6 ; Tiruvaṇṇāmalai, Tiruvanamalai Tq., N. Arcot Dt., T. Nadu St. **Dy.** Saṅgama, Dēvarāya, Ś. 1359 = 1437 A.D.

avasaravattin̤ai (T. *n.*), tax payable to the palace officer ; **text :** .... *nall erudu nal er̤umai nar̤ kiḍā* .... ***avasaravattin̤ai*** *uṭpaṭṭa palavarigaḷum uṭpaḍa* .... ; **tr.** taxes on quality bulls, quality buffalows, quality goats, presentations to be given to the Palace official and including other taxes ; *S.I.I.* VIII, No. 349, p. 188, l. 3 ; Śēndamaṅgalam, Tindivanam Tq., S. Arcot Dt., T. Nadu St. **Dy.** Saṅgama, Dēvarāya, Cy. yr. Saumya = 1429 A.D.

avishēkakkaikkāṇi (T. *n.*), see under abhishēka-kaikkāṇi.

āvu (K. *n.*), cow/cattle ; **text :** . . . *Muniya gauḍana maga Nāyanagauḍa* ***āvu****ge kadi koṇḍu svarggastanadaṁ* ; **tr.** Nāyanagauḍa son of Muniyagauḍa laid down his life while retrieving **cattle** (from the enemies) ; *E.C.* (R). X, Ak. 131, p. 172, ll. 2–3 ; Puralahaḷḷi, Arasikere Tq., Hassan Dt., Karn. St. **Misc.,** in characters of 16th–17th cent. A.D.

āvuge (K. *n.*), tax on potter's kiln ; **text :** *āvuge anāya . . . sahitavāgi ēnu baṁdadū . . . arasugaḷu .... yiḷihi koṭṭa darma* ; **tr.** the king exempted from the grant **taxes** such as one **levied on potter's kiln**, punitive tax etc. ; *K.I.* III, No. 6, p. 12, ll. 44–47 ; Iḍaguñji, Honnavar Tq., Karwar Dt., Karn. St. **Dy.** Āḷupa, Sōmidēvāḷpēndradēva, Cy. yr. Sarvajit = 1348 A.D.

āvupaṁna (K. *n.*), agricultural produce ; **text :** *Bhīmēśvara. dēvara naṁdādīvigegam ā sthaḷada* ***āvupaṁna****daḍake lekka oṁdake .... biṭṭa hāga-oṁdu* ; **tr.** for burning a perpetual lamp etc., in the temple of the god Bhīmēśvaradēva on each arecanut, the **agriucltural produce** one *hāga* (a kind of coin) of money was donated ; *S.I.I.* IX, pt. i, No. 293, p. 315, l. 26 ; Nīlagunda, Harapanahalli Tq., Bellary Dt., Karn. St. **Dy.** Kal. of Kal., Bijjaḷa, Cy. yr. Chitrabhānu = 1162 A.D.

avvai (T. *n.*), respectful address for women ; **text:** ..... *Gavurādēvi* ***avvai****gaḷ avasarattukku irayar* .... *Dēvarāya mahārāyar Tiruvaṇṇāmalai tānikarkku nirūpam* .... ; **tr.** the order issued to the temple officials of Tiruvaṇṇāmalai by Dēvarāya Mahārāya to the palace official of the **respectful** Gavurādēvi ; *S.I.I.* VIII, No. 160, p. 72, ll. 4–6 ; Tiruvaṇṇāmalai, Tiruvanamalai Tq., N. Arcot Dt., T. Nadu St. **Dy.** Saṅgama, Dēvarāya, Ś. 1359 = 1437 A.D.

āya (K. < Skt. *n.*), revenue income ; **text**[1] **:** . . . . *Goravaghaṭṭada keḷage khaṇḍugavedeya gadde* . . . *biṭṭaru illi puṭṭid****āya*** *mūlasthānadēvara nivēdyakkaṁ khaṇḍasphuṭitajīrṇōddhārakkaṁ allade per̤arggum salladu* . . ; **tr.** the **revenue income** from the paddy field of the extent of being sown with 1 *khaṁḍuga* (a grain measure) of seed located at the food of a hill called Goravaghaṭṭa is donated for the worship and other services of the main deity in the temple and not be utilised by any one else. ; *S.I.I.* IX, pt. i, No. 291, p. 311, ll. 22–24 ; Hirehaḍagalli, Hadagalli Tq., Bellary Dt., Karn. St. **Dy.** Chāḷ. of Kal., Vikramāditya VI, in characters of 11th–12th cent. A.D. ; **text[2] :** . . . . *Koṭṭiganūralu huṭṭida phalavellavaṁ sakaḷ**ā**ya sahita tri-bhāgaṁ māḍidalliya dēvarggoṁdu bhāgava brāhamaṇa bhōjanakkeraḍu bhāgavā* . . . . *naḍeyisuvaru* . . . ; **tr.** the revenue income from the village of Koṭṭiganūru derived from all products was divided into 3 portions, one portion meant for the deity of that place and 2 portions meant for the feeding of brāhmaṇas ; *S.I.I.* IX, pt. i, No. 254, p. 269, ll. 38–41 ; Koṭnakallu, Hadagalli Tq., Bellary Dt., Karn. St. **Dy.** Chāḷ. of Kal., Jayasiṁha II, reg. yr. 11 = 1148 A.D. ; **text[3] :** . . . . *maṭhake pradhān**āya**vāgi naḍasuva akki* mu 1 . . . . ; **tr.** the main **revenue income** for the maṭha is one *mu* (**muḍi** = a grain measure) of rice ; *S.I.I.* VII, No. 333, p. 185, l. 26 ; Mūḍakēri, Udipi Tq. and Dt., Karn. St. **Misc.,** Ś. 1470 = 1548 A.D.

āyādāya (K. < Skt. *n.*), income (from taxes etc.) ; **text :** . . . *Bāchaladēviyaru* . . *Kalidēvar-aṁgabhōga-raṁngabhōgake* . . . . *gāṇavāri gāṇaṁprati māna 1 asagarokkalu nibandi hiḍiyade sīre 1 upina kāvalideṟe pratyēkaṁ paṇa 5 uppu koḷaga 5 int-ivu modalāgi **āyādāya** sahitaṁ* . . . . . ; **tr.** for the services to the image of the god Kalidēva and for His entertainment, Bāchaladēvi granted the **revenue income** from each oil mill at the rate of 1 *māna* (a liquid measure), 1 saree from the washermen without affecting their income for each of the *kāvali* (pan) of salt *5 paṇas* (a coin denomination) *5 koḷaga* (a grain measure) of salt, etc. . . . ; *S.I.I.* IX, pt. i, No. 145, p. 128, ll. 25, 36–38, 39 ; Bāgaḷi, Harapanahalli Tq., Davanagere Dt., Karn. St. **Dy.** Chāḷ. of Kal., Vikramāditya VI, Ch. Vi. yr. 4 = 1079 A.D.

āyam (T. < Skt.), revenue income ; **text[1] :** . . . . *Tiruvuḷḷiyūr Īśvara bhaṭṭārarkku ūrōm Uḷḷiyūril koḷḷa uḍeya **āyam** . . . . Uḷḷiyūrāre śrīkōyil tirumaikkāppārāgavum* . . . ; **tr.** the inhabitants of the village Uḷḷiyūr granted to the god Īśvarabhaṭṭārar of that village the **income (from taxes etc.)** from that place and the inhabitants themselves will protect this grant ; *S.I.I.* VI, No. 324, p. 155, ll. 1–2, 4 ; Uttaramallūr, Madurantakam Tq., Chingleput Dt., T.N. St. **Dy.** Rāshṭr., Kṛishṇa III, reg. yr. 23 = 962 A.D. ; **text[2] :** . . . . *Tiruvēṅgaḍam uḍaiyāṉ* . . . . *Tiruvārādanaikkum śeñjikkuḷ naḍakkiṟa śukkiṟavāra śandai **āyam**mum Poṉpaṟṟigiṟāmaṁ oṉṟum* . . *naḍakkumbaḍikku kaṭṭaḷaiyiṭṭa śilāśāsanam*; **tr.** stone edict containing the order of the grant of the **revenue income** on weekly markets held on Fridays, the village of Poṉpaṟṟi (a number of other gifts are also recorded) for the worship of the god of Tiruvēṅgaḍam; *S.I.I.* XVII, No. 263, p. 105, ll. 3, 5, 9 ; Ginjee, Ginjee Tq., S. Arcot Dt., T. Nadu St. **Dy.** Tuḷuva, Sadāśiva, Ś. 1472 = 1550 A.D.

āyamu (Te. < Skt. *n.*), revenue income ; **text :** . . . *Divi Gaṇapatīśvara śrī Mahādēvaraku padinenimidi vishayamula ubhaya nānādēśiyu Naṅgēgaḍḍanichhina* ***āyamu*** *kalamunam pedda chinnamu* . . . . . ; **tr.** to the god Mahādēva of the Gaṇapatīśvara temple at Divi, the members of the merchant guild called Ubhayanānādēśi of the eighteen districtcts gave at Naṅgegaḍḍa the **revenue income** of the large coin of gold ; *Ep. Ind.* III, No. 15, p. 89, ll. 123–24, Gaṇapēśvaram, Masulipatnam Tq., Krishna Dt., A.P. St. **Dy.** Kākatīya, Gaṇapati, Ś. 1153 = 1231 A.D.

āyavargam (T. < Skt. *n.*), a group of revenues incomes ; **text :** (damaged) . . *aṉaittu* ***āyavargaṁ-gaḷum*** ; **tr.** all **groups of revenue incomes** ; *S.I.I.* XVII, No. 759, p. 362, l. 3, Tiruppāṟkaḍal, Walajapet Tq., N. Arcot Dt., T. Nadu St. **Dy.** Pāṇḍya, Sundarapāṇḍya I, reg. yr. 14 = 1264 A.D.

āyagāṟa (K. < Skt. *n.*), hereditary village servants/officials ; **text :** . . . (damaged) . *naṁma ūra prajegaḷu āyagāṟu muṁtāgi* ; **tr.** inhabitants and hereditary village servants/officials and others of our village ; *S.I.I.* IX, pt. ii, No. 528, p. 544, l. 31, Hāvinahāḷ Vīrāpura, Bellary Tq. and Dt., Karn. St., **Dy.** Tuḷuva, Kṛishṇadēvarāya, Ś. 1450 = 1529 A.D.

āyagāra (K. < Skt. *n.*), hereditary village servants/officials ; **text :** . . . *śānubhōgaru nāḍigaru 12 maṁdi āyagāraru* ; **tr.** Village Head, the head of the sub division and 12 heriditary village servants ; *E.C.* XI, No. 25, p. 253, ll. 63–64, Saṁtegōvi, Molakālmuru Tq., Chitradurga Dt., Karn. St. **Misc.,** Ś. 1587 = 1665 A.D.

ayanadīvige (K. < Skt. *n.*), lamp that goes on burning till the end of solstice ; **text :** . . . *udayapariyārara* ***ayana*** *dīvigegū dēvarige mālegū kūḍi haṁneraḍu hoṁnnanū. daṇiyara kayalū tandu koḍuvaru.* . . ; **tr.** 12 *hoṁnu* (gold coin) to be handed over to the owner for the **lamp that goes on burning until the end of a solstice** and for the garland of the deity ; *S.I.I.* IX, pt. ii, No. 407, p. 413, ll. 16–19, Kōṭēśvara, Kundapur Tq., Udupi Dt., Karn. St. **Dy.** Saṅgama, Bukka I, Ś. 1287 = 1364 A.D.

āyakaṭṭu (Te. *n.*), irrigated land in the vicinity of a water reservoir ; **text :** *ayakaṭni maḍisthaḷam* . . . ; **tr.** demarkated irrigated land in the vicinity of a water reservoir ; *I.A.P.* Cuddapah II, No. 84, p. 104, l. 21 ; Vanipeṁṭa, Proddatur Tq., Cuddapah Dt. , A.P. St. **Dy.** Tuḷuva, Kṛishṇadēvarāya, Ś. 1443 = 1521 A.D.

āyamēralu (Te. *n.*), portions of crop assigned at harvest time ; **text :** . . . *Tirumalareḍḍiṁgāru* . . . *Parachūri* . . . . . *vidvajjana mahajanālakunu ichchina* . . . . *vṛitti kshētralaku* . . . . ***āyamēralu*** . . . . . ; **tr.** Tirumalareḍḍi remitted all the taxes payable on **portions of crop assigned at harvest**

time to the learned *mahajana* (a local administrative body of the brāhmaṇa settlement) of the village Parachūru ; *S.I.I.* X, No. 586, p. 324, ll. 2, 4–5, 8–9 ; Parachūru, Bapatla Tq., Guntur Dt., A.P. St. **Misc.**, Ś. 1370 = 1448 A.D.

ayappaḍai (T. < Skt. *haya* + Tamil *paḍai*), cavalry ; **text :** (obscure) . . . ***ayappaḍai*** . . . ; **tr.** . . . cavalry . . . . ; *S.I.I.* VII, No. 1048, p. 506, l. 3 ; Kuḷambandal, Cheyyar Tq., N. Arcot Dt., T. Nadu St. **Dy.** Chōḷa, Rājādhirāja I, in characters of 11th cent. A.D.

aydondi (K. *n*.), 1/5th of tax ; **text :** (obscure) . . . . *Arasaṇṇaṁ* ***aydondi*** . . . . *biṭṭaṁ* . . . . ; **tr.** Arasaṇṇa exempted **1/5th of tax** ; *E.C.* (R) V, T. N. 146, p. 554, ll. 7–8 ; Vijayapura, T. Narasipura Tq., Mysore Dt., Karn. St. **Dy.** W. Gaṅga, Eṟeyappa, in characters of 9th cent. A.D.

ayigaṁḍuga (K. *n*.), five khaṁḍugas ; **text :** . . . ***ayigaṁḍuga*** *gadde* . . . . ; **tr.** paddy field of the extent of being sown with five *khaṁḍuga* (a grain measure) of seeds ; *E.C.* IX, Bng. 127, p. 48, l. 31, Koḍigehaḷḷi, Bangalore Tq. and Dt., Karn. St. **Dy.** Saṅgama, Dēvarāya, Ś. 1353 = 1431 A.D.

ayguḷa (K. *n*.), 5 *koḷaga* (a grain measure) ; **text:** . . . . *arasuṁ ūruṁ iḻdu* ***ayguḷa*** *kaḻaniyum koṭṭodu* . . . . ; **tr.** the king and the inhabitants of the village jointly gave paddy field of the extent of being sown with **5 *koḷaga* of seeds** ; *E.C.* X, Kol. 233, p. 56, ll. 6–8, : Mēdutaṁbihaḷḷi, Kolar Tq. and Dt, Karn. St. **Dy.** Noḷ. Pal, Noḷaṁbādhirāja, in characters of 9th century A.D.

ayigayi (K. *n*.), five arms' length ; **text :** (obscure) . . . . *hittilavu mūḍaluṁ paḍuvaluṁ* ***ayigayi*** *agalaṁ* . . . . ; **tr.** backyard measuring **five arms' length** from east to west ; *S.I.I.* XV, No. 233, p. 289, l. 77; Mangundi, Dharwar Tq. and Dt., Karn. St. **Dy.** Later Kadambas, Jayakēśi III, Cy. yr. Dundubhi = 1203 A.D.

ayiguḷa (K. *n*.), five times of a grain measure called *kuḷa* ; **text**[1] **:** . . . . *Kūchibhaṭṭara makkaḷu Mallijōyisarige . . . yereyalu gadde bījavari* ***ayiguḷa*** . . . . ; **tr.** black soil field of the extent of being sown with **five times of a grain measure called kuḷa** of seeds was given to Mallijōyisa son of Kūchibhaṭṭa ; *S.I.I.* IX, pt. ii, No. 440, p. 450, ll. 59–60 ; Rajabavanahaḷḷi, Harapanahalli Tq., Bellary Dt., Karn. St. **Dy.** Saṅgama, Dēvarāya, Ś. 1341 = 1419 A.D. ; **text**[2] **:** (damaged) . . *Chikkatiṁmapayanavaru* . . . . ***ayiguḷa*** *kshētravanu . . . koṭṭaru* . . ; **tr.** Chikkatiṁmapaya donated land to the extent of being sowed with five times of a grain measure called *kuḷa* of seeds ; *S.I.I.* IX pt. ii, No. 542, p. 561, l. 13 ; Chippagiri, Aluru Tq. Bellary Dt., Karn. St. **Dy.** Tuḷuva, Achyutarāya, Cy. yr. Khara = 1531 A.D.

āyiram aṟunūṟṟuvar (T. *n*.), administrative body of one thousand six hundred members ; **text :** . . . *Kulaśēkara chakkiravarttigaḷ* . . . . *naṉaichcharuḷa nāṉgu taḷiyum****āyiram aṟunūṟṟuvarum*** . . . . *kūḍiyirukka* . . . . . ; **tr.** when the emperor Kulaśekara was seated along with the four assemblies and the **administrative body of one thousand six hundred members** ; *T.A.S.* V, No. 13, pp. 44–45, ll. 15–17, 41–47, 56–57 ; Kollam, Tiruvalla Tq., Padma nabhapuram Dt. Ker. St. **Dy.** Chēra, Kulaśēkhara-chakravartti, Kollam 278, Ś. 1025 = 1103 A.D.

āyirattu ayinūṟṟuvar (T. *n.*), merchant guild of one thousand five hundred members ; **text** : . . . . *āmaṇakkaṁkoṭṭai vaṇḍi oṉṟukku kāśu pattum* . . . . *maṟṟum eppērppaṭṭa śarakkugaḷakkum* . . . *śamaiya piḍipāḍu paṇṇikuḍuttōm* ***āyirattu ayinūṟṟuvar****ōm.* ; **tr.** the **merchant guild of one thousand five hundred members** gave a conventional fee for commodities received for trade including at the rate of 10 *kāśu* (a coin) for a cart load of castor seeds ; *S.I.I.* VIII, No. 442, p. 232, ll. 15, 22 Pirāṉmalai, Tirupattur Tq., Ramnathapuram Dt., T. Nadu St. **comm. gld.**, in characters of 11th–12th cent. A.D.

āyirattirunūṟṟuvar (T. *n.*), an administrative body of one thousand two hundred members ; **text** : *Kāvēriyile irundu tīrttham prasādittaruḷinapōdu* ***āyirattirunūṟṟuvar****um Jananāta* . . . *chaturvvēdi maṅgaḷattu mahāsabhaiyōm Jananātha. Viṇṇagara ālvārkku dēvadānamāgavum Śamaṇapaḷḷi* . . . *kuḍuttōm* ; **tr.** when the holy water from the river Kāvēri was used for consecration, the **administrative body of one thousand two hundred members** donated the village Śamaṇapaḷḷi to the deity Janaṇāthaviṇṇagara Āḷvār as *dēvadāna* (land gifted to the temple) ; *E.C.* (R) V, T. N. 68, p. 459, ll. 1–2 ; Bannūru, T. Narasipur Tq., Mysore Dt., Karn. St. **Misc.**, in Kannaḍa characters of 11th cent. A.D.

ayivadāne (*aivattu+hāne*) (K. *n.*), , fifty *hāne* (a grain measure) ; **text :** . . . *ayivadāneya chatusīme vivara* . . . ; **tr.** details of the four boundaries of (the land on which can be sown seeds to the extent of) **fifty *hāne*** ; *S.I.I.* IX, pt. ii, No. 517, p. 532, ll. 10–11 ; Basarūru, Kundapur Tq., Udupi Dt., Karn. St. **Dy.** Tuḷuva, Kṛishṇadēvarāya, Ś. 1447 = 1525 A.D.

aymattal (K. *n.*), five *mattar* (a land measure) ; **text :** . . . . *Kumbiseyaṁ* . . . . ***aymattal*** *keyyaṁ koṭṭar* . . . ; **tr.** **five *mattar*** of land at Kumbise was given ; *E.C.* VIII, No. 85, p. 34, ll. 5, 7–8 ; Kuṁsi, Soraba Tq., Shimoga Dt., Karn. St. **Dy.** Rāshṭr, Amōghavarsha I, Ś. 799 = 876 A.D.

aynūru sāviradavaru (K.), administrative body of one thousand five hundred ; **text** : . . *nālkūra* ***ayinūru sāviradavar****a voḍaṁbaḍike-inda* . . . . . *koṭṭa vṛittiya vivara* ; **tr.** details of the land given with the agreement of the body of **one thousand five hundred members** of four villages; *S.I.I* VII, No. 198, p. 93, ll. 7, 10 ; Mūḍabidure, Karkala Tq., Udupi Dt., Karn. St. **Dy.** Saṅgama, Virūpāksha, Ś. 1384 = 1462 A.D.

aynūrva svāmigaḷ (K. *n.*), five hundred members of the mercantile guild (of Ayyāvoḷe) ; **text** : . *Bhagavatiya makkaḷu* . . . . *eṁṭunāḍa padinaṟuvaruṁ*

Ayyāvoḷe-puravarēśvararappa ***ainūrva-svāmigaḷ*** . . . . . ; **tr.** the devotees of the goddess Bhagavati viz., the guild of sixteen of eight divisions and the **five hundred svāmīs** who were the lords of the town of Ayyāvoḷe, a **mercantile guild** . . . . ; *S.I.I* IX pt. i, No. 139, p. 122, ll. 30–32, Hoḷalu, Hadagalli Tq., Bellary Dt., Karn. St. **Dy.** Chāḷ. of Kal., Sōmēśvara II, Ś. 996 = 1074 A.D.

aysaṁbara (K. *n.*), five kinds of spices viz., as Pepper, Cummin seeds, Coriander seeds, Mustard and Fenugreek (menthy) ; **text :** . . *paradēśigaḷu aḷava tūguva* ***aysaṁbaraṅgaḷaluṁ*** *eṇisuva davasaṁ māṟidalli koṭṭa hoṁge hāga 1.* . . . ; **tr.** the outsiders who measure and weigh the **five kinds of spices** viz., Pepper, Cummin seeds, Coriander seeds, Mustard and Fenugreek (menthy) have to pay a tax of 1 *hāga* (a coin) per one *hoṁnu* (gold coin) when they sell these spices ; *S.I.I* IX, pt. i, No. 297, p. 324, ll. 44–45, Kurugōḍu, Bellary Tq. and Dt., Karn. St. **Dy.** Kal. of Kal., Śaṅkhavarma, Ś. 1099 = 1177 A.D.

aysāvanta (K. *n.*), group of five chieftains ; **text:** ***aysāvaṁtaru*** *dēvaragghavaṇiya biṁdigege āvagegalana koṭṭaru*; **tr.** a **group of five chieftains** donated a pot burnt on the potter's kiln for collecting the sacred water for anointing the god's image ; *K.I.* VI, No. 73, p. 212, l. 75 ; Saundatti, Saundatti Tq. Belgaum Dt., Karn. St. **Dy.** Raṭṭas of Saundatti, Lakshmidēva, Ś. 1151 = 1228 A.D.

āyudha kāryyam (M. *n.*) activities connected with weapons/implements ; **text :** . . . *Mahadēvar-kōvilil mēlkōyinmayum ūrāṇmayum sthānam echchēṟum* ***āyudha kāryyattin*** *naḍannukoḷḷumāṟum cheyga* ; **tr.** the *Kōyiṇma* (temple officials), *ūrāṇma* (village officials), *sthāna* (temple establishment) as well as all other kinds of **activities connected with weapons/implements** pertaining to the temple of the god Mahādēva ***shall be attended to***. . . ; *T.A.S.* IV, pts. i and ii, No. 15, p. 88, ll. 15–16 ; Āṟṟūr, Padmanabhapuram Dt., Kēr St. **Dy.** Rulers of Vēṇāḍu, Śrī-vīra-Iravi-Udayamārttāṇḍavarman, Kollam 426, Ś. 1173 = 1251 A.D.

āyurvaidya (K. < Skt. *n.*), physician ; **text :** . . . . ***āyurvaidyana*** *haravari 1 kkaṁ kuḷa mū 20* . . . . . ; **tr.** tax on the cultivable land owned by the **physician** levied at the rate of one *kuḷa* (grain measure.) in the form of 20 *mū* (*mūḍe*, a grain measure.) ; *S.I.I* VII, No. 348, p. 205, l. 24, Chauḷikēri, Udupi Tq. and Dt., Karn. St. **Dy.** Saṅgama, Dēvarāya, Ś. 1353 = 1431 A.D.

ayvadiṁbar (K. *n.*), administrative body consisting of fifty members ; **text**[1] : . . *Saraṭapurada* ***ayvadiṁbar*** . . . *tuppadeṟenuḷidōr* ; **tr. the administrative body consisting of 50 members** of Saraṭapura remitted the tax on ghee ; *S.I.I.* XI, No. 12, p. 8, ll. 12–13, Soraṭūr, Gadag Tq. and Dt., Karn. St. **Dy.** Rāshṭr., Amōghavarsha I, Ś. 788 = 867-68 A.D. ; **text**[2] : . . . ***ayvadiṁbara*** *sannidhānadoḷ* . . . . *svayaṁbhū Kalidēvasvāmi* *agrāsanada brāhmaṇara sattrakke yeleya pēṟiṁgeyoṁdu. vīsaṁ . . . biṭṭar . .* ; **tr.** in the august presence of the **body consisting of fifty members** one *vīsa* (toll-revenue) per one head load of betel leaves was granted for the feeding of *brāhmaṇas* in the choultry of the temple of Svayaṁbhū Kalidēvasvāmi ; *S.I.I.* IX pt. i, No. 168, p. 162, ll. 30–33, Bāgaḷi, Harapanahalli Tq., Bellary Dt., Karn. St. **Dy.** Chāḷ. of Kal., Vikramāditya VI ; Ch. Vi. yr. 28 = 1103 A.D.

āyvattokkalu (K. *n.*), body of fifty agricultural tenants ; **text :** . . . *Bhaṁḍāri Chavuṁḍamayyam . . . . Kariguṁdavaṁ svabhūmiyāge dhārepaḍedu āvūra Dāsagauḍanu ūr**ayvattokkaluṁ** muṁtāgi dēvarige biṭṭa bhūmi . . . .* ; **tr.** land donated to the god by Chavuṁḍamayya who had received Kariguṁda as his own property and Dasagauḍa of that place as well as the **body of fifty agricultural tenants** of the village and others ; *E.C.* (R) X, Ak. 244, p. 314, ll. 36–38, Gōviṁdapura, Arasikere Tq., Hassan Dt., Karn. St. **Dy.** Hoy., Vishṇuvardhana, Ś. 1059 = 1136–37 A.D.

ayya (K. *n.*), father/honorifix suffix to a male name ; **text :** *Kaḷiṁgabbegaḷa* ***ayya*** *Pallahāraki*; **tr.** Pallahāraki the **father** of Kaḷiṁgabbe ; *E.C.* XI, Dvg. 17, p. 72, l. 8 ; Kāḍajji, Davanagere Tq. and Dt., Karn. St. **Dy.** Rāshṭr., Kṛishṇa III, Ś. 809 = 887 A.D.

ayyaṁgaḷ (K. *n.*), respectful suffix attached to male names ; **text :** *śrīmat Anantavīr**ayyaṁgaḷ*** ; **tr.** the illustrious Anantavīr**ayyaṁgaḷ** ; *I.A.* VI, No. 1, p. 102, l. 11 ; Perggūr, Kiggaṭnāḍu Tq., Kodagu Dt, Karn. St. **Dy.** W. Gaṅga, Satyavākya, Ś. 780 = 858 A.D.

ayyaṉmār (T. *n.*), elders of the brāhmaṇa community ; **text :** *ivviḷakku rakshippār Tiruchchuḻiyal* ***ayyaṉmār*** ; **tr.** the provision for this lamp is to be protected by the **elders of the *brāhmaṇa* community** of Tiruchchuḻiyal ; *S.I.I.* XIV, No. 79, p. 51, ll. 8–9 ; Paḷḷimaḍam, Aruppukkottai Tq., Ramanathapuram Dt, T. Nadu St. **Dy.** Pāṇḍya, Vīrapāṇḍya, reg. yr. 3+4 = 946 A.D.

ba (K. *n.*), grain and liquid measure = *baḷḷa* or *baṭṭalu* (a vessel) ; **text :** . . . . *akki* . . . *hesaru* . . . *tuppa mosaru* ***ba*** *1 aḷe* . . . *chhatrakke biṭṭaru* . . . ; **tr.** gave to the alms-house 1 ***ba*** of rice, green gram, ghee and curd . . . ; *S.I.I.* IX, pt. i, No. 245, p. 250, ll. 33–34 ; Chaṭnahaḷḷi, Harapanahalli Tq., Bellary Dt., Karn. St. **Dy.** Chāḷ. of Kal., Jagadēkamalla II, reg. yr. 9 = 1146 A.D.

bachchalu (K. *n.*), drain channel ; **text**[1] **:** . . . *dharmada bāḷa vivara* . . . . . ***bachchala*** *baḍagaṇa gaddeya bayalu* . . . . . ; **tr.** the details of the donated land . . . . the paddy field to the north of **drain channel** ; *S.I.I.* VII, No. 363 , p. 219, ll. 16–17 ; Maṇigārakēri, Udupi Tq. and Dt., Karn. St. **Dy.** Saṅgama, Harihararāya, Ś. 1317 = 1395 A.D. ; **text**[2] **:** . . . *Magavaṁṇa Ōjana gaḍiyiṁdaṁ baḍagalu harida* ***bachchal****iṁdaṁ* . . . *mūḍalu* . . . . ; **tr.** the paddy field to the east of the **drain channel** running north of the boundary of the field of Magavaṁṇa Ōja ; *S.I.I.* VII, No. 365, p. 221, ll. 15–16 ; Maṇigarakēri, Udupi Tq. and Dt., Karn. St. **Dy.** Saṅgama, Dēvarāya, Ś. 1342 = 1420 A.D.

bachchala bāḷu (K. *n.*), land cultivated with drain water ; **text :** . . . . *arasana* ***bachchala bāḷ****inalu* . . . . *mūḍe 150* . . . ; **tr.** 150 *mūḍe* (grain measure.) from the **land irrigated by the** king's **drain channel** ; *S.I.I.* VII, No. 330 , p. 180, ll. 29–30 ; Mūḍakēri, Udupi Tq. and Dt., Karn. St. **Dy.** Saṅgama, Bukkarāya II, Ś. 1281 = 1359 A.D.

bachchala-tōṭa (K. *n.*), grove land fed by the drain channel; **text :** . . . . ***bachchala*** *tōṭadiṁda ga 44* . . . . . ; **tr.** 44 *ga* (*gadyāṇa*, gold coin) from the **grove irrigated by the drain channel** ; *S.I.I.* VII, No. 330, p. 180, l. 34 ; Mūḍakēri, Udupi Tq. and Dt., Karn. St. **Dy.** Saṅgama, Bukkarāya II, Ś. 1281 = 1359 A.D.

bāchiviḍiya gaḷe (K. *n.*), land measure of the length of the handle of the carpenter's adze ; **text :** . . . . *Pārśvadēvargge* . . . . *samastaprajegaḷuṁ biṭṭa* . . . *vṛitti* . . . . ***bāchiviḍiya gaḷe****yiṁdaṁ kaṁba nālvattu* . . . . ; **tr.** to Pārśvadēva was granted by all the subjects forty *kaṁba* (land measure) of land measured by the **land measure of the length of the handle of the carpenter's adze ;** *E.C.* (R) X, Ak. 268, pp. 335–36, ll. 42, 44, 46 ; Bandūru, Arsikere Tq., Hassan Dt., Karn. St. **Dy.** Hoy., Vīra Ballāḷa II, Ś. 1091 = 1168–69 A.D.

bāchiviḍiya ghaḷe (K. *n.*), **text :** . . . ***bāchiviḍiya ghaḷe****yalu mattaru 6* . . . . ; **tr.** 6 *mattaru* (land measure) by the **land measure of the length of the handle of the carpenter's adze ;** *S.I.I.* XV, No. 164, p. 210, l. 37 ; Kundagōḷ, Hungund Tq., Bijapur Dt., Karn. St. **Dy.** Sēü. of Dēv., Siṁghaṇa, reg. yr. 21 = 1220 A.D.

bāchiviḍiya kōlu (K. *n.*), measuring rod of the length of the handle of the carpenter's adze ; **text :** . . . . *Biṭṭiyaṇa Heggaḍeyuṁ mūvaru gavuḍugaḷuṁ samasta prajaegaḷum mukhyavāgi ā ūra hiriya keṟeya keḷage* ***Bāchiviḍiya kōlalu*** *kaṁba 1* . . . . . *biṭṭa datti* ; **tr.** Biṭṭiyaṇṇa Heggaḍe, the three village headmean and all the subjects together gave as a grant 1 *kaṁba* of land measured by the **measuring rod of the length of the handle of the carpenter's adze** ; *E.C.* (R) VIII, Hn. 106, p. 316, ll. 36–38; Kittanakere, Holenarasipura Tq., Hassan Dt., Karn. St. **Dy.** Hoy., Ballāḷa II , Ś. 1095 = 1173 A.D.

bāḍa (K. *n.*), village ; **text**[1] : . . . . *daṇḍanāyaka Tikaṇṇa pramukha leṁka sāsirvaruṁ Armmeḷe Nellikudiru Sonna Poḻalguṁde Sūgūru Mōriṁgēṟi modalāgāṟumbāḍamuman aṇugajīvitavāgi* . . . *āḷuttaṁ* . . . . ; **tr.** while the thousand royal devotees led by *daṇḍanāyaka* Tikaṇṇa were administering the group of six **villages** Armmeḷe, Nellikudiri, Sonna, Poḻalguṁde, Sūgūru and Mōrigēṟi as their livelihood ; *S.I.I.* IX, pt. i, No. 101, p. 72, ll. 20–22 ; Morigēṟi, Hadagalli Tq., Bellary Dt., Karn. St. **Dy.** Chāḷ. of Kal., Āhavamalla, Ś. 967 = 1045 A.D. ; **text**[2] : . . . . *Kundūraynūrara baḷiya* ***bāḍaṁ*** *Dhāravāḍa* . . . . ; **tr.** the **village** of Dhāravāḍa which was included in Kundūru-500; *K.I.* V, No. 16 (2nd fragement), p. 58, l. 12 ; Dhārwar, Dharwar Tq. and Dt., Karn. St. **Dy.** Chāḷ. of Kal., Vikramāditya VI, Ch. Vi. yr. 42 = 1117 A.D.

baḍa (K. *adj.*), uncultivated land ; **text** : . . . . *biṭṭa keyi. . . . . Kōveyana hannasu* ***baḍa*** *bhū 40 mū* . . . . ; **tr.** the grant of **uncultivated land** belonging to Kōveya was of the extent of being sown with 40 *mū* (*mūḍe,* grain measure) of seeds ; *S.I.I.* IX, pt. i, No. 252, p. 265, ll. 43–44 ; Kuḍatini, Bellary Tq. and Dt., Karn. St. **Dy.** Chāḷ. of Kal., Jagadēkamalla II, Ch. Vi. yr. 10 = 1148 A.D.

bāḍage (K. *n.*), rent ; **text**[1] : . . . . *keyya guttageyiṁ maneya* ***bāḍage****yiṁ viśēshaṁ gadyāṇa dharaṇavāgi uḷideḍe pasidu baṁdavargaṁbaliya satravaṁ naḍesuvaru. . . . .* ; **tr.** in case any excess amount is available from the collection of the lease amount on the land and **rent** from the house such excess amount shall be used for running a feeding house for the hungry ; *S.I.I.* XX, No. 101, p. 129, ll. 54–55 ; Kāmadhēnu, Kalghatagi Tq., Dharwar Dt., Karn. St. **Dy.** Chāḷ. of Kal., Sōmēśvara III, Ch. Vi. yr. 54 = 1129 A.D. ; **text**[2] : . . . . *Kavatāḷa sīmeyalu aramaneya bhattagaḷige koṇḍu* ***bāḍage****yanū biṭevu* . . . . ; **tr.** we exempted from payment of **rent,** the paddy taken for the palace from Kavatāḷa division ; *S.I.I.* IX, pt. ii, No. 554, p. 574, ll. 9, 34–36 ; Kavatāḷa, Alur Tq., Bellary Dt., Karn. St. **Dy.** Tuḷuva, Achyutarāya, Ś. 1454=1533 A.D.

baḍagi (K. *n.*), carpenter ; **text**[1] : . . . . ***baḍagi*** *Kāmōjaṁge mattaru 6* . . . ; **tr.** the **carpenter** Kamōja was granted 6 *mattaru* (land measure) of land ; *K.I.* II, No. 34, p. 124, l. 414 ; Akkalkot, Akkalkot Tq., Sholapur Dt., Maha St. **Dy.** Sēü. of Dēv., Siṁghaṇadēva, reg. yr. 11 = 1223 A.D. ; **text**[2]: . . . . *khaṁḍasphuṭita iṭṭige sōdege akkasālikeya āchāritanakke Mariyāneyōjaṁge ga 12* ***baḍagi****ge ga 2 akkasālege ga 2 kuṁbāṟaru āḷu 2 kkaṁ ga 12 Nāyiṁdaṁge ga 4 asagaṁge ga 4* . . ; **tr.** 12

gadyāṇa (gold coin) are for bricks and mortar for repair works, 12 *gadyāṇa* to Maṟiyāneyōja for supervising smithy work, 2 *gadyāṇa* to the **carpenter**, 2 *gadyāṇa* to the smith, 12 *gadyāṇa* to three potters, 4 *gadyāṇa* to the barber, 4 *gadyāṇa* to the washerman ; . . . . *E.C.* IV (R) T. N. 96, p. 496, ll. 88–89 ; Sōmanāthapura, Bannur Tq., Mysore Dt., Karn. St. **Dy.** Hoy., Narasiṁha III, Ś. 1192 = 1270 A.D. and Cy. yr. Dhātṛi= 1276 A.D. **text**[3] : . . . . ***baḍagi*** *kammāṟarige . . . teṟuva aḍeya haṇa ardhaprahāra*. . . . ; **tr.** the **carpenter**s and smiths will have to pay only half the tax money on their anvils ; *S.I.I.* IX, pt. ii, No. 554, p. 575, l. 45 ; Kavutāḷaṁ, Adavani Tq., Kurnool Dt., A.P. St. **Dy.** Tuḷuva., Achyutarāya, Ś. 1454 = 1533 A.D.; **text**[4] : *ī śāsanava tiddida śilpi . .* ***baḍagi*** *. Demōjanu* ; **tr.** the (text of this) inscription has been engraved (on the stone) by the **carpenter** Dēmōja the artisan ; *S.I.I.* IX pt. ii, No. 666, p. 660, ll. 25 –26; Muttagi, Harapanahalli Tq., Bellary Dt., Karn. St. **Dy.** Tuḷuva, Sadāśiva, Ś. 1479 = 1557 A.D.

baḍagi-gadde (K. *n.*), carpenter's paddy field ; **text** : . . . . *Kaṁchavveyageṟeya gaddeyalli baḍagi Rebbōjage* ***baḍagi-gadde****yāgi koṭṭa gadde Kamma 50* . . . . ; **tr.** 50 *kamma* (land measure) of paddy field given to the carpenter Rebbōja as **carpenter's paddy field** out of the land in Kaṁchavveyageṟe; *S.I.I.* IX, pt. i, No. 178 , p. 173, l. 36 ; Bāgaḷi, Harapanahalli Tq., Bellary Dt., Karn. St. **Dy.** Chāḷ. of Kal., Vikramāditya VI, Ch. Vi. yr. 33 = 1108 A.D.

baḍagi kūṁṭe (K. *n.*), a village named after the carpenters ; **text** : *Kaṟekaṁṭhadēvarige . . . . Kaṁpaṇaṁ Tuṁbaḷa 30ṟa baḷiya bāḍam* ***Baḍagi kūṁṭe****ya manedeṟe . . . koṭṭar* . . . . ; **tr.** the house-tax from the **village named after the carpenters** as Baḍagi-kūṁṭe in the territorial division Tuṁbaḷa-30 was granted to the god Kaṟekaṁṭhadēva; *S.I.I.* IX, pt. i, No. 172 , p. 167, l. 17 ; Karakaṇṭhapura, Adavani Tq., Kurnool Dt., A.P. St. **Dy.** Chāḷ. of Kal., Vikramāditya VI, Ch. Vi. yr. 31 = 1106 A.D.

baḍagivola (K. < *n.*), land granted to carpenter ; **text** : . . ***badagivola****da saṁdinal ā īśānya guḍḍe*; **tr.** a mound to the north east of the alley of the **land granted to the carpenter** ; *S.I.I.* XX, No. 18, p. 17, l. 38 ; Saundatti, Parasgad Tq., Belgaum Dt., Karn. St. **Dy.** Chāḷ. of Kal., Taila II, Ś. 902 = 980 A.D.

badda (K. < Skt. *baddha, adj.*), belonging to ; **text** : . . . *Kṛishṇadēvara mūlada* ***badda*** *bāḷina vivara* ; **tr.** the details of the landed property originally **belonging to** the god Kṛishṇadēva ; *S.I.I.* VII, No. 299, p. 151, l. 13 ; Uḍupi., Udupi Tq. and Dt., Karn. St. **Dy.** Saṅgama, Harihara, Ś. 1317 = 1395 A.D.

baḍḍagi (K. *n.*), carpenter ; **text** : *Mārttaṁḍēśvara dēvara pūjāvidhānakkaṁ . . . Sōvimayyaṁge . . . biṭṭa keyiṁ* ***baḍḍagi*** *voladiṁ pattire . . . . navilumattar aydu* ; **tr.** six *navilumattar*(land measure) of land, adjoining the land given to Sōvimayya and the field belonging to the **carpenter,** was donated for the worship and other services to the god Mārttaṁḍēśvara ; *S.I.I.* IX, pt. i, No. 197, p. 194, ll. 44, 50 ; Kuḍatini, Bellary Tq. and Dt., Karn. St. **Dy.** Chāḷ. of Kal., Vikramāditya VI, Ch. Vi. yr. 44 = 1119 A.D.

baḍḍagivāḷu (K. *n.*), land donated to a carpenter for his livelihood ; **text :** . . . . ***baḍḍagivāḷa*** *Biṇṇōjage koṭṭa . . mattar 5* . . . . ; **tr.** Land donated to the **carpenter for his livelihood** was 5 *mattar* (land measure) ; *S.I.I.* IX, pt. i, No. 123, p. 105, l. 26 ; Donekallu, Gooty Tq., Anantapur Dt., A.P. St. **Dy.** Chāḷ. of Kal., Trailōkyamalla, Ś. 981 = 1059 A.D.

badde (K. *n.*), beautiful lady ; **text :** . . . . *Banavāsipuraparamēśvara* . . . . . . ***badde*** *Kandarpa* . . . *Māḷayya* . . ; **tr.** Māḷayya the Lord of Banavāsipura and a very cupid to **beautiful ladies** ; *S.I.I.* IX, pt. i, No. 57 , p. 32, l. 7 ; Kaḍabagere, Harapanahalli Tq., Bellary Dt., Karn. St. **Dy.** Rāshṭr, Indra III, Ś. 844 = 922 A.D.

baddha (K. *adj.*), attached to ; **text :** . . . . *Pāṁḍēśvaradoḷage tāvu* ***baddha*** *brahmadāyada mūlada bāḷu* . ; **tr.** land **attached to** us as original *brahmādāya* (land granted to brāhmaṇa) within Pāṁḍēśvara; *S.I.I.* VII, No. 363 , p. 219, ll. 8–9 ; Maṇigārakēri, Udupi Tq. and Dt., Karn. St. **Dy.** Saṅgama, Harihara, Ś 1317 = 1395 A.D.

baddha bhōjana (K. *n.*), meals served as per undertaking ; **text :** (damaged) . . . . *daṇiyaru tamma* ***baddha bhōjana*** *naḍavaṁtāgi* . . . . ; **tr.** so that the **meals** be **served as per the** donor's **undertaking** ; *S.I.I.* IX, pt. ii, No. 409 , p. 416, l. 26 ; Basarūru, Kundapur Tq., Udupi Dt., Karn. St. **Dy.** Saṅgama, Bukka, Ś 1287 = 1365 A.D.

baḍḍi (K. *n.*), interest ; **text**[1] **:** . . . . *Paradēsiyapanavara* . . . . *vaṁśōdbhavara vaśaṁ hoṁge hāga* ***baḍḍi****yaṁ dēvara bhaṁḍāravāgi koṭṭa gadyāṇaṁ mūru ā* ***baḍḍi****yiṁ nityapaḍiya soḍaraṁ salisuvaru.* . . . ; **tr.** three *gadyāṇa* (gold coin) accruing from the **interest** of one *hāga* (fraction of a coin) on one *hoṁnu* (gold coin) to be paid by the descendants of Paradēsiyapa was remitted to the treasury of the god and from that **interest** one lamp was to be lighted; *E.C.* V (R), TN. 64, p. 456, ll. 4–7 ; Bannūr, T. Narasipur Tq., Mysore Dt., Karn. St. **Misc.**, Cy. yr. Kāḷayukta = 1199 A.D. ; **text**[2] **:** . . . . *akki mūḍe 9kaṁ āda* ***baḍḍi*** *hā 3 ṟa mariyādeyalu bhatta mūḍe 2*. . . ; **tr.** for 9 *mūḍe* (grain measure) of rice the accruing **interest** is 3 *hāga* equivalent to 2 *mūḍe* of paddy ; *S.I.I.* VII, No. 351 , p. 209, l. 16 ; Chauḷikēri, Udupi Tq. and Dt., Karn. St. **Dy.** Saṅgama, Harihara, Ś. 1308 = 1386 A.D. ; **text**[3] **:** . . . . *Paḍuvakēriya halaru seṭṭikāṟaru* . . *Kōṭiyaka nāyakitiya kayyalū kaḍaṁgoṁḍudu* . . . *kāṭi ga 200* . . . *hoṁnnu ī hoṁnige* ***baḍḍi*** *prati varusha 1 ke* . . . *akki muḍi 13* . . . . ; **tr.** the *halaru* (an administrative body) *seṭṭikāṟaru* (trader's guild) had taken a loan of 200 *kāṭi ga* (quality gold coin) of gold from Kōṭiyakanāyakiti and the **interest** per annum on that gold was 13 *muḍi* (grain measure) of rice ; *S.I.I.* IX, pt. ii, No. 452, p. 462, l. 34–37 ; Basarūru, Kundapur Tq., Udupi Dt., Karn. St. **Dy.** Saṅgama, Mallikārjuna, Ś 1373 = 1450 A.D.

baḍi (K. < baḍḍi, *n.*), interest ; **text**[1] **:** . . . . *seṭṭiyaru koṭa kāṭi hoṁnu 110 idake* ***baḍi*** *nāghaṁḍugadali akki muḍi 9* . . . . ; **tr.** the seṭṭi donated 110 *kāṭi hoṁnu* (quality gold coin) which fetched an **interest** of 9 *muḍi* (grain measure) of rice measured by *nāghaṁḍuga* (grain measure) ; *S.I.I.* IX, pt. ii, No. 471, p. 486, ll. 49–50 ; Basarūru, Kundapur Tq., Udupi Dt., Karn. St. **Dy.** Sāḷuva, Narasingadēva, Ś 1404 = 1482 A.D. ; **text**[2] **:** *Kṛishṇadēvarige . . . . doḍavaraha ga 55 ayivataidu varahanu koṭṭu . . . ī hoṁnige saluva* ***baḍi*** *akkiyanū naivēdyanaṁdādīptige . . . māḍida . . . dharmaśāsana* . . . . ; **tr.** the pious donation made of fifty-five (55) *doḍavaraha* (coin of greater denomination) and the rice bought from the **interest** accruing from this gold, food offerings and perpetual lamp are to be provided to the god Kṛishṇadēva; *S.I.I.* VII, No. 302, p. 155, l. 25; Uḍupi, Udupi Tq. and Dt., Karn. St. **Misc.,** Ś. 1536 = 1614 A.D.

bāḍi (K. *n.*), hiring ; **text :** . . . . *Veṁkaṭappa nāyakayyanavaru . . . . . . Gaḷigekeṟe agrahāravanu jīrṇṇōddhāravanu māḍi ā grāmakke uṁṭāda* ***bāḍi*** *bēḍige kāṇike kaḍāya . . . . biṭṭi . . . . ivu modalāda ītibādhegaḷu ēnū ilā eṁdu . . . Viṭhala Bhaṭṭarige . . . . . . koṭevu* ; **tr.** We, Veṁkaṭappa nāyakayya renovated the brāhmaṇa settlement of Gaḷigekeṟe and after freeing it of all lets and hindrances such as **hiring**, demands, tributes, binding taxes . . . free labour, etc., donated it to Viṭhala Bhaṭṭa ; *E.C.* V, Kn. 104, p. 99, ll. 10, 15–19, 21 ; Gaḷigekere, Krishnarajanagara Tq., Mysore Dt., Karn. St. **Dy.** Āravīḍu, Śrīraṁga, Ś. 1478 = 1577 A.D.

bāḍibaḍita (K. *n.*), tautology term meaning lessening or reducing the income ; **text :** . . . *ī dēvādāyada mānyakke āvanānobba bāḍibaḍita tandavana bāyi koshṭa* . . . . ; **tr.** whosoever **lessens** the quantum of this grant to the temple, his mouth will become leprotic ; *S.I.I.* IX, pt. ii, No. 532 , p. 547, ll. 21–22; Adamankōṭṭai, Dharmapuri Tq., Salem Dt., T. Nadu St. **Dy.** Tuḷuva, Achyutarāya, Ś 1452 = 1530 A.D.

baḍige (K. *n.*), staff-bearer ; **text :** (damaged). . . *Hariyappa-oḍeyara* ***baḍige*** *. . . Chapparadahaḷḷiya Rāmagavuṁḍana maga . . . . . Sōyigauḍa* . . . . ; **tr.** Sōyigauḍa, the son of Rāmagavuṁḍa of Chapparadahaḷḷi who was the **staff-bearer** of Hariyappa-oḍeya ; *E.C.* IV (R), PP. 13, p. 515, ll. 2–4 ; Chapparadahaḷḷi, Piriyapattana Tq., Mysore Dt., Karn. St. **Misc.,** Ś 1266 = 1344 A.D.

baḍige kelasa (K. *n.*), carpenter's work; **text :** *ā maṭhada* ***baḍige kelasa****da besavittige varusha 1 ke bhatta mūḍe 9* ; **tr.** 9 *mūḍe* (grain measure) of paddy per year for one appointed for doing

carpenter's work ; *S.I.I.*VII, No. 330, p. 180, l. 25; Mūḍakēri, Udupi Tq. and Dt., Karn. St. **Dy.** Saṅgama, Bukkarāya, Ś. 1281 = 1359 A.D.

bāḍina sante (K. *n.*), vegetable market ; **text :** . . . . *satrakke biṭṭa dhammaveṁteṁdaḍe* . . . ***bāḍina santeya** heḍagegaḷalu nichcha bāḍu*. . . . ; **tr.** the donation given to the feeding house per day from the baskets of vegetables from the **vegetable market** . . . . ; *K.I.* II, No. 21, p. 82, ll. 21, 26 ; Telsang, Athani Tq., Belgaum Dt., Karn. St. **Dy.** Chāḷ. of Kal., Jagadēkamalla, reg. yr. 10 = 1147 A.D.

bāḍina vartane (K. *n.*), regularly (supplied) vegetable ; **text :** *śrōtriya agrahārada mahājanaṁgaḷige koṭṭa* . . . *śāsanada krama* . . . . *adhikāriya uḍugoṟe sēnabōyike **bāḍina vartane*** . . . . . . *muṁtāgi ēnuḷḷa sarvasvāmyavanū* . . . . *nīvu bhōgisibahudu* ; **tr.** as per the stone edict recorded, the *mahājana* (administrative body) of the settlement of the Vēdic *brāhmaṇas* were to enjoy all such privileges as the gifts to be given to the official, the village headmanship, the tax on loads of **regularly supplied vegetables**, etc. ; *S.I.I.* IX, pt. ii, No. 440 , p. 449, l. 27 ; Rajabavanahaḷḷi, Hirehadagalli Tq., Bellary Dt., Karn. St. **Dy.** Saṅgama, Dēvarāya, Ś. 1341 = 1419 A.D.

badu (K. *n.*), raised bank, a low ridge ; **text :** . . . . *bhūmiya chatusīme mūḍalu* . . . *haḷḷada mūḍaṇa **badu**hina naṭṭa kalu mēre* . . . . ; **tr.** of the four boundaries of the land, the stone planted on the **raised bank** to the east of the stream is the eastern boundary ; *S.I.I.* IX, pt. i, No. 343, p. 365, l. 56; Bennikal, Kudligi Tq., Bellary Dt., Karn. St. **Dy.** Hoy., Narasiṁha, Ś. 1148 = 1226 A.D.

bāḍu kāy (K. *n.*), raw vegetable ; **text :** . . . . *Bāḷguḷiya* . . . . *Kalidēvara sthaḷakke naḍeyisuva dharmma* . . . . *tuppa māna 1 soḷasa aḷe baḷḷa 3 **bāḍu kāy**ge vīsa 1 aḍake 25* . . . . ; **tr.** the god Kalidēva of Bāḷguḷi was provided one *soḷasa* (liquid measure) of ghee, 3 *baḷḷa* (liquid measure) of buttermilk, one *vīsa* (fraction of a coin) worth of **raw vegetables**, 25 arecanuts, etc. ; *S.I.I.* IX, pt. i, No. 258, p. 275, ll. 26–27 ; Bāgaḷi, Harapanahalli Tq., Bellary Dt., Karn. St. **Dy.** Chāḷ. of Kal., Jagadēkamalla II, reg. yr. 16 = 1153 A.D.

bāḍu kāyi (K. *n.*), raw vegetables; **text :** . . . . *Kalidēvara rātri naivēdyakkaṁ naḍavaṁtāgi*. . . . . ***bāḍu kāyi** lavaṇa* . . . *ghṛitakaṁ paṇa 1*. . . . ; **tr.** one *paṇa* (coin) was earmarked for getting **raw vegetables**, salt and ghee for offerings of food at night to the god Kalidēva ; *S.I.I.* IX, pt. ii, No. 640, p. 639, ll. 18–19 ; Bāgaḷi, Harapanahalli Tq., Bellary Dt., Karn. St. **Dy.** Tuḷuva, Sadāśiva, Ś. 1472 = 1550 A.D.

bādumbe (K. *n.*), a rural folk deity ; **text :** . . . *Sūrya dēvargge* . . . *biṭṭa bhūmi **Bāḍuṁbe**ya kaṭṭeyiṁ mūḍa* . . *keṅgāḍu mattar eraḍu* . . . ; **tr.** two *mattar* (land measure) of red forest soil to the east of the platform (on which) **the rural folk deity Bāduṁbe** (is installed) is donated to the

Sun god ; *S.I.I.* IX, pt. i, No. 329 , p. 346, l. 51–52, 55 ; Māgaḷa, Haḍagalli Tq., Bellary Dt., Karn. St. **Dy.** Hoy., Ballāḷa, Ś. 1131 = 1209 A.D.

bage (K. *n.*), different kinds (of lands) ; **text**[1] : . . . . *bittuva bedegaṇalu nāgaṁḍugada mūḍe 18 . . . . nāgaṇḍugada mūḍe 4 . . . . . nāgaṇḍugada mūḍe 5 antū* ***bage*** *3 ke bittuva mūḍe 27* . . ; **tr.** the **different kinds** of lands to be sown with seeds included that which was to be sown with 18 *mūḍe* (grain measure) of seeds measured by *nāgaṁḍuga* (four units of grain measure called *khaṁḍuga*), 4 *mūḍe* of seeds measured by *nāgaṁḍuga*, 5 *mūḍe* of seeds measured by *nāgaṁḍuga* thus amounting to lands of the extent of being sown with 27 *mūḍe* of seeds ; *S.I.I.* VII, No. 387, p. 243, ll. 11–13; Kōṭakēri, Udupi Tq. and Dt., Karn. St. **Dy.** Saṅgama, Bukkarāya, Ś. 1294 = 1372 A.D. ; **text**[2] : . . . . *dēvarige . . . naivēdyake . . . . bāḷehaṇṇu 8 . . . mēlōgara* ***bage*** *4* . . . . ; **tr.** for offerings to the deity 8 plaintain fruits and 4 **different kinds** of side dishes (were provided) ; *S.I.I.* IX, pt. ii, No. 547, p. 566, l. 5 ; Little Kāñchīpuram, Kanchipuram Tq., Chingleput Dt., T. Nadu St. **Dy.** Tuḷuva, Achyutarāya, Ś. 1454 = 1532 A.D. ; **text**[3] : . . . . *Toṟeyana bāḷinalu baha bhattada* ***bage****yakki 3 mūḍe* . ; **tr.** from the paddy field of Toreya 3 **different kinds** of rice amounting to 3 *mūḍe*; *S.I.I.* IX, pt. ii, No. 415, p. 421, ll. 20–21 ; Kōṭēśvara, Kundapur Tq., Udupi Dt., Karn. St. **Dy.** Saṅgama, Bukka, Ś. 1295 = 1373 A.D.

bageyavaru (K. *n.*), category of people ; **text** : . . . . *nālku* ***bageyavaru*** *Tirumaleya ūḷigavanū māḍabēku* . . . . ; **tr.** the four **categories of people** should perform menial services in Tirumale ; *S.I.I.* IX, pt. ii, No. 462, p. 474, l. 2 ; Tirupati, Chandrgiri Tq., Chittoor Dt., Karn. St. **Dy.** Sāḷuva, Narasiṅgadēva, Ś. 1389 = 1467 A.D.

bāgila gadde (K. *n.*), paddy field in front of main door of the house ; **text**[1] : (badly damaged) . . . . ***bāgila gadde*** . . . ; **tr. paddy field in front of main door of the house** ; *S.I.I.* VII, No. 358, p. 216, l. 14 ; Maṇigarakēri, Udupi Tq. and Dt., Karn. St. **Dy.** Saṅgama, Bukka, Ś. 1295 = 1373 A.D. ; **text**[2] : . . . . *daṇiyaru mūlavāgi koṁḍa bāḷu mane, maneya ṭhāvu bāvi* ***bāgila gadde*** . . . . . ; **tr.** the cultivable land, house, house site, well, **paddy field in front of main door of the house** was purchased with full ownership by the wealthy man ; *S.I.I.* IX, pt. ii, No. 415, p. 420, ll. 11–13 ; Kōṭēśvara, Udupi Tq. and Dt., Karn. St. **Dy.** Saṅgama, Bukka, Ś. 1295 = 1373 A.D.

bāgila gōpura (K. *n.*), gateway tower ; **text** : . . . . *Mayilappagaḷu . . . Penugoṁḍeya Chaṁnavīra bhadradēvarige māḍisida paḍuvaṇa* ***bāgila-gōpura****kke maṁgaḷa* ; **tr.** may the western **gateway tower** of the temple of the god Chaṁnavīra bhadradēva built by Mayilappa of Penugoṁḍe be auspicious ; *S.I.I.* VII, No. 565, p. 335, ll. 4–5 ; Penukoṁḍa, Penukonda Tq., Anantapur Dt., A.P. St. **Dy.** Saṅgama, Harihara,

Ś. 1314 = 1392 A.D.

bāgila haṇa (K. *n.*), house tax levied in cash ; **text:** (damaged). . . . *śrīkāryakke biṭṭa maṁṇu guḷi 1500 . . . . **bāgila haṇa**vana . . . . āvanā bhūmiyāḷuvaḍaṁ salisuvaru. . .* ; **tr.** 1500 *guḷi* (*q.v.*) of land was donated for services to the god from the income of **house tax levied in cash** and this must be maintained by whoever rules the land ; *E.C.* III, Nj. 327, pp. 390–91, ll. 20–24 ; Huṇasanāḷu, Nanjanagud Tq., Mysore Dt., Karn. St. **Dy.** Hoy., Vishṇuvardhana, Cy. yr. Tāraṇa = 1164 A.D.

bāgila koṭṭige (K. *n.*), shed in front of the main door of the farm house ; **text :** (text obscure) . . . . *bāḷa chatussīme. . . mūḍana **bāgila koṭṭige*** . . . . . ; **tr.** of the four boundaries on the east the **shed in front of the farm house** ; *S.I.I.* VII, No. 365, p. 222, l. 29 ; Maṇigārakēri, Udupi Tq. and Dt., Karn. St. **Dy.** Saṅgama, Dēvarāya, Ś. 1342 = 1420 A.D.

bāgilu (K. *n.*), door, entrance ; **text**[1] **:** . . . . . *mahārāyarige puṁṇyavāgabēkeṁndu **bāgila** Kṛishṇarāya-nāyakaru Doḍḍa Basavaṁṇana amritapaḍige koṭṭudu. . . .* ; **tr.** in order that merit may accrue to the emperor, the **door** keeper Kṛishṇarāyanāyaka made a donation of perpetual food offerings to the god Doḍḍa Basavaṁṇa ; *S.I.I.* IX, pt. ii, No. 524, p. 539, ll. 3–5 ; Kurugōḍu, Bellary Tq. and Dt., Karn. St. **Dy.** Tuḷuva, Kṛishṇadēvarāya, Ś. 1450 = 1528 A.D. ; **text**[2] **:** . . . *Varadarājaṁmana paṭaṇada mūḍalu Penugoṁḍe **bāgila** baḷiyalli . . Śrī-Raghunāthadēvaranu pratishṭeya māḍi. . .* ; **tr.** having installed the deity Raghunāthadēva near the **entrance** to the town of Penugoṁḍe to the east of Varadarājaṁmanapaṭaṇa ; *S.I.I.* IV, No. 245, p. 39, l. 7 ; Hampi, Hospet Tq., Bellary Dt., Karn. St. **Dy.** Tuḷuva, Achyutarāya, Ś. 1463 = 1541 A.D.

bāgilugaṭṭaḷe (K. *n.*), customary house tax ; **text :** . . . . *Tirumaleya Tātayyaṁgaḷu samastarājyada bhavya janaṁgaḷ-anumatadiṁda Beḷagoḷa tīrthadalli Vaishṇava aṁgarakshagōsuka samasta rājya doḷaguḷḷaṁtaha Jainaru **bāgilagaṭṭaḷe**yāgi mane manege varshakke 1 haṇa koṭṭu ā yettida hoṁniṁge dēvara aṁgarakshege yippattāḷanū saṁtaviṭṭu* . . . . . . ; **tr.** for the sake of protecting the Vaishṇava inhabitants of the holy place of Beḷaguḷa all the Jainas living in the entire kingdom gave one *haṇa* (coin) as **customary house tax** for each house and Tātayya of Tirumale, with the permission of the *bhavyajana* (Jaina laity) of the entire kingdom, appointed twenty persons as bodyguards ; *E.C.* II, Sb. 475, p. 286, ll. 21–25 ; Śravaṇabeḷagoḷa, Channarayapatna Tq., Hassan Dt., Karn. St. **Dy.** Saṅgama, Bukka I, Ś. 1290 = 1368 A.D.

bāgilu hoṁnu (K. *n.*), house tax levied in gold ; **text :** (text obscure). . . . . *Vāsudēva Uḍupa **bāgilu hoṁnu** 23* ; **tr. tax levied in gold on the house** of Vāsudeva Uḍupa is 23 coins ; *S.I.I.* IX, pt. ii, No. 516 , p. 533, l. 25 ; Basarūru, Kundapur

Tq., Udupi Dt., Karn. St. **Dy.** Tuḷuva, Kṛishṇadēvarāya, Ś. 1447 = 1525 A.D.

bāgu[1] (K. *n.*), fertile land situated at the bend of the river bank; **text**[1] : . . . . *Sōmēśvaradēvar-aṁgabhōgakkaṁ tapōdhanarāhāradānakkaṁ*. . . . . *Hagaraṇigana* ***bāgiṁ*** *paḍuvaṇa deseyali* . . . . . . *koṭṭa mattar 15* ; **tr.** 15 *mattar* (land measure) of land situated to the north of Hagaraṇiga's **fertile land situated at the bend of the river bank** was given for services to the god Sōmēśvaradeva and for free feeding of ascetics; *S.I.I.* IX, pt. i, No. 165, p. 158, ll. 41–42 ; Kuruvatti, Hirehadagalli Tq., Bellary Dt., Karn. St. **Dy.** Chāḷ. of Kal., Vikramāditya VI, Ch. Vi. yr. 24 = 1099 A.D. ; **text**[2] : . . . . . . *Svayaṁbhū mūlasthānadēvara pūje nivedyakkaṁ* . . . . . *biṭṭaru ūriṁ paḍuval Iṟuhegana* ***bāgim*** *baḍagalu Kōgaḷigaḍiṁbadalu* . . . . *keyi mattaru 6 kamma 800* . . . . ; **tr.** 6 *mattaru* (land measure) and 800 *kamma* (*q.v.*) of land measure by the measuring rod of Kōgaḷi to the north of the **fertile land situated at the bend of the river bank** and belonging to Iṟuhega to the west of the village ; *S.I.I.* IX, pt. i, No. 248 , p. 254, ll. 21–23 ; Alabūru, Harapanahalli Tq., Bellary Dt., Karn. St. **Dy.** Chāḷ. of Kal., Jagadēkamalla II, reg. yr. 10 = 1147 A.D.

bāgu (K. *n*), land with a slope ; **text** : . . . . . . *Śivāpurada polamēre pūrvva diśābhāgadoḷ kalmaḍuvum Koṁmadicheṟuvuṁ āgnēyadoḷ eṟeya* ***bāgum*** . . . ; **tr.** the boundaries of Śivāpura were marked by a stone cistern and the Kommadi tank on the eastern side and a **land with a slope** on the south east ; *S.I.I.* IX, pt. i, No. 121, p. 103, ll. 40–43 ; Śivapura, Nandikotkur Tq., Kurnool Dt., A.P. St. **Dy.** Chāḷ. of Kal., Traiḷōkyamalla, Ś. 980 = 1057 A.D.

Bāguḷi ēḷu gadyāṇa (K. *n.*), seven gold coins minted at Bāguḷi ; **text** : *Dharmmiyakkaṁ* . . . . *Lakshmīnārāyaṇadevaraṁgabhōgakkaṁ* . . . . *purāṇamaṁ hēḷalu orbba upādhyāyargge* ***Bāguḷi ēḷu gadyāṇa*** *poṁna jīvitakkaṁ* . . koṭṭu . . . . ; **tr.** Dharmmiyakka having provided for services to the god Lakshmīnārāyaṇa . . . . . granted **seven gold coins minted at Bāguḷi** fot the livelihood of the teacher teaching *Purāṇa* ; *S.I.I.* IX, pt. i, No. 267, p. 286, ll. 61–62 ; Bāgaḷi, Harapanahalli Tq., Bellary Dt., Karn. St. **Dy.** Chāḷ. of Kal., Jagadēkamalla II, Ś. 1082 = 1160 A.D.

bāhattaraniyōgādhipati (K. Pkt.+Skt. *n*), head of seventy two government departments ; **text**[1] : . . . *mahāpradhānaṁ* . . . ***bāhattaraniyōgādhipati****yappa Banavasenāḍa daṁḍanāykaṁ* . . . *Kēsimayyaṁ* . . . . . ; **tr.** Kēsimayya the army general of Banavasenāḍu is the chief minister, **head of the seventy two government departments** ; *K.I.* IV, No. 14, p. 40, l. 10 ; Haḷeniḍnēgila, Hirekerur Tq., Belgaum Dt., Karn. St. **Dy.** Kal of Kal., Rāya murāri Sōvidēva, Ś. 1094 = 1172 A.D. ; **text**[2] : . . . . *mahāpradhānaṁ* ***bāhattaraniyōgādhipati*** *bīḍina rakshapāḷakaṁ Udayādityadēvarājya* *samuddharaṇaṁ taḷāri Chidepanāyaka* . . ; **tr.** the town watchman Chidepanāyaka, the redeemer of the of the principality of Udayādityadeva, who was the Chief Minister, the **head of the seventy-two government departments** and was the protector of the capital city ; *S.I.I.* IV, No. 798, p. 271, ll. 57–58 ; Tāḍapatri, Tadapatri Tq., Anantapur Dt., A.P. St. **Dy.** Pāṇḍya chfs. of Kalukaḍepura, Udayāditya, Ś. 1130 = 1208 A.D.

bāhattaraniyōgādhishṭāyaka (K. < Pkt.+Skt *n.*), head of seventy -two government departments ; **text** : . . . *mahāpradhānaṁ* . . . ***bāhattara-niyōgādhishṭāyakaṁ*** . . . *Barmmaṇayyaṁgaḷ* . . ; **tr.** Barmmaṇayya the chief minister and **head of the seventy-two government departments** ; *K.I.* IV, No. 11, pp. 31–32, ll. 5, 7–8 ; Hirēhaḷḷi, Byadagi Tq., Dharwar Dt., Karn. St. **Dy.** Chāḷ. of Kal., Jagadēkamalla II, in characters of 12th cent. A.D.

bāhattaraniyōgigaḷ (K. *n.*), officers of the seventy-two government departments ; **text**[1] **:** (text damaged) . . . *mahā-pradhānaṁ Siṁgaṇasāhaṇi* ***bāhattarniyōgigaḷ*** . . . . ; **tr.** the chief minister Siṁghaṇasāhani who was **an officer of the head of the seventyt-wo government departments** ; *S.I.I.* VII, No. 274, p. 141, ll. 9–10 ; Kaup, Udupi Tq. and Dt., Karn. St. **Dy.** Āḷupa., Sōyideva, Ś. 1247 = 1325 A.D. ; **text**[2] **:** . . . . ***bāhattaraniyōgigaḷa*** *jīvitavarggakkeyuṁ* . . . . . ; **tr.** for the livelihood of the **officers of the seventy-two government departments** ; *E.C.* V, T.N. 96, p. 493, l. 33 ; Sōmanāthapura, T. Narasipur Tq., Mysore Dt., Karn. St. **Dy.** Hoy., Narasiṁha III, Ś. 1198 = 1276 A.D.

bahiḥpuram (K. *adj.*), surrounding outskirts of a city ; **text :** . . . *tamāḷatāḷavakuḷa drumalōlōdhralavaṅga bhūruhāvaḷigaḷin-īkshiparggatimanōharavalte* . . . . ***bahiḥpuraṁ*** *karaṁ* . . . . ; **tr.** were not the **surrounding outskirts of the city** with rows of trees and plants such as tamāḷa, tāḷa, vakuḷa, lōdhra and clove a feast to the eyes of the beholders ? ; *S.I.I.* IX, pt. i, No. 297, p. 323, l. 16 ; Kurugōḍu, Bellary Tq. and Dt., Karn. St. **Dy.** Kal. of Kal., Śaṅkhavarmadēva, Ś. 1099 = 1177 A.D.

bāhiri (K. < Skt. *vyavahārin*, *n*), a professional (trader's) surname ; **text :** (text damaged) . . . . . *Sōvaṇṇa* ***bāhiriya*** *maḷige* . ; **tr.** the shop of Sōvaṇṇa-**bāhiri** ; *S.I.I.* VII, No. 288, p. 145, ll. 22–23 ; Udyāvara, Udupi Tq. and Dt., Karn. St. **Dy.** Saṅgama, Dēvarāya, Ś. 1351 = 1429 A.D.

bahirvvanaṁ (K. *adj.*), copse on the outskirts of a village/town ; **text :** . . . . *tōṁṭamuṁ* . . . . *tāvaregoḷaṁ keṟe bāvigaḷiṁ* ***bahirvvanaṁ*** *īleyanuṁṭumāḍuvudu nōḷpara chittadoḷāvakālamuṁ* . . . . ; **tr.** the **copse on the outskirts of the town** with its groves, lotus pond, tank and wells always create delight in the minds of the beholders ; *S.I.I.* IX, pt. i, No. 246, p. 256, ll. 26–27 ; Kōlūr, Bellary Tq. and Dt., Karn. St. **Dy.** Chāḷ. of Kal.,

Jagadēkamalla II, Reg. yr. 10 = 1147 A.D.

bahitra (K. *n.*), boat ; **text :** . . . . ***bahitra**da Nāraṇaverggaḍe* . . . . ; **tr.** Nāraṇaverggaḍe, the supervisor of the ferrying of **boats** ; *E.C.* VII, Ng. 118, p. 121, l. 57–58. ; Haṭṭaṇa, Nagamangala Tq. Mandya Dt., Karn. St. **Dy.** Hoy., Ballāḷa, Ś. 1100 = 1178 A.D.

bahumāna (K. *n.*), presentation ; **text :** (fragmentary) . . . . *dāyādigaḷu dēvara gade nāṭikoṇḍu tamma pālanu tegedukoṇḍu grāmada . . . Giriyōja Ēkadase ātage **bahumāna**va māḍi* . . . . ; **tr.** kinsmen having cultivated the land belonging to the god and having taken their portion of the yield, they made a **presentation** to Giriyoja-Ekadase of the village ; *S.I.I.* IX, pt. ii, No. 688., p. 680, l. 9 ; Śriraṁgapura, Kalyanadurga Tq., Anantapur Dt., A.P. St. **Dy.** Āravīḍu, Śrīraṁgarāya, Ś. 1506 = 1584 A.D.

bāhuvalayam (T. < Skt. *n.*), gold armlet ; **text :** . . . . ***bāhuvalayam** oṉṟu poṉ eṇbattoṉbadiṉ kaḻañjēy mañjāḍiyum* . . . . ; **tr.** one **armlet** containing eightynine *kaḻañju* (gold coin) and one *mañjāḍi* (weight of gold) of **gold**; *S.I.I.* II, No.7, p. 79, ll. 4–5 ; Tañjāvūr, Tanjavur Tq. and Dt., T. Nadu St. **Dy.** Chōḷa, Rājarāja I, reg. yr. 29 = 1014 A.D.

baige (K. *n.*), evening ; **text :** *Lakhumidēvanāyakaru Kalināthadēvarige* . . . . ***baige** obaḷa akkiya pāyasa* . . . . *naḍasuvaru* ; **tr.** Lakhumidēvanāyaka will offer sweet porridge prepared from one *baḷḷa* (grain measure) of rice during the **evening** service of the god Kalināthadēva; *S.I.I.* IX, pt. i, No. 376, pp. 392–93, ll. 6–7, 11–12 ; Neraniki, Aluru Tq., Bellary Dt., Karn. St. **Dy.** Sēü. of Dēv. Rāmachandra, Ś. 1198 = 1276 A.D.

baigu (K. *n.*), evening ; **text :** *Mahāpradhānaṁ Anaṁtapāḷadaṁḍarasaru* . . . . . . *Tripurāṁtaka dēvara* . . . . . ***baigina** naivēdyakkaṁ **baigina** pūjegaṁ Chāpalamaḍuge chatussīma sahitaṁ* . . . . *biṭṭaru* . . . . ; **tr.** the Chief Minister Anaṁtapāladaṁḍarasaru donated the village of Chāpalamaḍuge along with its four boundaries for the performance of the **evening** food offering and **evening** worship of the god Tripurāṁtakadēva; *S.I.I.* IX, pt. i, No. 212, pp. 213–14, ll. 12–13, 16–20; Tripurāntakam, Markapuram Tq., Kurnool Dt., A.P. St. **Dy.** Chāḷ. of Kal., Vikramāditya VI, Ch. Vi. yr. 51 = 1126 A.D.

bhaktādāya (K. < Skt *n.*), income from grains ; **text :** . . . . *Rāmayyavoḍeyara makkaḷu Hiriyavīrayyavoḍeyarige koṭṭa* . . . *Attivāḷa grāma* . . . . *ā grāmakke saluva sakala suvarṇādāya **bhaktādāya** ēnuṁṭāda svāmyavanu āgumāḍikoṁḍu teṟuva guttigeya hoṁnu ga 30* . . . ; **tr.** a lease amount of gold *ga* (gadyāṇa, gold coin) of 30 was paid after taking over the village of Attivāḷagrāma given to Hiriyavīrayya voḍeya son of Rāmayyavoḍeya with the stipulation that he will enjoy all the incomes including the **income from** gold and **grains** ; *E.C.* (R) III, Nj. 389, p. 424, ll. 5–8, 11–12 ; Hattavāḷu, Nanjanagud Tq., Mysore

Dt., Karn. St. **Dy.** Umm. Chfs., Tipparasa, Ś. 1425 = 1502 A.D.

bāl̤ (K. *n.*), livelihood ; **text :** (text obscure). . . . *Śaṁkaraṁ nār̤gāmuṇḍugeye Gāḍiyammanā* ***bāl̤****aṁ paripālisi nile paḍedōṁ* . . . ; **tr.** While Śaṁkara was holding the office of the head of the Subdivision *(Nār̤gāmuṇḍugeye)*, he obained the land meant for the **livelihood** of Gāḍiyamma as a permanent gift ; *K.I.* I, No. 15, p. 17, ll. 15–16 ; Shiggāon, Shiggaon Tq., Dharwar Dt., Karn. St. **Dy.** Rāshṭr., Amōghavarsha I, in characters of 9th century A.D.

bala, baḷa (K. < Skt. *n.*), army ; **text**[1] **:** . . . . *sanmantri mitra kōśa dēśa durga* ***bala*** *samētanumāgi rājyaṁ geyvutirdā Rājēṁdra* ; **tr.** Rājēṁdra was ruling, endowed with good counsel, friends, treasury, principality, fortress and **army** ; *S.I.I.* VII, No. 207, p. 103, l. 31; Mūḍabidure, Karkala Tq., Udupi Dt., Karn St. **Dy.** Sāḷva, Mallēśvara, in characters of 15th cent. A.D. ; **text**[2] **:** . . . . *ubhaya****baḷa*** *raṇāchāryyanachaḷitadhairyyaṁ.* ; **tr.** he who was respected by both the **armies** and was firm in bravery ; *S.I.I.* IX, pt. i, No. 143., p. 126, ll. 10–11 ; Chinnatumbaḷam, Adavani Tq., Kurnool Dt., Karn. St. **Dy.** Chāḷ. of Kal., Vikramāditya VI, Ch. Vi. yr. 4 = 1079 A.D. ; **text**[3] **:** (damaged) . . . *raṇadhīraṁ para****baḷa*** *sādhakaṁ* . . . . **tr.** one who is brave in war and is adept in trouncing the enemy's **army** ; *S.I.I.* IX, pt. i, No. 97, p. 67, ll. 7–8 ; Kaṭṭebennūru, Hadagalli Tq., Bellary Dt., Karn. St. **Dy.** Chāḷ. of Kal., Jagadēkamalla, in characters of 11th century A.D.

baḷa[1] (K. *n.*), donation of an already donated land; **text :** . . . . *Kāvagauḍaṁ taṁna hāgada* ***baḷa****doḷage biṭṭa mattareraḍu* . . . ; **tr.** Kāvagauḍa **donated** two *mattar* (land measure) of land from out of the **already donated land** in his possession ; *K.I.* I, No. 24, p. 35, ll. 19–20 ; Sirasaṁgi, Saundatti, Belgaum Dt., Karn. St. **Dy.** Chāḷ. of Kal., Jagadēkamalla II, Cy. yr. Vibhava = 1148 A.D.

baḷa[2] (K. *n.*), a unit of grain measure ; **text :** . . *dēvara paḍi hotare o****baḷa*** *akki* . . . ; **tr.** one who takes the responsibility of offering service to the deity shall give rice equivalent to one **unit of grain measure** called baḷa ; *S.I.I.* IX, pt. i, No. 376, p. 392, l. 9 ; Neraniki, Aluru Tq., Bellary Dt., Karn. St. **Dy.** Sēü. of Dēv., Rāmachandra, Ś. 1198 = 1276 A.D.

bālikā (Pkt. *n.*), daughter ; **text :** . . . . *Ujanikā Mahārāja* ***bālika*** *Mahādēvi Ujanikā Rudradharabhaṭṭārikā* . . . . . ; **tr.** Rudradhara bhaṭṭārikā, a mahārāja's **daughter** from Ujani ; *Ep. Ind.* XX, No. 1, p. 19, ll. 3–4 ; Nāgārjunikoṇḍa, Palnad Tq., Guntur Dt., A.P. St. **Dy.** Ikshvāku, Siri Vīrapurusadata, reg. yr. 6, in characters of 3rd cent. A.D.

bāḷu (K. *n*), cultivable land ; **text**[1] **:** . . . *1 kāṭi hoṁnanu Lakhamāseṭṭiya makkaḷige koṭṭu* . . . . . *ā* ***bāḷ****anu koṇḍevāgi ā* ***bāḷa*** *gaddegaḷa vivara* . . . ; **tr.** the details of the paddy fields within the

cultivable property bought after paying 1 *kāṭi* (quality gold) of gold to the children of Lakhamāseṭṭi ; *S.I.I.* VII, No. 183, p. 79, l. 10 ; Mangalore, Mangalore Tq. D. K. Dt., Karn. St. **Dy.** Saṅgama, Harihara, Ś. 1318 = 1396 A.D. ; **text**[2] **:** . . . . . *Mūvaṇaseṭṭi āhāradānakke biṭṭa bāḷa teṟu beḷi ga nālku* . . . ; **tr.** the tax on the **cultivable land** donated by Mūvaṇaseṭṭi for food offering is four silver *ga* (gadyāṇa, a coin) ; *K.I.* III, pt. i, No. 11, p. 31, ll. 20–21 ; Kaikaṇi, Bhatkal Tq. and Dt., Karn. St. **Dy.** Tuḷuva, Kṛishṇadēvarāya, Ś. 1465 = 1542 A.D.

bāḷabaḷi (K. *n.*), a festival ; **text :** . . . *aidusthaḷadavaru pavitrada parvake nōḍalu baṁdu* . . . . . ***bāḷabaḷi** harvadali* . . . *hāgamaṁ Chandrabhūshaṇadēvargge* . . . *koṭṭaru* . . . . . ; **tr.** the pilgrims who had come from five places to witness the holy **festival** made a grant of one *hāga* (fraction of coin) to Chaṁdrabhūshaṇadēva during the **festival** days ; *K.I.* V, No. 32, p. 131, ll. 57–58 ; Dharwāḍa, Dharwar Tq. and Dt., Karn. St. **Dy.** Chāḷ. of Kal., Sōmēśvara IV, reg. yr. 28 = 1215 A.D.

bāḷgachchu (K. *n.*), reward for one's livelihood ; **text :** . . . *Būtuganuṁ Maṇaleraṁ tanna munde nindiṟidudarkke mechchi Ātukūr panneraḍuṁ Beḷvolada Kāḍiyūrumaṁ **bāḷgachchu** koṭṭaṁ* . . . ; **tr.** Būtuga as an appreciation for the way in which Maṇelera fought in his presence gave him as **reward for his livelihood** the sub-division of Ātukūr 12 and Kāḍiyūru in Beḷvola ; *E.C.* (R) VII, Mu. 42, p. 277, ll. 21–23 ; Ātakūr, Maddur Tq., Mandya Dt., Karn. St. **Dy.** Rāshṭr., Kṛishṇa III, Ś. 872 = 949 A.D.

bāḷa gadde (K. *n.*), paddy field gifted for one's livelihood ; **text :** . . . *mūru ṭhāvina **bāḷa gadde** mu 4* . . . ; **tr.** 4 *mu* (*muḍi*, land of the extent of being sown with 4 *muḍi* of seeds) of **paddy field gifted for one's livelihood** in three places ; *S.I.I.* VII, No. 390, p. 249, l. 44 ; Hosakēṟi, Udupi Tq. and Dt., Karn. St. **Misc.**, in characters of 14th century A.D.

bāḷa gaḍi (K. *n.*), boundary of the land gifted for one's livelihood ; **text :** . . . *maṭhada bāḷina vivara mūḍalu* . . . *Uḍuvara baḷiyavara **bāḷa gaḍi**yiṁdaṁ* . . . *paḍuvalu* . . . ; **tr.** the details of the eastern boundary of the land gifted to the *maṭha* (religious institution) lay to the west of the **boundary of the land gifted** to the family of Uḍuvaru **for** their **livelihood** ; *S.I.I.* VII, No. 344, p. 198, ll. 38–39, 40–42, 47 ; Chauḷikēri, Udupi Tq. and Dt., Karn. St. **Dy.** Saṅgama, Harihara I, Ś. 1314 = 1392 A.D.

baḷagāṟa (K. *n.*), bangle seller ; **text :** . . . ***baḷagāṟara** Mallaseṭṭi* . . . ; **tr.** Mallaseṭṭi of the profession of **bangle seller** ; *E.C.* (R) VII, Md. 71, p. 246, ll. 10–11 ; Kannalli, Mandya Tq. and Dt., Karn. St. **Dy.** Hoy., Sōmēśvara, Ś. 1173 = 1251 A.D.

baḷagāra (K. *n.*), bangle seller ; **text :** . . . *baḍagalu **baḷagāra** baḷiyavara gaḍiyiṁdaṁ teṁkalu* . . . ; **tr.** on the north, to the south of the boundary of the land belonging to the family of the **bangle seller** ; *S.I.I.* IX, pt. ii, No. 424, p. 431, l. 13 ; Basarūru, Kundapur Tq., Udupi Dt., Karn. St. **Dy.** Saṅgama, Harihara, Ś. 1323 = 1401 A.D.

baḷagāra sthaḷa (K. *n.*), village(s) of bangle manufacturers ; **text :** . . . ***baḷagārasthaḷa****ṁgaḷu Senavaḷḷi Kallakunduruge Niṯṯurugaḷ . . . koṭṭaru .* . . ; **tr.** Senavaḷḷi, Kallakunduruge and Niṯṯuru were **villages** granted to **bangle manufacturers** ; *K.I.* II, No. 40, p. 141, l. 14 ; Belgaum, Belgaum Tq. and Dt., Karn. St. **Dy.** Sēü. of Dēv., Kandharadēva, Ś. 1184 = 1261 A.D.

bāḷa gēṇi (K.), lease payment on cultivable tenanacy land ; **text :** (obscure) . . . *maṭhakke koṭṭa* . . . . ***bāḷa gēṇi*** . . . . ; **tr. lease payment on the cultivable land** gifted to the *maṭha* (religious institution) ; *S.I.I.* VII, No. 389, p. 245, ll. 11–12 ; Bārakūru, Udupi Tq. and Dt., Karn. St. **Dy.** Tuḷuva, Sadāśiva, Ś. 1491 = 1569 A.D.

bāḷakaru (K. < Skt. *n.*), children ; **text :** . . . *anyāyadin ī dharmavanaḷidavarge . . . . gō brāhmaṇarumaṁ . . . strī* ***bāḷakaru****maṁ koṁda . . pātakarappar* . . . ; **tr.** those who flout the provisions of this grant would have in effect killed cows, brāhmaṇas, women and **children** ; *S.I.I.* IX, pt. i, No. 102, pp. 75–76, ll. 29–30 ; Mailāra, Hadagalli Tq., Bellary Dt., Karn. St. **Dy.** Chāḷ. of Kal., Trailōkyamalla, Ś. 968 = 1046 A.D.

baḷaṁbe (K. *n*), hay-stack ; **text :** *Kaṟekaṇṭhēśvaradēvara gītavādyanṛityakkaṁ Baḍagikūṇṭeya manedeṟe holadeṟe* . . . . . ***baḷaṁbe****ya teṟe* . . . . *koṭṭar*; **tr.** donated the tax incomes from houses, fields, **hay-stacks**, etc. (other tax incomes and land grants are also mentioned) for the singing, playing on instruments and dance performance in front of the god Kaṟekaṇṭhēśvara; *S.I.I.* IX, pt. i, No. 172 , p, 167, ll. 15–16, 18, 22 ; Karakaṇṭhapura, Adavani Tq., Kurnool Dt., A.P. St. **Dy.** Chāḷ. of Kal., Vikramāditya VI, Ch. Vi. yr. 31 = 1106 A.D.

baḷaṁjigaru (K. *n.*), merchants ; **text :** *Kaṟekaṇṭhadēvara . . . . . . aṁgabhōgakkaṁ . . . . taḷada* ***baḷaṁjigaruṁ*** *nānādēsigaḷumiḷdu koṭṭar arisinada hēṟu 1 rkke pala 5 śuṇṭhiya hēṟiṁge pa 5* . . . . ; **tr.** the **merchants** of the place and members of the Trade Guild which was engaged in trade in different countries gave 5 *pala* (grain measure) per load of turmeric and 5 *pa* (*s. a. pala*) per load of ginger, etc., for the enjoyment of the god Kaṟekaṇṭhadēva ; *S.I.I.* IX, pt. i, No. 172, p. 167, ll. 15–16, 31–32 ; Karakaṇṭhapura, Adavani Tq., Kurnool Dt., Karn. St. **Dy.** Chāḷ. of Kal., Vikramāditya VI, Ch. Vi. yr. 31 = 1106 A.D.

bālapaṇa, bālavaṇa (K. *n.*), tax on cattle ; **text**[1]**:** (damaged). . . . . . *holeyara* ***bālapaṇa****vanettuvalli Sāgatavalliya holeyara* ***bālavaṇa****vanu . . Lakshmināryaṇa dēvara . . . . naṁdādīvigege . . . koṭṭan*. . . . ; **tr.** he (name lost) gave the **tax on cattle** collected from the outcastes of Sāgatavaḷḷi for the perpetual lamp of the god Lakshmīnārāyaṇa while collecting tax on cattle from outcastes ; *E.C.* (R) X, Chnp. 22, p. 436, ll. 14–17, 20 ; Sāgatavaḻḻi, Channarayapatna Tq., Hassan Dt., Karn. St. **Dy.** Hoy., Ballāḷa II, Cy. yr. Krōdhana = 1205 A.D.

bālaśikshā (Skt. *n.*), teaching children ; **text** : . . . . . *purāṇa* ***bālaśikshā****rthaṁ pratyēkaṁ nivartana trayaṁ*. . . . ; **tr.** three *nivartana* (a land measure) of land each for reciting purāṇa texts and for **teaching the children** ; *K.I.* IV, No. 54, p. 112, ll. 69–70 ; Hulgūr (Deposited in KRIM, Dharwar), Dharwar Tq. and Dt., Karn. St. **Dy.** Sēü. of Dēv., Siṅghaṇa, Ś. 1167 = 1245 A.D.

bālasikshe (K. < Skt. *n.*), teaching of children ; **text**[1] : . . . *Beḻḻūralli hēḷuva Rugvēdada khaṁḍikaā Yajurvēdada khaṁḍikā bhaṭṭavṛitti bālasiksheya* . . . . . *mahājanaṁgaḷu* . . . *naḍesikoḍuvaru* . . . . . ; **tr.** the *mahājana* (a body brāhmaṇas) will enable the running of the school of Rugvēda, Yajurvēda and also allot the shares to the brāhmaṇas and **teaching of children** ; *E.C.* (R) VII, Ng. 74, p. 68, l. 48 ; Beḻḻūru, Nagamangala Tq., Mandya Dt., Karn. St. **Dy.** Hoy., Narasiṁha III, Ś. 1113 = 1271 A.D. ; **text**[2] ; . . . . *ga 12 nū ā khaṁḍikā* ***bālaśikshe*** *upādyara jīvitakke varishamprati tamma tamma makkaḷu makkaḷudappade eṁdeṁdiṁgaṁ koḍutta baharu* . . . . ; **tr.** the parents of all the children shall pay without fail 12 ga (*gadyāṇa*, a gold coin) every year for the livelihood of the teacher in the school for **teaching of children** ; *E.C.* (R) IV, T. N. 238, p. 619, ll. 42–44 ; Taḍimālingi, T. Narasipura Tq., Mysore Dt., Karn. St. **Dy.** Hoy., Narasiṁha., Ś. 1212 = 1290 A.D.

bālavaṇa (K. *n.*), tax on cattle ; **text** : . . . *Koṁganāḍa suṁkada Haṁpaṁṇa Guṁmaṁṇa Basavaṁṇanavaru Rāmanāthadēvara naṁdādīvigevu Dēvarahaḷi Kōṭehaḷa maggadere āḍuderẹ* ***bālavaṇa*** *kabba maduve* . . . . . *koṭṭa datti* . . ; **tr.** Haṁpaṁṇa, Guṁmaṁṇa and Basavaṁṇa of the Customs department of Koṁganāḍu donated tax on looms, tax on goats, **tax on cattle,** tax on sugarcane and tax on marriages for burning a perpetual lamp for the god Rāmanāthadēva ; *E.C.* (R) VIII, Ag. 45, p. 143 , ll. 7–9, 11–12, 23–24 ; Rāmanāthapura, Arakalagudu, Tq., Hassan Dt., Karn. St. **Dy.** Hoy., Narasiṁha III , Ś. 1197= 1275 A.D.

bālavaṇaderẹ (K. *n.*), tax on cattle ; **text** : . . . *heggaḍe Hiriyaṁṇa Perumāḷanāyakaṁgaḷu Chikkabeḷugaliya hogederẹ,* ***bālavaṇaderẹ****yoḷage Eḻḻēśvaradēvara nandādīvigege varushanibaṁdhi yāgi koṭṭa pa 3* . . ; **tr.** the village headman Hiriyaṇṇa and Perumāḷanāyaka gave 3 *pa* (*paṇa*, a coin) annually from the smoke tax and **tax on cattle** levied from the village of Chikkabeḷugali for a perpetual lamp for the god Eḻḻēśvaradēva ; *E.C.* (R) VIII, HN. 72, p. 40, ll. 10–11; Yellēśpura, Holenarasipura Tq., Hassan Dt., Karn. St. **Dy.** Hoy., Sōmēśvara, Ś. 1159= 1238 A.D.

bālavaṇamu (K. *n.*), tax on cattle ; **text** : . . . . .

Duddhayya Indavali modalāge panneraḍu maṇḍaliga pulluḷvu ***bālavaṇamu*** *māyila-deṟegaḷuman . . . biṭṭa idu ballahana datti* . . ; **tr.** Duddhayya granted to twelve *maṇḍalika* (subordinate ruler) including that of Indavali tax on cultivating land for grazing, **tax on cattle** and the tax called *māyiladeṟe* ; this is the emperor's grant ; *S.I.I.* IX, pt. i, No. 54 , p. 30, l. 6 ; Rāmadurga, Alur Tq., Bellary Dt., Karn. St. **Dy.** Rāshṭr., Amōghavarsha, in charactes of 9th cent. A.D.

bālavṛiddha (K. *n.*), young and old ; **text :** (damaged) . . . *gaḷdeyaṁ* ***bāla vṛiddha*** *sahitaṁ neredu Piṭṭayyanuṁ Chāmayyanuṁ Vishṇuvina śrīpadavaneydugeṁdu . . ittar* **tr.** the paddy field was donated by Piṭṭayya and Chāmayya accompanied by the **young and old** so that the two may attain the feet of Lord Vishṇu ; *S.I.I.* IX, pt. i, No. 28, p. 15, ll. 27–35 ; Madhudi, Madakasira Tq., Anantapur Dt., A.P. St. **Dy.** Noḷ. Pal., Noḷaṁbādhi rāja, Ś. 881 = 959 A.D.

bāḷe (K. *n.*), plantain fruit ; **text[1] :** . . . *bāḷe sunimbe māduphalamīḷe . . . . tāvaregoḷaṁ keṟe bāvigaḷiṁ bahirvvanaṁ līḷeyanuṁṭumāḍuvudu nōḷpara chittadoḷāvakālamuṁ*; **tr.** the groves on the town's outskirts are always a source of delight to the onlookers with **plantains,** lemons, citrons, citrus fruits and with its lotus pond, tank and wells ; *S.I.I.* IX, pt. i, No. 249, p. 255, l. 25–27 ; Kōlūr, Bellary Tq. and Dt., Karn. St. **Dy.** Chāḷ. of Kal., Jagadēkamalla II, Reg. yr. 10 = 1147 A.D. ; **text[2] :** . . . *teṁgu kauṁgu māü mādaḷe atti jaṁbu niṁbe kaṁkēli nelli* ***bāḷe*** *rastāḷe dāḷiṁbaṁ modalāda phalatarugaḷiṁ palavuṁ pūgiḍaṁgaḷiṁ beḷaṁguva tōṁṭa* . . ; **tr.** the grove which was splendid with its coconut and arecanut trees, as well as fruit-yielding trees such as mango, citron, fig, rose-apple, purple-berry, lemon, a superior variety of **plantain,** pomegrenate and varieties of flower plants ; *S.I.I.* IV, No. 267, pp. 64–65, ll. 89–90 ; Hampi, Hospet Tq., Bellary Dt., Karn. St. **Dy.** Saṅgama, Dēvarāya, Ś. 1332 = 1410 A.D ; **text[3] :** . . . . ***bāḷe****ya maṁṇina keḷagṇa gadde* . . ; **tr.** the paddy field to the east of the soil of the plantain (grove) ; *S.I.I.* VII, No. 345, p. 199, l. 20 ; Chauḷikēṟi, Udupi Tq. and Dt., Karn. St. **Dy.** Sāḷuva, Narasiṁha, Ś. 1424 = 1502 A.D. ; **text[4] :** . . . *ā bhūmiya gadeya vivarā . . . Baṁkana gade* ***bāḷe****ya hāḷi saha* . . . . ; **tr.** the details of the boundary of the paddy field in that area include the paddy field of Baṁka and the **plantain** field; *S.I.I.* IX, pt. ii, No. 674, p. 667, l. 31 ; Śaṁkaranārāyaṇa, Kundapur Tq., Udupi Dt., Karn. St. **Dy.** Tuḷuva, Sadāśiva, Ś. 1485 = 1562 A.D.

bāḷele (K. *n.*), plantain leaf; **text :** (badly damaged) . . . *maṭhadalli uṁba brāhmaṇa ja 12 jana . . . huḷi meṇasu* ***bāḷele*** . . . ; **tr.** for the 12 *brāhmaṇa* to be fed in the *maṭha* (religious institution.) . . . . tamarind, chillies, **plantain leaves** ; *S.I.I.* VII, No. 387, p. 244, l. 69 ; Kōṭakēri, Udupi Tq. and Dt., Karn. St. **Dy.** Saṅgama, Bukkarāya, Ś. 1294 =

1372 A.D.

baḷegāra (K. *n.*), bangale seller ; **text[1] :** *Basarūra* ***baḷegāra*** *. . . Nāraṇaseṭṭi barasida . . śāsana . .* ; **tr.** the stone inscription got engraved by Nāraṇaseṭṭi the **bangle-seller** of Basarūru ; *S.I.I.* IX, pt. ii, No. 446, p. 455, l. 7 ; Basarūru, Kundapur Tq., Udupi Dt., Karn. St. **Dy.** Saṅgama, Dēvarāya, Ś. 1358 = 1436 A.D. ; **text[2] :** . . . . ***baḷegāra****na holakke vāyavya* . ; **tr.** to the north-west of the field of the **bangle-seller** ; *E.C.* (R) V, T. N. 16, p. 376, l. 637; Tirumakūḍalu Narasīpura, T. Narasipura Tq., Mysore Dt, Karn. St. **Dy.** Woḍ. of Mys., Kṛishṇarāja, Ś. 1671 = 1749 A.D.

bāḷehaṁ (K. *n.*), abridged form of *bāḷehaṁṇu*, banana ; **text:** *Rāmachaṁdradēvarige. . . . . naivēdyake samarpista . . . . bella 50 kabbu teṁginakā 6 yeḷanīru 6* ***bāḷehaṁ*** *10* . . ; **tr.** for the food offerings of the god Rāmachaṁdra jaggery, 50 sugarcanes, 6 tender coconuts and 10 **bananas** were donated ; *S.I.I.* IV, No. 250, p. 42, l. 8 ; Hampi, Hospet Tq., Bellary Dt., Karn. St. **Dy.** Tuḷuva, Kṛishṇadēvarāya, Ś. 1443 = 1521 A.D.

bāḷe haṁṇu (K. *n.*), banana ; **text :** *. . . dēvarige . . . naivēdyake . . . hālu . . . tuppa . sakhare . . .* ***bāḷe-haṁṇu*** *8* . . . . ; **tr.** milk, ghee, sugar, 8 **bananas** were donated for making offerings to the god ; *S.I.I.* IX, pt. ii, No. 547, p. 566, l. 5 ; Little Kāñchīpuram, Kanchipuram Tq., Chingleput Dt., T. Nadu St. **Dy.** Tuḷuva, Achyutarāya, Ś. 1454 = 1532 A.D.

bāḷe kaṁbha (K. *n.*), plantain trunk (used for decoration on festive occasions) ; **text :** (obscure) *. . . Viṭhaladēvara . . . naivēdyakke . . . kuṁbārūpa* ***bāḷe-kaṁbha*** *saha ga 83* . . . . . ; **tr.** for erecting a *pandal* with **plantain trunks** for the god Viṭṭhala 83 *ga* (*gadyāṇa,* gold coin) were given ; *S.I.I.* IX, pt. ii, No. 653, p. 648, l. 5 ; Hampi, Hospet Tq., Bellary Dt., Karn. St. **Dy.** Tuḷuva, Sadāśiva, Ś. 1476 = 1554 A.D.

bāḷeya haṁṇu (K. *n.*), banana ; **text :** . . . *Vināyakadēvarige dinaṁprati naḍasuva pañcha-kajhāyake kabbu* ***bāḷeya haṁṇu*** *teṁginakāyi kaḍale bella . . . . Chauḷiyakēriya ayivaru halaru naḍasikoḍuvaru* ; **tr.** for the daily offering of a sweet dish containing five ingredients, the *ayivaru halaru* (a body of 5 members) of Chauḷiyakēri will provide sugarcane, **bananas** fruits, coconuts, chick-pea and jaggery ; *S.I.I.* VII, No. 342, p. 195, ll. 19–20 ; Chauḷikēri, Udupi Tq. and Dt., Karn. St. **Dy.** Saṅgama, Harihara, Ś. 1318 = 1396 A.D.

bāḷeya tōṭa (K. *n.*), plantain grove ; **text :** . . . *Kaṁpileyalū Sātāsirumayana* ***bāḷeya tōṭa*** *sthaḷada gadde* . . . ; **tr.** the paddy field in the vicinity of the **plantain grove** of Sātāsirumaya at Kaṁpile ; *S.I.I.* IV, No. 245, p. 39, l. 20 ; Hampi, Hospet Tq., Bellary Dt., Karn. St. **Dy.** Tuḷuva, Achyutarāya, Ś. 1463 = 1541 A.D.

bāḷgaḷchu (K. *n.*), (1) grant given to a warrior for his livelihood at the end of a battle for his bravery by washing his sword; (2) grant given to a warrior in appreciation of bravery shown in the battle field ; **text**[1] **:** *Kēkaya Pallavaraṁ kādeṟidu pettajayan ā Vija arasange bāḷgaḻchu Palmaḍiüṁ Mūḻivaḷḷiyuṁ koṭṭār* ; **tr :** the villages of Palmaḍi and Mūḻivaḷḷi were **granted** to Vijā arasa **after washing his sword in appreciation of his victory at the end of the battle** against the Kēkaya and Pallava adversaries ; (alternatively, *bāḷgaḻchu* could also mean earning a livelihood from *bāḷ* < *bāḻ* = *livelihood* + *gaḻchu* > *gaḷisu* = *earn*) ; M.A.R. 1936, No. 16. l. 12 ; Halmiḍi, Belur Tq., Hassan Dt., Karn. St. Kad. of Ban., Mṛigēśavarman, C. 450 A.D. ; **text**[2] **:** (damaged) .... *vānaradhvajan* . ... ***bāḷgaḻchu*** *goṭṭan* ..... ; **tr.** registers a gift of **bāḷgaḻchu** by some person who bore the title *vānaradvhaja* ; *E.C.* VIII, Hn. 99, p. 311, ll. 4–5 ; Honnāvara, Hassan Tq. and Dt., Karn. St. **Dy.** W. Gaṅga, Nītimārga, in characters of 10th cent. A.D.

baḷi (K. *n.*), lineage; **text :** ..... *Hāluḷigana* ***baḷi****ya Kōṭīsara Bhāratana aḷiya Māṇinaṁdariya kaiyali* .... *koṁḍa bāḷina vivara ;* **tr.** the details of the land bought from Māṇinaṁdari the son-in-law of Kōṭīsara Bhārata of the **lineage** of Hāluḷiga ; *S.I.I.* VII, No. 391, p. 250, l. 9 ; Maṇigārakēṟi, Udupi Tq. and Dt, Karn. St. **Dy.** Saṅgama, Harihara, Ś. 1312 = 1390 A.D.

baḷi gadde (K. *n.*), ancestral paddy field ; **text :** ..... ***baḷi gadde****ya vivara hariva sāliṁda paḍuvalu adara Takkaḷa gaḍiyiṁ baḍagalu Maṇigārakēriya halara gaḍiyiṁ mūḍalu Nāru Bāleseṭṭiya gaḍiyiṁ teṁkalu yiṁtī gaḍiyoḷage gadde mu 1;* **tr.** the details of the boundaries of the **ancestral paddy field** with a sowable capacity of 1 *mu* (*muḍi,* a grain measure) of seeds are the lane to the west, the boundary of the field of Takkaḷu to the north, to the east of the lands belonging to the *halaru* (an administrative body) of Maṇigārakēri and to the south of the lands belonging to Nāru Bāḷeseṭṭi ; *S.I.I.* VII, No. 389, p. 246, l. 19 ; Hosakēri, Udupi Tq. and Dt, Karn. St. **Dy.** Tuḷuva, Sadāśiva, Ś. 1491 = 1569 A.D.

baḷigāṟa (K. *n.*), close confidant ; **text :** ... *Pallavādityaṁ* .... ***baḷigāṟa*** *Karavayya-mummaḍigavaṟe Pallavāditya Noḷaṁbaseṭṭiyendu pesaraṁ dayageydu paṭṭaṁgaṭṭi* ; **tr.** Pallavāditya having crowned his **close confidant** Karavayya-mummaḍigavaṟe with the honorific name of Pallavāditya-Noḷaṁbaseṭṭi ; *S.I.I.* IX, pt. i, No. 41, p. 24, ll–12 ; Nelapalli, Punganur Tq., Chittoor Dt, A.P. St. **Dy.** Noḷ. Pal., Iṟivanoḷaṁba Pallavāditya, in characters of 9th century A.D.

bāḷike (K. *n.*), landed property; **text**[1] **:** *Baṁgamañjuva modalāda hiriyaru lōkabeṭṭeṁba* ***bāḷike****yanu bāḷi bandalli* .... ; **tr.** while Baṁgamañjuva and other elders were enjoying their livelihood from the **landed property** called lōkabeṭṭu ; *S.I.I.* IX, pt. ii, No. 460, p. 472, ll. 11–12; Poḷali Ammunaje, Mangalore Tq., D. K. Dt, Karn. St. **Dy.** Saṅgama, Mallikārjuna, Ś. 1387 =

1465 A.D. ; **text**[2] : . . . . . *chhatrada maṭhada dharmmakke barasida* **bāḷike***ya śilā śāsana* . . . ; **tr.** the stone edict registering the **landed property** for charitable purposes in the *maṭha* (religious institution) of the choultry; *S.I.I.* VII, No. 346, p. 201, ll. 10–11; Chauḷikēri, Udupi Tq. and Dt., Karn. St. **Dy.** Saṅgama, Virūpāksha, Ś. 1397 = 1475 A.D.

balikkal (T. *n.*), stone sacrificial altar ; **text :** . . . . *Nārāyaṇam Paśupati birāmaṇi Śēndaṅkuṉṟappoḻi paṇṇuvitta* ***balikkal*** . . . ; **tr.** the **stone sacrificial altar** got made by the lady of the highest caste Śēndaṅkuṉṟappoḻi, the wife of Nārāyaṇam Paśupati; *S.I.I.* VII, No. 169, p. 70, ll. 1–2 ; Tellicherry, Kottayam Tq., Kozhikode Dt., Ker. St. **Misc.,** in characters of 13th cent. A.D.

bāḷina tōṭa (K. *n.*), garden land as means of subsistence ; **text :** . . . . *Kaṁchayichchuvana kayya koṁḍa* ***bāḷina tōṭa*** . . . . ; **tr.** the **garden land** purchased fron Kaṁchayichchuva **as means of subsistance** ; *S.I.I.* VII, No. 330, p. 180, ll. 35–36 ; Mūḍakēri, Udupi Tq. and Dt., Karn. St. **Dy.** Saṅgama, Bukkarāya, Ś. 1281 = 1359 A.D.

bali pīṭham (Skt. *n.*)**, bali pīṭam** (T. < Skt. *n.*), sacrificial altar ; **text :** . . . *Kuṉṟagōpaḥ* . . . . *upalamayaṁ kārayamāsa* ***pīṭham balyartham*** . . . . . *Iḻiyilkōṭṭu mudiyaṉ Kuṉṟaṅgōpaṉ śeyvichcha* ***bali pīṭam*** . . ; **tr.** Kuṉṟagōpa caused to be made a stone **sacrificial altar** ; the elder Kuṉṟangōpan of Iḻiyilkōṭṭu caused the stone **sacrificial altar** to be made ; *T.A.S.* IV, No. 37, p. 143, ll. 5, 7–9 ; Pākōḍu (Kuḻittarai), Ker. St. **Misc.,** Kali 4044 = 943 A.D. (bilinguial text).

balishṭa māḍu (K. < Skt. *vb.*), to strengthen ; **text:** (obscure) . . . . . . *keṟemānya māḍida krama* . . . *Amitagaṭṭi ādiyāgi Hirigereyoḷuvaraṁ* ***balishṭa māḍi*** . . . . ; **tr.** the purpose of the grant was **to strengthen** the inner parts of the big tank ; *S.I.I.* IX, pt. ii, No. 710, p. 696, ll. 7–8 ; Bāgaḷi, Harapana halli Tq., Bellary Dt., Karn. St. **Misc.,** in characters of 12th cent. A.D.

bāḷisi koḍu (K. *vb.*), restore the right of enjoyment ; **text :** . . . . . . *yī ṭāvige oḷage baṁdu horaganyaru tāgu taḍava māḍidare nāvu pariharisi* ***bāḷisi koḍu****vevu* . . . . . . ; **tr.** if any outsider should intrude into this place and hinders or delays implementation, we shall set right the intrusion and **restore** your **right of enjoyment** ; *S.I.I.* IX, pt. ii, No. 460, p. 472, l. 23; Poḷali Ammunaje, Mangalore Tq., D. K. Dt., Karn. St. **Dy.** Saṅgama, Mallikārjuna, Ś. 1387 = 1465 A.D.

baḷiya hoṁnu (K. *n.*), gold belonging to the family ; **text :** . . . . *Śāṁtigrāmada Varada Narasiṁhadēvarge Vīra Ballāḷadēvaru ā Śāṁtigrāmada siddhāyada modala hoṁnoḷage* . . . *pūrvāyaṁ mattu apūrvāyaṁ voḷagāgi grāmakke śrīkaraṇada Bōva maryādeya* ***baḷiya hoṁnu*** *sahita Achalaprakāsasvāmigaḷa kayyalu tāmraśāsanaṁ koṭṭaru* . . . . ; **tr.** Vīra-Ballāḷadēva donated to the God Varada Narasiṁha of Śāṁtigrāma gold collected as permanent tax and taxes already being levied and taxes to be levied in future as also the **gold belonging to the family** of the chief accountant Bōva of Śāṁtigrāma ; *E.C.* (R) VIII, Hn. 160, p. 392, l. 23 ; Śāṁtigrāma, Hassan Tq. and Dt., Karn. St. **Dy.** Hoy., Vīra Ballāḷa, Ś. 1138 = 1215 A.D.

baḷiyavaru (K. *n.*), persons of the same lineage ; **text :** . . . . . . *Kanakara **baḷiyavara*** . . . ; **tr. persons belonging to the same lineage** as Kanaka; *S.I.I.* VII, No. 390, p. 248, ll. 7–8 ; Hosakēri, Udupi Tq. and Dt., Karn. St. **Misc.,** in characters of 15th cent. A.D.

baḷḷa (K. *n.*), grain measure ; **text[1] :** . . *Sivenāyakaṁge* . . . . *kūḻge ōr**baḷḷa** koṭṭa stithiyakku* . . . . ; **tr.** the grant of one *baḷḷa* (**grain measure**) of grain made to Sivenāyaka for his livelihood ; *S.I.I.* IX, pt. i, No. 55, p. 31, ll. 11–13; Maṁchāle, Adavani Tq., Kurnool Dt., A. P. St. **Dy.** Rāshṭr., Kṛishṇa II, Ś. 815 = 893 A.D. ; **text[2] :** (damaged) . . . . *Dēmēśvara dēvaraṁgabhōgakkaṁ* . . . . *oṁdu **baḷḷa**maṁ biṭṭaru* . . . . ; **tr.** gave one *baḷḷa* of grain for services to the god Dēmēśvara ; *S.I.I.* IX, pt. i, No. 118, p. 97, ll. 47, 58; Hirehaḍagalli, Hadagalli Tq., Bellary Dt., Karn. St. **Dy.** Chāḷ. of Kal., Trailōkyamalla, Ś. 978 = 1057 A.D. ; **text[3] :** . . . *Rasabaṁḍanūṟu bhūmige eraḍu **baḷḷa*** . . . . ; **tr.** for the produce from the land of Rasabaṁḍanūru two *baḷḷa* (of grain has to be paid as tax) ; *E.C.* IV, Yl. 1, p. 272, ll. 88–89 ; Yeḷandūru, Yelanduru Tq., Chamarajanagara Dt., Karn. St. **Dy.** Hadināḍu chiefs, Muddabhūpa, Ś. 1576 = 1654 A.D.

ballaha (K. < Skt. *vallabha, n.*), the emperor of Karnataka ; **text :** (obscure) *Bhaṭārara maga Duddhayya* . . . . *koṭṭa stiti* . . . . *idu **ballaha**na datti* . . . . ; **tr.** the **emperor's** son Duddhayya made this grant. This is the **emperor's** grant ; *S.I.I.* IX, pt. i, No. 54, p. 30, ll. 3, 4, 7 ; Rāmadurga, Alur Tq., Bellary Dt., Karn. St. **Dy.** Rāshṭr., Amōghavarsha, in characters of 9th cent. A.D.

ballāḷu (K. *n.*), powerful executive ; **text[1] :** . . *aṟuvattu **ballāḷu**gaḷu* . . . . *nāyakaru oḷagāda samasta kaṭṭaḷeyavaru* . . . ; **tr.** all the customary royal officials including sixty **powerful executives**, the *nāyakas* etc. ; *S.I.I.* VII, No. 350, p. 207, l. 11–12 ; Chauḷikēri, Udupi Tq. and Dt., Karn. St. **Dy.** Saṅgama, Harihara, Ś. 1321 = 1399 A.D. ; **text[2] :** . . . . . *adhikārigaḷu nālvaru **ballāḷu**gaḷayvaru horahinavaru sthaḷada sēnabōvaru appaṇekāraneṁbivaru kūḍi* . . . . *Chaṁḍōgra pārśvadēvara śrīkāryakke* . . . *koṭṭa kshētra* . . . ; **tr.** the land given for services to Chaṁḍōgra-pārśvadēva jointly by the four official, six **powerful executives**, outsiders, the accountant of the village and the officer dealing with royal orders ; *S.I.I.* VII, No. 211, pp. 106–07, ll. 6–8; Mūḍabidure, Udupi Tq. and Dt., Karn. St. **Dy.** Saṅgama, Bukkarāya, Ś. 1329 = 1407 A.D.

baḷḷi (K. *n*), creeper ; **text[1] :** (badly damaged) . . . . . . ***baḷḷi**ya tōṇṭamumirkhkhaṇḍuga*. . . . ; **tr.**

also two *khaṇḍuga* (a land measure) of the garden of **creepers** ; *S.I.I.* IX, pt. i, No. 98, p. 64, l. 27 ; Sogi, Bellary Tq. and Dt., Karn. St. **Dy.** Chāḷ. of Kal, Jagadēkamalla, Ś. 960 = 1038 A.D. ; **text[2] :** .. *pannirmattaru sāyira **baḷḷiya** ēlakkiya tōṇṭamuṁ koṭṭar* .... ; **tr.** donated 12 *mattars* (land measure) of garden land growing one thousand **creepers** of cardamom ; *E.C.* XI, Chit. 26, p. 18, l. 16 ; Goḍabanāḷu, Chitradurga Tq. and Dt., Karn. St. **Misc.,** in characters of 9th century A.D.

bāḷu[1] (K. *n.*), land gifted for livelihood, land gifted for maintenance ; **text[1] :** .. *baḍḍagivāḷa Biṇṇōjage koṭṭa matta 5 akkasālevāḷu **bāḷige** matta 5* ... ; **tr.** land gifted to the carpenter Biṇṇōja is 5 *matta* (*mattar,* a land measure) and **land gifted for the livelihood** of the metal-smith is 5 *matta* ; *S.I.I.* IX, pt. i, No. 123, p. 105, l. 26 ; Doṇekallu, Anantapur Tq. and Dt., A. P. St. **Dy.** Chāḷ. of Kal., Trailōkyamalla II, Ś. 981 = 1059 A.D. ; **text[2] :** . *Hittilakēṟiya Uttarēśvaradēvara **bāḷu*** .... ; **tr. land gifted for the maintenance** of the temple of the god Uttarēśvara of Hittilakēṟi; *S.I.I.* IX, pt. i, No. 371, p. 389, ll. 54–55 ; Yēṇigi, Hadagalli Tq., Bellary Dt., Karn. St. **Dy.** Sēü. of Dēv, Kannaradēva, Ś. 1181 = 1259 A.D. ; **text[3] :** *Sōvaṁṇa Bākaṁṇanavaru .. dēvasvada bāḷa mēle agra nākakke varuśa 1 ke nāgaṁḍugadalu nūṟanālvattu mūḍe baha **bāḷanu** arthava koṭṭtu* .. . *koṁḍu agra nālkakke tāvu koṭṭaru* ...... ; **tr.** Sōvaṁṇa and Bākaṁṇa **gifted** to the temple **land** which yields hundred and forty *mūḍe* (grain measure) per year after purchasing the same by paying cash **for the maintanence** of the temple's programme of feeding four members of the highest caste ; *S.I.I.* VII, No. 312, p. 163, ll. 8–13 ; Mūḍakēri, Udupi Tq. and Dt., Karn. St. **Dy.** Hoy., Kikkāyitāyi, Ś. 1258 = 1336 A.D. ; **text[4] :** ... *Ādidēvarige Janni Śivaṁṇanāykaru ātana taṁma Yīśvarasēnabōvara maga Dēvaṁṇasēnabōva* .... *biṭṭa **bāḷu*** ; **tr.** the **land gifted for the maintenance** of the temple of Ādidēva by Janni Śivaṁṇanāyaka, his younger brother Yīśvarasēnabōva and his son Dēvaṁṇasēnabōva ; *S.I.I.* VII, No. 368, p. 224, ll. 17–18 ; Maṇigārakēri, Udupi Tq. and Dt., Karn. St. **Dy.** Saṅgama, Mallikārjuna, Ś. 1375 = 1453 A.D. ; **text[5] :** ... *brāhamaṇa bhōjana dina 1 ke jana 6 lekkadalu* . ... *biṭṭa **bāḷa** vivara* ...... ; **tr.** the details of the **land gifted for the maintenance** of the feeding of six numbers of brāhmaṇas ; *S.I.I.* VII, No. 366, p. 223, ll. 13–14; Maṇigārakēri, Udupi Tq. and Dt., Karn. St. **Dy.** Tuḷuva, Sadāśiva, Ś. 1486 = 1564 A.D.

bāḷu[2] (K. *n.*), sword ; **text :** .. *Nāgaguṭṭarasaṁ* .... ***bāḷam** kiḻtu naḍadu palaraniridu sattoḍe* ... ... ; **tr.** Nāgaguṭṭarasa having died after drawing his **sword** and walking towards the enemy and stabbed a number of persons ; *E.C.* X, Kol. 200, p. 46, ll. 8–9, 11–13 ; Nukkanahaḻḻi, Kolar Tq. and Dt., Karn. St. **Dy.** Bāṇa, Bāṇarasa, in characters of

9th century A.D.

bāḷu[3] (K. *vb.*), reside ; **text :** .. *mūḍaṇa maneyanu Mūḍakēri halaru* ***bāḷuvaru*** .... ; **tr.** the *halaru* (an administrative body) of Mūḍakēri will **reside** in the eastern house ; *S.I.I.* IX, pt. ii, No. 457, p. 468, ll. 19–20 ; Basarūru, Udupi Tq. and Dt., Karn. St. **Dy.** Saṅgama, Mallikārjuna, Ś. 1377 = 1455 A.D.

bāḷu gadde (K. *n.*), paddy field given as livelihood; **text :** . . . ***bāḷu-gadde*** . . . . *mu 13* . . . . . . *Sōmanāthadēvarigu Maṇigāṟakēriya halarige Saṁkarahaṁde arthaparitsēdyavāgi tegedukoṁḍu mūlaparichchhēdyavāgi koṭṭanu* ; **tr.** Saṁkarahaṁde bought with cash 13 *mu* (*muḍi,* a grain measure) of **paddy field given as means of livelihood** and gave it on permanent basis to the god Sōmanāthedēva and the *halaru* (an administrative body) of Maṇigāṟakēri ; *S.I.I.* VII, No. 359, p. 216, ll. 8, 10, 13–16; Maṇigārakēri, Udupi Tq. and Dt., Karn. St. **Misc.,** in characters of 15th cent. A.D.

bāḷuka (K. *n.*), fruits and vegetables preserved like pickles, etc. ; **text :** *Hariyaṁṇagaḷu* . . *mahājanaṁgaḷige* . . . . *koṭṭa śrōtriya agrahāra dānaśilāśāsanada kramaveṁteṁdare* . . . . . *kereya keḷage gadde beddalu aḍakeyamara teṁginamara* . . . . . . ***bāḷuka*** *huṇaseya haṇṇu* . . . . *muṁtāgi yēnuḷa sarvasvāmyavanū* . . . . *nimma saṁtānaparaṁpareyāgi bhōgisibahudu* . . . . ; **tr.** as per the order issued by Hariyaṁṇa, the *mahājana* (an administrarive body) were granted as a *vaidika* brāhmaṇa settlement ; you are to enjoy hereditarily all the privileges such as exemption from all taxes such as on the wet land under the tank, dry land, arecanut, coconut trees, **fruits and vegetables preserved like pickles**, tamarind fruit, etc. ; *S.I.I.* IX, pt. ii, No. 440, p. 449, ll. 7–8, 12–13, 23, 27–30 ; Rajabavanahaḷḷi, Harapanahalli Tq., Bellary Dt., Karn. St. **Dy.** Saṅgama, Dēvarāya, Ś. 1341 = 1419 A.D.

baḷukunīru (K. *n.*), a kind of tax ; **text :** . . . . *Timminayakaru Tiruvadiya Vīraṭadēvarige* . . . . *vasaṁta ubhayake koṭṭadu Mosukoḷattūra* . . . . . . *grāmada chatusīmege saluva* . . . . *māvaḍe kuḷavaḍe* . . . . ***baḷukunīru*** . . . . . *modalāda hala upādhigaḷu* . . . . . . ; **tr.** Timmināyaka gave, for performing the spring festival for the god Vīraṭadēva of Tiruvadi, several incomes from taxes on animals, land and **tax called *baḷukunīru*** ; *S.I.I.* IX, pt. ii, No. 466, p. 480, l. 6 ; Tiruvadi, Cuddalore Tq., S. Arcot Dt., Karn. St. **Dy.** Sāḷuva, Narasiṁha, Ś. 1391 = 1472 A.D.

bamaṇa (Pkt. *n.*), member of the highest caste ; **text :** . . . . *samaṇa* ***bamaṇa*** *kavaṇa* . . . . . ; **tr.** Samaṇa, **member of the highest caste** and those that are miserable ; *Ep. Ind.* XX, No. 1, p. 16, l. 8 ; Nāgārjunikoṇḍa, Palnad Tq., Guntur Dt., A.P. St. **Dy.** Ikshvāku, Siri Vīrapurusadata, reg. yr. 6, in characters of 3rd cent. A.D.

baṁḍe (K. *n.*), boulder ; **text**[1] **:** . . . . *mūḍalu*

Virupājiya bhāviya ***baṁḍe****ya śāsana mēre. . . .* ; **tr.** on the east the inscribed **boulder** of the well of Virupāji is the boundary; *S.I.I.* IX, pt. ii, No. 535, p. 551, l. 28 ; Lēpākshi, Hindupur Tq., Anantapur Dt., A.P. St. **Dy.** Tuḷuva, Achyutarāya, Ś. 1453 = 1531 A.D. ; **text[2] :** *. . . . baḍagalū agasara bāviya baḷiya* ***baṁḍe*** *mēre. . . . . . .* ; **tr.** on the north the **boulder** by the side of the washermen's well is the boundary ; *S.I.I.* IX, pt. ii, No. 668, p. 661, l. 2 ; Hampi, Hospet Tq., Bellary Dt., Karn. St. **Dy.** Tuḷuva, Sadāśiva, Ś. 1480 = 1559 A.D.

bāṁdhava (K. < Skt. *n.*), person of great intimacy; **text :** . . *Ravidaṁḍanāyakaṁ . . . apāraguṇaṁ jagadēka* ***bāṁdhavaṁ*** *. . . . . . . ;* **tr.** the General Ravi, of excellent qualities, was a unique **person of great intimacy** to the world ; *S.I.I.* IX, pt. i, No. 158, p. 142, l. 23 ; Hūvina-Haḍagalli, Hadagalli Tq., Bellary Dt., Karn. St. **Dy.** Chāḷ. of Kal., Vikramāditya VI, Ch. Vi. yr. 15 = 1090 A.D.

baṁdhugaḷu (K. < Skt. *n.*), kinsmen ; **text[1] :** . *tannoppuva gōtramuṁ ishṭaśishṭaruṁ* ***baṁdhugaḷuṁ*** *divijēṁdravibhavadiṁ Chaṁdaya maṁgaḷadoḷire sukhadiṁdaṁ* ; **tr.** when Chaṁdaya was leading a happy and auspicious life with excellent lineage whose members were of his high standard, and with people who were likeable and good and with his **kinsmen** ; *S.I.I.* IX, pt. i, No. 298, p. 328, ll. 100-106; Nāgēnahaḷḷi, Rayadurga Tq., Bellary Dt., Karn. St. **Dy.** Kal. of Kal., Saṅkama, Ś. 1118. = 1196 A.D. ; **text[2] :** (fragmentary) *. . . . ī bāḷiṁge Māṇinaṁdariya akka Sādhakagōvitiya saṁbaṁdha . . . . . bāḷiṁge oḷage* ***baṁdhugaḷu*** *horage anyaru āru vakra naḍa . . . .* ; **tr.** in the land belonging to Sādhakagōviti, the elder sister of Māṇinaṁdari, either her **kinsmen** therein or outsiders shall not cause any hindrance ; *S.I.I.* VII, No. 391, p. 250, ll. 19–20; Maṇigārakēri, Udupi Tq. and Dt., Karn. St. **Dy.** Saṅgama, Harihara, Ś. 1321 = 1390 A.D.

baṁdhujana (K. < Skt. *n.*), kinsmen; **text[1] :** . . . . ***baṁdhujan****āśrayanāśritajanakaḷpavṛiksha . . . . perggaḍe Kālidāsayyaṁgaḷu* ; **tr.** the headman Kāḷidāsayya who was a refuge to his **kinsmen** and was like wish–fulfilling tree to his dependants; *S.I.I.* IX, pt. i, No. 102, p. 75, ll. 19, 21 ; Mailāra, Hadagalli Tq., Bellary Dt., Karn. St. **Dy.** Chāḷ. of Kal., Traiḷōkyamalla, Ś. 968 = 1046 A.D. ; **text[2]:** (incomplete)*svakulōddhārakaṁ* ***baṁdhujana*** *chiṁtāmaṇi . . . Ghanagiri Udayādripramukhādi anēkadurga prajā rakshakaṁ* ; **tr.** the promoter of his own lineage, who was concerned about the welfare of his **kinsmen** and was the protector of the subjects living in many forts such as Ghanagiri and Udayādri ; *S.I.I.* IX, pt. ii, No. 507, p. 521, ll. 22–23, 24–25; Chōḷasamudram, Hindupur Tq., Anantapur Dt., A.P. St. **Dy.** Tuḷuva, Kṛishṇadēvarāya, Ś. 1439 = 1517 A.D.

baṁdhuvargga (K. < Skt. *n.*), kinsmen ; **text :** *dvitīyaLakshmīsamāne . . parirakshitātmīya* ***baṁdhuvargge*** *manunītimārgge . . . piriyarasi*

Padmalapaṭṭamahādēvi ; **tr.** the crowned queen Padmale who was like a second (goddess) Lakshmī, who was the protector of her **kinsmen** and who followed the path of Manu's code of ethics ; *S.I.I.* IX, pt. i, No. 330, p. 348, l. 20 ; Hirēhaḍagalli, Hadagalli Tq., Bellary Dt., Karn. St. **Dy.** Hoy., Ballāḷa, Ś. 1133 = 1212 A.D.

baṁḍi (K. *n.*), cart ; **text :** . . . . *Svayaṁbhu Kalidēvara sthaḷakke naḍeyisuva dharma* . . . . *nellakki koḷaga 1* . . . *tuppa māna 1* . . . *aḍake 25 yele 50 aḍugarbbu tiṁgaḷiṁge **baṁḍi** 1*. . . . . . ; **tr.** the donations for sacred service to be conducted at the temple of Svayaṁbhu Kalidēva included 1 *koḷaga* (a grain measure) of rice, 1 *māna* (a liquid measure) of ghee, 25 betelnuts, 50 betel leaves, 1 **cart**(-load) of firewood per month, etc. ; *S.I.I.* IX, pt. i, No. 258, p. 275, ll. 24, 26–27; Bāgaḷi, Harapanahalli Tq., Bellary Dt., Karn. St. **Dy.** Jagadēkamalla II, Reg. yr. 16 = 1153 A.D.

baṁḍi dāri (K. *n.*), cart track ; **text :** . . . . . . *paḍuva **baṁḍi-dāri*** . . . . . ; **tr.** the **cart track** to the west ; *E.C.* II, Sb. 444, p. 272 l. 77 ; Śravaṇabeḷagoḷa, Channarayapatna Tq., Hassan Dt., Karn. St. **Dy.** Hoy., Ballāḷa II, Ś. 1104 = 1181 A.D.

baṁḍi haṇa (K. *n.*), tax levied on carts ; **text :** (damaged and incomplete) *Rāghavadēvara palakisēvegāgi* . . . . *Dhārāpurada çhāvaḍiyali voppi sarvaru varushakke **baṁḍi-haṇa**va pallakisēve* . . . . ; **tr.** for performing the palanquin service to the god Rāghavadēva, all (devotees) met at the village office and agreed to donate per year **tax levied on carts** ; *S.I.I.* IX, pt. ii, No. 644, p. 642, ll. 19–21, 43–45; Dharāpuram, Dharāpuram Tq., Coimbatore Dt., T. Nadu St. **Dy.** Tuḷuva, Sadāśiva, Ś. 1473 = 1551 A.D.

baṁdisu (K. < Skt. *vb.*), to construct ; **text :** . . *mummaḍi Trikāḷayōgimunīṁdrar* . . . *Rāma koṇḍamaṁ **baṁdisi**dar*. . . . . . ; **tr.** the ascetic Trikāḷayōgi caused this tank called Rāmakoṁḍa **to be constructed** ; *S.I.I.* IX, pt. i, No. 403, p. 409, l. 4 ; Rāmatīrtham, Vijayanagaram Tq., Vishakha patnam Dt., A.P. St. **Dy.** E. Chāḷ., Bhīma III, in characters of 12th cent. A.D.

baṁdu iha vokkalugaḷu (K. *n.*), tenants who have migrated from elsewhere ; **text :** *Krushṇa-rāyadēvamahārāyarugaḷa hesarali kaṭṭida pēṭeyali **bandu iha vokkalugaḷu*** . . . . . . ; **tr. tenants who had migrated from elsewhere** and had settled down in the market town established in the name of Krushṇarāyadēvamahārāya ; *S.I.I.* IX, pt. ii, No. 516, p. 531, ll. 4–5 ; Velpamaḍugu, Gooty Tq., Anantapura Dt., A.P. St. **Dy.** Tuḷuva, Krishṇadēvarāya, Ś. 1446 = 1525 A.D.

baṁgāṟa (K. *n.*), jewel ; **text :** . . . . *rāya**baṁgāṟa*** . . . . *Vikramādityanaṁkakāṟa* . . . . . . *Kaligabhūpa* ; **tr.** Kaligabhūpa, the **jewel** of a ruler, the follower of Vikramāditya ; *S.I.I.* IX, pt. i, No. 161, p. 148, ll. 22–24 ; Chinna Tumbaḷam, Adavani Tq., Kurnool Dt., A.P. St.

Dy. Chāḷ. of Kal., Vikramāditya VI, Ch. Vi. yr. 17 = 1092 A.D.

baṁgārujalapoṁtakalaśālu (Te. *n.*), gold-gilded pinnacles ; **text :** . . . . . *Ahōbaḷēśvarula Diguva Tirupatini pedda gōpurānaku* ***baṁgārujalapoṁtakalaśālu*** *ēḍuṁnu viṁjāmarālu reṁḍuṁnu . . . . . . samarppiṁchina vivaraṁ* ; **tr.** details regarding the donation of seven **gold-gilded pinnacles** for the big tower and two fly whisks to the temple of the god Ahōbaḷēśvara at Diguva Tirupati ; *S.I.I.* XVI, No. 310, p. 317, ll. 15–17; Chinna Ahōbaḷam, Sirvel Tq., Kurnool Dt., A.P. St. **Dy.** Āravīḍu, Venkaṭapati, Ś. 1531 = 1609 A.D.

baṁṭar (K. *n.*), cultivators ; **text :** (fragmentary) . . . . *Meḷavāḍiya* **baṁṭar** ; **tr.** the **cultivators** of Meḷavāḍi ; *S.I.I.* IX, pt. i, No. 399, p. 407, l. 10 ; Poḷali Ammunaje, Mangalore Tq., D.K. Dt., Karn. St. **Dy.** Āḷupa, Paṭṭigadēva, in characters of 10th cent. A.D.

baṁṭu (Te. *n.*), confidant ; **text :** . . . . *Narasānāyaniṁgāru tama* ***baṁṭu*** *bokkasaṁ Timmānāyaniṁgāri mariṁdi Suṁkayya Muttukūri Cheṁnakēśvaradēvaraku . . . . ichchina dharmmaśāsanaṁ*; **tr.** the pious grant made to the god Cheṁnakēśvara by Suṁkayya, the son-in-law of Treasurer Tiṁmānāyaka, the **confidant** of Narasānāyaka; *S.I.I.* XVI, No. 37, p. 39, l. 14 ; Mutukūru, Pulivendla Tq., Cuddappah Dt., A.P. St. **Dy.** Tuḷuva, Immaḍi Narasiṁha, Ś. 1415 = 1493 A.D.

bana (K. *n.*), copse ; **text**[1] **:** . . *Sattiyūra Mahādēvarge* ***bana****da Bhaḷāriya baḍagaṇa deseyalu eraḍu khaṁḍuga vedegadde . . . . viṭṭar . . .* ; **tr.** two *khaṁḍuga* (a grain measure) of sowable paddy field situated to the north of the **copse** enshrining the goddess was donated to the god Mahādēva of Sattiyūru ; *S.I.I.* IX, pt. i, No. 99, p. 69, ll. 20–21, 24; Sattūru, Harapanahalli Tq., Bellary Dt., Karn. St. **Dy.** Chāḷ. of Kal., Sōmēśvara I, Ś. 966 = 1044 A.D. ; **text**[2] **:** *parvatada mūḍana deseyoḷu Hiḍiṁbavanamā* ***bana****doḷage Svayaṁbhu Kalidēvasvāmiyeṁbudu ā dēvargge dēgulavaṁ māḍisidaḷu Hiḍiṁbe . . . . .* ; **tr.** within the **copse** called Hiḍiṁbavana to the east of the mountain Hiḍiṁbe constructed the temple for the god Svayaṁbhu Kalidēvasvāmi ; *S.I.I.* IX, pt. i, No. 126, p. 108, ll. 26–28 ; Uchchaṁgidurga, Harapanahalli Tq., Bellary Dt., Karn. St. **Dy.** Chāḷ. of Kal., Āhavamalla, Ś. 986 = 1064 A.D. ; **text**[3] **:** . . . *baḻḻeya keṟeya teṁkaṇa kōḍiya Baḷariya* ***bana*** . . . . . . ; **tr.** the **copse** of the goddess Bhaḷari in the corner on the south of the baḻḻeya tank ; *E.C.* II, Sb. 476, p. 290, l. 62 ; Śravaṇabeḷagoḷa, Channarayapatna Tq., Hassan Dt., Karn. St. **Dy.** Hoy., Narasiṁha I, in characters of 12th cent. A.D.

bānagadde (K. *n.*), paddy field depending on rain water ; **text :** . . *koḷake bayalalli . . . . brahmadāya mūlada bāḷa halagadde* ***bānagadde*** . . . . ; **tr.** the cultivable paddy field and the **paddy field**

depending upon rain situated in the field called *koḷakebayalu*; *S.I.I.* VII, No. 389, p. 245, l. 12 ; Hosakēri, Udupi Tq. and Dt., Karn. St. **Dy.** Tuḷuva, Sadāśiva, Ś. 1491 = 1569 A.D.

bānagēḍu (K. *n.*), failure of rains ; **text**[1] : (damaged) .. *varushaṁprati* ***bānagēḍu*** *baragēḍu* ... *yeṁnade* .... *naḍasi baharu* .... ; **tr.** they should continue to meet the provisions of the grant without giving excuses of **failure of rains**; *S.I.I.* VII, No. 385, p. 241, ll. 32–33 ; Kōṭakēri, Udupi Tq. and Dt., Karn. St. **Dy.** Saṅgama, Dēvarāya, Ś. 1347 = 1425 A.D. ; **text**[2] : *Beṁmaṇaseṭṭi tānu taṁna makkaḷa kāla tanaka 4 muḍi taḷavanū gēṇige bitti varushaṁprati* ***bānagēḍu*** *baṟagēḍu yeṁnade 12 muḍi akkiyanū Rudrapūjege naḍasi baharu* ; **tr.** until the times of his children Beṁmaṇaseṭṭi shall cultivate on lease the land sowable with 4 *muḍi* (a grain measure) of seeds and shall supply 12 *muḍi* of rice every year for the performance of Rudrapūjā without adducing reasons of **failure of rains** ; *S.I.I.* IX, pt. II, No. 444, p. 454, ll. 34–36; Basarūru, Kundapur Tq., Udupi Dt., Karn. St. Dy. Saṅgama, Devarāya, Ś. 1356 = 1433 A.D.

banaguttige (K. *n.*), quit rent on groves ; **text :** .. *Maṇalige nāḍoḷagaṇa Cheṁḍanahaḷḷiya grāma 1 Mūganāḍoḷagaṇa Haradananūrapurda grāma antū ubhayaṁ grāma 2 ṟoḷagaṇa gadde* ... *aṟuvaṇavanu* ***banaguttige*** ..... *ēnuṁṭāda sarvamānyavanu* ... *pūjārigaḷu āgumāḍikoṁbadu* ; **tr.** one village of Chaṁḍanahaḷḷi in Maṇalige nāḍu and one village of Haradanūrapura in the Mūganāḍu, in these two villages, the priests can enjoy the wetlands, tax levied on ploughs and **quit rent on the groves** ; *E.C.* VIII, Al. 41, p. 458, ll. 33–36 ; Pāḷya, Alur Tq., Hassan Dt., Karn. St. **Dy.** Saṅgama, Bukkarāya I, Ś. 1283 = 1360 A.D.

baṇaja (K. *n.*), merchant ; **text :** .. *nāḍa* ***baṇaja*** *dharmmētakke biṭṭa datti* ..... ; **tr.** the grant made by the **merchant** of the *nāḍu* (a territorial division) for the charity water-lift ; *S.I.I.* IX, pt. i, No. 190, p. 185, l. 23 ; Peddahotūru, Gooty Tq., Anantapur Dt., A.P. St. **Dy.** Chāḷ. of Kal., Vikrmāditya VI, Ch. Vi. yr. 38 = 1113 A.D.

baṇaja varttane (K. *n.*), merchants' profession ; **text :** *Kirugasūra grāmadiṁda aramanege Beḷakavāḍiya ṭhāṇeyakke* ... *saluvanthā magga* . . . *gāṇa* ... ***baṇaja varttane*** *muṁtāgi prāku prāmāṇuvina suṁka varaha ga 6* ... *Vaidyanātha dēvarige koḍuvudu. eṁdu Daṁṇāyaka voḍeyara rāyasa* .... ; **tr.** as per the order of Daṁṇāyakavoḍeya six *varaha* of *ga* (*gadyāṇa*, a gold coin) of tax collected at the rate fixed previously on loom, oil mill, **merchants' profession** etc. payable in the divisional office at Beḷakavāḍi from Kiragusūr village for the palace .... are to be paid to the god Vaidyanātha ; *E.C.* VII, Ml. 102, p. 405, ll. 11–14 ; Kiragasūru, Malavalli Tq., Mandya Dt., Karn. St. **Dy.** Saṅgama, Dēvarāya II, Ś. 1362 = 1440 A.D.

bāṇasa (K. *n.*), large kitchen ; **text :** ..... ***bāṇasa***

upakaraava beḷaguvaru jīvitaga 5 . . . . ; **tr.** for the livelihood of those who clean the utensils in the **large kitchen** *ga.* (*gadyāṇa*, gold coin) are set aside ; *E.C.* (R) VIII, HN 95, p. 59, ll. 60–61 ; Māvanūru, Holenarasipura Tq., Hassan Dt., Karn. St. **Dy.** Hoy., Narasiṁha, Ś. 1204 = 1282 A.D.

bāṇasi (K. *n.*), cook ; **text :** . . *Jainagēhamaṁ* . . . . . *Duddamalladēvana* ***bāṇasi*** *Jakkayaṁ māḍisidaṁ* . . . ; **tr.** the Jaina temple was caused to be built by Jakkayya the **cook** of Duddamalladēva ; *E.C.* VIII, Ag. 139, pp. 190–91, ll. 1–3 ; Suḷagūḍu Sōmavāra, Arakalagud Tq., Hassan Dt., Karn. St. **Misc.**, in characters of 11th cent. A.D. ; **text[2] :** . . . *Tribhuvanachūḍāmaṇichaityālayada mukhamaṁṭapamaṁ* . . . . . *māḍisidarā Bhavyajanaṁgaḷāreṁdoḍe* . . . . . ***bāṇasi*** *Maindisettiyarige bhāge 1* . . . . ***bāṇasi*** *Paibhaseṭṭige bhāge 1.* . . . . ; **tr.** the Jaina builders of the *mukhamaṁṭapa* (front hall) of the Tribhuvana chūḍāmaṇichaityālaya included, among others, the **cook** Maindiseṭṭi with one share . . . . the **cook** Paibhaseṭṭi with one share (of contribution) ; *S.I.I.* VII, No. 197, p. 91, ll. 4, 8 ; Mūḍabidure, Karkala Tq., Udupi Dt., Karn. St. **Dy.** Saṅgama, Dēvarāya, Ś. 1373 = 1451 A.D.

bāṇasiga (K. *n.*), cook ; **text :** . . ***bāṇasigaru*** *hattu ardhakkaṁ gadyāṇaṁ nālvatteraḍu* . . . . ; **tr.** forty two *gadyāṇa* (gold coins) were set aside for payment to 10 and odd **cooks** ; *E.C.* V, T. N. 88, p. 480., l. 83 ; Sōmanāthapura, Tirumakudalu Narasipura Tq., Mysore Dt., Karn. St. **Dy.** Hoy., Narasiṁha III, Cy. yr. Dhātṛi = 1276 A.D. ; **text[2] :** (damaged) . . . . *Kṛishṇarāyanāyakaru* . . . . *mahādēvarige* . . . *dēvara abhishēka maṁtrapushpa* ***bāṇasiga*** *viniyōgada* . . . . *Seṭiyhaḷiya grāmavanu kōṭeü* . . ; **tr.** Kṛishṇarāyanāyaka granted the village of Seṭihaḷḷi for providing anointment, worship with flower, preparation of food by **cook** for offering to the god Mahādēva ; *E.C.* (R) IV, PP. 123, p. 571, ll. 4–5, 7–10 ; Śeṭṭihaḷḷi, Piriyapatna Tq., Mysore Dt., Karn. St. **Dy.** Tuḷuva, Krishṇadēvarāya, in characters of 16th cent. A.D.

bāṇasiverggaḍe (K. *n.*), headman of royal kitchen; **text :** . . . . . *mahāpradhānaṁ daṁḍanāyaka* ***bāṇasiverggaḍe*** *Anaṁtayya* . . . . . ; **tr.** the chief minister and army head Anaṁtayya who was the **headman of the royal kitchen** ; *K.I.* IV, No. 3, p. 17, ll. 11–12 ; Sātēnahaḷḷi, Hirekerūr Tq., . Dharwar Dt., Karn. St. **Dy.** Chāḷ. of Kal., Vikramāditya VI, Ch. Vi. yr. 39 = 1114 A.D.

baṇḍārappottagam (T. < Skt. *n.*), Registrar of the treasury ; **text :** . . . . . *Kaṭṭi Nakkaṉ Iraṉaṉ* ***baṇḍārappottagamāga*** . . . . . . ; **tr.** with Kaṭṭi Nakkaṉ Iraṉaṉ as the **Registrar of the treasury** ; *S.I.I.* XIV, No. 95, p. 61, l. 10 ; Ambāsamudram, Ambasamudram Tq., Tirunelveli Dt., T. Nadu St. **Dy.** Pāṇḍya, Vīrapāṇḍya, reg. yr. 12 = 959 A.D.

bānaṁ (K. *n.*), a vessel with wide mouth ; **text:** . . . . . *davasakke hoṁge* ***bānaṁ*** *oṁdu baṇaṁjigar*

. . . *biṭṭa dharmavappudu* . . . . ; **tr.** the merchants gave as an act of charity one **vessel with wide mouth** for storing grains worth one *homnu* (a gold coin) . . . . ; *S.I.I.* IX, pt. i, No. 141, p. 124, l. 30 ; Nīlagunda, Harapanahalli Tq., Bellary Dt., Karn. St. **Dy.** Chāḷ. of Kal., Vikramāditya VI, Ch. Vi. yr. 4 = 1079 A.D.

banaṁ (K. *n.*), grove ; **text :** . . *kaḷaveyiṁ gaḷdeyiṁgaṇgoḷisuva* . . . ***banaṁ*** . . . . ; **tr.** the **grove** which was pleasing to look at with black berry shrubs and paddy fields. . . ; *S.I.I.* IX, pt. i, No. 158, p. 144, ll. 49–50 ; Hūvinahaḍagalli, Hadagalli Tq., Bellary Dt, Karn. St. **Dy.** Chāḷ. of Kal., Vikramāditya VI, Ch. Vi. yr. 15 = 1090 A.D.

baṇaṁbe (K. *n.*), hay-stack ; **text :** (damaged) . . *biṭṭa tōṁṭaṁ Māṇikēśvarada mattaroṁdu* . . . . . . *manege **baṇaṁbe**gaṁ tōṁṭakkaṁ* . . . . ; **tr.** gift of one *mattar* (a land measure) of garden measured by the Māṇikēśvara pole, for the house, a **hay-stack** and a grove. . . ; *K.I.* VI, No. 15, p. 42, l. 24 ; Malghāṇ, Sindagi Tq., Bijapur Dt., Karn. St. **Dy.** Chāḷ. of Kal., Vikramāditya VI, Ch. Vi. yr. 26 = 1101 A.D.

baṇaṁbeya nivēśana (K. *n.*), site of a hay stack; **text :** . . *19 kai agala 20 kai nīḷada **baṇaṁbeya nivēśana** oṁdu* . . . . . . ; **tr.** one **site of a hay stack** measuring 19 arms in width and 20 arms in length ; *K.I.* VI, No. 15, p. 41 , l. 16 ; Malghāṇ, Sindagi Tq., Bijapur Dt., Karn. St. **Dy.** Chāḷ. of Kal., Vikramāditya VI, Ch. Vi. yr. 26 = 1101 A.D.

baṇaṁjiga (K. *n.*), merchant ; **text :** . . . . *Mudiyanūroḷ peṁpaggaḷada **baṇaṁjiga**nene Kētiseṭṭiya pogaḷadarār* . . . . ; **tr.** who indeed does not praise the great **merchant** Kētiseṭṭi in Muḍiyanūru ? . . . . ; *S.I.I.* IX, pt. i, No. 296, p. 320, l. 27 ; Kurugōḍu, Bellary Tq. and Dt., Karn. St. **Dy.** Kal. of Kal., Sōvidēva, Ś. 1097 = 1176 A.D.

baṇaṁjigar (K. *n.*), traders ; **text**[1] **:** . . *taḷada **baṇaṁjigar**uṁ nānādēsigaḷuvirdu dēvargge* . . . *biṭṭa dharma* . . . . . ; **tr.** the donation jointly made by the **traders** of the place and the *nānādēsigaḷ* (merchants doing business in various countries) ; *S.I.I.* IX, pt. i, No. 141, p. 124, l. 29 ; Nīlagunda, Harapanahalli Tq., Bellary Dt., Karn. St. **Dy.** Chāḷ. of Kal., Vikramāditya VI, Ch. Vi. yr. 4 = 1079 A.D. ; **text**[2] **:** . . *ī staḷada hēṟuva **baṇaṁjigaru** ṭhāṇavāga paṇa oṁdu koḍuvaru* . . . . . ; **tr.** the **traders** who pick up their loads from this place shall give one *paṇa* (a coin) as their share to that place ; *K.I.* VI, No. 42, p. 128, l. 16; Raṭṭihaḷḷi, Hirekerur Tq., Dharwar Dt., Karn. St. **Dy.** Sēü. of Dēv., Siṅghaṇa II, Cy. yr. Hēmaḷaṁbi = 1237 A.D.

baṇaṁjigar ainūrbaru (K. *n.*), merchant guild of five hundred members ; **text :** . . . . *samasta **baṇaṁjigar ainūrbaru**virdu biṭṭa dharma* . . . . ; **tr.** grant made by the entire **merchant guild of five hundred members** ; *S.I.I.* IX, pt. i, No. 144, p. 124, l. 30 ; Nīlagunda, Harapanahalli Tq., Bellary Dt., Karn. St. **Dy.** Chāḷ. of Kal., Vikramāditya

VI, Ch. Vi. yr. 4 = 1079 A.D.

baṇaṁjudharmma (K. *n.*), traders' code of ethics; **text** : . . . . . *nayavinayavijñānavīrāvatāra* ***baṇaṁjudharmma****pratipāḷana* . . . . *Ayyāvoḷey ainūrvvarsvāmigaḷu* ; **tr.** Ayyāvoḷeyainūvvar svāmigaḷ, who were (all) the very incarnation of polity, humility, knowledge and bravery and who were upholders of the **traders' code of ethics** ; *S.I.I.* IX, pt. i, No. 391, p. 402, ll. 2, 4–6 ; Kuruvatti, Harapanahalli Tq., Bellary Dt., Karn. St. **Dy.** Gutta, Vikramāditya II, Ś. 1104 = 1181 A.D.

baṇaṁjuvaṭṭaṇa (K. *n.*), commercial town ; **text**[1] : . . . . *Kūṁḍi mūṟusāsiradoḷage hanneraḍakkaṁ modala bāḍaṁ* ***baṇaṁjuvaṭṭanaṁ*** . . . . . *Tēridāḷa* . . . . . ; **tr.** Tēridāḷa, the **commercial town**, which was the leading town among the twelve villages of Kūṁḍi-three thousand ; *K.I.* V, No. 98, p. 298, l. 4 ; Tērdāḷ, Jamakhandi Tq., Bijapur Dt., Karn. St. Comm. gld., Ś. 1104 = 1181 A.D. ; **text**[2] : . . *Nāgarakhaṁḍaveppattaṟa baḷiya bāḍaṁ* ***baṇaṁjuvaṭṭanaṁ*** *Sātēnahaḷḷi* . . . . ; **tr.** Sātēnahaḷḷi, the **commercial town**, a place included in Nāgarakhaṁḍa-seventy ; *K.I.* IV, No. 1, p. 7, ll. 42–43 ; Sātēnahaḷḷi, Hirekerur Tq., Dharwar Dt., Karn. St. **Dy.** Hoy., Ballāḷa, Ś. 1126 = 1204 A.D.

bāṇe (K. *n.*), bucket ; **text** : . . *ōjugaḷu dharmaḍōṇige nīra etuva kabiṇada ētada* ***bāṇe*** . . . . . . *tappade naḍasibāhevu* . . . . ; **tr.** we the artisans shall fulfill our undertaking of supplying an iron **bucket** to bale out water for the charity water-trough ; *S.I.I.* IX, pt. ii, No. 670, p. 663, ll. 21–23; Chatradahaḷḷi, Hadagalli Tq., Bellary Dt., Karn. St. **Dy.** Tuḷuva, Sadāśiva, Ś. 1481 = 1559 A.D.

baṇṇige (K. *n.*), dyeing ; **text** : . . *Bālachandradēvara guḍḍa heggaḍe Challayanu Māṟikaliya Trikūṭa Jinālayakke* . . . . *maduve* ***baṇṇige*** . . . . *volagāgi samasta suṅkavaṁ*. . . . *biṭṭar* . . . . ; **tr.** Heggaḍe Challaya lay desciple of Bālachaṁdradēva remitted for the Trikūṭa Jinālaya of Māṟikali all the custom dues including those on marriage, **dyeing** etc. ; *E.C.* VIII, Hn. 174, p. 411, ll. 73–75 ; Markuli, Hassan Tq. and Dt., Karn. St. **Dy.** Hoy., Vīraballāḷa, Ś. 1095 = 1173 A.D. ; **baṇṇigedeṟe** (K. *n.*) ; tax on dyeying ; **text**[1] : . . . . *Mallugidēva pramukha karaṇaṁgaḷu Beḷuhaḍeya dēviṁgeṟege āvūra* ***baṇṇigedeṟe****ya biṭṭar* . . ; **tr.** clerks led by Mallugidēva donated the **tax on dyeing** (for the maintenance) of the Dēviṁgeṟe tank at Beḷuhaḍe; *K.I.* V, No. 39, p. 157, l. 6 ; Belhōḍ, Gadag Tq. and Dt., Karn. St. **Dy.** Kal. of Kal., Saṅkama, reg. yr. 3 = 1178 A.D. ; **text**[2] : (damaged and incomplete) . . . . ***baṇṇigedeṟe****ya heggaḍe Biṭiyaṇṇa* . . . ; **tr.** Biṭṭiyaṇṇa the officer in charge of collecting the **tax on dyeing** . . . . . ; *E.C.* (R) VIII, Hn. 26, p. 258, l. 2 ; Doḍḍagaddavaḷḷi, Hassan Tq. and Dt., Karn. St. **Dy.** Hoy., Narasiṁha II, Cy. yr. Sarvajit = 1227 A.D.

baṇṭaṁ (K. *n.*), confidant ; **text** : . . . . *mahāsāmantaṁ Kannana* ***baṇṭaṁ*** . . . . *nerevoḍe* ***baṇṭaṁ*** . . . *Sōbhanarasar* ; **tr.** Sōbhanarasar, the

confidant of *mahāsāmanta* (Great feudatary) Kanna and the **confidant** of those who were close to him ; *S.I.I.* XI, No. 47, p. 33, ll. 7–8 ; Hosūru, Gadag Tq. and Dt., Karn. St. **Dy.** Chāḷ. of Kal., Taila II, Ś. 915 = 994 A.D.

barada (K. *indec.*), written ; **text :** .... *haṁneraḍu maṁdi brāhmaru bhōjanava māḍuvadakke muṁna* ***barada*** *akkiya mūḍe 120* .... ; **tr.** 120 *mūḍe* (a grain measure) of rice for feeding twelve *brāhmaṇas* as was **written** earlier ; *S.I.I.* VII, No. 385, p. 241, ll. 27–28 ; Kōṭakēri, Udupi Tq. and Dt., Karn. St. **Dy.** Saṅgama, Dēvarāya, Ś. 1347 = 1425 A.D.

barada kallu (K. *n.*), inscribed stone ; **text :** ... *Kuṁdāpurada grāmake varushavoṁdakke ikkuva samudāya gadyāṇa 140 eṁdu* ***barada kallu*** .. ; **tr. inscribed stone** registering the fact that the annual tax to be paid by the village of Kuṁdāpura is 140 collective *gadyāṇa* (gold coins) ...... ; *S.I.I.* IX, pt. i, No. 396, p. 406, ll. 14–17; Kōṭēśvara, Kundapur Tq., Udupi Dt., Karn. St. **Dy.** Āḷupa, Paṭṭamahādēvi and Pāṁḍyadēva, Ś. 1184 = 1262 A.D.

baradāta (K. *n.*), he who engraved (the stone inscription) ; **text :** ..... *ī śāsanava* ***baradāta*** *kallukuṭiga Kaṁnapanu* .... ; **tr. he who engraved** this inscription is the stone mason Kaṁnapa ... ... ; *S.I.I.* VII, No. 382, p. 238, ll. 134–37; Koṭakēri, Udupi Tq. and Dt., Karn. St. **Dy.** Saṅgama, Dēvarāya, Ś. 1356 = 1434 A.D.

baradava (K. *n.*), he who engraved (the stone inscription) ; **text** (badly damaged) ... *baradava* ..... *Tippayya*; **tr.** (the stone inscription) has been **engraved** by Tippayya ; *S.I.I.* VII, No. 387, p. 245, l. 77; Kōṭakēri, Udupi Tq. and Dt., Karn. St. **Dy.** Saṅgama, Bukkarāya, Ś. 1294 = 1372 A.D.

bar̤adukoḍu (K. *vb.*), give in writing ; **text :** .. .. *hattu hoṁnanū Maṇigār̤akēriya Sōmanāthadēvarige Sōyidēvarasaru* ... ***bar̤adu koṭṭaru*** ..... ; **tr.** Sōyidēvarasa **gave in writing** ten gold (coins) to the god Sōmanātha of Maṇigār̤akēri ...... ; *S.I.I.* VII, No. 354, p. 212, ll. 12–15; Maṇigār̤akēri, Udupi Tq. and Dt., Karn. St. **Dy.** Āḷupa, Sōyidēva, Ś. 1238 = 1316 A.D.

bar̤agēḍu (K. *n.*), drought ; **text**[1] **:** .... *Kṛishṇa Maṁḍachaṁge* .... *mūlavāgi* ... *koṭṭaru ā Maṁḍachanu bānagēḍu* ***bar̤agēḍu*** *yeṁnade* .... *nāgaṁḍugadalu* ..... *akki mūḍe 10 nū* ... *Bārakūrige taṁdu hāi'kuvanu* ... ; **tr.** ... Krishṇa Maṁḍacha was given (land) on permanent lease; that Maṁḍacha shall supply 19 *mūḍe* (a grain measure) of rice to Bārakūru without adducing excuse of failure of rains or **drought** ; *S.I.I.* VII, No. 319, p. 169, l. 26; Mūḍakēri, Udupi Tq. and Dt., Karn. St. **Dy.** Saṅgama, Bukkarāya, Ś. 1293 = 1371 A.D. ; **text**[2] **:** .... *Beṁmaṇaseṭṭi tānu taṁna makkaḷa kāla tanaka 4 muḍi taḷavanū gēṇige bitti varushaṁprati bānagēḍu* ***bar̤agēḍu*** *yeṁnade 12 muḍi akkiyanū Rudrapūjege* ...... *naḍasibaharu*; **tr.** Beṁmaṇaseṭṭi shall cultivate on lease land of the extent of being sown with 4 *muḍi* (a grain measure) of seeds and shall give 12 *muḍi* of rice every year for Rudrapūjā until the times of self and his sons without adducing excuse of **drought** ; *S.I.I.* IX, pt. ii, No. 444, p. 454, ll. 34–36 ; Basarūru, Kundapur Tq., Udupi Dt., Karn. St. **Dy.** Saṅgama, Dēvarāya, Ś. 1356 = 1433 A.D.

baragu (K. *n.*), Indian millet ; **text :** ... *Durgādēviya dēguladalu agrake maḍagida* .... **baragina** *gadde 3 mūḍe bittuvudu* .. ; **tr.** 3 *mūḍe* (a grain measure) of seeds of **Indian millet** shall be sown on the wet field for providing food for *brāhmaṇas* in the temple of Durgādēvi ; *S.I.I.* VII, No. 223, p. 112, l. 20; Prāṁta, Mudabidure Tq., Udupi Dt., Karn. St. **Dy.** Āḷupa, Kulaśēkhara, Ś. 1127 = 1205 A.D.

baraha[1] (K. *n.*), writing ; **text**[1] **:** .... *Mallappagaḷa* **baraha** ... ; **tr.** the **writing** of Mallappa ; *S.I.I.* VII, No. 342, p. 196, ll. 25–26 ; Chauḷikēri, Udupi Tq. and Dt., Karn. St. **Dy.** Saṅgama, Harihara, Ś. 1318 = 1396 A.D. ; **text**[2] **:** .... *yiṁtī śāsanada vakkaṇeya Aṁṇasāmaṁta- heggaḍeyara sēnabōva dēvarasara* **baraha** ... ; **tr.** the **writing** of the text of the inscription is by Dēvarasa, the *Sēnabōva* (Village Accountant) of Aṁṇasāmaṁtaheggaḍe.. .. ; *S.I.I.* VII, No. 198, p. 93, l. 13 ; Mūḍabidure, Karkala Tq., Udupi Dt., Karn. St. **Dy.** Saṅgama, Virūpāksha, Ś. 1384 = 1462 A.D.

baraha[2] (K. *n.*), signature ; **text :** .... *Nārāyaṇa dēvara saṁnidhiyali baradu naṭṭa śilāśāsana* ..... *iṁtappudakke Nāgarasara* **baraha** ... ; **tr.** the inscribed stone slab has been set up in the proximity of the god Nārāyaṇa ; this is Nāgarasa's **signature** in confirmation; *S.I.I.* VII, No. 350, p. 208, ll. 41–42 ; Chauḷikēri, Udupi Tq. and Dt., Karn. St. **Dy.** Saṅgama, Harihara, Ś. 1321 = 1399 A.D.

Bārakanūra gadyāṇa (K. *n.*), gold coin minted at Bārakūru ; **text**[1] **:** ...... ***Bārakanūra gadyāṇa*** *50 Maṅgaḷūra gadyāṇa 50 iṁtu eraḍu gadyāṇa 100* ... ; **tr. 50 *gadyāṇa* (gold coin) minted at Bārakanūru** and 50 *gadyāṇa* minted at Mangalūru adding up to 100 **gadyāṇa** ..... ; *S.I.I.* VII, No. 223, p. 112, l. 24 ; Prāṁta, Udupi Tq. and Dt., Karn. St. **Dy.** Pāṇḍya, Kulaśēkhara, Ś. 1127 = 1205 A.D.

bārakkūli (T. *n.*), freight charges ; **text :** .... (badly damaged) .... ***bārakkūli*** .... ; **tr. freight charges** ... ; *S.I.I.* XXII, No. 278, p. 220, l. 25 ; Tirumālapuram, Walajapet Tq., North Arcot Dt., T. Nadu St., **Dy.** Chōḷa, Rājarāja I, in characters of 10th-11th Cent. A.D.

Bārakūra gadyāṇa (K. *n.*), gold coin minted at Bārakūru ; **text :** .... *ā satrada mēlu vechakke* ...... *varusha 1 kke* ***Bārakūra ga*** *68* ..... ; **tr.** for the additional expenditure of the choultry per year 68 *ga* (*gadyāṇa*, **gold coin**) **minted at Bārakūru** are earmarked..... ; *S.I.I.* VII, No. 330, p. 180, ll. 27–28 ; Mūḍakēri, Udupi Tq. and Dt., Karn. St. **Dy.** Saṅgama, Bukkarāya, Ś. 1281 = 1359 A.D.

Bārakūra kaṁchina hāne (K. *n.*), bronze measure

standardized in Bārakūru territory ; **text :** . . . . ***Bārakūra*** ***kaṁ**chi**na*** ***hāne**ge ota baha akki hāne 16* . . . . ; **tr.** 16 *hāne* (a grain measure) of rice measurable with the **bronze measure standardized in Bārakūru territory**. . . . .; *S.I.I.* VII, No. 385, p. 241, ll. 31–32 ; Kōṭakēr̤i, Udupi Tq. and Dt., Karn. St. **Dy.** Saṅgama, Dēvarāya, Ś. 1347 = 1425 A.D.

Bārakanūra kāṭi gadyāṇa (K. *n.*), pure gold coin minted at Bārakūru ; **text :** . . . *kuḷavāgi tamma baha* ***Bārakūra kāṭi gadyāṇa*** *100* . . . ; **tr.** 100 **pure gold coin minted at Bārakūru** received by me as revenue income . . . . ; *S.I.I.* VII, No. 303, pp. 155, l. 6 ; Udupi, Udupi Tq. and Dt., Karn. St. **Dy.** Saṅgama, Harihara, in characters of 14th cent. A.D.

Bārakūra parivartana (K. *n.*), exchange rate for Bārakūru coins ; **text :** (damaged) . . . . . . *ī sarvasvavanu biḍāruvāravāgi Chikadaṁṇaṁdaru* ***Bārakūra parivartana**ke saluva doḍa va ga 81* . . . . . *tegedukoṁḍaru* . . . . . ; **tr.** Chikadaṁṇaṁdaru had taken all these movable and immovable assets (listed in the inscription) by paying *va* (*varaha*, a coin) *ga* (*gadyāṇa*, gold coin) at the prevailing **exchange rate for Bārakūru coins** ; *S.I.I.* IX, pt. ii, No. 525, p. 540, ll. 15, 18 ; Basarūru, Kundapur Tq., Udupi Dt., Karn. St. **Dy.** Tuḷuva, Kṛishṇadēvarāya, Ś. 1451 = 1528 A.D.

Bārakūra tāra (K. *n.*), silver/copper coin minted at Bārakuru ; **text :** (damaged) . . . . . . ***Bārakūra tāra*** *20* . . . *dēvālyadalu taṁdukoḍuvanu* . . . . . . ; **tr.** he will bring **20 silver/copper coins minted at Bārakūru** and give it to the temple . . . ; *S.I.I.*VII, No. 231, p. 117, ll. 16–17; Kāntāvara, Mudabidure Tq., Udupi Dt., Karn. St. **Dy.** Saṅgama, Harihara, in characters of 14th cent. A.D.

barasi koḍu (K. *vb.*), give in writing; **text :** *haṁnoṁdu hoṁnige baṁda kuḷāgrada ter̤ina hoṁnanu* . . . . *sōmanāthadēvarigū Ādiparamēśvararigū* . . . . *dharmakke biṭṭu* ***barasi koṭṭa*** *śilāśāsana* . . . . . ; **tr.** pious charity **given in writing** on a stone slab to the gods Sōmanātha and Ādiparamēśvara of the tax income in gold on eleven *hoṁnu* (gold coins) . . . . . ; *S.I.I.* VII, No. 368, p. 224, ll. 14–15 ; Maṇigār̤akēri, Udupi Tq. and Dt., Karn. St. **Dy.** Saṅgama, Mallikārjuna, Ś. 1375 = 1453 A.D.

barasida (K. *indec.*), got written ; **text :** . . . . *brāhmaṇa bhōjanakke dāna* . . . *koṭu* ***barasida*** *śilāśāsana* . . . . ; **tr.** stone inscription **got written** registering a grant given for feeding brāhmaṇas ; *S.I.I.* VII, No. 385, p. 240, ll. 9–10; Kōṭakēri, Udupi Tq. and Dt., Karn. St. **Dy.** Saṅgama, Dēvarāya, Ś. 1347 = 1425 A.D.

bar̤a siḍilu (K. *n.*), dry thunderbolt ; **text :** . . . ***bar̤a siḍilu*** *pagege tannam mar̤evokka naraṁge vajrapaṁjaraṁ* . . . . . ; **tr.** a strong shelter to those who seek his refuge on being struck like a **dry thunderbolt** by his enemy ; *S.I.I.* IX, pt. i, No. 249, p. 256, ll. 44–45; Kōlūr, Bellary Tq. and Dt., Karn. St. **Dy.** Chāḷ. of Kal., Jagadēkamalla II,

reg. yr. 10 = 1147 A.D.

bare[1] (K. *vb.*), to write ; **text**[1] **:** . . . . . . *perggaḍe Kāḷidāsayya* ***bare****daṁ* . . . . . ; **tr.** the headman Kāḷidāsayya **wrote** . . . . . ; *S.I.I.* IX, pt. i, No. 89, p. 60, ll. 29–30; Bāgaḷi, Bellary Tq. and Dt., Karn. St. **Dy.** Chāḷ. of Kal., Jagadēkamalla II, Ś. 957 = 1035 A.D. ; **text**[2] **:** . . . . . *siḷāsāsanadoḷu Manu munigaḷa vākyamanaṟiye Nāgaṁma* ***bare****daṁ* . . . . . ; **tr.** Nāgaṁma **wrote** (the text of) this inscription expounding the utterances of Manu and the seers; *S.I.I.* IX, pt. i, No. 102, p. 77, ll. 52–53 ; Mailāra, Bellary Tq. and Dt., Karn. St. **Dy.** Chāḷ. of Kal., Āhavamalla, Ś. 968 = 1046 A.D.

bare[2] (K. *n.*), hillock ; **text :** . . . . *paḍuvalu* ***bare****ya baḷiya gaddeyiṁdaṁ mūḍalu* . . . . . ; **tr.** on the west, to the east of the wet field by the side of the **hillock** . . ; *S.I.I.* VII, No. 347, p. 204, l. 21; Chauḷikēri, Udupi Tq. and Dt., Karn. St. **Dy.** Saṅgama, Harihara, Ś. 1309 = 1387 A.D.

bareda (K. *indec.*), written ; **text :** . . *ī śasanadoḷ* ***bareda*** *stithiyaṁ pālippōr Anaṁtaśivaruṁ Laguḷīśvararuṁ* . . . . . ; **tr.** the conditions **written** in this inscription are to be protected by the Anaṁtīśvaras and Lakuḷīśvaras ; *S.I.I.* IX, pt. i, No. 19, p. 9, ll. 20–22 ; Hēmāvati, Kalyanadurga Tq., Anantapur Dt., A. P. St. **Dy.** Noḷ. Pal., Mahēndra I, in characters of 9th cent. A.D.

barepa (K. *n.*), writing ; **text :** . . . *Kōvarājana* ***barepa*** ; **tr.** the **writing** of Kōvarāja; *S.I.I.* IX, pt. i, No. 157, p. 140, l. 71 ; Konakoṇḍla, Gooty Tq., Anantapur Dt., A.P. St. **Dy.** Chāḷ. of Kal., Vikramāditya VI, Ch. Vi. yr. 12 = 1088 A.D.

bārika (K. *n.*), village sentry ; **text**[1] **:** (damaged) . . . . *samasta* . . . . . . *birudaruṁ bīravaṇigaruṁ* ***bārika*** . . . *gāvuṁḍugaḷuṁ* . . . . *Beḷupāḍiya* . . . *Mūlasthānadēvargge* . . . *biṭṭaru* . . . . ; **tr.** all title-holders, warriors-cum-traders, **village sentry**, village headmen granted (details lost) to the god Mūlasthānadēva of Beḷupāḍi ; *K.I.* V, No. 37, p. 151, ll. 37–38 ; Beḷhōḍ, Gadag Tq. and Dt., Karn. St. **Dy.** Kal. of Kal., Rāyamurāri Sōvidēva, reg. yr. 8 = 1174 A.D. ; **text**[2] **:** . . . . *agasa nāyiṁda* ***bārika*** . . . *muṁtāda samasta birugaḷige jōḷada Kaḍāyavanu hākalilla.* . . . . . ; **tr.** persons of lower positions such as washermen, barbers and **village sentries** have not been subjected to compulsory levy of millet ; *S.I.I.* IX, pt. ii, No. 554, p. 575, ll. 42–44 ; Kavatāḷaṁ, Adavani Tq., Kurnool Dt., A.P. St. **Dy.** Tuḷuva, Achyutarāya, Ś. 1454 = 1533 A.D.

baruhu (K. *n.*), a ridge raised along the field ; **text :** . . . . *paḍuvaṇa sīme Kariya Rāmaṇana hakkala* ***baruhu*** . . . . ; **tr.** the western boundary is **the ridge raised along the** fallow **field** of Kariya Rāmaṇa ; *K.I.* V, No. 32, p. 133, l. 76 ; Dharwar, Dharwar Tq. and Dt., Karn. St. **Dy.** Kād. of Goa, Jayakēśi III, reg. yr. 28 = 1215 A.D.

basadi (K. < Skt. *n.*), Jaina temple ; **text**[1] **:** . . . . *basadige seṭṭiyarpannasigar gāvuṇḍugaḷ modalāgi mānykāṟaru śrāhege pariyāra gadyāṇavantiṟuvar.* . . . . . ; **tr.** those donees who enjoy the gifted lands such as the *seṭṭi* (agriculturists), the *pannasiga* (those enjoy 50 shares of the gift lands) and the village head men shall each pay to the **Jaina temple** as compensation one *gadyāṇa* (gold coin) ; *S.I.I.* IX, pt. i, No. 77, p. 48, ll. 22, 30 ; Kōgaḷi, Bellary Tq. and Dt., Karn. St. **Dy.** Chāḷ. of Kal., Āhavamalla, Ś. 914 = 992 A.D. ; **text**[2] : . . . . . . *Tāṭipāṟapurada Chaṁdranātha Pāruśvanātha* . . . . . **basadi***ya khaṁḍasphuṭita jīrṇṇōddhārakaṁ dēvarashṭavidhārchchanegaṁ āhāradānakaṁ* . . . . . *biṭṭa vṛiṭṭi* ; **tr.** the grant given for the repairs and renovation of the **Jaina temple** and for the eight types of worship of Chaṁdranātha and Pāruśvanātha and for free feeding ; *S.I.I.* IV, No. 798, p. 271, ll. 42–43, 53 ; Tāḍapatri, Tadapatri Tq., Anantapur Dt., A.P. St. **Dy.** Kalukaḍepura Chfs., Udayāditya, Ś. 1130 = 1208 A.D.

basanigar (K. *n.*), persons addicted to vices ; **text:** . . . . **basanigar***ggaṁ kaḷkuḍivavarggaṁ vṛittilōpaṁ* . . . . ; **tr.** those who are **addicted to vices** and those who imbibe intoxicating drinks are barred from receiving gift shares ; *S.I.I.* IX, pt. i, No. 117, p. 93, ll. 37–38 ; Kōgaḷi, Bellary Tq. and Dt., Karn. St. **Dy.** Chāḷ. of Kal., Sōmēśvara, Ś. 977 = 1055 A.D.

basaṁta (K. < Skt. *vasanta*), spring season ; **text :** . . . . . . *phaḷaṁgaḷalu sōneye sōne enalu nirutam* **basaṁtaṁ**. . . . . ; **tr.** the **spring season** was truly characterised by the sap oozing from the stalks of plucked fruits ; *S.I.I.* IX, pt. i, No. 267, p. 284, l. 26 ; Bāgaḷi, Hirehadagalli Tq., Bellary Dt., Karn. St. **Dy.** Chāḷ. of Kal., Jagadēkamalla, Ś. 1082 = 1160 A.D.

basavitti (K. *n.*), lady dedicated to religious institution ; **text :** . . . . . . *maṭhava bōharisuva* **basavitti***ya jana oṁdakkaṁ varisa oṁdakkaṁ akki mūḍe eraḍu hāne hattu* . . . . . ; **tr.** for the feeding of one **lady dedicated to the religious institution** for cleaning the same one *mūḍe* (a grain measure) and ten *hāne* (a grain measure) of rice were earmarked per year. . . . . ; *S.I.I.* IX, pt. ii, No. 417, p. 423, ll. 38–39; Kōṭēśvara, Kundapur Tq., Udupi Dt., Karn. St. **Dy.** Saṅgama, Harihara, Ś. 1300 = 1378 A.D.

basir peṇḍir (K. *n.*), pregnant women ; **text :** . . . . *idanaḷidōṁ* . . . . . . *sāsirvvar* **basir peṇḍir***uma sāyira keṟeyumanaḷidōna lōkakke salgu* . . . . ; **tr.** whoever destroys this (grant) will be condemned to the same world destined for those who would have killed one thousand **pregnant women** and destroyed thousand tanks ; *S.I.I.* IX, pt. i, No. 40, p. 23, ll. 12–15 ; Kalugōḍu, Rayadurga Tq., Bellary Dt., Karn. St. **Dy.** Noḷ-Pal., Maydammarasa, Ś. 899 = 977 A.D.

basti (K. *s.a. basadi < Skt. vasati, n.*), Jaina temple ; **text**[1] **:** . . . . *teṁkalu* **basti***ya mekkeya gaḍiyiṁdaṁ baḍagalu* . . . . ; **tr.** on the south the northern boundary is the low-yielding elevated land of the **Jaina temple** ; *S.I.I.* VII, No. 383,

p. 238, l. 9; Kōṭakēri, Udupi Tq. and Dt., Karn. St. **Misc.,** Ś. 1336 = 1414 A.D. ; **text**[2] : . . . . *Paḍuvakēriyoḷage Cheṁnappaseṭṭiheggaḍe gaḍiyiṁda baḍaga***basti***ya bāḷagaḍiyiṁda teṁka gadde* . . . ; **tr.** within the bounds of Paḍuvakēri, the wet field to the south of the land belonging to the **Jaina temple** and to the north of the land belonging to Cheṁnappaseṭṭiheggaḍe ; *S.I.I.* VII, No. 375, p. 230, ll. 18–19, 26–27 ; Maṇigāṟakēri, Udupi Tq. and Dt., Karn. St. **Dy.** Āravīḍu, Śrīraṁga, Ś. 1502 = 1580 A.D.

baṭe (K. wrong for *baṭṭe, n.*), pathway ; **text** : . . . . *Vaṁganūra* ***baṭe****ya Rāvikūḍe* . . . . ; **tr.** the **pathway** leading from Vaṁganūru to Rāvikūḍe ; *S.I.I.* IV, No. 798, p. 271, l. 55 ; Tāḍapatri, Tadapatri Tq., Anantapur Dt., A.P. St. **Dy.** Kalukaḍepura chfs., Udayāditya, Ś. 1130 = 1208 A.D.

battada maṇṇu (K. *n.*), land measure ; **text** : . . . . *Maṇiliya Sattiyāramaṇa kaṭṭāri kāḷēgadali kalnāḍu paḍeda innūru battada maṇṇaṁ* . . ; **tr.** Sattiyāramaṇa of Maṇili fought in a dagger fight and obtained two hundred ***batta* of land** as *kalnāḍu* (installed hero-stone) ; *E.C.* (R) III, Hg. 110, p. 507, ll. 8–14 ; Maḷali, H. D. Kote Tq. Mysore Dt., Karn. St. **Dy. Misc.,** in characters of 10th cent. A.D.

baṭṭalu (K. *n.*), metal plate ; **text**[1] : . . . . ***baṭṭala*** *tāṁbūlaṁbaḍevantī maryāde* . . . . ; **tr.** this honour of receiving arecanuts and betel nuts offered in a **metal plate** ; *S.I.I.* IX, pt. i, No. 77, p. 49, l. 35 ; Kōgaḷi, Bellary Tq. and Dt., Karn. St. **Dy.** Chāḷ. of Kal., Āhavamalla, Ś. 914 = 992 A.D.; **text**[2] : . . . . *Tribhuvanachūḍāmaṇichaityālayakke* . . . . . . ***rajata****da pari pariya* ***baṭṭala****ṁ* . . . *Bhairavēśvaran ittaṁ* . . . . . ; **tr.** Bhairavēśvara donated different types of **silver plates** to the Tribhuvanachūḍāmaṇi chaityālaya ; *S.I.I.* VII, No. 202, p. 98, l. 50 ; Mūḍabidure, Karkala Tq., Udupi Dt., Karn. St. **Dy.** Saṅgama, Dēvarāya, Ś. 1351 = 1429 A.D.

baṭṭe (K. *n.*), pathway ; **text**[1] : . . . . *Ātukūriṁge pōda* ***baṭṭe*** . . . . . ; **tr.** the **pathway** leading to Ātukūru ; *S.I.I.* IX, pt. i, No. 119, p. 100, l. 40 ; Kottapalle, Nandikotkur Tq., Kurnool Dt., A.P. St. **Dy.** Chāḷ. of Kal., Trailōkyamalla, Ś. 980 = 1057 A.D. ; **text**[2] : . . . . . *teṁka Bāḷguḷiya* ***baṭṭe****yiṁ mūḍalu* . . . . ; **tr.** in the south, to the east of the **pathway** leading to Bāḷguḷi ; *S.I.I.* IX, pt. i, No. 158, p. 144, l. 54 ; Hirēhadagaḷḷi, Bellary Tq. and Dt., Karn. St. **Dy.** Chāḷ. of Kal., Vikramāditya VI, Ch. Vi. yr. 15 = 1090 A.D. ; **text**[3] : . . . *baḍagaṇa* ***baṭṭe****ya kāluveya usubu* . . . ; **tr.** the sandbank of the canal along the northern **pathway**; *S.I.I.* IX, pt. ii, No. 440, p. 449, l. 34 ; Rajabavanahaḷḷi, Harapanahalli Tq., Bellary Dt., Karn. St. **Dy.** Saṅgama, Dēvarāya, Ś. 1341 = 1419 A.D.

baṭṭi (K. *n.*), pathway ; **text** : . . . . *Haḍuvalu* . . . . *Māvinakereya gaddeyoḷagāgi Beḷagoḷakke hōda* ***baṭṭi*** *gaḍi* . . . . . ; **tr.** proceeding through the wetland of the Māvinakeṟe tank, the **pathway**

leading to Beḷagoḷa is the boundary ; *E.C.* (R) II, Sb. 82, p. 65, l. 44; Chikkabeṭṭa (Śravaṇabeḷagoḷa), Channarayapatna Tq., Hassan Dt., Karn. St. **Dy.** Hoy., Vishṇuvardhana, Ś. 1039 = 1118 A.D.

bavara (K. *n.*), battle ; **text:** . . . *Muṁmuri daṁḍaṁgaḷ* . . . . . *āṭanda* ***bavara****kke nāṭakaṁ nalivaruṁ* . . . . ; **tr.** (the members of the merchant guild called) *Mummuridaṁḍa* . . . . . treated as a joyful play **battle** thrust upon them . . . ; *S.I.I.* IX, pt. i, No. 296, p. 320, ll. 23–24; Kurugōḍu, Bellary Tq. and Dt., Karn. St. **Dy.** Kal. of Kal., Sōvidēva, Ś. 1097 = 1176 A.D.

bavara gaṁḍa (K. *n.*), great in war ; **text :** (damaged) . . . . *Chikkakāṭayya sargatanāge* . . . ***bavara gaṁḍa*** *taḻara Makayya kalla nilisida* . . . ; **tr.** Chikkakāṭayya having died in a battle, the village watchman Makayya, who was **great in war** set up the herostone ; *E.C.* (R) IX, Skl. 32, p. 519, ll. 4–6 ; Chikkanāyakanahaḷḷi, Sakaleshpura Tq., Hassan Dt., Karn. St. **Dy.** W. Gaṅga, Nītimahārāja, Cy. yr. Bhāva = 1034 A.D.

bāvi, bhāvi (K. *n.*), well ; **text**[1] **:** . . . . . . *Baṇṭarasarā koṭṭudu* . . . . *Dharmmabhaṭārargge* . . . . . *nelanu keṟeyu* ***bāvi****yu* . . . . ; **tr.** Baṇṭarasa gave to god Dharmmabhaṭāra land, tank, **well**, etc. ; *S.I.I.* IX, pt. i, No. 48, p. 28, ll. 15–16; Chippagiri, Alur Tq., Bellary Dt., Karn. St. **Dy.** Chal. of Bād., Vijayāditya, in characters of 8th cent. A.D. ; **text**[2] **:** . . . . . *Sōmaṇanu tammavve Kētagaüṁḍi svargaste ahaṁtāgi dharmmakke agaḷisida* ***bhāvi*** *ikkida tōpu* . . . . ; **tr.** on the death of his mother Kētagaüṁḍi Sōmaṇa carried out the charitable work of sinking a **well** and planted the grove ; *E.C.* III, Nj. 296, p. 368, ll. 9–11 ; Doḍḍahomma, Nanjanagud Tq., Mysore Dt., Karn. St. **Dy.** Hoy., Ballāḷa, Ś. 1219 = 1296 A.D. ; **text**[3] **:** . . . . *Duggaseṭṭiyaru* . . . . . *naṁma mūlada bāḷu mu 9 hā 25 ashṭaroḷagaṇa kaḷa maneṭhāvu* ***bāvi*** . . . . . . ; **tr.** Duggaseṭṭi' s original land yielding 9 *mu (muḍi,* a grain measure*)* and *25 hā* (*hāne,* a grain measure) within which were located a threshing floor, a house site and a **well** ; *S.I.I.* VII, No. 345, p. 200, l. 21 ; Chauḷikēri, Udupi Tq. and Dt., Karn. St. **Dy.** Tuḷuva, Narasiṁha, Ś. 1424 = 1502 A.D. ; **text**[4] **:** . . . . *Karakaṁṭhēśvara svāmige* . . *Mallaṇṇanavara maga Naṁjuṁḍdaseṭṭi* . . . ***bāvi*** *sēvārtha* . . . . . ; **tr.** the **well** is the pious gift of Naṁjuṁḍaseṭṭi the son of Mallaṇṇa to the god Karakaṁṭhēśvara . . . . ; *E.C.* (R) IV, PP. 119, p. 569, ll. 2–3 ; Kaṁpalāpura, Piriyapattana Tq., Mysore Dt., Karn. St. **Misc.**, Cy. yr. Prabhava = 1687 A.D.

bāvi hūḷuvudu (K. *indec.*), well getting filled up with silt ; **text :** *mūṟu vrittiyalu* . . . . . ***bāvi hūḷi****dare tōḍuvudakke* . . . . *eraḍu bhāge saluvudu* . . . . . . ; **tr.** out of the three *vritti* (lands) two shares will be spent on desilting the **well** when it **gets silted** ; *S.I.I.* IX, pt. ii, No. 436, p. 446, ll. 21, 25–26 ; Malapanaguḍi, Hospet Tq., Bellary Dt., Karn. St. **Dy.** Saṅgama., Dēvarāya, Ś. 1333 = 1412 A.D.

bāvulu (Te. *n.*), wells ; **text :** . . . . *kāluvalu cheruvulu* ***bāvulu*** . . . ; **tr.** canals, tanks, **wells** ; *S.I.I.* XVI, No. 38, p. 41, ll. 24–25 ; Rāmāpuram, Gooty Tq., Anantapur Dt., A.P. St. **Dy.** Sāḷuva, Narasiṁha II, Ś. 1419 = 1497 A.D.

bayakār̤a (K. *n.*), musician ; **text¹ :** . . . . ***bayakāra*** *Rāmappayyanavaru* . . . *kaṭṭisida* . . . *ker̤e*. . . . ; **tr.** the tank got constructed by the **musician** Rāmappayya . . . ; *S.I.I.* IX, pt. ii, No. 593, p. 606, l. 3 ; Chikkakeriyaginahaḷḷi, Kudligi Tq., Bellary Dt., Karn. St. **Dy.** Tuḷuva, Achyutarāya, Ś. 1461 = 1539 A.D. ; **text² :** . . . ***bayakāra*** *Rāmappayyanavaru* . . . . *kaṭṭisida Bālakṛishṇadēvara guḍi* ; **tr.** the temple of the god Bālakṛishṇa caused to be built by the **musician** Rāmappayya. . . . . ; *S.I.I.* IX, pt. ii, No. 660, p. 653, ll. 2–4 ; Huliguṁṭa, Kudligi Tq., Bellary Dt., Karn. St. **Dy.** Tuḷuva, Sadāśiva, Ś. 1478 = 1556 A.D.

bayalu (K. *n.*), open field ; **text¹ :** . . . . *paṭṭamahādēvi Śāntaladēviyaru tāvu* . . . . . *māḍisida Savati gaṁdha vāraṇabasadige* . . . . *Gaṁgasamudrada keḷagaṇa naḍu**bayal**aivattu koḷaga gardde tōṭavṁ* . . . . . *biṭṭa datti* ; **tr.** the crowned queen Śāntaladēvi made a grant of fifty *koḷaga* (a land measure) of wetland in the middle of the **open field** below the reservoir Gaṁgasamudra to the Savatigaṁdhavāraṇabasadi built by her; *E.C.* II, Sb. 162, p. 105, ll. 50–52; Chikkabeṭṭa (Śravaṇabeḷagoḷa), Channarayapatna Tq., Hassan Dt., Karn. St. **Dy.** Hoy., Vishṇuvardhana, Ś. 1045 = 1123 A.D. ; **text² :** . . . . *Kukkuḍeyoḷage koḷaga **bayal**a gēṇiyiṁda dēvara muṁdaṇa raṁgavallige naḍava bhatta mūḍe 24* . . . . ; **tr.** 24 *mūḍe* (a grain measure) of paddy procured from the lease of the **open field** is granted towards meeting expenses for drawing decorative designs in front of the deity. . . . ; *S.I.I.* VII, No. 329, p. 179, ll. 16–17 ; Mūḍakēri, Udupi Tq. and Dt., Karn. St. **Dy.** Saṅgama, Bukkarāya, Ś. 1282 = 1360 A.D.

bayala gadde (K. *n.*), wet land in an open field; **text :** . . . . *koṁḍa kshētrada vivara* . . . *paḍuvaluḷḷa* ***bayala gadde*** . . . *mūḍaṇa dikkinalu* ***bayala gadde*** . . . . ; **tr.** the details of the land bought include the **wet land in the open field** in the west and the **wetland in the open field** in the east . . . ; *S.I.I.* VII, No. 270, p. 139, ll. 16, 20; Yermāḷ, Udupi Tq. and Dt., Karn. St. **Dy.** Saṅgama, Harihara, Ś. 1342 = 1402 A.D.

bēḍa (K. *n.*), hunter ; **text :** . . . . . . *Kaliyuga Bhīma mahārājana rājyadoḷ* ***bēḍa****ra Bīrammana pariyoḷ Nallūraḷivinuḷ* . . . *Doragundayya* . . . . *svargakke sandan ātana magan Er̤eyaṁga* . . . *kallaniṟisidaṁ* . . . . ; **tr.** hero stone set up by Er̤eyaṁga in memory of his father Doragundayya who died when the **hunter** Bīramma attacked the village Nallūru during the reign of Kaliyuga Bhīma ; *E.C.* VIII, Al. 35, p. 455, ll. 3–6 ; Nallūru, Alur Tq., Hassan Dt., Karn. St. **Dy.** Nallūr Chfs., Kaliyuga Bhīma, Ś. 909 = 987 A.D.

beḍaṁgu (K. *n.*), beauty ; **text :** . . . . . . *mogasiri*

Lakshmige Vāgdēvige buddhi Nijēśvaraṁge hitasiddhiyenal sogayisire rūpumati kāryyagati ***beḍaṁg****amardudā mahāsatigeṁtu* . . . . . ; **tr.** 'thus indeed did shine her rich face equal to that of the goddess of wealth, her wisdom equal to that of the goddess of learning, her work for the welfare of her husband and her **beauty**, wisdom and way of working ; *E.C.* (R) IX, Bl. 16, p. 12, l. 15 ; Bēlūr, Belur Tq., Hassan Dt., Karn. St. **Dy.** Hoy., Vishṇuvardhana, Ś. 1039 = 1117-18 A.D.

bedakāru (K. *n.*), seeds ; **text :** . . . . *bittuva* ***bedakāru*** *mūḍe 6* . . . . . ; **tr.** the seeds for sowing are 6 *mūḍe* (a grain measure) ; *S.I.I.* VII, No. 183, p. 79, l. 11 ; Mangalore, Mangalore Tq., D. K. Dt., Karn. St. **Dy.** Saṅgama, Harihara, Ś. 1318 = 1396 A.D.

beddalu (K. *n.*), rain fed agricultural land ; **text[1]:** . . . . *Toṁḍeyahāḷa Harada gāvuṁḍanu* . . . . *kaṭṭisida kere etisida dēvālayakke gadde khaṁ 4* ***beddale****yu tribhāga* . . . . . *saluvantāgi biṭṭa datti.* . . . . ; **tr.** Haradagāvuṁḍa of Toṁḍeyahāḷu granted to the tank constructed and the temple built by him, 4 *khaṁ* (*khaṁḍuga*, a land measure) of wet land and 3 shares of **rain fed agricultural land**; *E.C.* (R) IV, Hs. 9, p. 487, l. 1; Toṁḍāḷu, Hunsur Tq., Mysore Dt., Karn. St. **Dy.** Hoy., Narasiṁha I, Ś. 1089 = 1167 A.D. ; **text[2] :** . . . *bīḍina dakshiṇada koḷadoḷage* ***beddala*** *kaṁma 50* . . . ; **tr.** 50 *kaṁma* (a land measure) of **rain fed agricultural land** under the tank of the house ; *K.I.* V, No. 19, p. 79, l. 11 ; Mangalore, Mangalore Tq., D. K. Dt., Karn. St. **Dy.** Saṅgama, Harihara, Ś. 1318 = 1396 A.D. ; **text[3] :** . . . . *Dēvarāyavoḍeyaru* . . . . *Śivayōgivoḍeyarige* . . . . *Muḍukanapurada grāmavanu nāvu nimage* . . . . *koṭṭevāgi ā grāmada chatusīmeya voḷagāda gadde* ***beddalu*** *tōṭa* . . . . *ivu muṁtāda ēnuṁṭāda payirugaḷanu āgumāḍi nimma putrapautra pāraṁparyavāgi* . . . . *anubhavisikoṁḍu bahiri.* . . . . ; **tr.** We Dēvarāyavoḍeya granted to you, Śivayōgivoḍeya, the village of Muḍukanapura with the stipulation that you may enjoy all the produces of the wet land, **rain fed agricultural land**, garden, etc., within the four boundaries of the said village along with your sons, grandsons and decendants ; *E.C.* (R) V, TN. 103, p. 501, ll. 6–7, 8–9, 11, 13–14, 16–18. ; Muḍukanapura, T. Narasipura Tq., Mysore Dt., Karn. St. **Dy.** Āravīḍu, Veṁkaṭapati, Ś. 1520 = 1598 A.D.

beddala bhūmi (K. *n.*), rain fed agricultural land; **text :** . . . . *Paṁchaliṁga* . . . . *svāmiyavara paḍitarake Taḷakāḍa* . . . . . ***beddalabhūmi****yanu Basavaliṁgaṁṇanu koṭṭanu* . . . . . ; **tr.** Basavaliṁgaṁṇa made a grant of **rain fed agricultural land** at Talakāḍu for offerings to the god Paṁchaliṁga ; *E.C.* (R) V, T.N. 187, p. 580, ll. 6–7, 9–10 ; Talakāḍu, T. Narasipura Tq., Mysore Dt., Karn. St. **Dy.** Woḍ. of Mys., Chāmarāja, Ś. 1555 = 1633 A.D.

beddale (K. *n.*), rain fed agricultural land ; **text :** . . . . *Noḷaṁbamahādēviyar* . . . . . . *Hosageṟeya*

Mahādēvarge nivēdyakkaṁ pūjisuvargaṁ grasakkaṁ biṭṭa gaḻde mattar ondu **beddale** *mattar panneraḍu.* . . . . ; **tr.** Noḷaṁbamahādēvi granted one *mattar* (a land measure) of wet land and twelve *mattar* of **rain fed agricultural land** for the food offerings to the god Mahādēva of Hosageṟe and to the priest and for feeding ; *S.I.I.* IX, pt. i, No. 110, p. 85, ll. 12, 14–16 ; Punabagaṭṭa, Harapanahalli Tq., Bellary Dt., Karn. St. **Dy.** Chāḷ. of Kal., Sōmēśvara I, Ś. 974 = 1052 A.D.

bede (K. *n.*), wet land prepared for sowing ; **text**[1] **:** *Maṇaliya maṁṭapada kelasakke* . . . . *biṭṭa bhūmi* . . . . ***bede*** *koḷaga 10 gadde* . . . . . ; **tr.** 10 *koḷaga* (a grain measure) of **wet land prepared for sowing** was granted for the construction of the *maṁṭapa* at Maṇali ; *E.C.* (R) V, Kn. 9, p. 8, l. 5–6, 9 ; Maḷali, K.R. Nagara Tq., Mysore Dt., Karn. St. **Dy.** Hoy., Vishṇuvardhana, Ś. 1058 = 1136 A.D. ; **text**[2] **:** *Kēśavanāthadēvara dēvadānada* . . . . . *Śrīvaishṇavarige mārikoṁḍa maṁṇanettisi māḍida gadde ko 10* . . ***bede*** . . . . . ; **tr.** 10 *ko* (*koḷaga,* a grain measure) of **wet land prepared for sowing** was sold to Śrīvaishṇavas of the god Kēśavanātha after ploughing ; *E.C.* (R) III, Nj. 347, p. 402, ll. 9–11, 13–15 ; Heḍatale, Nanjanagud Tq., Mysore Dt., Karn. St. **Dy.** Hoy., Ballāḷa III, Ś. 1236 = 1314 A.D.

bedegadde (K. *n.*), wet land prepared for sowing ; **text :** *Rākaṁṇṇa* . . . . *Moḍiyahaḷiyalli koḍageyāgi hola maṁṇu nūru eraḍu salage* ***bedegadde*** *yishṭu eṁdeṁdigū saluvudu* . . . . ; **tr.** one hundred *maṁṇu* (a land measure) of dry land and two *salage* (a land measure) of sowing capacity of **wet land prepared for sowing** at Moḍiyahaḷḷi belong to Rākaṁṇṇa as a permanent grant ; *E.C.* (R) IV, Ko. 62, p. 440, ll. 11, 32–38 ; Kāmagere, Kollegala Tq., Mysore Dt., Karn. St. **Dy.** Saṅgama, Prince Kaṁpaṇa, Ś. 1276 = 1354 A.D.

bedegaḻde (K. *n.*), wet land prepared for sowing; **text :** *kalukuṭiga Māṇikāchārige aiguḷa ga* ***bede-gaḻde****yu beḻdele mattaru eraḍu.* . . . ; **tr.** to the stone mason Māṇikāchāri were given wet land of the extent of being sown with *aiguḷa* (a grain measure of five units of *kuḷa*) of seeds for the *wet land prepared for sowing* and two *mattar* (a land mesure) of rain fed agricultural land ; *S.I.I.* IX, pt. i, No. 112, p. 87, ll. 26–27 ; Nandikamba, Harapanahalli Tq., Bellary Dt., Karn. St. **Dy.** Chāḷ. of Kal., Sōmēśvara I, Ś. 974 = 1053 A.D.

bedemaṇṇu (K. *n.*), wet land prepared for sowing; **text :** (damaged) . . . *koḷaga* ***bede-maṇṇu*** . . . . ; **tr. wet land prepared for sowing** (of the extent of being sown with one *koḷaga* (a grain measure) of seeds ; *E.C.* (R) V, T.N. 142, p. 552, l. 16 ; Vijayapura, T. Narasipura Tq., Mysore Dt., Karn. St. **Dy.** Chōḷa, Rājēndra I, reg. yr. 6 = 1017-18 A.D.

bēḍige (K. *n.*), requisitioned cess ; **text**[1] **:** (damaged)

. . *nāvu terigeyanu koṁḍu . . . kāṇike* ***bēḍige*** *. . . . āvudu yilla . . . .* ; **tr.** we having collected tax, there are no presents, **requisitioned cess,** etc. ; *E.C.* (R) III, Nj. 292, p. 365, ll. 23–24 ; Dāsanūru, Nanjanagud Tq., Mysore Dt., Karn. St. **Misc.,** Ś. 1449 = 1527 A.D. ; **text**[2] **:** *. . . . ī sīmāpradēśa . . . . . grāmaṁgaḷa . . . . . gadde beddalu tōṭa . . . . magga manevaṇa . . . . kāṇike* ***bēḍige*** *. . . . ivu modalāda . . sakalasvāmyavanū . . . . mahājanaṁgaḷu . . . . . . śāśvatavāgi . . . . . . anubhavisikoṁḍu baharu . . .* ; **tr.** the *mahājana* (body of brāhmaṇas) will enjoy permanently the revenue incomes such as from wet lands, dry land, groves, tax on handlooms, house tax, tributes, **requisitioned cess,** etc., from the villages within this territory ; *E.C.* (R) V, My. 99, p. 222, ll. 410, 412, 416, 418 ; Mysore, Mysore Tq. and Dt., Karn. St. **Dy.** Woḍ. of Mys., Chikkadēvarāja Woḍeyar, Ś. 1595 = 1674 A.D.

bēḍike (K. *n.*), requisitioned cess ; **text :** (fragmentary) , ... *Kōṭeyakala grāmadalu . . . .* ***bēḍike*** *. . roka 127 . . .* ; **tr.** the **requisitioned cess** from the village of Kōṭeyakalu amounting to 127 *roka* (a coin) ; *S.I.I.* IX, pt. ii, No. 604, p. 612, ll. 14–15 ; Kōṭakalu, Adavani Tq., Kurnool Dt., A.P. St. **Dy.** Tuḷuva, Sadāśiva, Ś. 1465 = 1542 A.D.

bēḍigeya kammaṭa (K. *n.*), mint supplying coins on requisition ; **text :** *. . . aśēsha Kottaḷiyumirdu Kammaṭēśvaradēvara naṁdādīvigege biṭṭa datti* ***bēḍigeya kammaṭa****dalu daḷake vīsa 1. . . . . .* ; **tr.** the entire Kottaḷi guild assembled and granted to the god Kammaṭēśvaradēva for a perpetual lamp 1 *vīsa* (fraction of a coin) per *daḷa* (bundle of coins) from the **mint supplying coins on requisition** ; *S.I.I.* IX, pt. i, No. 262, p. 278, ll. 15–18 ; Korrevu, Madakasira Tq., Anantapur Dt., A.P. St. **Dy.** Chāḷ. of Kal., Jagadēkamalla II, in characters of 12th century A.D.

bēḍuge (K. *n.*), requisitioned cess ; **text :** *. . . dēvarige nīrukūli . . .* ***bēḍuge*** *manevaṇa . . . . mukhyvāgi . . . . ī dēvara vokkalu . . . . biṭṭa datti . . . . .* ; **tr.** the tenants of the temple land donated to the god water fetching wages, **requisitioned cess,** house tax, etc., ; *E.C.* IV, Ch. 3, pp. 7–8, ll. 13–18 ; Chāmarājanagara, Chamarajanagara Tq. and Dt., Karn. St. **Dy.** Hoy., Narasiṁha III, Ś. 1203 = 1281 A.D.

beḍuṁgoḷu (K. *n.*), a kind of minor tax ; **text :** *. . . . . Heggaḍe Nāchimayya Vijayanārāyaṇadēvara haṁnneraḍūraluṁ haḷḷigaḷaluṁ kāṇike . . . .* ***beḍuṁgoḷu*** *. . . . . . voḷagāda samasta kirukuḷavellavaṁ . . . . . Ballāḷadēvan biṭṭan . . . .* ; **tr.** Ballāḷadēva granted to the god Vijayanārāyaṇa all the minor taxes including tributes, **kind of minor tax called beḍuṁgoḷu** collected from the 12 towns and villages belonging to that god ; *E.C.* (R) IX, Bl. 17, p. 18, ll. 2–3 ; Bēlūru, Belur Tq., Hassan Dt., Karn. St. **Dy.** Hoy., Ballāḷa II, Ś. 1095 = 1174 A.D.

bēgāra (K. *n.*), free labour ; **text :** *. . . . . ā* *grāmakke uṁṭāda .. bēḍige kāṇike kāḍāya ...* ***bēgara*** *suṁka yivu modalāda yīti bādhegaḷu ēnu illa eṁdu .... nāvu nimage Rāmāpuraveṁba agrahāravanu koṭṭevu ....* ; **tr.** we gave you as a grant the brāhmaṇa settlement Rāmāpura exempting it from payment of all taxes such as requsitioned cess, tributes, compulsory tax, tax on **free labour,** etc. ; *E.C.* (R), Kn. 104, p. 99, ll. 17–18, 23–25 ; Galigēkere, Krishnarajanagara Tq., Mysore Dt., Karn. St. **Dy.** Āravīḍu, Śrīraṁga, Ś. 1498 = 1577 A.D.

bēhara (K. *n.*), services to the god ; **text :** .... *Sōmanāthadēvara* ***bēhara*** *naḍavaḍe ī agra naḍavudu* ... ; **tr.** as part of the **services to the god** Sōmanātha, there will be feeding of brāhmaṇas; *S.I.I.* VII, No. 312, p. 163, ll. 13–14 ; Mūḍakēri, Udupi Tq. and Dt., Karn. St. **Dy.** Hoy., Vīraballāḷa, Ś. 1258 = 1336 A.D.

bēhāra (K. < Skt. *vyavahāra, n.*), trade ; **text :** ..... *nūlu sīreya* ***bēhāra****vū Mūrukēriyavarige saluvudu* ... ; **tr.** the right of **trade** in cotton sarees is the privilege of the traders of Mūrukēri; *S.I.I.* VII, No. 309, p. 160, ll. 32–33, ; Mūḍakēri, Udupi Tq. and Dt., Karn. St. **Dy.** Saṅgama, Dēvarāya, Ś. 1353 = 1431 A.D.

bēhāri (K. < Skt. *vyavaharin, n.*), trader ; **text**[1] **:** .... *Boppeya* ***bēhāri****ya kaiyyalu mūlava koṁḍa bāḷu* ..... ; **tr.** land purchased on permanent basis from the hands of the **trader** Boppeya; *S.I.I.* VII, No. 330, p. 180, ll. 30–31 ; Mūḍakēri, Udupi Tq. and Dt., Karn. St. **Dy.** Saṅgama, Bukkarāya, Ś. 1281 = 1359 A.D. ; **text**[2]**:** ..... *seṭṭikāṟa* ***bēhāri*** *kayya āruvārava māḍikoṇḍa tāru* .... ; **tr.** a type of land taken on lease from the **trader** belonging to the seṭṭi community; *S.I.I.* VII, No. 389, p. 247, ll. 43–44 ; Hosakēri, Udupi Tq. and Dt., Karn. St. **Dy.** Tuḷuva, Sadāśiva, Ś. 1491 = 1569 A.D.

bēhārigaḷu (K. < Skt. *n.*), traders ; **text :** ...... *chatrake davasava hākuva* ***behārigaḷu*** .... ; **tr. traders** who supply grains to the choultry ; *S.I.I.* IV, No. 265, p. 59, l. 20 ; Hampi, Hospet Tq., Bellary Dt., Karn. St. **Dy.** Tuḷuva, Sadāśiva, Ś. 1467 = 1545 A.D.

beḷageygaḷu (K. *n.*), fields with standing crops ; **text :** ..... *kaṭṭisida keṟe manōmudadiṭṭārave pasiyalīyadikkuva satra biṭṭa* ***beḷageygaḷ****eṟe-Vaṟavaṭṭige māḍida. dharmaṁ* .... ; **tr.** the pious charities of Kalidēvaseṭṭi include the construction of a tank, the setting up of a beautiful garden, a choultry for feeding the hungry, **fields with standing crop** and road-side sheds for free supply of water and butter milk to travellers ; *S.I.I.* IX, pt. i, No. 296, p. 321, ll. 48–49 ; Kuṟugōḍu, Bellary Tq. and Dt., Karn. St. **Dy.** Kal. of Kal., Sōvidēva, Ś. 1097 = 1176 A.D.

beḷatige akki (K. *n.*), white rice ; **text :** (damaged) ..... ***beḷatige akki*** .... ; **tr. white rice** ; *S.I.I.* VII, No. 299, p. 153, l. 55 ; Udupi, Udupi Tq. and Dt., Karn. St. **Dy.** Saṅgama, Harihara,

Ś. 1317 = 1395 A.D.

beḻdele (K. *n.*), rain fed agricultural land ; **text :** *kalukuṭiga Māṇikāchārige aiguḷa ga bedegaḻdeyu **beḻdele** mattaru eraḍu.* . . . ; **tr.** to the stone mason Māṇikāchāri were given wet land of the extent of being sown with *aiguḷa* (a grain measure of five units of *kuḷa*) of seeds for the wet land prepared for sowing and two *mattar* (a land mesure) of **rain fed agricultural land** ; *S.I.I.* IX, pt. i, No. 112, p. 87, ll. 26–27 ; Nandikamba, Harapanahalli Tq., Bellary Dt., Karn. St. **Dy.** Chāḷ. of Kal., Sōmēśvara I, Ś. 974 = 1053 A.D.

bēḷe (K. *n.*), half of a *hāga*, a coin of fractional denomination ; **text**[1] **:** . . . .*vokkalalu hāga talehoṟege **bēḷe*** . . . ; **tr.** per tenant one *hāga* (a coin of fractional denomination) one ***bēḷe*** **(= half a *hāga*)** per head load ; *S.I.I.* IX, pt. i, No. 76, p. 47, l. 22 ; Bāgaḷi, Harapanahalli Tq., Bellary Dt., Karn. St. **Dy.** Chāḷ. of Kal., Āhavamalla, Ś. 913 = 991 A.D. ; **text**[2] **:** . . . *aḍakeya hēṟigoṁdu **bēḷe**yaṁ biṭṭaru* . . . . . ; **tr.** for every load of arecaunut **half of a hāga coin of fractional denomination** was granted ; *K.I.* IV, No. 34, p. 79, l. 27 ; Nūlgēri, Hirekerur Tq., Dharwar Dt., Karn. St. **Dy.** Chāḷ. of Kal., Vikramāditya VI, Ch. Vi. yr. 33 = 1109 A.D. ; **text**[3] **:** (damaged) . . . *bhattada hēṟiṁge vīsa eleya hēṟiṁge **bēḷe*** . . . . ; **tr.** one *vīsa* (a coin of fractional denomination) for a load of paddy and one **half of a hāga coin of fractional denomination** for a load of (plantain) leaves ; *K.I.* VI, No. 42, p. 128, l. 17 ; Raṭṭihaḷḷi, Hirekerur Tq., Dharwar Dt., Karn. St. **Dy.** Sēü. of Dēv., Siṅghaṇa II, Cy. yr. Hemaḷaṁbi = 1237 A.D.

beḷe (K. *n.*), agricultural crop ; **text**[1] **:** . . . *chatussīmeyoḷaguḷḷa* . . . . ***beḷeda** bāḷu nāgaṁḍugada mūḍe 12* . . . . . ; **tr.** the land within the four boundaries with standing **agricultural crop** amounting to 12 *mūḍe* (a grain measure) measured by nāgaṁḍuga (four units of a *khaṁḍuga* grain measure) ; *S.I.I.* IX, pt. ii, No. 409, p. 416, l. 18 ; Kōṭēśvara, Kundapur Tq., Udupi Dt., Karn. St. **Dy.** Saṅgama, Bukka, Ś. 1287 = 1365 A.D. ; **text**[2] **:** . . *ī mūṟu vṛittiya **beḷe**ya ādāyavanu mūru bhāgava māḍi* . . . . ; **tr.** having divided the income from the standing **agricultural crop** into three shares to be distributed to three shareholders ; *S.I.I.* IX, pt. ii, No. 436, p. 445, ll. 21–22 ; Malapanaguḍi, Hospet Tq., Bellary Dt., Karn. St. **Dy.** Saṅgama, Dēvarāya, Ś. 1333 = 1412 A.D.

bele (K. *n.*), cost ; **text :** (fragmentary) . . . . *Kāṁchīpurada* . . . . *Varadarājadēvara* . . . . *puṇyakōṭiya vimānava chiṁnava hāsuvadakke lōveyiṁda mēle kaḷasa paryaṁtaralū muṭṭida aparaṁjiya tūṁkada* . . . . . ***bele** ga* . . . . *nū pādarasa tūkakke **bele** ga.* . . *nū* . . *koṭṭu* . . . . *vimānavanu aparaṁjiya chiṁnadalū hāśistevu.* ; **tr.** for gilding the *puṇyakōṭi vimāna* of the temple of Varadarāja at Kāṁchīpura from frame to the pinnacle, the **cost** of copper was *ga* (*gadyāṇa*, a gold coin) (amount not specified) and for the mercury **cost** of *ga* (amount not specified) and the guilding of the *vimāna* with gold was done ; *S.I.I.* IX, pt. ii, No. 499, p. 514, l. 3 ; Little Kāñchīpuram, Kancheepuram Tq., Chingleput Dt., T. Nadu St. **Dy.** Tuḷuva, Kṛishṇadēvarāya, Ś. 1436 = 1514 A.D.

beḷegey (K. *n.*), field with standing agricultural crop ; **text :** . . . *Ballakuṁde . . . nāḍoḷ tiḷigoḷadim* ***beḷegeyyiṁ*** *Yoruvāy . . . . . sogayisutirkkuṁ . . . .* ; **tr.** Oruvāyi, located within Ballakuṁdenāḍu was resplendent with clear tanks, **field with standing agricultural crops**, etc. ; *S.I.I.* IX, pt. i, No. 322, pp. 337–38, ll. 10, 20–22 ; Oruvay, Bellary Tq. and Dt., Karn. St. **Dy.** Sinda, Rāchamalla II, Cy. yr. Ānanda = 1195 A.D.

beḷeva bhūmi (K. *n.*), cultivable land ; **text :** . . . . . *vṛittige erppattu Tōhige pravishṭavāgi . . . ūra muṁdaṇa Brahmadēvana keṟeyuṁ . . . haḷḷada kālveyuṁ aṁteraḍaṟa nīruvaḷiyiṁ* ***beḷeva bhūmi*** *enituṁṭanitumaṁ . . . . . koṭṭaru . . . . .* ; **tr.** all the **cultivable land** being irrigated by two sources of water viz., the tank called Brahmadēva and the lower canal were granted after dividing them into seventy shares ; *S.I.I.* IX, pt. i, No. 250, p. 260, ll. 54–57 ; Peddatumbaḷam, Adavani Tq., Kurnool Dt., A.P. St. **Dy.** Chāḷ. of Kal., Jagadēkamalla II, reg. yr. 11 = 1148 A.D.

beḷgalmoṟaḍi (K. *n.*), white boulder ; **text :** . . . *pūrvasyāṁ diśi . . . beḷgalmoṟaḍi . . . .* ; **tr.** on the east white boulder (as the boundary mark) ; *E.C.* VII, Ng. 149, p. 146, l. 61 ; Dēvarahaḷḷi, Nagamangala Tq., Mandya Dt., Karn. St. **Dy.** W. Gaṅga., Śrīpurusha, Ś. 698 = 776 A.D.

beḷgoḍe (K. *n.*), white parasol (a mark of honour/ distinction) ; **text :** . . . . . . *Ravidaṇḍanāyakaṁ . . . . . taḷedaṁ* ***beḷgoḍe*** *mahāḍaṁbaraṁ chāmaraṁ . . . enipa mahīśa chinhamaṁ . .* ; **tr.** Ravidaṇḍa-nāyaka enjoyed the honour of being endowed with royal insignia such as **white parasol**, great pomp, fly whisk, etc. ; *S.I.I.* IX, pt. i, No. 158, p. 142, l. 21 ; Hūvinahaḍagalli, Hadagalli Tq., Bellary Dt., Karn. St. **Dy.** Chāḷ. of Kal., Vikramāditya VI, Ch. Vi. yr. 15 = 1090 A.D.

bēli[1] (K. *n.*), a land measure ; **text**[1] **:** *Gaṁgapayyagaḷu . . . . māḍisida basadige biṭṭa datti . . . keṟeya gadde 30 salageyyuṁ ā keṟeyiṁ baḍagalu ēriya beddale* ***bēli*** *2 . . . . .* ; **tr.** the grant given to the *basadi* built by Gaṁgapayya included 30 *salage* (a land measure) of wet land under the tank, 2 **bēli** (a land measure) of rain fed agricultural land under the lake to the north of that tank ; *E.C.* (R) V, My. 207, p. 311, ll. 8–9, 10–13 ; Kumārabīḍu, Mysore Tq. and Dt., Karn. St. **Dy.** Hoy., Vishṇuvardhana, Ś. 1044 = 1121 A.D.; **text**[2] **:** *Rāmanāthadēvargge . . . . Beḷatulavāḍiya ā . . . bhūmiyoḷage . . . biṭṭa maṇṇu* ***bēli****yoṁdu alliya mūligarige biṭṭa* ***bēli*** *1 . . . . .* ; **tr.** one **bēli** (a land measure) of land at Beḷatulavāḍi was granted to the god Rāmanāthadēva and one **bēli**

of land was granted to the permanent resident of that place ; *E.C.* (R) III, Gu. 47, p. 41, ll. 6–7, 10, 13–15 ; Beḷachalavāḍi, Gundlupet Tq., Mysore Dt., Karn. St. **Dy.** Hoy., Narasiṁha I, Cy. yr. Khara = 1171 A.D.

bēli[2] (K. *n.*), fence ; **text**[1] : . . . . . . *Jōḷiyara gaḍiya* ***bēli****yiṁdam baḍagalu* . . . . ; **tr.** to the north of the **fence** of the boundary of the land of Jōḷiyaru ; *S.I.I.* IX, pt. ii, No. 409, p. 416, l. 10 ; Kōṭēśvara, Kundapur Tq., Udupi Dt., Karn. St. **Dy.** Saṅgama, Bukka, Ś. 1287 = 1365 A.D. ; **text**[2]: . . . . . . *Kaṁnaṁbāḍī kāluve Teṁkavāri ērikeḷage ī tōṭada* ***bēli*** *baḷiya mūḍa mukhavāgi neṭṭa kallu* . . . . . . ; **tr.** stone set up facing the east near the **fence** of the garden under the Teṁkavāri lake formed by the Kaṁnaṁbāḍi canal ; *E.C.* (R) V, Kn. 117, p. 126, ll. 208–09 ; Māchanahaḷḷi, Krishnarājanagar Tq., Mysore Dt., Karn. St. **Dy.** Woḍ. of Mys., Krishṇarāja II, Ś. 1663 = 1741 A.D.

bella (K. *n.*), jaggery ; **text** : . . . . *Chauḷikēriya Mūrukēriya samasta halaru sahavāgi voḍaṁbaṭṭu āḍuva bēhārada kaṭṭaḷe ghaṭṭada mēlaṇiṁdalū hādiya bēhāradiṁdalū bahanthā akki* . . . *kaḍale uddu hesaru* . . . ***bella*** . . . . *sahavāda talevoṟeyalu baṁdaṁthādanu eraḍu kēriyavarū sariyāgi hāyikkikoṁḍu namma namma kēriyalū bēhārava māḍuvevu* . . . ; **tr.** *samasta halaru* (body of tradesmen) of Chauḷikēri and Mūrukēri entered into an agreement that head loads of articles such as rice, . . . chick-pea, common pulse, green-gram, . . **jaggery** etc., coming from above the ghats and available for trade enroute are to be equally shared and sold in their respective areas ; *S.I.I.* VII, No. 340, p. 193, ll. 13–14, 15–21 ; Chauḷikēri, Udupi Tq. and Dt., Karn. St. **Dy.** Saṅgama, Dēvarāya, Ś. 1353 = 1431 A.D.

beḷḷākaraṇe (K. *n.*), a kind of tax ; **text** : . . . . *Nārāyaṇabhaṭṭaru eṟadu koṭṭa sthalaṁgaḷiṁge* . . . . . *kāṇike khaḍḍāya* ***beḷḷākaraṇe*** *beḷudaṇḍa* . . . . . *modalāgi āvudu salla* . . ; **tr.** there shall be no taxation such as tribute, compulsory revenue, **tax called beḷḷākaraṇe**, beḷudaṁḍa, etc., on the lands which have been donated by Nārāyaṇabhaṭṭa ; *K.I.* I, No. 53, pp. 128-29, ll. 25–28 ; Bailūr, Bhatkal Tq. and Dt., Karn. St. **Dy.** Saṅgama, Dēvarāya II, Ś. 1355 = 1433 A.D.

bella suṁka (K. *n.*), taxes on production of jaggery ; **text** : . . . . . . *Triyaṁbakadēvarige Koṁgina sīmeyali naḍadu baha grāmagaḷa sthaḷa suṁka magga mane* ***bella suṁka*** . . . *biṭṭaru* . . . ; **tr.** to the god Triyaṁbakadēva were granted tax incomes collected from the villages of Koṁginasīme such as local tax, tax on handlooms, house tax, **tax on the production of jaggery**, etc. ; *E.C.* (R) III, Gu. 150, p. 119, ll. 98–99 ; Triyaṁbakapura, Gundlupet Tq., Mysore Dt., Karn. St. **Dy.** Tuḷuva, Kṛishṇadēvarāya, Ś. 1443 = 1521 A.D.

beḷḷi (K. *n.*), silver ; **text** : . . . . . *Kṛishṇarāyaru Virūpākshadēvarige samarpisida nāgābharaṇa 1*

. . . . *beḷḷiya āratiya halage 34* . . . . ; **tr.** Kṛishṇarāya donated to the god Virūpāksha 1 *Nāgābharaṇa* and among other things 34 **silver** plates for waving the lamp before the god ; *S.I.I.* IX, pt. ii, No. 493, p. 507, ll. 53–55, 57–58 ; Hampi, Hospet Tq., Bellary Dt., Karn. St. **Dy.** Tuḷuva, Kṛishṇadēvarāya, Ś. 1435 = 1513 A.D.

beḷḷi ga (K. *n.*), silver coin ; **text :** . . . . *Pāriśva dēvarie . . . varusha 1 kke **beḷḷi** ga. 1* . . ; **tr.** one **silver** *ga* (*gadyāṇa*, a **coin**) was granted per year to the god Pārśvanātha ; *K.I.* I, No. 51, p. 122, ll. 23, 28 ; Kaikiṇi, Bhatkal Tq. and Dt., Karn. St. **Misc.**, in characters of 15th cent. A.D.

beḷmoṛaḍi (K.), white boulder ; **text :** . . . . . *Kaḍekoḷaṁ Khāravuraṁ Taṁḍeyada mukkōḍu mūḍa mogade pōgi **beḷmoṛaḍi*** . . . . ; **tr.** going towards the east, the trijunction of Kaḍekoḷa Khāravura and Taṇḍeya, going towards the north the **white boulder** ; *E.C.* (R) V, My. 102, p. 237, ll. 7–8 ; Mysore, Mysore Tq. and Dt., Karn. St. **Dy.** W. Gaṅga, Chāgipermmāḍi, in characters of 11th cent. A.D.

beḷudaṇḍa (K. *n.*), a kind of tax ; **text :** . . . . *Nārāyaṇabhaṭṭaru eṛadu koṭṭa sthalaṁgaḷiṁge* . . . . . *kāṇike khaḍḍāya beḷḷākaraṇe **beḷudaṇḍa*** . . . . . *modalāgi āvudu salla* . . ; **tr.** there shall be no taxation such as tribute, compulsory revenue, beḷḷākaraṇe, **beḷudaṁḍa,** etc., on the lands which have been donated by Nārāyaṇabhaṭṭa ; *K.I.* I, No. 53, pp. 128-29, ll. 25–28 ; Bailūr, Bhatkal Tq. and Dt., Karn. St. **Dy.** Saṅgama, Dēvarāya II, Ś. 1355 = 1433 A.D.

beṁche (K. *n.*), a small pond, reservoir ; **text**[1] **:** . . . . . . *Tuṟuhaṁpeyalli baḍagaṇa **beṁche**yim baḍagalu* . . . . . . ; **tr.** to the north of the **small pond** on the northern side of Tuṟuhaṁpe ; *S.I.I.* IX, pt. i, No. 367, p. 385, l. 28 ; Chinnatumbalam, Adavani Tq., Kurnool Dt., A.P. St. **Dy.** Sēü of Dēv., Jaitugi, Ś. 1151 = 1229 A.D. ; **text**[2] **:** . . . . . . *Rāchahaḷḷiya araḷīmarakke paḍuvalu chikka **beṁche** mēre* . . . . ; **tr.** the boundary on the west of the Pipal tree of Rāchahaḷḷi is the **small reservoir** ; *S.I.I.* IX, pt. ii, No. 535, p. 551, l. 26 ; Lēpākshi, Hindupur Tq., Ananthapur Dt., A.P. St. **Dy.** Tuḷuva, Achyutarāya, Ś. 1453 = 1531 A.D.

beṁkoḷuvana kōlu (K. *n.*), the measuring rod named after the title **Beṁkoḷva** of the king ; **text :** (badly damaged). . . . . . . ***Beṁkoḷuvana kōlalu*** *matta 40* . . . . ; **tr.** 40 *matta* (*mattar*, a land measure) of land measured by **the measuring rod named after the title *Beṁkoḷva* of the king** ; *S.I.I.* XV, No. 166, p. 213., l. 43 ; Yāḷvār, Bagevadi Tq., Bijapur Dt., Karn. St. **Dy.** Sēü of Dēv., Siṅghaṇa, Ś. 1144= 1222 A.D.

beṁkoḷvanaruvattunālgēṇa ghaḷe (K. *n.*), measuring rod, 64 spans in length, named after the title Beṁkoḷuva of the king ; **text :** (damaged). . . . . . ***beṁkoḷuvanaruvattunāḷgēṇa ghaḷeya*** *bhūmi mattarāṟu* . . . . ; **tr.** 6 *mattar* (a land measure) of land measured by the **measuring**

rod, 64 spans in length, named after the title Beṁkoḷva of the king ; *S.I.I.* IX, pt. i, No. 230, p. 235, ll. 22–23 ; Rāmadurga, Alur Tq., Bellary Dt., Karn. St. **Dy.** Chāḷ. of Kal., Bhūlōkamalla, reg. yr. 8 = 1134 A.D.

beṁṇe (K. *n.*), butter ; **text :** . . . . *mūḍalu* ***beṁṇeya** Bhaṁḍāriyavara aṁgaḍiyē . . . gaḍi* . . ; **tr.** on the east, the boundary is the shop of Bhaṁḍāri selling **butter** ; *S.I.I.* VII, No. 349, p. 207, ll. 15–16 ; Chauḷikēri, Udupi Tq. and Dt., Karn. St. **Dy.** Saṅgama, Bukkarāya, Ś. 1328 = 1406 A.D.

beṁnirkke (K. *n.*), a kind of tax ; **text :** . . . . . . *Māblayyana baḷada . . . . . ippatteraḍu mattar keyge **beṁnirkke** yilla* . . . . ; **tr.** the tax called ***beṁnirkke*** is not to be levied on the twenty two *mattar* (a land measure) of land gifted to Mābalayya ; *K.I.* II, No. 10, p. 31, l. 21 ; Lakkuṇḍi, Gadag Tq. and Dt., Karn. St. **Dy.** Kal. of Kal., Āhavamalla, reg. yr. 2 = 1180 A.D.

bēṁṭekāṟa (K. *n.*), hunter ; **text**[1] **:** . . . *Banavāsi-puravarādhīśvaraṁ . . . . nuḍidaṁte gaṁḍa* . . . ***bēṁṭekāṟa** Ghaṭṭidēva.* . . ; **tr.** Ghaṭṭidēva, the lord of Banavāsipura, one who practiced what he spoke and a **hunter** ; *S.I.I.* IX, pt. i, No. 242, p. 247, ll. 10–12 ; Aṁbali, Kudligi Tq., Bellary Dt., Karn. St. **Dy.** Chāḷ. of Kal., Jagadēkamalla II, Ś. 1065 = 1143 A.D. ; **text**[2] **:** . . . . . . *gaja **bēṁnṭekāra** śrīmad Dēvarāya-mahārāya* . . . . . . ; **tr.** the illustrious king Dēvarāya who was an expert elephant **hunter** ; *S.I.I.* VII, No. 202, p. 95, l. 15 ; Mūḍabidure, Karkala Tq., Udupi Dt., Karn. St. **Dy.** Saṅgama, Dēvarāya, Ś. 1351 = 1429 A.D.

berasi (K. indec.), merging together ; **text :** . . . . . *Tripurāṁtakadēvara aṁgaraṁgabhōgakkaṁ mattaṁ āchārya tapōdhana adhyayana śuśrūsha brāhmara aśana āchchādanakkaṁ* . . . . . *Madumaṁchchi Pālūrgaḷum aṁtu **berasi** 44 ūrggaḷum chatussīme sahita* . . . . *biṭṭaru.* . . . . . ; **tr. merging together** 44 villages such as Madhumaṁchchi and Pālūr they were donated along with the their boundaries duly demarcated for service to the god Tripurāntakadēva and for the preceptor, ascetics, students, nurses and for the feeding and clothing of the brāhmaṇas ; *S.I.I.* IX, pt. i, No. 204, pp. 203–04, ll. 26–29, 62–65 ; Tripurāntaka, Markapur Tq., Kurnool Dt., A.P. St. **Dy.** Chāḷ. of Kal., Tribhuvanamalla, Ch. Vi. yr. 47 = 1122 A.D.

berddale (K. *n.*), wet land made ready for sowing; **text :** . . . . . . *Chaṁdrabhūshaṇapaṁḍitara kālam karchchi* . . . . *biṭṭa **berddale** matta 5 piriya keṟeya keḷage 10 koḷagaveregaddeyuṁ . . . biṭṭa* . . . . ; **tr.** after laving the feet of Chaṁdrabhūshaṇa paṁḍita 5 *matta* (*mattar,* a land measure) of **wet land made ready for sowing** and a blacksoil field under the big tank with the sowing capacity of 10 *koḷaga* (a grain measure) of seeds was granted ; *S.I.I.* IX, pt. i, No. 113, p. 88, ll. 13–15 ; Hirēmagalagēri, Harapanahalli Tq., Bellary Dt.,

Karn. St. **Dy.** Chāḷ. of Kal., Jagadēkamalla, Ś. 975 = 1054 A.D.

berikeya bhūmi (K. *n.*), land of mixed soils ; **text :** . . . . . . *Śaṁkaradēvara paḍuvabhāgadalli* ***berikeya bhūmi****ya chatusīmeya vivara* . . . . ; **tr.** the details of the four boundaries of the **land of mixed soils** on the western portion of the temple of the god Śaṁkaranārāyaṇa ; *S.I.I.* IX, pt. ii, No. 609, p. 616, ll. 11–12 ; Śaṁkaranārāyaṇa, Kundapur Tq., Udupi Dt., Karn. St. **Dy.** Tuḷuva, Sadāśiva, Ś. 1466 = 1544 A.D.

besa[1] (K. *n.*), order ; **text :** . . . . . *Pāṇḍya dēvara* ***besadiṁ*** *daṁḍanāyakaṁ* . . . . . . *Perggaḍe Attimarasaṁ mūrulakshadaḍakeya perjjuṁkamaṁ biṭṭaru* . . . . ; **tr.** on the **orders** of Pāṇḍyadēva, the army commander and headman Attimarasa donated the major tax on three lakh arecanuts ; *S.I.I.* IX, pt. i, No. 118, p. 98, ll. 65–66 ; Hirehaḍagalli, Hadagalli Tq., Bellary Dt., Karn. St. **Dy.** Chāḷ. of Kal., Tribhuvanamalla, Ch. Vi. yr. 31 = 1107 A.D.

besa[2] (K. *n.*), a kind of tax ; **text :** . . . . . *Kūtanapurada ūramuṁde neḍesikoṭṭa śilāśāsana* . . . . *pūrvamariyādi yidallade* . . . . *birāḍa kāṇike kaḍḍāya biṭṭi* ***besa*** *sollige Mallige yāvudu yillaveṁdu naḍesikoṭṭa śilāśāsana* . . . . ; **tr.** this stone inscription was set up in front of Kūtanapura recording the continuation of exemption from payement of taxes previously made, in addition to such taxes as on agriculatural product, presents, forced labour, free labour, **kinds of taxes** called **besa**, *sollige* and *mallige* ; *E.C.* (R) IV, Ch. 300, p. 194, ll. 20–23 ; Kūtanapura, Chamarajanagar Tq. and Dt., Karn. St. **Dy.** Umm. Chfs., Chikkarāya, Ś. 1432 = 1511 A.D.

besadāḷu (K. *n.*), servant who carries out orders ; **text :** . . . *Kiriya Ponnayya Ballahana* ***besadāḷu*** ; **tr.** Kiriya Ponnayya, the **servant who carries out the orders** of Ballaha (< Skt., *Vallabha*, Karnataka Emperor) ; *S.I.I.* IX, pt. i, No. 25, p. 13, l. 7 ; Maḍakasira, Madakasira Tq., Anantapur Dt., A.P. St. **Dy.** Noḷ. Pal., Dilīparasa, Ś. 870 = 948 A.D.

besade (K. *n.*), on the orders of ; **text :** . . . *Permānanḍigaḷa* ***besade*** *Mahārājar Pulināḍān eṟiyaḻvēḻdoḍe* ; **tr. on the orders of** Perumānaḍi when Mahārāja marched against Pulināḍu ; *S.I.I.* IX, pt. i, No. 20, p. 10, ll. 5–6 ; Kaḷakattūr, Punganur Tq., Chittoor Dt., A.P. St. **Dy.** Noḷ. Pal., Mahēndra I, in characters of 9th cent. A.D.

besagey[1] (K. *vb.*), to engrave ; **text :** . . . . *idam* ***besagey****dōn Kritayugachōḻa* ; **tr.** Kritayugachōḻa **engraved** the text of the inscription ; *S.I.I.* IX, pt. i, No. 40, p. 23, ll. 19–22 ; Kalugōḍu, Rayadurg Tq., Bellary Dt., Karn. St. **Dy.** Noḷ. Pal., Maydamma, Ś. 899 = 977 A.D.

besagey[2] (K. *vb.*), to order ; **text :** (damaged) . . *Hōsaḷa* . . . . *Vīranārasiṁhadēvarasaru* . . . .*chatusīmeyiṁdoḷagāda maṁṇanu mahājanakke* ***besagey****dire* . . . . ; **tr.** while Hoysaḷa Narasiṁha-dēvarasa has **order**ed the grant of land within four demarcated boundaries to the *mahājana* (administrative body of brāhmaṇas) ; *E.C.* IV, Yl. 15, p. 282, ll. 1–2, 14–16 ; Honnūru, Yalandur Tq., Mysore Dt., Karn. St. **Dy.** Hoy., Narasiṁha, Ś. 1204 = 1283 A.D.

besaṁ (K.), a kind of tax ; **text :** . . . . . *seṭṭiyargaṁ Pannasiggargaṁ gāvuṇḍugaḷgaṁ biṭṭi koṭṭaṇaṁ bīḍu* ***besaṁ*** *poṟagu*. . . . . . ; **tr.** the taxes on free labour, on those who pound paddy, house tax, and **a kind of tax** called **besa** to be collected by the *seṭṭi* (traders), the donees of land grants and the *gāvuṁḍu* (village headmen) are exempt ; *S.I.I.* IX, pt. i, No. 77, pp. 48–49, ll. 25–26 ; Kōgaḷi, Hadagalli Tq., Bellary Dt., Karn. St. **Dy.** Chāḷ. of Kal., Āhvamalla, Ś. 914 = 992 A.D.

besaṁgey (K. *vb.*), to engrave ; **text :** . . . . . *idaṁ baredān Āychavemma* ***besaṁgey****da Maṇiyammōjar*. . . . . . ; **tr.** this inscription was composed by Āychavemma and **engraved** by Maṇiyammōja ; *S.I.I.* IX, pt. i, No. 30, p. 17, ll. 1–4 ; Kambadūru, Kalyandurg Tq., Anantapur Dt., A.P. St. **Dy.** Noḷ. Pal., Iṟiva-Noḷaṁba, Ś. 887 = 965 A.D.

besamakkaḷu (K. *n.*), servants who carry out orders ; **text :** . . . . . *Kētaiyaṁgaḷu Nulagēriya* . . . *turuva koṁḍu hōhaṁdu avara kūḍe kādi* . . . *sattu svargaṁbaḍadaru adake mechi Sātagāvuḍa praje* ***besamakkaḷuṁ*** *mukyavāgi* . . . . *ātana makkaḷige netarugeyi gade kaṁba 12* . . . *mane koṭu salisuvaru* . . . . . ; **tr.** when Kētayya was rustling the cattle from the village of Nulagēri, the copper smith Kalōja fought against him and died. In appreciation of this mortyrdom Sātagāvuḍa, the subjects and the **servants who carry out orders** donated to his children as a reward for shedding blood 12 *kaṁba* (a land measure) of wet land and a house; *K.I.* IV, No. 35, p. 80, ll. 3–10 ; Nūlgēri, Hirekerur Tq., Dharwar Dt., Karn. St. **Dy.** Sēü. of Dēv, Siṅghaṇa, in characters of 11th-12th century A.D.

besanu (K. *n.*), work ; **text :** . . . . . *khaṇḍasphuṭitaṁ modalāgellā* ***besanumaṁ*** *naḍeyisuva rūvāri Muchchōjaṁge mattar panneraḍu* ; **tr.** 12 *mattar* (a grain measure) of land earmarked for the sculptor who supervises all **works** connected with renovation ; *S.I.I.* IX, pt. i, No. 101, p. 73, ll. 54–55 ; Mōrigēri, Hadagalli Tq., Bellary Dt., Karn. St. **Dy.** Chāḷ. of Kal., Āhavamalla, Ś. 967 = 1045 A.D.

besavakkaḷu (K. *n.*), servants who carry out orders ; **text :** (damaged). . . . *Bairamaṁgalada aśēshamahājanaṁgaḷu* . . . . . ***besavakkaḷu*** *Uppiligarige* . . . *biṭṭa kodaṁge* . . . . . *siddhāya sēse*. . . . ; **tr.** the entire administrative body of brāhmaṇas of Bairamaṁgala and those **servants who carry out orders** made a grant of income from fixed tax and *sēse* tax to the Uppiliga community ; *E.C.* IV, Yl. 15, p. 282, ll. 7–9, 17 ; Honnūru, Yalandur Tq., Mysore Dt., Karn. St. **Dy.** Hoy., Narasiṁha, Ś. 1204 = 1283 A.D.

besavēḍu (K. *vb.*), to obtain the master's order ; **text :** . . . . *Gajāṁkusa Chōḷana mēge daṇḍu* *vōgalu Dilīpa Noḷaṁba daṇḍinalu kūḍi Ibīḻida Kāḷagadalu āḻdana* **besavēḍi** *sattaṁ Ponnayya* ; **tr.** when the army was attacking Gajāṁkusa Chōḻa, Ponnayya who was a soldier of the army of Dilīpa Noḷaṁba **obtained his master's order** to fight and died in the battle ; *S.I.I.* IX, pt. i, No. 25, p. 13, ll. 7–9 ; Maḍakasira, Madakasira Tq., Anantapur Dt., A.P. St. **Dy.** Noḷ. Pal., Dilīparasa, Ś. 870 = 948 A.D.

besavokkalu (K. *n.*), agricultural labourers ; **text:** . . . . . *Maleyūra grāma 1 ra chatussīmeyoḷaguḷḷa gadde beddalu tōṭa . . . kuṁbāradere . . . dēvadāna* . . . . **besavokkalu** . . . . . . *muṁtāgi prāku maryāde ēnuḷḷa sarvasvāmyavanū anubhavisikoṁba Maleyūra grāma* ; **tr.** the village of Maleyūru will continue to enjoy all the privileges of wetland, rain fed agricultural land, groves, tax on potters, the *dēvadāna* (gift to temples) lands and the **agricultural labourers** within the four boundaries of Maleyūru ; *E.C.* IV, Ch. 372, p. 246, ll. 12–18 ; Maleyūru, Chamarajanagar Tq. and Dt., Karn. St. **Dy.** Saṅgama, Dēvarāya II, Ś. 1344 = 1422 A.D.

besavitti (K. *n.*), maid servant ; **text :** . . . *maṭhada kasava kaḷava* **besavittige** *bhatta mūḍe 5* . . . . . ; **tr.** 5 *mūḍe* (a grain measure) of paddy for the **maid servant** removing garbage from the *maṭha* (religious institution) ; *S.I.I.* VII, No. 329, p. 179, ll. 29–30 ; Mūḍakēṟi, Udupi Tq. and Dt., Karn. St. **Dy.** Saṅgama, Bukkarāya, Ś. 1282 = 1360 A.D.

besta (K. *n.*), fisherman ; **text :** . . . *Kōnēṭi Timmarājayyanavaru taṁma daḷavāyi Yallappanāyakarige uṁbaḷiyāgi koṭṭa Kasavāpuradalli yiha* **besta** *bōvugaḷige . . . terige horige kraya sidhāya biṭi birāḍagaḷa biḍisidaru.* ; **tr.** on the village Kasavapura gifted to his army commander Yellappanāyaka by Kōnēṭi Timmarājayya taxes such as tax on load, fixed tax, tax on free labour and house tax were remitted in favour of **fishermen** and palanquin bearer communities ; *S.I.I.* IX, pt. ii, No. 624, p. 629, ll. 8–12, 17–18 ; Kasavapuram, Gooty Tq., Anantapur Dt., A. P. St. **Dy.** Tuḷuva, Sadāśiva, Ś. 1469 = 1547 A.D.

bēṭe (K. *n.*), hunting ; **text :** . . . . *ā grāmakke uṁṭāda . . . bāḍi bēḍige kāṇike kaḍāya kūṭa* **bēṭe** *biṭṭi . . . . . yivu modalāda yīti bādhegaḷu ēnu ila eṁdu . . . . Veṁkattappanāyaka ayyanavaru . . . . . Viṭhalabhaṭṭarige Rāmāpuraveṁba agrahāravanu koṭṭevu* ; **tr.** Veṁkaṭappanāyaka ayya made a gift of *agrahāra* Rāmāpura to Viṭhalabhaṭṭa with the exemption of taxes such as on hiring out, requsitioned cess, tribute, compulsory tax, assembly, **hunting**, free labour ; *E.C.* (R) V, Kn. 104, p. 99, ll. 17–25 ; Gaḷigekeṟe, Krishṇarājanagara Tq., Mysore Dt., Karn. St. **Dy.** Āravīḍu, Śriraṁga, Ś. 1498 = 1577 A.D.

beṭṭa (K. *n.*), hill ; **text**[1] **:** *teṁkalu . . . . Hiriya dēvara* **beṭṭa***kkaṁ hōda hebbaṭṭeye gaḍi* . . . . . ; **tr.** on the south the boundary is the major road proceeding from the **hill** named after Hiriyadēva; *E.C.* II, Sb. 547, p. 336, ll. 43–44 ; Sāṇēnahaḷḷi,

Channarayapatna Tq., Hassan Dt., Karn. St. **Misc.**, Gaṁgarāja, Ś. 1041 = 1119 A.D. ; **text**[2] **:** . . . . *Heggoṭhārada Sinda* ***beṭṭakke*** *teṅkalu neṭṭiruva vāmana mudre kallu* . . . . . ; **tr.** the stone with the figure Vāmana set up to the south of the **hill** called Sinda of the village Heggoṭhāra ; *E.C.* V, My. 99, p. 220, l. 343–44 ; Mysore, Mysore Tq. and Dt., Karn. St. **Dy.** Woḍ. of Mys., Chikkadēvarāja, Ś. 1595 = 1674 A.D.

beṭṭadakāvalu (K. *n.*), tax to be paid for grazing cattle on the hill ; **text :** . . . . . . *Dēvarāja oḍeyaru* . . . . *Rudrākshi oḍeyarige Goṁdiganahaḷḷiya grāmake saluva gadde beddalu tōṭa* . . . . *kuṁbāṛadeṛe* . . . ***beṭṭada kāvalu*** . . . *muṁtāda* . . . . *sarvasvāmyavanu anubhavisuviri eṁdu koṭṭa liṁgamudre śilāśāsana*. . . . . ; **tr.** Dēvarāja oḍeya granted the village of Goṁdiganahaḷḷi to Rudrākshi oḍeya with all the revenue incomes such as on wet land, rain fed land, groves, tax on potters, **tax to be paid for grazing cattle on the hill**, etc., as recorded in the stone inscription with the figure of a *liṁga* on top ; *E.C.* (R) III, Gu. 176, p. 138, ll. 5-7, 9, 11–12, 16–18 ; Śivapura, Gundlupete Tq., Mysore Dt., Karn. St. **Dy.** Umm. Chfs., Dēvarāja oḍeya, Ś. 1391 = 1469 A.D.

beṭṭina gadde (K. *n.*), wet land lying at a higher level ; **text :** . . . . *agaḷiṁda voḷage* ***beṭṭina gadde*** *1 kkaṁ bīja baḷḷa mūvattara lekkadalu batta mūḍe 2* . . . . . ; **tr.** on the inner side of the trench one piece of **wet land lying at a higher level** of the extent of being sown with 2 *mūḍe* (a grain measure) of paddy calculated at 30 *baḷḷa* (grain measure.) for each *mūḍe* ; *Ep. Ind.* XX, No. 8, p. 94, ll. 37–38 ; Kāpu, Udupi Tq. and Dt., Karn. St. **Dy.** Keḷadi, Sadāśivanāyaka, Ś. 1479 = 1556 A.D.

beṭṭina bāḷu (K. *n.*), cultivable wet land at a raised level granted for maintenance ; **text :** . . . . *maṭhadalu uṁba brāhmara jana prati divasadalu ja 6 kkaṁ biṭṭa bāḷu haṁdeṭina voḷage* ***beṭṭina bāḷu*** . . . . . . ; **tr.** for the **maintenance** of the free feeding of 6 brāhmaṇas in the *maṭha* (religious institution) every day, **cultivable wet land at a higher level** was granted to the religious institution; *S.I.I.* VII, No. 360, p. 217, ll. 10–12 ; Maṇigārakēri, Udupi Tq. and Dt., Karn. St. **Dy.** Saṅgama, Virupākшarāya, Ś. 1398 = 1476 A.D.

beṭṭina makki (K. *n.*), poor quality of land lying at a higher level for cultivating paddy ; **text :** . . . . *Mākabeya* ***beṭṭina makki*** *mū 5*. . . . . ; **tr.** **poor quality of land lying at a higher level for cultivating paddy** belonging to Makabbe, of the extent of being sown with 5 *mū* (*mūḍe*, a grain measure) of seeds ; *S.I.I.* VII, No. 319, p. 169, ll. 21–22 ; Mūḍakēri, Udupi Tq. and Dt., Karn. St. **Dy.** Saṅgama, Bukka, Ś. 1293 = 1371 A.D.

beṭṭina pore (K. *n.*), a hillock with poor soil with a kind of wild shrubs ; **text :** (obscure) . . . . . . *Maddūra sīme mūḍāy* ***beṭṭina pore****ye* . . . ;

tr. the boundary of Maddur is to the east **a hillock with poor soil with a kind of wild shrubs** ; *E.C.* (R) III, Hg. 90, p. 498, ll. 27–28 ; Saragūru, H.D. Kote Tq., Mysore Dt., Karn. St. **Dy.** W. Gaṅga, Śrīpurusha, in characters of 9th cent. A.D.

beṭṭu (K. *n.*), field situated at a higher level depending on rain water ; **text**[1] : .... *mane bhāvi kuṁṭe* ***beṭṭu*** *iṁtī sarvasvava ... seṭṭiyaru Timirēśvara dēvarige .... koṭṭaru ....* ; **tr.** the *seṭṭi* granted to the god Timirēśvaradēva a house, a well, a pond, **field situated at a higher level depending on rain water**, etc. ; *S.I.I.* IX, pt. ii, No. 416, p. 421, ll. 8–10 ; Bantwal Muda, Mangalore Tq., D.K. Dt., Karn. St. **Dy.** Saṅgama, Bukka, Ś. 1299 = 1377 A.D. ; **text**[2] : .... ***beṭṭiṁ****dalū saluva akki khaṁḍuga 132* ; **tr. field situated at a higher level depending on rain water** yielding 132 *khaṁḍuga* (a grain measure) of rice ; *S.I.I.* VII, No. 248, p. 126, l. 19 ; Hiriyaṁgaḍi, Karkala Tq., Udupi Dt., Karn. St. **Dy.** Kaḷasa-Kārkaḷa, Vīra Pāṇḍya, Ś. 1467 = 1545 A.D.

bevahāra (K. < Skt. *vyavahāra, n.*), business transaction ; **text :** ..... *nūlu sīreya* ***bevahāra****vū. Mūrukēriyavarige saluvudu* ... ; **tr.** the right of conducting **business transaction** in cotton sarees is the previlege of the people of Mūrukēri; *S.I.I.* VII, No. 309, p. 160, ll. 32–33 ; Mūḍakēri, Udupi Tq. and Dt., Karn. St. **Dy.** Saṅgama, Dēvarāya, Ś. 1353 = 1431 A.D.

bevahāri (K. *n.*), merchant ; **text :** (damaged). .... *Hemmaragāla* ***bevahāri*** *Gaṅgara Mādhava seṭṭiya maga Masaṇāḍeseṭṭige Bīmasamudrada mūdaṇa kōḍiyali* (further details lost) .... ; **tr.** records some grant of land in the eastern corner of Bhīmasamudra made to Masaṇāḍeseṭṭi son of Gaṅgara Mādhavaseṭṭi, the **merchant** of Hemmaragāla ; *E.C.* (R) III, Nj. 329, p. 392, ll. 10–11 ; Hemmaragāla, Nanjanagud Tq., Mysore Dt. Karn. St. **Dy.** Hoy., Ballāḷa III, Ś. 1213 = 1292 A.D.

bevasāya (K. *n.*), cultivation ; **text :** (damaged) ..... ***bevasāya****va māḍuvaṁthā vokkalugaḷige ... .* ; **tr.** to the tenants who do the work of **cultivation** ; *S.I.I.* IX, pt. ii, No. 666, p. 660, ll. 10–11; Muttigi, Harapanahalli Tq., Bellary Dt. Karn. St. **Dy.** Tuḷuva, Sadāśiva, Ś. 1479 = 1557 A.D.

bhāga (K. < Skt. *n.*), share ; **text :** (damaged) .... *Gaḷḷagēśvaradēvarge biṭṭar ī bhūmi dēvarigoṁdu* ***bhāgam*** *maṭakkeraḍu bhāga ...* ; **tr.** (of the granted land) one **share** was earmarked for the god Gaḷḷagēśvara and two **shares** for the religious institution ; *S.I.I.* IX pt. i, No. 126, p. 108, ll. 15–16 ; Ucchangidurga, Harapanahalli Tq., Bellary Dt., Karn. St. **Dy.** Chāḷ. of Kal., Āhavamalla, Ś. 986 = 1064 A.D.

bhāge (K. *n.*), share ; **text**[1] : .... *ūroḍeyara śrīmānyada bhūmi ..... Aṇṇayyanappayyana* ***bhāge*** *mattaru nālku kaṁbha nālnūṟaivattu* ... ; **tr.** out of the gift land belonging to the headman of the village Aṇṇayyanappayya's **share** is four *mattar* (a land measure) and four hundred and fifty *kaṁbha* (a land measure) ; *S.I.I.* IX pt. i, No. 329, p. 346, ll. 57–58 ; Māgaḷa, Hadagalli Tq., Bellary Dt., Karn. St. **Dy.** Hoy., Ballāḷa II, Ś. 1131 = 1209 A.D. ; **text**[2] **:** .... *Tribhuvana Chūḍāmaṇi Chaityālayada mukha maṁṭapamaṁ .... māḍisidar ā bhavya janaṅgalāreṁdoḍe .... Chaḷaseṭṭiyarige* ***bhāge*** *1 .... sēnāpatiyarige* ***bhāge*** *1 Cheṁñana Dēvati seṭṭiyarige* ***bhāge*** *1* .... ; **tr.** the Jaina laity built the front hall of the Tribhuvana Chūḍāmaṇi Chaityālaya with the contribution of one **share** from Chaḷaseṭṭi, one **share** from Sēnāpati, one **share** from Cheṁñana Dēvati seṭṭi, etc.(in the same fashion a number of other contributors are mentioned) ; *S.I.I.* VII, No. 197, p. 91, ll. 3–4 ; Mūḍabidure, Karkala Tq., Udupi Dt., Karn. St. **Dy.** Saṅgama, Dēvarāya, Ś. 1373 = 1451 A.D.

bhāgi (K. *n.*), share (in land) ; **text :** (damaged) .... *brammadāyada .... bayala oḷage tamage baṁda* ***bhāgi****yali naḍava akki mūḍe 2* ... ; **tr.** 2 *mūḍe* (a grain measure) of rice realised from the **share** out of the field forming part of *brahmadāya*; *S.I.I.* VII, No. 374, p. 229, ll. 9, 11; Maṇigarakēri, Udupi Tq. and Dt., Karn. St. **Dy.** Tuḷuva, Achyutarāya, in characters of 16th cent. A.D.

bhagini (K. < Skt. *n.*), sister ; **text :** .... *Anantapāla chamūnāthana* ***bhagini*** *Kṛishnarājana sati* ..... *Padmaladēvi* ... ; **tr.** Padmaladēvi, the wife of Kṛishṇarāja and the **sister** of the army commander Anantapāla ; *S.I.I.* IX, pt. i, No. 213, p. 215, l. 54 ; Tripurāntakam, Markapur Tq., Kurnool Dt., A.P. St. **Dy.** Chāḷ. of Kal., Tribhuvanamalla, Ch. Vi. yr. 51 = 1126 A.D.

bhāgini (K. *n.*), wife ; **text :** .... *Kētiseṭṭigam* ***bhāgini*** *Chandikabbegogedirda sutarge eṇeyār lōkadoḷ* ... ; **tr.** who indeed are the equals to the sons born to Kētiseṭṭi and his **wife** Chandikabbe; *S.I.I.* IX, pt. i, No. 296, p. 320, l. 28 ; Kuṟugōḍu, Bellary Tq. and Dt., Karn. St. **Dy.** Kal. of Kal., Sōvidēva, Ś. 1097 = 1176 A.D.

bhaishajya śāstra (K. < Skt. *n.*), science of medicine ; **text :** .... *āhārābhaya* ***bhaishjya śāstra*** *dānadatta avadānaruṁ .... Vēṇupurada yeṁṭu praje seṭṭikāṟaru* .... ; **tr.** the eight seṭṭikāras of Vēṇupura known for free feeding, refuge, the **science of medicine** and making gifts ; *S.I.I.* VII, No. 196, pp. 90–91, ll. 24–25 ; Mūḍabidure, Karkala Tq., Udupi Dt., Karn. St. **Dy.** Saṅgama, Dēvarāya, Ś. 1351 = 1429 A.D.

bhaitra (K. *n.*), ship ; **text :** ... *Ayyāvaḷe ayinūrvvar svāmigaḷu .... Nēmitīrthēśvarana .. ... ashṭavidhārchane .... naḍavantāgi nūrippattettu katte kōṇa bhaṇḍi* ***bhaitra*** *dōṇi pēṟi jaḷasthaḷa jātreyalu naḍevaḍam suṁka parihāravāgi koṭṭaru* .... ; **tr.** the five hundred *svāmis* of Ayyāvoḷe granted tax incomes on one hundred twenty bulls, donkeys, buffalloes, carts, **ships**, boats, etc., carrying merchandice in caravans for the eight types of worship to be offered to Nēmitīrthēśvara ; *K.I.* V, No. 98, p. 298, ll. 3, 6–8 ; Tērdāḷ, Jamakhandi

Tq., Bijapur Dt., Karn. St. **Comm. gld.**, Ś. 1104 = 1181 A.D.

bhājana (K. < Skt. *n.*), vessel ; **text :** .... *Naṟugundadoḷ negaḻda mūlastānadarkaṁge beḻḻiya kaṇ taṁbrada* ***bhājanaṁ*** .... *ittan* .... *Mamma* ... ; **tr.** Mamma donated to the Sun god of the main shrine in Naṟugunda silver eyes, copper **vessel,** etc. ; *K.I.* V, No. 11, p. 35, ll. 27–29 ; Naragunda, Naragunda Tq., Dharwar Dt., Karn. St. **Dy.** Chāḷ. of Kal., Vikramāditya VI, Cy. yr. Kāḷayukta = 1078 A.D.

bhaktādāya (K. *n.*), income from pulses ; **text :** .... *sakala suvarṇādāya* ***bhaktādāya*** *ēnuṁṭāda svāmyavanu āgumāḍikoṁḍu teruva guttigeya hoṁnu ga. 30* ; **tr.** the lease amount of 30 *ga* (*gadyāna*, gold coin) to be paid for enjoying all incomes in gold and all **incomes from pulses**, etc. ; *E.C.* III, Nj. 389, p. 424, ll. 11–12 ; Hattavāḷu, Nanjanagudu Tq., Mysore Dt., Karn. St. **Misc.**, Ś. 1424 = 1502 A.D.

bhaḻara (K. < Skt. *bhaṭāra, n.*), priest ; **text :** .. ... *tiruvārādhanegeyva* ***bhaḻarar****gge* .... *pattu koḷaga bhattavaṁ koḍuvar* ... ; **tr.** for the **priest** who performs the worship of the deity 10 *koḷaga* (a grain measure) of paddy is granted ; *E.C.* (R) III, Nj. 241, p. 328, ll. 7–13 ; Nagarle, Nanjanagudu Tq., Mysore Dt., Karn. St. **Dy.** Chōḷa, Rājēndra, reg. yr. 16 = 1027-28 A.D.

bhaḷāri[1] (Te. < *Skt. Bhaṭāri, n.*), goddess ; **text :** *Gaṭṭuyabōyunakun aidu maṟuturu* ***bhaḷāri*** *guḍi mundaṭa chēni* .... *ichchiri* .... ; **tr.** granted five *maṟuturu* (a land measure) of land in front of the temple of **goddess** to Gaṭṭuyabōyu ; *I.A.P.*, pt. i, No. 92, p. 117, ll. 7–9 ; Kōḍūru, Kamalapuram Tq., Cuddappah Dt., A.P. St. **Misc.**, Ś. 878 = 956-57 A.D.

bhaḷāri[2] (K. < Skt. *Bhaṭāri, n.*), goddess ; **text :** ... *Kañchagāra Beḷagaliya* ... *Śivālayakke naḍeva piriyakōla kariya matta 18* .... ***bhaḷārige*** *matta 6.* .... ; **tr.** 18 *matta* (*mattar*, a land measure) of black soil measured by the big measuring rod to the Śiva temple and 6 *matta* of land to the **goddess** ; *S.I.I.* IX, pt. i, No. 74, p. 45, ll. 5–7 ; Kaṁchagāra-Beḷagallu, Alur Tq., Bellary Dt., Karn. St. **Dy.** Chāḷ. of Kal, Āhavamalla, Ś. 903 = 981 A.D.

bhalluṁke daṁḍa (K. *n.*), (commercial guild's) staff with the emblem of the bear ; **text :** ... ***bhalluṁke daṁḍa*** *hastarumappa* ...... *Ayyāvoḷeyainūrvar svāmigaḷu* ..... ; **tr.** the commercial guild called Five Hundred Svāmis of Ayyāvoḷe carrying a **staff with the emblem of the bear** ; *S.I.I.* IX, pt. i, No. 391, p. 402, ll. 4–5 ; Kuṟuvatti, Harapanahalli Tq., Bellary Dt., Karn. St. **Dy.** Guttas of Guttavoḷaḷ, Vikramāditya II, in characters of 12th century A.D.

bhalluṁki daṇḍa (K. *n.*), (commercial guild's) staff with the emblem of the bear ; **text :** ... . ***bhalluṁki daṇḍa*** *hastar Aiyyāvoḷeya puraparamēśvarar* ; **tr.** the lords of the city of

Aiyyāvoḷe (a commercial guild) bearing the **staff with the emblem of the bear** ; *K.I.*, IV, No. 55, p. 125, ll. 8–9 ; Bēḍkīhāḷ, Chikkodi Tq., Belgam Dt., Karn. St. **Dy.** Chāḷ. of Kal., Iṛivabeḍeṅga Satyāśraya, Ś. 922 = 1000 A.D.

bhaṁḍa[1] (K. < Skt. *n.*), goods ; **text :** . . . . *Mahādēvadēvargge Duggatiya taḷada **bhaṁḍa**dalu sārigeyoḷoṁdu lakka aḍakeya suṁkava nivēdyake biṭṭaru* . . . . . ; **tr.** from among the **goods** available in Duggati while it is transported the tax on arecanuts is granted to the feeding of the god Mahādēva ; *S.I.I.* IX, pt. i, No. 215, p. 218, l. 39 ; Duggavatti, Harapanahalli Tq., Bellary Dt., Karn. St. **Dy.** Chāḷ. of Kal., Tribhuvanamalla, Ś. 1049 = 1126 A.D.

bhaṁḍa[2] (K. < Skt. *n.*), any object which is weighed ; **text :** (obscure) . . . *tūguva **bhaṁḍa**ke hoṁge hāga 1* . . . . ; **tr.** for **any object which is weighed** costing one *hoṁnu* (a gold coin) will attract a tax 1 *hāga* (1/4 of a gold coin) ; *S.I.I.* IX, pt. i, No. 145, p. 128, l. 36 ; Bāgaḷi, Harapanahalli Tq., Bellary Dt., Karn. St. **Dy.** Chāḷ. of Kal., Vikramāditya VI, Ch. Vi. yr. 4 = 1079 A.D.

bhaṁḍa[3] (K. < Skt. *n.*), merhandise ; **text**[1] **:** . . . . *nānādēsi mummuri daṁḍaṁgaḷu samasta **bhaṁḍa**vaṁ māṟidātanalli oṁdu hoṁge kāṇiyoṁdu māṟugoṁḍātanalli oṁdu hoṁge kāṇiyoṁdu.* . . . ; **tr.** the *nānādēsi* and *mummaḍidaṁda* guild members, while selling all the merchandise will pay one *kāṇi* (a fraction of a coin denomination) per *hoṁnu* (a gold coin) as tax and the buyer will pay one *kāṇi* for one of merchandise purchased ; *S.I.I.* IX, pt. i, No. 295, p. 318, ll. 29 ; Bāpuram, Adavani Tq., Kurnool Dt., A.P. St. **Dy.** Chāḷ. of Kal., Sōmēśvara, Ś. 1093 = 1172 A.D. ; **text**[2] **:** . . . . *mūvattettina suṁka vokkaludeṟe bīravaṇa yāva **bhaṁḍa**vaṁ hiḍidu naḍedadaṁ* . . . . . *Kōṇavatteya saṁteyadāya* ; **tr.** tax from the market of Kōṇavatte levied on thirty oxen, tenancy cess, tax paid by the people for the maintenance of the army and for the transport of any **merchandise**; *K.I.* IV, No. 1, p. 13, l. 102 ; Sātēnahaḷḷi, Hirekerur Tq., Dhārwar Dt., Karn. St. **Dy.** Hoy., Ballāḷadēva, Ś. 1126 = 1204 A.D.

bhaṁḍāra (K. < Skt. *n.*), treasury ; **text**[1] **:** . . . . *samasta durgaṁgaḷali **bhaṁḍāra**gaḷa parama viśvāsi* . . . . *Gōpināyaka* . . . . . ; **tr.** Gōpināyaka, the supreme trustee of the **treasuries** in all the forts ; *S.I.I.* VII, No. 575, p. 343, ll. 5–7 ; Penukoṇḍa, Penukonda Tq., Anantapur Dt., A.P. St. **Dy.** Saṅgama, Harihara, Ś. 1314 = 1392 A.D. ; **text**[2] **:** . . *Goravūra grāmavu jīrṇavāgi idali Tiṁmaṇa daṁṇāyakarige biṁnahaṁ māḍi aramaneyiṁda dhaṁma sahāyavāgi **bhaṁḍāra**diṁda koḍisida Vōsanada grāmadiṁda ga 125* . . . . ; **tr.** since the village Gorūru had been in ruins, having appealed to Tiṁmaṇadaṁṇāyaka, a grant of 125 *ga* (*gadyāṇa*, gold coin) collected from the village Vōsana was taken from the palace **treasury** for salvaging the village ; *E.C.* (R) VIII, Hn. 201,

p. 425, ll. 2–5 ; Gorūru, Hassan Tq. and Dt., Karn. St. **Misc.**, Cy. yr. Vyaya = 1466 A.D. ; **text**[3] : . . *Uḷuvareya grāma mūlakrayake saluva arthavanū . . . . . namma* ***bhaṁḍāra****ke tegedukoṇḍu ā grāmavanu namage mūlavāgi biṭṭukoṭṭa* (text stops here) ; **tr.** the original price of the village Uḷavari was remitted into our **treasury** and that village was handed over to us on a permanent basis ; *K.I.* VI, No. 70, p. 192, ll. 12–13 ; Uḷavari, Ankola Tq., Karwar Dt., Karn. St. **Dy.** Tuḷuva, Sadāśiva, Ś. 1473 = 1550 A.D.

bhaṁḍāra grāma (K. < Skt. *n.*), village belonging to royal treasury ; **text :** (damaged). . . . *Kaṇiyakala* ***bhaṁḍāra-grāma*** . . . . . . ; **tr.** Kaṇiyakal, a **village belonging to the royal treasury** ; *S.I.I.* IX, pt. ii, No. 506, p. 519, ll. 7–8 ; Kaṇekkal, Rayadurga Tq., Bellary Dt., Karn. St. **Dy.** Tuḷuva, Kṛishṇadēvarāya, Ś. 1438 = 1516 A.D.

bhaṁḍāra staḷa (K. < Skt. *n.*), place belonging to the palace treasury ; **text :** . . . . *aramaneya* ***bhaṁḍāra-staḷ****ada Kaṁdāvurada grāmada* . . . ; **tr.** village Kaṇḍāvuragrama, the **place belonging to the palace treasury** ; *S.I.I.* IX, pt. ii, No. 476, p. 491, l. 10 ; Basarūru, Kundapur Tq., Udupi Dt., Karn. St. **Dy.** Sāḷuva, Narasiṁha, Ś. 1428 = 1506 A.D.

bhaṁḍāravāḍa (K. < Skt.), treasury building ; **text :** . . . . ***bhaṁḍāravāḍake*** *saluva Mūḍanāḍa modala grāma Velupaḍige*. . . . . . . ; **tr.** the chief village Velupaḍige belonging to Mūḍanāḍu which was attached to the **treasury building** ; *S.I.I.* IX, pt. ii, No. 516, p. 531, l. 3 ; Velpamadugu, Gooty Tq., Anantapur Dt., A.P. St. **Dy.** Tuḷuva, Kṛishṇadēvarāya, Ś. 1446 = 1525 A.D.

bhaṁ ḍāri[1] (K. < Skt. *n.*), treasurer ; **text :** . . . . *Ballāḷana* ***bhaṁḍāri*** *Siṁganam bayasadarāru* . . . . ; **tr.** who does not like Siṁga, the **treasurer** of Ballāḷa ; *S.I.I.* IX, pt. i, No. 329, p. 345, l. 26 ; Māgaḷa, Hadagalli Tq., Bellary Dt., Karn. St. **Dy.** Hoy., Ballāḷa, Ś. 1131 = 1209 A.D.

bhaṁḍāri[2] (K. < Skt. *prn.*), inherited professional surname ; **text :** . . . . *baḍaga Beṁmaṇa* ***bhaṁḍāri****ya gaḍiyiṁ teṁka* . . . . . ; **tr.** on the north to the south of the boundary of (land belonging to) Beṁmaṇa **bhaṁḍāri** ; *S.I.I.* IX, pt. ii, No. 448, p. 457, l. 14 ; Basarūru, Kundapur Tq., Udupi Dt., Karn. St. **Dy.** Saṅgama, Dēvarāya, Ś. 1363 = 1442 A.D.

bhaṁḍasāli (K. < Skt. *n.*), warehouse ; **text :** . . ***bhaṁḍasāli****yiṁda bhatta mūḍe eppattu* . . . . ; **tr.** 70 *mūḍe* (a grain measure) of paddy from the warehouse ; *S.I.I.* IX, pt. ii, No. 417, p. 422, l. 14; Kōṭēśvara, Kundapur Tq., Udupi Dt., Karn. St. **Dy.** Saṅgama, Harihara, Ś. 1300 = 1377 A.D.

bhaṁḍi dāri (K.), cart track ; **text**[1] **:** . . . *paḍuva* ***bhaṁḍi dāri*** . . . ; **tr.** the cart track to the west ; *E.C.* II, Sb. 444, p. 272 l. 77 ; Śravaṇabeḷagoḷa, Channarayapatna Tq., Hassan Dt., Karn. St. **Dy.** Hoy., Ballāḷa II, Ś. 1104 = 1181 A.D. ; **text**[2] **:** . . . ***bhaṇḍi dāri****ya Gavarahaḷiya ōṇiyim baḍagalu* . .

.... ; **tr.** to the north of the lane of Gavarehaḷḷi off the cart track ; *E.C.* (R) IV, Yl. 168, p. 371, l. 37; Ālakere, Yalandur Tq., Chamarajanagara Dt., Karn. St. **Dy.** Tuḷuva, Kṛishṇadēvarāya, Ś. 1441 = 1519 A.D.

bhaṁḍidere (K. *n.*), tax on carts ; **text :** ...... *Dharmapurada śrī Kēśavadēvariṁge ā vūra .... gāṇadere kuṁbāradeṟe asagadeṟe ....* ***bhaṁḍidere*** *....... nāvidadere intinisara teṟeyanu biṭṭaru.......* ; **tr.** the **taxes on** oil mills, potters, washermen, **carts**, barbers, etc. collected from Dharmapura were donated to the god Kēśavadēva; *E.C.* (R) IV, Hs. 24, p. 499, ll. 39–41 ; Dharmapura, Hunasur Tq., Mysore Dt., Karn. St. **Dy.** Hoy., Narasiṁha I, Ś. 1084 = 1162 A.D.

bhaṁḍi gaḍahu (K. *n.*), ferry for carts ; **text :** .... *Sōmanapura ūra muṁdaṇa ōṇiyiṁ aravaṭṭige āladiṁ Mālaṁgi* ***bhaṁḍigaḍahina*** *koḷḷiyiṁda mūḍalu hoḷeyiṁda teṁkalu* ..... ; **tr.** from the lane in front of the village Sōmanapura, from road side shed where water, buttermilk, etc., are offered free to travellers, to the east of the gulf of the Mālaṁgi ferry for carts ; *E.C.* (R) V, T. N. 225, p. 605, ll. 15–16; Kaliyūr, T. Narasipura Tq., Mysore Dt., Karn. St. **Dy.** Tuḷuva, Krishṇadēvarāya, Ś. 1445 = 1521 A.D.

bhaṁḍikāṟa (K. *n.*), cartman ; **text :** ... *Hadināḍasīme prabhu Dēvappagaüḍara makkaḷu Rājanāyakaru ī kaṭṭeyalli Naṁdyāla sīme* ***bhaṁḍikāṟara*** *kailli kaṭṭisida vadaü 2* ..... ; **tr.** Rājanāyaka son of Dēvappagauḍa, the chief of Hadināḍasīme caused two dykes in this tank to be constructed by the **cartmen** of Naṁdyālasīme; *E.C.* (R) IV, Yl. 176, p. 376, ll. 2–5 ; Gaṇiganūru, Yalandur Tq., Chamarajanagar Dt., Karn. St. **Dy.** Hadināḍu Chfs., Dēvappagauḍa, in characters of 16th cent. A.D.

bhaṁḍi vaṭṭe (K. *n.*), cart road ; **text :** ..... *teṁkalu* ***bhaṇḍivaṭṭe*** .. ; **tr.** to the south the **cart road** ; *S.I.I.* IX, pt. i, No. 165, p. 159, ll. 69–70; Kuṟuvatti, Harapanahalli Tq., Bellary Dt., Karn. St. **Dy.** Chāḷ. of Kal., Vikramāditya VI, Ch. Vi. yr. 24 = 1099 A.D.

bhaṁḍiya bhattada suṁka (K. *n.*), levy on cart load of paddy ; **text:** (damaged) ***bhaṇḍiya-bhattada suṁka*** .... ; **tr. levy on card load of paddy** ; *S.I.I.* IX, pt. ii, No. 438, p. 446, l. 15 ; Kadiri, Kadiri Tq., Anantapur Dt., A.P. St. **Dy.** Saṅgama, Dēvarāya, Cy. yr. Hēmaḷambi = 1418 A.D.

bhaṁgāru vāhanālu (Te. *n.*), golden vehicles ; **text :** .... *paṁchapātralu .... Tirumaṁjena biṁdelu ...* ***bhaṁgāru vāhanālu*** *..... modalaina tirupaṇulu chēyiṁchi* ...; **tr.** having done such pious deeds like donating 5 vessels, vessels for sacred bathing, **golden vehicles,** etc. ; *S.I.I.* XVI, No. 295, p. 300, ll. 8–9 ; Śrīmushṇam, Chidambaram Tq., S. Arcot Dt., T. Nadu St. **Dy.** Āravīḍu, Śrīraṁga I, Ś. 1505 = 1584 A.D.

bhāṇasa verggaḍe (K. *n.*), headman of the royal

kitchen ; **text :** . . . . . . *mahāpradhānaṁ* ***bhāṇasa verggaḍe*** . . . *Anaṁtapāḷayya daṁḍanāyakaru* . . . . . ; **tr.** Anaṁtapāḷayya the general who was the chief minister and the **headman of the royal kitchen** ; *S.I.I.* IX, pt. i, No. 153, p. 136, l. 66 ; Ambali, Kudligi Tq., Bellary Dt., Karn. St. **Dy.** Chāḷ. of Kal., Vikramāditya VI, Ś. 1004 = 1083 A.D.

bhāṇasu verggaḍe (K. *n.*), headman of the royal kitchen ; **text :** . . *mahāpradhānaṁ daṁḍanāyaka* ***bhāṇasu verggaḍe*** *maneverggaḍe sēnādhipati daṁḍanāyakan Anaṁtapāḷayyaṁgaḷu* . . . . . ; **tr.** the chief minister, army head, head of the royal household and army commander General Anaṁtapāḷayya who was the **head of the royal kitchen** ; *S.I.I.* IX, pt. i, No. 224, p. 229, ll. 16–18; Sindavala, Bellary Tq. and Dt., Karn. St. **Dy.** Chāḷ. of Kal., Bhūlōkamalla, reg. yr. 5 = 1130 A.D.

bhaṇḍa (K. < Skt. *n.*), goods ; **text :** (damaged). . . . *Beḷvaladiṁ baṁda* ***bhaṇḍa****kke hejjuṁkamaneide koḷvar* . . . . ; **tr.** the major tax levied on **goods** imported from Beḷvala is to be collected ; *K.I.*, V, No. 16, p. 59, l. 19 ; Dharwar, Dharwar Tq. and Dt., Karn. St. **Dy.** Chāḷ. of Kal., Vikramāditya VI, Ch. Vi. yr. 42 = 1117 A.D.

bhaṇḍāram (T. < Skt. *n.*), treasury ; **text :** . . . . . . *Maṇikaṇṭaṉ* . . . . . *Kīḻappēṟūr Uḍaya Kaḍambaṉāḍum Perumaṉṉūrum* . . . . ***bhaṇḍāra****ttil niṉṟeḍuttu koḍutta achchu yiruṉūṟṟināl ppadiṉṉum cheluttumāṟu kalppichcha nel yiruṉūṟṟinālppadu paṟa* . . . . ; **tr.** the **treasury** paid 240 *achchu* (a coin) on certain lands in Kaḍaṁbanāḍu and Perumaṉṉūr belonging to Maṇikaṇṭan of Kīḻappērūr and from these lands 240 *paṟa* (a grain measure) has to be measured ; *T.A.S.* V, pts. i to iii, No. 24, p. 80, ll. 16–17 ; Kiḷimāṉūr, Trivandrum Tq. and Dt., Ker. St. **Dy.** Rulers of Vēṇāḍu, Mārttāṇḍavarma tiruvaḍi, Kollam 343 = 1167-68 A.D.

bhaṇḍi (K. *n.*), cart ; **text :** . . . *Ayyāvaḷe ayinūrvvar svāmigaḷu* . . . . *Nēmitīrthēśvarana* . . . . . *ashṭavidhārchane* . . . . *naḍavantāgi nūrippattettu katte kōṇa* ***bhaṇḍi*** *bhaitra dōṇi pēṟi jaḷasthaḷa jātreyalu naḍevaḍam suṁka parihāravāgi koṭṭaru* . . . . ; **tr.** the five hundred *svāmis* of Ayyāvoḷe granted tax incomes on one hundred twenty bulls, donkeys, buffalloes, **carts**, ships, boats, etc., carrying merchandice in caravans for the eight types of worship to be offered to Nēmitīrthēśvara ; *K.I.*, V, No. 98, p. 298, ll. 3, 6–8 ; Tērdāḷ, Jamakhandi Tq., Bijapur Dt., Karn. St. **Comm. gld.**, Ś. 1104 = 1181 A.D.

bhaṇḍiya bhatta (K. *n.*), cart load of paddy ; **text:** . . . . ***bhaṇḍiya bhatta*** *koḷaga 1* . . . .; **tr.** **cart load of paddy** measuring 1 *koḷaga* (a grain measure) ; *S.I.I.* IX, pt. i, No. 233, p. 239, l. 59 ; Eraḍukere, Kalyandurga Tq., Anantapur Dt., A.P. St. **Dy.** Chāḷ. of Kal., Jagadēkamalla, Ś. 1060 = 1139 A.D.

bhāra (K. *indec.*), load ; **text :** . . . . *arasugaḷuṁ* *pradhānaruṁ Kārakaḷada halaruṁ ubhaya nānādēsigaḷuṁ biṭṭa suṁka .... meṇasina-**bhāra**kke suṇṭiya **bhāra**kke bhattada hērige akkiya hērige . . . . . ivu modalāda sarva suṁka ivu dēvara bhōgake naḍavudu. . . .* ; **tr.** all the revenue incomes from the **load**s of pepper, ginger, paddy, rice etc were donated for services to the deity by the ruler, the minister and the *halaru* (an administrative body) of Kārakaḷa ; *S.I.I.* VII, No. 247, p. 125, ll. 31–34 ; Kārkaḷa, Karkala Tq., Udupi Dt., Karn. St. **Dy.** Hoy., Ballāḷa, Ś. 1256 = 1334 A.D.

bharaṇa (K. *n.*), a land measure ; **text :** . . . . *hiriyakeṟeya tuṁbina hariya eraḍu **bharaṇa** tōṭa . . . . .* ; **tr.** one grove on land measuring two *bharaṇa* (land measure) under the sluice of the big tank ; *K.I.* IV, No. 2, p. 15, l. 17 ; Sātēnahaḷḷi, Hirekerur Tq., Dharwar Dt., Karn. St. **Dy.** Sēü of Dēv, Siṁhaṇa, reg. yr. 31 = 1241 A.D.

bharaṇada kōḷu (K. *n.*), a rod for measuring land ; **text :** . . . . *Nagarēśvaradēvargge . . . . . bharaṇada kōloḷ . . . . biṭṭa nela mattaru 60 . . .* ; **tr.** 60 *mattar* (land measure) of land **measured by the *bharaṇa* rod** was donated to the god Nagarēśvara; *S.I.I.* XX, No. 19, p. 19, ll. 37, 39–40 ; Rūgi, Indi Tq., Bijapur Dt., Karn. St. **Dy.** Chāḷ. of Kal., Ayyaṇadēva, Ś. 936 = 1015 A.D.

bharaṇaṁ (K. *n.*), responsibility ; **text :** (damaged) . . . *ī dēvabhōga . . . . Dēvayyanu Muttayyanu Nāraṇōjaru yiṁti mūvattirvara **bharaṇaṁ*** ; **tr.** the responsibility of protecting this donation to the god lies with 32 persons including Dēvayya, Muttayya, Nāraṇōja ; *S.I.I.* IX, pt. i, No. 28, p. 15, first face top, ll. 1–2, 6–12 ; Madhudi, Madakasira Tq., Anantapur Dt., A.P. St. **Dy.** Noḷ. Pal., Nolaṁbādhirāja, Ś. 881 = 959 A.D.

bharaṇaṁgey (K. *vb.*), to protect ; **text :** . . . . *ūraṁ vidvajjanakkādaradoḷ bharaṇaṁgeydu . . .* ; **tr.** having protected the village in favour of the learned inhabitants ; *S.I.I.* XI, No. 45, p. 32, l. 48; Kurahaṭṭi, Navalgunda Tq., Dharwar Dt., Karn. St. **Dy.** Chāḷ. of Kal., Āhavamalla, Ś. 902 = 980 A.D.

bharata (K. *n.*), the subject of fine arts ; **text:** . . . . ***bharata** vyākaraṇa. āgama smṛiti purāṇa . . . . vistararu . . . . .* ; **tr.** exponent of **the subjects of fine arts**, grammar, doctrinal works, religious codes, mythology, etc. ; *S.I.I.* IX, pt. i, No. 267, p. 284, ll. 32–33 ; Bāgaḷi, Harapanahalli Tq., Bellary Dt., Karn. St. **Dy.** Chāḷ. of Kal., Jagadēkamalla II, Ś. 1082 = 1160 A.D.

bhāravaḍḍige (K. *n.*), beam ; **text :** . . . *Śrīraṁga daṁṇāyakara paṭṭa sāhaṇi Maṁḍalasāhaṇi mādisida **bhāravaḍḍige** . . . .* ; **tr.** records the provision of a **beam** by Maṁḍalasāhaṇi, the *paṭṭa sāhaṇi* (chief of the horse-stable) of Śrīraṁga daṁṇāyaka ; *E.C.* IV, Yl. 56, p. 302, l. 2 ; Maddūru, Yelandur Tq., Mysore Dt., Karn. St. **Misc.**, Ś. 1165 = 1243 A.D.

bhartāra (K. *n.*), husband ; **text :** . . . *Nālikabbe taṁna **bhartāra**ṁge koṁḍakuṁḍeya tīrthadalu*

Chaṭṭa Jinālayameṁdu . . . māḍisida basadi . . . ; **tr.** the temple called Chaṭṭa Jinālaya was got constructed by Nālikabbe in memory of her **husband** at the holy place of Koṁḍakuṁde ; *S.I.I.* IX, pt. i, No. 150, p. 132, ll. 22–24 ; Konakoṇḍla, Gooty Tq., Anantapur Dt., A.P. St. **Dy.** Chāḷ. of Kal., Vikramāditya VI, Ch. Vi. yr. 6 = 1081 A.D.

bhaṭa (K. *n.*), soldier ; **text :** . . . . *nal**bhaṭa**ranēkaraṁ bharade sīḻdu . . . . Kalināga gauṁda* ; **tr.** Kalināga gauṁda having forcefully killed a number of good **soldiers** (in the enemy army) ; *E.C.* (R), XII, Tk. 9, p. 343, ll. 45–46 ; Amṛitāpura, Tarikere, Tq., Chickmagalur Dt., Karn. St. **Dy.** Hoy., Ballāḷa, Ś. 1128 = 1205 A.D.

Bhaṭāra[1] (K. *n.*), deity ; **text :** . . . . *Ballahana daṁḍanāyaka Kōṭayya . . Vishṇu grihamanettise Vishṇu **bhaṭāra**ge koṭṭa maṇṇu . . . . pannīrkhaṁḍuga* . . . ; **tr.** Kōṭaiah, the army commander of the emperor (*Ballaha*) constructed a temple for Vishṇu and donated 12 *khaṁḍuga* (land to the extent of being sown with 12 khaṁḍuga of seeds) of land to Vishṇu ***bhaṭāra*** ; *S.I.I.* IX, pt. i, No. 33, p. 19, ll. 3–5, 7–11 ; Agaḷi, Madakasira Tq., Anantapur Dt., A.P. St. **Dy.** Noḷ. Pal., Noḷambādhirāja, in characters of 10th cent. A.D.

bhaṭāra[2] (K. *n.*), learned brāhmaṇa ; **text :** . . . . *Noḷaṁbādhirājar Piriyameḻpiya . . . . Bāḷasōma**bhaṭārar**ge . . . . siddhāyava . . . biṭṭar* . . . ; **tr.** Noḷaṁbādhirāja granted to the **learned brāhmaṇa** Bāḷasōma of Piriyameḻpi, income from fixed tax ; *S.I.I.* IX, pt. i, No. 32, p. 18, ll. 6–12 ; Gollapuram, Hindupur Tq., Anantapur Dt., A.P. St. **Dy.** Noḷ. Pal., Noḷaṁbādhirāja, in characters of 10th cent. A.D.

bhaṭārar[1] (K. *n.*), learned person ; **text :** . . . *Rudrarāsi **bhaṭārar** pōgi chakravartiyaṁ kaṇḍaravattiru mattar keyyaṁ . . . sāsanaṁbadedar* . . . . ; **tr.** the **learned person** Rudrarāsi met the emperor and obtained an order for the grant of sixty two *mattar* (a land measure) of wet land ; *S.I.I.* IX, pt. i, No. 65, p. 37, ll. 19–21 ; Kuḍatini, Bellary Tq. and Dt., Karn. St. **Dy.** Rāshṭr., Kṛishṇa III, Ś. 870 = 947 A.D.

Bhaṭārar[2] (T. *n.*), deity ; **text :** . . . *Nalvayalūr kūṟṟattu dēvadāṉam Uṟumūr śiṟuttirukkōyil **bhaṭārar**kku . . . . kuḍutta āḍu toṉṉūru* . . . . ; **tr.** Ninety sheep were donated to the **deity** in the small temple of Uṟumūr a *dēvadāna* (land grant to temple) of Nalvayalūrkūṟṟam; *S.I.I.* XIX, No. 135, p. 69, ll. 2–4 ; Eṟumbūr, Chidambaram Tq., S. Arcot Dt., T. Nadu St. **Dy.** Chōḷa, Parakēsarivarman, in characters of 11th cent. A.D.

bhaṭāriyār (T. *n.*), (Jaina) goddess, village goddess; **text**[1] **:** . . . *iru kaḷaiñju niṟai uḍaiya poṟpūv oṉṟu **bhaṭāriyār**kku* . . . ; **tr.** one gold flower weighing two *kaḷaiñju* (gold coin) was donated to the **(Jaina) goddess** ; *T.A.S.* IV, No. 40, p. 148, ll. 10–12 ; Chitaral, Vilavangod Tq., Padmanabhapram Dt., Ker. St. **Dy.** Āy, Vikramāditya Varaguṇa, reg. yr. 17+4, in characters of 11th cent. A.D. ; **text**[2] **:**

. . . . . *Mārakabbe* ***bhaṭārige*** *mattar panneraḍu maneyoṁdu* . . . . . ; **tr.** 12 *mattar* (a land measure) and one house granted to the **village goddess Mārakabbe** ; *Ep. Ind.* XX, No. 6, p. 67, l. 23 ; Kōṭa umachigi, Gadag Tq. and Dt., Karn. St. **Dy.** Chāḷ. of Kal., Vikramāditya VI, Ś. 934 = 1012 A.D.

bhaṭṭa[1] (K. < *Skt. n.*), learned brāhmaṇa ; **text**[1] : . . . *Kañchagāra Beḷagaliya* . . . *Śivālayakke naḍeva piriyakōla kariya matta 18* . . . . ***bhaṭārige*** *matta 6.* . . . ***bhaṭṭa****geyi matta 6.* ; **tr.** 18 *matta* (*mattar*, a land measure) of black soil measured by the longer measuring rod to the Śiva temple and 6 **matta** of land to the goddess and six *matta* of wet land to the **learned brāhmaṇa** ; *S.I.I.* IX, pt. i, No. 74, p. 45, ll. 5–7 ; Kañchagāra-Beḷagallu, Alur Tq., Bellary Dt., Karn. St. **Dy.** Chāḷ. of Kal, Āhavamalla, Ś. 903 = 981 A.D. ; **text**[2] : . . . *iṁtappudakke* . . . *Mādhavana voppa Yaḍahāḍiya* ***bhaṭṭa****ra oppa* . . . . . ; **tr.** the signatories to this grant are Mādhava and the **learned brāhmaṇa** of Yaḍahāḍi ; *S.I.I.* VII, No. 361, p. 218, l. 30 ; Maṇigarakēri, Udupi Tq. and Dt., Karn. St. **Dy.** Saṅgama, Mallikārjuna, Ś. 1385 = 1463 A.D. ;

bhaṭṭa[2] (Skt. *n.*), inherited professional surname ; **text**[1] : . . . *Brahmadēva****bhaṭṭā****nāṁ nivartana saptakaṁ* . . . . ; **tr.** seven *nivartana* (a land measure) of land to Brahmadēva**bhaṭṭa** ; *K.I.* IV, No. 54, p. 111, l. 44 ; Hulgūr, Shiggaon Tq., Dharwar Dt., Karn. St. **Dy.** Sēü. of Dēv., Siṁghaṇa, Ś. 1167 = 1245 A.D. ; **text**[2] : . . . *Jāvagalla purāṇada Kēśava****bhaṭṭa****ra kṛiti* . . . . . ; **tr.** the work of Kēśava**bhaṭṭa** an exponent of Purāṇa belonging to Jāvagallu ; *S.I.I.* VII, No. 565, p. 336, ll. 11–12 ; Penukoṇḍa, Penukonda Tq., Anantapura Dt., A.P. St. **Dy.** Saṅgama, Harihara, Ś. 1314 = 1392 A.D. ; **text** : *ī pramāṇiṁge sākshigaḷu* . . . . *Narahari****bhaṭṭa****ru* . . . . . . ; **tr.** (one of the) witness(es) for this stipulation is Narahari-**bhaṭṭa** . . . . ; *S.I.I.* VII, No. 357, p. 215, ll. 20, 22 ; Maṇigāṛakēri, Udupi Tq. and Dt., Karn. St. **Dy.** Saṅgama, Dēvarāya, Ś. 1343 = 1421 A.D.

bhatta (K. *n.*), paddy ; **text**[1] : . . *Gavarēśvara dēvarge* . . . . *ainūrvarumiḻdu* . . . . *aṁgaḍiyalu soṭige* ***bhatta****ma biṭṭar* . . . . ; **tr.** the five hundred (commercial guild) assembled and donated one *soṭige* (a grain measure) of **paddy** from the shop to the god Gavarēśvara ; *S.I.I.* IX, pt. i, No. 139, p. 122, ll. 37, 40 ; Hoḷalu, Hadagalli Tq., Bellary Dt., Karn. St. **Dy.** Chāḷ. of Kal., Sōmēśvara II, Ś. 996 = 1074 A.D. ; **text**[2] : (incomplete) . . . *kaḷadalu mūguḷa* ***bhattaṁ*** . . ; **tr.** from the wetland three *kuḷa* (a grain measure) of **paddy** ; *E.C.* (R) VIII, Hn. 14, p. 250, l. 56; Muguḷūru, Hassan Tq. and Dt., Karn. St. **Dy.** Hoy., Vishṇuvardhana, Cy. yr. Prabhava = 1147 A.D. ; **text**[3] : . . . . *Sōvaṁṇa Bākaṁṇanavaru agra nākakke varsha 1 ke nāgaṁḍugadalu nūṛanālvattu mūḍe* ***bhatta*** *baha bāḷanu* . . . . *koṭṭaru* . . . . ; **tr.** Bākaṁṇa and Sōvaṁṇa donated land yielding one hundred forty *mūḍe* (a grain measure) of **paddy** measured by *nāgaṁḍuga* (a grain measure of 4 units of **khaṁḍuga**) for feeding four brāhmaṇas for one year ; *S.I.I.* VII, No. 312, p. 163, ll. 8, 10–11, 12–13 ; Mūḍakēri, Udupi Tq. and Dt., Karn. St. **Dy.** Hoy., Ballāḷa, Ś. 1258 = 1336 A.D. ; ; **text**[4] : ..... *Mēkaṁṭana maneyiṁdaṁ mūḍalu* ...... *gadde 1 kkaṁ bittuva bede* ... *nāghaṁḍugadalu mu 2 kaṁ naḍasuva gēṇi* ***bhatta*** *nāghaṁḍugadalu mu 15* .... ; **tr.** on the paddy field located to the east of the house of Mēkaṁṭa, of the extent of being sown with 2 *mu* (=*muḍi*, a grain measure) measured by *nāghaṁḍuga* (4 units of grain measure *khaṁḍuga*), the produce of **paddy** being 15 *mu* ; *S.I.I.* VII, No. 353, pp. 211–12, ll. 15–17 ; Maṇigāṟakēri, Udupi Tq. and Dt, Karn. St. **Dy.** Saṅgama, Harihara, Ś. 1312 = 1390 A.D. **text**[5] : ... *Uḍupina dēvarige teṟuva dēvasvada* ***bhatta*** .. ; **tr.** the **paddy** supplied as *dēvasva* (gift to a temple) to the deity in Udupi ; *S.I.I.* VII, No. 372, p. 228, l. 57 ; Maṇigarakēri, Udupi Tq. and Dt., Karn. St. **Dy.** Saṅgama., Dēvarāya, Ś. 1359 = 1437 A.D.

bhattādāya (K. *n.*), income from paddy ; **text**[1] : (incomplete) ... *Puṇajūra grāmake sērida gadde beddalu tōṭa* .... *gōmāḷa* ..... *suṁka suvarṇādāya* ... ***bhattādāya*** *modalāda sarvasvāmya* ... *āgumāḍi ā grāmakke saluva kuḷa ga. 44* ..... ; **tr.** the wet fields, rain fed fields, groves, pasture land, taxes, income in gold, **income from paddy** and all other such incomes to be enjoyed on payment of tax of 44 *ga* (*gadyāṇa*, gold coin) ; *E.C.* IV, Ch. 240, p. 148, ll. 13–17 ; Puṇajūru, Chamarajanagara Tq. and Dt., Karn. St. **Dy.** Saṅgama, Dēvarāya II, Ś. 1351 = 1429 A.D. ; **text**[2] : *keṟeya teṁkaṇa kōḍivoḷagaṇa* ***bhattādāya*** ; **income derived from paddy** grown on the wetland located at the outlet of the tank; *E.C.* IX, Nlm. 53, p. 74, ll. 23–25 ; Mudda- liṁganahaḷḷi, Nelamangala Tq., Bangalore Dt., Karn. St. **Dy.** Saṅgama, Bukka, Ś. 1398 = 1465 A.D. ; **text**[3] : .. *Upparikeya maṭhada* ... *Mādēvarige* ... *Bāṇagavāḍi* ... *grāmakke saluva* ... *kere gadde beddalu tōṭa* .. *kirukuḷa suvarṇādāya suṁka* ***bhattādāya*** .... *ēnuṁṭāda sarvasvāmyavanu* ... *āgumāḍi* ... *sukhadali iruviri eṁdu koṭṭa dānaśāsana* ...... ; **tr.** as per the donative inscription set up, the tank, wet lands, rain fed lands, groves, minor taxes, income from gold, taxes, **income from paddy,** etc. are to be happily enjoyed by Mādēva, the pontiff of Upparikeya *maṭha* (religious institution); *E.C.* IV, Ch. 229, p. 140, ll. 12, 14, 18–27, 30–31 ; Bānagavāḍi, Chamarajanagara Tq. and Dt., Karn. St. **Dy.** Tuḷuva, Sadāśiva, Ś. 1485 = 1563 A.D.

bhaṭṭagaḷ (T. *n.*), learned brāhmaṇas ; **text** : .. *Rūparnārāyaṇachaturvēdimaṁgalattu* ***bhaṭṭagaḷ****ukku* .... *Poṉṉuḷāṉ kuḍutta pariśu.* ... ; **tr.** the grant made by the Poṉṉuḷāṉ to the **learned brāhmaṇas** of Rūpanārāyaṇachaturvēdimaṅgalam ; *S.I.I.* VIII, No. 89, p. 47, ll. 2–3 ; Tiruvaṇṇāmalai, Tiruvanna malai Tq., N. Arcot Dt., T. Nadu St. **Dy.** Hoy., Ballāḷa, Ś. 1262 = 1341 A.D.

bhattagāve[1] (K. < Skt. *n.*), village granted for meritorious service; **text.** *mahāsāhaṇādhipati Sauchayanāyakar* ..... ***bhattagāve*** *Eleyapasuṇḍiyaṁ āḷdu sukhadinire* ; **tr.** while *mahāsāhaṇādhipathi* (the great cavalry head) was happily ruling over Eleyapasuṇḍi, **a village granted to him for meritorious service** ; *S.I.I.* XI, pt. i, No. 63, p. 52, ll. 8–10, Asuṁḍi, Gadag Tq. and Dt., Karn. St., Chāḷ. of Kal., Jagadēkamalla I, Ś. 948 = 1026 A.D.

bhattagāve[2] (K. *n.*), paddy growing village ; **text :** .. *Rudradēvarasaru Beḷvoladoḷeseva palavuṁ* ***bhattagāve****gaḷaṁ Koḷanūrmmūvattumaṁ Beṇṇedaḍi yerpattumaṁ .... rakshisuttamire* ..... ; **tr.** while Rudradēvarasa was protecting the several **paddy growing villages** in Beḷvola, Koḷanūr-30 and Beṇṇedaḍi-70 ; *K.I.* V, No. 24, p. 91, ll. 23–25 ; Naragunda, Naragund Tq., Dharwar Dt., Karn. St. **Dy.** Chāḷ. of Kal., Sōmēśvara III, reg. yr. 13 = 1138 A.D.

bhattagrāma[1] (K. < Skt. *n.*), village granted for meritorious service ; **text :** .... *mahāmaṁḍaḷēśvaraṁ Gaṁḍarāditya arasar* ... *taṁma* ***bhattagrāma*** *Naṟuguṁdamaṁ* ...... *rājyaṁ geyyuttire*.. .. ; **tr.** while *mahāmaṇḍaḷēśvara* (subordinate ruler) Gaṁḍarāditya arasa was administering Naṟuguṁda, a **village granted** to him **for meritorious service** ; *S.I.I.* IX, pt. i, No. 105, p. 80, ll. 7–9; Kanchagāra Beḷagallu, Alur Tq., Bellary Dt., Karn. St. **Dy.** Chāḷ. of Kal., Trailōkyamalla, Ś. 969 = 1047 A.D.

bhattagrāma[2] (K. *n.*), paddy growing village ; **text :** ... *Tekkekallu panneṟaḍaroḷagaṇa* ***bhatta-grāma*** *Siriguppe* .... ; **tr.** Siriguppe, the **paddy growing village** in the subdivision Tekkekallu–12 ; *S.I.I.* IX, pt. i, No. 159., p. 146, l. 11 ; Siruguppa, Bellary Tq. and Dt., Karn. St. **Dy.** Chāḷ. of Kal., Vikramāditya VI, Ch. Vi. yr. 16 = 1091 A.D.

bhaṭṭaguttar (K. *n.*), bards in the royal court ; **text :** ... *bhaṭṭaguttaru eraḍakkaṁ gadyāṇaṁ ippattu* ...... ; **tr.** twenty *gadyāṇa* (gold coin) for two **bards in the royal court** ; *E.C.* V, T.N. 88, p. 480, l. 82 ; Sōmanāthapura, T. Narasipura Tq., Mysore Dt., Karn. St. **Dy.** Hoy., Narasiṁha III, Cy. yr. Dhātri = 1276 A.D.

bhaṭṭaguttike (K. *n.*), contract for the office of temple service ; **text :** .. *mahājanaṁgaḷu Chakravartti daṁṇṇāyakarige koṭṭa dēvara* . ***bhattaguttike****ya niyōga 1 ke jīvita ga 5* ... ; **tr.** for the livelihood of 1 **contracted to the office of temple service**, the *mahājana* (brāhmaṇa administrative body) granted to Chakravarti daṁṇṇāyaka 5 *gadyāṇa* (gold coin) ; *E.C.* (R) VII, Ng. 76, p. 75, ll. 88–89 ; Beḷḷūru, Nagamangala Tq., Mandya Dt., Karn. St. **Dy.** Hoy., Narasiṁha III, Ś. 1231 = 1309 A.D.

bhattavaṭṭi aṁgaḍi (T. < Skt.), paddy shop ; **text :** ... ***bhattavaṭṭiyaṁgaḍi****ya nakharaṁgaḷu varshaṁprati chaitrakke hāgamaṁ mattaṁ paitrakke hāgamāṁ biṭṭar* ..... ; **tr.** a group of merchants owning **paddy shops** donated from their shops every year one *hāga* (a coin denomination) for the *Chaitra* festival and one *hāga* for the religious festival ; *S.I.I.* XV, No. 135, p. 177, ll. 54 ; Lakkuṇḍi, Gadag Tq. and Dt., Karn. St. **Dy.** Kal. of Kal., Saṁkhama, Ś. 1100 = 1179 A.D.

bhaṭṭa vṛitti (K. < Sky. *n.*), land granted for the livelihood of brāhmaṇas **text**[1] **:** (damaged) . . . . . . *eḷppattu guḷagaḷde bhaṭṭa vritti* . . . ; **tr.** 70 *guḷa* (a land measure) of wet **land granted for the livelihood of brāhamaṇa** ; *E.C.* (R) V, T.N. 47, p. 447, ll. 3–4 ; Bannūru, T. Narasipur Tq., Mysore Dt., Karn. St. **Misc.,** in characters of 9th cent. A.D. ; **text**[2] **:** . . . . *Nyāsaṁ Prābhākaravuvaṁ vakkhaṇisi guṇaśāsanadiṁ uṇba* ***bhaṭṭa vṛitti*** *mattar ayvattu mane voṁdu* . . . . . ; **tr.** 50 *mattar* (a land measure) of land and one house **granted for the livelihood of brāhmaṇas** in return for performing the duties of expounding *Nyāsa* and *Prābhākara*; *Ep. Ind.* XX, No. 6, p. 67, ll. 23–24 ; Kōṭavumachigi, Gadag Tq. and Dt., Karn. St. **Dy.** Chāḷ. of Kal., Vikramāditya VI, Ś. 934 = 1012 A.D. **bhaṭṭavṛitti** (T. < Skt. *n.*), land granted for the livelihood of the brāhamaṇas ; **text :** (damaged) . . . *maṉai oṉṟuṁ* ***bhaṭṭavṛitti*** *āga sarvamānyam iṟaiyili-āga* . . . . *kuḍuttōm* . . .; **tr.** one house was given as tax free **grant for the livelihood of learned brāhmaṇas** ; *S.I.I.* VII, No. 60, p. 26, l. 3 ; Puttūr, Arni Tq., N. Arcot Dt., T. Nadu St. **Dy.** Saṅgama, Harihara, Ś. 1299 = 1377 A.D.

bhaṭṭavrittimānyam (Te. < Skt. *n.*), tax free land granted to brāhmaṇa for his livelihood ; **text :** . . . . . *Aṁgalrājugāri vṛittimānyaṁ Alamūru* . . ; **tr.** Alamūru the **village granted tax free to the Brāhmaṇa** Aṁgalarāju **for his livelihood** ; *S.I.I.* XVI, No. 174, p. 181, l. 2 ; Chinna Ahōbilam, Sirvel Tq., Kurnool Dt., A.P. St. **Dy.** Tuḷuva, Sadāśiva, Ś. 1472 = 1550 A.D.

bhattāya (K. < Skt. *n.*), tax on income from paddy ; **text :** (damaged) . . . *siddhāya bhattāya* . . . . *anyāyameṁbuvaṁdu āgadaṁte* . . . . *khaṁḍikakke* . . . *biṭṭa mattaru nālvattu*. . . . ; **tr.** forty *mattaru* (a land measure) was donated to the school with the exemption of fixed tax, **tax on income from paddy** and punitive tax, etc. ; *S.I.I.* IX, pt. i, No. 162, p. 151, ll. 12–13 ; Slab kept in Madras Museum, Chennai Tq. and Dt., T. Nadu St. **Dy.** Chāḷ. of Kal., Vikramāditya VI, Ch. Vi. yr. 18 = 1093 A.D.

bhaṭṭōpādhyāya (T. < Skt.), inherited professional surname of learned brāhmaṇa teacher ; **text**[1] **:** . . *Bāguḷiya mahājanamayvadiṁbaru purāṇada Īśvara-****bhaṭṭōpādhyā****yarige Sōvanāyaka koṭṭa kaṭṭada kereya keḷagaṇa tōṁṭa 60 ma Kalidēvara brahmapurigaḷāgi śrīmānyavāgi salisuvaru* . . . . ; **tr.** the 50 *mahajana* (the brāhmaṇa administrative body) gave as a donation to Kalidēva a grove of 60 *ma* (*mattar*, a land measure) after converting it into a *brahmapuri* (brahmaṇa settlement) below the tank of the land given by Sōvanāyaka to Īśvara**bhaṭṭōpādhyāya** an exponent of purāṇas ; *S.I.I.* IX, pt. i, No. 192, p. 188, ll. 44–47 ; Bāgaḷi, Harapanahalli Tq., Bellary Dt., Karn. St. **Dy.** Chāḷ. of Kal., Vikramāditya VI, Ś. 1020 = 1098 A.D. ; **text**[2] (Skt.) **:** . . . *Viṭhṭhala* ***bhaṭṭōpādhyāyā****nāṁ pratyēkaṁ nivartana chatushkkaṁ* . . . . ; **tr.** our *nivarttana* (a land measure) individually given to Viṭhṭhala**bhaṭṭōpādhyāya** ; *K.I.* IV, No. 54, p. 111, ll. 43-44 ; Hulgūr, Shiggaon Tq., Dharwar Dt., Karn. St. **Dy.** Sēü of Dēv., Siṅghaṇa, Ś. 1167 = 1245 A.D.

bhavana (K. < Skt.), temple ; **text :** . . . . . *Dharmmabuddhi Kūchigoḷadoḷ . . . Śivana* ***bhavana****maṁ māḍisidaṁ* . . . ; **tr.** Dharmmabuddhi got constructed the **temple** of Śiva at Kūchigoḷa; *S.I.I.* IX, pt. i, No. 247, p. 252, l. 31 ; Śrīnivasapura, Harapanahalli Tq., Bellary Dt., Karn. St. **Dy.** Chāḷ. of Kal., Jagadēkamalla, Cy. yr. Prabhava = 1147 A.D.

bhavaṁti (K. *n.*), court yard in the centre of the building ; **text :** . . . . . *Tribhuvana chūḍāmaṇi eṁba Chaityālayada keḷagaṇa neleya* ***bhavaṁti*** . . . . ; **tr.** the **court yard in the centre** of the ground level of the Tribhuvana chūḍāmaṇi chaityālaya ; *S.I.I.* VII, No. 199, p. 94, l. 2 ; Mūḍabidure, Karkala Tq., Udupi Dt., Karn. St. **Misc.**, Ś. 1409 = 1487 A.D.

bhāvi (K. < Skt.), well ; **text :** . . . . . *teṁkaṇa baḍagaṇa eraḍu* ***bhāvi****ya nīru* . . . ; **tr.** water from two **wells** one in the south and the other in the north ; *S.I.I.* VII, No. 365, p. 222, l. 30 ; Maṇigarakēri, Udupi Tq. and Dt., Karn. St. **Dy.** Saṅgama, Dēvarāya, Ś. 1342 = 1420 A.D.

bhāvi mānya (K. < Skt.), land given as gift for sinking a new well ; **text :** . . . . . ***bhāvi mānya****da kramaveṁteṁdare* . . . . *bhāvi khilavāgi* . . . *irlāgi hostāgi bhāvi agudu* . . . *holanu* . . . . . *anubhavisuvudu* . . . . ; **tr.** the procedure for **land given as gift for sinking a new well** is that, a new well should be dug up in place of the fully silted old well in order to enjoy the grant ; *S.I.I.* IX, pt. ii, No. 691, p. 682, ll. 10, 15, 16 ; Beludōṇa, Adavani Tq., Kurnool Dt., A.P. St. **Dy.** Āravīḍu, Venkaṭapatirāya, Ś. 1514 = 1592 A.D.

bhavya (Skt. *n.*), Jaina laity; **text :** . . . . *saṁtataṁ* ***bhavya****sēvyaḥ* . . . . . *vijayatē Vāsupūjya bratīṁdraḥ* . . . . . ; **tr.** victorious is the great ascetic Vāsupūjya who is ever adored by the **Jaina laity** ; *E.C.* (R) VIII, Hn. 15, p. 251, ll. 13–15; Muguḷūru, Hassan Tq. and Dt., Karn. St. **Misc.**, Cy. yr. Hēmaḷaṁbi = 1177 A.D.

bhavyajana (K. *n.*), Jaina laity ; **text :** . . . . *Tirumaleya Tātayyaṁgaḷu samastarājyada* ***bhavya janaṁ****gaḷ-anumatadiṁda Beḷagoḷa tīrthadalli Vaishṇava aṁgarakshagōsuka samasta rājya doḷaguḷḷaṁtaha Jainaru bāgilagaṭṭaḷeyāgi mane manege varshakke 1 haṇa koṭṭu ā yettida hoṁniṁge dēvara aṁgarakshege yippattāḷanū saṁtaviṭṭu* . . . . . ; **tr.** for the sake of protecting the Vaishṇava inhabitants of the holy place of Beḷaguḷa all the Jainas living in the entire kingdom gave one *haṇa* (a coin) as customary house tax for each house and Tātayya of Tirumale, with the permission of the **Jain laity** of the entire kingdom, appointed twenty persons as bodyguards ; *E.C.* II, Sb. 475, p. 286, ll. 21–25 ; Śravaṇabeḷagoḷa, Channarayapatna Tq., Hassan Dt., Karn. St. **Dy.** Saṅgama, Bukka I, Ś. 1290 = 1368 A.D.

bhavya janaṁgaḷu (K. < Skt. *n.*), Jaina laity ; **text :** .... *chaityālayada mukhamaṁṭapamaṁ. ..... māḍisidarā* ***bhavya janaṁgaḷ*** ... ; **tr.** the **Jaina laity** caused to be constructed the front hall of the Jaina temple ; *S.I.I.* VII, No. 197, p. 91, ll. 2, 3 ; Mūḍabidure, Karkala Tq., Udupi Dt., Karn. St. **Dy.** Saṅgama, Dēvarāya, Ś. 1373 = 1451 A.D.

bhēri (K. < Skt. *n.*), a musical instrument of the shape of kettle drum, percussion instrument ; **text :** (damaged)..... *Mahādēvarige Timmaṇaseṭi tāṁbara* ***bhēriya*** *kāṇikeyāgi māḍisi koṭanu* ... ; **tr.** Timmaṇaseṭi got prepared a copper **kettle drum** and donated it as his tribute to the god Mahādēva ; *S.I.I.* IX, pt. ii, No. 683, p. 676, l. 39–40 ; Basarūru, Kundapur Tq., Udupi Dt., Karn. St. in characters of 16th cent. A.D.

bhēshajagaḷ (K. < Skt. *n.*), medicines ; **text :** . ... *sarva jīvamaṁ ... rakshisi rōgadoḷuṁdidarge ...* ***bhēshajagaḷ****aṁ biḍadittu mudadi māḷpanu Bhairavabhūvarēśvaraṁ.* ... ; **tr.** the kind Bhairava happily provides without let ***medicines*** for all those affected by illness ; *S.I.I.* VII, No. 202, p. 97, ll. 36–37 ; Mūḍabidure, Karkala Tq., Udupi Dt., Karn. St. **Dy.** Kaḷasa-Kārkaḷa, Bhairava, Ś. 1351 = 1429 A.D.

bhikshā vṛitti (K. < Skt. *n.*), land granted for the maintenance of ascetics ; **text :** (fragmentary) .. ... ***bhikshā-vṛitti*** ..... ; **tr. land granted for the maintenance of ascetics** ; *S.I.I.* IX, pt. ii, No. 438, p. 447, l. 48 ; Kadiri, Kadiri Tq., Anantapur Dt., A.P. St. **Dy.** Saṅgama, Dēvarāya, Cy. yr. Hemaḷaṁbi = 1418 A.D.

bhōgada sūḷe (Skt.+K. *n.*), a dancer in the service of god ; **text :** ***bhōgada sūḷe****yargge ... biṭṭa mane panneraḍu* .... ; **tr.** tweleve houses were given for the residence of **dancers in the service of god** ; *S.I.I.* XX, No. 35, p. 39, ll. 12–13 ; Kalkēri, Hangal Tq., Dharwar Dt., Karn. St. **Dy.** Chāḷ. of Kal., Sōmēśvara I, Ś. 977 = 1055 A.D.

bhōgadavaru (K. < Skt. *n.*), women dedicated to temple ; **text :** ... ***Bhōgadavari****ge Kaṁnnegeṟe Dummasamudradalu sa. 1* .. ; **tr.** the **women dedicated to the temple** were granted 1 *sa* (a land measure) of land under the new tank called Dummasamudra ; *E.C.* VII, Ng. 130., p. 126, l. 5 ; Doḍḍajaṭaka, Nagamangala Tq., Mandya Dt., Karn. St. **Dy.** Hoy., Ballāḷa II, Ś. 1101 = 1179 A.D.

bhōgam (T. < Skt. *n.*), yield, produce ; **text :** *Sonnamahādēviyār .... kuḍutta poṉ ... ainnūṟṟu eḻukaḻañjarai .... ippoṉ mudal aḻiyāmai idaṉāl* *vanda* ***bhōgam*** *uṇṇapperuvārgaḷāga vaittadu. . .* ; **tr.** Sonnamahādēvi made a grant of five hundred seven and a half of *kaḻañju* (gold coin); this gold has been endowed without any reduction in future and should be utilized to secure crop **yields** for feeding ; *S.I.I.* XIX, No. 383., p. 202, ll. 4–5 ; Śembiyanmādēvi, Nāgapattinam Tq., Tanjavur Dt., T. Nadu St. **Dy.** Chōḷa, Uttamachōḷa, reg. yr. 15 = 986 A.D.

bhōgam mēḷālu (Te. < Skt. *n.*), dance troupe ; **text :** *idēvuni* . . . . ***bhōgam mēḷālu*** *39* . . . ; **tr.** for this god there were 30 **dance troupes** ; *I.A.P.* Cuddapah II, No. 75, p. 92, l. 14 ; Dēvuni Cuddapah, Cuddapah Tq. and Dt., A.P. St. **Dy.** Tuḷuva, Kṛishṇadēvarāya, Ś. 1439 = 1517 A.D.

bhōga pātra (K. < Skt.), women dedicated to the service of god ; **text :** *Mahādēvarige* ***bhōga-pātra****da dharmake māḍidu sidhāya . . . kāṭi ga. 111* . . ; **tr.** for the maintenance of **women dedicated to the service of god** Mahādēva, the fixed tax of 111 *kāṭi ga* (*kāṭi gadyāṇa*, pure gold coin) was donated ; *S.I.I.* IX, pt. ii, No. 456, p. 467, ll. 8–9 ; Basarūru, Kundapur Tq., Udupi Dt., Karn. St. **Dy.** Saṅgama, Mallikārjuna, Ś. 1374 = 1451 A.D.

bhōgisu (K. < Skt. *vb.*), to enjoy ; **text :** *uḍugoṟe biṭṭi koṭṭaṇa . . . . sēnabōyike . . . muṁtāgi ēnuḷḷa sarva svāmyavanū nīvu. . . . . .* ***bhōgisa****bahudu. . . . .* . ; **tr.** you may enjoy all privileges such as gifts, free labour, shelter, headship of the village, etc. ; *S.I.I.* IX, pt. ii, No. 440, p. 449, ll. 26–30 ; Rajabavanahalli, Harapanahalli Tq., Bellary Dt., Karn. St. **Dy.** Saṅgama, Dēvarāya, Ś. 1341 = 1419 A.D.

bhōjana (K. < Skt. *n.*), free feeding ; **text :** *pratidinavū āṟu praje brāhmaṇa* ***bhōjana****kkeṁdu kaṭṭisida maṭha . . . .* ; **tr.** a religious institution built for the daily **free feeding** of six brāhmaṇas ; *S.I.I.* VII, No. 344, p. 197, ll. 12–13 ; Chauḷikēri, Udupi Tq. and Dt., Karn. St. **Dy.** Saṅgama, Harihara, Ś. 1314 = 1392 A.D.

bhṛitya (K. < Skt. *n.*), devotee ; **text :** *Dēmēśvara dēva sadanamaṁ . . . māḍisidaṁ Dēmēśvaradēva****bhṛityan*** *Udayāditya . . .* ; **tr.** Udayāditya, a devotee of Dēmēśvara got constructed a temple for the god Dēmēśvara ; *S.I.I.* IX, pt. i, No. 118, p. 98, ll. 67–68 ; Hirehaḍagalli, Hadagalli Tq., Bellary Dt., Karn. St. **Dy.** Chāḷ. of Kal., Vikramāditya VI, Ch. Vi. yr. 31 = 1107 A.D.

bhṛityaṁ (K. < Skt. *n.*), servant ; **text :** *svajana-vatsaḷaṁ svāminī* ***bhṛityaṁ*** *Dovayyaṁ perggadetanaṁ geye. . .* ; **tr.** when Dōvayya who was loved by his own people and who was the **servant** of the queen was holding the office of headman ; *S.I.I.* IX, pt. i, No. 64, p. 36, ll. 8–9 ; Bāgaḷi, Harapanahalli Tq., Bellary Dt., Karn. St. **Dy.** Rāshṭr., Kṛishṇa III, Ś. 868 = 944 A.D.

bhū dakshiṇe (K. < Skt. *n.*), land given in the form of fee to the officiating priest ; **text :** (damaged) *Iksvāku chakravartti aśvamēdha* *yāgadali śōḍasha ṛitviggaṇagaḷige* ***bhū dakshiṇe****yāgi koṭṭu agarhāravāgi māḍi* .... ; **tr.** the Ikshvāku emperor after performing the horse sacrifice **gave land in the form of fee** to the 16 **officiating priests** and converted the gift land into a brāhmaṇa settlement ; *K.I.* II, No. 40, p. 140, ll. 6–7 ; Belgaum, Belgaum Tq. and Dt., Karn. St. **Dy.** Sēū. of Dēv. Kandharadēva, Ś. 1184 = 1261 A.D.

bhū dāna (K. < Skt. *n.*), gift of land ; **text**[1] : . . . . *Kulaśēkarachchaturvvēdimaṅgalattu bhaṭṭargaḷukku* . . . . *aṇaittēvai uḻḻiṭṭa aṇaittu upādhigaḷuṁ uṭpaḍa* . . . . ***bhūdāṇa****māga*. . . . *iṟaiyiliyāga tandōm.*; **tr.** we made a **gift of land** as tax free grant and also granted taxes collected such as the one levied for the maintenance of the dam etc. to the *brāhmaṇas* of the *agrahāra* called Kulaśēkara chchaturvēdimaṅgalam ; *S.I.I.* VII, No. 145, p. 63, ll. 3, 12–13 ; Vṛiddhāchalam, Vriddhachalam Tq., S. Arcot Dt., T. Nadu St. **Dy.** Chōḷa, Kōnēriṉmaikoṇḍāṉ, reg. yr. 4+1, in characters of about 12th cent. A.D. ; **text**[2] : *Sōvaṁṇagaḷa makkaḷu Nārāyaṇa dēvagaḷige koṭṭa* ***bhūdāna*** . . . . ; **tr.** the **gift of land** to Nārāyaṇadēva made by the sons of Sōvaṁṇana ; *S.I.I.* VII, No. 364, p. 220, ll. 9–10 ; Maṇigārakēri, Udupi Tq. and Dt., Karn. St. **Dy.** Sāḷuva, Narasiṁha, Ś. 1421 = 1499 A.D. ; **text**[3] : *karaṇaṁ Basavarasaru* . . . *naṭṭuva Nāgayyanavarige koṭṭa* ***bhūdāna*** . ; **tr.** the **gift of land** made by the clerk Basavarasa to the male dancer Nāgayyanavaru ; *S.I.I.* IX, pt. ii, No. 498, p. 511, l. 7, 9–10 ; Cheruvu-Beḷagallu, Kurnool Tq. and Dt., A.P. St. **Dy.** Tuḷuva, Kṛishṇadēvarāya, Ś. 1436 = 1514 A.D. ; **text**[4] (Te. < Skt. *n.*) : . . . *avasaraṁ Chaṁdraśēkharayyavāru Basavamaṭhaṁ Rāchūṭi Vīraṇṇoḍeyalaku ichchina* ***bhū dāna*** *dharma śāsanaṁ* . . . . ; **tr.** the palace official Chaṁdraśēkharayya made a **gift of land** to Rāchūṭi Vīraṇṇoḍeya of Basavamaṭha ; *S.I.I.* XVI, No. 86, p. 102, ll. 2–3 ; Śrīśailam, Nandikotkur Tq., Kurnool Dt., A.P. St. **Dy.** Tuḷuva, Kṛishṇadēvarāya, Ś. 1451 = 1529 A.D.

bhūdāna iṟaiyili (Te. < Skt. *n.*), tax free land gift; **text :** *ivvagarattil bhaṭṭargaḷakku kuḍutta innilam tāṉ vēṇḍum aṇaittu payirgaḷam śeydukoṇḍu vēṇḍum phalavṛikshaṅgaḷum veittukoṇḍu chandrādityavat śella* ***bhūdāna iṟaiyili****yāga anubhavikka kaḍavargaḷāgavum* .... ; **tr.** the brāhmaṇas of this agara (brahmaṇa settlement) have been given land on which they can cultivate all sorts of crops and grow whatever fruit trees they need and shall enjoy these things till the moon and sun lasts, the **land gift** having been declared **tax free** ; *S.I.I.* VII, No. 24, p. 10, ll. 4–5 ; Tāramaṅgalam, Omalur Tq., Salem Dt., T. Nadu St. **Dy.** Pāṇḍya, Sundarapāṇḍya, reg. yr. 13, in characters of 12th cent. A.D.

bhūgata (K. < Skt. *n.*), to go underground, to hide oneself ; **text :** *Achyutarāya mahārāyarū* . . . *śaraṇāgatarāgi baṁda pāḷayada nāyaka makkaḷanu pālisi* ***bhūgata****rāgidda maṁneyaranu rakshisi* . . ;

tr. the emperor Achyutarāya having protected the feudal chieftains who had taken refuge and having protected the minor feudatories who had **gone underground** ; *S.I.I.* IX, pt. ii, No. 547, p. 566, ll. 1–2 ; Little Kāñchpuram, Kanchipuram Tq., Chengleput Dt., T. Nadu St. **Dy.** Tuḷuva, Achyutarāya, Ś. 1454 = 1532 A.D.

bhujabalappudumāḍai (Skt.+T. *n.*), new coin issued after the title *bhujabala* ; **text :** *Śivabhūtan Madiśūdanavāṉavarnāyakaṉ . . . pakkal kaikkoṇḍa* ***bhujabalappudumāḍai*** *24 . . . immāḍai iruvvattunālukkum ittirunaṉḍāviḷakku iraṇḍum . . . erippadāga śilālēkai paṉṉikkuḍuttōm* ; **tr.** we registered in an inscriptions the arrangment made for burning 2 perpetual lamps using 24 **new coins issued after the title bhujabala** donated by Śivabhūtan Madiśūdanavāṉavarnāyakaṉ ; *S.I.I.* XVII, No. 724, p. 346, ll. 3, 5–6 ; Tirumullaivāyal, Saidapet Tq., Chingleput Dt., T. Nadu St. **Dy.** Chōḷa, Kulōttuṅga III, reg. yr. 21 = 1198-99 A.D.

bhuje (K. < Skt. *n.*), arm's length ; **text :** . . . *Rēvagāvuṁḍaṁ māḍisida Śivālayaṁgaḷge pūje punaskāra nivēdya jīrṇṇōddhārakkameṁdu biṭṭa bhūmi 56 gēṇu ghaḷeyim nīḷada* ***bhujeyaṁ*** *dviguṇisiy-agaladoḷ-oṁdaṁ kūḍi guṇisuvī kramadaḷateyalu. . . . . . . koṭṭaru. . .* ; **tr.** for the conduct of worship, other services, offering of food and repair works in the Śiva temples built by Rēvagāvuṁḍa, land measured by the measuring rod of the length of 56 *gēṇu* (a span's length) in **arm's length** and double of that in breadth, thus being the method of calculating the area of gift land ; *S.I.I.* IX, pt. i, No. 249, pp. 257–58, ll. 75–77 ; Kōlūr, Bellary Tq. and Dt., Karn. St. **Dy.** Chāḷ. of Kal., Jagadēkamalla II, reg. yr. 10 = 1147 A.D.

bhuktānubhōgaṁ (K. < Skt. *n.*), possessing and enjoying ; **text :** *Kuṟuṁgōḍa mūnūrvvar mahājanaru . . . . Dēkammana dēgulake . . . aruvattirmattar keyyaṁ . . . . koṭṭu* ***bhuktānubhōgaṁ*** *bhōgisuttire . . . .* ; **tr.** when the temple of the goddess Dēkamma was possessing and enjoying 62 *mattar* (land measure) of land donated to the temple by the *mahājana* (*brāhmaṇa* administrative body) of Kuṟuṁgōḍu ; *S.I.I.* IX, pt. i, No. 65, p. 37, ll. 6–10; Kuḍatini, Bellary Tq. and Dt., Karn. St. **Dy.** Rāshṭr., Kṛishṇa III, Ś. 870 = 947 A.D.

bhūmi (K. < Skt. *n.*), land ; **text**[1] **:** *Agaḷiya mahājanamirppattiṁbarum* ***bhūmi****yoḷāda anyāyamaṁ kāvudu . . . .* ; **tr.** the *mahājana* (a brāhmin administrative body) of Agaḷi shall protect this **land** from injustice ; *S.I.I.* IX, pt. i, No. 33, p. 19, ll. 39–43 ; Agaḷi, Madakasira Tq., Anantapur Dt., A.P. St. **Dy.** Noḷ. Pal., Noḷaṁbādhirāja, in characters of 10th cent. A.D. ; **text**[2] **:** . . . *Ṭhāvaseṭṭiya keṟe ēṟiya Kēśavēśvara dēvara* ***bhūmi****yiṁ baḍagalu . . . .* ; **tr.** to the north of the **land** belonging to the god Kēśavēśvara located on the tank bund of Ṭhāvaseṭṭi ; *K.I.* V, No. 25, p. 96, l. 25 ; Kolhāpur, Kolhapur Tq. and Dt., Maha. St., **Dy.** Chāḷ. of Kal., Jagadēkamalla II, Cy. yr. Siddhārthi = 1139 A.D.

bhūmidāna (K. < Skt. *n.*), gift of land ; **text**[1] **:** (damaged) *annaṁ . . . gōdāna* ***bhūmidāna*** *. . . kanyādānaṁgaḷan atyōnnatadiṁ māḍisida* . . . ; **tr.** he made great acts of charity such as free food, **gift of lands**, cows, getting girls married, etc. ; *E.C.* (R) VI, Kr. 62, p. 44, ll. 31–32 ; Hubbanahaḷḷi, Krishnarajapet Tq., Mandya Dt., Karn. St. **Dy.** Hoy., Vishṇuvardhana, Ś. 1059 = 1140 A.D. ; **text**[2] (Skt. *n.*) **:** *pavitrē Hēmakūṭataṭē . . . . tatra kurvan mahādānaṁ Tulāpurushasaṁjñitaṁ* ***bhūmidāna*** . . . . . ; **tr.** he made a **gift of land** while performing the great ritual of *Tulāpurusha* (weighing oneself against valuables) *dāna* at the foot of Hēmakūṭa hill ; *E.C.* (R) III, Gu. 147, p. 105, ll. 36–38 ; Triyaṁbakapura, Gundlupet Tq., Mysore Dt., Karn. St. **Dy.** Saṅgama, Mallikārjua, Ś. 1369 = 1448 A.D.

bhūmi pramāṇam (T. < Skt. *n.*), deed of land ownership ; **text :** . . . . . *Rājarāja śambuvarāyarkku nāṅgaḷ bhūmipramāṇam paṇṇikuḍutta pariśu* . . ; **tr.** the **deed of land ownership** given by us to Rājarājaśambuvarāyar ; *S.I.I.* XVII, No. 244, p. 95, l. 7 ; Mēlśēvūr, Ginjee Tq., S. Arcot Dt., T. Nadu St. **Dy.** Chōḷa, Rājādhirāja II, reg. yr. 13 = 1175 A.D.

bhūparivartana (K.), conversion of land ; **text :** . . . . . *Viṭhaladēvara śrībhaṁḍārake . . . . koṭa* ***bhūparivartanada*** . . . *śilāśāsana* . . . . ; **tr.** stone inscription recording the **conversion of land** granted to the temple treasury of the god Viṭhala; *S.I.I.* IX, pt. ii, No. 668, p. 661, l. 1 ; Hampi, Hospet Tq., Bellary Dt., Karn. St. **Dy.** Tuḷuva, Sadāśiva, Ś. 1480 = 1559 A.D.

bhūruha (K. *n.*), tree ; **text :** . . . . . *tamāla* . . . *vakuḷa . . .* ***bhūruhā****vaḷigaḷan īkshiparge ati manōharavalte bahiḥpuram* . . . . . ; **tr.** the outskirts were pleasing to those who look at it with its rows of **trees** such as *tamāḷa, vakuḷa,* etc. ; *S.I.I.* IX, pt. i, No. 297, p. 323, l. 16 ; Kurugōḍu, Bellary Tq. and Dt., Karn. St. **Dy.** Kal. of Kal., Śankhavarma, Ś. 1099 = 1177 A.D.

biḍāra (K. *n.*), house tax ; **text :** *mahājanaṁgaḷige koṭṭa Śrōtriya-agrahāra dānaśilāśāsanada kramaveṁteṁdare* . . . ***biḍāra****. aṁgajāvige* . . . *adhikāriya uḍugoṟe sēnabōyike* . . . *muṁtāgi ēnuḷa sarvvasvāmyavanu nīvu . . . āgumāḍikoṁḍu bhōgisibahudu* . . . ; **tr.** as per the grant of the brāhamaṇa settlement Śrōtriya-agrahāra given to the *mahājana* (an administrative body), they were to enjoy all revenue incomes such as **house tax** and those imposed on bodyguards doing duty by turns, gifts given to the officials and tax on the office of the village head, etc. ; *S.I.I.* IX, pt. ii, No. 440, pp. 448–49, ll. 12–13, 26–30, Rājabāvanahaḷḷi, Harapanahalli Tq., Bellary Dt., Karn. St. **Dy.** Saṅgama, Dēvarāya, Ś. 1341 = 1419 A.D.

biḍāra vāra (K. *n.*), land lease ; **text :** . . . . . ***biḍāru-vāra****vāgi irisi tegedu koṭadu Bārakūra parivartanege saluva doḍḍa varaha 55* . . . . . ; **tr.** 55 *doḍḍa varaha* (bigger denomination of a coin) convertible at Bārakūru was given for a land **lease** ; *S.I.I.* VII, No. 345, p. 200, ll. 29–30 ; Chauḷikēri, Udupi Tq. and Dt., Karn. St. **Dy.** Sāḷuva, Narasiṁha, Ś. 1424 = 1502 A.D.

biḍāruvāra patra (K. *n.*), land lease deed ; **text** : (incomplete). . . . *Tiṁmayyaseṭṭige Kandavarada grāmiṇi Aṁṇauḍupara koṭṭa* ***biḍāruvārada patra****.* . . . ; **tr.** land lease deed given by Aṁṇauḍupa, the village head of Kandavara to Tiṁmayyaseṭṭi ; *S.I.I.* IX, pt. ii, No. 665, p. 650, ll. 14–15 ; Basarūru, Kundapur Ta., Udupi Dt., Karn. St. **Dy.** Tuḷuva, Sadāśiva, Ś. 1476 = 1564 A.D.

bide kāru (K. *n.*), seeds sowing implement ; **text** : *Kaṁṇūru haravayyalu kaṭivaṭṭa meṁba . . .* ***bidekāru*** *mū 12* . . ; **tr.** in Kaṁṇūru, 12 *mū* (*mūḍe* a grain measure) of seeds is to be sown with the sowing implement in the filed Kaṭiveṭṭa ; *S.I.I.* VII, No. 177, p. 75, l. 11 ; Mangalore, Mangalore Tq. and Dt., Karn. St. **Dy.** Āḷupa, Pāṇḍya Baṅkidēva, Ś. 1225 = 1303 A.D.

bīdi (K. *n.*), street ; **text :** ***bīdi****ya bāgila gadeya gaḍiyiṁda mūḍana nela* ; **tr.** land to the east of the boundary of the wet land facing the front door ; *S.I.I.* IX, pt. ii, No. 457, p. 469, l. 52 ; Basarūr, Kundapur Tq., Udupi Dt., Karn. St. **Dy.** Saṅgama, Mallikārjuna, Ś. 1377 = 1455 A.D.

bīḍike (K. *n.*), residence ; **text** : . . . . *mahāmaṁḍalēśvaraṁ Vaṁkaṇa-chōḷa mahārājaru Haṁḍakallu Kannenāḍu Rēnāḍu . . . Naṁdyāleya* ***bīḍike****yalu rājyam geyyuttamire*. . . . . . . ; **tr.** when subordinate ruler Vaṁkaṇa mahārāja was ruling over Haṁḍakallu, Kannenāḍu, Rēnāḍu etc. from his residence at Nandyale ; *S.I.I.* IX, pt. i, No. 231, p. 236, ll. 6–9 ; Kolimiguṇḍla, Koilkuntla Tq., Kurnool Dt., A.P. St. **Dy.** Chāḷ. of Kal., Bhūlōkamalla, Ch. Vi. yr. 58 = 1134 A.D.

bidir (K. *n.*), bamboo ; **text :** (damaged). . . . *bidira tāḷa pushpada tōṭada bhūmi* . . . ; **tr.** the land of bamboo, palamaira and flower garden ; *E.C.* (R) IV, Yl. 8, p. 277, l. 2 ; Yaḷandūru, Yalandur Tq., Mysore Dt., Karn. St. **Misc.,** in characters of 17th cent. A.D.

bidirameḷe (K. *n.*), bamboo bush ; **text :** . . . . *teṁkalū Hebbaḷḷave Heb ballave yelle īsānya mūle bidarameḷe* . . . . ; **tr.** in the south the big stream is the boundary and in the north east the bamboo bush ; *E.C.* (R) III, Hg. 17, p. 442, l. 15 ; Haramaraḷi, Heggadadevanakote Tq., Mysore Dt., Karn. St. **Dy.** Woḍ. of Mys., Dēvarāja Voḍeya, Ś. 1591 = 1669 A.D.

bidira paḷavu (K. *n.*), old bamboo bush ; **text :** . . . . *Śivapurada polamēre* . . . *nairutyadalu bidira paḷalu* . . . . ; **tr.** boundary of the land at Śivapura is the old bamboo bush in the south west ; *S.I.I.* IX, pt. i, No. 121, p. 103, ll. 36, 45–46 ; Śivapura, Nandikotkur Tq., Kurnool Dt., A.P. St. **Dy.** Chāḷ. of Kal., Traiḷōkyamalla, Ś. 980 = 1057 A.D.

bīdi vīdi (K. *n.*), street after street (a tautology) ; **text :** . . . . . . *kērigēri janadiṁ sale tiṁtiṇi* ***bīdi vīdi*** . . . . *negaḷda Bāguḷi* . . . . ; **tr.** Bāguḷi was characterised by crowds of people in quarter after quarter and in street after stree ; *S.I.I.* IX, pt. i, No. 267, p. 284, l. 30 ; Bāgaḷi, Harapanahalli Tq., Bellary Dt., Karn. St. **Dy.** Chāḷ. of Kal., Jagadēkamalla II, Ś. 1082 = 1160 A.D.

bīḍu (K. *n.*), (royal) camp ; **text**[1] : . . . . . . *Āhavamalladēvar . . . nūrā-aivatt-**āne**yuman Roddada bīḍinoḷ-koṇḍu* . . . ; **tr.** Āhavamalladēva having captured 150 **elephant**s while **camp**ing at Rodda; *S.I.I.* IX, pt. i, No. 77, pp. 47–48, ll. 2, 4 ; Kōgaḷi, Hadagalli Tq. and Dt., Karn. St. **Dy.** Chāḷ. of Kal, Sōmēśvara I, Ś. 914 = 992 A.D. ; **text**[2] : . . . . *mahā pradhānaṁ bāhattara niyōgādhipati bīḍina rakshapāḷakaṁ . . . . taḷāri Chidapanāyaka . . . koṭa gade 10 koḷagada bede* . . . . ; **tr.** the chief minister, head of the 72 goverment departments and the protector of the royal camp donated land of the extent of being sown with 10 *koḷaga* (grain measure) of seeds ; *S.I.I.* IV, No. 798, p. 271, ll. 57–59 ; Tāḍapatri, Tadapatri Tq., Anantapur Dt., A.P. St. **Dy.** Tāḍapatri Chfs., Udayāditya, Ś. 1130 = 1208 A.D. ; **text**[3] : (damaged). . . . . *sahita Madhupaṁgigaḷa **bīḍiṁ**daṁ baḍagalu* . . . . . ; **tr.** to the west of the residence of Madhupaṁgi ; *S.I.I.* IX, pt. ii, No. 435, p. 444, l. 16 ; Kōṭēśvara, Kundapur Tq., Udupi Dt., Karn. St. **Dy.** Saṅgama, king's name lost, Ś. 1333 = 1411 A.D.

bīḍudāṇa (K. *n.*), residential headquarters ; **text** : . . . . *Maṁgaḷivēḍaṁ bīḍudāṇaṁ tanagene jesamaṁ tāḷdidam Krishṇarāja*. . . . ; **tr.** the famous Krishṇarāja had made Maṁgaḷivēḍa his own residential headquarters ; *S.I.I.* XX, No. 133, p. 170, ll. 15–16 ; Chaḍachaṇ, Indi Tq., Bijapur Dt., Karn. St., **Dy.** Kal. of Kal., Kannamarasa, Ś. 988 = 1067 A.D.

bīgamudre (K. *n.*), locking up the door and sealing by lack ; **text** : . . . . *Viṭhaladēvarada bhaṁḍārada Hire Timmayage . . . koṭa grāma Kaṁpile māgaṇēlu Sāyaṇāpuravanu . . . svāmi nānābharaṇa **bīga** mudrēnu kādukoṁḍu sukhadalyu yirōdu* . . . . . ; **tr.** Hire Timmaya of the temple treasury of Viṭhaladēva was granted the village of Sayaṇāpura in Kaṁpilamāgaṇe with the stipulation that he should guard the **door** of the shrine Svāmi Nānābharaṇa **locked up and sealed by lack** ; *S.I.I.* IV, No. 277, p. 72, ll. 5–6 ; Hampi, Hospet Tq., Bellary Dt., Karn. St. **Dy.** Tuḷuva, Kṛishṇadēvarāya, Ś. 1435 = 1513 A.D.

bīja (K. *n.*), seed ; **text** : . . . . *keṟeya keḷage gadde bīja khaṇḍuga 2* . . . . ; **tr.** *2 khaṇḍuga* (a grain measure) of **seed** to be sown on the wet land below the tank ; *S.I.I.* IX, pt. i, No. 232, p. 237, l. 24–25 ; Ubacherla, Gooty Tq., Anantapur Dt., A.P. St., **Dy.** Chāḷ. of Kal., Bhūlōkamalla, reg. yr. 10 = 1135 A.D.

bījavari (K. *n.*), extent of land in terms of the amount of seeds required for sowing ; **text** : . . . . . . *satakhaṁḍada gadde **bījavari** khaṁḍuga 1 koḷaga 5* . . . . ; **tr.** wet **land** called satakhaṁḍa **of the extent of being sown with** 1 *khaṁḍuga* and 5 koḷaga of **seeds** ; *S.I.I.* IV, No. 260, p. 57, l. 78 ; Hampi, Hospet Tq., Bellary Dt., Karn. St. **Dy.** Kuṟugōḍu Chfs., Mādeya nāyaka, Ś. 1121 = 1199 A.D. ; **text**[2] : . . . . *dēvālyada beṭṭina baḍagalu bittuva* ***bījavari*** *hāne nālvattaṟa lekkadalu nālvattu muḍe gadde* . . . . . ; **tr.** to the north of the reclaimed land of the temple forty mūḍe of, wet **land** each **sowable with** forty hāne (grain measure) of **seeds** ; *S.I.I.* IX, pt. ii, No. 470, p. 484, ll. 32–34 ; Kollūru, Kundapur Tq., Udupi Dt., Karn. St. **Dy.** Saṅgama, Virūpāksha, Ś. 1404 = 1482 A.D.

bījavonnu (K. *n.*), capital deposit of gold for earning interest ; **text** : . . . . *Dēvaṇṇanu uttarāyaṇa saṁkramaṇadalu adhikārōgaṇege hoṁge hāga voṁda vṛiddhiyaṁ bījavoṁnāgi mahājanaṁgaḷige naḍasuvaṁtāgi koṭṭa ga 2* . . . . . . ; **tr.** Dēvaṇṇa granted 2 *gadyāṇa* (gold coin) as ***capital deposit*** with the *mahājana* (brāhmaṇa administrative body) in order that from the interest thereon at the rate of one *hāga* (fraction of a oin) for a *hon* (a gold coin) they might provide for extra feeding on the day of Uttarāyaṇa saṁkramaṇa ; *E.C.* (R) IX, Bl. 15, p. 10, ll. 4–6 ; Bēlūr, Belur Tq., Hassan Dt., Karn. St., **Misc.**, Ś. 1163 = 1241 A.D.

bijayṁgey (K. *vb.*), military campaign ; **text** : (damaged) . . . . *Vijayādityadēvar* . . . . . *dakshiṇa diśāvarakke* ***bijayaṁgeyutta*** . . . ; **tr.** when the king Vijayāditya was proceeding on a **military campaign** to the south ; *S.I.I.* IX, pt. i, No. 127, p. 109, ll. 5, 8 ; Morigēri, Hadagalli Tq., Bellary Dt., Karn. St. **Dy.** Chāḷ. of Kal., Āhavamalla, Ś. 986 = 1064 A.D.

bīḷa gadde (K. *n.*), neglected cultivable wet land **text** : . . . . *mūḍalu paḍuvalu* ***bīḷa gade*** . . . . . ; **tr. neglected cultivable wet land** on the east and west ; *S.I.I.* IX, pt. ii, No. 609, p. 616, l. 13 ; Śankaranārāyaṇa, Kundapur Tq., Udupi Dt., Karn. St. **Dy.** Tuḷuva, Sadāśiva, Ś. 1466 = 1544 A.D.

bīḷavṛitti (K. *n.*), a fief granted by a king to his subordinate ; **text**[1] : . . . . *Noḷaṁba Pallava Permānaḍidēvar . . . Kadaṁbaṟige sāyiramumaṁ* ***bīḷa vṛitti****yināḷuttamire* . . . . ; **tr.** when Noḷaṁba Pallava Permānaḍidēvar was administering Kadaṁbarige 1000 as **a fief granted by a king to his subordinate** ; *S.I.I.* IX, pt. i, No. 109, p. 84, ll. 9–11 ; Talakallu, Haḍagalli Tq., Bellary Dt., Karn. St. **Dy.** Chāḷ. of Kal., Traiḷōkyamalla, Ś. 974 = 1052 A.D. ; **text**[2] : . . . . . . *Joyimayyarasar Sindavāḍi sāsiramam* ***bīḷānu vṛitti****yim* . . . . *sukhadin arasugeyye*. . . . ; **tr.** while Joyimayyarasa was administering happily Sindavāḍi 1000 as **a fief granted to his subordinate by the king** ; *S.I.I.* IX, pt. i, No. 143, p. 126, ll. 14–16 ; Chinnatumbuḷam, Adavani Tq., Kurnool Dt., A.P. St. **Dy.** Chāḷ. of Kal., Vikramāditya VI, Ch. Vi. yr 4 = 1079 A.D

bilkaḍe (K. *n.*), a kind of tax ; **text**[1] : . . . . *Mallahāṇiyuṁ Poleyama Gāvuṇḍanu niḷdu tamma naḍeva* ***biḷkaḍe*** *yeraḍaṟoḷameraḍu lakavaḍakeya suṁkamaṁ keṟeya kalukaṭṭiṅge biṭṭaru* . . . . ; **tr.**

Mallahāṇi and Poleyama Gāvuṇḍa assembled together and granted for the stone construction of the tank tax on 2 lakhs of betel nuts out of the **bilkaḍe tax** due to them ; *K.I.* II, No. 8, p. 23, ll. 29–32 ; Tiḷivaḷḷi, Hangal Tq., Dharwar Dt., Karn. St. **Dy.** Chāḷ. of Kal, Bhuvanaikamalla, Ś. 993 = 1072 A.D. ; **text**[2] : . . . . *Hānuṁgallaynūrara hejjuṅka* ***biḷkaḍe****ya suṁkigaru* . . . ; **tr.** officials in charge of collecting major taxes and **bilkaḍe tax** in Hanuṁga 500 ; *K.I.* V, No. 19, p. 67, ll. 18–19 ; Hangal, Hangal Tq., Dharwar Dt., Karn. St. **Dy.** Chāḷ. of Kal, Vikramāditya VI, Ch. Vi. yr. 45 = 1121 A.D.

bilkoḍe (K. *n.*), sales tax ; **text :** . . . . *Sādēśvara dēvargge nandādīvigegeraḍuṁ* ***bilkoḍe*** *herjjuṁkavintinitaṟa teṟeyaṁ . . . . parihāravāagi biṭṭa gāṇadokkaloṁdu* . . . ; **tr.** records the gift of an oil mill free from sales tax and major taxes for a perpetual lamp to god Sādēśvara ; *K.I.* VI, No. 20, p. 46, ll. 12–16 ; Chinnamuḷugunda, Hirekerur Tq., Dharwar Dt., Karn. St. **Dy.** Chāḷ. of Kal, Vikramāditya VI, Ch. Vi. yr. 47 = 1122 A.D.

bīḷkuṁṭe (K. *n.*), abandoned land/tank ; **text :** . . . . *Svāmidēvara . . . jātrege baṁda kappaḍigaḷa sattrakke Mallarasa biṭṭa keyi* ***bīḷkuṁṭe****ya dāriyim baḍaga* . . . . ; **tr.** land granted by Mallara lying to the north of the road leading to the abandoned tank for the choultry meant for the benefit of barely clothed devotees coming to the festival of the god Svāmidēva ; *S.I.I.* IX, pt. i, No. 252, p. 265, ll. 37–39 ; Kuḍatini, Bellary Tq. and Dt., Karn. St. **Dy.** Chāḷ. of Kal, Jagadēkamalla II, reg. yr. 10 = 1148 A.D.

billa bēṭe (K. *n.*), hunting with bows and arrows; **text :** . . . . ***billa bēṭeya*** *Chikeyanāyaka Aṁkeyakkanu samasta prajegavuḍugaḷu Amṛitēśvaradēvarige . . . nāku salage gadde koḍageya kaḷadu . . . biṭṭaru* . . . ; **tr.** Chikeyanāya who **hunts with bows and arrows**, Aṁkayakka and all the inhabitants and village headmen jointly donated four salage (a land measure) of wet land after excluding already donated land to the god Amritēśvara ; *E.C.* (R) VIII, Ag. 35, p. 136, ll. 13–15, 18–20 ; Doḍḍamagge, Arakalagud Tq., Hassan Dt., Karn. St. **Dy.** Koṅgāḷva, Rājēndra, Ś. 1135 = 1213 A.D.

bīḷu (K. *n.*), fallow land ; **text :** . . . . *Urvakoṁḍeya sīmege saluva Velupaḍigeya grāmada holanu . .* ***bīḷu*** *bidu iralāgi nāvu nimage koṭa sāguvaḷiya vivara* . . . ; **tr.** details of cultivation rights given to you for cultivating the **lands** at Velupaḍige which has been lying **fallow** ; *S.I.I.* IX, pt. ii, No. 633, p. 634, ll. 3–4 ; Velpumaḍugu, Gooty Tq., Anantapur Dt., A.P. St. **Dy.** Tuḷuva, Sadāśiva, Ś. 1470 = 1548 A.D.

bīḷu daṁḍa (K. *n.*), fine on land left uncultivated; **text :** . . . . *bīḷu daṁḍa . . . apūrvāya ēnu baṁdaḍaṁ . . . paṁchāḷa naḍasuva dharmakke saluvudu* . . .; **tr.** fine on land left uncultivated and taxes to be imposed in future are donated for the conduct of pious deed by the five classes of artisans ; *E.C.* IX (s), No. 92, p. 89, ll. 31–32, 34–35 ; Kānakānahaḷḷi, Kanakanahalli Tq., Bangalore Dt., Karn. St. **Dy.** Hoy., kings name lost, in characters of 14th century A.D.

biḷuvaḍike (K. *n.*), a kind of levy ; **text :** . . . . *Māreya sāvaṁtana taṁma Masaṇeya sāvaṁtanuṁ . . . mukhyavāgi . . . Beṁṇeūrasthaḷadalu . . . . neredu ā vūra . . . . Virūpākshadēvarigaṁ Haṁnirbbaru mahājanaṁgaḷigaṁ tamma biḷuvaḍide mukhyavāgi kabbilavaḍike āvudubaṁdaḍaṁ . . . . biṭṭa dharma* . . . ; **tr.** a number of persons including Māreta sāvaṁta and his younger brother Masaṇeya sāvaṁta assembled at Beṇṇevūru and granted the sales tax including the tax on fishermen and any other such income to the god Virūpākshadēva ; *S.I.I.* IX, pt. i, No. 351, p. 372, ll. 7–12 ; Beṇṇehaḷḷi, Harapanahalli Tq., Bellary Dt., Karn. St. **Dy.** Hoy., Narasiṁha III, Cy. yr. Chitrabhānu = 1282 A.D.

binnaha (K. *n.*), supplication ; **text :** . . . *ā mūru grāmada brāhmaṇariṁge . . . śatru baṁdare arasiṁge biṁnahaṁ māḍi . . . halarū pālisikoṁḍu baharu* . . . ; **tr.** if enemies come to attack the brāhamaṇa residents of the three villages, the *halaru* (administrative body) shall make a **supplication** to the king and protect them ; *S.I.I.* VII, No. 339, p. 192, ll. 14–15 ; Chauḷikēri, Udupi Tq. and Dt., Karn. St. **Dy.** Saṅgama, Bukkarāya, Ś. 1338 = 1416 A.D.

binnāṇi (K. < Skt. Vijñāni, *n.*), skilled person, also occurs as a male surname ; **text :** . . . . . *Gōviṁda **binnāṇi** grāma bhaṭṭara baraha* . . ; **tr.** the writing of the village brāhmaṇa Gōviṁda who was a skilled person ; *S.I.I.* IX, pt. ii, No. .430, p. 439, ll. 39–40 ; Vaḍērahōbḷi, Kundapur Tq., Udupi Dt., Karn. St. **Dy.** Saṅgama, Bukka II, Ś. 1328 = 1406 A.D.

binnapa (K. *n.*), supplication ; **text**[1] **:** . . . . *Kōgaḷi ainūṟvan Ādityavarmmarasa āḷuttamire suṁkadanyāya peṟchidaḍe . . . ainūṟvarum pōgi . . . . . Āhavamalladēvara śrīpādaṁgaḷge . . . **binnapa**ṁ geydaḍe . . . Kannaradēvana maryyādeyalāda suṁkada maryyādeyaṁ tappade naḍeyimeṁdu biṭṭan* ; **tr.** when there were unjustified excessive taxation, while Āditya-varmmarasa was administering Kōgaḷi 500, the body of 500 merchants made a supplication to the emperor Āhavamalla who ordered that the same taxation as was introduced by Kannaradēva shall continue ; *S.I.I.* IX, pt. i, No. 76, p. 47, ll. 7–9, 10–11, 13–15 ; Bāgaḷi, Harapanahalli Tq., Bellary Dt., Karn. St. **Dy.** Chāḷ. of Kal., Āhavamalla, Ś. 913 = 991 A.D. ; **text**[2] **:** . . . . *Vīranoḷaṁba Gaṭṭidēva . . . Kammāṟa cheṟuvina Chaṭṭagāvuṇḍa Piriyanāmagāvuṇḍa Māchigavuṇda. . . intī halavara **binnapa**diṁ . . . mūlasthāna dēvargge biṭṭa kariya nela mattaru 12.* . . . ; **tr.** on the supplication of Chaṭṭagāvuṇḍa, Piriyanāmagāvuṇḍa, Māchigāvuṇḍa and others of Kammār̤acher̤uvu Vīranoḷaṁba Gaṭṭidēva granted to the god Mūlasthānadēva 12 *mattar* (land measure) of black soil land ; *S.I.I.* IX, pt. i, No. 114, p. 88-89, ll. 8, 12-13, 17–18 ; Kammarachodu, Ālūr Tq., Bellary Dt., Karn. St. **Dy.** Chāḷ. of Kal., Sōmēśvara I, Ś. 976 = 1054 A.D.

binuder̤e (K. *n.*), a kind of tax ; **text :** (damaged and incomplete) . . . . *gadde beddalu tōṭa* . . . ***binudere*** . . . ; **tr.** tax on wet land, dry land, groves and the tax called **binuder̤e**, etc. ; *E.C.* (R) III, Nj. 305, p. 374, ll. 10–11. ; Chuṁchanahaḷḷi, Nanjanagud Tq., Mysore Dt., Karn. St. **Misc.**, Ś. 1419 = 1496 A.D.

binuga[1] (K. *n.*), artisan ; **text :** . . . . ***binuga****gaḷige ār̤ugeyagala ippattu kaiyuddadali manegaḷanu māḍisi* . . . ; **tr.** having built houses measuring 6 cubits wide by 20 cubits long for **artisans** ; *E.C.* (R) IV, Yl. 62, p. 306, ll. 27–28 ; Maddūru, Yalandur Tq., Mysore Dt., Karn. St. **Dy.** Hoy., Ballāḷa III, Ś. 1250 = 1328 A.D.

binuga[2] (K. *n.*), low profession ; **text :** . . . . *nāyiṁda bārika maḍiyavaru muṁtāda samasta* ***binuga****gaḷige jōḷada kaḍāyavanu hākalilla* . . . . ; **tr.** compulsory levy on Jawar was not imposed on all men of **low profession** such as barbers, watchmen, washermen, etc. ; *S.I.I.* IX, pt. ii, No. 554, p. 575, ll. 42–44 ; Kavutāḷṁ, Adavani Tq., Kurnool Dt., A.P. St. **Dy.** Tuḷuva, Achyutarāya, Ś. 1454 = 1533 A.D.

binugu (K. *n.*), a kind of tax ; **text**[1] **:** . . . . *Kumara Hariharāyaroḍeyaru Kanakagiriya Vijayanātha dēvarige . . . koṭṭa dharma śāsana . . Kolagaṇada bhāgeya Maleyūra grāma 1 ra . . . . gadde beddalu tōṭa . . . . dēvadāna* ***binugu*** . . . . *muṁtāgi . . . . . ēnuḷḷa sarvasvāmyavanu anubhavisikoṁba Maḷeyūra grāma 1ra Kāluvaḷḷi Huṇusūrapurada grāma 1 ubhayaṁ grāma 2* . . . ; **tr.** the details of the grant made by prince Harihararāyavoḍeya to the god Vijayanātha of Kanakagiri is as follows : the wet land, dry land, groves, the tax called ***binugu*** etc. including all incomes have to be enjoyed by the village Maleyūru and its hamlets Huṇusūrapura amounting to 2 villages on behalf of the god ; *E.C.* (R) IV, Ch. 372, pp. 246–47, ll. 8–9, 12–19 ; Maleyūru, Chamarajanagara Tq. and Dt., Karn. St. **Dy.** Saṅgama, Dēvarāya II, Ś. 1344 = 1422 A.D. ; **text**[2] **:** . . . . *gadde beddalu tōṭa* . . . . ***binugu*** . . . . *Gobūra Raṁgarājayyanavaru Terakaṇāṁbeya Varadarājadēvarige rathōtsavakke koṭṭa Arakalavāḍiya grāma* . . . ; **tr.** revenue incomes such as on wet land, dry lands, groves, a king of tax called ***biṇugu*** etc. from the village of Arakalavāḍi were granted for the car festival of the god Varadarāja of Terakaṇāṁbe by Raṁgarājayya of Gobūru ; *E.C.* (R) IV, Ch. 301, p. 195, ll. 9–10, 12–14 ; Arkalavāḍi, Chamarajanagara Tq. and Dt., Karn. St. **Dy.** Tiḷuva, Sadāśiva, Ś. 1477 = 1555 A.D.

binugudeṟe (K. *n.*), a kind of tax ; **text :** . . . *samasta gavudagaḷu Tammaḍināḍiṁge kuḷa* . . . . ***binugudeṟe*** . . . *Aṇilēśvara dēvarige koṭṭa śilāśāsana* . . . . ; **tr.** stone edict registering the grant of tax income such as tax on land and a tax called binugudeṟe Tammaḍināḍu given by all the village headmen to the god Aṇilēśvara ; *E.C.* (R) IV, Ch. 260, p. 160, ll. 18, 23–24 ; Haradanahaḷḷi, Chamarajanagara Tq. and Dt., Karn. St. **Dy.** Saṅgama, Bukka II, Ś. 1290 = 1368 A.D.

biṇugudere (K. *n.*), a kind of tax ; **text :** . . . (text damaged) *Kuṁtūra grāmada gade bejjalu tōṭa* . . . . *manevaṇa* . . . ***biṇugudere*** *kuṁbāradeṟe* . . . *ēnu uḷadanu āgumāḍikoṁḍu* . ; **tr.** whatever revenue incomes are available from the village of Kumtūru such as wet land, dry lands, groves, house tax, **a kind of tax biṇugudere**, etc. ; *S.I.I.* IX, pt. ii, No. 701, p. 689, ll. 8–12 ; Kuṁthūru, Kollegal Tq., Chamarajanagar Dt., Karn. St. **Dy.** Umm. Chf., Chikkarāya II, Ś. 1434 = 1512 A.D.

binugu praje (K. *n.*), men of low profession ; **text :** . . . . *Moḍehaḷḷiyalli* . . . . *kammāra teḷḷiga nāvida asaga noḷagāda* ***biṇugu praje***. . . ; **tr.** men of lower professions such as blacksmith, oil monger, barber, washemen of Moḍehaḷḷi ; *E.C.* (R) IV, Ko. 62, p. 440, ll. 14–17 ; Kāmagere, Kollegal Tq., Chamarajanagar Dt., Karn. St. **Dy.** Saṅgama, Bukka, Ś. 1276 = 1354 A.D.

biṇugu praje (K. *n.*), labourer ; **text :** . . . *nānājātiya* ***biṇugu praje****yanu āḷikoṁḍu nioṁma putra pautra pāraṁparyavāgi* . . . *Chikkarāya sāgaraveṁba grāmavanu anubhavisikoṁḍu bahiri eṁdu Chikkarāyaru* . . . *Nāgabhaṭṭarige agrahāravāgi koṭṭu* . . *neḍisikoṭṭa śilāśāsana* . . . ; **tr.** stone edict set up registering the grant of the agrahāra Chikkarāyasāgara as a permanent gift to Nāgābhaṭṭa for all privileges including the authority over the **labourers** of different castes ; *E.C.* (R) VII, Ml. 106, p. 409, ll. 28–32 ; Muṭṇahaḷḷi, Malavalli Tq., Mandya Dt., Karn. St. **Dy.** Tuḷuva, Narasiṁha, Ś. 1428 = 1506 A.D.

bīra (K. *n.*), soldier maintained by commercial guilds ; **text :** . . . . *gavaṟegaḷum gātrigaḷum vēḷakāṟarum* ***bīra****rum bīravaṇigarum*. . . . . ; **tr.** the *gavaṟe, gātriga, vēḷakāṟa, bīravaṇiga* and their **soldier maintained by commercial guilds** ; *S.I.I.* IX, pt. i, No. 118, p. 97, ll. 55 ; Hirehadagalli, Hadagalli Tq., Bellary Dt., Karn. St. **Dy.** Chāḷ. of Kal., Traiḷōkyamalla, Ś. 978 = 1057 A.D.

birāḍa (K. *n.*), a kind of tax ; **text**[1] **:** *Mahābala-bhaṭṭaru* . . . . *Mādaṁṇagaḷa magaḷu Virupāyigaḷige teṟuva akara asaṁtāya biṭṭi* ***birāḍa*** . . . . *koṭaru* . . . . . . ; **tr.** Mahābalabhaṭṭa gave to Virupāyi the daughter of Mādaṁṇa, the revenue **incomes** such as those collected from **a tax called** ***birāḍa*** etc. ; *K.I.* VI, No. 62, p. 169, ll. 18–20 ; Babbarawāḍa, Ankola Tq., Karwar Dt., Karn. St. **Dy.** Saṅgama, Harihara II, Ś. 1324 = 1401 A.D. ; **text**[2] **:** . . . . *ā Kūtanapurada* *ūramunde neḍesikoṭṭa śilāśāsana stānamāṁnya pūrva mariyādi yiddallade* ***birāḍa*** *kāṇike kadāya biṭṭi . . . . yilla . . . .* ; **tr.** a stone edict was set up in front of Kūtanapura according to which besides the sthānamānya and grants previously made, the tax ***birāḍa***, presents, forced labour, free labour, etc. were exempted ; *E.C.* (R) IV, Ch. 300, p. 194, ll. 20–23 ; Kūtanapura, Chamarajanagara Tq. and Dt., Karn. St. **Dy.** Umm. Chf., Chikkarāya Ś. 1432 = 1511 A.D. ; **text**[3] : . . . *Kelumane* ***birāḍa*** *chika ga. 11* . . ; **tr.** the ***birāḍa*** **tax** on Kelumane is 11 smaller gold coins ; *K.I.* V, No. 73, p. 275, l. 26 ; Siddāpur, Siddapur Tq., Karwar Dt., Karn. St. **Dy.** Bīligi Chfs., Ghaṁṭēṁdra II, Ś. 1573 = 1651 A.D.

bīragallu (K. *n.*), hero stone ; **text**[1] : . . . . . . *Doḍḍagauḍanamaga Māchagavuḍanu raṇadoḷage kāduvali hoydu dēvalōkaprāptanāda . . . . ī* ***bīragallu*** *. . . Tiruvaṁṇama gavuḍanu pratishṭeya māḍidanu . . . .* ; **tr.** Machegowḍa son of Doḍḍagavuḍa while fighting a battle fell and attained the world of the gods ; *E.C.* (R) VIII, Al. 4, p. 436, ll. 6–7. . . ; Marusu, Alur Tq., Hassan Dt., Karn. St. **Dy.** Hoy., Narasiṁha III, Ś. 1200 = 1277 A.D. ; **text**[2] : . . . *Turakaru Dōrasamudrakke yethi bandalli Duddana Naḍegōṭeya . . . . Baicheya nāyakanu . . . . ubhaya daḷa mechchi hoydāḍi biddalli ātana tamma Pāḍināyaka . . . . yettisida* ***bīragallu*** *. . . . . . .* ; **tr.** a hero stone set up by Pāḍināyaka younger brother of Baicheyanāyaka of Naḍegōṭe in Dudda, who fought a battle to the appreciation of both the sides when the Muslims had attacked Dōrasamudra and fell ; *E.C.* (R) VIII, Hn. 138, p. 359, ll. 4–9 ; Dudda, Hassan Tq. and Dt., Karn. St. **Dy.** Hoy., Ballāḷa III, Cy, yr. Saumya = 1310 A.D.

birāmaṇi (T. *n.*), a brāhmaṇa wife ; **text** : . . . *Peruṅkavuśiyaṉ Iravi . . . ivaṉ birāmaṇi Śivakāma Sundari* . . ; **tr.** Śivakāmasundari the brāhmaṇa wife of Peruṅkavisian Iravi ; *S.I.I.* VIII, No. 708, p. 359, l. 74 ; Chidambaram, Chidambaram Tq., S. Arcot Dt., T. Nadu St. **Dy.** Kāḍava, Kōopperuṅjiṅga, reg. yr. 3 = 1245 A.D.

bīravaṇa[1] (K. *n.*), tax on bundle of betel leaves ; **text** : . . . *Sōmēśvara dēvara naṁdādīvigege . . . .* ***bīravaṇa****mumaṁ biṭṭugoṭṭa yī dharmmamaṁ pratipāḷisidavaṁge mahāpuṇyavakku . . . . . .* ; **tr.** whoever protects the grant of the **tax** income **on bundles of betel leaves** for the lighting of a perpetual lamp for the god Sōmēśvara will earn great merit ; *K.I.* VI, No. 27, p. 60, ll. 17–18, 20–23 ; Chinna Muḷugunda, Hirekerur Tq., Dharwar Dt., Karn. St. **Dy.** Chāḷ. of Kal., Jagadēkamalla II, reg. yr. 4 = 1142 A.D.

bīravaṇa[2] (K. *n.*), toll on transport ; **text** : . . . *muṁmuri daṁḍam SeṭṭIguttaruṁ Buyyārastaḷdalli irdokkalalli ettu kōṇa kattegaḷa sārige* ***bīravaṇa****vaṁ dēvara chaitra pavitrakke biṭṭaru . . .* ; **tr.** Muṁmuri daṁḍa (a comm. gld) and Seṭṭiguttar (a comm. gld) granted the toll on transportation of bullocks, buffaloes, donkeys, etc. for the services of the god ; *S.I.I.* XX, No. 138, p. 176, ll. 23–25 ; Bhūyār, Indi Tq., Bijapur Dt., Karn. St. **Dy.** Kal. of Kal., Bijjaḷa, reg. yr. 7 = 1162 A.D.

bīravaṇiga (K. *n.*), trade guild dealing with betel leaves . . . ; **text :** . . . *muvattāru bīḍugaḷa seṭṭiyaruṁ seṭṭiguttaruṁ* . . . ***bīravaṇigaruṁ*** . . . . *intu samasta nānā dēśigaḷuṁ* . . ; **tr.** merchant guilds doing business in different lands and hailing from 36 trade centres including seṭṭis (comm. gld.), seṭṭIguttar (comm. gld.), **trade guild dealing with betel leaves**, etc ; *K.I.* V, No. 64, p. 41, l. 41–43 ; Gōlihaḷḷi, Khanapur Tq., Belgaum. Dt., Karn. St. **Dy.** Kād. of Goa, Śivachitta Vīra Permāḍidēva, reg. yr. 17 = 1163 A.D.

birudaṅka bhīma (K. *n.*), a hero who is comparable to Bhīma ; **text :** . . . *(damaged) birudaṅka-bhīma* . . . . ; **tr. a hero who is comparable to Bhīma** ; *S.I.I.* IX, pt. i, No. 163, p. 152, l. 15 ; Halagondi, Hadagalli Tq., Bellary Dt., Karn., **Dy.** Chāḷ. of Kal., Vikramāditya VI, Ch.Vi. Yr. 17 = 1093 A.D.

birudiṅa aṁkamāle (K. *n.*), a panegyric of epithets; **text :** . . . *birudina aṁka-māle* . . . . ; **tr.** a panegyric of epithets ; *S.I.I.* IX, pt. i, No. 276, p. 297, l. 32 ; Mannēra-masalavāḍa, Harapanahalli Tq., Bellary Dt., Karn. St. **Dy.** Kal. of Kal., Sōvidēva, reg. yr. 4 = 1183 A.D.

birudu (K. *n.*), a hereditary or conferred title ; **text :** . . . . *birudara javaṁ* ***biruda*** *manneya* . . . *Udayāditya Sindarasaru* . . . . ; **tr.** Udayāditya Sindarasa who was like the god of death for title holder and was himself bore the title of a subordinate ruler ; S.I.I. IX, pt. i, No. 100, p. 70, ll. 13–14, 16 ; Hāvinahāḷu Vīrapura, Bellary Tq. and Dt., Karn. St. Dy. Chāḷ. of Kal., Āhavamalla, Ś. 967 = 1045 A.D.

birudumāḍa (Te. *n.*), coin bearing a title ; **text :** . . . . *Bhāvanārāyaṇadēvaraku* . . . . *akahaṁḍavartti dīpamunakuṁ beṭṭina* ***birudumāḍa****lu paṁḍreṁḍu vīniṁjēkōni* . . . . *Permmāḍi aradiviyayuṁ* . . . *Nāgadēvaṇḍu aradiviyayunumgāniddaṟumgūḍi* . . . *nēyi vōyaṅgalavāru* . . . . . ; **tr.** for lighting a perpetual lamp for the god śrī Bhāvanārāyaṇadēva twelve coins bearing a title were granted. With this amount Permmāḍi and Nāgadēva each provided ghee for two half perpetual lamps ; *S.I.I.* VI, No. 151, p. 76, ll. 8–12 ; Bāpaṭla, Bapatla Tq., Guntur Dt, A.P. St. **Dy.** Chōḷa, Rājarāja, Ś. 1076 = 1154 A.D.

biṟumagatti (T. < *brahmahatya n.*), killing of a brahman, great sin ; **text :** . . . . *inda daṉmattukku agutam paṉṉiṉavaṉ* . . . . ***biṟumagatti*** *paṉṉiṉa dōshattilum pōgakkaḍavāṉ* . . . . ; **tr.** he who hinders the implementation of the act of charity would have, in effect, committed the sin of having killed brāhmaṇas ; *S.I.I.* VIII, No. 424, p. 223, ll. 26–29, 39–43 ; Tiruvādavūr, Melur Tq., Madurai Dt., T. Nadu St. **Dy.** Nāyakas of Madurai, Viśvanātha, Cy. yr. Rākshasa, date not verifiable.

bisa (K. *n.*), a kind of tax ; **text :** .... *Maddūra Mādarasayya .... ā haḻḻiyalu suṁka suvarnnādāya gadde beddalu .... magga manevaṇa ...* ***bisa*** *yēnuḷa sarvasvāmyavanu ... sukhadiṁ anubhavisuviri* ... ; **tr.** Maddūra Mādarasayya was given for his enjoyment all the tax incomes, gold income, wet lands, tax on looms, dry lands, house tax and a **tax** called **bisa** ; *E.C.* (R) IV, Yl. 169, pp. 371–72, ll. 8, 20–25 ; Malhārapāḷya, Yelandur Tq., Mysore Dt., Karn. St. **Dy.** Tuḷuva, Achyutarāya, Ś. 1452 = 1531 A.D.

bīsu (K. *vb.*), to grind into flour ; **text :** ... hiṭṭu kuṭṭōdu gōdhi **bīsu**va kūli hoṟegūli .. ; **tr.** wages for pounding to powder, **grinding** wheat **into flour** and for headload ; S.I.I. IX, pt. ii, No. 653, p. 648, l. 5 ; Hampi, Hospet Tq., Bellary Dt., Karn. St. **Dy.** Tuḷuva, Sadāśiva, Ś. 1476 = 1554 A.D.

bitanake (K. *prn.*), for sowing ; **text :** ... nālku sīmeyiṁdoḷage bitaṇake mu 4 gade ... ; **tr. for sowing** seeds on wet land of the extent of being sown with 4 *mu* (*muḍi*, a grain measure) within the four boundaries ; *S.I.I.* IX, pt. ii, No. 512, p. 526, l. 24 ; Basarūru, Kundapur Tq., Udupi Dt., Karn. St. **Dy.** Tuḷuva, Kṛishṇadēvarāya, Ś. 1442 = 1520 A.D.

bitta (K. *n.*), seeds for sowing ; **text :** ...... *Kōṭīśvaradēvarige arasu bhaṁḍāri taṁna vūra Mādavakallaṁbiya kayyalu tā koṁḍa ...... nāgaṁḍugadalu* ***bitta*** *bittuva gadde mū 8* ... ; **tr.** for donating to the Kōṭīśvaradēva, the royal treasurer bought from Mādhava Kallaṁbi residing in his village wet land of the extend of being sown with 8 *mu* (*mūḍe*, a grain measure) ; S.I.I. IX, pt. ii, No. 407, p. 414, ll. 21–25 ; Kōṭēśvara, Kundapur Tq., Udupi Dt., Karn. St. **Dy.** Saṅgama, Bukka, Ś. 1287 = 1364 A.D.

bittalaṇḍe (K. *n.*), land below the tank granted for its maintenance ; **text :** ... *Kallaḷūra keṟeya keḻaguḻḷa* ***bittalaṇḍe****yam keṟege ikkadandu .. pāpakke salvaṁ* ... ; **tr.** he who fails to earmark the land below the tank at Kallaḻūru for the maintenance of the tank would have committed a sin ; S.I.I. IX, pt. i, No. 34, p. 20, ll. 7–10, 12 ; Kallūru, Hindupur Tq., Anantapur Dt., A.P. St. **Dy.** Noḷ. Pal., Noḻaṁbādhirāja, in charactersof 10th cent. A.D.

bittalaṭṭe (K. *n.*), land below the tank granted for its maintenance ; **text :** ... *keṟeya keḻage* . ... *bittalaṭṭeyuṁ khaṇḍuga gaḻdeyuṁ keṟege salgu* ... ; **tr.** land for the maintenance of the tank and one khaṇḍuga (a grain mesure) of wet land are earmarked for the tank ; *S.I.I.* IX, pt. i, No. 27, p. 14, ll. 6–9 ; Hindūpur, Hindupur Tq., Anantapur Dt., A.P. St. **Dy.** Noḷ. Pal., Dilīparasa, in characters of 10th century A.D.

bittarisu (K. *vb.*), to extend ; **text :**. ... *pūgitaru saṁkuḷadōṁṭaṁ* ***bittarisal*** *mūnūṟu kammaṁ sale biṭṭaru* ... ; **tr.** three hundred *kamma* (a land measure) of land was donated in order **to extend**

the grove of groups of arecanut and other trees; *S.I.I.* IX, pt. i, No. 153, p. 136, l. 61 ; Aṁbali, Kudligi Tq., Bellary Dt., Karn. St. **Dy.** Chāḷ. of Kal., Vikramāditya VI, Ś. 1004 = 1083 A.D.

biṭṭi (K. *n.*), free labour ; **text**[1] **:** (fragmentary) . . . . . *Dēvaṇṇayyaṁ Beḷvola mūnūṟu nāḍāḷe* . . . . *nīruṇi suṁkaṁ* ***biṭṭi*** *modalāgi ellamaṁ biṭṭōm* . . ; **tr.** when Dēvaṇṇayya was administering the division Beḷvola-300, the tax on water for irrigation and free labour were donated ; S.I.I. XI, No. 15, p. 11, ll. 4–5 ; Chiñchli, Gadag Tq. and Dt., Karn. St. **Dy.** Rāshṭr., Amōghavarsha I, Ś. 793 = 871 A.D. ; **text**[2] **:** . . . *Tippaṇṇavoḍeyaru SeṭṭIganapālayada Janārdanadēvarige* . . . *Chaṁḍanahaḷḷiya grāma 1* . . . . *Haradanūrapurada grāma aṁtū ubhayaṁ grāma* . . . . *ā 2 haḷi dēvadānavāgi* . . . . . ***biṭṭi koṭṭaṇa muṁtāgi sarva bādāparihāra*** . . . ; **tr.** taxes on free labour and mortar for pounding paddy were donated without let or hindrance from the two villages of Chaṁḍanahaḷḷi and Haradanūrapura to the god Janārdana of Seṭṭiganapāḷaya by Tippaṇṇavoḍeya ; *E.C.* (R) VIII, Al. 41, p. 458, ll. 31–33, 48. ; Pāḷya, Alur Tq., Hassan Dt., Karn. St. **Dy.** Saṅgama, Bukka I, Ś. 1283 = 1360 A.D. ; **text**[3] **:** (fragmentary) . . . . *suṁkavilla kāṇike bēḍige* ***biṭṭi*** *besa āvudu yilla* . . . . ; **tr.** no taxation and no other revenue incomes such as tribute, requisition tax, tax on free labour, tax called besa are also exempt ; *E.C.* III, Nj. 292, p. 365, ll. 23–24 ; Dāsanūru, Nanjanagud Tq., Mysore Dt., Karn. St. **Dy.** Tuḷuva, Kṛishṇadēvarāya, Ś. 1449 = 1527 A.D. ; **text**[4] **:** . . . *Arekuṭhārada Vīrabhadradēvarige* . . . *Haṁgaṟeyapurada grāmavanu koṭṭevāgi* . . . prāku saluva . . . . gadde beddalu tōṭa . . ***biṭṭi*** . . . . *muṁtāda* . . . *svāmyavellā* . . . . salluvudu ; **tr.** we having donated the village of Hangaṟapura to the god Vīrabhadra of Arekoṭhāra, all the revenue incomes already collected such as on wet lands, dry lands, groves, free labour, etc., will continue to be enjoyed ; *E.C.* (R) IV, Ch. 1, p. 4, ll. 11, 14 ; Chāmarājanagara, Chamarajanagar Tq. and Dt., Karn. St. **Dy.** Āravīḍu, Veṁkaṭapati, Ś. 1527 = 1605 A.D.

biṭṭi biḍāra (K. *n.*), free accommodation ; **text :** . . . . *Koṅganāḍoḷagaṇa Hebbāleyanu* . . . *nāḍadhikārigaḷu muṁtāgi āru biṭṭi* ***biḍāra****veṁnu hokkaḍe husidaṁ keḍahuüdu*. . . . ; **tr.** the officer of the nāḍu and any other officer while visiting the village Hebbale in Koṅganāḍu will be at fault if he seeks free accommodation ; *E.C.* (R) VIII, Ag. 15, p. 111, ll. 7–12 ; Hebbāle, Arakalagudu Tq., Hassan Dt., Karn. St. **Dy.** Hoy., Narasiṁha I, Cy. yr. Bahudhānya = 1159 A.D.

biṭṭi birāḍa (K. *n.*), free labour (tautology) ; **text :** . . . *grāmagaḷalū idaṁta nāyiṁdarige terige horige* ***biṭṭi-birāḍa*** *āvudu illa* . . . ; **tr.** for the barbers living in the villages taxes, taxes on loads and taxes on **free labour** and all such other taxes are not to be levied ; *S.I.I.* IX, pt. ii, No. 625,

p. 629, ll. 11-13 ; Gadekallu, Gooty Tq., Anantapur Dt., A.P. St. Dy. Tuḷuva, Sadāśiva, Cy. yr. Plavaṁga = 1547 A.D.

biṭṭiya bhaṇḍi (K. *n.*), free cart service ; **text :** . . . . . . *Mahālakshmīdēvi, Mahākāḷidēvi Bhūtanāthadēvara Gaddumbaḷḷi Niḍiviḍiya siddhāya* . . . ***biṭṭiya-bhaṇḍi*** . . . . *koṭṭigedere* . . . . . *ivoḷagāgi muṁde huṭṭuva apūrvaya vellavum* . . . *māṇisi* . . . . *biṭṭu* . . . . *koṭṭa śāsanaṁ* . . . ; **tr.** stone edict registering the grant of all revenue incomes from compulsory tax, **free cart services**, tax on cowshed as well as taxes which may be levied in future were made to the goddesses Mahālakshmī, Mahākāḷī and god Bhutanāthadēva of Gadduṁbaḷḷi; *E.C.* (R) VIII, Hn. 41, p. 267, ll. 8–15 ; Doḍḍagaddavaḷḷi, Hassan Tq. and Dt., Karn. St. **Dy.** Hoy., Ballāḷa II, Cy. yr. Raudri = 1200 A.D.

bittu (K. *vb.*), sowing of seeds ; **text**[1] : . . . *Sājirāṇanu Pannirppaḷḷiyolu* . . . . *nālgaṁḍugada padinālku mūḍe* ***bittuva*** *mekke bhūmiya* artthamaṁ goṭṭanitaṁkoṁḍu . . . . . ; **tr.** Sājirāṇa having purchased the entire low yielding high land of the extent of being **sown** with 14 *mūḍe* (a grain measure) **of seeds** measured by *nālgaṁḍuga* (four units of the land measure *khaṁḍuga*) at Pannirppaḷḷi *S.I.I.* VII, No. 367, p. 231, ll. 12–14 ; Kōṭakēri, Udupi Tq. and Dt., Karn. St. **Dy.** Āḷupas, Kavi Āḷupēndra, Ś. 1077 = 1155 A.D. ; **text**[2] : (damaged) . . . *gaḍiyoḷage* ***bittuva*** *gade muḍe 1 idakke*. . . . . . ; **tr.** wet land of the extent of being **sown** with 1 *muḍe* (a grain measure) **of seeds** within the boundary ; *S.I.I.* VII, No. 375, p. 230, l. 16 ; Maṇigārakēri, Udupi Tq. and Dt., Karn. St. **Dy.** Āravīḍu, Śrīraṁgarāya, Ś. 1502 = 1580 A.D.

bittu bāḷu (K. *n.*), cultivable land as means of livelihood ; **text :** . . . *mane ṭāü saha bittu bāḷu mu 3 gadde* . . . . ; **tr.** house site and **cultivable** wet **land** of the extent of being sown with 3 *mu* (*muḍi,* a grain measure) of seeds **as means of livelihood** ; *S.I.I.* VII, No. 343, p. 196, l. 14 ; Chauḷikēri, Udupi Tq. and Dt., Karn. St. **Dy.** Tuḷuva, Krishṇadēvarāya, Ś. 1447 = 1525 A.D.

bittuva gēṇikāra (K. *n.*), lease holder who actualy cultivaes ; **text :** . . . . . . *bāḷanū tōṭavanū hiḍidu* ***bittuva gēṇikārarū*** *oppāne tuppavanū kāla kālake naḍasi baharu* . . . . . ; **tr.** the lease holder who actually cultivates the wet land given for his livelihood and also the grove will contribute from time to time one *hāne* (liquid measure) of ghee ; *S.I.I.* IX, pt. ii, No. 448, p. 458, ll. 23–24 ; Basarūru, Kundapur Tq., Udupi Dt., Karn. St. **Dy.** Saṅgama, Dēvarāya, Ś. 1363 = 1442 A.D.

bittu kaṭṭu (K. *n.*), wet land below the tank granted for its maintenance ; **text :** . . . *Saṁbayyaṁ BidiRūranāḷuttiṛdu keṛege* ***bittukaṭṭaṁ*** *biṭṭa* . . . ; **tr.** while Saṁbayya was administering Bidirūṛu, he granted **wet land below the tank for its maintenance** ; *E.C.* X, Mb. 126, p. 98, ll. 16–18 ; Yedarūṛu, Mulubagilu Tq., Kolar Dt., Karn. St. **Dy.** Noḷ. Pal., Iṛiva Noḷaṁba, Ś. 883 =

961 A.D.

bittu vaṭa (K. *n.*), wet land below the tank granted for its maintenance ; **text:**. . . . . *ūruṁ mahājanavu Varuṇaśiva bhaṭārarumiḻdu kerege* ***bittu vatava*** *koṭṭu* . . . ; **tr.** the village, the mahājana (administrative body) and Varuṇaśiva bhaṭāra being present, they granted wet land below the tank for its maintenance ; *S.I.I.* IX, pt. i, No. . . , p. 13, l. 39 ; Guṇimōrubāgal, Madakasira Tq. Anantapur Dt., A.P. St. **Dy.** Noḷ. Pal., Aṇṇayadēva, Ś. 858 = 936 A.D.

bittu vāṭa (K. *n.*), wet land below the tank granted for its maintenance ; **text :**. . . . . *Vāraṇāsiyuṁ kavilayanaḻida keṟeya* ***bittuvāṭa****muṁ kere koḍaduṇḍavanu* . . . ; **tr.** he who fails to grant the **wet land below the tank for its maintenance** and instead enjoys the fruits of cultivation himself, would have, in effect, the sin of killing tawny cows in Vāraṇāsi ; *E.C.* (R) V, T.N. 320, pp. 670–71, ll. 10-12 ; Basavanahaḻḷi, T. Narasipura Tq., Mysore Dt., Karn. St. **Dy.** W. Gaṅga, Satyavākya, in characters of 10th cent. A.D.

bittu vaṭṭa (K. *n.*), wet land under the tank for its maintenance ; **text :** *Kāreyavanāḷva Jayasēna bhaṭararuṁ pannirvarumiḻdu Nāgavarmmana kaṭṭIsida Dēvigeṟegaṁ piriyakereguṁ* ***bittuvaṭṭa****vaṁ koṭṭaru.* . . . ; **tr.** Jayasēnabhaṭara who administering Kāreya and the administrative body of twelve members having assembled **granted wet land below the tanks** Dēvigeṟe and piriyakeṟe **for their maintenance** were present ; *E.C.* (R) III, Nj. 282, p. 359, ll. 6–9 ; Kārya, Nanjanagud Tq., Mysore Dt., Karn. St. **Dy.** W. Gaṅga, Satyavākya, Ś. 890 = 968 A.D.

bīya (K. *n.*), tax in kind in the form of rice ; **text :** . . . *ī basadiya vṟittiyallavakkaṁ . . . . kāṇike sēse . . .* ***bīya*** *modalāga . . . sarvabādhāparihāravaṁ māḍidar* . . ; **tr.** for all the provisions of the Jaina temple they granted with the exemption of all let or hindrance incomes such as tributes, tax called sēse and **tax in kind in the form of rice** ; *E.C.* VIII, Ngr. 36, p. 365, ll. 154–55, 159 ; Kōḍūru, Nagara Tq., Shimoga Dt., Karn. St. **Dy.** Chāḷ. of Kal., Vikramāditya VI, Ś. 999 = 1077 A.D.

biyyaṁ (Te. *n.*), rice ; **text :** (incomplete) . . . *dadhyōdana paḷyālu . . . .* ***bīyaṁ*** *yenimidi muṁttalu perugu nālugu muṁttalu* . . . ; **tr.** curd rice, vegetable preparation, eight *muṁtta* (a grain measure) of **rice** four *muṁtta* (liquid measure) of ghee, etc. ; *S.I.I.* XVI, No. 40, p. 44, ll. 42–44 ; Nandalūru, Rajamept Tq., Cuddapah Dt., A.P. St. **Dy.** Tuḷuva, Narasiṁha II, Ś. 1423 = 1501 A.D.

bōgāṟa (K. *n.*), bronze smith ; **text**[1] **:** . . . *Kōgaḷiya . . . . Pārśvadēvarige* ***bōgaṟa*** *Chauvuḍayyana heṁḍati Māyidēvi akshayabhaṁḍāravāgi koṭṭa ga 1* ; **tr.** 1 *ga* (*gadyāṇa,* a gold coin) given a permanent endowment by Mayidēvi wife of Chauvuḍayya the **bronze smith** ; *S.I.I.* IX, pt. i, No. 347, p. 370,

l. 31 ; Kōgaḷi, Hadagalli Tq., Bellary Dt., Karn. St. **Dy.** Hoy., Rāmanātha, Cy. yr. Dhātu= 1276 A.D. ; **text**[2] : . . . ***bōgār̤a*** *Baṁma seṭṭi* . . . . ; **tr.** Baṁmaseṭṭi the ***bronze smith*** ; *E.C.* (R) IV, Ko. 56, p. 434, l. 36 ; Siṁganallūru, Kolllegal Tq., Chamarajanagar Dt., Karn. St. **Dy.** Saṅgama, Harihara, Ś. 1330 = 1408 A.D. ; **text**[3] : . . . . ***bōgar̤ana*** *bāḷa paḍuvalu muḍi 1* . . ; **tr.** 1 *muḍi* (land measure) to the west of the land enjoyed for his livelihood by the **bronze smith** ; *S.I.I.* VII, No. 345, p. 200, ll. 24–25 ; Chauḷikēri, Udupi Tq. and Dt., Karn. St. **Dy.** Tuḷuva, Narasiṁma II, Ś. 1424 = 1502 A.D.

bōgār̤ader̤e (K. *n.*), tax on bronze smiths ; **text** : . . . . . *beṭṭada kāvalu* ***bōgar̤ader̤e*** *gaṇākārader̤e* . . . . ; **tr.** tax for grazing on the hill, **tax on bronze smiths**, professional tax, etc. ; *E.C.* (R) III, Gu. 134, p. 97, ll. 15–16 ; Triyaṁbakapura, Gundlupet Tq., Mysore Dt., Karn. St. **Dy.** Tuḷuva, Kṛishṇadēvarāya, Ś. 1444 = 1521 A.D.

bōgār̤ader̤ige (K. *n.*), tax on bronze smiths ; **text** : . . . *beṭṭada kāvalu* ***bōgar̤ader̤ige*** *gaṇā-chāriderige* . . . . ; **tr.** tax for grazing on the hill, **tax on bronze smiths**, professional tax, etc. ; *E.C.* (R) III, Gu. 136, p. 100, ll. 17 ; Triyaṁbakapura, Gundlupet Tq., Mysore Dt., Karn. St. **Dy.** Tuḷuva, Kṛishṇadēvarāya, Ś. 1435 = 1513 A.D.

bōgār̤ike (K. *n.*), tax on bronze smiths ; **text** : . . . . *gadde beddalu tōṭa* . . . . *kammārader̤e kuṁbārader̤e* ***bōgār̤ike*** . . . ; **tr.** tax on wet lands, dry lands, groves, . . tax on black smiths, tax on potters, **tax on bronze smiths**, etc. ; *E.C.* (R) III, Gu. 39, p. 32, ll. 5–6 ; Rāghavāpura, Gundlupet Tq., Mysore Dt., Karn. St. **Dy.** Chikkarāya, Umm. Chfs., Ś. 1429 = 1507 A.D.

bōgiyār (T. < Skt. *bhōga, n.*), mistress ; **text** : . . . . . *Mahādēvarkku Chōḷapperumānaḍigaḷ* ***bōgiyār*** *Naṅgai Śāttaperumān̤ār noṇḍāviḷakkin̤ukku kuḍutta pon̤ muppadin kaḷañju* . . ; **tr.** 30 *kaḷañju* (gold coin) of gold given for a perpetual lamp by Naṅga Śāttaperumān̤ār, the **mistress** of Chōḷaperumānaḍigaḷ to the god Mahādēva ; *S.I.I.* XIII, No. 247, p. 131, ll. 1–3 ; Tillaistānam, Thanjavur Tq. and Dt., T. Nadu St. **Dy.** Chōḷa, Āditya I, reg. yr. 14 = 885 A.D.

bōharisu (K. *vb.*), clean ; **text**[1] : . . . *rājāṁgaḷa* ***bōharisu****va dāsige iṁmāna akkiya prasāda paḍi saluvudu* . . . ; **tr.** the maid servant who **cleans** the main courtyard would get two *māna* (grain measure) of offered food ; *E.C.* (R) XII, Kd. 126, p. 137, l. 64–65 ; Bāṇūru agrahāra, Kadur Tq., Chickmagalur. Dt., Karn. St. **Dy.** Hoy., Ballāḷa III, Ś. 1213 = 1291 A.D. ; **text**[2] : . . . *maṭhava* ***bōharisu****va basavittiya jana oṁdakkaṁ varisa oṁdakkaṁ akki mūḍe eraḍu hāne hattu* . . . . . . ; **tr.** two *mūḍe* (a grain measure) and ten *hāne* (a grain measure) of rice per year for one temple mistress who is to **clean** the monastery ; *S.I.I.* IX, pt. ii, No. 417, p. 423, ll. 38–39 ; Kōṭēśvara, Kundapur Tq., Udupi Dt., Karn. St. **Dy.** Saṅgama, Harihara, Ś. 1300 = 1377 A.D.

bokkasa (K. *n.*), treasury (of a temple) ; **text[1] :** . . . . *.guḍiya nervāhadivaru stānikaru . . . pālu 5, dēvara* ***bokkasa****ke palu 1 . . .* ; **tr.** the administrative officials of the temple get 5 shares and 1 share goes to the temple **treasury** ; *S.I.I.* IX, pt. ii, No. 607, p. 615, ll. 8–9 ; Hampi, Hospet Tq., Bellary Dt., Karn. St. **Dy.** Tuḷuva, Sadāśiva, Ś. 1465 = 1543 A.D. ; **text[2] :** . . *Nālku sāvirada yiṁnūra aravattēḷu varahavu aidu haṇavaṁnu vartaka Koḷāgālada Vīraseṭṭi mukāṁtara* ***bokkasa****kke . . . vopistiyāda kāraṇa ī gadde huṭuvaḷiyaṁnnu ninage krayabhūdānavāgi koḍisi iruvadu . . .* ; **tr.** you having paid to the **treasury** through Vīraseṭṭi, the trader of Koḷāgāla, a sum of four thousand two hundred fifty seven *varaha* (coin) and five *haṇa* (coin), you have been given the wet land through a sale deed to enjoy the produce therefrom ; *E.C.* (R) IV, Yl. 145, p. 354, ll. 16–20 ; Agara, Yalandur Tq., Mysore Dt., Karn. St. **Dy.** Woḍ. of Mys., Kṛishṇarājavoḍeya, Ś. 1694 = 1763 A.D.

bōva (K. *n.*), community of palanquin bearers ; **text :** . . . ***bōva*** *maryādeya baḷiya hoṁnu . . . . .* ; **tr.** customary payment in gold to be made to the **community of palanquin bearers** ; *E.C.* (R) VIII, Hn. 160, p. 392, ll. 27–28 ; Śāntigrama, Hassan Tq. and Dt., Karn. St. **Dy.** Hoy., Vīra Ballāḷa II, Ś. 1138 = 1215 A.D.

bōva (K. *prn.*), suffix to the proper names of the community of palanquin bearers ; **text :** . . . *arasumaneyalli Sūra****bōva****na maga Mayada****bōva*** *Saudare Bīra****bōva*** *Heggaḍe maneya. Naṁna****bōva****na maga Aya****bōva****. . . . . .* ; **tr.** Mayada**bōva**, the son of Sūra**bōva** and Saudare Bīra**bōva** of the palace, Aya**bōva** the son of Nanna**bōva** of the house of the village headman ; *S.I.I.* IX, pt. i, No. 350, p. 372, ll. 4–5 ; Beṇṇehaḷḷi, Harapanahalli Tq., Bellary Dt., Karn. St. **Dy.** Hoy., Narasiṁha III, Cy. yr. Chitrabhānu = 1282 A.D.

brāhmaru, brahmaru (K. *n.*), brāhmaṇas ; **text[1] :** . . . . . . *yī dharmakke aḷupidavaru Vāraṇāsiyalu gōvanū.* ***brāhma****ranu vadhisida doshadalu hōharu . . .* ; **tr.** whoever flouts the provisions of this grant would have, in effect, committed the sin of killing cows and **brāhmaṇas** in Vāraṇāsi ; *S.I.I.* VII, No. 351, p. 210, ll. 46–47 ; Chauḷikēri, Udupi Tq. and Dt., Karn. St. **Dy.** Saṅgama, Harihara, Ś. 1308 = 1386 A.D. ; **text[2] :** . . . *Rājādiya* ***brahmaru*** *Aṁṇaheggaḍeya oppa . . . . .*; **tr.** the signature of approval of the **brāhmaṇa** Aṁṇaheggaḍe of Rājādi ; *S.I.I.* VII, No. 336, p. 190, l. 19 ; Chauḷikēri, Udupi Tq. and Dt., Karn. St. **Dy.** Saṅgama, Dēvarāya, Ś. 1380 = 1458 A.D.; **text[3] :** . . . *Ayyappanavaru taṁma tāyi mājiyara kayyalu Chōḷiyakēriya Kallaṁgereya taṁma tōṭada maṭhada chhatradalli uṁba* ***brahmaru*** *12 aḍuvavanobba aṁtū 13 kaṁ māḍida dharmada bāḷina vivara. . . .*; **tr.** details of the charitable grant of land for sustenance made by Ayyappa through his mother Maji for feeding 12 **brāhmaṇas** and one cook, totalling 13 persons at the choultry in the *maṭha* (religious institution) located in his grove in Kallaṁgere of Chōḷiyakēri ; *S.I.I.* VII, No. 387, p. 243, ll. 7–9 ; Kōṭakēri, Udupi Tq. and Dt., Karn. St. **Dy.** Saṅgama, Bukkarāya, Ś. 1294 = 1372 A.D.

brahmachāri (Skt. *n.*), celibate ; **text :** .... *Sōhilaḥ* ***brahmachāriṇaḥ*** *Ādibhaṭṭāraka pratimēyaṁ* ... ; **tr.** the image of Ādibhaṭṭāraka was made by **celibate** Sōhila ; *K.I.* V, No. 87, p. 286, ll. 1–3 ; Ellōra, Aurangabad Tq. and Dt., Mahā. St. **Misc.**, in characters of 9th cent. A.D.

brahmadāya, brahmādāya (K. < Skt. *n.*), village gifted to the brāhmaṇas ; **text[1] :** (damaged) ... *hattukēriya halaru* .... *Kārakaḷada Kadurabelaṁbeṭṭina taṁma* ***brahmādāya***.... ; **tr. village gifted to** the **brāhmaṇas** in Kadurabelaṁbeṭṭu of Kārakaḷa the *halaru* (administrative body of brāhmaṇas) of hattukēri (ten quarters) ; *S.I.I.* VII, No. 314, p. 165, ll. 5–7 ; Bārakūru, Udupi Tq. and Dt., Karn. St. **Dy.** Āḷupa, Dattāḷupa, in characters of 9th cent. A.D.; **text[2] :** .... *dina 1 kaṁ obba brāhmaṇa uṁba hāge māḍida dharma Taṁtrāḍi voḷage baddha* ***brahmadāya*** *mūlada bāḷu* ... *gadde 2* ; **tr.** 2 wet fields orignally attached to the **village gifted to the brāhmaṇas** in Taṁtrāḍi was gifted for feeding 1 brāhmaṇa per day ; *S.I.I.* VII, No. 319, p. 169, ll. 12–14 ; Mūḍakēri, Udupi Tq. and Dt., Karn. St. **Dy.** Saṅgama, Bukka, Ś. 1293 = 1371 A.D. ; **text[3] :** ... *dēvādāya* ***brahmādāya*** *sarvamānya* ... *pūrva mariyādeyeṁdu koṭṭa Koḷogālada sthaḷada śilāsāsana* ; **tr.** the **grants of village gifted to** god and **brāhmaṇa** that have come down by tradition are tax free. Thus has been issued the stone edict of the Koḷagāla-sthaḷa ; *E.C.* IV, Ko. 1, p. 397, ll. 14–16 ; Koḷḷegāla, Kollegala Tq., Chamarajanagar Dt., Karn. St. **Dy.** Tuḷuva, Sadāśiva, Ś. 1491 = 1569 A.D. ; **text[4] :** .... *Narasiṁhadēvarige saluva Sālagrāmada* ... *kāluve keḷagana dēvādāya* ***brahmādāya****da gadde* ; **tr. village given as gift to the** god and the **brāhmaṇas** below the canal in the village of Sālagrāma belonging to the god Narasiṁhadēva ; *E.C.* V, Kn. 53, p. 51, ll. 7–10 ; Sāligrāma, Krishnarajanagara Tq., Mysore Dt., Karn. St. **Misc.**, Ś. 1574 = 1652 A.D.

brahmadēya (K. < Skt. *n.*), village gifted to brāhamaṇas ; **text :** ... *Raṇavikramayyaṁ Ārida gōtram Parapadibhaṭṭarge Kuḷanelūra* ***brahmadēyaṁ*** *koṭṭaṁ* ; **tr.** Raṇavikramayya **gifted village to the brāhmaṇa** Parapadibhaṭṭa of Hārita gōtra at Kuḷanelūru ; *E.C.* V, Kn. 105, p. 102, ll. 68–69; Gaḷigēkere, Krishnarajanagara Tq., Mysore Dt., Karn. St. **Dy.** W. Gaṅga, Śiva- māra I, in characters of 9th cent. A.D.

brahmadēya iraiyili (Skt.+T. *n.*), tax free land gifted to brāhamaṇas ; **text :** (damaged) *Kampayanūṟ* ... *chatuppēdi bhaṭṭagaḷkku* ... ***brahmadēya iraiyil****yākkiyaruḷi* ... ; **tr.** having gifted to the brāhmaṇas learned in the four vēdas, the village of Kampayanūṟ as a **tax free land**

gifted to a brāhmaṇa settlement ; *E.C.* (R) IV, Yl. 98, p. 326, l. 29 ; Yaḷandūru, Kollegala Tq., Chamarajanagar Dt., Karn. St. **Dy.** Chōḷa, Kulōttuṅga I, reg. yr. 34 = 1104 A.D.

brahmadēya kiḻavargaḷ (Skt.+T. *n.*), elders of the village gifted to the brāhmaṇas ; **text :** . . . *Mahādēvarkku* . . . . *niśadam Uḻakkeṇṇaiyāl iravum pagalum oru nandāviḷakkerivadurkku* . . . . *aṭṭuvōmānōm Kōḍiyālattu ūrkiḻārmakkaḷum* ***brahmadēyakiḻavargaḷum*** *ūrōmum.* ; **tr.** the elders of the village, **elders of the village gifted to the brāhmaṇas** and the villagers jointly undertook to supply one *uḻakku* (liquid measure) of oil for burning a perpetual lamp day and night for the god Mahādēva ; *S.I.I.* XIII, No. 126, p. 65, ll. 1, 2–3, 4–5 ; Tiruchchatturai, Tanjavur Tq. and Dt., T. Nadu St. **Dy.** Chōḷa, Gaṇḍarāditya, reg. yr. 5 = 955 A.D.

brahmadēyam (T. < Skt. *n.*), village gifted to brāhamaṇas ; **text**[1] **:** . . . . *Rājarājavaḷanāṭṭu Nāñji nāṭṭu* ***brahmadēyam*** *Suchīndirattu emberumāṉ* ; **tr.** the god of Suchīndira in the **village granted to the brāhmaṇas** in Nāñjināḍu within Rājarājavaḷanāḍu; *T.A.S.* IV, pts. i and ii, No. 29, p. 129, ll. 6–8 ; Suchīndram, Agasteesvaram Tq., Kanyakumari Dt., T. Nadu St. **Dy.** Chōḷa., Rājarāja I, reg. yr. 14 = 999 A.D. ; **text**[2] **:** . . . . *Damanūrnāṭṭu* ***brahmadēyam*** *Kāyvāṉtaṇḍalamāgiya chaturvēdimaṅgalam* ; **tr.** Kāyvaṉtaṇḍalam, the chaturvēdimaṅgalam which is a **village gifted to brāhmaṇas** in Damanūrnāḍu ; *S.I.I.* III, pts. i and ii, No. 77, p. 173, l. 3 ; Kāvantaṇḍalam, Kanchipuram Tq., Chingleput Dt., T. Nadu St. **Dy.** Chōḷa, Rājēndra, reg. yr. 4 = 1016 A.D.

brahmahatti (T. < Skt. *n.*), killing of brāhmaṇas; **text :** . . . *idu mārumavaṉ Geṅgaikaraiyil kurāṟ paśu koṉṟrāṉ* ***brahmahatti*** *koḷvāṉ* . . . .; **tr.** he who goes against this grant, would have, in effect, killed tawny cows on the banks of the Ganges and would have incurred the sin of **having killed brāhmaṇas** ; *S.I.I.* VII, No. 9, p. 4, l. 4 ; Kambayanallūr, Uttangarai Tq., Salem Dt., T. Nadu St. **Dy.** Hoy., Viśvanātha, reg. yr. 2, in characters of 13th-14th century A.D.

brahma kshētra (K. < Skt. *n.*), land dedicated to brāhmaṇas ; **text :** (damaged). . . . . *nāvu nāḍāgi ī brāhmaṇarige* . . . . *koṭṭa dāna śilā śāsana ī* ***brahma kshētravu*** ; **tr.** this **land dedicated to brāhmaṇas** has been given by us to the brāhmaṇas when we had assembled as a *nāḍu* (assembly of the territory) ; *S.I.I.* IX, pt. ii, No. 421, p. 429, ll. 133–35, 137–39 ; Modalli, Kollegal Tq., Chamarajanagar Dt., Karn. St. **Dy.** Saṅgama, Harihara, Ś. 1313 = 1392 A.D.

brāhmaṇa chhatra (K. < Skt. *n.*), choultry for free lodging and feeding of brāhamaṇas ; **text :** . . . *Naṁjalugūḍa Naṁjuṁḍēśvaradēvara saṁnidhiyalli naḍavaṁthā chhatrada* . . . . *jaṁgama chhatrada* . . . . ***brāhmaṇa chhatradae*** *Liṁgappa* . . . . .; **tr.** Liṁgappa of the **choultry for free**

lodging and feeding of brāhmaṇas, the choultry for free lodging and feeding of Vīraśaiva ascetics and the choultries functioning in the august presence of the god Naṁjuṁḍēśvara of Naṁjalugūḍu ; *S.I.I.* IX, pt. ii, No. 545, p. 564, ll. 11–12, 14 ; Eraganahaḷḷi, Gopichettipalyam Tq., Coimbatore Dt., T. Nadu St. **Dy.** Tuḷuva, Achyutarāya, Ś. 1454 = 1532 A.D.

brāhmaṇa vṛitti (K. < Skt. *n.*), (house site) gifted to a brāhmaṇa ; **text :** .... *nivēsanamaṁ* ***brāhmaṇa vṛitti****yāgi* ... *māḍi*...; **tr.** having **gifted** the house-site **to a brāhmaṇa** ; *S.I.I.* VIII, No. 363, p. 194, ll. 9–10 ; Gooty, Gooty Tq., Anantapur Dt., A.P. St. **Dy.** Chāḷ. of Kal., Jagadēkamalla, reg. yr. 5, in characters of 12th century A.D.

brāhmaṇarāśakkāṇam (T. < Skt. *n.*), share of the brāhmaṇas and of the king ; **text :** ..... *ivvūr peṟṟa parichāram chekkum taṟiyum* .... ***brāhmaṇarāśakkāṇamum*** ..... *tāmē uṇṇappeṟuvārāguvam*....; **tr.** (the donees) shall enjoy the excemption obtaining in this village without paying for the oil mills and looms, the **share of the brāhmaṇas and of the king** ; *S.I.I.* II, pts. iii, iv and v, No. 73, p. 352, ll. 122–23, 131, 132 ; Kaśākkuḍi, Pondicherry Tq. and Dt., Pondicherry St. **Dy.** Pallava, Nandivarman II, reg. yr. 22 = 753 A.D.

brāhmaṇi (T. < Skt. *n.*), brāhmaṇa wife ; **text[1] :** .... *Kuṭṭūr Narāyaṇaṉ Daśapuriyaṉ* ***brāhmaṇi*** *pakkal vilaikoṇḍuḍaiya* ... *nilamarai mā*.....; **tr.** half *mā* (land measure) of land purchased from the **brāhmaṇa wife** of Nārāyaṇaṉ Daśapuriyan of Kuṭṭūr ; *S.I.I.* III, pts. iii and iv, No. 111, p. 246, l. 6 ; Tiruppālatturai, Tiruchirapalli Tq. and Dt., T. Nadu St. **Dy.** Chōḷa, Gaṇḍarāditya, reg. yr. 8 = 958 A.D. ; **text[2]** (K. < Skt. *n.*), **:** ...... *Rudrachaṭṭōpādyāyaru biṭṭa dharma matta avara* ***brāhmaṇi*** *Machiyabbēru* .... *Sōmayājigaḷa dēvālyakke* ... *biṭṭa gadyāṇa 250* ....; **tr.** Rudrachaṭṭōpādhyāya and his **brāhmaṇa wife** Māchiyabbe made a gift of 250 *gadyāṇa* (gold coin) to the temple of Sōmayāji ; *K.I.* V, No. 17, p. 61, ll. 11–13, 19 ; Tiḷivaḷḷi, Hangal Tq., Dharwar Dt., Karn. St. **Dy.** Chāḷ. of Kal., Vikramāditya VI, Ch. Vi. yr. 42 = 1118 A.D. ; **text[3] :** ..... *baḍagalu Bāchaṇabāsiriya* ***brāhmaṇi****ge barada bāḷiṁdaṁ mūḍalu*.... ; **tr.** in the north, to the east of the land registered in the name of the **brāhmaṇa wife** of Bāchaṇabāsiri ; *S.I.I.* VII, No. 346, p. 202, l. 37 ; Chauḷikēri, Udupi Tq. and Dt., Karn. St. **Dy.** Saṅgama, Virūpāksha, Ś. 1397 = 1475 A.D.

brahmapura (K. < Skt. *n.*), brāhmaṇa settlement; **text :** .... *idān dēvargallade peṟarkoḷvōr Śivaḷḷiya* ***Brahmapura****manaḷida mahāpātakanakku* ...; **tr.** whoever takes away this grant from the god and misappropriates would have committed, in effect, the sin of having destroyed the **brāhamaṇa settlement** of Śivaḷḷi ; *S.I.I.* VII, No. 284, p. 144, ll. 5–6; Udayāvara, Udupi Tq. and Dt., Karn. St.

Dy. Āḷupa, Raṇasāgara, in characters of 8th century A.D.

brahmapuri, brāhmapuri (K. < Skt. *n.*), village inhabited by the brāhmaṇas ; **text[1] :** . . . . ***brahmapuri**ya brāhmaṇarige mattaru 10*. . .; **tr.** 10 *mattar* (a land measure) of land granted to the brāhmaṇas of the **village inhabited by the brāhmaṇas** ; *S.I.I.* IX, pt. i, No. 240, p. 245, l. 13; Guruzala, Adavani Tq., Kurnool Dt., A.P. St. **Dy.** Chāḷ. of Kal., Jagadēkamalla, reg. yr. 5 = 1142 A.D. ; **text[2] :** . . . . *Maṁnneya Kupparasaru . . . Saṁgamēśvaradēvara **brāhmapuri**ya brāhmaṇaru eṁṭu manisyarige ita ma. 50*. . .; **tr.** 50 *ma* (*mattar*, land measure) of land was gifted to 8 persons who were residing in the **village inhabited by the brāhmaṇas** and belonging to the god Saṁgamēśvara by the chief Kupparasa ; *K.I.* II, No. 33, pp. 121–22, ll. 21, 25–27 ; Akkalkōṭ, Akkalkot Tq., Sholapur Dt., Mahā. St. **Dy.** Sēü. of Dēv, Siṁhaṇa, reg. yr. 11 = 1211 A.D.

brahmasthānam (T. < Skt. *n.*), a place where brāhmaṇas usually assembled and discussed village affairs ; **text[1] :** . . . *Veḷichchēri mahāsabhaiyōm emmūr **brahmasthāna**ttu kūṭṭam kuṟaivara kūḍi irund viṟkinṟa nilam* . . .; **tr.** the land being sold when the *mahāsabhā* (administrative body of brāhmaṇas) of Veḷichchēri had met in full quorum in our **place where we usually assemble and discuss village affairs** ; *S.I.I.* III, pts. iii and iv, No. 116, p. 252, ll. 2–4 ; Vēḷachchēri, Saidapet Tq., Chingleput Dt., T. Nadu St. **Dy.** Chōḷa, Sundarachōḷa, reg. yr. 7 = 964 A.D. ; **text[2] :** . . . *Māgaṇūrnāṭṭu . . . Rājachūḍāmaṇichaturvvēdimaṅgalattu mahāsabhaiyōm emmūr **brahmasthāna**ttē . . . kūṭṭa kkuṟaivaṟa kūḍi irundu. . . . Kāmakōṭi viṇṇagar Āḷvārkku iṟaiyiḻichchikkuḍutta nilam*. . . .; **tr.** land made tax free donated to the god Kāmakōṭi Viṇṇagar Āḷvār by the administrative body of brāhmaṇas who had met in full quorum in our **place where we usually assemble and discuss village affairs** in Rājachūḍāmaṇi chaturvvēdimaṅgalam in Māgaṇūrnāḍu ; *S.I.I.* III, pts. i and ii, No. 28, p. 55, ll. 7–8 ; Manimaṅgalam, Kanchipuram Tq., Chingleput Dt., T. Nadu St. **Dy.** Chōḷa, Rājādhirāja, reg. yr. 29 = 1047 A.D.

brahmasva (K. < Skt. *n.*), land holding of brāhmaṇas ; **text :** . . . . *Kēśava āhitāgñigaḷa kayyalu maṭhada mūḍalu koṁḍa bāḷu **brahmasva** nāgaṁḍugadalu mūḍe 1* . . . .; **tr.** the **land holding of the *brāhmaṇa*** Kēśava āhitāgñi situated to the east of the *maṭha* (religious institution) and measuring 1 *mūḍe* (grain measure) measured by four units of the grain measure called *khaṁḍuga*; *S.I.I.* VII, No. 387, p. 243, ll. 29–30 ; Kōṭakēri, Udupi Tq. and Dt., Karn. St. **Dy.** Saṅgama, Bukkarāya, Ś. 1294 = 1372 A.D.

budha jana (K. < Skt. *prn.*), learned men ; **text:** . . . *samasta bhuvanāśrayan samasta **budha-janā**śrayan Āhavamalla* . . . . . ; **tr.** Āhavamalla who was a refuge of the entire world and who was a refuge of **learned men** ; *S.I.I.* IX, pt. i, No. 127, p. 109, l. 1 ; Morigēri, Hadagalli Tq., Bellary Dt., Karn. St. **Dy.** Chāḷ. of Kal., Āhavamalla, Ś. 986 = 1064 A.D. ; **text**[2] : .... *āśrita* ***budhajana*** *sudhe ... Lakmādēviyarasi....* ; **tr.** Lakmādēviyarasi who was like nectar to the **learned men** who seek her refuge ; *S.I.I.* IX, pt. i, No. 273, p. 293, ll. 42–43, 55–56 ; Malayanur, Kalyanadurga Tq., Anantapur Dt., A.P. St. **Dy.** Chāḷ. of Kal., Jagadēkamalla, Ś. 1101 = 1179 A.D.

budhivantaru (K. *n.*), body of learned men ; **text:** ..... *prati amāvase prati dvādaśiyali obbobba brāhmaṇa bhōjana naḍeyabahudu ī dharma naḍavaṁtāge ... nālvaru seṭṭikāraru* ***budhivaṁtaru*** *samasta halara kaiyiyali ..... bittuva ... bhatta muḍe mūṟanu Taṁgāyiseṭṭiti ... koṭṭaru ...* ; **tr.** Taṁgāyiseṭṭi granted through the four *seṭṭikāras* (administrative body of traders) *budhivaṁtaru* (**body of learned men**) and *samasta halaru* (an administrative body) so that on every *amāvāsya* and *dvādaśi* day one brāhmaṇa can be fed ; *S.I.I.* VII, No. 379, p. 235, ll. 12–16, 23, 26–27 ; Kōṭakēri, Udupi Tq. and Dt. Karn. St. **Dy.** Saṅgama, Harihara, Ś. 1304 = 1382 A.D.

byavahāra (K. < *Skt. vyavahāra, n.*), business transaction ; **text**[1] : .... *Kalidēva seṭṭiya ... byavasāya* ***byavahāra****ventene ...* ; **tr.** to describe the agricultural profession and business transactions of Kalidēva ; *S.I.I.* IX, pt. i, No. 296, p. 320, ll. 39-40 ; Kurugōḍu, Bellary Tq. and Dt., Karn. St. **Dy.** Kal. of Kal., Sōvidēva, Ś. 1097 = 1176 A.D. ; **text**[2] : .... Tīkiseṭṭiyaru ***byavahāra*** *mārgadiṁ ... Kēdārēśvaradēvara śrīkāryakkeṁdu koṁḍa eremattar eraḍu ...* ; **tr.** Tīkiseṭṭi bought by way of **business transaction** two mattar (a land measure) of black soil for offering services to the god Kēdārēśvara ; *S.I.I.* XX, No. 198, p. 246, l. 22–24; Lakshmēśvara, Shirahatti Tq., Dharwar Dt., Karn. St. **Dy.** Sēü of Dēv., Siṁghaṇa, Ś. 1149 = 1227 A.D.

byavahāri (K. *n.*), trader ; **text** : ... *Kāḷiseṭṭi oḷagāda samasta* ***byavahāri****gaḷuṁ brāhmaṇa mannēra upādhyara māṇi ...* ; **tr.** all the **traders** including Kāḷiseṭṭi, the brāhmaṇas, the chieftains and the teacher's assistant ; *S.I.I.* IX, pt. ii, No. 433, p. 442, ll. 37–38 ; Siṅganallūr, Chamarajanagar Tq. and Dt., T. Nadu St. **Dy.** Saṅgama, Dēvarāya, Ś. 1330 1408 A.D.

byavasāya (K. < Skt. *vyavahāra, n.*), agricultural profession ; **text**[1] : .... *Kalidēva seṭṭiya ... byavasāya* ***byavahāra****ventene ...* ; **tr.** to describe the **agricultural profession** and business transactions of Kalidēva ; *S.I.I.* IX, pt. i, No. 296, p. 320, ll. 39–40 ; Kurugōḍu, Bellary Tq. and Dt., Karn. St. **Dy.** Kal. of Kal., Sōvidēva, Ś. 1097 = 1176 A.D.

chādaṇam (T. < Skt. *śāsanaṁ, n.*), document ; **text :** . . . . *ich***chādaṇam** *eḻudiṇamaikku ivvūr madhyasthaṉ Śiṟiyapiḷḷai eḻuttu* . . . . ; **tr.** this is the signature of Śiṟiyapiḷḷai, the arbitrator, attesting to the writing of this **document** ; *S.I.I.* VIII, No. 194, p. 96, ll. 27–28 ; Anbil, Tiruchirapalli Tq. and Dt. T. Nadu St. **Dy.** Hoy., Vīrarāmanātha, reg. yr. 8 = 1262 A.D.

chadiram (T. *n.*), land area having four equal sides ; **text :** (damaged) *nālāṅkaṇṇāṟṟu mūṉṟāñ***chadiram** . . . ; **tr.** the third **land area having four equal sides** irrigated by the fourth canal ; *S.I.I.* IV, No. 226, p. 35, l. 12 ; Chidambaram, Chidambaram Tq., S. Arcot Dt., T. Nadu St. **Dy.** Chōḷa, Kulōttuṅga I, reg. yr. 5 = 1075 A.D.

chaḍiya dāri (T. *n.*), foot path ; **text :** *Īśānya* ***chaḍiya dāri*** . . . ; **tr.** (the boundary) on the north east is the **foot path** ; *E.C.* (R) V, Hn. 61, p. 47, l. 42 ; Heragu, Hassan Tq. and Dt., Karn. St. **Dy.** Hoy., Ballāḷa, Ś. 1139 = 1217 A.D.

chadura (K. *n.*), square segment of land ; **text :** . . . *Virūpākshadēvara keyiṁ mūḍalā* . . . . . *kennela* ***chadura****da matta 1* . . . ; **tr.** one *matta* (land measure) of **square segment of** red soil **land** to the east of the land belonging to the god Virūpāksha ; *S.I.I.* IX, pt. i, No. 253, p. 267, ll. 89–93 ; Oruvay, Bellary Tq. and Dt., Karn. St. **Dy.** Chāḷ. of Kal., Jagadēkamalla II, Ś. 1071 = 1149 A.D.

chāga (K. < Skt. *tyāga, n.*), generosity ; **text :** . . . . *Vīraballāḷadēvara* . . . . . *pādapadmōpa–jīvigaḷappāneyamāvaṁtara kulada chalada* ***chāga****meṁtene* . . . ; **tr.** the elephant driver to describe whose family's predilections for generosity and devotion at the lotus feet of Vīraballāḷa ; *E.C.* (R) X, Ak. 214, p. 263, ll. 27, 30 ; Muduḍi, Arasikere Tq., Hassan Dt., Karn. St. **Dy.** Hoy., Ballāḷa II, Ś. 1117 = 1195 A.D.

chaitya gṛiha[1] (K. < Skt. *n.*), memorial temple ; **text :** . . *Chaṁgāḷvannija satigĒchabbarasige parōksha vinayanimittaṁ* . . . ***chaitya gṛiha****man māḍisidaṁ* . . . ; **tr.** Chaṁgāḷva got the **memorial temple** constructed for the salvation of his wife Ēchabbarasi ; *E.C.* (R)VIII, Ag. 140, p. 191, ll. 5–6 ; Suḷagōḍusōmavāra, Arakalagudu Tq., Hassan Dt., Karn. St. **Dy.** Chaṅgālva, Matsyabhūpāḷaka, in characters of 11–12th cent. A.D.

chaitya gṛiha[2] (K. < Skt. *n.*), Jaina temple ; **text:** . . . . . *māḍisidar*. . . . . *Śāṁtināthajinapa śrīgēhaman mērunagēṁdrara* ***chaitya gṛiha****diṁ mēleṁbinaṁ* . . *Barmmadēvavibhugaḷ* ; **tr.** Lord Barmmadēva got this temple of Śāṁtināthajina constructed to rival with the **Jaina temple** on mount Mēru; *S.I.I.* VII, No. 724, p. 366, ll. 36–39 ; Sēḍam, Sedam Tq. Gulbarga Dt. Karn. St. **Dy.** Chāḷ. of Kal., Bhūlōkamalla, in characters of 12th cent. A.D.

chaityālaya (K. < Skt. *n.*), Jaina temple ; **text**[1] **:** . . . . . . *Pōchāṁbike Beḷagoḷada tīrtthaṁ modalādanēka tīrtthagaḷoḷu palavu* ***chaity-ālaya****ṁgaḷa māḍisi mahādānaṁgeydu* . . . . ;

tr. Pōchāṁbike got constructed several **Jaina temples** in holy places including Beḷagoḷa and made grants ; *E.C.* (R) II, Sb. 136, p. 84, l. 28; Śravaṇabeḷagoḷa, Channarayapatna Tq., Hassan Dt., Karn. St. **Dy.** Hoy., Vishṇuvardhana, Ś. 1043 = 1120 A.D. ; **text**[2] : . . . . *Ādivāra udayavāda aydu ghaḷigeyalli kāikaṇiyoḷu* ***chaityālayakke*** *kesaṟugallanikki* . . ; **tr.** having laid the foundation stone for the **Jaina temple** at Kāikaṇi at the fifth *ghaḷige* (a span of 24 minutes) after sun rise ; *K.I.* I, No. 41, p. 95, l. 11 ; Kaikiṇi, Bhatkal Tq. and Dt., Karn. St. **Dy.** Saṅgama, Dēvarāya I, Ś. 1338 = 1417 A.D. ; **text**[3] : . . . . *Śrīmān Nāraṇanāyakō vyarachayach****chaityālayaṁ*** *dharmmadaṁ* . . ; **tr.** the illustrious Nāraṇanāyaka got constructed the merit-yielding **Jaina temple**; *K.I.* III, pt. i, No. 17, p. 67, l. 20 ; Bhaṭkal, Bhatkal Tq. and Dt., Karn. St. **Dy.** Sāḷuva chfs., Chenna Bhairādēvi, Ś. 1471 = 1549 A.D.

chākkaikkūttu (T. *n.*), a kind of folk dance ; **text :** . . . *aśvati tiruviḻāvukku vandu* ***chākkaikkūttu*** *āḍakkaḍava Aḍalaiyūr chākkai* ; **tr.** the ***chākkai*** troupe of Aḍalaiyur which goes to the festival on the occasion of Aśvini asterism to perrform the **folk dance** ; *S.I.I.* XIX, No. 171, p. 87, ll. 8–11 ; Kīḻappaḻuvūr, Udaiyarpalayam Tq., Tiruchirapalli Dt., T. Nadu St. **Dy.** Chōḷa, Parakēsari, reg. yr. 6, in characters of 10th century A.D.

chākkaimār virutti (M. *n.*), maintenance of those who perform (the folk dance) *chākkaikkūttu*; **text :** . . . . ***chākkaimār virutti*** *Nagarūr vaṭṭattil Cheṅgaiyūrālkkoḻḻunel panniru paṟai arai* . . . . . ; **tr.** for the **maintenance of the *chākkaimār* who perform (the folk dance Chākkaikkūttu)** twelve and a half *paṟai* (a grain measure) of paddy from Cheṅgaiyūr in Nagarūr division was earmarked ; *T.A.S.* IV, No. 7, p. 52, ll. 95–96 ; Kollūrmaḍam, Ker. St. **Dy.** Rulers of Vēṇāḍu, Udayamārttāṇḍavarma Tiruvaḍi, Kollam 364 = 1188 A.D.

chakkaram paṇam (T. *n.*), a type of circular coin ; **text :** . . . . . . *ivvūr pāḍikāvalukku nichchayitta aṉṟāḍuvaḻaṅgum* ***chakkaram paṇam*** *300* ; **tr.** for the payment for persons doing watch and ward duty, a payment of 300 **coins of circular type** was decided upon from coins in valid currency ; *I.P.S.*, No. 703, p. 485, ll. 4–5 ; Kāraiyur, Tirumayyam Tq., Pudukkottai Dt., T. Nadu St. **Dy.** Saṅgama, Dēvarāya, Ś. 1354 = 1432 A.D.

chakke (K. *n.*), (sandal wood) piece ; **text :** . . . . *dēvarige* . . . *samarpista śrīgaṁdhada* ***chakke*** *16 karpūrada kudiru 6* . ; **tr.** 16 **pieces** of sandal wood and six *kudiru* (a measure of weight) of camphor were offered to the god ; *S.I.I.* IX, pt. ii, No. 551, p. 571, l. 4 ; Little Kāñchīpuram, Kanchipuram Tq., Chingleput Dt., T. Nadu St. **Dy.** Tuḷuva, Achyutarāya, Ś. 1454 = 1532 A.D.

chakkili (T. *n.*), member of the cobbler community; **text :** . . . . *Tiruvaṇṇāmalai uḍaiyanāyanār kōyililē* *chakkilikku deriśaṉam kāṭṭi tōlālē śeyda tiruvaḍinilai;* **tr.** a footrest made of leather for the god Tiruvaṇṇāmalai uḍaiyanāyanār was got done after arranging for the seeing of the deity by a member of the **cobbler community** ; *S.I.I.* VIII, No. 151, p. 68, l. 4; Tiruvaṇṇāmalai, Tiruvannamalai Tq., North Arcot Dt., T. Nadu St. **Dy.** Chōḷa, Kulōttuṅga III, reg. yr. 24 = 1202 A.D.

chakkiliyar (T. *n.*), members of the cobbler community ; **text :** . . . . *Marundanum Maṭṭaiyāṇḍānum* . . . . . . *Piḷḷaiyār śrīpādam viṭṭu ōḍippōnōmāgil eṅgaḷ miṉāṭṭimārai* ***chakkiliyār****kku kuḍuttuppāttirundōmāvōm* . . . ; **tr.** if we, Marundan and Maṭṭaiyāṇḍāṉ should run away from this god Piḷḷaiyār, we would have in effect handed over our wives to the **members of the cobbler community** and will be haplessly watching ; *S.I.I.* VIII, No. 86, p. 46, l. 4; Tiruvaṇṇāmalai, Tiruvannamalai Tq., North Arcot Dt., T. Nadu St. **Dy.** Chōḷa, Rājarāja III, reg. yr. 5 = 1221 A.D.

chakra (K. *n.*), village watchman ; **text :** . . . *Kaḍalegāla* ***chakra****na koḍageya holada hērobbe*. . . . . ; **tr.** the big heap of stones in the gift land of the **village watchman** of Kaḍalegala ; *E.C.* (R) IV, Ch. 104, p. 60, l. 65; Mūḍalagrahāra, Chamarajanagar Tq. and Dt., Karn. St. **Dy.** Tāyūr chfs., Perumāḷadēva, Ś. 1335 = 1413 A.D.

chakradhvaja (K. *n.*), banner with the emblem of discus ; **text :** . . . . ***chakra dhvaja****virājar* . . . . *Kuṟugōḍa Paṭṭaṇasvāmigaḷ* ; **tr.** the merchant guild of Kuṟugōḍu which had its **banner with the emblem of discus** ; *S.I.I.* IX, pt. i, No. 297, p. 324, ll. 34, 38–39 ; Kurugōḍu, Bellary Tq. and Dt., Karn. St. **Dy.** Kal of Kal., Śaṅkhamadēva, Ś. 1099 = 1177 A.D.

chakra ga (K. *n.*), circular gold coin ; **text :** . . . . . . *Varadarājadēvarige samarpista kāṇike* . . . ***chakra ga*** *415* ; **tr.** 415 **circular gold coins** were donated to the god Varadarāja. . . . ; *S.I.I.* IX, pt. ii, No. 547, p. 566, l. 3 ; Little Kāñchīpuram, Kanchipuram Tq., Chingleput Dt., T. Nadu St. **Dy.** Tuḷuva, Achyutarāya, Ś. 1454 = 1532 A.D.

chakrakalu (K. *n.*), boundary stone with mark of discus, a weapon of Vishṇu ; **text :** (damaged) . . . . *baḍagalu rājabīdige hattira naṭṭa* ***chakrakalu*** *1 adake teṅkalu* **. . . .** ***chakra kalu*** *1* . . . . . ; **tr.** on the north, boundary **stone with the mark of discus, a weapon of Vishṇu,** to its south a similar boundary stone ; *S.I.I.* IX, pt. ii, No. 534, p. 548, ll. 8–11; Kamalāpura, Hospet Tq., Bellary Dt., Karn. St. **Dy.** Tuḷuva, Achyutarāya, Ś. 1454 = 1531 A.D.

chakralāṁchhanapuṟālu (Te. *n.*), boundary stones with mark of discus ; **text :** (damaged) . . . . . . *dhārāpūrvakamu sēsi nālvu dikkulayaṁdu* ***chakralāṁchhanapuṟālu*** *pāṁtipeṭṭiṁchu* . . . . . ; **tr.** having set up **boundary stones with the mark of the discus,** a weapon of Vishṇu, on four sides . . ; *S.I.I.* VI, No. 1203, p. 487, ll. 9–10; Siṁhāchalam, Vishākhapatnam Tq. and Dt., A.P.

St. **Misc.**, Ś. 1148 = 1226 A.D.

chakravarti (K. *n.*), emperor ; **text**[1] : .... *Rudrarāśibhaṭārar pōgi* ***chakravarti****yaṁ kaṇḍaruvattirmmattar keyyaṁ ... parihāraṁ ... paḍedar* .... ; **tr.** Rudrarāśibhaṭāra went and met the **emperor** and got 62 *mattar* (a land measure) of land as compensation; *S.I.I.* IX, pt. i, No. 65, p. 37, ll. 18–20 ; Kuḍatini, Bellary Tq. and Dt., Karn. St. **Dy.** Rāshṭr., Kṛishṇa III, Ś. 870 = 947 A.D. ; **text**[2] : .... *śrīmatu YādavaNārāyaṇa pratāpa****chakravartti*** *Hoyisaṇa Vīra Ballāḷa* .... ; **tr.** the illustrious and valourous Hoysaḷa **emperor** Vīra-Ballāḷa, who was the very Nārāyaṇa of the Yādava clan; *S.I.I.* IX, pt. i, No. 335, p. 356, l. 2 ; Taḷūru, Hospet Tq., Bellary Dt., Karn. St. **Dy.** Hoy., Ballāḷa, Cy. yr. Bahudhānya = 1218 A.D.; **text**[3] : .... *Jinarathayātrāpravarttana Kaliyuga* ***chakravartti****yuṁ Hiraṇyachaityālayanirmāpakanuṁ* ..... *Sāḷuvamalla* ; **tr.** Sāḷuvamalla who was verily an **emperor** of the Kali age, who set in motion the journey of the chariot of the Jaina faith, who had constructed a golden Jaina temple; *S.I.I.* VII, No. 207, p. 103, l. 44 ; Mūḍabidure, Karkala Tq., Udupi Dt., Karn. St. **Dy.** Nagire Chfs., Bhairavadēva, Ś. 1384=1462 A.D.

chakravartidatti (K. *n.*), emperor's gift ; **text** : . ... *Āhavamalladēvaṁge binnapaṁgeydu* ***chakravartidatti*** *prakhyātamappa śāsanamaṁ* ... *paḍedu* .... ; **tr.** having made a request to Āhavamalladēva and obtaining an edict well known as **'emperor's gift'** ; *S.I.I.* XI, No. 52, p. 42, l. 53; Lakkuṁḍi, Gadag Tq. and Dt., Karn. St. **Dy.** Chāḷ. of Kal., Iṟivabeḍeṁga Satyāśraya, Ś. 929 = 1007 A.D.

chakrēśvara (K. *n.*), emperor ; **text** : ...... *Āhavamalladēvanesedaṁ Chāḷukya****chakrēśvara*** . .... ; **tr.** there flourished Āhavamalladēva the **emperor** of the Chāḷukya dynasty ; *S.I.I.* IX, pt. i, No. 118, p. 95, l. 14 ; Bāgaḷi, Hirehadagalli Tq., Bellary Dt., Karn. St. **Dy.** Chāḷ. of Kal., Trailōkyamalla, Ś. 978 = 1057 A.D.

chakri (K. *n.*), emperor ; **text**[1] : (damaged) .. .... *Sōbhanarasaṁ māḍisi Sōbhanēśvaramanoppise Bhāvaśivar maṭhamaṁ puramaṁ mukhasāle māḍamaṁ māḍisi* ***chakri****yoḷ paḍedu śāsanamaṁ* . ... ; **tr.** Śōbhanarasa having built the temple of Śōbhanēśvara and having handed it over to Bhāvaśiva, the latter got built a monastery, founded a township, and built a frontal upper floor (for the temple) and obtained a stone edict (registering gifts) from the **emperor** ; *S.I.I.* XI, No. 64, p. 54, ll. 13–15 ; Muḷugunda, Gadag Tq. and Dt., Karn. St. **Dy.** Chāḷ. of Kal., Jayasiṁha II, Ś. 950 = 1028 A.D. ; **text**[2] : ...... *Chāḷukyavaṁśa samudbhūtar anēkarāḷdaravaroḷ tāṁ* ***chakri*** *Sōmēśvaraṁ* .... ; **tr.** a number of kings hailing from the Chāḷukya family had ruled and among them was the **emperor** Sōmēśvara ; *S.I.I.* IX, pt. i, No. 249, p. 255, l. 8 ; Kōlūr, Bellary Tq. and Dt., Karn. St. **Dy.** Chāḷ. of Kal., Jagadēkamalla II, reg. yr. 10 =

1147 A.D.

chaladaṁkakāṟa (K. *n.*), hero who fights with grit and valour (a title) ; **text :** . . . . . . *parasainyamaṁ peṟaṁgeḍeguḍadaṭṭi kolva chalamāḷda chalaṁ* ***chaladaṁkakāṟana*** . . . ; **tr. Chaladaṁkakāra** (hero who fights with grit and valour) who chased and killed, unassisted, the enemy's army; *E.C.* II, Sb. 163, p. 107, ll. 24–25 ; Śravaṇabeḷagoḷa, Channarayapatna Tq., Hassan Dist, Karn. St., **Dy.** W. Gaṅga, Gaṅga Gaṅgēya, Ś. 904 = 982 A.D.

chaladaṁka Rāma (K. *n.*), hero who fights with grit and valour like the (legendary) Rāma ; **text :** . . *bhujabalavīranasahāyaśūra* ***chaladaṁka Rāma*** . . . *Hoysaḷa Vīraballāḷadēva* . . . . ; **tr.** a warrior who fights with the strength of his arms, unassisted fighter, **hero who fights with grit and valour like the (legendary) Rāma** ; *E.C.* (R) X, Ak. 224, p. 222, ll. 14–15; Gījihaḷḷi, Arasikere Tq., Hassan Dt., Karn. St. **Dy.** Hoy., Ballāḷa II, Ś. 1123=1200 A.D.

chalavādi (K. *n.*), a subsect among the scheduled caste community ; **text :** . . . . *dēvadāyada saṁteya dānakke aḷupidavaru* . . . . . ***chalavādi*** *saṁgeḍi paṁtagāṟarigū* . . . . *bāyi koshṭa* . . . . ; **tr.** those who oppose the grant of the toll revenue raised from the market as a gift to the god Bhairavadēva including those belonging to the **subsect among the scheduled caste**, the saṁgēḍi and paṁtagāṟa communities will suffer from oral leprosy ; *S.I.I.* IX, pt. ii, No. 532, p. 547, ll. 14, 20, 22 ; Adamaṉkōṭṭai, Dharmapuri Tq., Salem Dt., T. Nadu St. **Dy.** Tuḷuva, Achyutarāya, Ś. 1452 = 1530 A.D.

cheliviṁdramānya (Te. *n.*), tax free land with facility for irrigation during summer ; **text :** . . . . . . *Vēmula Rāghavayyaṁgāru* . . . . *Tammaḷa Vīrayyaku* . . . . . *reṁḍu kuchcheḷḷu kshētraṁ* ***cheliviṁdramānyaṁgānu*** . . . . *yistimi ganuka anubhaviṁchi bratikēdi* . . . ; **tr.** Vēmula Rāghavayya donated **tax free land with facility for irrigation during summer** to TammaḷaVīrayya so that he can enjoy the same for his subsistence ; *S.I.I.* XVI, No. 288, p. 293, ll. 21, 25, 31–32, 35–36 ; Koṇḍēpāḍu, Guntur Tq. and Dt., A.P. St. **Dy.** Āravīḍu, Śrīraṅga I, Ś. 1498 = 1576 A.D.

chālumūla samasta pekkaṁḍru (Te. *n.*), a commercial guild ; **text :** (incomplete) . . . . . . *Ayyāvaḷi mukhyamaina* ***chālumūla samasta pekkaṁḍra*** *muṁdaṭānu nirnayapeṭi sāgiṁchina vivaraṁ* . . . ; **tr.** details of the grant made as decided in the presence of the **Commercial guild called Chālumūla samasta pekkaṁḍru** led by the Ayyāvaḷi guild; *I.A.P.* Cuddapah II, No. 93, p. 119, ll. 17–19 ; Virūru, Siddhavatam Tq. Cuddapah Dt., A.P. St. Comm. gld., Ś. 1449 = 1527 A.D.

chālumūla samasta samaya pekkaṁḍru (Te. *n.*), a merchant guild consisting of members of all faiths ; **text :** . . . . . ***Chālumūla samasta samaya pekkaṁḍra*** *paṁpunānu* . . . . . *ī grāma prajālu* *ichē dommaripannu*; **tr.** on the advice of the merchant guild called Chālumūla samasta samaya pekkaṁḍru, the residents of the village donated the tax calleld *dommaripannu* ; *S.I.I.* XVI, No. 225, pp. 232–33 , ll. 10, 12–13, 19–21 ; Ainavōlu, Guntur Tq. and Dt., A.P. St. **Dy.** Tuḷuva, Sadāśiva, Ś. 1480 = 1558 A.D.

chālumūla samasta yāṁbhaiyāru dēśālavāru (Te. *n.*), a merchant guild consisting of members hailing from 56 countries ; **text :** (badly damaged) . . . . ***chālumūla samasta yāṁbhaiyāru dēśālavāru*** . . . . . *kūḍi kūrchuṁḍi vichāriṁchukonna vivaramu* . . . ; **tr.** details of enquiries conducted by the **merchant guild consisting of members from 56 contries** while they were seated in quorum ; *S.I.I.* XVI, No. 315, p. 322, ll. 10–11, 12–13; Nārāyaṇavanaṁ, Puttur Tq., Chittoor Dt., A.P. St. **Dy.** Āravīḍu, Veṅkaṭapati, Ś. 1542 = 1620 A.D.

chālumūla ubhaya nānādēśāla pekkaṁḍru (Te. *n.*), the itenerant group of merchants belonging to various countries ; **text :** (damaged) . . . . . . ***chālumūla ubhaya nānādēśāla pekkaṁḍru*** . . . ; **tr. itenerant group of merchants belonging to various countries** ; *S.I.I.* X, No. 567, p. 314, l. 17 ; Taṅgēḍa, Palnad Tq., Guntur Dt., A.P. St. **Dy.** Reḍḍis, Komaragiri Reddi, in characters of 14th cent. A.D.

chāmara (K. *n.*), fly-whisk (as an insignia) ; **text**[1] **:** . . . . . . *Kāṁchanakaḷaśa*. . . . *chchhatra* ***chāmara*** . . . . . *bhērīravādi rājachinhabirājitar* . . . ; **tr.** adorned with such royal insignia as golden pinnacle, parasol, **fly-whisk**, trumpet sound, etc. ; *S.I.I.* V, No. 848, p. 344, l. 28 ; Hūli (near Saundatti), Saundatti Tq., Belgaum Dt., Karn. St. **Dy.** Chāḷ. of Kal., Tribhuvanamalla, Ś. 1019 = 1097 A.D. ; **text**[2] **:** . . . . . *dēvarige* ***chāmara****vanikkuva* . . . . . . *jana eraḍakkaṁ prati dina oṁdakkaṁ akki nāḍahāne eraḍu* . . . ; **tr.** for the two persons who fan the **fly-whisk** before the god two *nāḍa hāne* (a grain measure., measured by the standard vessel in vogue in that territory) of rice was set aside ; *S.I.I.* IX, pt. ii, No. 417, p. 423, l. 36 ; Kōṭēśvara, Udupi Tq. and Dt., Karn. St. **Dy.** Saṅgama, Harihara, Ś. 1300 = 1377 A.D.

chāmarai (T. *n.*), flywhisk (an emblem of royalty); **text :** . . . . . *taviśum* ***chāmaraiyum*** *śivigaiyuntimilaiyum kōyilum pōṉagamum kāḷamuṅkaḷir̤r̤uṉir̤aiyuñChembiyaṉr̤amiḻavēḷeṉṉuṅ kulappiyarum per̤r̤a Vikki Aṉṉaṉ* ; **tr.** Vikki Aṉṉaṉ who had received a throne, **fly-whisk**, palanquin, drum, mansion, allowance, bugle, an army of male elephants and the hereditary title of Śembiyaṉ Tamiḻavēḷ ; *S.I.I.* III, pt. III, No. 89, p. 221, ll. 3–6 ; Tillaisthānam, Tanjavur Tq. and Dt., T. Nadu St. **Dy.** Chōḷa, Āditya I, reg. yr. 9 = 880 A.D.

chamarīdhvaja (K. *n.*), fly-whisk made of the bushy tail of yak; **text:** . . . . . . ***chamarīdhvaja*** *virājitar* . . . . . . ; **tr.** resplendant with the banner having **flywhisk made of the bushy tail of**

yak ; *S.I.I.* IX, pt. i, No. 101, p. 72, ll. 17–18 ; Mōrigēri, Bellary Tq. and Dt., Karn. St. **Dy.** Chāḷ. of Kal., Āhavamalla, Ś. 967 = 1045 A.D.

chaṁdrana kal (K. *n.*), stone slab bearing the figure of a moon ; **text:** . . . . *ā keyge* . . . *nairutyadoḷ* ***chaṁdrana kal*** . . . . ; **tr.** the south west boundary for this field is the **stone slab bearing the figure of a moon** ; *Ep. Ind.* XVI, No. 9, p. 56, ll. 32–33 ; Muḷugunda, Mulugunda Tq., Gadag Dt., Karn. St. **Dy.** Chāḷ. of Kal., Sōmēśvara I, Ś. 995 = 1053 A.D.

chamūnātha (K. *n.*), army chief ; **text :** . . . . . . *Ravi* ***chamūnātha*** . . . ; **tr.** Ravi who was the **army chief** ; *S.I.I.* IX, pt. i, No. 158, p. 142, l. 31 ; Huvinahadagalli, Bellary Tq. and Dt., Karn. St. **Dy.** Chāḷ. of Kal., Vikramāditya VI, Ch. Vi. yr. 15 = 1090 A.D.

chamūpa (K. *n.*), army chief ; **text**[1] **:** . . . . . . *Ravi* ***chamūpa****narddhāṁgi* . . . *Rebbāṁbike* . . ; **tr.** Rebbāṁbike the wife of Ravi, the **army chief** ; *S.I.I.* IX, pt. i, No. 158, p. 143, l. 40 ; Huvinahadagalli, Bellary Tq. and Dt., Karn. St. **Dy.** Chāḷ. of Kal., Vikramāditya VI, Ch. Vi. yr. 15 = 1090 A.D. ; **text**[2] **:** . . . . . . *Vināyakadēvarggā* . . . . . *Basava* ***chamupaṁ*** . . . *koṭṭa keyi* . . *ma 2* . . . ; **tr.** Basava the **army chief** donated 2 *ma* (*mattar*, a land measure) of land to the god Vināyaka ; *S.I.I.* IX, pt. i, No. 334, p. 355, ll. 12–15 ; Oruvay, Bellary Tq. and Dt., Karn. St. **Dy.** Hoy., Ballāḷa II, Cy. yr. Īśvara = 1217 A.D.

chāmūpati (K. *n.*), army chief ; **text :** (damaged) . . . . . ***chamupati*** *Mallikārjunaṁ tanagaṁ Hēmāchalakkam sthirateye sahaja* . . . ; **tr.** Mallikārjuna, the **army chief** (considered) that firmness is the common characterstic of self and the mount Mēru ; *K.I.* II, No. 24, p. 92, ll. 45–46 ; Rāmatīrtha, Athani Tq., Belgaum Dt., Karn. St. **Dy.** Kal. of Kal., Bijjaḷa, Ś. 1089 = 1166 A.D.

chaṇḍai (T. *n.*), leather purcussion instrument ; **text :** . . . . . . *ittēvarkkuch* ***chaṇḍai*** *koṭṭuvadāga vaittamaiyil* . . . ; **tr.** having arranged for the beating of the **leather purcussion instrument** for the god ; *S.I.I.* VIII, No. 739, p. 378, ll. 9–10 ; Tiruvāmāttūr, Villuppuram Tq., S. Arcot Dt., T. Nadu St., **Dy.** Chōḷa, Parāntaka I, in characters of 9th century A.D.

chaṇḍirai (T. *n.*), a kind of tax ; **text :** . . . . *Rājarājēśvaramuḍaiyār* . . . . *Tirunāḷaikku Mahāmēruviṭaṅkaṉpaḷḷi nañjai puñjai nāṟpāl ellaiyum* ***chaṇḍirai*** *koḷḷakkaḍava dānam* . . . . ; **tr.** for the celebrations of the auspicious day in the temple of Rājarājēśvaramuḍaiyār wet lands, dry lands and the income from **taxes** like **chaṇḍirai** were granted at Mahāmēruviṭaṅkaṉpaḷḷi ; *E.C.* (R) V, T.N. 188, p. 580, ll. 5–11 ; Talakāḍu, T. Narasipur Tq., Mysore Dt., Karn. St. **Dy.** Hoy., Narasiṁha, in characters of the 13th-14th century A.D.

chandana (K. *n.*), sandal tree ; **text :** . . . . *lateya maṁṭapadiṁ* . . . . *misupa*

***chandana**dimdelevaḷḷiyiṁ niraṁtaravesedirpa pūgavanadiṁ Pūvinapaḍaṁgile oppuvadāvakālamuṁ* . . . . . ; **tr.** the village of Pūvinapaḍaṁgile was ever pleasing with its arbours, glowing **sandal trees** and arecanut groves, etc. ; *S.I.I.* IX, pt. i, No. 371, pp. 387–88, ll. 14–15 ; Yēṇigi, Hadagalli Tq., Bellary Dt., Karn. St. **Dy.** Sēü of Dēv., Kandhara, Ś. 1181 = 1259 A.D.

chandana nandana (K. *n.*), sandal wood grove ; **text :** . . . . . *Malayagiri* ***chandana-nandana*** . . . ; **tr.** in the **sandal wood grove** of the Malaya mountain ; *S.I.I.* IX, pt. i, No. 292, p. 313, l. 33 ; Bāgaḷi, Harapanahalli Tq., Bellary Dt., Karn. St. **Dy.** Pāṇḍya, Vijayapāṇḍya, in characters of 12th century A.D.

Chaṇḍēśvara (T. *n.*), accountant deity in the Śiva temple ; **text :** . . . . . *Tiḍalāykkiḍanda nilattil* ***Chaṇḍēśvara*** *dēvariḍai nāṉ vilai koṇḍu vaśakkiṉa nilam* . . . . ; **tr.** land lying at an elevation bought by payment by me from the ***accountant deity Chaṇḍēśvara*** and duly reclaimed ; *S.I.I.* VIII, No. 677, p. 340, ll. 6–7 ; Allūr, Tiruchirapalli Tq. and Dt., T. Nadu St. **Dy.** Chōḷa, Rājēndra I, reg. yr. 4 = 1016 A.D.

Chaṇḍēśvara vilaippramāṇam (T. *n.*), sale deed approved in the name of accountant deity Chaṇḍēśvara ; **text :** . . . . . ***Chaṇḍēśvara vilaippramāṇaṁ*** *paṇṇi kuḍuttāpaḍi* . . . ; **tr.** according to the **sale deed approved in the name of the account deity Chaṇḍēśvara** ; *S.I.I.* VII, No. 108, p. 45, ll. 2–3 ; Tiruvottūr, Cheyyar Tq., N. Arcot Dt., T. Nadu St. **Misc.,** in characters of 12th century A.D.

Chaṇḍēśvara peruvilai (T. *n.*), land auctioned in the name of the accountant deity Chaṇḍēśvara at highest cost decided upon ; **text :** . . . . *karaṁbum tirutti* . . . *payirśeyyumiḍuttu* . . . ***Chaṇḍēśvara-peruvilai*** *āga nichchaiyitta mūlāndikkollaikku paṇam 15*. . . ; **tr.** having reclaimed uncultivated land and cultivating crops thereon, the **land auctioned in the name of accountant deity Chaṇḍēśvara at highest cost decided upon** for the land *mūlāndikkollai* is 15 *paṇam* (coin) ; *S.I.I.* VIII, No. 72, p. 40, ll. 2–3 ; Tiruvaṇṇāmalai, Tiruvannamalai Tq., N. Arcot Dt., T. Nadu St. **Dy.** Saṅgama, Virūpāksha, Ś. 1311 = 1389 A.D.

Chaṁdrada koḍe (K. *n.*), white umbrella ; **text:** . . . . . *paḍedam* . . . . *rājachihnavan* . . . ***chaṁdrada koḍe****yaṁ* . . . *Śōbhanagauṁḍan* . . . ; **tr.** Śōbanagauṁḍa earned the honour of being endowed with a **white umbrella** ; *K.I.* IV, No. 10, p. 27, ll. 19–20 ; Hirēhaḷḷi, Byādagi Tq., Dharwar Dt., Karn. St. **Dy.** Chāḷ. of Kal., Vikramāditya VI, Ch. Vi. yr. 45 = 1121 A.D.

chapara, chappara (K. *n.*), pandal ; **text**[1] **:** . . . . *tērabīdiya Parāṁkuśamaṁṭapada muṁde* ***chapara*** *ikki ā maṁṭapada chaparavanu siṁghārisuvudake saha koṭadu gade bījavari kha 1/2*. . . . . . ; **tr.** in front of the *Parāṁkuśamaṁṭapa* in the car street, a **pandal** was erected and for decorating that pandal one wet land with the sowable capacity of 1/2 *kha* (*khaṁḍuga*, a land measure) of seeds was granted ; *S.I.I.* IX, pt. ii, No. 668, p. 661, l. 3 ; Hampi, Hospet Tq., Bellary Dt., Karn. St. **Dy.** Tuḷuva, Sadāśiva, Ś. 1480 = 1559 A.D. ; **text**[2] : ..... *prativarusha Tirumale tīrthayātreyanu māḍi* ... ***chappara*** .. *nīnu horisikoṁḍu* ... *naḍavadakkāgi kaṭaḷe*.. ... ; **tr.** after you perform your annual pilgrimage to Tirumale you will errect a **pandal** as per the established custom ; *S.I.I.* IX, pt. ii, No. 687, p. 679, ll. 31–38 ; Pailabanda, Madakasira Tq., Anantapur Dt., A.P. St. **Dy.** Niḍugal chfs., Timmaṇa Nāyaka II, Cy. yr. Svabhānu = 1584 A.D.

chappara mānya (K. *n.*), grant made for errecting pandal ; **text :** ..... *Immaḍi Tiṁmaṇa nāyakaru* .... *koṭa* ***chappara mānyada*** .. *Narasāṁbudhikuṁṭeya Kāṇāchi* .... ; **tr.** Immaḍi Tiṁmaṇa nāyaka **granted** the ancestral rights over the Narasāṁbudhikuṁṭe tank **for the erection of pandals** ; *S.I.I.* IX, pt. ii, No. 687, p. 679, ll. 21–26 ; Pailabanda, Madakasira Tq., Anantapur Dt., A.P. St. **Dy.** Niḍugal chfs., Timmaṇa Nāyaka II, Cy. yr. Svabhānu = 1584 A.D.

charādāya (K. < *Skt. n.*), revenue income from tax on moveable properties ; **text**[1] : ... *Somayyadēva Voḍeyarige* ... *Tagavūra grāmada suṁka suvarṇādāya gadde toṭa viśēsha* ***charādāya*** *modalāgi* .... *anubhavisi bahiri* ...... ; **tr.** the revenue income, income in gold, wet lands, groves, income from special **tax on moveable properties** etc., from the village of Tagavūra were granted to Sōmayyadēva Voḍeya ; *E.C.* (R) IV, Ko. 11, p. 406, ll. 15–16, 22–23, 25–26 ; Tagarapura, Kollegal Tq., Chamarajanagar Dt., Karn. St. **Dy.** Tuḷuva, Kṛishṇadēvarāya, Ś. 1437 = 1514A.D. ; **text**[2] : ... *Arakalavāḍiya* .... *grāmakke saluva gadde beddalu tōṭa* ...... ***charādāya*** .... *Raṁgarājayyanavaru Terakaṇāṁbiya Varadarājadēvarige koṭṭaru*..... ; **tr.** Raṁgarājayya granted to the god Varadarāja of Terakaṇāṁbi, all revenue **incomes from** the village of Arakalavāḍi such as on wet lands, dry lands, groves and **moveable properties** ; *E.C.* (R) IV, Ch. 301, p. 195, ll. 7–8, 9–10, 12–14 ; Arakalavāḍi, Chamarajanagar Tq. and Dt., Karn. St. **Dy.** Tuḷuva, Sadāśiva, 1477 = 1555 A.D. ; **text**[3] : ...... *śilāparivēshṭitaṁgaḷāgi grāmaṁgaḷa gadde beddalu tōṭa* .... *grāmādāya* ***charādāya*** *horādāya ivu modalādavanu* ... *mahājanaṁgaḷu* ... *anubhavisikoṁḍu baharu* ..... ; **tr.** the *mahājana* (*brāhmaṇa* administrative body) shall enjoy all the revenue incomes from wet lands, dry lands, groves, **revenue income from** villages, demarked by boundaries stones, **tax on moveable properties** and the revenue from the incoming articles ; *E.C.* (R) V, My. 99, p. 222, ll. 410–11, 414, 416, 418 ; Mysore, Mysore Tq. and Dt., Karn. St. **Dy.** Woḍ. of Mys., Dēvarāja, Ś. 1595 = 1674 A.D.

charakkarai (T. *n.*), store keeper ; **text :** (damaged) .... *Dēsinārāyaṇapperumāḷ* .... ***charakkarai*** *paṇam*...... ; **tr.** money (*paṇam*) for the store keeper of the Dēśinārāyaṇapperumāḷ temple ; *E.C.* (R) IV, Ko. 99, p. 468, ll. 10, 13 ; Muḍigoṇḍa, Kollegal Tq., Chamarajanagar Dt., Karn. St. **Misc.**, in characters of 13-14th cent. A.D.

charukuḍumuka (Te. *n.*), a vessel for keeping boiled rice etc., for food offerings to the deity; **text** : .... *Narasiṁhanāthuniki .... **charukuḍumuka.** 3* .. ; **tr.** 3 **vessels for keeping boiled rice for the food offerings to the god** Narasiṁhanātha; *S.I.I.* VI, No. 709, p. 267, ll. 5, 10–11 ; Siṁhāchalam, Vishakhapatnam Tq. and Dt., A.P. St. **Misc.**, Ś. 1338 = 1416 A.D.

chalāvuṇapporuṭchelavōlai (M. *n*), document evidencing the payment of the price ; **text** : .. .... *iduvē vilaiyāvaṇach**chalāvuṇapporuṭchelev-ōlai**yāvidāgavum iśaindu ikkāśu aṟupadum koṇḍu viṟṟu ippaḍi kallilum chembilum veṭṭa-kkaḍavidāguvam* ...... ; **tr.** this shall be the **deed evidencing the payment of sale amount** fixed at the documentary office and it shall be engraved on stone and copper ; *T.A.S.* IV, No. 31, p. 133, ll. 21–22 ; Suchīndram, Agastheeśvaram Tq., Kanyakumari, T. Nadu St. **Dy.** Chōḷa-Pāṇḍya, Jaṭāvarman, reg. yr. 25 = 1043 A.D.

chatra (K. *n.*), free feeding house ; **text**[1] : (damaged) .... *basadige biṭṭa **chatrakke** maneyonduman ā mahājanam.* .... *rakshisuvaru.* .. ; **tr.** the *mahājana* (an administrative body) will take care of the house allotted for the **free feeding house** of the Jaina temple ; *K.I.* V, No. 10, p. 31, ll. 21–22 ; Naragunda, Naragund Tq., Dharwar Dt., Karn. St. **Dy.** Chāḷ. of Kal., Sōmēśvara II, Ś. 996 = 1074 A.D. ; **text**[2] : .... *Jēvurageya* .... *Bīchayyanu krayavaṁ koṁḍu **chatrakke** biḍalu* .... *mattar nālvattu* ; **tr.** Bīchayya paid and bought 40 *mattar* (a land measure) of land for donating it to the **free feeding house** ; *K.I.* II, No. 28, p. 105, ll. 13–14, 16 ; Akkalkōṭ, Akkalkot Tq., Sholapur Dt., Maha. St. **Dy.** Kal. of Kal., Saṅkhamadēva, Ś. 1102 = 1180 A.D.

chaṭṭagey (K. *n.*), land granted for the maintenance of students ; **text** : .... *bhaḷārige matta 6 bhaṭagey matta 6 chaṭṭageyi mattar 6 perggaḍegey matta 8* .... ; **tr.** 6 *matta* (*mattar*, a land measure) of land for the godess, 6 *matta* of land for the teachers maintenance, 6 *matta* of **land for the student's maintenance** and 8 *matta* for the maintenance of the headman (were granted) ; *S.I.I.* IX, pt. i, No. 74, p. 45, ll. 7–8 ; Kaṁchagāra-Belagullu, Alur Tq., Bellary Dt., Karn. St. **Dy.** Chāḷ. of Kal., Āhavamalla, Ś. 903 = 981 A.D.

chattakkūli (M. *n.*), cart charges ; **text** : .... (badly damaged) *niśadam padinkalamāga ēḻunāḷaikku eḻubadim kalam **chattakkūli*** .... ; **tr.** at the rate of 7 *kalam* (grain measure) per day amounting to 70 *kalam* per seven days cart charges included. .... ; *S.I.I.* XIX, No. 194, p. 100, ll. 15–18 ; Vēdāraṇyam, Tirutturaipundi, Tanjavur Tq. and Dt., T. Nadu. St. **Dy.** Chōḷa, Parakēsari-varma, reg. yr. 8 = 985 A.D.

chaṭṭar (T. *n*.), vēdic student ; **text :** (damaged) . . . *paṇimakkaḷ* ***chaṭṭarai*** *piḷaikkappeśuvār oṟu kāśu daṇḍappaḍuvāra* . . ; **tr.** the servants who speak ill of the **vēdic students** will be subjected to a fine of one *kāśu* (a coin) ; *T.A.S.* I, No. 1, p. 9, ll. 7–8 ; Tiruvananthapuram, Tiruvananthapuram Tq. and Dt., Ker. St. **Dy.** Āy, Karunandaḍakkan, reg. yr. 9 = 866 A.D.

chaṭṭavritti (K. *n*.), land given for the maintenance of students ; **text :** (damaged). . . *Kalidēva svāmidēvara* . . . . . *dēgulakkaṁ māṭakkaṁ* ***chaṭṭavritti*** *bālaśikshe initumaṁ naḍeyisuvantāgi* . . . *biṭṭar* . . ; **tr.** (**land**) was **granted** to the temple of Kalidēvasvāmi for the structure of the temple, **for the maintenance of students**, for the education of children, etc.; *S.I.I.* XI, No. 171, p. 220, ll. 87-89; Nāvaḷḷi, Navalgunda Tq., Dharwar Dt., Karn. St. **Dy.** Chāḷ. of Kal., Vikramāditya VI, Ch. Vi. yr. 46 = 1121 A.D.

chaṭṭi, cheṭṭi (T. *n*.), mud pot ; **text[1] :** ***chaṭṭi*** *irubadukkum pēragal nāṟpadukkum śiṟṟagal irubadukkum nellu aiṅguruṇi* . . . ; **tr.** 5 *kuruṇi* (a grain measure) of paddy being the cost of 20 **mudpots**, forty earthern lamps and 20 small earthern lamps ; *S.I.I.* VIII, No. 66, p. 34, l. 10 ; Tiruvaṇṇāmalai, Tiruvannamalai Tq., N. Arcot Dt., T. Nadu St. **Dy.** Chōḷa, Rājēndra, reg. yr. 18 = 1030 A.D. ; **text[2] :** (incomeplete) . . *pāṉai* ***cheṭṭi*** *tirumañjaṉakkuḍam* . . . *ivayum vēṇḍuvaṉa kuraiyvaruttu* . . . . ; **tr.** earthen vessel, **mudpot,** vessel used for bathing the image of the deity etc., in sufficient numbers ; *S.I.I.* VII, No. 470, p. 292, l. 4 ; Achcharapākkam, Madhurantakam Tq., Chingleput Dt., T. Nadu St. **Dy.** Saṅgama, Bukka, Ś. 1298 = 1376 A.D.

chaṭṭichchōṟu (T. *n*.), food kept in earthern pot ; **text :** *Tiruvaṇṇāmalai Uḍaiyār* . . . *Tiruvēṭṭai irundaruḷi irundāl peruntiruvamirdu śeidaruḷavum aḍiyārkku* ***chaṭṭichchōṟu*** *praśādam śeidaruḷavum kuḍuttapoṉ ēḻu kaḷañju* . . . . ; **tr.** seven *kaḷañju* of gold coin was given for food offerings to the god Tiruvaṇṇāmalai Uḍaiyār when He goes for hunting expedition and for the supply of **food kept in earthern pots** to be supplied to the devotees ; *S.I.I.* VIII, No. 66, p. 34, l. 7 ; Tiruvaṇṇāmalai, Tiruvannamalai Tq., N. Arcot Dt., T. Nadu St. **Dy.** Chōḷa, Rājēndra, reg. yr. 18 = 1030 A.D.

chaṭṭōpādhyāya (K. < Skt. *prn*.), a surname (literally meaning teacher of students) ; **text :** *mahāgrāmaṁ Piriyakereyūra* . . . . *Vasudēva* ***chaṭṭōpādhyā****yar* . . . . . . ; **tr.** Vāsudēva chaṭṭōpādhyāya of Piriyakereyūru, a great village ; *K.I.* IV, No. 32, p. 72, l. 14 ; Bāḷaṁbīḍ, Hirekerur Tq., Dharwar Dt., Karn. St. **Dy.** Chāḷ. of Kal., Vikramāditya VI, Ch. Vi. yr. 12 = 1088 A.D.

chatuḥsainya (K. *n*.), four wings of an army ; **text:** . . . . *raṇadoḷ teṁkaṇa rāyanaṁkada* ***chatuḥsainy****ōtkaraṁ* . . . ; **tr.** who exterminated the warriors of the **four wings of the army** of the southern ruler in the battle ; *E.C.* XI, Dvg. 25, p. 86, l. 56 ; Harihara, Harihara Tq., Davanagere Dt., Karn. St. **Dy.** Hoy., Narasiṁha, Ś. 1145 = 1225 A.D.

chaturāghāṭa (K. < Skt. *n.*), four boundaries ; **text :** ..... *Bhāskarāchāryara pādaprakshāḷanaṁ geydu dānasvarūpavāgi ... koṭṭa mattarāṟu adakke* ***chaturāghāṭa*** *veṁteṁdaḍe* . . . ; **tr.** 5 *mattar* (land measure) of land given in the form of donation to Bhāskarāchārya after laving his feet; the details of the **four boundaries** of the land (details follow) ; *S.I.I.* XV, No. 220, p. 268, ll. 32–34 ; Muḷugunda, Gadag Tq. and Dt., Karn. St. **Dy.** Hoy., Ballāḷa II, Ś. 1128 = 1207 A.D.

chaturanga bala (K. < Skt. *n.*), traditional four divisions of the army ; **text :** .... *Tauḷa vaṁśābdhichandra ..... sakalalōka rakshakaṁ . . . . ati bahaḷa* ***chaturaṅgabala*** *samōpētam . . . Kṛishṇarāyamahārāyar* ; **tr.** Kṛishṇarāyamahārāya who was a like a moon raisen in the sea of Tauḷa family who was the protector of all the world and who was possessed of the **traditional four divisions of the army** ; *S.I.I.* IX, pt. ii, No. 507, p. 520, ll. 3, 9–10, 15 ; Chōḷasamudram, Hindupur Tq., Anantapur Dt., A.P. St. **Dy.** Tuḷuva, Kṛishṇadēvarāya, Ś. 1439 = 1517 A.D.

chaturasra (K. < Skt. *adj.*), with four boundaries; **text :** ..... *aṟavaṁṭageya udakadānakkaṁ . . . . . . biṭṭa . . .* ***chaturasra*** *Kōgaḷiya gaḍiṁbadalu mattaru 1 . . .* ; **tr.** 1 *mattar* (land measure) of land **with four boundaries** measured by the measuring rod called *gaḍiṁba* of Kōgaḷi was donated for the road side shed for free distribution of water and buttermilk to travellers ; *S.I.I.* IX, pt. i, No. 332, p. 352, ll. 30, 34–35 ; Muttagi, Harapanahalli Tq., Bellary Dt., Karn. St. **Dy.** Hoy., Ballāḷa II, Ś. 1136 = 1213 A.D.

chaturāśraya (K. < Skt. *n.*), four boundaries ; **text :** ..... *Kapilasiddha Mallēśvaradēvara kshētrada* ***chaturāśrayada*** *nālkuṁ dese* .. ; **tr.** four sides of the **four boundaries** of the field belonging to Kapilasiddha Mallēśvaradēva ; *E.I.* XXIII, No. 30, p. 195, ll. 47–48 ; Saṅgūr, Haveri Tq. and Dt., Karn. St. **Dy.** Sēü of Dēv., Mahādēva, Ś. 1186 = 1265 A.D.

chaturbhāga (K. < Skt. *n.*), one fourth share ; **text :** ..... *dharmakartake baha* ***chāturbhāgakke*** *uṁṭāda prasādavanu . . . brāhmarige sattravāgi ikki bahudu* .... ; **tr.** the **one fourth share** of the offerings alloted to the trusty shall be distributed free among the brāhmaṇas . . . ; *S.I.I.* IX, pt. ii, No. 551, p. 572, l. 7 ; Kāḷahasti, Chandragiri Tq., Chittoor Dt., Karn. St. **Dy.** Tuḷuva, Achyutarāya, Ś. 1484 = 1562 A.D.

chaturdaśa vidyā (K. < Skt. *n.*), fourteen traditional branches of knowledge ; **text :** ..... *mahāgrahāraṁ Māṁgoḷadūroḍeya pramukha mahājanavinnūrvar* ***chaturdaśa vidyā*** *pāragar āśritajana kalpadrumar* ... .. ; **tr.** two hundred *mahājana* (a brāhmaṇa administrative body) including the head of the village of the great brāhmaṇa settlement Māṁgoḷa, who were experts in the **fourteen traditional branches of knowledge** and were like the wish-fulfilling tree for people who seek their help ; *S.I.I.* IX, pt. i, No. 195, p. 190, ll. 15–19 ; Rangapura, Hadagalli Tq., Bellary Dt., Karn. St. **Dy.** Chāḷ. of Kal., Vikramāditya VI, Ch. Vi. yr. 41 = 1116 A.D.

chaturthāṁśa (K. < Skt. *n.*), one-fourth portion ; **text :** ..... *ī grāmada **chaturthāṁśa**vanū koṁḍu Dīkshitaru muṁtāda 4 nālku bage avarindalū ... . Sōmayājigaḷige sallisi koṭṭu* .. ; **tr.** one-fourth portion of this village bought from Dikshitar and others and was donated to Sōmayāji ; *S.I.I.* IX, pt. ii, No. 587, p. 602, ll. 15, 17, 18, 23 ; Lēpākshi, Hindupur Tq., Anantapur Dt., A.P. St. **Dy.** Tuḷuva, Achyutarāya, Ś. 1460 = 1538 A.D.

chaturvēdi maṁgaḷa (K. < Skt. *n.*), brāhmaṇa settlement ; **text[1] :** .... *Gaṇḍarāditya **chaturvēdi maṁgaḷa**da nūṟaṁippadiṁbaruṁ alliya telligaraivattokkaluṁ muṁmuridaṁḍamuṁ*.... ; **tr.** one hundred and twenty *mahājana* (administrative body) of the **brāhmaṇa settlement** named after the chōḷa king Gaṇḍarāditya and all the fifty oil mongers of that place and the trade guild called *mumuridaṇḍa* etc. ; *S.I.I.* IX, pt. i, No. 139., p. 122, ll. 33–35 ; Hoḷalu, Hadagalli Tq., Bellary Dt., Karn. St. **Dy.** Chāḷ. of Kal., Sōmēśvara II, Ś. 996 = 1074 A.D. ; **text[2] :** (T. < Skt. *n.*), ... *Tribhuvanamādēvich **chaturvēdimaṅgala**ttu Tirumēṟkōylilāṉa .... Vaṇḍuvarai Perumāḷukku tiruviḍaiyaṭṭam kīḻkaṟaikaḷani kuḻi ... 1100* ... ; **tr.** 1100 *kuḻi* (land measure) of land granted to the Vaishṇava shrine of Vaṇḍuvaṟai pperumāḷ in the temple of Tirumēṟkōyil ; *E.C.* (R) IV, Ko. 4, p. 399, ll. 4–11 ; Koḷḷēgāla, Kollegal Tq., Chamarajanagar Dt., Karn. St. **Dy.** Hoy., Narasiṁha, Cy. yr. Tāraṇa = 1224 A.D.

chatussīme, chatusīme (K. < Skt. *n.*), four boundaries ; **text[1] :** .... *Nāraṇaseṭṭige koṭṭa mūla śāsanada kramaveṁteṁdare ... Koṁgāḷiya beṭina bayalina **chatussīme**ya vivara* ...... ; **tr.** the details of the **four boundaries** as detailed in this inscription of the elevated land at Koṁgāḷi given as a permanent grant to Nāraṇaseṭṭi ; *S.I.I.* IX, pt. ii, No. 449., p. 458, ll. 9–10 ; Basarūru, Kundapur Tq., Udupi Tq. and Dt., Karn. St. **Dy.** Saṅgama, Dēvarāya, Ś. 1366 = 1444 A.D. ; **text[2] :** ***chatusīme**gaḷige Vāmanamudreya kallugaḷanū naḍisikoṭṭevu* .. ; **tr.** we set up stone slabs with the figure Vāmana etched to mark the four boundaries ; *E.C.* VIII, Tīr. 190, p. 688, l. 28; Mahishi, Teerthahalli Tq., Shimoga Dt., Karn. St. **Dy.** Saṅgama, Dēvaraāya, Ś. 1327 = 1405 A.D.

chatussīmāghāṭa (K. < Skt. *n.*), area with specified boundaries on all four sides ; **text :** . .... *Kaḍalevāḍada **chatussīmāghāṭa** jalapāshāṇa sahitamāgi .... Sōvarāsipaṁḍitadēvargge koṭṭaru* ... ; **tr.** whole **area** of Kaḍalevāḍa was granted to Sōmarāsipaṁḍitadēva **with specified boundaries**

on all four sides ; *S.I.I.* XX, No. 158, pp. 201–202, ll. 42, 47–48 ; Kaḍalēvāḍ, Sindhagi Tq., Vijapur Dt., Karn. St. **Dy.** Kal. of Kal., Sōvidēva, Ś. 1097 = 1176 A.D.

chāvaḍi (K. < Skt. *n.*), place where the village assembly meets ; **text**[1] : . . . . *iṁnṳ̄ra eṁṭūvare hoṁnnanu Bārakūra* ***chāvaḍi****ya vahige tegesi ī dharmake . . . . dēvasvavāgi koṭṭevu . . . . .* ; **tr.** we gave as a gift to a temple two hundred eight and a half gold coins after entering the details in the ledger of the place where the assembly meets in Bārakūru ; *S.I.I.* IX, pt. ii, No. 451, p. 461, ll. 16–17 ; Kōṭēśvara, Kundapur Tq., Udupi Dt., Karn. St. **Dy.** Saṅgama, Dēvarāya, Ś. 1369 = 1447 A.D.; **text**[2] : . . . . *Terakaṇāṁbeya* ***chāvaḍi****ge chikkapārupatyagā̤raru . . . .* ; **tr.** the junior overseer of the **place where the village assembly meets** in Terakaṇāṁbe ; *E.C.* (R) III, Gu. 119, p. 89, ll. 14–15 ; Terakaṇāṁbi, Gundlupete Tq., Mysore Dt., Karn. St. **Dy.** Tuḷuva, Kṛishṇadēvarāya, Ś. 1442 = 1521 A.D. ; **text**[3] (M. *n.*), (obscure) . . . *ambalattil . . . . . .* ***chāvaḍi****yum keṭṭi . . . .* ; **tr.** having built the **place where the assembly meets** (in the vicinity of) public hall ; *T.A.S.* V, No. 25, p. 88, ll. 96, 98–99 ; Tiruvidāṅgōḍu, Ker. St. **Misc.**, Kollam 864 = 1688 A.D.

chaudhore (K. *n.*), officer of an administrative division ; **text** : . . . . *nāḍa maṁneyaruṁ* ***chaudhore****gaḷuṁ prabhu gāvuṇḍagaḷuṁ iḻdu koṭṭar . . . . dharmamaṁ* ; **tr.** the feudal lords of the territorial division, **officers in charge of administrative division**, the chiefs and headmen together made the donation ; *S.I.I.* IX, pt. i, No. 172, p. 167, ll. 35–36, 37 ; Karakaṁṭapura, Adavani Tq., Kurnool Dt., A.P. St. **Dy.** Chāḷ. of Kal., Vikramāditya VI, Ch. Vi. yr. 31 = 1106 A.D.

chaushashṭi kaḷā (Te. *n.*), sixty four arts ; **text** : . . . . ***chaushashṭi kaḷā****nvita vasumatī gīrvāṇar* ; **tr.** highly learned men on earth who were very proficient in the **sixty four arts** ; *S.I.I.* VII, No. 723, p. 364, l. 25 ; Sēḍam, Sedam Tq., Gulbarga Dt., Karn. St. **Dy.** Chāḷ. of Kal., Vikramāditya VI, Ch. Vi. yr. 48 = 1123 A.D.

chaushashṭi vidyā (K. *n.*), sixty four branches of knowledge ; **text** : . . . ***chaushashṭi vidyā*** *pravīṇarāda vidvajjanārādharāda Gōvindayya Kēśavayya . . . . Basavayya Dakshiṇāmūrti Suṁkada Vallabhayya . . . . jana aivaru . . . .* ; **tr.** five persons viz., Goviṁdayya, Kēśavayya, Basavayya, Dakshiṇāmūrti and Vallabhayya the tax collector who were highly proficient in **sixty four branches of knowledge** and were refuge to scholars ; *S.I.I.* IX, pt. ii, No. 652, p. 647, ll. 9–11 ; Rāguḷapāḍu, Gooty Tq., Anantapur Dt., A.P. St. **Dy.** Tuḷuva, Sadāśiva, Ś. 1476 = 1554 A.D.

chauvala (K. *n.*), fraction of a coin ; **text** : . . . . *mataru 30 ā mūvatta̤roḷage ippattanālkakaṁ aruvaṇa matarige* ***chauvala*** ; **tr.** 30 *matar* (*mattar*, a land measure) of land ; out of the 30 *matars*, 24 were subjected to a collection of tax on ploughs in the form a fraction of a coin called *chauvala* ; *S.I.I.* XI, No. 68, p. 59, l. 13 ; Tammadahaḍḍi, Muddebihal Tq., Bijapur Dt., Karn. St. **Dy.** Chāḷ. of Kal., Jayasiṁha II, in characters of 11th cent. 1033 A.D.

chavaradava (K. *n.*), barber ; **text :** . . . *Yareyūra gaddeyalli* . . . . ***chavaradava**rige 1 khaṁḍuga gāreyavarige 1 khaṁḍuga hūvāḍigarige 1 khaṁḍuga* . . . ; **tr.** from the wet lands of Yareyūru 1 *khaṁḍuga* (a land measure) for the barber, 1 *khaṁḍuga* for the mason and 1 *khaṁḍuga* for the florist were earmarked ; *E.C.* (R) IV, Yl. 1, p. 272, ll. 74–77 ; Yaḷandūru, Yalandur Tq., Chamarajanagar Dt., Karn. St. **Dy.** Hadināḍu Chfs., Muddabhūpa, Ś. 1576 = 1654 A.D.

chāvupila (M. *n.*), defilement on death ; **text :** . . . . ***chāvupila** uoṇḍāyāl 16 nāḷ anṟu Muttanayaṉār pilakūri uṉṉumāṟu* . . . ; **tr.** if any defilement on death occurs the Muttanayaṉār shall for 16 days mention the same and obtain the customary food ; *T.A.S.* IV, No. 42, p. 150, ll. 23–27 ; Chitarāl, Vilavangod Tq., Padmanabhapuram Dt., Ker. St. **Misc.**, Kollam 540 = 1364 A.D.

chaluvānaprajegaḷu (K. *n.*), commoners ; **text :** . . . . *Prasanna Sōmaśēkhasvāmiyavarige* . . . *Aṁkanahaḷḷi Hosūru sthaḷakke saluva grāmagaḷa gavuḍa prajegaḷu brāhmaṇaru seṭṭigaḷu pūjārigaḷu māṁnyagāraru kavadadavaru **chaluvāna prajegaḷu** muṁtāgi tamma sēvārthavāgi koṭṭa vivara* . . . ; **tr.** the village officials, brāhmaṇas, merchants, temple priests, holders of tax free grants, mechanics, commoners and others of the villages belonging to Aṁkanahaḷḷi and Hosūru sthaḷa made grants to the god Prasanna Sōmaśēkhara ; *E.C.* IV, Ch. 218, p. 133, ll. 7, 8–10 ; Hosūru, Chamarajanagar Tq. and Dt., Karn. St. **Dy.** Woḍ. of Mys., Kṛishṇarāja voḍeya, Ś. 1680 = 1759 A.D.

chēdiya (K. < Pkt. *n.*), Jaina temple ; **text :** . . . . *Jēbuḷagērige Kaliyammagāmuṇḍugeydī **chēdiya**mān māḍisidān* . . . . . . ; **tr.** While Kaliyamma was holding the office of headmanship of Jēbuḷagēri, he got this **Jaina temple** constructed; *S.I.I.* XI, No. 5, p. 3, ll. 6–9 ; Aṇṇigēri, Navalgunda Tq., Dharwar Dt., Karn. St. **Dy.** Chal. of Bād., Kīrtivarmman, reg. yr. 6 = 750 A.D.

chekkālai (T. *n.*), oil mill ; **text :** (damaged) . . . . . . *Tiruviḍaimarudil **chekkālai**chchēri iṟubadin kaḻañju poṉ kuḍuttoōm* . . . . . ; **tr.** the residents of the street with the **oil mills** have given twenty *kaḻañju* (a gold coin) of gold ; *S.I.I.* XIX, No. 92, p. 47, l. 5 ; Tirumalai, Polur Tq., N. Arcot Dt., T. Nadu St. **Dy.** Chōḻa, Parāntaka I, reg. yr. 4 = 911 A.D.

chekkār (T. *n.*), oil mongers ; **text :** . . . . ***chekkār**kkum ivargaḷ anusārattuḷḷārkkum irubadu manai* . . . . . . ; **tr.** twenty houses were given to the oil mongers and their dependants ; *S.I.I.* XVII, No. 588, p. 255, ll. 3–4 ; Tiruvārūr, Nagapattinam Tq., Tanjavur Dt., T. Nadu St. **Dy.** Chōḻa, Rājādhirāja II, reg. yr. 5 = 1167 A.D.

chekkiṟai (T. *n.*), tax on oil mills ; **text :** . . . *chekkiṟai* . . . . . . *taṭṭāṉppāṭṭam* . . . . . *maṟṟum eppērpaṭṭa varivugaḷum viṭṭa* . . . . . ; **tr.** all taxes including the **tax on oil mills**, tax on goldsmiths were gifted ; *E.C.* X, Bow. 68 b, p. 92, ll. 7–8, 10–11 ; Yalavahaḷḷi, Bowringpet Tq., Kolar Dt., Karn. St., **Misc.**, in characters of the 14th cent. A.D.

chekku (T. *n.*), oil mill ; **text**[1] **:** . . . *turavu kiṇaṟu iḻittapperuvadāgavum peruñ***chekku** *iḍappeṟuvadu āguvam* . . ; **tr.** the big irrigation tank has got to be dug and the big **oil mill** has to be established; *S.I.I.* II, pts. iii and iv, No. 98, p. 509, ll. 60–61 ; Vēlūrpāḷaiyam, Arakonam Tq., N. Arcot Dt., T. Nadu St. **Dy.** Pallava, Nandivarman II, reg. yr. 6 = 735 A.D. ; **text**[2] **:** (incomplete) . . . . . *Mādēvarkku dēvadānamāga tirunandāviḷakkukku* ***chekkoṉṟum*** . . . . . . ; **tr.** one **oil mill** for burning the perpetual lamp as a gift to the temple of Mahādēva ; *E.C.* X, Sdl. 84, p. 117, ll. 27–29 ; Chiḷakalamērperu, Sidlaghatta Tq., Kolar Dt., Karn. St. **Dy.** Chōḷa, Kulōttuṅga I, reg. yr. 3 = 1053 A.D.

chekkukkaḍamai (T. *n.*), tax on oil mills ; **text:** . . . *Āvattukāttaruliya nayiṉār* . . . . *vāśal paṇam veṭṭivary* . . . ***chekkukkaḍamai*** . . . *utpaṭṭa pala varigaḷum* . . . . . . *anubhavittukkoḷḷavum.* . . . . . ; **tr.** the god Āvattukāttaruḷiya nayiṉār shall enjoy (many gifts are mentioned) tax incomes such as house tax, tax on free labour, **tax on oil mills** and all such various tax incomes ; *S.I.I.* VIII, No. 349, p. 188, ll. 1, 3 ; Śēndamaṅgalam, Tindivanam Tq., S. Arcot Dt., T. Nadu St. **Dy.** Saṅgama, Dēvarāya II, Ś. 1352 = 1429 A.D.

cheliviṁdramānya (Te. *n.*), tax free land with facility for irrigation during summer ; **text :** . . . . . . *Vēmula Rāghavayyaṁgāru* . . . . *Tammaḷa Vīrayyaku* . . . . . *reṁḍu kuchcheḷḷu kshētraṁ* ***cheliviṁdramānyaṁ****gānu* . . . . *yistimi ganuka anubhaviṁchi bratikēdi* . . . ; **tr.** Vēmula Rāghavayya donated **tax free land with facility for irrigation during summer** to TammaḷaVīrayya so that he can enjoy the same for his subsistence ; *S.I.I.* XVI, No. 288, p. 293, ll. 21, 25, 31–32, 35–36 ; Koṇḍēpāḍu, Guntur Tq. and Dt., A.P. St. **Dy.** Āravīḍu, Śrīraṅga I, Ś. 1498 = 1576 A.D.

cheluvāna hēru (K. *n.*), load of sundry items ; **text :** . . . . ***cheluvāna hērina*** *vartakara vappita* . . . . . ; **tr.** the signature of approval of the merchants selling loads of sundry items ; *E.C.* (R) IV, Ch. 250, p. 154, ll. 42–43 ; Veṅkaṭayyanachchatra, Chamarajanagara Tq. and Dt., Karn. St. **Comm. gld.**, Ś. 1655 = 1733 A.D.

cheṁbina patra (K. *n.*), copper plate charter ; **text :** . . . . *Kārakaḷada aydusāvira halara maṭadalli makkaḷa ōdisuvātana svāsthege kshētradalli koṭṭaru ā kshētrada vivaravanu* ***cheṁbina patra****dalli nōḍikaṁbudu* . . . . . ; **tr.** land was given as property to the person teaching children by the five thousand *halaru* (an administratrive body); the details of the land given may be verified from the **copper plate charter** ; *S.I.I.* VII, No.

243, p. 121, ll. 8–11 ; Hiriyangaḍi, Karkala Tq., Udupi Dt., Karn. St. **Misc.,** Ś. 1501 = 1579 A.D.

cheṁbu[1] (T. *n.*), copper vessel ; **text**[1] **:** (damaged). . . . *cheṁbiṉāl taḷigai* . . . . ; **tr.** items cooked in **copper vessel** ; *S.I.I.* XXII, pt. i, No. 187, p. 151, ll. 9–10 ; Grāmam, Tirukkoyilur Tq., S. Arcot Dt., T. Nadu St. **Dy.** Chōḷa, Parāntaka I, reg. yr. 31 = 938 A.D.

cheṁbu[2] (K. *n.*), pinacle on the temple tower ; **text :** . . . . *ī hoṁnu Mahādēvara* ***cheṁbi****na oḍila honna kaḷaśake māḍida dharma*. . . . . . . ; **tr.** this gold granted to the god Mahādēva is meant for the gold plating of the **pinacle on the temple of the tower** ; *S.I.I.* IX, pt. ii, No. 450., p. 460, ll. 21–22; Basarūru, Kundapur Tq., Udupi Dt., Karn. St. **Dy.** Saṅgama, Dēvarāya, Ś. 1366 = 1444 A.D.

cheṁbu[3] (T. *n.*), copper sheet ; **text :** . . . . *ippaḍikku* ***chembi****lum kallilum veṭṭikkoḷga* . . . . . ; **tr.** you may thus get (the details of) the grant engraved on **copper sheet** as well as stone ; *S.I.I.* VIII, No. 245, p. 136, ll. 18–19 ; Tirumiyachchūr, Nannilam Tq., Tanjavur Dt., T. Nadu St. **Dy.** Pāṇḍya, Sundara Pāṇḍya, reg. yr. 4, in characters of 13th cent. A.D.

chemmāra (K. *n.*), cobbler ; **text :** (damaged) . . . . . *teṁkalu keḷagaṇa Mallagaddeyim baha* ***cheṁmāra****ra ōṇiyim mū* . . . ; **tr.** in the south to the east of the **cobbler's** lane deviating from the wet land of Malla at a lower level ; *S.I.I.* IX, pt. ii, No. 465, p. 478, l. 9 ; Basarūru, Kundapur Tq., Udupi Dt., Karn. St. **Dy.** Saṅgama, Virūpāksha, Ś. 1395 = 1472 A.D.

cheṁta (Te. *n.*), the adjoining site of a place ; **text :** (incomplete) . . . *cheṟupiḷavāri* ***cheṁta*** *kha 1* . . . . . ; **tr.** 1 *kha* (*khaṁḍuga*, a land measure) of land belonging to the Cheṟupiḷavāru is **the adjoining site** (of the land in question) ; *S.I.I.* X, No. 510, p. 278, ll. 21 ; Mōgallu, Bhimavaram Tq., W. Godavari Dt., A.P. St. **Dy.** Pōti chfs., Pedapōti Reḍḍi, Ś. 1237 = 1315 A.D.

chennel (M. *n.*), quality paddy ; **text :** (damaged) . . . . ***chennel*** *muppattaṟu kalam* . . . ; **tr.** thirty six *kalam* (a grain measure) of quality paddy ; *T.A.S.* V, pt. i, No. 13, p. 45, ll. 82–83 ; Kollam, Kollam Tq and Dt., Ker. St. **Dy.** Chēra, Irāmar-tiruvaḍi kōyiladhikārigaḷ, Kollam 278 = 1103 A.D.

chennīrpoduviṉai (T. *n.*), free labour for maintaining irrigation canal ; **text :** *innilañchuṭṭi* ***chennīrpoduviṉai*** *śeyyādadāguvum* . . . . ; **tr.** for this land there should be no **free labour for the maintenance of the irrigational canal** ; *S.I.I.* XVII, No. 643, p. 296, l. 6 ; Śrīnivāsanallūr, Musiri Tq., Tiruchirapalli Dt., T. Nadu St. **Dy.** Chōḷa, Parāntaka I, reg. yr. 20 = 926–27 A.D.

chēnu (Te. *n.*), cultivable land ; **text :** . . . . *pushpālatōtaku na 2 nē varipolamuku 2 nē verasi na 4* ***chēnu*** . . ; **tr.** 4 *na* (*nakara*, a land measure) of **cultivable land,** 2 *na* for flower 2 *na* of paddy field ; *S.I.I.* XVI, No. 8, p. 8, ll. 9–10; Tripurāntakam, Markapur Tq., Kurnool Dt., A.P.

St. **Dy.** Saṅgama, Harihara II, Ś. 1308 = 1386 A.D.

cheppēḍu (T. *n.*), copper plate ; **text :** . . . . *ippaḍikku* ***cheppēḍilum*** *kallilum eḻuttu veṭṭikoṇḍu aruḷa kaḍavārgaḷāgavum* . . . . . ; **tr.** thus will (the details of the record) be engraved on **copper plate** and stone as a favour ; *S.I.I.* VIII, No. 227, p. 122, l. 20 ; Tiruvalañjuḻi, Kumbhakonam Tq., Tanjavur Dt., T. Nadu St. **Dy.** Chōḷa, Rājādhirāja II, reg. yr. 8 = 1170 A.D.

cheppu nāḻi (T. *n.*), grain measure made of copper ; **text :** (incomplete). . . *nilam 30 māvuṅgoṇḍu nittam* ***cheppu nāḻi****yāl iru nāḻi ariśi* . . . *Tiruvēngaḍattāḻvārkku* . . . . . ; **tr.** 30 *mā* (a land measure) of land was bought for supplying 2 *nāḻi* (a grain measure) of rice measured by the **grain measure made of copper** to the god Tiruvēṅgaḍattāḻvār ; *T.A.S.* IV, No. 6, p. 21, ll. 5–6 ; Suchīndram, Agasteesvaram Tq., Kanyakumari Dt., T. Nadu St. **Dy.** Rulers of Vēṇāḍu, Kōdai Kēraḷavarman, Kollam 325+1 = 1151 A.D.

cheppu pattiram (T. *n.*), copper plate document; **text :** . . . . *evvagaipaṭṭa iṟaiyum Terisāppaḷḷiyārkku viḍupērāgach****cheppuppattirañ****cheydaṭṭi kuḍuttēṉ* . . . . . ; **tr.** I have given as part of the grants made in kind and privileges, every kind of tax to the people of Terisāppaḷḷi as registered in the **copper plate document** ; *T.A.S.* II, No. 9, p. 68, ll. 13–14; Kōṭṭayam, Kottayam Tq. and Dt., Ker. St. **Dy.** Chēra, Sthāṇu Ravi, reg. yr. 5, in characters of 10th century A.D.

chēri (T. *n.*), street, ward ; **text**[1] **:** . . . . *śrī bhuvana chūḷāmaṇich****chēri*** . . . . . ; **tr. street** named śrībhuvanachūḷāmaṇi ; *S.I.I.* XIII, No. 249, p. 132, l. 4 ; Uḍaiyārguḍi, Chidambaram Tq., S. Arcot Dt., T. Nadu St. **Dy.** Chōḷa, Rājakēsarivarman, reg. yr. 14 = 969 A.D. ; **text**[2] **:** . . . . *Kachchippēṭṭu Kambuḻaṉpāḍiyum Adimāṉappāḍiyum ivv iraṇḍu* ***chēri****yum* . . . . ; **tr.** the two **wards** Kambuḻaṉpāḍi and Adimāṉappāḍi of Kachchippēḍu ; *S.I.I.* III, No. 128, p. 269, l. 24 ; Madras Museum, Madras Tq. and Dt., T. Nadu St. **Dy.** Chōḷa, Uttamachōḷa, reg. yr. 16 = 987 A.D.

cheṟuvu[1] (T. *n.*), plot of land ; **text**[1] **:** . . . . *biramadēyamāyina aṟubadu* ***cheṟuvu****kkukkiḻakkum* . . . . ; **tr.** to the east of the sixty **plots of land** belonging to the *brāhmadēya* (brāhmaṇa settlement) ; *S.I.I.* II, No. 98, p. 516 (tamil portion); Bāhūr, Pondichery Tq. and Dt., T. Nadu St. **Dy.** Pallava, Nrupatuṅga, reg. yr. 8 = 854 A.D. ; **text**[2] **:** (damaged) . . . . *śeṟai eṉṟu pērkūvappaḍum nilam* ***cheṟuvu*** *aiñjum* . . . . ; **tr.** five **plots of land** called by the name of . . . . śeṟai ; *S.I.I.* XXII, No. 185, p. 150, l. 6 ; Grāmam, Tirukkoyilur Tq., S. Arcot Dt., T. Nadu St. **Dy.** Chōḷa, Parāntaka I, reg. yr. 35 = 942 A.D. ; **text**[3] **:** . . . *vaḍapāṟkellai Kōvaṉ* ***cheṟuvuṁ*** *Karuṇākaraṉ* ***cheṟuvuṁ*** . . . ; **tr.** the northern boundaries are the **plot of land** belonging to Kōvaṉ and the **plot of land** belonging to Karuṇākaraṉ ; *S.I.I.*

VII, No. 96, p. 39, l. 8 ; Tiruvottūr, Cheyyar Tq., N. Arcot Dt., T. Nadu St. **Dy.** Chōḷa, Vikramachōḷa, reg. yr. 6 = 1124 A.D.

cheṟuvu[2] (K. *n.*), tank ; **text**[1] : .... *Kūlichchēvagaṉ paṟṟum* .... ***cheṟuvum*** ... ; **tr.** the land of the servant on wages and the **tank** ; *E.C.* X, Kol. 120, p. 30, l. 2 ; Kolar, Kolar Tq. and Dt., Karn. St. **Dy.** Chōḷa, Uttamachōḷa Vīragaṅgaṉ, Ś. 1100 = 1178. A.D. ; **text**[2] (Te. *n.*), : ... *paḍumaṭi pedda* ***cheṟuvu*** *kaṭṭa mīdanu*.... ; **tr.** on the land of the big **tank** in the west ; *I.A.P. Cuddapah* II, No. 34, p. 39, ll. 13–14 ; Pendlimarri, Kadapa Tq. and Dt., A.P. St. **Dy.** Saṅgama, Dēvarāya I, Ś. 1334 = 1413 A.D. ; **text**[3] : ... *polamulōṁgala kāluvalu* ***cheruvulu*** *bāvulu kāḍāraṁbha sahā* .... *ādāyamu ēmi galaviṁnni* .... *Rāmayadēvuniki samarpistimi* .... ; **tr.** we granted to god Ramayadēva, lands, income from canals, **tanks**, wells, reclaimed forest lands, etc. ; *S.I.I.* XVI, No. 38, p. 41, ll. 24–29 ; Rāmāpuram, Gooty Tq., Anantapur Dt., A.P. St. **Dy.** Sāḷuva, Narasiṁha II, Ś. 1419 = 1497 A.D.

cheṟvukaṭṭukavulu (Te. *n.*), agreement for renovation of an irrigation tank ; **text** : .... *Bālayamodali nānānāyakulku ichchina* ***cheruvukaṭṭakāvalu***.... ; **tr.** the terms of **agreement** given by Balaya to a number of nāyakas **for the renovation of the irrigation tank** ; *S.I.I.* X, No. 771, p. 405, l. 7 ; Basinikoṇḍa, Madanapalle Tq., Chittor Dt., A.P. St. **Misc.**, Ś. 1614 = 1692 A.D.

chētulu (Te. *n.*), a measure of length ; **text** : (damaged) ... *nūṁṭa muppayi* ***chētulu*** ... ; **tr.** one hundred thirty **chētulu** (a measure of length, in present day terms a length of 24 inches) of land ; *S.I.I.* IV, No. 276, p. 71, l. 2 ; Hampi, Hospet Tq., Bellary Dt., Karn. St. **Dy.** Kōnēti chfs., Śrīraṁgayyadēva, in characters of 15th cent. A.D.

chettalnīkku (T. *vb.*), to remove husk ; **text** : ..... *poṉ aṟubadiṉ kaḷañjukkum* .... *nel* .. *Tirumālpēṟuḍaiyār kōyilil* ... *koḍuvandu puḻudiyum* ***chettal****um nīkkii tūyavākki* .... ; **tr.** buying paddy for 60 *kaḷañju* (gold coin) of gold, transporting it to the hall of the temple of Tirumālpēṟuḍaiyār and purifying the paddy by **removing** dust and **husk** ; *S.I.I.* XXII, pt. i., No. 281, p. 222, ll. 22–26 ; Tirumālpuram, Walajapet Tq., N. Arcot Dt., T. Nadu St. **Dy.** Chōḷa, Rājarāja I, reg. yr. 12 = 996-97 A.D.

cheṭṭi (T. < Skt. *śrēshṭhin, n.*), merchant ; **text** : .. *paḍaivīṭṭil irukkum* ***cheṭṭi****gaḷil* ... *vaṇigar Aḻagapperumāḷ* .... ; **tr.** the trader Aḻagapperumāḷ, one among the merchants in the army camp ; *S.I.I.* VIII, No. 161, p. 73, l. 3 ; Tiruvaṇṇāmalai, Trivunnamalai Tq., N. Arcot Dt., T. Nadu St. **Dy.** Saṅgama, Mallikārjuna, Ś. 1375 = 1457 A.D.

cheṭṭigaḷ vāṇigar pērkaḍamai (T. *n.*), tax levied on traders and merchants ; **text** : .. *taṟi iṟai taṭṭārpāṭṭaṁ* .... *podumakkaḷ pērkaḍamai* ***cheṭṭigaḷ vāṇigar pērkaḍamai***.... *maṟṟum eppērapaṭṭa* . .... *varigaḷum uṭpaḍa* ... *iṟayiliyāga kuḍuttēṉ* ; **tr.** I gave as a tax free gift revenue incomes from handlooms, tax on goldsmiths, tax on the public and **tax on merchants and traders** as well as all other tax incomes ; *S.I.I.* VII, No. 107, p. 45, ll. 17–20 ; Tiruvattūr, Cheyyar Tq., N. Arcot Dt., T. Nadu St. **Dy.** Pāṇḍya, Sundarapāṇḍya, reg. yr. 12, in characters of 12th centurty A.D.

cheṭṭiputtiraṉ (T. *n.*), one group belonging to the 500 guilds ; **text :** . . . *samaiyattaṉmai iṉidu naḍādirikiṉṟa cheṭṭiyum* ***cheṭṭiputtiraṉum*** *gavaṟaiyum* . . . ; **tr.** the merchants, **the group belonging to the 500 commercial guilds** and the *gavaṟai* (a comm. gld.) who had properly observed the code of ethics ; *Āvaṇam* II, No. 3, p. 7, ll. 10–12 ; (now deposited in Tirumalaināyaka Mahalal) Madurai, Madurai Tq. and Dt., T. Nadu St. **Dy.** Chōḷa-Pāṇḍya, Vikrama, reg. yr. 26, in characters of 11th century A.D.

cheṭṭiṟai (T. *n.*), tax levied on merchants ; **text :** . . . ***cheṭṭiṟai*** *maṉai iṟai chekkiṟai taṟi iṟai taṭṭārpāṭṭam* . . . ; **tr.** tax on merchants, house tax, tax on oil mills, tax on handlooms, tax on gold smiths ; *S.I.I.* VIII, No. 313, p. 170, ll. 8–9 ; Tiruvadi, Cuddalore Tq., S. Arcot Dt., T. Nadu St. **Misc.** in characters of 11-12th century A.D.

cheṭṭiyaḷ (M. *n.*), merchants ; **text :** . . . *Mērpaḍi kōvil chāntikkāṟar piḷḷaimār talattār kōvilkkuḍiyāna* . . . . . *nāṭṭār Koṭṭāṟu* ***cheṭṭiyaḷ*** *nagarattār vaḻipāḍāga tanda paṇam 4422* ; **tr.** 4422 *paṇam* (coin) given as service (to the deity) by the worshipping priests, the *piḷḷaimār*, the *talattār*, the temple ryots, the *nāṭṭār*, the ***merchants*** of Koṭṭāṟu and the citizens ; *T.A.S.* IV, pts. i and ii, No. 23, p. 114, ll. 31–34 ; Kanyākumāri, Kanyakumari Tq. and Dt., T. Nadu St. **Dy.** Rulers of Travancore, Balarāmavarman, Kollam 936, Ś. 1682 = 1760 A.D.

chey (T. *n.*), cultivable land one *vēli* in extent ; **text[1] :** . . *nilam pattu cheyuṁ koṇḍu niśadi iraṇḍu nondā viḷakku* . . *erippippōm āṉōm*. . . . ; **tr.** we agree to burn daily two perpetual lamps with the income from 10 **chey** (**cultivable land one** ***vēli*** **in extent**) of land ; *S.I.I.* III, No. 113, p. 250, ll. 9–10 ; Tillaisthānam, Tanjavur Tq. and Dt., T. Nadu St. **Dy.** Chōḷa, Āditya I, reg. yr. 13 = 884 A.D. ; **text[2] :** . . *Aṇukkanambi* ***cheykku*** *vaḍakkum* . . . ; **tr.** to the north of the **chey** (**cultivable land one** ***vēli*** **in extent**) belonging to Aṇukkanambi; *S.I.I.* III, No. 24, p. 45, l. 6 ; Karuvūr, Karuvur Tq., Tiruchirapalli Dt., T. Nadu St. **Dy.** Chōḷa, Kulōttuṅga III, reg. yr. 25 = 1203 A.D.

chhatra[1] (K. *n.*), umbrella ; **text :** (damaged) . . *Pāṇḍyāṁta gṛihīta suvarṇṇa* ***chhatra*** *dhvaja virājamānaṁ* . . . *Bōḻaga*. . . . ; **tr.** Bōḻaga who had wrested the golden **umbrella** and banner from the Pāṇḍya king ; *S.I.I.* XI, No. 41, p. 26, ll. 22–23 ; Nāgāvi, Gadag Tq. and Dt., Karn. St. **Dy.** Rāshṭr., Koṭṭigadēva, Ś. 891 = 969 A.D.

chhatra[2] (K. *n.*), choultry where travellers are provided with free lodging and food ; **text :** . . . . *Noḷaṁbaseṭṭiyum Padmāvatiyabbeyuṁ parōkshavinayakkeṁdu biṭṭa* ***chhatra***. . . . . ; **tr.**

the **choultry where travellers are provided with free lodging and food** was donated by Noḷaṁbaseṭṭi and Padmāvatiyabbe for their salvation ; *S.I.I.* IX, pt. i, No. 130, p. 113, l. 24 ; Kōgaḷi, Hadagalli Tq., Bellary Dt., Karn. St. **Dy.** Chāḷ. of Kal., Sōmēśvara I, in characters of 11th cent. A.D.

chhatra[3] (K. *n*.), free feeding house ; **text**[1] **:** . . . *Ayyappanavaru tamma tāyi Mājiyara kayyalu Chōḷiyakēriya Kallaṁgereya taṁma tōṭada maṭhada* ***chhatra****dalli uṁba brāhmaru 12 aḍuvavanobba antu 13 kkaṁ māḍida dhama* . . . . ; **tr.** Ayyappa through his mother Māji made a grant of lands for feeding 12 brāhmaṇas and one cook totalling 13 persons to be fed in the **free feeing house** located in the *maṭha* (religious institution) of his grove ; *S.I.I.* VII, No. 387, p. 243, ll. 7–9 ; Kōṭakēṟi, Udupi Tq. and Dt., Karn. St. **Dy.** Saṅgama, Bukka, Ś. 1294 = 1372 A.D. ; **text**[2] **:** *Narasarāja mahīpālanu purōhita Liṁgabhaṭṭara mukhāṁtaravāgi Kāśiyalli māḍuvaṁta dharmagaḷu Viśvēśvara modalāda dēvategaḷige abhishēka pūje* . . . . *ī māsatrayadalli sthānadāna nityadalli nūru brāhmaṇarige mṛishṭāṁna* ***chatra*** . . . . ; **tr.** king Narasarāja made gift through his priest Liṁgarājabhaṭṭa in order to maintain several charities at Kāśi including the anointment and worship of gods like Viśvēśvara and others, for feeding delicious meal for hundred brāhmaṇas daily for 3 months in the **free feeding house** ; *E.C.* (R) IV, Ch. 171, p. 104, ll. 2, 10–17 ; Hoṅganūru, Chamarajanagar Tq. and Dt., Karn. St. **Dy.** Woḍ. of Mys., Narasarāja, in characters of 17th century A.D.

chhatra dharmma (K. *n*.), grant for the choultry for free feeding ; **text :** . . ***chhatra-dharmma*** *yatibhōjana adhyayana* . . . . *māḍida dharmmasthaḷada vivara* . . . . ; **tr.** the details of the place **granted for choultry for free feeding,** for feeding the ascetics, for maintenance of students, etc. ; *K.I.* VI, No. 69, pp. 188-189, ll. 21–22 ; Mīrjan, Kumta Tq., Karwar Dt., Karn. St. **Dy.** Tuḷuva, Kṛishṇadēvarāya, Ś. 1449 = 1526 A.D.

chhatrada koḷaga (K. *n*.), standard grain measure of the choultry ; **text :** . . nālvatta salige bhatta yidū ***chhatrada koḷaga****dalū nālvattu khaṁḍuga* . . . . . ; **tr.** the forty ***salige*** (a grain measure) of paddy is equal to forty *khaṁḍuga* (a grain measure) of the *koḷaga* (a **grain measure**) **standardized** by the **choultry** ; *E.C.* VIII, Tīr. 33, p. 470, l. 42; Kāḷammanaguḍi, Tirthahalli Tq., Shimoga Dt., Karn. St. **Misc.,** in characters of 15th century A.D.

chhatra maṭha (K. *n*.), free feeding house-cum-monastery ; **text :** . . *Duggaseṭiyaru taṁma gurugaḷaha Puṁṇyaśravaṇavoḍeyara nirūpadalu māḍida* ***chhatra maṭha****da dharmmakke barasida śilāśāsanada* . . . . ; **tr.** stone edict got written by Duggaseṭṭi for the grant made by him to the **free feeding house-cum-monastery** on the orders of his preceptor Puṁṇyaśravaṇavoḍeya ; *S.I.I.* VII,

No. 345, p. 199, ll. 9–10 ; Chauḷikēri, Udupi Tq. and Dt., Karn. St. **Dy.** Sāḷuva, Narasiṁha, Ś. 1424 = 1502 A.D.

chhāyā paṭimā (Pkt. *n.*), memorial image; **text :** . . . . . *Kalakasa* ***chhāyā paṭimā*** . . . . ; **tr.** the memorial image of Kalaka ; *Ep. Ind.* XXXVII, No. 22, p. 132, l. 1 ; Beḷavāḍigi, Chitapur Tq., Gulbarga Dt., Karn. St. **Misc.,** in characters of 3rd cent. A.D.

chibilaṁgaḍi (K. *n.*), shops dealing with bamboo articles ; **text :** . . ***chibilaṁgaḍi****yavaru koḍuva dhūpada kāṇike* . . . . ; **tr.** the donation of incense made by the owners of the shops dealing with bamboo articles ; *S.I.I.* IV, No. 255, p. 49, l. 25; Hampi, Hospet Tq., Bellary Dt., Karn. St. **Dy.** Tuḷuva, Kṛishṇadēvarāya, Ś. 1435 = 1513 A.D.

chikka pārupatyagāṟaru (K. *n.*), junior manager; **text :** . . *Terakaṇāṁbeya chāvaḍige* ***chikka pārupatyagāṟaru*** . . . *Āḷvāradēvara rathōtsavanu* . . . *naḍesi bahiri.* . . . ; **tr.** the **junior manager** of the village assembly of Terakaṇāṁbi will organize the car festival of the god Āḷvāradēva ; *E.C.* (R) III, Gu. 119, p. 89, ll. 14–16; Terakaṇāṁbi, Gundlupet Tq., Mysore Dt., Karn. St. **Dy.** Tuḷuva, Kṛishṇadēvarāya, Ś. 1442 = 1521 A.D.

chikka gadyāṇa (K. mentioned as chiga. *n.*), gold coin of a smaller denomination ; **text :** . . *Taṁmaṇa nāyana makki mu nālkakkake teṟu* ***chi ga*** *nālku* . . . . ; **tr.** for four *mu* (*muḍi*, land of the extend of being sown with four *muḍi* of seeds) the tax is four **gold coin of a smaller denomination** ; *K.I.* III, No. 11, p. 31, ll. 21–22; Kaikiṇi, Bhatkal Tq. and Dt., Karn. St. **Dy.** Haive chfs., Kṛishṇadēvarasa, Ś. 1465 = 1542 A.D.

chikka tāra (K. *n.*), silver coin of a smaller denomination ; **text :** . . . . *Telligēśvara dēvaraṁ* . . . . *pratishṭheya māḍi* . . . *Telligaru* . . . . . ***chikka tārava*** *teṟuvaru* . . . . ; **tr.** having installed the deity Telligēśvara, the oil mongers shall give a **silver coin of smaller denomination** to the deity ; *S.I.I.* IX, pt. i, No. 336, p. 357, ll. 20, 26 ; Kuḍatini, Bellary Tq. and Dt., Karn. St. **Dy.** Hoy., Ballāḷa II, Ś. 1140 = 1219 A.D.

chikka voḍeya (K. *n.*), junior prince ; **text :** . . . . . . *Varadādēvi aṁmanavaru Komāra Veṅkaṭādri* ***chikka voḍeyarū*** *tulāpurusha* . . . *sahasra gōdāna* . . . *muṁtāda dānagaḷanu māḍi* . . . . . *Varadarāja dēvarige samarpista kāṇike* . . . . . ; **tr.** tribute paid to the god Varadarāja by Varadādēvi ammanavaru and her son the **junior prince** Veṁkaṭādri after they had performed religious acts such as *tulāpurusha*, a gift of thousand cows, etc. ; *S.I.I.* IX, pt. ii, No. 547, p. 566, l. 2 ; Little Kāñchīpuram, Kanchipuram Tq., Chengleput Dt., T.Nadu St. **Dy.** Tuḷuva, Achyutarāya, Ś. 1454 = 1532 A.D.

chilpi āchāryulu (T. *n.*), master sculptor ; **text :** . . . . ***chilpi āchāryulu*** *Śāṁttōja koḍuku Guḍḍōjanaku kha 2. akkasāla Baiyyapōju koḍuku prōlōjunaku kha 1* . . . . *vrittulu.* . . . . ; **tr.** 1 *vritti* (share) of the extent of 2 *kha* (*khaṁḍuga*, a grain measure) to Guḍḍōja son of the **master sculptor** Śāṁttōja and 1 *vritti* to Prōlōju son of Baiyyapōju; *S.I.I.* X, No. 396, p. 209, ll. 1–2 ; Malkāpuram, Guntur Tq. and Dt., A.P. St. **Dy.** Kākatīya, Rudramadēvi, Ś. 1183 = 1261 A.D.

chiluvāna hadike (K. *n.*), minor tax ; **text :** . . . . . *Śivapuradalli . . . iddaṁtaha kabbilada hadike voḷagāda* ***chiluvāna hadike****yanu . . . . Sōmanāthadēvarige . . . koṭṭu barasida sāsana* . . ; **tr.** stone edict got written registering the donation of **minor taxes** such as tax on hunters from the village Śivapura to the god Sōmanāthadēva ; *E.C.* V, Chnp. 268, p. 707, ll. 12–14, 16–17 ; Vura, Channarayapatna Tq., Hassan Dt., Karn. St. **Misc.,** Cy. yr. Siddhārthi, in characters of 12th century A.D.

chiluvāna kāṇike (K. *n.*), minor tax ; **text[1] :** . . . . . . *davasādāya hoge kāṇike muṁtāda* ***chiluvāna kāṇike*** *nīve . . . anubhavisikoṇḍu baraluḷḷavaru eṁdu Kṛishṇappanāyakarayanavaru . . . . Manjunāthadīkshitaravarige koṭa . . . tāṁra śāsana* . . . . ; **tr.** copper plate charter given to Manjunāthadīkshita by Kṛishṇappanāyakaya stipulating that he may enjoy all **minor tax** incomes such as tax on tobacco and income from sale of grains ; *E.C.* (R) VIII, HN. 47, p. 26, ll. 50–52, 54, 57–58 ; Hoḷenarasīpura, Holenarasipura Tq., Hassan Dt., Karn. St. **Dy.** Nāyakas of Maṇināgapura, Kṛishṇappanāyaka, Ś. 1484 = 1563 A.D. ; **text[2] :** . . *sakala suvarṇādāya davasādāya hoge kāṇike muṁtāda* ***chiluvāna-kāṇike****gaḷu* . . . . ; **tr.** minor taxes including income from all types of gold, tax on grains, tax on tobacco, etc. ; *E.C.* (R) VIII, Ag. 20, p. 124, ll. 128–30 ; Kaṁchēnahaḷḷi, Arakalagudu Tq., Hassan Dt., Karn. St. **Dy.** Hoḷenarasīpura chfs., Narasiṁhanāyaka, Ś. 1587 = 1665 A.D.

chiluvāna suṁka (K. *n.*), tax on sundry articles ; **text[1] :** . . . . ***chiluvāna suṁka*** . . . *yeletaragu mādāṟike taḷavārike uppina kāvali* . . . . ; **tr.** remitting the taxes on **sundry articles,** dry leaves, basket making, watch and ward, saltpan etc. ; *E.C.* IV, Ch. 302, p. 196, ll. 14–15 ; Dāsanapura, Chamarajanagar Tq. and Dt., Karn. St. **Dy.** Tuḷuva, Achyutarāya Ś. 1458 = 1536 A.D. ; **text[2] :** . . *chatusīmeyoḷagāda gadde beddalu kaṭṭe kāluve aṇe achchukaṭṭu . . . . taḷavārike . . . .* ***chiluvāna-suṁka*** *. . . ivu modalu . . . Hasanada śrī Virūpāksha dēvarige . . . śāsana pratishṭeyanu māḍidaru* ; **tr.** an inscribed slab was set up registering the grant of income from **minor taxes** such as on wet land, dry lands, ponds, canals, dams, partitioned area of arable land, watch and ward, etc.; *E.C.* (R) VIII, Hn. 2, p. 215, ll. 16–24 ; Hāsana, Hassan Tq. and Dt., Karn. St. **Dy.** Tuḷuva, Sadāśiva, Ś. 1485 = 1563 A.D.

chilvari (T. *n.*), minor taxes ; **text :** . . . ***chilvari*** *peruvari eppērppaṭṭadum . . . . suvāmi abiśekatukku viṭṭa paḍi* . . . . . ; **tr.** the **minor taxes** and major taxes and all others of the same type were donated for the anointment of the god ; *T.A.S.* V, No. 64 (II), p. 194, ll. 7–8 ; Vindaṉūr *alias* Śāmbūrvaḍagarai, Shenkottai Tq., Tirunelveli Dt., T. Nadu St. **Dy.** Nāyakas of Madurai, Muttu Vīrappanāyaka, Ś. 1527 = 1605 A.D.

chiṁna (K. *n.*), gold ; **text :** . . . . *Svāmidēvargge varsha nibandhadiṁ teruva gadyāṇa panneraḍu gaḷaṁtigeyalu puṭṭidāyadoḷage Lokkiyu navilumāgi ponnavaṇa* ***chiṁna****manāydu* . . . ; **tr.** having selected the **gold** in the form of *Lokki* and *Navilu* gold coins from the income accuring through the endowment of 12 *gadyāṇa* (a gold coin) of gold endowed annually in the name of the god Svāmidēva ; *S.I.I.* IX, pt. i, No. 164, p. 155, ll. 26–28 ; Kuḍatini, Bellary Tq. and Dt., Karn. St. **Dy.** Chāḷ. of Kal., Vikramāditya VI, Ch. Vi. yr. 23 = 1098 A.D.

chiṁna bhaṁḍāra (K. *n.*), treasury of gold ; **text**[1] **:** . . . *Keḷadi Vekaṭappanāyakara mudreyāgi* ***chiṁna bhaṁnḍāra****da Vōbarasayyagaḷa makkaḷu. Rāmakrishṇappavoḍeyaru* . . . . ; **tr.** Rāmakrishṇappavoḍeya son of Vobarasayya who was in charge of the **treasury of gold** belonging to Veṁkaṭappanāyaka, the Keḷadi ruler ; *S.I.I.* VII, No. 297, p. 149, ll. 12–13 ; Uḍupi, Udupi Tq. and Dt., Karn. St. **Dy.** Āravīḍu, Veṁkaṭapatirāya, Ś. 1536 = 1614 A.D. ; **text**[2] **:** . . . . *Kṛishṇarāya mahārāyara* ***chiṁna bhaṁḍāra****da Tiṁmarasarau* . . . . ; **tr.** Timmarasa of the **treasury of gold** belonging to the emperor Kṛishṇadēvarāya ; *S.I.I.* IX, pt. ii, No. 522, p. 538, ll. 6–7 ; Guḍihaḷḷi, Harapanahalli Tq., Bellary Dt., Karn. St. **Dy.** Tuḷuva, Kṛishṇadēvarāya, Ś. 1449 = 1527 A.D.

chiṁnada barahada hachaḍa (K. *n.*), cloth with goldern embroider ; **text :** . . . *Varadarājadēvarige samarpista kāṇike* . . . . ***chiṁnnada barahada hachaḍa*** *11 chiṁnada barahada sīre 3* . . . ; **tr.** 11 pieces of **cloth with golden embroidary** and 3 pieces of cloth with gold designs were presented to the god Varadarāja; *S.I.I.* IX, pt. ii, No. 547, p. 566, ll. 2–3 ; Little Kāñchīpuram, Kancheepuram Tq., Chingleput Dt., T. Nadu St. **Dy.** Tuḷuva, Achyutarāya, Ś. 1454 = 1532 A.D.

chiṁnavarada (K. *n.*), gold merchant ; **text :** . . . . . . *Urusaṇaseṭṭiyara maga heggaḍe baḷiya* ***chiṁnavarada*** *Nāgaṁṇa seṭṭiyaru* . . . ; **tr.** Nāgaṁṇaseṭṭi a **gold merchant** belonging to heggaḍe lineage and son of Urusaṇaseṭṭi ; *S.I.I.* VII, No. 372, p. 226, l. 7 ; Maṇigārakēri, Udupi Tq. and Dt., Karn. St. **Dy.** Saṅgama, Dēvarāya, Ś. 1359 = 1437 A.D.

chinnada barahada sīre (K. *n.*), piece of cloth with golden designs ; **text :** . . . . *Varadarāja dēvarige samarpista kāṇike* . . . . *chiṁnnada barahada hachaḍa 11* ***chinnada barahada sīre*** *3* . . . ; **tr.** 11 pieces of cloth with golden embroidary and 3 **pieces of cloth with gold designs** were presented to the god Varadarāja ;

S.I.I. IX, pt. ii, No. 547, p. 566, ll. 2–3 ; Little Kāñchīpuram, Kancheepuram Tq., Chingleput Dt., T. Nadu St. **Dy.** Tuḷuva, Achyutarāya, Ś. 1454 = 1532 A.D.

chinnada baṭṭalu (K. *n.*), golden bowl ; **text :** . . . . *Kāḷahastīśvaradēvarige samarpista* . . . . ***chinnada baṭṭalu** 1* . . . ; **tr.** one **golden bowl** presented to the god Kāḷahastīśvara ; *S.I.I.* IX, pt. ii, No. 487, p. 500, ll. 2, 4 ; Kāḷahasti, Chandragiri Tq., Chittoor Dt., A.P. St. **Dy.** Tuḷuva, Kṛishṇadēvarāya, Ś. 1434 = 1513 A.D.

chinnnada hū (K. *n.*), golden flower ; **text :** . . . . *Kāḷahastīśvara dēvarge samarpista* . . . . . ***chinnada hū*** . . . ; **tr. golden flower** presented to the god Kāḷahastīśvara ; *S.I.I.* IX, pt. ii, No. 551, p. 571, ll. 2, 4 ; Kāḷahasti, Chandragiri Tq., Chittoor Dt., A.P. St. **Dy.** Tuḷuva, Achyutarāya, Ś. 1484 = 1562 A.D.

chinnnada kambi (K. *n.*), golden band ; **text :** . . . . *Kāḷahastīśvara samarpista* . . . . . ***chinnada-kambi*** . . . ; **tr. golden band** presented to the god Kāḷahastīśvara ; *S.I.I.* IX, pt. ii, No. 551, p. 571, ll. 2, 4 ; Kāḷahasti, Chandragiri Tq., Chittoor Dt., A.P. St. **Dy.** Tuḷuva, Achyutarāya, Ś. 1484 = 1562 A.D.

chinnageyika (K. *n.*), retail gold merchants ; **text:** . . . . *brāhmaṇarachigārakke **chinnageyika**da haradarali tiṅgaḷiṁge pratyēka hāgavondu* . . . ; **tr.** for the payment of brāhmaṇas one *hāga* (a fractional denomination of a coin) each every month from the **retail gold merchants** ; *K.I.* II, No. 21, p. 82, l. 26–27 ; Telsang, Athani Tq., Belgaum Dt., Karn. St. **Dy.** Chāḷ. of Kal., Jagadēkamalla, reg. yr. 10 = 1147 A.D.

chiṉṉaṅgaḷ (T. *n.*), ornaments ; **text :** . . . . *śrī Rājarāja Īśvaramuḍaiya paramasvāmikkukkuḍutta poṉṉiṉ **chiṉṉaṅgaḷ** āḍavallāṉ eṉṉum kallāl niṟaiyeḍuttu* . . . ; **tr.** to the supreme Lord Rājarāja Īśvara gold **ornaments** which were weighed by the stone *āḍavallān* were given ; *S.I.I.* II, No. 1, 7th Section, p. 4, ll. 2–3 ; Tañjāvūr, Tanjavur Tq. and Dt., T. Nadu St. **Dy.** Chōḷa, Rājarāja I, reg. yr. 26 = 1011 A.D.

chippiga (K. *n.*), tailor ; **text :** . . . . ***chippigara** aṁgaḍi vaṁdakke haṇa 1/2* . . . ; **tr.** for each shop of the **tailors** 1/2 *haṇa* (coin) of tax ; *E.C.* (R) X, Ak. 134, p. 174, l. 27–28 ; Tirupati, Arsikere Tq., Hassan Dt., Karn. St. **Misc.**, Ś. 1666 = 1744 A.D.

chiṟai (T. *n.*), barrage ; **text :** . . . . . *teṉṉellai **chiṟaikku** vaḍakku* . . . ; **tr.** the southern boundry is to the north of the **barrage** ; *T.A.S.* V, No. 14, p. 46, l. 3 ; Kollam, Kollam Tq. and Dt., Ker. St. **Misc.**, Kollam 513 = 1337-38 A.D.

chīralamōpu (Te. *n.*), bundle of sarees ; **text :** (incomplete) . . . . ***chīralamōpu** 1* . . . ; **tr.** one **bundle of sarees** ; *S.I.I.* X, No. 239, p. 121, l. 22; Āchanta, Narasapuram Tq., W. Godawari Dt., A.P. St. **Misc**, in characters of 13th cent. A.D.

chiṟpāchāriyaṉ (T. *n.*), master sculptor ; **text :**

. . . . *ippaḍi kallil veṭṭinēṉ ivvūr* ***chiṟpāchāriyaṉ*** *Vichchādiraṉ uyyavandāṉ* . . . . ; **tr.** (the text of this inscription) was thus engraved on stone by the **master sculptor** Vichchādiraṉ Uyyavandāṉ ; *S.I.I.* VIII, No. 423, p. 223, l. 35 ; Tiruvādavūr, Melur Tq., Madurai Dt., T, Nadu St. **Dy.** Pāṇḍya, Sundarapāṇḍya I, reg. yr. 15 = 1231 A.D.

chiṟṟambalattu kōl (T. *n.*), standard measuring rod of the Chidambaram temple ; **text :** . . . . *nilaṉ* ***Chiṟṟambalattu kollāl*** *iraṇḍāyiraṅkuḻi* . . . ; **tr.** land of the extent of 2000 *kuḻi* (a land measure) measured by the **standard measuring rod of the Chidambaram temple** ; *S.I.I.* III, No. 55, p. 110, ll. 39–41 ; Tiruvallam, Chittoor Tq. and Dt., A.P. St. **Dy.** Chōḷa, Rājendra I, reg. yr. 4 = 1016 A.D.

chittaisu (K. *vb.*), to rule with concern ; **text**[1] **:** . . . *Dēvarāyamahārāyaru* . . . . . *sakala sāmrājyavanū* ***chittaisu****tiha kāladali* . . . ; **tr.** when the emperor Dēvarāya was **ruling with concern** over the entire empire ; *S.I.I.* IX, pt. ii, No. 448, p. 457, ll. 5–6 ; Basarūru, Kundapur Tq., Udupi Dt., Karn. St. **Dy.** Saṅgama, Dēvarāya, Ś. 1363 = 1442 A.D. ; **text**[2] **:** . . . . . *Kṛishṇarāyamahārāyaru Vijeyanagariya siṁhāsanadalū* ***chittaisi*** . . . . *sakala varṇadharmāśramavanu pratipālisuttiha kāladalū* . . . . ; **tr.** while the emperor Kṛishṇrāya was ruling with concern safeguarding all the *varṇa* (traditional classes) and *āśrama* (stages of life) ; *S.I.I.* IX, pt. ii, No. 520, p. 536, ll. 6–8 ; Voḍerahobli, Kundapur Tq., Udupi Dt., Karn. St. **Dy.** Tuḷuva, Kṛishṇadēvarāya, Ś. 1448 = 1526 A.D.

chittayisu (K. *n.*), having made up one's mind ; **text :** . . . . . . *Achyutarāya* . . . . *Tiruvaḍirājyakke* . . . *maṁneyaranū daḷavāḍavanū* . . . *kaḷihi* ***chittayisi*** *Tiruvaḍi kayya kappavanū tegadukoṇḍu* . . . . . . ; **tr.** Achyutarāya having made up his mind to send subordinate chiefs and a regiment to Tiruvaḍirājya, he extracted tributes from the Tiruvaḍi ruler ; *S.I.I.* IX, pt. ii, No. 547, p. 566, l. 2 ; Little Kāñchīpuram, Kanchipuram Tq., Chingleput Dt., T. Nadu St. **Dy.** Tuḷuva, Achyutarāya, Ś. 1454 = 1532 A.D.

chiṭi (Te. *n.*), liquid measure ; **text :** . . . . *neyyi* ***chiṭlu*** *3 bellaṁ pa 7* . . . . ; **tr.** 3 *chiṭi* (liquid measure) of ghee and 7 *pa* (*pala*, a measure of weight) of jaggery ; *S.I.I.* XVI, No. 248, p. 254, l. 27 ; Pedda-Ahōbalaṁ, Sirvel Tq., Kurnool Dt., A.P. St. **Dy.** Tuḷuva, Sadāśiva, Ś. 1482 = 1560 A.D.

chitra lipi (K. *n.*), calligraphical writing ; **text :** . . . . *chhappannadēśa* ***chitra lipi*** *lēkha kōvidaṁ* . . . *Koṁḍamarasayya* . . . . ; **tr.** Koṁḍamarasayya was an expert in **calligraphical writing** of alphabets used in 56 kingdoms ; *S.I.I.* IX, pt. ii, No. 507, p. 521, ll. 26–28 ; Chōḷasamudram, Hindupur Tq., Anantapur Dt., A.P. St. **Dy.** Tuḷuva, Kṛishṇadēvarāya, Ś. 1439 = 1517 A.D.

chitramēḻi (T. *n.*), ornamental plough (symbol of agricultural guild) ; **text :** . . . . *śeṅgōlē muṉṉāgavuñ* ***chitramēḻi****yē daivamāgavum* . . . ; **tr.** (the **agricultural**

guild for which) the scepter was primary and the **ornamental plough** was the divinity ; *S.I.I.* VII, No. 129, p. 54, l. 6 ; Tirukkōyilūr, Tirukkoyilur Tq., S. Arcot Dt., T. Nadu St. **Misc.**, Com. gld., in characters of 12th century A.D.

chittiramēl̤i periyanāḍu (T. *n.*), major agricultural guild having ornamental plough as its symbol ; **text :** . . . . . . ***chittiramēl̤i periyanāṭṭōm*** *vaittukkuḍutta pariśu* . . . . . ; **tr.** the grant made by the **major guild of agriculturists who have an organmental plough as their symbol** ; *S.I.I.* VII, No. 129, p. 54, l. 7 ; Tirukkoyilūr, Tirukkoyilur Tq., S. Arcot Dt., T. Nadu St. **Agri. gld.,** in characters of 12th century A.D.

chittiramēl̤i Vin̤n̤agar (T. *n.*), Vishṇu temple built by the agricultural guild having ornamental plough as its symbol ; **text :** . . . . . . *el̤ubattoṇbadu nāṭṭu paḍin̤enbhūmi* ***chittiramēl̤i Vin̤n̤agar*** . . . ; **tr.** the temple of Vishṇu built by the **agricultural guild having ornamental plough as its symbol** and spread over 79 lands in 18 countries ; *S.I.I.* VII, No. 129, p. 54, l. 8 ; Tirukkōyilūr, Tirukkoyilur Tq., S. Arcot Dt., T. Nadu St. **Agri. gld.** in characters of 12th century A.D.

chittirakūṭam (T. *n.*), painted hall ; **text :** . . . . *Duggaḍibhaṭṭan̤ brāhmaṇi Kandichhān̤iyēn̤ ivvūr kaṇapperumakkaḷ eḍupitta chittirakūṭattukku kuḍuttēn̤ Nārāyaṇasvāmigaḷukku Tiruviḷakkukkāga pattu pon̤ kuḍuttēn̤* . . . ; **tr.** I Kandichhān̤i the brāhmaṇa wife of Duggaḍibhaṭṭa donated 10 gold coins for burning a perpetual lamp to the god Nārāyaṇasvāmi in the **painted hall** built by the elders of the assembly of the village ; *S.I.I.* VI, No. 354, p. 166, ll. 1–2 ; Uttaramallūr, Madurantakam Tq., Chingleput Dt., T. Nadu St. **Misc.**, in characters of 12th century A.D.

chīvigai (T. *n.*), palanquin ; **text :** . . . . *taviśuṅ chāmaraiyuṅ* ***chīvigai****yum timilaiyum kōyilum* . . . . *Chembiyan̤ramil̤avēḷennum kulappyarum per̤r̤a Vikkian̤n̤an̤.* . . . ; **tr.** Vikkian̤n̤an̤ who has received a feudatory throne, flywhisk, **palanquin,** drum, mansion, . . . and the hereditory title of Chembiyan̤ramil̤avēḷ ; *S.I.I.* III, No. 89 , p. 221, ll. 3–6 ; Tillaisthānam, Tanjavur Tq. and Dt., T. Nadu St. **Dy.** Chōḷa, Āditya I, in characters of 9th cent. A.D.

chōḷaman̤ (T. *n.*), jowar growing land ; **text :** . . . . *Kar̤aikkaṇḍaiyyan̤ Mādēvarkku dānamāga viṭṭa* ***chōḷaman̤*** *irukaṇḍugam* . . . . . ; **tr.** Kar̤aikkaṇḍaiyyan donated to the god Mahādēva **jowar growing land** of the extent of being sown with two *khaṇḍuga* (a greain measure) of seeds ; *E.C.* (R) IV, No. Ko. 65, p. 446, ll. 8–10 ; Śāgyam, Kollegal Tq., Chamarajanagar Dt., Karn. St. **Dy.** Chōḷa, Rājādhirāja I, reg. year 28 = 1045-46.

chōra yūtha (K. *n.*), a band of thieves ; **text :** . . . . *Basaveyanāyakaṁ* . . . . ***chōra yūtha****maṁ pesavarigeydu* . . . . *surāṁganeyar* . . . *koṁḍupōdar* . . . . ; **tr.** Basaveyanāyaka having fought against a **band of thieves**, he was accompanied to the heavens by divine damsels ; *S.I.I.* IX, pt. i, No. 321, p. 337, ll. 13–14 ; Hoḷal, Hadagalli Tq., Bellary Dt., Karn. St. **Dy.** Hoy., Ballāḷa II, Ś. 1116 = 1194 A.D.

chōṟu (T. *n.*), food ; **text**[1] : (fragmentary and incomplete) *puḍavaikkuñ**chōṟu**kkumāga* ..... ; **tr.** for providing cloths and food ; *S.I.I.* XIII, No. 295, p. 157, l. 10 ; Tiruppaḻanam, Tanjavur Tq. and Dt., T. Nadu St. **Dy.** Chōḷa, Āditya I, reg. yr. 21, in characters of 9th century A.D. ; **text**[2] : .... *diṉappaḍiyāgachchilavu naḍakkumbaḍikku Nāchchiyārkku nittaṟpaḍi naḍandu pōdum kālai-sandi pūjaiyil .... nāḷoṉṟukku kaṟpitta **chōṟu** kuruṇi* .. ; **tr.** the expenditure for the conduct of the daily morning service of the goddess Nāchchiyār is on one *kuṟuṇi* (grain measure) of rice per day for cooked **food** ; *T.A.S.* IV, No. 66, p. 196, ll. 17–23 ; Kanyākumāri, Kanyakumari Tq. and Dt., T. Nadu St. **Dy.** Nāyakas of Madurai, Muttu Vīrappanāyakkar, Ś. 1529, Kollam 782 = 1607 A.D.

chūḍāgāra mahādhikāra (Skt. *n.*), Superintendent of the treasury of ornaments ; **text** : .... ***chūḍāgāra mahādhikāra*** *mahitaḥ* ... *Mārābhidhānaḥ* ; **tr.** the **superintendent of the treasury of ornaments** by name Mārā ; *S.I.I.* X, No. 73, p. 30, ll. 26–28, 30–33 ; Tangēḍumalli, Narasaraopet Tq., Guntur Dt., A.P. St. **Dy.** Chōḍa Chfs., Kannaradēva, Ś. 1037 = 1115 A.D.

chūḍāmaṇi (K. *n.*), crest jewel ; an eminent person ; **text** : .... *Jōisa-**chūḍāmaṇi** Chāvuṁḍayya bareda* .... ; **tr.** written by Chāvuṁdayya, a **crest jewel** among astrologer ; *S.I.I.* IX, pt. i, p. 62, ll. 49–50 ; Oruvayi, Bellary Tq and Dt., Karn. St. **Dy.** Chāḷ. of Kal., Jagadēkamalla, Ś. 958 = 1036 A.D.

chūrṇa bhaṁgāra (K. *n.*), gold powder ; **text** : ... *Lokkiyu navilumāgi pannavaṇa chinnamanāydu kaḷedu nindatappa **chūrṇa bhaṁgāraṁ*** ... ; **tr.** the **gold powder** which results after the minting of gold coins of Lokki and Navilu ; *S.I.I.* IX, pt. i, No. 164, p. 155, ll. 27–29 ; Kuḍatini, Bellary Tq. and Dt., Karn. St. **Dy.** Chāḷ. of Kal., Vikramāditya VI, Ch. Vi. yr. 23 = 1093 A.D.

dabbaṇigader̤e (K. *n.*), tax on professions using pack needles ; **text :** . . . . *mēdaralli dabbaṇige der̤eya nōḍikoṁbaru Beḷḷakaṭṭeya kōḍiya gaḷ̤de motta ondu* . . . . ; **tr.** those who take care of the **tax on professions using pack needles** among the basket makers are given one *mattar* (land measure) of wet land at the corner of Beḷḷakaṭṭe ; *S.I.I.* IX pt. i, No. 170, p. 165, ll. 25–26 ; Aṁbali, Kudligi Tq., Bellary Dt., Karn. St. **Dy.** Chāḷ. of Kal., Vikramāditya VI, Ch. Vi. yr. 30 = 1106 A.D.

daḍa (K. *n.*), bank of a tank ; **text :** . . . . *Taṁmaṇakoṁga tōḍisida ker̤eya mūḍaṇa* ***daḍa*** . . . . . . ; **tr.** the eastern **bank of the tank** got excavated by Taṁmaṇakoṁga ; *S.I.I.* IX pt. ii, No. 457, p. 469, ll. 43–44 ; Basarūru, Kundapur Tq., Udupi Dt., Karn. St. **Dy.** Saṅgama, Mallikārjuna, Ś. 1377 = 1455 A.D.

dakshiṇabhujādaṁḍa (K. < Skt. *adj.*), he who was verily the right hand (a title) ; **text :** *Achyutadēvarāyamahārāyara* ***dakshiṇabhujādaṁḍa*** *bhaṁḍārada Timmapa Ayyanavaru* ; **tr.** Timmapa Ayya of the treasury **who was verily the right hand** of the emperor Achyutadēvarāya ; *S.I.I.* IX pt. ii, No. 553, p. 573, ll. 5–7 ; Kuḍatini, Bellary Tq. and Dt., Karn. St. **Dy.** Tuḷuva, Achyutarāya, Ś. 1454 = 1532 A.D.

dakshiṇadōrddaṁḍa (K. < Skt. *adj.*), he who was verily the right hand (a title) ; **text :** . . . . *Mudiyappanāyakēṁdranu rājyavanāḷuttāyiralu ātaṁge* ***dakshiṇadōrddaṁḍa****vāda* . . . . . *daḷavāyi Paramaśivappa* . . . . ; **tr.** while Mudiyappa-nāyakēṁdra was ruling, the army commander Paramaśivappa was **verily his right hand** man ; *E.C.* XVI, Chnk. 1, p. 1, ll. 9–12 ; Jōgihaḷḷi, Chikkanayakanahalli Tq., Tumkur Dt., Karn. St. **Dy.** Chikkanāyakanahaḷḷi Chfs., Rāmadēvarāya, Ś. 1544 = 1622 A.D.

dakshiṇai (T. < Skt. *n.*), priestly fee ; **text :** . . *tirunayana mōksham paṇṇu* . . . . *kku* ***dakshiṇai****kku kkāśu araikkāl* . . . . ; **tr.** three fourth of a *kāśu* (a coin denomination) given as **priestly fee** for conducting a ritual called *tirunayana mōksha* in the temple ; *E.C.* X, Kol. 108, p. 39 ; Kōlār, Kolar Tq. and Dt., Karn St. **Dy.** Chōḷa, Kulōttuṅga I, reg. yr. 2 = 1072 A.D.

dakshiṇamēru viṭaṅkaṉ (T. < Skt. *n.*), a weighing stone used in the Rājarājēśvara temple of Tañjāvūr (during the time of Rājarāja to weigh golden jewels, ornaments, etc.) ; **text :** . . . . *Rājarājīśvaram Uḍaiyār kōyilil* . . . . . . *chapputtirumēṉigaḷ* . . . . . *muḷattāl aḷandum ratnaṅgaḷ* ***dakshiṇamēru viṭaṅkan*** *eṉṉum kallāl niṟai eḍuttum* . . . ; **tr.** in the temple of the god Rajarājīśvara, the images were measured by the cubit measure and jewels had been **weighed by the stone called dakshiṇamēru viṭaṅkan** ; *S.I.I.* II, No. 48, p. 194, ll. 4–5, 7–9 ; Tañjāvūr, Tanjavur Tq. and Dt., T. Nadu St. **Dy.** Chōḷa, Rājarāja I, reg. yr. 29 = 1014 A.D.

dakshiṇe (K. < Skt. *n.*), priestly fee ; **text :** . . . . *brāhmara* ***dakshiṇe****ge gadyāṇam āṟu haṇavāṟu* *āchāryara* ***dakshiṇe****ge gadyāṇaveraḍu haṇa oṁdu.* . . . ; **tr. priestly fee** of six *gadyāṇa* (gold coin) and six *haṇa* (coin) for the brāhmaṇa and **priestly fee** of two *gadyāṇa* and one *haṇa* for the preceptor ; *E.C.* (R) V, T.N. 88, p. 480, ll. 74–75 ; Sōmanāthapura, T. Narasipura Tq., Mysore Dt., Karn St. **Dy.** Hoy., Narasiṁha III, Cy. yr. Dhātṛi = 1276 A.D.

daḷa[1] (K. *n.*), bundle of coins ; **text :** . . . . *achchina ṭaṁkasāleyalu* ***daḷa****kke vīsa 2* ; **tr.** 2 *vīsa* (coin) for preparing one **bundle of coins** in the mint with its mould ; *S.I.I* IX, pt. i, No. 228, p. 233, l. 11 ; Peddatuṁbaḷam, Adavani Tq., Kurnool Dt., A.P. St. **Dy.** Chāḷ. of Kal., Bhūlōkamalla, Ch. Vi. yr. 58 = 1133 A.D.

daḷa[2] (K. < Skt. *n.*), army ; **text :** . . . . *Chāḷukya chakravatti Tribhuvanamalla Permāḍidēvana* ***daḷaṁ*** . . . . ; **tr.** the **army** of the Chāḷukya emperor Tribhuvanamalla Permmāḍidēva ; *E.C.* (R) II, No. 82, p. 64, l. 21 ; Śravaṇabeḷagoḷa, Channarayapatna Tq., Hassan Dt., Karn. St. **Dy.** Chāḷ. of Kal., Vikramāditya VI,. Ś. 1039 = 1118 A.D.

daladadhikāra (K. < Skt. *n.*), head of the infantry division ; **text :** . . . . *Achchutarāyara* ***daladadhikāra*** *Bayiranagaḷavara maga Siṁgaya kaṭisida kaṁba* . . . . ; **tr.** a supporting pillar constructed by Siṁgaya the son of Bayirana who was the **head of the infantry division** of Achyutarāya ; *E.C.* XII, Tmk. 71, p. 56, ll. 4–5 ; Koṭnahaḷḷi, Tumkur Tq. and Dt., Karn. St. **Dy.** Tuḷuva, Achyutarāya, Ś. 1459 = 1537 A.D.

daḷamukhya (K. < Skt. *n.*), chief of the infantry division ; **text :** . . . . *rājadhāni Dōrasamudrakke sēvuṇa* ***daḷamukhya*** *Sāḷuva Tikkama Jayidēva Haripāḷyaruṁ Guṇaganeyiṁ. naḍadubaṁdu biṭṭalli. . . Nōbeyanu Sēvuṇavalavaṁ koṁdu . . . . suralōka prāptanāda* ; **tr.** when Sāḷuva Tikkama, the **chief of the infantry division** marched from Guṇagane against the capital city of Dōrasamudra along with Jayidēva and Haripāḷya, Nōbeya drove the enemey in the course of the battle and died ; *E.C.* (R) IX, Bl. 430, pp. 403-404, ll. 4–6, 9, 11–12 ; Kaṭṭēsōmanahaḷḷi, Belur Tq., Hassan Dt., Karn. St. **Dy.** Hoy., Narasiṁha III, Ś. 1199 = 1276 A.D.

daḷavāḍa (K. < Skt. *n.*), regiment ; **text :** . . . . *Achyutarāyamahārāyaru* . . . . *Tiruvaḍiyarājyakke maṁneyaranū* ***daḷavāḍa****vanū kaḷuhisalāgi Tiruvaḍiya keiyyalu kappavanu tegedukoṁḍu* . . . ; **tr.** Achyutaraya having sent the subordinate chiefs and a **regiment** to the kingdom of Tiruvaḍi and having collected tributes (from the ruler of that kingdom); *S.I.I.* IX, pt. ii, No. 551, pp. 570–71, ll. 1, 2 ; Kāḷahasti, Chandragiri Tq., Chittoor Dt., A.P. St. **Dy.** Tuḷuva, Achyutarāya, Ś. 1454 = 1532 A.D.

daḷavāyi (K. < Skt. *n.*), army commander; **text**[1] **:** . . . . *mahārāyara kāryake kartarāda* ***daḷavāyi*** *Channamanāykara makkaḷu* ***daḷavāyi*** *Kṛishṇappanāykaru* . . . . ; **tr.** the personal secretary of the emperor and **army commander**

Channamanāyaka's son Krishnappanāyaka (also an) **army commander** ; *S.I.I.* IX, pt. ii, No. 605, p. 613, ll. 4–5 ; Koṇḍāpuram, Hindupur Tq., Anantapur Dt., A.P. St. **Dy.** Tuḷuva, Sadāśiva, Ś. 1465 = 1543 A.D. ; **text**[2] : . . . *Kaṁṭhīrava Narasarājoḍeyaravaru prithivirājyaṁgeyyutiralu Hurada prabhu Mādhavanāyakara kumāraru* ***daḷavāyi*** *Liṁgarājayyanavaru* . . . ; **tr.** the **army commander** Liṁgarājayya son of Mādhavanāyaka the administrator of Hura while Kaṁṭhīrava Narasarājoḍeya was ruling over the earth ; *E.C.* (R) III, Hg. 116, p. 510, ll. 9–12 ; Narasīpura, Heggadadevanakote Tq., Mysore Dt., Karn. St. **Dy.** Woḍ. of Mys., Narasarājoḍeya, Ś. 1576 = 1655 A.D.

dāḷi (K. < Skt. *n.*), invasion ; **text :** . . . . *gagana taḷaṁbaraṁ negeda* ***dāḷi****ya dhūḷige berchi . . . vanāntaramaṁ puge guhāntarmaṁ puge* ; **tr.** the enemies having ran into the forest and having hidden themselves in caves out of fear created by the dust which arose sky-high during the **invasion** ; *S.I.I.* XI, No. 147, p. 179, l. 10 ; Chikkahandigoḷ, Gadag Tq. and Dt., Karn. St. **Dy.** Chāḷ. of Kal., Vikramāditya VI, Ch. Vi. yr. 24 = 1099 A.D.

dāḷikrama (K. < Skt. *n.*), strategy of military campaign ; **text :** . . . . *arasar* ***dāḷikrama****doḷ Śivāpan piḍidu maguḷe bandu Pūvinapadaṁgaḷiy-appayaṇavīḍinoḷ*. . . . ; **tr.** as part of the **strategy of** the ruler's **military campaign** he captured Sivāpan and returned to the camp at Pūvinapaḍaṁgaḷi ; *S.I.I.* IX, pt. i, No. 101, p. 72, l. 29 ; Mōrigēri, Hadagalli Tq., Bellary Dt., Karn. St. **Dy.** Chāḷ. of Kal., Āhavamalla, Ś. 967 = 1045 A.D.

damagoḷaga (K. < Skt.+K. *dharmagoḷaga, n.*), measure of capacity of grains given for pious purposes to the god ; **text :** . . . *Kalidēvara naṁdādīvigege gāṇa 1 dēvagoḷaga* ***damagoḷaga****vaṁ dhānyadali kuḷavaṁ Kētayanāyakanu aṟuvattokkalumirddu koṭṭaru*. . . . ; **tr.** Kētayanāyaka and the body of sixty tenants jointly gave one oil mill and from the produce on land **one measure of capacity of grains to the god as a pious gift** ; *S.I.I.* IX, pt. i, No. 88, p. 59, ll. 23–25 ; Chimnahaḷḷi, Hadagalli Tq., Bellary Dt., Karn. St. **Dy.** Chāḷ. of Kal., Jagadēkamalla, Ś. 956 = 1034 A.D.

ḍāmara (K. *n.*), attacking ; **text :** . . . . . *śrī Āhavamalladēvar . . . . chōṟāri māri* ***ḍāmarō****pasarggaṁgaḷamaṟgisi nānādēsādhīsaraṁ vasagataṁ māḍi* . . . . ; **tr.** Āhavamalladēva having **attack**ed and subdued the evil enemy Chōṟa (Chōḷa) and having won over rulers of different countries ; *S.I.I.* IX, pt. i, No. 77, p. 47 ll. 2–3 ; Kōgaḷi, Hadagalli Tq., Bellary Dt., Karn. St. **Dy.** Chāḷ. of Kal., Āhavamalla, Ś. 914 = 992 A.D.

daṁḍa[1] (Skt. *n.*), measuring rod ; **text :** . . . *Rāmēśvarāya samadāyi Suvarṇavāḍagrāmādhikāri* . . . . . . ***daṁḍāt*** *sā pañcha viṁśati nivarttana saṁmitā bhūḥ* . . . . . ; **tr.** 25 *nivarttana* (land measure) of land measured by the **measuring**

rod was granted by headman of Survarṇavāḍa village to the god Rāmēśvara ; *K.I.* II, No. 24, p. 91, ll. 34–35 ; Rāmatīrtha, Athani Tq., Belgaum Dt., Karn. St. **Dy.** Kal. of Kal., Bijjaḷa, Ś. 1089 = 1166 A.D.

daṁḍa[2] (Skt. *n.*), punitive tax ; **text**[1] : . . . *Ēṇige nāmadhēyaṁ grāmaṁ* . . . . *śulka* . . . . ***daṁḍādi*** *sakala dravyōpārjanōpētaṁ* . . . . . *śatāya daśabhyaścha* . . . . . *mahābrāhmaṇēbhyah* . . . . *dattavān;* **tr.** he gave the village named Ēṇige to one hundred and ten great brāhmaṇas along with revenue incomes such as taxes, **punitive tax**es, etc ; *K.I.* II, No. 29, p. 110, ll. 64–65, 69–70, 73; copper plates stored in Kannada Research Institute, Dharwar, Dharwar Tq. and Dt., Karn. St. **Dy.** Kal. of Kal., Bijjaḷa, Ś. 1104 = 1182 A.D. ; **text**[2] (K. *n.)* : . . . *Dōsahaḷḷiya* ***daṁḍa****varu arasugaḷige teṟuvevu* . . . . ; **tr.** we will remit to the king **punitive tax**es collected from Dōsahaḷḷi ; *S.I.I.* IX, pt. ii, No. 433, p. 442, ll. 53–54 ; Siṁganallūru, Kollegala Tq., Chamarajanagara Dt., Karn. St. **Dy.** Saṅgama, Dēvarāya, Ś. 1330 = 1408 A.D.

daṁḍādhikāri (Te. < Skt. *n.*), magistrate ; **text :** (damaged) *dakshiṇa* ***daṁḍādhikāru****laina śrīkaraṇa Mahānāḍa sēnāpatulu*. . . . ; **tr.** Mahānāḍa sēnāpati the accounts officer and **magistrate** of the sourthern region ; *S.I.I.* V, No. 1284, p. 470, l. 16–17 ; Śrīkūrmam, Srikakulam Tq. and Dt., A.P. St. **Misc.,** Ś. 1157 = 1235 A.D.

daṁḍādhipa (K. < Skt. *n.*), army general ; **text**[1] : . . . . *gāṁbhīryadiṁ sauryyadiṁ Baladēvaṁge samānamapparoḷarē mattanya* ***daṁḍādhipa****ru* . . . . . . ; **tr.** in statelyness and bravery is there any other **army commander** who can rival Baladēva; *E.C.* II, No. 175, p. 127, ll. 26-27 ; Śravaṇabeḷagoḷa, Channarayapatna Tq., Hassan Dt., Karn. St. **Misc.,** Ś. 1061 = 1139 A.D. ; **text**[2] : . . . *śrīmad Baicha* ***daṁḍādhipa*** . . . . . . ; **tr.** the illustrious **army commander** Baicha ; *S.I.I.* VII, pt. i, No. 212, p. 107, l. 11 ; Mūḍabidure, Karkala Tq., Udupi Dt., Karn. St. **Dy.** Tuḷuva, Kṛishṇadēvarāya, Ś. 1437 = 1515 A.D.

daṁḍādhīśaṁ (K. < Skt. *n.*), army commander ; **text** : . . . *jagadoḷatiśayamideṁisalu* . . . . *Sivapuramaṁ sogayisuva* . . . . . *Jōgadēva* ***daṁḍādhīśaṁ*** . . . . ; **tr.** the **army commander** Jōgadēva founded the township called Sivapura which shone as a wonder of the world ; *K.I.* I, No. 30, pp. 68–69, ll. 33–34 ; Munavaḷḷi, Saundatti Tq., Belgaum Dt., Karn. St. **Dy.** Sēü. of Dēv., Singhaṇa, Ś. 1145 = 1222 A.D.

daṁḍādhishṭhāyaka (K. < Skt. *n.*), army commander ; **text :** . . . ***daṁḍādhishṭhāyaka*** *kammaṭada Māchayyaṁgaḷu* . . . . . ; **tr.** Māchayya of the mint who was also an **army commander**; *E.C.* (R) VIII, Hn. 131, p. 352, l. 1 ; Kōravangala, Hassan Tq. and Dt., Karn. St. **Misc.,** Cy. yr. Jaya = 1174 A.D.

daṁḍadōsha (K. < Skt. *n.*), income from fines ; **text** : . . . *Daṁḍanāyakaṁ Mādhava bhaṭṭar* . . .

Urigeṟeyalu māṟuveleya paṁnāyamuman . . . . *vokkaldeṟe* ***daṁḍadōsha*** *intinituvan* . . . . *biṭṭar* . . . . . . ; **tr.** the army commander Mādhava bhaṭṭa donated (among many other incomes) the income from the sale of betel leaves in Urigeṟe, tenants' tax and **income from fines** for offences, etc. ; *Ep. Ind.* XVI, No. 8, pp. 33–34, ll. 33–34, 38, 40, 42 ; Lakshmēśvara, Shirahatti Tq., Dharwar Dt., Karn. St. **Dy.** Chāḷ. of Kal., Vikramāditya VI, reg. yr. 27 = 1102 A.D.

daṁḍanātha (K. < Skt. *n.*), army commander ; **text**[1] **:** . . . *bittariparār aggaḷa Bhāskara* ***daṁḍanātha*** *naṁ* . . . . ; **tr.** who indeed can describe the greatness of the **army commander** Bhāskara . . ; *S.I.I.* XX, No. 46, p. 53, l. 32 ; Guḍigēri, Shirhatti Tq., Dharwar Dt., Karn. St. **Dy.** Chāḷ. of Kal., Sōmēśvara II, Ś. 994 = 1072 A.D. ; **text**[2] **:** . . . *Tuḷukaṭakaṁ virōdamanoḍarchhalu Maṁgapa* ***daṁḍanāthanuṁ*** . . . . *Hayiva bhūbhūjanu pēḷalu pōgiye kādi geldanu* . . . . ; **tr.** . . in order to put down the enmity of the Tuḷu kingdom, the ruler of Hayive ordered his **army commander** Maṁgapa to fight against the enemy and he won the battle . . . . ; *K.I.* I, No. 36, sections 3 and 4, p. 85, ll. 11–12 ; Kaikiṇi, Bhatkal Tq. and Dt., Karn. St. **Dy.** Nagire chfs., Hayivarasa, Cy. yr. Bahudhānya = 1398 A.D.

daṁḍanāyaka (K. < Skt. *n.*), army commander ; [This word and its cognates occur in a large number of South Indian inscriptions] ; **text :** . . *samastapraśastisahitaṁ* . . . . *śrīmad* ***daṁḍanāyakam*** *Kariya Kēśirājayyaṁgaḷu Siṁdavāḍi sāyiranāḷuttire* . . . . ; **tr.** while Kariya Kēśirājayya, endowed with all the epithets and an **army commander** was ruling over Siṁdavāḍi - 1000 . . ; *S.I.I.* IX, pt. i, No. 295, p. 317, ll. 6–8 ; Bāpuram, Advani Tq., Kurnool Dt., A. P. St. **Dy.** Kal. of Kal., Sōmēśvara, Ś. 1098 = 1172 A.D.

daṁḍapāṭa (Te. *n.*), territorial division ; **text :** . . . *Rājamahēndrvarapu* ***daṁḍapāṭa*** *21 sthalāla baḷiṁjapekkaṁḍru* . . . . . . ; **tr.** the commercial guilds in 21 centres of the **territorial division** called Rājamahēndravara ; *S.I.I.* X, No. 739, p. 386, ll. 12–13 ; Drākshārāma, Ramachandrapuram Tq., E. Godavari Dt., A.P. St. **Dy.** Gajapati, Mukuṁda Gajapati., in characters of 16th century A.D.

daṁḍe (K. *n.*), bank (of canal or river) ; **text :** . . . *modala kāluve* ***daṁḍe****ya gadde* . . . . ; **tr.** wet field on the **bank** of the first **canal** . . ; *E.C.* XVI, Chnk. 53, p. 4, ll. 15–16 ; Chikkanāyakanahaḷḷi, Chikkanayakanahalli, Tumkur Dt., Karn. St. **Dy.** Āravīḍu, Veṁkaṭapati, Ś. 1559 = 1637 A.D.

daṁḍe beṭṭu (K. *n.*), elevated land adjoining river bank; **text :** . . . *Ayiraḍiya oḷagaṇa* ***daṁḍe beṭṭi****nalu* . . . . *baddha brahmdāyada mūlada bāḷu* . . . . ; **tr.** the land originally given for the livelihood of inhabitants of the brāhmaṇa settlement on the **elevated land adjoining river bank** within Ayiraḍi . . . ; *S.I.I.* VII, No. 356, p. 213, ll. 7–8 ; Maṇigārakēri, Udupi Tq. and Dt., Karn. St. **Dy.** Saṅgama, Harihara, Ś. 1316 = 1394 A.D.

daṁḍēśa (K. *n.*), army commander ; **text :** .. *Kasapa* ***daṁḍēśana*** *sabheyoḷ maṁtri mukhyanene negaḷdaṁ sajjanutan Aṁmmaṇa****daṁḍēśan*** .... ; **tr.** Aṁmmaṇa, the **army commander** who is respected by good persons flourished as a chief minister in the assembly of the **army commander** Kasapa . . . ; *S.I.I.* XX, No. 137, p. 174, ll. 16–17 ; Lakshmēśvara, Shirahatti Tq., Dharwar Dt., Karn. St. **Dy.** Kal. of Kal., Bijjaḷa, Ś. 1083 = 1161 A.D.

daṁḍeyaḍḍaṇa (K. *n.*), shield ; **text :** . . . *raṇadoḷ teṁkaṇarāyanaṁkada chatuḥsainyōtkaraṁ* ***daṁḍeyaḍḍaṇa****vītaṁ* . . . ; **tr.** he was verily the **shield** for the enitre army of the southern lord in battle fields ; *E.C.* XI, Dvg. 25, p. 86, ll. 56–57 ; Harihara, Harihara Tq., Davanagere Dt., Karn. St. **Dy.** Hoy., Narasiṁha, Ś. 1146 = 1224 A.D.

daṁḍige (K. *n.*), palanquin ; **text :** *Hoṁnappana magaḷu Bayichavvege* ***daṁḍigeya*** *Bīyake koṭṭa Tāvarekeṟe hola*.... ; **tr.** the field at Tāvarekeṟe given to Bayichavve, the daughter of Hoṁnappa for procuring rice therefrom for maintaining a **palanquin** . . . ; *E.C.* IX, Mgd. 81, p. 131, ll. 7–9; Baichaguppe, Magadi Tq., Bangalore Dt., Karn. St. **Dy.** Hoy., Ballāḷa, Cy. yr. Vikrama = 1340 A.D.

daṁḍige uṁbaḷi grāma (K. *n.*), village granted for the livelihood of palanquin bearers ; **text :** *Gaṁgappanāykarige koṭa* .... ***daṁḍige uṁbaḷi grāma****da śilālēkhanada vivara* . . . ; **tr.** details registered in the inscription regarding **the village granted for the livelihood** of Gaṁgappanāyka the **palanquin bearer** . . . ; *E.C.* XII, Tmk. 59, p. 52, ll. 6–8 ; Vaṁchihaḻḻi, Tumkur Tq. and Dt., Karn. St. **Dy.** Tuḷuva, Achyutarāya, Ś. 1465 = 1543 A.D.

daṁḍinabhyāgate (K. *n.*), tax levied for maintaining the army ; **text :** *dēvadānada sthaḷaṁgaḷigevū* .... *Perumāḷadēva daṁṇṇāykara Koḍagiya sthaḷaṁgaḷigevū* .... *āneya sēse kudureya sēse* ***daṁḍinabhyāgate*** ... *nallettu nalleṁmme* .. ... *intivoḷagāda ellā bādheyanu* .... *pariharsi* .. ... *koṭṭaru* ... ; **tr.** all the places belonging to the grant made to deities and all the gift lands belonging to Perumāḷadēva daṁṇṇāyka, taxes such as on elephants, on horses, **tax levied for maintaining the army**, taxes on quality bullocks, quality buffaloes, etc., were exempted ; *E.C.* (R) VII, Ng. 73, p. 63, ll. 47, 48, 50 ; Beḻḻūru, Nagamanagala Tq., Mandya Dt., Karn. St. **Dy.** Hoy., Narasiṁha III, Ś. 1206 = 1284 A.D.

daṁḍinagōva (K. *n.*), protector of the army (a title) ; **text :** ***daṁḍinagōva*** *Kuppadēvarasaru Puligeṟe mūnūru Kōgaḷi ayinūṟu Māsavāḍi nūṟanālvattanāḷuttaṁ* .... ; **tr.** while Kuppadēvarasa, the **protector of the army** was administering Puligeṟe-300, Kōgaḷi-500 and Māsavāḍi-140 . . . ; *S.I.I.* XI, No. 30, p. 18, ll. 11–13 ; Mēvuṇḍi, Mundaragi Tq., Dharwar Dt., Karn. St. **Dy.** Rāshṭr., Kṛishṇa II, recopied in 12th century characters.

daṁḍinahodake (K. *n.*), tax levied for maintaining the army ; **text :** *yellā dēvadāna Koḍagiya sthaḷaṁgaḷa . . . . kiṟukuḷa . . . . āneya sēse kudureya sēse* ***daṁḍinahodake*** *. . . voḷagāda yellā tereyanū . . . . . mahājanaṁgaḷu pariharsi . . . koṭṭaru* . . . ; **tr.** in the case of all grants made to temples and other grants of lands, taxes such as minor taxes, taxes on elephants and horses, **tax levied for maintaining the army**, etc., were exempted by the *mahājana* (administrative body) while making the grants ; *E.C.* (R) VII, Ng. 76, p. 73, ll. 56–57, 58 ; Beḷḷūru, Nagamanagala Tq., Mandya Dt., Karn. St. **Dy.** Hoy., Narasiṁha III, Ś. 1206 = 1284 A.D.

daṁḍina kāṇike (K. *n.*), contribution towards the maintenance of the army ; **text :** *Uruvakoṁḍeya sīmeyoḷagaṇa . . . . . agrahāragaḷali taḷavārike bēḍike . . .* ***daṁḍina-kāṇike*** *. . . modalāda . . . kāṇike kappagaḷu . . . biṭu . . . . hākisikoṭṭa dharmaśilāśāsana* ; **tr.** a stone edict registering the pious act of exempting the inhabitants of the *agrahāras* in Uruvakoṁḍe-sīme from such taxes as village watch and ward, requisitioned tax, **contribution towards the maintenance of the army**, etc ; *S.I.I.* IX, pt. ii, No. 663, p. 657, ll. 7, 16, 20, 26 ; Pennahobilam, Gooty Tq., Ananatapur Dt., A.P. St. **Dy.** Tuḷuva, Sadāśiva, Ś. 1478 = 1556 A.D.

daṁḍinokkalu (K. *n.*), army cantonment ; **text :** *Telligēśvaradēvargge . . .* ***daṁḍinokkaluṁ*** *taḷadokkaluṁ devasavaḷaveṁṇe gāṇadalli soḷasaveraḍu* ; **tr.** each family in the **army cantonment** and the township should each day measure out two *soḷasa* (a liquid measure) of oil from the oil mills as donation to the god Telligēśvara ; *Ep. Ind.*, XX, No. 12, p. 117, ll. 47, 48–49 ; Beṇachamaṭṭi, Ron Tq., Dharwar Dt., Karn. St. **Dy.** Kal. of Kal., Bijjaṇa, Ś. 1088 = 1167 A.D.

daṁḍudōva (Te. *n.*), road used by the army ; **text :** (damaged) . . . . . . *Hālaharavi polamulō* ***daṁḍudōvanu*** *paradēśi brāhmala satrānakunnu . . . . . Haḷigēra grāmamaṁdu . . . . amara uṁbaḷiki pāliṁchina* . . . ; **tr.** a permanent grant of land in the village of Haligēra for the free feeding choultry for the itinerant brāhmaṇas who travel on **road used by the army** across the field called Hālaharavi ; *S.I.I.* XVI, No. 247, p. 253, ll. 9–10, 13 ; Haḷigēra, Alur Tq., Bellary Dt., Karn. St. **Dy.** Tuḷuva, Sadāśiva, Ś. 1482 = 1560 A.D.

daṁḍuhōgu (K. *vb.*), march one's army against ; **text :** (badly damaged) . . . . . . *Bukkarāyanu Ōrugalla dēsakke* ***daṁḍuhōda****lli Kottakoṁḍadalli Turukaru tāgidali . . . . . Rāmadēvanu kādi svargastanāda* . . . ; **tr.** while Bukkarāya **marched his army against** Orugalladēsa the muslims attacked him at Kottakoṁḍa and Rāmadēva fought and died in the ensuing battle ; *E.C.* XII, Chnk. 15, p. 212, ll. 3–4, 11–12 ; Doḍḍatekkalavaṭṭa, Chikkanayakanahalli Tq., Tumkur Dt., Karn. St.

Dy. Saṅgama, Harihara, Ś. 1306 = 1384 A.D.

daṁḍumānyamu (Te. *n.*), grant for the maintenance of an army ; **text :** (badly damaged) . . . . . . *Bōlavaram grāmāna* ***daṁḍumānyamu*** . . . . ; **tr.** (perhaps) **grant** of the village Bōlavaram **for the maintenance of an army** ; *S.I.I.* X, No. 773, p. 406, ll. 9–10 ; Bollavaram, Nandikotkur Tq., Kurnool Dt., A.P. St. **Dy.** Mughal, Aurangazeb, Ś. 1619 = 1697 A.D.

daṁḍutōva (Te. *n.*), road used by the army ; **text :** (damaged) . . . . . . ***daṁḍutōva****nu vachche paradēśi brāṁhmala sūdrulaku anna satturuvu peṭi aṁduku Aligēra grāmaṁ . . . . tāmraśāsanaṁ yiṁpiṁchi dhāravōśiri* . . . ; **tr.** the village of Aligēra was granted with the libation of water to the charity feeding house for the benefit of the itinerant brāhmaṇas and śūdras travelling through the **road used by the army** ; *S.I.I.* XVI, No. 273, pp. 279–80, ll. 4–8 ; Hālaharavi, Alur Tq., Bellary Dt., Karn. St. **Dy.** Tuḷuva, Sadāśiva, in characters of 16th cent.

daṁma (K. < Skt. *dramma, n.*), gold coin; **text**[1] **:** . . . . . *pariyāra irmattargge ondu* ***daṁma*** . . . ; **tr.** a compensation of one **gold coin** for two *mattar* (a land measure) of land ; *S.I.I.* XI, No. 12, p. 9, l. 22 ; Soraṭūr, Gadag Tq. and Dt., Karn. St. **Dy.** Rāshṭr., Amōghavarsha, Ś. 788 = 867 A.D. ; **text**[2] (Te. < Skt. *dramma, n.*) **:** (badly damaged). . . . . *prati* ***daṁma****niluvakoka vīsamu* . . . . ; **tr.** one *vīsa* on the sale price of each **gold coin** ; *S.I.I.* X, No. 505, p. 273, l. 26 ; Mācherla, Palnad Tq., Guntur Dt., A.P. St. **Dy.** Kākatīya, Pratāparudra, Ś. 1235 = 1313 A.D.

daṁṇāyaka (K. < Skt. *n.*), an army-cum-revenue officer ; **text :** . . . . *mahāpradhānaṁ Pōlāḷva****daṁṇāyaka****ra sēnabōva* . . . . *Dēvaṇṇanu* ; **tr.** Dēvaṇṇa the village accountant of the chief minister Pōlāḷva who was **an army-cum-revenue officer** ; *E.C.* (R) IX, Bl. 15, p. 10, ll. 3–4 ; Bēlūru, Belur Tq., Hassan Dt., Karn. St. **Misc.,** Ś. 1163 = 1241 A.D.

daṁṇṇāyaka (K. < Skt. *n.*), chief of the army ; **text :** *Paṁchaliṁgadēvarige* . . . . *Siṁghaṇadēvara sarbbādhikāri Puruśōttama* ***daṁṇṇāyakara*** *niyāmadiṁ Jōgadēva . . . Kaḻḻavoḷeyaṁ māḍikoṭṭu* . . . . ; **tr.** Jōgadēva made a grant of the village Kaḻḻavoḷe on the orders of the **chief of the army** Purushōttama, an officer with over all powers under the emperor Siṁghaṇadēva. . . ; *K.I.* I, No. 30, p. 68, ll. 25, 26–28 ; Munavaḻḻi, Saundatti Tq., Belgaum Dt., Karn. St. **Dy.** Sēü. of Dēv., Siṁghaṇa, Ś. 1145 = 1222 A.D.

daṁti (K. *n.*), elephant ; **text :** (fragmentary) . . *arātigaḷa* ***daṁti*** . . . . ; **tr. elephant** of the enemies . . . ; *E.C.* (R) X , Ak. 16, p. 22, l. 18 ; Arasīkere, Arasikere Tq., Hassan Dt., Karn. St. **Dy.** Hoy., Vīraballāḷa, Ś. 1111 = 1189 A.D.

danabaḷa (K. < Skt. *n.*), tax on cattle ; **text :** . . . . *Tipparasaruṁ* . . . *Goṇamahadēviyuṁ* . . . . *Huluṁgūra haṁnnirvvaru gāvuṁḍu samasta praje* *nakhara mummuridaṁḍaṁgaḷige* .... ***danabaḷa****varu* *biṭṭaru* .... ; **tr.** Tipparasa and Goṇamahadēvi granted to the body of twelve, the village heads, all the inhabitants, the merchants and the merchant guild the income from **tax on cattle** ; *S.I.I.* XV, No. 596, p. 390, l. 8 ; Kuṇṭōji, Muddebihal Tq., Bijapur Dt., Karn. St. **Misc.,** in characters of 12th cent. A.D.

dānachintāmaṇi ghaḷe (K. < Skt. *n.*), measuring rod named after the title *dānachintāmaṇi* ; **text :** (badly damaged) .... ***dānachintamaṇiya ghaḷe*** .... ; **tr. measuring rod named after the title dānachintāmaṇi** ; *S.I.I.* XV, No. 596, p. 390, l. 8 ; Kuṇṭōji, Muddebihal Tq., Bijapur Dt., Karn. St. **Misc.,** in characters of 12th cent. A.D.

dānādhikāri (Skt. *n.*), officer in charge of grants and endowments ; **text :** .. *Kāshmīrabhaṭṭa Mallayapaṁḍitēna* ***dānādhikāriṇā*** *likhitamidaṁ* .... ; **tr.** this charter was written by Mallaya paṁḍita who was a brāhmaṇa from Kāshmīra and was the **officer in charge of grants and endowments** ; *Ep. Ind.* XII, No. 19, p. 155, ll. 86–87 ; Nīlagunda, Harapanahalli Tq., Bellary Dt., Karn. St. **Dy.,** Chāḷ. of Kal., Vikramāditya VI, Ch. Vi. yr. 48 = 1123 A.D.

dānādhikrayayōgya (K. < Skt. *n.*), grant given with right to gift or sell ; **text :** .... *Maṇiyapākagrāmake saluva sarvvavu* .... *Visaṇarāvuttaru Nārāyaṇabhaṭarige* .... *niṁma putrapautra pāraṁpareyāgi* .... ***dānādhikraya yōgya****vāda sukhadalū anubhavisūdū eṁdu koṭa dānapaṭṭe* .. ; **tr.** Visaṇarāvuta **granted** through this donative edict, all privileges in the village of Maṇiyapāka to Nārāyaṇabhaṭa to be enjoyed by him and his descendants with the **right to gift or sell** ; *S.I.I.* IX, pt. ii, No. 515, p. 530, ll. 37–38, 46–48, 50–53 ; Chaṭnahaḷḷi, Harapanahalli Tq., Bellary Dt., Karn. St. **Dy.** Tuḷuva, Krishṇadēvarāya, Ś. 1446 = 1524 A.D.

dānādi vinimaya vikrayaṅgaḷ (M. < Skt. *n.*), (right to) gift, barter or sell ; **text :** .... *Kākkūr nañjai pūñjai varṇādāyam* .... *svāmyaṅgaḷukku* ***dānādi vinimaya vikrayaṅgaḷ****ukku yōgyamāga* .. .. *Kulaśēkharapperumāḷavargaḷ naḍattugira Irāmēśvarakaṭṭaḷettanmattukku* .... *anubhavittukkoḷvārgaḷāgavum* ; **tr.** Kākkūr shall be enjoyed together with its wet and dry lands, its perquisites in gold, etc., with the right to dispose them of in **gifts, barter, or sale** by Kulaśēkharapperumāḷ for conduct of services in Rāmēśvaram ; *T.A.S.* V, No. 4, p. 15, ll. 46–53 ; Tiruvanantapuram, Tiruvanantapuram Tq. and Dt., Ker. St. **Dy.** Sētupati, Muttu Rāmaliṅga Vijaya Raṅganātha Sētupati , Kollam 945, Ś. 1691 = 1769 A.D.

dānakraya (K. < Skt. *n.*), monetary value of the gift ; **text :** .. *Bijjarasa Achyutadēvaṁgaḷu*. ... ... *Talavāgilahaḷḷiya* .... ***dānakraya****vāgi* .... *koṭṭaru* .... ; **tr.** Bijjarasa Achyutadēva granted the village of Talavāgilahaḷḷi after fixing its monetary value ; *S.I.I.* IX, pt. i, No. 352, p. 372, ll. 2–4 ; Nīlagunda, Harapanahalli Tq., Bellary Dt., Karn. St. **Misc.**, Cy. yr. Kīlaka = 1309 A.D.

dānamāṇaṅṅal (M. < Skt. *n.*), grants ; **text :** *Bālamārttāṇḍavarmmar . . . . namakku avakā śamāyiṭṭu anubavichchu varunna vattu kīrttiyaṅṅaḷum* ***dāṇamāṇaṅṅaḷum*** *eppērppaṭṭadum Perumāḷ śrībhaṇḍārattilekku . . . . eḻudikkoḍuttār* ; **tr.** Bālamārttāṇḍavarmmar gave away in writing to the temple treasury of the god Perumāḷ all the property, duties, **grants**, etc. hitherto hereditarily enjoyed by him ; *T.A.S.* V, No. 6, p. 27, ll. 5–7 ; Tiruvananthapura, Tiruvananthapuram Tq. and Dt., Ker. St. **Dy.** Rulers of Travancore, Bālamārttāṇḍavarmmar, Kollam 925 = 1750 A.D.

dānamānyaṁ (K. < Skt. *n.*), tax free gift of land; **text**[1] **:** (badly damaged) . . . ***dānamānyaṁ*** *koṭṭa key mattar* . . . . ; **tr. tax free gift of** *mattar* (land measure) of **land** ; *S.I.I.* IX, pt. i, No. 71, p. 44, l. 14 ; Bāgaḷi, Bellary Tq. and Dt., Karn. St. **Dy.** Rāshṭr., Khoṭṭigadēva., Ś. 894 = 972 A.D. ; **text**[2] (T. < Skt. *n.*) **:** . . . . . *inda rājyattu dēvadānam tiruviḍaiyāṭṭam maḍappuṟam paḷḷichchandamāṇa* ***dāṇamānyaṅ****gaḷil* . . . . ; **tr.** we have made a **tax free gift of lands** in our kingdom remitting all kinds of taxes such as on gift to temples, gift made for the entertainment of the deity, gift made for the temple kitchen and gift made to the Jaina temple ; *E.C.* X, Chik. 20, p. 123, ll. 24–28; Nandi, Chikkaballapur Tq., Kolar Dt., Karn. St. **Dy.** Hoy., Ballāḷa, Ś. 1224 = 1302 A.D.

dānamūla (K. < Skt. *n.*), right over a gifted land; **text :** *dānamūligaḷanoḍaṁbaḍsi avara* ***dānamūla****vanu toḍesi* . . . ; **tr.** having cancelled the **right over a gifted land** with the consent of those who were holding right over gifted land ; *E.C.* (R) VIII, Tīr. 196, p. 691, ll. 20–21 ; Aṁbigere, Tirthahalli Tq., ShimogaDt., Karn. St. **Dy.** Saṅgama, Harihara, Ś. 1307 = 1395 A.D.

dānamūli (K. < Skt. *n.*), holder of the right over gifted land ; **text :** ***dānamūli****gaḷanoḍaṁbaḍsi avara dānamūlavanu toḍesi* . . . ; **tr.** having cancelled the right over a gifted land with the consent of the **holders of the right over the gifted land** . . . ; *E.C.* (R) VIII, Tīr. 196, p. 691, ll. 20–21 ; Aṁbigere, Tirthahalli Tq., Shimoga Dt., Karn. St. **Dy.** Saṅgama, Harihara, Ś. 1307 = 1395 A.D.

dānapatraṁ (Te. < Skt. *n.*), gift deed ; **text :** . . . . . . *Kṛishṇamarājuṁgāru* . . . ***dānapatraṁ*** *yichchi samarpiṁchina chēnu kha 1/2* . . . . . . ; **tr.** 1/2 *kha* (*khaṁḍuga*, land of the extent of being sown with half *khaṁḍuga* of seeds) of land given by Kṛishṇamarājuṁgāru through a **gift deed** ; *S.I.I.* XVI, No. 261, p. 267, ll. 23–24 ; Pedda Ahōbalaṁ, Sirvel Tq., Kurnool Dt., A.P. St. **Dy.** Tuḷuva, Sadāśiva, Cy. yr. Rudhirōdgārin = 1563 A.D.

dānapaṭṭe (K. < Skt. *n.*), gift deed ; **text :** . . . *Koṁḍappavoḍeyaru Tirumaladēvarige koṭṭa*

dānapaṭṭe . . . . ; **tr.** the **gift deed** given by Koṁḍapavoḍeya to Tirumaladēva ; *S.I.I.* IX, pt. ii, No. 555, p. 576, ll. 13–14 ; Basarūru, Kundapur Tq., Udupi Dt., Karn. St. **Dy.** Tuḷuva, Achyutarāya, Ś. 1454 = 1533 A.D.

dāṉappiramāṇam (T. < Skt. *n.*), gift deed; **text[1] :** . . . . . *nañjey puñjey nāṟpāl ellaiyuḷ kīḻnōkkiṉa kiṇaṟum mēlnokkiṉa maramum maṟṟum eppēṟpaṭṭaṉavum* . . . . . *śellakkaḍavadāga* . . . . ***dāṉappiramāṇam*** *paṇṇikkuḍuttōm* . . . . ; **tr.** we gave all the lands within the four boundaries including wet and dry lands . . . . . trees grown over and wells dug below the ground level by executing a **gift deed**; *E.C.* X, Mal. 43, pp. 102–03, ll. 11–17 ; Mākārahaḷḷi, Malur Tq., Kolar Dt., Karn. St. **Dy.** Hoy., Vīra Rāmanātha, in characters of 13th cent. A.D. ; **text[2] :** . . . . ***dāṉappira-māṇamāga*** *viṭṭtukkuḍutta nilam* . . . . ; **tr.** land given through the **gift deed**; *T.A.S.* V, No. 25, p. 86, ll. 23–25 ; Tiruvidāṅgōḍu, Ker. St. **Misc.,** Kollam 864 = 1688 A.D.

dānasāle, dānaśāle (K. < Skt. *n.*), charity feeding house ; **text[1] :** . . . *Padmabbarasiyar tamma basadige* ***dānasālege*** . . . *Mārasiṅghayyaṁ kereyaṁ biṭṭaṁ* ; **tr.** Mārasiṅghayya granted a tank to the **charity feeding house** attached to the Jaina temple constructed by Padmabbarasi ; *S.I.I.* XI, No. 38, p. 24, ll. 6–7, 11, 13 ; Naregal, Ron Tq., Dharwar Dt., Karn. St. **Dy.** Rāshṭr., Kṛishṇa III, Ś. 873 = 950 A.D. ; **text[2] :** . . . ***dānaśālege*** *haḷḷivayala gaddeya krayada maulya ga 70* . . . ; **tr.** the value of the wet land called *haḷḷivayalu* donated to the **charity feeding house** was 70 *ga* (*gadyāṇa*, gold coin) ; *E.C.* (R) I, Cg. 19, p. 16, ll. 48–51 ; Aṁjanagiri, Madikeri Tq., Kodagu Dt., Karn. St. **Misc.,** Ś. 1465 = 1543 A.D.

dānaśilāśāsana (K. < Skt. *n.*), stone inscription recording a grant ; **text :** . . . *samasta praje gāvuṇḍagaḷu koṭṭa* ***dānaśilāśāsana*** . . . ; **tr. stone inscription recording the grant** made by all the inhabitants and village headmen ; *S.I.I.* IX, pt. ii, No. 421, p. 426, ll. 19–21 ; Modalli, Kollegal Tq., Chamarajanagar Dt., Karn. St. **Dy.** Saṅgama, Harihara, Ś. 1313 = 1392 A.D.

dānaśilā tāmbra śāsana (K. < Skt. *n.*), stone and copper plate inscriptions recording the details of grant ; **text :** . . . *dharṁmma sākshiyāgi oḍaṁbaṭṭu koṭṭa* ***dānaśilā tāṁbra śāsana*** . . . . . ; **tr.** with the consent of the witnesses, the pious grant the **stone and copper plate inscriptions recording the details of grant** were given ; *E.C.* VIII, Tīr. 130, p. 593, ll. 50–51 ; Hosakoppa, Tirthahalli Tq., Shimoga Dt., Karn. St. **Dy.** Saṅgama, Harihara, Ś. 1327 = 1405 A.D.

dānavinōdana ghaḷe (K. < Skt. *n.*), measuring rod named after the epithet *dānavinōda* ; **text :** *mūvattaidu gēṇa* ***dānavinōdana ghaḷe****yoḷ biṭṭa mattar aivattu* . . . ; **tr.** fifty *mattar* (a land measure) of land measured by the **measuring rod named after the epithet *dānavinōda*,** having a standard length of 35 spans, was granted ; *Ep. Ind.* XII, No. 32, p. 283, ll. 238–39 ; Yēvūr, Shorapur Tq., Gulbarga Dt., Karn. St. **Dy.** Chāḷ. of Kal., Vikramāditya VI, Ch. Vi. yr. 2 = 1077 A.D.

daṇāyaka (K. *n.*), army commander ; **text**[1] **:** . . . . . . *Kēteya* ***daṇāyaka****ru* . . . . *nambiyaru tamna magana hesaraniṭṭudakke* . . . . *koṭṭa maṇṇu* . . . . ; **tr.** Kēteya, the **army commander** made a gift of land to the temple priest who performed the naming ceremony of his son ; *E.C.* (R) III, Gu. 74, p. 58, ll. 6–12 ; Ballahaḷḷi, Gundlupet Tq., Mysore Dt., Karn. St. **Misc.,** Ś. 1258 = 1336 A.D. ; **text**[2] **:** . . . . *Bukkaṁṇa oḍeyara nirūpadiṁ* . . . . *mahāpradhānaṁ Malleya* ***daṇāyaka****ru Bārakūra rājyavanāḷuva kāladalu* . . . . ; **tr.** when the chief minister and **army commander** Malleya was administering Bārakūrarājya on the orders of Bukkaṁṇa oḍeya. . . . . ; *S.I.I.* VII, No. 322, p. 171, ll. 6–8 ; Mūḍakēri, Udupi Tq. and Dt., Karn. St. **Dy.** Saṅgama, Bukka, Ś. 1282 = 1360 A.D.

daṇāyakara sāmya (K. *n.*), landed property of the army commander ; **text :** (damaged) . . . . *keṟeya keḷage gadde beddalu* . . . . *siddhāya* . . . ***daṇāyakara sāmya*** . . . . *mumtāgi ēnuḷadanu nīvu āgumāḍikomḍu* . . . *saluvamtāgi* . . . *koṭṭa* . . . *dāna śilāśāsana* ; **tr.** stone inscription recording the grants of the wet land below the tank, dry lands, fixed tax, **landed property of the army commander**, etc., including whatever other benefits are available were granted ; *S.I.I.* IX, pt. ii, No. 440, p. 449, ll. 23, 24, 27–28, 29–31 ; Rajabavanahaḷḷi, Harapanahalli Tq., Bellary Dt., Karn. St **Dy.** Saṅgama, Dēvarāya, Ś. 1341 = 1419 A.D.

daṇāyini varttana (Te. *n.*), regular tax levied for the maintenance of army commander ; **text :** . . . *Ghamḍikōṭaku achēṭi durgga varttana* ***daṇāyini varttana*** *bēḍige kāṇika* . . . . *modalainavi yemnigalavu amnimni* . . . . *Mōpūri Bhairavēśvaruniki* . . . . *dhāravōsi ichchina dharmaśāsanaṁ* . . . ; **tr. regular tax** income such as for the maintenance of the fort, **for the maintenance of the army commander**, requisitioned tax, tribute, etc. were donated to the god Bhairavēśvara of Mōpūru with the libation of water ; *S.I.I.* XVI, No. 139, p. 151, ll. 15–17, 25, 29 ; Mōpūru, Pulivendla Tq., Cuddapah Dt., A.P. St. **Dy.** Tuḷuva, Sadāśiva, Ś. 1466 = 1545 A.D.

daṇḍa[1] (K. *n.*), standard measuring rod ; **text :** (damaged) . . . . *Satyāśraya dattiya paḍeda Kuṟugōḍa vyavaste entendoḍe padineṇṭu gēṇa 18 kōlu* . . . . . ***daṇḍa*** . . . . . . ; **tr.** for the grants made in the name of Satyāśraya, the **standard measuring rod** for Kuṟugōḍu is the use of the measuring rod of 18 spans ; *S.I.I.* IX, pt. i, No. 53, p. 30, ll. 1–3 ; Kurugōḍu, Bellary Tq. and Dt., Karn. St. **Dy.** Chal. of Bād., Satyāśraya, in characters of the 8th cent. A.D.

daṇḍa[2] (Skt. *n.*), fine ; **text :** . . . *Rāmēśvarāya samadāyi Suvarṇavāḍagrāmādhikāri patimukhya mahājanairyā* . . . . . *tasmin samuttha* ***daṇḍāt*** *sā* *pañchaviṁśati nivarttana saṁhitā bhūḥ* . . . . . ; **tr.** 25 *nivarttana* (land measure) of land was purchased out of the **fines** realized which was donated by the *mahājana* (administrative body) led by the headman (*grāmādhikāri*) of Suvarṇavāḍa to the god Rāmēśvara ; *K.I.* II, No. 24, pp. 91–92, ll. 34–35 ; Rāmatīrtha, Athani Tq., Belgaum Dt., Karn. St. **Dy.** Kal. of Kal., Bijjaḷa, Ś. 1089 = 1166 A.D.

daṇḍādāya (K. < Skt. *n.*), income from fines ; **text :** . . . *Baḍagikūṇṭeya manedeṟe holadeṟe* . . . . ***daṇḍādāya****vintinitttumaṁ* . . . . *dēvara nivēdyakke* . . . . . *koṭṭar* . . . . . ; **tr.** income from house tax, tax on fields, **income from fines**, etc., from the village of Baḍagikūṇṭe were granted for offering food services to the deity ; *S.I.I.* IX, pt. i, No. 172, p. 167, ll. 17–19, 22 ; Karakanṭhapura, Adavani Tq., Kurnool Dt., A.P. St. **Dy.** Chāḷ. of Kal., Vikramāditya VI, Ch. Vi. yr. 31 = 1106 A.D.

daṇḍādhinātha (K. < Skt. *n.*), army commander ; **text :** *samagra maṁtri perarilleṁdiṁtu* . . . . *charitrakke mechchi piriduṁ koṇḍāḍe* ***daṇḍādhinātha****roḷiṁtorvvane jīya bāppenisidaṁ śri Bhīma daṇḍādhipa*. . . . ; **tr.** a perfect counsellor among the most capable of fitting and reliable deliberations, there are no others equal to him and being pleased at his conduct, abundantly praises him, hence the blessed **army commander** Bhīma alone among the generals is addressed with great approval and admiration; *Ep. Ind.* XVI, No. 8, pp. 32-33, l. 6–8 ; Lakshmēśvara, Shirahatti Tq., Dharwar Dt., Karn. St. **Dy.** Chāḷ, of Kal., Vikramāditya VI, Ch. Vi. yr. 27 = 1102 A.D.

daṇḍādhipaṁ (K. < Skt. *n.*), army commander ; **text :** *samagra maṁtri perarilleṁdiṁtu* . . . *charitrakke mechchi piriduṁ koṇḍāḍe daṁḍādhinātharoḷiṁtorvvane jīya bāppenisidaṁ śri Bhīma****daṇḍādhipaṁ***. . . . ; **tr.** a perfect counsellor among the most capable of fitting and reliable deliberations, there are no others equal to him and being pleased at his conduct, abundantly praises him, hence the blessed **army commander** Bhīma alone among all the army commanders is addressed with great approval and admiration; *Ep. Ind.* XVI, No. 8, pp. 32–33, ll. 6–8 ; Lakshmēśvara, Dharwar Dt., Karn. St. **Dy.** Chāḷ, of Kal., Vikramāditya VI, Ch. Vi. yr. 27 = 1102 A.D.

daṇḍadōsha (K. < Skt. *n.*), income from fines ; **text :** . . . *Chōḷēśvaradēvaraṁgabhōgakkaṁ* . . . *Niḍuguṟute* . . . . . *nidhinidhāna nikshēpaṁ* . . . . *sahasra daṁḍadōshaṁ modalāge* . . . . *biṭṭukoṭṭa* . . . . . . ; **tr.** village of Niḍuguṟute was granted for the services to the god Chōḷēśvara along with privileges such as hidden treasure trove, underground deposits, thousand varities of **income from fines**, etc., ; *E.C.* XI, Chdg. 34, p. 25, ll. 28, 34–36 ; Gārēhaṭṭi, Chitradurga Tq. and Dt., Karn. St. **Dy.** Chāḷ. of Kal., Vikramāditya VI, reg. yr. 48 = 1123 A.D.

daṇḍakāṇam (T. *n.*), imposing of fine ; **text :** .

. . . *Nār̤āyaṇan Mādhavan* ***daṇḍakāṇam*** *paṭṭu vara ivanum aḍaivillādu pōga* . . . ; **tr.** Nār̤āyaṇan Mādhavan who was **imposed a fine** had run away ; *S.I.I.* XIII, No. 260, p. 138, ll. 3–4 ; Tiruppūndurutti, Tanjavur Tq. and Dt., T. Nadu St. **Dy.** Chōḷa, Sundara, reg. yr. 15 = 981 A.D.

daṇḍakkur̤r̤am (T. *n.*), fine for wrong doing ; **text:** (damaged) . . . . *dēvarkku* . . . . *Kārtigai viḷakku iḍa* . . . . *ney tūṇi* . . . *ivvūr* ***daṇḍakkur̤r̤amum*** *pīḍiligai variyum. koṇḍu* . . . *Īśānaśivanum Brahmaśivanum uḷḷiṭṭa dēvakanmigal śeyvippārgaḷāgavum* . . . . ; **tr.** the temple servants including Īśānaśiva and Brahmaśiva shall purchase one *tūṇi* (a liquid meausre) of ghee from the fine on wrong doings and the income from the donation box for burning a lamp in the month of *Kārtigai* to the god ; *S.I.I.* XVII, No. 243, p. 93, ll. 43–45 ; Mēlśēvūr, Gingee Tq., S. Arcot Dt., T. Nadu St. **Dy.** Chōḷa, Rājarāja I, reg. yr. 18 = 1002-03 A.D.

daṇḍam (T. < Skt. *n.*), fine ; **text**[1] : . . . ***daṇḍam*** *uḷḷiṭṭa eppēr̤paṭṭa man̤r̤upāḍum ērikkē kuḍuttēn̤ Nambiyamallanēn̤* . . . . ; **tr.** I, Nambiyamalla gave all the **fines** including the ones in cash for the maintenance of the tank ; *S.I.I.* III, pts. iii and iv, No. 93, p. 226, ll. 28–32 ; Ner̤kun̤r̤am, Vandavasi Tq., N. Arcot Dt., T. Nadu St. **Dy.** Chōḷa, Āditya I, reg. yr. 24 = 895 A.D. ; **text**[2] : (damaged) . . . . . . *niśadam irubattunālēkāl* ***daṇḍam*** *paḍuvadāgavum* . . . . ; **tr.** will be subjected to a **fine** of twenty four and a quarter (in cash) daily . . . ; *S.I.I.* VII, No. 73, p. 31, l. 14; Śīyamaṅgalam, Vandavasi Tq., N. Arcot Dt., T. Nadu St. **Dy.** Chōḷa, Kulōttuṅga II, reg. yr. 3 = 1139 A.D.

daṇḍanāyaka (K. < Skt. *n.*), army commander ; **text**[1] : *Kāreyavanāḷva Jayasēnabhaṭararuṁ pannirvarum* . . . ***daṇḍanāyaka*** *Chikeyanumiḷdu Nāgavarmmana kaṭṭisida Dēviger̤egaṁ piriyakeregaṁ bittuvaṭṭavaṁ koṭṭaru.* . . . . ; **tr.** Jayasēnabhaṭara who was administering Kāreya and the administrative body of twelve members and the **army commander** Chikeya met together and granted wet land below the tanks Dēviger̤e and *piriyaker̤e* excavated by Nāgavarma, for their maintenance ; *E.C.* (R) III, Nj. 282, p. 359, ll. 5–9 ; Kārya, Nanjanagud Tq., Mysore Dt., Karn. St. **Dy.** W. Gaṅga, Satyavākya, Ś. 890 = 968 A.D. ; **text**[2] : . . *chakravartti Sōmēśvaradēvaṁ Kīrtidēvana mēle piridumākshēpaṁ geydu pannirvarsāmantara* ***daṇḍanāyakan*** *Udayādittyaṁ muntāge mahādaṇḍaṁ* . . . . . *bandu Banavāseya Kōṭeyaṁ mutti* . . . ; **tr.** having greatly objected to the attitude of Kīrtidēva, the emperor Sōmēśvara along with the **army commander** Udayāditya, the head of 12 feudatories lead a great army and laid siege to the fort of Banavāse . . . . ; *K.I.* V, No. 7, sections iv and v, p. 21, ll. 25–27 ; Tamaḍi Kallāḷa, Siddapur Tq., Karwar Dt., Karn. St. **Dy.** Chāḷ. of Kal., Sōmēśvara II, Ś. 993 = 1071 A.D. [This word and its cognates occur in a large number of South Indian inscriptions].

daṇḍanāyaka kaṇkāṇi (T. < Skt.+T. *n.*), supervisory army commander ; **text :** . . . ***daṇḍanāyaka kaṇkāṇi*** *Chōḷamaṇḍalattu . . . Viḷānāṭṭu . . . . Vēṭṭaṉ Pañchanadivāṇaṉ* . . . . . . ; **tr.** Vēṭṭaṉ Pañchanadivāṇaṉ of Viḷānāḍu in Chōḷamaṇḍala who was the **supervisory army commander** ; *E.C.* X, Kol. 107, p. 18, ll. 5–6 ; Kōlār, Kolar Tq. and Dt., Karn. St. **Dy.** Chōḷa, Rājēndra, reg. yr. 3, 1054 A.D.

daṇḍanāyakam (T. < Skt. *n.*), army commander ; **text :** . . . *Śuchīndramuḍaiya paramasvāmigaḷukku* ***daṇḍanāyakam*** . . . . . *Karikālachōḷa Vaidumbarāyaṉ* . . . . . . *oru tirunandāviḷakkerivadāga vaitta śāvāmūvāppērāḍu aimbadu* . . . . . ; **tr.** fifty irreducible number of sheep were donated to the temple of the god of Śuchīndram for the burning of one perpetual lamp by the **army commander** Karikālachōḷa Vaidumbarāyaṉ . . ; *T.A.S.* IV, No. 33, p. 137, ll. 9–10, 14–18 ; Śuchīndram, Agastee–svaram Tq., Kanyakumari Dt., T. Nadu St. **Dy.** Chōḷa-Pāṇḍya, Jaṭāvarman, reg. yr. 3 = 1021 A.D.

daṇḍanāyakiti (K. < Skt. *n.*), female army commander ; **text :** . . . . . *mahānāyaki* ***daṇḍanāyakiti*** *Ratnadēviakkaṁgaḷ* . . . ; **tr.** Ratnadēvi akka the great leader and **female army commander** . . . . ; *S.I.I.* IX, pt. i, No. 223., p. 227, l. 20 ; Rāgimasaḷavāḍa, Harapanahalli Tq., Bellary Dt., Karn. St. **Dy.** Chāḷ. of Kal., Vikramāditya VI, Ch. Vi. yr. 52 = 1127 A.D.

daṇḍapati (Skt. *n.*), army commander ; **text :** . . *Kāṁchyāspade dakshiṇadigramaṇyāḥ kartuṁ ratiṁ* ***daṇḍapatiḥ****prayuktaḥ* . . . . . ; **tr.** an **army commander** was entrusted with the task of occupying the city of Kāṁchi which was the glory of the south ; *Ep. Ind.* XXXVI, No. 8, p. 66, ll. 14–15 ; Rāmēśvara, Proddatur Tq., Cuddapah Dt., A.P. St. **Dy.** Rāshṭr, Gōviṁda III, in characters of 9th-10th cent. A.D.

daṇḍaṭṭu (K. < Skt.+K. *vb.*), chase away the enemy army ; **text :** . . . . . *Rājamallanarapa* ***daṇḍaṭṭi*** *Pērūroḻiḻdu . . . Īsaragaṇḍa . . . . sattu padeda Kalnāḍu* . . . ; **tr.** herostone set up to commemorate the death of Īsaragaṇḍa when the king Rājamalla was camping at Pērūru after he **chased away the enemy army** ; *E.C.* (R) VII, Md. 81, p. 250, ll. 5–7 ; Kottatti, Mandya Tq. and Dt., Karn. St. **Dy.** W. Gaṅga, Rāchamalla, Ś 899 = 977 A.D.

daṇḍavāṇi (T. *n.*), standard gold ; **text :** . . . . . . *Uḍaiyār bhaṇḍārattu poṉ koṇḍu śeyda tiruppaṭṭigai oṉṟu* ***daṇḍavāṇi****kkukkāl māṟṟuttaṉṉiya poṉ kaḻañjē mukkālē mūṉṟu mañjāḍi kuṉṟi* . . . . . ; **tr.** one sacred girdle made of gold taken from the treasury of the Lord and containing ten *kaḻañju* (gold measure) and three *mañjāḍi* (gold measure) and one *kuṉṟi* (gold measure) which was a quarter inferior in fineness to the **standard gold** called **daṇḍavāṇi** . . . . ; *S.I.I.* II, pt. i, No. 3, p. 21, ll. 2nd section 13–15, 3rd section 1–4 ;

Tanjāvūr, Tanjavur Tq. and Dt., T. Nadu St. **Dy.** Chōḷa, Rājarāja I, reg. yr. 29 = 1014 A.D.

daṇḍāya (K. < Skt. *n.*), income from punitive tax; **text**[1] **:** (badly damaged) . . . . . *kir̤uder̤e* ***daṇḍāyam-*** *eṁbivu modalāge* . . . ; **tr. income** from minor taxes, **from punitive tax**, etc., ... ; *S.I.I.* XI, No. 40., p. 25, l. 12 ; Narsalgi, Bagewadi Tq., Bijapur Dt., Karn. St. **Dy.** Rāshṭr., Kṛishṇa III, Ś. 886 = 965 A.D. ; **text**[2] **:** . . . *dēvargge siddhāyaṁ kir̤uder̤e* . . . . . . *manevaṇaṁ* ***daṇḍāyaṁ*** . . . . *biṭṭar* . . . . ; **tr.** revenue incomes such as from fixed taxes, minor taxes, house tax, **income from punitive tax**, etc., were granted to the god. . . . ; *K.I.* I, No. 17, p. 24, ll. 34–35 ; Shiggaon, Shiggaon Tq., Dharwar Dt., Karn. St. **Dy.** Chāḷ. of Kal., Sōmēśvara I, Ś. 977 = 1055 A.D.

daṇḍāyada heggaḍe (K. < Skt. *n.*), officer who collects incomes from fines ; **text :** . . . ***daṇḍāyada heggaḍe*** *Mādimayya* . . . . ; **tr.** Mādimayya the **officer who collects income from fines** ; *E.C.* XII, Tpt. 66, p. 157, ll. 9–10 ; Śivara, Tiptur Tq., Tumkur Dt., Karn. St. **Dy.** Hoy., Narasiṁha, Ś. 1084 = 1163 A.D.

daṇḍiga (K. *n.*), soldier ; **text :** (badly damaged). . . . . ***daṇḍigar****aniriva vikramōttuṅga* . . . *Siṁgaṇadēvar*. . . ; **tr.** Siṁgaṇadēva of excellent bravery who pierces the (enemy) **soldier**. . . . . ; *S.I.I.* IX, pt. i, No. 124, p. 106, l. 9 ; Hirēmagaḷagēri, Harapanahalli Tq., Bellary Dt., Karn. St. **Dy.** Chāḷ. of Kal., Trailōkyamalla, Ś. 981 = 1059 A.D.

daṇḍikai jīvitam (T. < T.+Skt *n.*), endowment for the maintenance of palanquin bearers ; **text :** *Uttamanambikku koḍutta paṭṭaiyam nammuḍaiya rāyasapramāṇappaḍi taṉakku* ***daṇḍikai jīvita****ttukkukkuḍutta Tiruchirāpaḻḻi uśāvaḍi* . . . ; **tr.** the territory of Tiruchirāpaḻḻi given to Uttamanambi through an **endowment** deed **for** his **maintenance as a palanquin bearer**. . . . . ; *S.I.I.* XXIV, No. 319, p. 327, ll. 1–2 ; Śrīrangam, Tiruchirapalli Tq. and Dt., T. Nadu St. **Dy.** Saṅgama, Vijayabhūpati, Cy. yr. Śubhakṛit = 1423 A.D.

daṇḍiṁ munnir̤ivōṁ (K. *n.*), he who fights at the vanguard of the army (a title) ; **text :** . . . *Akaḷaṁka Mahēsvaraṁ* ***daṇḍiṁ munnir̤ivōṁ*** . . . . . . *Narasiṁgayya* . . . . ; **tr.** Narasiṁgayya who used to **fight at the vanguard of the army** and who had the title of *Akaḷaṁka Mahēśvara* ; *E.C.* (R) V, Mys. 223, p. 321, ll. 5–6 ; Kukkarahaḻḻi, Mysore Tq. and Dt., Karn. St. **Dy.** Chāḷ. Chfs., Narasiṁgayya, in characters of 10th cent. A.D.

daṇḍu (K. *n.*), army ; **text :** *Siṅgamadēva Er̤emmana maga Paḍiganoṁba ā* ***daṇḍi****noḷ kādi sattān*. . . . . . ; **tr.** Paḍiganoṁba son of Siṅgamadēva Er̤emma died fighting against an **army** . . . . ; *S.I.I.* IX, pt. i, No. 61, p. 35, ll. 16–22 ; Sirastahaḻḻi, Harapanahalli Tq., Bellary Dt., Karn. St. **Dy.** Rāshṭr., Gōvinda IV, Ś. 853 = 931 A.D.

daṇḍuvēḻ (K. *vb.*), declare war ; **text :** *Er̤eyapparasar* . . . . *Bīramahēndranoḷkādalendu*

*Ayyappadēvaṁge .... **daṇḍuvē l̤doḍe** Tuṁbepāḍiyoḷ kādi ... satta.......* ; **tr.** when Er̤eyapparasara **declared war** against Bīramahēndra, Ayyappadēva was deployed to fight and he fought a battle in Tumbepāḍi and died ; *E. C.* IX, Bng. 83, p. 30, ll. 2, 3–5 ; Bēgūr, Bangalore Tq. and Dt., Karn. St. **Dy.** W. Gaṅga, Er̤eyapparasa, in characters of 9th century A.D.

daṇḍuvōgu (K. *vb.*), march one's army against ; **text :** *.... Ballahana besadāḷu gajāṁkuśa Chōḷana mēge **daṇḍuvōgalu** Dilīpa Noḷaṁba daṇḍinalu kūḍi Ibīl̤ida kāḷegadalu āḷdana besavēḍi sattam Ponnyya ....* ; **tr.** when Ballaha **marched his army against** Gajāṁkuśa Chōḷa, Dilīpanoḷaṁba joined his forces and in the battle of Ibīl̤i, Ponnayya begged his master for permission to fight and laid down his life ; *S.I.I.* IX, pt. i, No. 25, p. 13, ll. 7–9 ; Maḍakasira, Madakasira Tq., Anantapur Dt., A.P. St. **Dy.** Rāshṭr., Kṛishṇa III (Ballaha), Ś. 870 = 948 A.D.

daniyaru (K. *n.*), master ; surname suffixed to male name ; **text**[1] **:** (damaged) *Śivarātrige dēvarige .... mālegū kūḍi haṁneraḍu honnanū **daniyara** kayyalu taṁdu koḍuvaru....* ; **tr.** they will bring and hand over to the **master** 12 gold coins for the provision of garlands to the deity on the day of Śivarātri..... ; *S.I.I.* IX, pt. ii, No. 407., p. 413, ll. 15, 17–19 ; Kōṭēśvara, Kundapur Tq., Udupi Dt., Karn. St. **Dy.** Saṅgama, Bukka, Ś. 1287 = 1364 A.D. ; **text**[2] **:** (damaged) *yī dharmavanū Yīśvara **daniyara** makkaḷu Divākara **daniyaru** ādiyāgi naḍesi pālisi baharu ..* ; **tr.** this pious charity shall be conducted and also protected by Divākara**daniyaru** son of Yīśvara**daniyaru**; *S.I.I.* IX, pt. ii, No. 407., pp. 413–14, ll. 19–21 ; Kōṭēśvara, Kundapur Tq., Udupi Dt., Karn. St. **Dy.** Saṅgama, Bukka, Ś. 1287 = 1364 A.D.

daṇṇāyaka (K. < Skt. *n.*), military-cum-revenue officer ; **text :** *mahāpradhānaṁ kumāra Lakshmīdhara **daṇṇāyaka** ....* ; **tr.** the chief minister and prince Lakshmīdhara, who was the **military-cum-revenue officer ....** ; *E.C.* (R) IX, Bl. 2, p. 4., l. 1 ; Bēlūru, Belur Tq., Hassan Dt., Karn. St. **Dy.** Hoy., Ballāḷa II, in characters of 12th-13th cent. A.D.

daṇṇāyakitti (K. < Skt. *n.*), wife of the army commander; **text :** *... Kāḷavve **daṇṇāyakitti**yararamaneya baḍagaṇa bēli....* ; **tr.** the northern fence of the palace of Kāḷavve, the **wife of the army commander....** ; *E.C.* (R) XII, Tk. 10, p. 344, ll. 4–5 ; Amṛitāpura, Tarikere Tq., Chikkamagaluru Dt., Karn. St. **Misc.,** in characters of 13th cent. A.D.

daṇṇāyakkan̤ (T. < Skt. *n.*), army commander ; **text :** *... Chikkadēvaṇa **daṇṇāyakkan̤** Aṇṇāmalaidēvar ...* ; **tr.** Chikkadēvaṇa *alias* Aṇṇāmalaidēvar, the **army commander** ; *E.C.* X, Kol. 18, p. 2, ll. 8–9 ; Kalluhaḷḷi, Kolar Tq. and Dt., Karn. St. **Dy.** Hoy., Rāmanātha, Ś. 1216 = 1293 A.D.

daṇṇāyakkar (T. < Skt. *n.*), army commander (in respectful plural) ; **text :** . . . *Pōśaḷa Vīravallāḷa Dēvar kumāraṉ Periya Vallappa* ***daṇṇāyakkar*** *vāḷukkum tōḷukkum jayamāga.* . . . ; **tr.** so that the sword and shoulders of Periya Vallappa, the **army commander,** son of Pōśaḷa Vallāḷadēva may be victorious . . . . ; *E.C.* X, Kol. 54, p. 8, ll. 5–7 ; Holērahaḷḷi, Kolar Tq. and Dt., Karn. St. **Dy.** Hoy., Ballāḷa, Kali 4440 = 1339 A.D.

danta (K. < Skt. *n.*), tusk of the elephant ; **text :** . . . *yidirādaribhūpāḷara madadāneya kombanuḍidu* ***danta****da baḷeyaṁ biduvina muttina hāramanodavida jayavadhuge tuḍisuvaṁ Narasiṁhaṁ* . . . . ; **tr.** Narasiṁha breaks the tusks of the rutting elephants of the opposing hostile kings and adorns the goddess of victory with the bangles prepared out of the **tusks** and the garlands prepared from the pearls in the frontal globe of the elephants . . ; *E.C.* (R) X, Ak. 227, p. 278, ll. 10–11 ; Muruṇḍi, Arasikere Tq., Hassan Dt., Karn. St. **Dy.** Hoy., Ballāḷa II, Ś. 1096 = 1174 A.D.

dāra (K. *n.*), sculpture ; **text :** . . . *Moraḍiyiṁ baḍagalu kaṁba nānūṟu* . . . . . *yiṁtū* ***dāra****va māḍidātanu Mārōjana maga rūvāri Mākōja* . . . ; **tr.** the sculptor Mākōja son of Mārōja prepared the **sculpture** of four hundred pillars to the north of the heap of stones ; *E.C.* (R) X , Ak. 213, p. 262, ll. 13–14 ; Bāgaḍe, Arasikere Tq., Hassan Dt., Karn. St. **Misc.,** Ś. 1161 = 1239 A.D.

darasaka (Te. < Skt. *dvāraśākhā n.*), the stone beam over the door way ; **text :** . . . *Mrōpūri Bhairavuni maṁḍapamu* . . . . *vakili* ***darasakulu*** *pratishṭa chēyiṁchenu* . . . ; **tr.** I got installed **the stone beam over the door way** of the hall of the god Bhairava of Mrōpuru . . . ; *S.I.I.* X, No. 498, p. 268, l. 19 ; Mōpuru, Pulivendla Tq., Cuddapah Dt., A.P. St. **Dy.** Te. Ch., Brammidēva, Ś. 1231 = 1309 A.D.

dāri (K. *n.*), road ; **text**[1] **:** . . . . *Nelkudureya Kalidēvargge Kēteyanāyakaṁ* . . . . *koṭṭa keyi Sonnada* ***dāri****yindaṁ mūḍalu* . . . ; **tr.** the land donated by Kētayanāyaka to the god Kalidēva of Nelkudure lay to the east of the **road** leading to Sonna . ; *S.I.I.* IX, pt. i, No. 88, p. 59, ll. 15–18 ; Chimnahaḷḷi, Hadagalli Tq., Bellary Dt., Karn. St. **Dy.** Chāḷ. of Kal., Jagadēkamalla, Ś. 956 = 1034 A.D. ; **text**[2] **:** . . . *Koṭūra* ***dāri****ya guḍḍada huṭaṟe* . . . ; **tr.** a natural boulder belonging to the hillock on the **road** to Koṭūru . . . . ; *S.I.I.* IX, pt. ii, No. 440, p. 448, l. 19 ; Rajabavanahaḷḷi, Harapanahalli Tq., Bellary Dt., Karn. St. **Dy.** Saṅgama, Dēvarāya, Ś. 1341 = 1419 A.D.

dāri gadde (K. *n.*), wet land situated by the side of the road ; **text :** . . . *dhāreyaneredu koṭa* . . . . ***dāri gadde*** *mu. 2* . . . . ; **tr. wet land situated by the side of the road** of the extant of being sown with 2 *mu* (*muḍi,* a grain measure) of seeds was donated ; *S.I.I.* VII, No. 334, p. 188, l. 46 ; Mūḍakēri, Udupi Tq. and Dt., Karn. St. **Dy.** Saṅgama, Virūpāksha, Ś. 1391 = 1469 A.D.

darśana pāga (K. *n.*), a lesser denomination of the coin called *pāga* ; **text :** (badly damaged) . . . . ***darśana pāga** 1* . . . . ; **tr.** one coin of **a lesser denomination of the coin called** ***pāga.*** . . . ; *S.I.I.* XV, No. 16, p. 15, l. 29 ; Madanabhāvi, Dharwar Tq. and Dt., Karn. St. **Dy.** Chāḷ. of Kal., Bhūlōkamalla, Ch. Vi. Yr. 52 = 1128 A.D.

dārukarma (K. < Skt. *n.*), carpentry ; **text :** . . . *dēvāyatanamaṁ **dārukarma**vishṭakākarma śilākarmaṁgaḷeṁdoṁdoṁdakke saharādhika guṇaphaḷadāyigaḷeṁdu śilākarmmadiṁ dēvāyatanamaṁ nirmisuvapakramamanettikoṁḍu* ; **tr.** since construction of a temple through **carpentry**, with bricks and with stones were each in that order a thousand times more meritorious, the task of building the temple with stone was taken up; *K.I.* I, No. 25, p. 47-48, ll. 69–70 ; Sirasangi, Saundatti Tq., Belgaum Dt., Karn. St. **Dy.** Chāḷ. of Kal., Sōmēśvara IV, Ś. 1108 = 1186 A.D.

dāsa (K. < Skt. *n.*), devotee ; **text :** . . . . *Lakshmīnarasiṁha dēvara . . . . . pratishṭhākāladalu Siṁdaviya svāmigaḷa **dāsa** . . . . . Viśvanāthadēvanu . . . . koṭṭa kaṁba hanneraḍu* . . . . ; **tr.** Viśvanāthadēva, the **devotee** of the religious leader of Siṁdavi donated twelve *kaṁba* (a land measurre) of land at the time of the installation of the deity Lakshmīnarasiṁha ; *E.C.* (R) X, Ak. 232, p. 285–86, ll. 35, 38, 40 ; Hāranahaḷḷi, Arasikere Tq., Hassan Dt., Karn. St. **Dy.** Hoy., Narasiṁha II, Ś. 1156 = 1234 A.D.

daśaka (K. < Skt. *n.*), groups of ten ; **text :** . . . . . . *Bīcharasayyaṁgaḷu taṁmma semmina oṁdu vṛittige ā **daśakada** mahājanaṁgaḷanoḍaṁbaḍisi hasugeyaṁ dhruva üṁḍigeyāgi . . . koṭṭaru* . . . ; **tr.** Bīcharasayya after obtaining the consent of the *mahājana* (an administrarive body) divided into **groups of ten**, gave his portion of the property as a permanent gift ; *S.I.I* IX, pt. i, No. 295, p. 318, ll. 25–26 ; Bāpuram, Adavani Tq., Kurnool Dt., A.P. St. **Dy.** Kal. of Kal., Sōmēśvara, Ś. 1093 = 1172 A.D.

daśamūla harītaki (T. < Skt. *n.*), medicine prepared from ten different roots ; **text :** . . . *āturaśālai Vīraśōḻanil āṇḍoṉṟil iḍum marundu . . . . . . **daśamūla harītaki** paḍiy yoṉṟum. . .* ; **tr.** in the hospital named after Vīraśōḻa one measure of medicine prepared from ten different roots was stored per year ; *Ep. Ind.* XXI, No. 38, p. 240, l. 46 ; Tirumukkūḍal, Madhurantakam Tq., Chingleput Dt., T. Nadu St. **Dy.** Chōḷa, Vīrarājēndra, in characters of 11th cent. A.D.

dasaṟāḍlu (Te. *n.*), temple servants ; **text :** . . . *Bejavāḍa Rājanārāyaṇadēvaraku Kulōttuṅga-chōḍayadēvamahārāyalu . . . . kolichina . . . . **dasaṟāḍlu** jana 2* . . . . ; **tr.** two **temple servants** were dedicated to the god Rājanārāyaṇa of Bejavāḍa by Kulōttuṅgachōḍamahārāya . . . . . ; *S.I.I.* X, No. 740, p. 386, ll. 1–4, 10, 27 ; Yenikepāḍu, Masulipatam Tq., Krishna Dt., A.P. St. **Dy.** Te. Ch., Kulōttuṅgachōḍadēva, in characters of

13th century A.D.

daśa tāḷa lakshaṇa (K. < Skt. *n.*), ten features of iconography ; **text :** . . . *daśatāḷa-lakshaṇaṁ kaṇgesedire satkāṁsyadiṁda Chaṁdraprabharaṁ hostāgi māḍisidar* . . . ; **tr.** the sculptors prepared the bronze image of Chaṁdraprabha afresh in conformity with the **ten features of iconography** . . . ; *S.I.I.* VII, No. 196, p. 91, l. 31 ; Mūḍabidure, Karkala Tq., Udupi Dt., Karn. St. **Dy.** Saṅgama, Dēvarāya, Ś. 1351 = 1429 A.D.

dasavaṁda (K. < Skt. *n.*), tax at the rate of 10%; **text :** (corrupt) . . . *nīra tidi haridu yeshṭu gade huṭidarū tidida tidida sthaḷadalū nālku beḷeda bhāga māṁnyavanū anubhavisi* . . . . ***dasavaṁda****vanū tiruchikoṁḍu mikkāda gadeyanū eṁdeṁdigū nimma sāguvaḷiyāgi naḍesi bahiri* . . . ; **tr.** after improving the irrigation canal, watever number of lands are reclaimed with yielding four crops on the gift land, you will enjoy all the produce from all the reclaimed field after paying the **tax at the rate of 10% of the produce** . . . . ; *E.C.* X, Mb. 172, p. 113, ll. 15–16 ; Rājaguṇḍlahaḷḷi, Mulabagilu Tq., Kolar Dt., Karn. St. **Misc.**, Ś. 1419 = 1496 A.D.

dasavanda (K. < Skt. *n.*), grant of 1/10th portion of land ; **text :** . . . *keṟeyanu hostāgi kaṭṭida saṁmandha ā keṟeya keḷage sarvamānyavāgi koṭa gaddeya* . . . ***dasavanda*** *keṟeya keḷagaṇa* . . . *bittida bījavari kha 1 kke* . . . . ; **tr. 1/10th portion of land** below the tank, of the extent of being sown with 1 *kha* (*khaṁḍuga*, a grain measure) of seed was granted in connection with the construction of a tank . . ; *S.I.I.* IX, pt. ii, No. 501, p. 516, l. 10 ; Uravakoṇḍa, Gooty Tq., Anantapur Dt., A.P. St. **Dy.** Tuḷuva, Kṛishṇadēvarāya, Ś. 1439 = 1516 A.D.

daśavandam[1] (K. < Skt. *n.*), 1/10 of any kind of property ; **text :** . . . . . *kavartteyoḷaputrika dravyada* ***daśavandadoḷaṁ*** *puṭṭida dravyaṁ* . . . ; **tr. 1/10 of the** confiscated **property** of persons dying intestate . . . . ; *Ep. Ind.* XX, No. 6, p. 68, l. 40–41 ; Kōṭavūmachgi, Gadag Tq. and Dt., Karn. St. **Dy.** Chāḷ. of Kal., Vikramāditya V, Ś. 934 = 1012 A.D.

daśavandam[2] (T. < Skt. *n.*), remission of 1/10th of the share of the produce ; **text :** (badly damaged). . . . . . . *kachchāṇamum māḍaikkūli* ***daśavandamum*** . . . . ; **tr.** taxes such as *kachchāṇa* and *māḍaikkūli* and **remission of 1/10th of the share of the produce** . . ; *E.C.* (R) IV, Yl. 98, p. 326, l. 30 ; Agara, Yalandur Tq., Mysore St. **Dy.** Chōḷa., Kulōttuṅga I, Reg. yr. 34 = 1104 A.D.

daśavandha (K. < Skt. *n.*), remission of 1/10th of the revenue ; **text :** . . . . *prabhugaḷge aḷadu koṇḍa bhūmige nūṟakke hattarōpādiya* ***daśavaṁdha****manikki*. . . . . . ; **tr.** remitted 1/10th of the revenue on the corn field after measuring it for the Lord ; *Ep. Ind.* XVI, No. 8 C., p. 48, l. 52; Lakshmēśvara, Shirahatti Tq., Dharwar Dt., Karn. St. **Dy.** Chāḷ. of Kal., Jagadēkamalla II,

reg. yr. 10 = 1147 A.D.

dasavandhamu (Te. < Skt. *n.*), remission of 1/10 of the income ; **text :** . . . . *Guṁḍramarireddi Gurijāla Pittireddi Kōṭakaṁnāṭireddi* . . . . *mukhyamaina vīralakichchina* ***dasavandhamu*** *śāsanapatraṁ* . . . . ; **tr.** the stone edict recording the **remission 1/10 of income** from land granted to soldiers including Guṁdramarireddi, Pittireddi of Gurijāla, Kōṭakaṁnāṭireddi . . ; *I.A.P. Cuddapah* II, No. 34, p. 39, ll. 5–7, 9–12 ; Peṇḍlimarri, Cuddapah Tq. and Dt., A.P. St. **Dy.** Saṅgama, Dēvarāya, Ś. 1334 = 1412 A.D. [Note : Dasavanda and its variants derived from Sanskrit *daśabandha* occur in South Indian Inscriptions denoting land granted to cultivators at a deduction of 1/10 of revenue for construction and upkeep of tanks, etc., and for completion of any public work].

dāsipatra (K. < Skt. *n.*), deed enforcing bonded labour ; **text :** . . . *Bīrammana kulamanituṁ* ***dāsipatra****kke niṁdar*. . . . . . ; **tr.** the entire family of Bīramma agreed to abide by the **deed enforcing** them to **bonded labour** . . ; *S.I.I.* XI, No. 49, p. 58, ll. 24–25 ; Kalkēri, Hangal Tq., Dharwar Dt., Karn. St. **Dy.** Chāḷ. of Kal., Sōmēśvara II, Ś. 998 = 1076 A.D.

dāsugaḷa terige (K. < Skt. *n.*), tax on fishermen ; **text :** . . . *beṭṭada kāvalu bōgāra deṟe* . . . . ***dāsugaḷa terige*** . . . . *asagara terige nāyiṁdara terige kuṁbhāra terige*. . . . . . ; **tr.** tax to be paid for grazing cattle on the hill, tax on bronze smiths, **tax on fishermen**, tax on washermen, tax on barbers, tax on potters, etc. . . ; *E.C.* (R) III, Gu. 134, p. 97, ll. 15–17 ; Triyaṁbakapura, Gundlupet Tq., Mysore Dt., Karn. St. **Dy.** Tuḷuva, Kṛishṇadēvarāya, Ś. 1444 = 1521 A.D.

dātārar (K. < Skt. *n.*), donors ; **text :** . . . *intinitumaṁ modalaṁ kiḍalīyade vṛiddhiyoḷe dharmaṁ tamma santatiyavar naḍeyisuvar kkiḍisadantu Brahmapuriya mahājanamuṁ sāsirvvaruṁ parirakshisuvar upēkshegeyyadavar tāve* ***dātāra****rappar*. . . . . . ; **tr.** if the *mahājana* and the thousand (an administrative body of the brāhmaṇa settlement) do not allow this grant to be misappropriated and instead ensure its further growth through their descendants these bodies would, in effect, be deemed as the actual **donors**; *S.I.I.* XI, No. 64, pp. 54–55, ll. 30–32 ; Muḷugunda, Gadag Tq. and Dt., Karn. St. **Dy.** Chāḷ. of Kal., Jayasiṁha II, Ś. 950 = 1028 A.D.

datti (K. < Skt. *n.*), grant ; **text**[1] **:** . . . *Satyāśraya* ***datti****ya paḍeda Kuṟuṁgōḍa vyavaste* . . . . ; **tr.** the arrangment made in the village of Kuṟuṁgōḍu with reference to the **grant** given by Satyāśraya . . . ; *S.I.I.* IX, pt. i, No. 53, p. 30, ll. 1–2 ; Kurugōḍu, Bellary Tq. and Dt., Karn. St. **Dy.** Chal. of Bād., Satyāśraya, in characters of 8th century A.D. ; **text**[2] **:** (damaged) . . . *Kuruḷa Kāmaseṭṭiya Kāmēśvarade* . . . . ***datti*** . . . *rājamāna ayvattu mattar* . . . . . ; **tr.** grant of fifty *mattar* (a land measure) of land measured by the *rājamāna* (a standard royal measure) granted by Kāmēśetti of Kuruḷa to the god Kāmēśvara ; *S.I.I.* IX, pt. i, No. 60, p. 34, l. 9 ; Doddimakala, Adavani Tq., Kurnoll Dt., A.P. St. **Dy.** Rāshṭr., Gōvinda IV, Ś. 852 = 931 A.D. ; **text**[3] : . . . . . *Ballāḷadēvaru* . . . . . *Heragina basadige* . . . . . . *biṭṭa* ***datti*** . . . ; **tr. grant** made by Ballāḷadēva to the Jaina temple at Heragu ; *E.C.* (R) VIII, Hn. 147, pp. 378–79, ll. 3, 4, 7 ; Heragu, Hassan Tq. and Dt., Karn. St. **Dy.** Hoy., Ballāḷa, Cy. yr. Jaya = 1174 A.D.

davaṇiga (K. *n.*), trader ; **text :** . . . *Lokkiguṇḍiya jōḷadaṁgaḍiya* ***davaṇiga*** *mahājanaṁ* . . *Maruḷēśvaradēvarige angaḍiyal aravānaṁgoḷva saṁṭṭuga bhattamaṁ koṭṭaru.* . . . . ; **tr.** each of the mahājana **traders** of Jowar shops of Lokkiguṇḍi granted to the god Maruḷēśvara paddy measuring one half of *māna* (a grain measure) . . ; *K.I.* II, No. 10, p. 31, ll. 14–16 ; Lakkuṇḍi, Gadag Tq. and Dt., Karn. St. **Dy.** Chāḷ. of Kal., Vikramāditya VI, Ch. Vi. yr. 4 = 1079 A.D.

davasa (K. *n.*), food grains ; **text**[1] : . . . *ainūrvvaru mukhyavāgi ā staḷada gavaregaṁḍaruṁ mummuri daṁḍaṁgaḷuṁ koṭṭa dharma* . . . . ***davasa*** *vikrayakke arevīsa* . . . ; **tr.** the merchant guilds such as *gavaregaṁḍa* and *mummuridaṁḍa* lead by the *ainūrvvar* (a mercantile gld. of five hundred). made a gift of half *vīsa* (a coin) on the sale of **food grains** as an act of piety ; *S.I.I.* XI, No. 69, p. 60, ll. 30–33 ; Rājūr, Ron Tq., Dharwar Dt., Karn. St. **Dy.** Chāḷ. of Kal., Jagadēkamalla I, Ś. 955 = 1033 A.D. ; **text**[2] : . . . *Kṛishṇāpurada pēṭheya* ***davasa****daṁgaḍigaḷa toḍeyada bageyallū saluva ghaṭivaraha* . . . ; **tr.** in the manner of **food grains** shops located in the Kṛishṇāpura market not being destroyed pure gold coins were donated . . ; *S.I.I.* IV, No. 262, p. 58, l. 1 ; Hampi, Hospet Tq., Bellary Dt., Karn. St. **Dy.** Tuḷuva, Achyutarāya, Ś. 1455 = 1533 A.D.

davasada suṁka (K. *n.*), tax on food grains ; **text :** . . . *Sōmēśaṁge* . . . . *perjjuṁkadoḍeyar irvvarmmudadiṁdittar****davasada suṁka****maṁ* . . . ; **tr.** the two officers in charge of collecting major taxes were pleased to donate the **tax** income **on food grains** to the god Sōmēśa ; *S.I.I.* IX, pt. i, No. 165, p. 159, l. 63 ; Kuruvatti, Harapanahalli Tq., Bellary Dt., Karn. St. **Dy.** Chāḷ. of Kal., Vikramāditya VI, Ch. Vi. yr. 24 = 1099 A.D.

davasādāya (K. *n.*), income from food grains ; **text :** . . . *Veṁkaṭēśvarasvāmi dēvatā kaṭṭaḷe* . . . . . . *Gōviṁdapurada* . . . *sakala suvarṇādāya* . . . ***davasādāya*** . . . . *muṁttāda utpatyavanū* . . . . *barasi koṭṭa bhūdāna śāsana*. . . . ; **tr.** an edict of land grant got written registering the grant (among many other things) of income from all types of gold and **income from food grains** to the god Veṁkaṭēśvara as per the customary practice ; *E.C.* (R) XII, Tk. 53, pp. 388-89, ll. 15, 48, 56 ; Tarīkere, Tarikere Tq., Chickamagaluru Dt., Karn. St. **Misc.**, Ś. 1603 = 1681 A.D.

davasa dhānya (K. + Skt. *n.*), food grains ; **text :** . . . . . . *Hoṁnakahaḷḷiyeṁba grāmadiṁ bhaṁḍārakke tettu baha samasta* . . . . ***davasa dhānya*** . . . *kammāradeṟige* . . . . *modalāda samasta terige* . . . . . *ellvanū* . . . *biṭu agrahāravāgi* . . . *koṭevu*. . . . ; **tr.** we gave the village of Hoṁnakahaḷḷi as an *agrahāra* after remitting all taxes payable to the treasury such as income from tax on **food grains**, tax on blacksmith, etc. ; *E.C.* III, Gu. 26, p. 25, ll. 15–16, 17, 19 ; Hoṇakanahaḷḷi, Gundlupete Tq., Mysore Dt., Karn. St. **Dy.** Tuḷuva, Narasiṁha, Ś. 1427 = 1506 A.D.

davasāya (K. + Skt. *n.*), income from food grains; **text :** . . . *Kalināthadēvara* . . . *nivēdyakkaṁ biṭṭa dattiyā Pāṇḍyanāḍa Paḍikēṇisthaḷada Kōgaḷināḍa* ***davasāyadoḷage*** *variśaṁprati nibaṁdhavāgi saluva gadyāṇaveraḍu* . . . . ; **tr.** two *gadyāṇa* (gold coin) each year out of the **income from food grains** from Kōgaḷināḍu in Paḍikēṇi sthaḷa of Pāṇḍyanāḍu were endowed for the services of the god Kalināthadēva. . . ; *S.I.I.* IX, pt. i, No. 341, p. 361, ll. 8–10 ; Sōgi, Hadagalli Tq., Bellary Dt., Karn. St. **Dy.** Hoy., Narasiṁima II, Ś. 1148 = 1226 A.D.

davasāyada herggaḍe (K. *n.*), revenue official in charge of collecting tax on food grains ; **text :** . . . ***davasāyada hergaḍe*** *Mākimayya* . . . . ; **tr.** Mākimayya, the revenue official in charge of collecting tax on food grains . . ; *E.C.* VIII, Sb. 170, p. 70, ll. 15–16 ; Mūḍigrāma, Soraba Tq., Shimoga Dt., Karn. St. **Dy.** Chāḷ. of Kal., Vikramāditya VI, Ch. Vi. yr. 50 = 1126 A.D.

davasāyada suṁka (K. *n.*), tax on income from sale of food grains ; **text :** . . . *Banavāsi pannirchchāsirada* ***davasāyada suṁka***. . . . ; **tr.** **the tax on income from sale of food grains** in the territorial division Banavāsi-12000. . . ; *E.C.* VIII, Sor. 288, p. 183, ll. 13–14 ; Elevāḷa, Soraba Tq., Shimoga Dt., Karn. St. **Dy.** Chāḷ. of Kal., Vikramāditya VI, Ch. Vi. yr. 13 = 1088 A.D.

dāyadeṟe (K. < Skt. *n.*), tax on gifts and presents; **text :** . . . *haṁneraḍūralū haḷḷigaḷaluṁ* . . . . . . ***dāyadeṟe*** . . . *nallettu* . . *oḷagāda samasta kiṟukuḷavellavaṁ* . . . *Vijayanārāyaṇadēvara śrīpādadalu* . . . . *Ballāḷadēva biṭṭan* . . . . ; **tr.** Ballāḷadēva granted to the god Vijayanārāyaṇadēva all minor taxes including the **tax on gifts and presents** collected from 12 townships and villages; *E.C.* (R) IX, Bl. 17, p. 18, ll. 2, 3 ; Bēlūr, Belur Tq., Hassan Dt., Karn. St. **Dy.** Hoy., Ballāḷa II, Ś. 1095 = 1174 A.D.

dāyādi (K. < Skt. *n.*), descendants from the same original male stock ; **text :** . . . . . . *Sōmayājigaḷu tāvu taṁma strī putra jñāti sāmaṁta* ***dāyādyānumatadim*** . . *krayadānavāgi koṭa krayadānapatra* . . . . . ; **tr.** a sale deed for the gift by sale made by Sōmayāji with the consent of the women folk, male relatives, subordinates and the **descendants from the same original male stock** . . . ; *S.I.I.* IX, pt. ii, No. 582, pp. 598-99, ll. 33–34 ; Lēpākshi, Hindupur Tq., Anantapur Dt., A.P. St. **Dy.** Tuḷuva,

Achyutarāya, Ś. 1459 = 1537 A.D.

dāyadramma (K. < Skt. *n.*), a kind of tax collected in cash ; **text :** . . . *dēvargge siddhāyaṁ kirudeṟe kiṟukuḷaṁ* ***dāyadramma*** *manevaṇaṁ* . . . . . *biṭṭar* . . . . . . ; **tr.** grants of fixed tax, minor tax, minor cess, **a kind of tax collected in cash,** house tax etc., were donated to the god ; *K.I.* I, No. 17, p. 24, ll. 34–35 ; Shiggaon, Shiggaon Tq., Dharwar Dt., Karn. St. **Dy.** Chāḷ. of Kal., Sōmēśvara I, Ś. 977 = 1055 A.D.

dāyādyulu (Te. < Skt. *n.*), descendants from the same original male stock ; **text :** . . . *Hanumaṁttadēvaru pratishṭhachēsi* . . . *nalutūmu chēnu dēvara nivēdyānaku* . . . . ***dāyādyula*** *sammatin ichchēvu* . . . . ; **tr.** I have given four *tūmu* (land measure) of land with the consent of **descendants from the same original male stock** for offerings to the god Hanumaṁtta ; *I.A.P.* Cuddapah II, No. 42, p. 48, ll. 5–10 ; Chilamakūru, Kamalapuram Tq., Cuddapah Dt., A.P. St. **Misc.,** Ś. 1364 = 1441 A.D.

dayirya koḍagi (K. *dhairya°* *n.*), grant for bravery ; **text :** . . . *Haṭṭiyūra Vīrappaṁge koṭṭa śāsana krama* . . . . *Hullūra nāḍalu Toravasamudrada grāma 1 nū niṁnna dayirya koḍagiyāgi koṭṭevu* . . . . . . ; **tr.** we granted to you, Vīrappa of Haṭṭiyūru, for your bravery one village named Toravasamudra in Hullūranāḍu as per the inscription set up ; *E.C.* X, Ml. 87, pp. 171–72, ll. 14–22 ; Koranahaḷḷi, Malur Tq., Kolar Dt., Karn. St. **Dy.** Saṅgama, Harihara, Ś. (wrong for Kali year) 4444 = 1343 A.D.

dēḍamagga (K. *n.*), weaver's loom ; **text :** (damaged) . . . . *suṁkada Māyidēva daṁḍanāyakaru* . . . *Kalidēvara dēvakāryakkeṁdu biṭṭa āya* . . . . *baḍagi 1 kammāra 1 sammagāra 1 asaga 1* ***dēḍamagga*** . . . ; **tr.** the revenue official Māyidēva daṁḍanāyaka donated to the god Kalidēva for His worship income from taxes on the carpenter, the blacksmith, the cobbler, the washerman and the **weaver's loom** ; *S.I.I.* XX, No. 178, p. 225, ll. 44–46 ; Hipparagi, Sindagi Tq., Bijapur Dt., Karn. St. **Dy.** Kal. of Kal., Bhillama, Ś. 1115 = 1193 A.D.

dēgula (K. < Skt. *n.*), temple ; **text :** . . . . *Ballahana dayeyiṁ Kōgaḷi ayinūṟumaṁ Māsiyavāḍi nūranālvattuman āḷuttamirddu* . . . . *nijarājadhāni Meḻuviḍuvinoḷ* . . . . . ***dēgula****maṁ māḍi* . . . . . . ; **tr.** while administering the territorial divisions Kōgaḷi-500 and Māsiyavāḍi-140 through the favour of the emperor, he (name lost) built a **temple** in his own capital city Meḻuviḍuvu ; *S.I.I.* XI, No. 22, pp. 13–14, ll. 7–9 ; Mēvuṇḍi, Mundaragi Tq., Dharwar Dt., Karn. St. **Dy.** Rāshṭr., Kṛishṇa II, Ś. 818 = 897 A.D.

dēhāra (K. < Skt. *n.*), temple ; **text**[1] **:** . . . . *ūriṁgīśānyada paḷḷada baḍagaṇa taḍiya piriya* ***dēhāra****da keyi teṅkaṇa sīme* . . . . ; **tr.** the southern boundary is the land belonging to the big **temple** on the banks of the rivulet to the northeast of the village ; *S.I.I.* XI, No. 65, p. 56, ll. 49–50 ; Hosūr, Gadag Tq. and Dt., Karn. St. **Dy.** Chāḷ. of Kal., Jagadēkamalla, Ś. 950 = 1029 A.D. ; **text**[2] : . . . *Hoysaḷa Vīranārasiṁhadēvaru Pāṁḍyanamēle digvijayamumaṁ māḍalōsuga* . . . *Ravitadāṇada kuppadalu* . . . . . ***dēhārada*** *vaḍḍōlagada dharmma prasaṁgadalu* . . . . ; **tr.** when the Hoysaḷa king Vīranarasiṁhadēvarasa, in order to carry out expedition against the Pāṁḍya was camping at Ravitadāṇadakuppa and was holding a religious audience in the **temple** ; *E.C.* (R) X, Ak. 232, p. 285, ll. 31–32 ; Hāranahaḷḷi, Arasikere Tq., Hassan Dt., Karn. St. **Dy.** Hoy., Narasimha II, Ś. 1156 = 1234 A.D.

dekhkhādekhkhiyoḷu kādu (K. *vb.*), get involved in intense fight ; **text** : . . . . ***dekhkhādekhkhiyoḷu kādi*** *taḷtiṟidu geldu turaga daḷamaṁ taṁda pagemechche gaṁḍa* . . . . ; **tr.** he who was appreciated even by his enemies after his **intense involvement in a battle** which he won and captured the cavalry ; *S.I.I.* IX, pt. i, No. 343, p. 363, l. 22; Bennikal, Kudligi Tq., Bellary Dt., Karn. St. **Dy.** Hoy., Narasiṁha II, Ś. 1148 = 1226 A.D.

dēnagavaḷe (K. *n.*), good quality crop ; **text** : . . . . . . *Mādhavēśvaradēvara* . . . . . . *naivēdyakke* ***dēnagavaḷe*** *nellu baḷḷa 2* . . . . ; **tr.** 2 *baḷḷa* (a grain measure) of **good quality crop** of paddy for food offerings to the god Mādhavēśvara ; *S.I.I.* XV, No. 241, p. 300, ll. 67, 68 ; Niḍugundi, Ron Tq., Dharwar Dt., Karn. St. **Dy.** Kal. of Kal., Bijjaḷa, Ś. 1096 = 1174 A.D.

dēsa, dēśa (K. < Skt. *n.*), country ; **text**[1] : . . . *Kuntaḷa* ***dēsa****da mahā agrahāra Beluhūra* . . . . ; **tr.** Beluhūru the great brāhmaṇa settlement in Kuntaḷa **country** ; *E.C.* (R) IX, Bl. 4, p. 4, l. 1 ; Bēlūru, Belur Tq., Hassan Dt., Karn. St. **Dy.** Hoy., Vishṇuvaradhana, in charactes of 12th century A.D. ; **text**[2] : . . . . *sanmantri mitra kōśa* ***dēśa*** *durga bala samētanumāgi rājyaṁ geyvutirdā Rājēṁdra* ; **tr.** Rājēṁdra was ruling, endowed with good counsel, friends, treasury, **country**, fortress and army ; *S.I.I.*VII, No. 207, p. 103, l. 31; Mūḍabidure, Karkala Tq., Udupi Dt., Karn St. **Dy.** Sāḷva, Mallēśvara, in characters of 15th cent. A.D.

dēśa bhāga (K. < Skt. *n.*), specific region of a kingdom; **text** : . . . . *Timmōja Koṁḍōja Bhadrōjagaḷu muṁtāda* ***dēśa bhāga****da nāyiṁdarige biṭṭu Koṭṭūrasīmeya nāyiṁdarige teṟige kaṁdāya biṭi* . . . *yēnū illa eṁdu koṭṭa sāsana* . . . . ; **tr.** a stone edict registering the details of the barbers including Timmōja, Koṁḍōja Bhadrōja and the barbers of Koṭṭūrusīme, **a specific region of the kingdom** being exempted from paying tax, revenue tax, tax on free labour, etc. ; *S.I.I.* IX, pt. ii, No. 628, p. 631, ll. 13–18 ; Koṭṭūru, Kudligi Tq., Bellary Dt., Karn. St. **Dy.** Tuḷuva, Sadāśiva, Ś. 1469 = 1548 A.D.

dēśa bhāshe (K. < Skt. *n.*), vernacular of a given region ; **text** : . . . . *datta grāmasya sīmādi* *likyatē* ***dēśabhāshayā*** . . . . ; **tr.** the boundaries of the granted village are enumerated in the **vernacular of the given region** ; *E.C.* (R) III, Gu. 112, p. 82, ll. 15–16 ; Lakkūru, Gundlupet Tq., Mysore Dt., Karn. St. **Dy.** Woḍ. of Mys., Dēvarājavoḍeya, Ś. 1586 = 1665 A.D.

dēśadavaru (K. < Skt. *n.*), subjects of the kingdom; **text :** . . . . *ī dharmmavanu arasu prati ivaru* ***dēśadavara*** *ubhayānumatadiṁda māḍida dharmakke maṁgaḷa* . . . . ; **tr.** may this grant made with the consent of the king and the **subjects of** his **kingdom** be asupicious ; *S.I.I.* VII, No. 255, p. 129, ll. 20–21 ; Vēṇūr, Karkala Tq., Udupi Dt., Karn. St. **Misc.**, Ś. 1544 = 1622 A.D.

dēśādhikāraṁ (K. < Skt. *n.*), administration of a territory ; **text :** . . . . *daṇḍanātha Ammaṇṇa daṇṇāyakaru* . . . . *samasta* ***dēśādhikāraṁ*** *māḍuttavire* . . . . . . ; **tr.** while the army commander Ammaṇṇa daṇṇāyaka was **administering the** entire **territory** ; *S.I.I.* IX, pt. i, No. 339, p. 359, ll. 16–17, 18–19 ; Anijigere, Harapanahalli Tq., Bellary Dt., Karn. St. **Dy.** Hoy., Narasiṁha, Ś. 1145 = 1222 A.D.

dēśādhipati (K. < Skt. *n.*), lord of the region ; **text :** (incomplete) . . . . *ī dharmavaṁ* . . . . *tappade muṁde muṁde naḍeva* ***dēśādhipati****yu sthānada kartaru naḍesi* . . ; **tr.** this grant shall be continued successively by the **lord of the region** and the officials of the temple in future too ; *S.I.I.* VII, No. 269, p. 138, ll. 43–46 ; Palimāru, Udupi Tq. and Dt., Karn. St. **Misc.**, in characters of 16th century A.D.

dēśādhīśvara (K. < Skt. *n.*), ruler of a kingdom; **text :** (damaged) . . . . . . *samasta* ***dēśādhīśvarara*** *negaḻteyuṁ nijaprabhāvamuṁ* . . . ; **tr.** the fame and the genuine influence of all the **rulers of kingdoms** ; *S.I.I.* VII, No. 327, p. 178, ll. 10–11 ; Mūḍakēri, Udupi Tq. and Dt., Karn. St. **Dy.** Āḷupas, Baṁkidēva, in characters of 11th century A.D.

dēsai (K. wrong for *dēsāyi, n.*), fief holder ; **text:** *Bhīmappa* ***dēsai*** *kaṭikoṭa kere* . . . ; **tr.** tank constructed by the **fief holder** Bhīmappa ; *S.I.I.* XV, No. 674, p. 422, ll. 3–6 ; Gaddanakēri, Bagalkot Tq., Bijapur Dt., Karn. St. **Misc.**, in characters of 15th century A.D.

dēśāmātya (Skt. *n.*), minister of the kingdom ; **text :** (damaged) *Ravivarmadharmamahārājaḥ* . . . . . . *ātmanaḥ priya vaidyasya Nīlakaṁṭhākhya* ***dēśāmātya****sya Mahādēvāyatanāya sārēgrāme* . . . *baṁdupukkōli kshētrē* . . . *nivarttana chatushṭayaṁ dattavān*. . . ; **tr.** Ravivarma gave four *nivarttana* (a land measure) of land in the plough-land called *baṁdupukkōli* situated in the village of Sāre to the temple of Mahādēva belonging to his beloved physician Nīlakaṁṭha, who was the **minister of the kingdom** ; *Ep. Ind.* XVI, No. 19, pp. 266–67, ll. 4, 12–16 ; Sirsi, Sirsi Tq., N. Kanara Dt., Karn. St. **Dy.** Kad. of Ban., Ravivarma, reg. yr. 35, in characters of 5th-6th century A.D.

dēśāṁtrigaḷ (K. < Skt. *n.*), pilgrims from other regions ; **text :** . . . . *Kamaḷanābhatīrttharu staḷāṁtarake hōdaḍe* ***dēśāṁtrigaḷige*** *baḷinaḍeyāgi naḍasuvaru* . . . . . . ; **tr.** whenever the saint Kamaḷanābhatīrttha is away on pilgrimage, the food will be distributed among the **piligrims from other regions** ; *E.C.* (R) IX, Bl. 8, p. 6, ll. 11–13 ; Bēlūru, Belur Tq., Hassan Dt., Karn. St. **Misc.,** Ś. 1199 = 1277 A.D.

dēśāntarigaḷ (T. < Skt. *n.*), pilgrims from other regions ; **text :** . . . . *uchchisandi amudu* ***dēśāntarigaḷ****ukku oḍukku* . . . ; **tr.** the food preparaed for offering to god during the midday service is to be set apart for **pilgrims from other regions** ; *E.C.* X, Bow. 33, p. 84, l. 3 ; Kasabayahaḷḷi, Bowringpet Tq., Kolar Dt., Karn. St. **Dy.** Hoy., Vīra Rāmanātha, Ś. 1215 = 1293 A.D.

dēśāntiri (T. < Skt. *n.*), pilgrim from other region; **text :** . . . *Tiruvābaraṇaṅgaḷum* . . . *saṟva kaiṅkaryyamum* . . . . . ***dēśāntiri*** *Narasiṅgayaṅgār kaiyyilē Teḷḷiyasiṅgapperumāḷ koṇḍaruḷiṉār* . . . ; **tr.** Teḷḷiyasiṅgapperumāḷ was pleased to bestow on Narasiṅgayaṅgār a **pilgrim from other region** all the ornaments and all temple services . . . . ; *S.I.I.* VIII, No. 538, p. 275, ll. 6–7 ; Chennai, Chennai Tq. and Dt., T. Nadu St. **Dy.** Tuḷuva, Sadāśiva, Ś. 1486 = 1564 A.D.

dēśarakshakaṁ (K. < Skt. *n.*), protector of the country ; **text :** . . . . *Pāpakallakulatilakaṁ* . . . . ***dēśarakshakaṁ*** *Pāṇḍyāntagṛihīta suvarṇṇachhatra dhvaja virājamānaṁ* . . . . *Bōḷuga* . . ; **tr.** Bōḷuga, the crest jewel of Pāpakallakula, the **protector of the region** who had wrested the golden umbrella and the banner of the Pāṇḍya king ; *S.I.I.* XI, No. 41, p. 25, ll. 21–23 ; Nāgāvi, Gadag Tq. and Dt., Karn. St. **Dy.** Rāshṭr., Koṭṭiga, Ś. 891 = 969 A.D.

dēśayi (Te. *n.*), fief holder ; **text :** *māyi Kollāpuraṁ* ***dēśayi*** . . . . ; **tr.** a **fief holder** officiating in the temple of the goddess Mahālakshmi in Kollāpur; *E.C.* XII, Tmk. 51, p. 48, ll. 15–16 ; Kōḷāla, Tumkur Tq. and Dt., Karn. St. **Misc.,** Ś. 1438 = 1516 A.D.

dēsi (K. *n.*), mercantile guild ; **text :** . . . *agrahāraṁ Tuṁbuḷadalu taṁbuligaruṁ* ***dēsi****yuṁ biṭṭa dharmmaṁ* . . . ; **tr.** the grant given by the betel merchants and the **mercantile guild** in the brāhmaṇa settlement of Tuṁbuḷa ; *S.I.I.* IX, pt. i, No. 239, p. 244, ll. 16–17 ; Chinnatuṁbaḷam, Adavani Tq., Kurnool Dt., A.P. St. **Dy.** Chāḷ. of Kal., Jagadēkamalla II, reg. yr. 5 = 1142 A.D.

dēsiga (K. *adj.*), outsiders ; **text :** . . . . *Bāḷguḷiya Telidēvasvāmige* . . . . *Lōgēśvarada* . . . . *bhūmiyaṁ dēvara nivēdyakkaṁ* . . . . ***dēsiga*** *chhātra bhōjanakkaṁ* . . . *kuḍe* . . . ; **tr.** the land in Lōgēśvara having been donated to the god Telidēvasvāmi of Bāḷguḷi for the deity's food offerings and for feeding **outsiders**, students, etc.; *S.I.I.* IX, pt. i, No. 80, p. 51, ll. 12–15, 16, 18 ;

Bāgaḷi, Harapanahalli Tq., Bellary Dt., Karn. St. **Dy.** Chāḷ. of Kal., Jayasiṁha II, Ś. 940 = 1018 A.D.

dēsiya daṇḍanāyaka (K. *n.*), regional army commander ; **text :** . . . . *maṁnneya Virupa dēvarasaruṁ avara hiriya heggaḍe* ***dēsiya daṇḍanāyaka*** *Nannarasaruṁ pramukha karaṇaṁgaḷuṁ* . . . ; **tr.** the feudatory chief Virupadēvarasa, his senior official Nannarasa, who was the **regional army commander** and the senior clerks ; *S.I.I.* XV, No. 58, p. 81, ll. 118–120; Miṇajigi, Muddebihal Tq., Bijapur Dt., Karn. St. **Dy.** Chāḷ. of Kal., Sōmēśvara IV, Ś. 1107 = 1184 A.D.

dettu (T. wrong for *dattu, n.*), adoption ; **text :** . . . . *Peṟṟayiṉār magaḷ Nallayiṉār taṅgachchi uḷḷiṭṭāraiyum Iraviśēkharaṉ uḍaiyāraiyum uḍaiyadāga* **dettu** *ākki* . . . ; **tr.** Peṟṟayiṉār's daughter Nallayiṉār and her younger sister and Raviśēkharaṉ uḍaiyār were **adopted** as heirs ; *T.A.S.* IV, pts. i and ii, No. 44, p. 155, ll. 12–13 ; Āṟṟūr, Ker. St. **Dy.** Kīḻappērūr, Ravivarmaṉ, Kollam 821 = 1646 A.D.

dēvabhaṁḍāra (K. < Skt. *n.*), temple treasury ; **text :** . . . . ***dēvabhaṁḍāra****diṁ aramanege saluva saṁbaḷa saradigaḷiṁge biṭṭudu ga 15* . . . . . ; **tr.** from the **temple treasury** an amount of 15 *ga* (*gadyāṇa*, gold coin) was given for the salary etc. of palace officials ; *E.C.* (R) IV, Ch. 259, p. 159, ll. 6–8 ; Haradanahaḷḷi, Chamarajanagar Tq. and Dt., Karn. St. **Misc.**, in characters of 14th-15th cent. A.D.

dēvabhōga (K. < Skt. *n.*), rent free land granted to temple ; **text :** . . . . *Bhīmēśvarake* . . . . *Āneūroḷ koṭṭa* ***dēvabhōga*** *kaṇḍuga gaḷdeyu* . . . ; **tr. rent free** wet **land** of one *kaṇḍuga* (a land measure) **granted to the temple** of Bhīmēśvara in Āneūru;. *E.C.* X, Chin. 49, p. 315, ll. 9–11 ; Ānūru, Chintamani Tq., Kolar Dt., Karn. St. **Dy.** Noḷ. Pal., Iṟiva Noḷaṁba, Ś. 873 = 951 A.D.

dēvabrāhmaṇadattulu (Te. < Skt. *n.*), the gifts granted to the gods and brāhmaṇas ; **text :** . . . . *samasta saṁtānaṁbulu* ***dēvabrāhmaṇadattulu*** *samasta dharmmaṁbuluṁbratipāliṁchchi.* ; **tr.** having protected all the lineages, all the **gifts made to the gods and brāhmaṇas** and all the pious acts of charity ; *S.I.I.* VI, No. 628, p. 232, ll. 134–36 ; Konidēna, Narasaraopet Tq., Guntur Dt., A.P. St. **Misc.**, Ś. 1146 = 1224 A.D.

dēvabrāhmaṇavṛittulu (Te. < Skt. *n.*), shares of gift lands earmarked for deities and brāhmaṇas ; **text :** . . . . *nēla* ***dēvabrāhmaṇavṛittulu*** *peṭṭinavi* . . . . ; **tr. gift lands earmarked** as **shares for deities and brāhmaṇas** ; *S.I.I.* XVI, No. 90, p. 9, l. 16 ; Mudivēḍu, Madanapalle Tq., Chittoor Dt., A.P. St. **Dy.** Saṅgama, Harihara II, Cy. yr. Īśvara = 1397 A.D.

dēvadāna (K. < Skt. *n.*), donation made to temple; **text**[1] **:** . . . *ī* ***dēvadāna****vanaḷidavaru* . . . . *kavileyaṁ Bāṇarāsi Gaṁgeya taḍiyalaḷidaru* . . . ; **tr.** whoever destroys this **donation made to a temple** would have, in effect, destroyed tawny cows on the banks of the river Gaṁgā at Vāraṇāsi ; *E.C.* (R) X, Ak. 190, p. 247, ll. 10–12 ; Bāgavāḷu, Arasikere Tq., Hassan Dt., Karn. St. **Dy.** Hoy., Vinayāditya, Cy. yr. Bahudhānya = 1098-99 A.D. ; **text**[2] **:** *yī yellā* ***dēvadāna*** *koḍagiya sthalaṁgaḷa . . . . yellā teṟeyanū yellā bādheyanū . . . . pariharisi . . . . koṭṭaru . . .* ; **tr.** all these **donations made to the temples** and other land gifts were exempted from all taxes and all hindrances ; *E.C.* (R) VII, Ng. 76, p. 73, ll. 56, 57–58 ; Beḷḷūru, Nagamanagala Tq., Mandya Dt., Karn. St. **Dy.** Hoy., Ballāḷa, Ś. 1231 = 1309 A.D. [this term occurs in a large number of South Indian Inscriptions].

dēvadāṉa iṟaiyili (T. < Skt.+T. *n.*), tax free gift of land to temple ; **text**[1] **:** *. . . . kaṇakkiṉpaḍi nilamaippaśāna mudal* ***dēvadāṉa-iṟaiyili****yāga vēṟu piṟinda Tirunīṟṟuchōḷanallūr taranpeṟṟa nīrnilam nāṟpattu oṉbadiṟṟu vēli. . . . .* ; **tr.** forty nine *vēli* (a land measure) of quality wet **land** in Tirunīṟṟuchōḷanallūr which has been separated and declared as a **tax free gift to the temple** ; *S.I.I.* VII, No. 816, p. 414, l. 6 ; Villiyanūr, Pondicherry Tq. and Dt., T. Nadu St. **Dy.** Chōḷa, Kulōttuṅga I, reg. yr. 13 = 1083 A.D. ; **text**[2] **:** *. . . . uḷḷūr dēvargaḷ* ***dēvadāna-iṟaiyili****yāy varugiṟa nilam nīkki. . . . .* ; **tr.** having excluded the **tax free gifts of land to** the deities of the village; *S.I.I.* VIII, No. 85, p. 46, ll. 4–5 ; Tiruvaṇṇāmalai, Tiruvannamalai Tq. and Dt., T. Nadu St. **Dy.** Chōḷa, Rājarāja III, reg. yr. 30 = 1246 A.D.

dēvadāṉam (T. *n.*), land/village donated to a temple ; **text**[1] **:** *. . . . Aimpūṇiyum Viḷattūrum iddēvar* ***dēvadāṉam*** *Amaruṉṟimaṅgalamum Viḍēlviḍugu Vikkiramādittachchaturvēdimaṅgala meṉṉum pērāl yēkagrāmamākki . . . . .* ; **tr.** having merged into one **village**, the three villages of Aimpūṇi, Viḷattūr, Amaruṉṟimaṅgaḷam and renaming the same as Viḍēlviḍugu Vikkiramāditta-chchaturvēdimangalam, it was **donated to the temple** ; *S.I.I.* III, pt. i & ii, No. 43, p. 93, ll. 6–12, 16 ; Tiruvallam, Tanjavur Tq. and Dt., T. Nadu, St. **Dy.** Gaṁga-Pallava, Vijayanandi Vikramavarmaṉ, reg. yr. 62, in characters of 9th century A.D. ; **text**[2] **:** *. . . . Kshētrapāla Piḷḷaiyārkku Chikkadēvadaṉṉāyakkaṉ Iṉṉāyaṉār* ***dēvadānamāna*** *Kaḷḷipaḷḷitirumaḷaiviḷāgattil . . . . eppērpaṭṭa varigaḷum . . . . Irāmanāthadēvar vāḷukkuntōḷukkum naṉṟāga . . . . kuḍuttēṉ . . . .* ; **tr.** I, Chikkadēvadaṉṉāyakkaṉ granted all the tax incomes to the kitchen at Kaḷḷipaḷḷi which is a **village donated to the temple** of the god Kshētrapāla Piḷḷaiyār so that the sword and the shoulders of the king Rāmanātha may flourish ; *E.C.* X, Kol. 18, p. 2, ll. 5–6, 8–11, 17–19, 22–23; Kalluhaḷḷi, Kolar Tq. and Dt., Karn. St. **Dy.** Hoy., Rāmanātha, Ś. 1216 = 1293 A.D. ; **text**[3] **:** *. . . . Kaḍigaippaṭṭinattu periya kuḷattiṉ kīḻ Ūḍuppaḷḷippaṟṟuḍaṉ kūṭṭi . . .* ***dēvadāṉam*** *taḍi oṉṟu . . .* ; **tr. land donated to a temple** after merging Ūḍupaḷḷipaṟṟu under the big tank and Kaḍigaipaṭṭiṉam measuring in all one *taḍi* (a land measure) ; *T.A.S.* IV, No. 17, p. 95, l. 6 ; Suchīndram, Agasteesvaram Tq., Kanyakumari Dt., T. Nadu St. **Dy.** Rulers of Travancore, Vīra Rāma Rāmavarman, Kali yr. 4572 = Kollam 646 = 1471 A.D. [this term occurs in a large number of South Indian Inscriptions].

dēvadānappaṟṟu (T. < Skt.+T. *n.*), temple holding the lands gifted to it ; **text :** . . . . *Tiruvaṇṇāmalai uḍaiyanāyaṉār* ***dēvadānappaṟṟu*** . . . ; **tr.** the **temple** of the god Tiruvaṇṇāmalai uḍaiyanāyaṉār **holding the lands gifted to it** ; *S.I.I.* VIII, No. 90, p. 48, l. 4 ; Tiruvaṇṇāmalai, Tiruvannamalai Tq., N. Arcot Dt., T. Nadu St. **Dy.** Kāḍava, Kōpperuñjiṅga, reg. yr. 5, in characters of 13th cent. A.D.

dēvadāsi (K. < Skt. *n.*), female dedicated to the service of the temple ; **text :** . . . *Bannikeṟeyalu kalukuṭiga kāḷōja dēvadāsigaḷge biṭṭa beddale gaḷeyalu mattar ondu* . . . ; **tr.** one *mattar* (land measure) of dry land measured by the *gaḷe* (measuring rod) was granted to the females dedicated to the service of the temple by the stone mason Kāḷōja in Bannikeṟe ; *E.C.* (R) XIII, No. 7, p. 6, ll. 55–56 ; Ālahaḷḷi, Shimoga Tq. and Dt., Karn. St. **Dy.** Chāḷ. of Kal., Vikramāditya VI, Ch. Vi. yr. 37 = 1112 A.D.

dēvadatti (K. < *Skt. n.*), grant given to temple ; **text :** (beginning lost) . . . . *Kaḍagahaḷiya samastaprajegaḷa kayyalu Mādirājaya* ***dēvadatti****yāgi* . . . . *koṭṭa gadde hiriya keṟe keḷage yikhaṁḍuga* . . . . *Brahmabhaṭṭarige koṭṭaru* ; **tr.** Mādirājaya **granted** two *khaṁduga* (grain measure, i.e., **land** of the extent of being sown with 2 *khaṁḍuga* of seeds) to the (**temple** priest) Brahmabhaṭṭa and handed them over to the inhabitants of the village Kaḍagahaḷi ; *E.C.* (R) VIII, Hn. 53, p. 271, ll. 1–2, 3 ; Kaḍaga, Hassan Tq. and Dt., Karn. St. **Misc**, in characters of 15th cent. A.D.

dēvadāya (K. < Skt. *n.*), grant of land/village to the temple ; **text :** (damaged) . . . *Ummattūra Naṁjarāja voḍeyaru dharmavāgi Terakaṇāṁbiya pārupatyāgāra Chikkanaṁjayyanavarige nirūpava koṭṭu* . . . . . *tēra kāṇikeya* . . . . *dharma śilāśāsana mūlasthānadēvara tēra kāṇikege* ***dēvadāya*** *brahmadāya grāmagaḷu* . . . *Piriyūru Puragaḷu modalāda grāmagaḷiṁ* . . . ; **tr.** the Superintendent of Terakaṇāṁbi Chikkanaṁjayya granted for the merit of Naṁjarāyavoḍeya, the Ummattūr Chief, incomes from **villages granted to temples**, villages granted to brāhmaṇas, other villages such as Piriyūru, Pura, etc. for conducting the car festival of the temple of Mūlasthānadēva ; *E.C.* (R) III, Gu. 114, p. 86, ll. 5, 6–9 ; Terakaṇāṁbi, Gundlupet Tq., Mysore Dt., Karn. St. **Dy.** Umm. Chfs., Vīranaṁjarāya, Ś. 1426 = 1504 A.D.

dēvadāyamu (Te. < Skt. *n.*), land granted to temple ; **text :** . . . . . *Bayyappanāyani ayyavāru*

Būdigumma sīmalōni Yaraguḍi ***dēvadāya*** *brahmadāyaṁ vāriki ichina dharma śāsanamu* . . ; **tr.** the edict of charity recording the **grant of land to the temple** and land to the brāhmaṇas at Yeraguḍi in Būdigumma-sīma by Bayyappanāyani ayyavāru ; *S.I.I.* XVI, No. 124, p. 138, ll. 4–7 ; Yerṟaguḍi, Kalyanadurga Tq., Anantapur Dt., A.P. St. **Dy.** Tuḷuva, Achyutarāya, Ś. 1464 = 1541 A.D.

dēvaḍi (K. *n.*), temple pavilion ; **text :** . . *kaṁmaṁ hattumaṁ* . . . *Prasaṁnakēśavadēvara pūjārigaṁ dēvara* ***dēvaḍigaḷaṁ*** *kaṭṭalu* . . . . . *koṭṭaru* . . . . ; **tr.** ten *kaṁma* (land measure) of land was donated to the priest of the temple of Prasaṁnakēśava for constructing **pavilions** in the **temple** ; *S.I.I.* XV, No. 545, pp. 367–68, ll. 8, 10; Muttagi, Bagewadi Tq., Bijapur Dt., Karn. St. **Dy.** Chāḷ. of Kal., Jagadēkamalla, Cy. yr. Pārthiva = 1165 A.D.

dēvaḍichchi (M. *n.*), maid servant of the temple; **text :** . . . . *tiru amardiṉṉu nel kuṭṭuvidum kaiviḷakku piḍippidum śeyigiṉṟa* ***dēvaḍichchi****gaḷkku yirunnāḻi arichchōṟu* . . . . ; **tr.** for the **maid servants of the temple** doing the jobs of pounding rice and holding the hand lamps two *nāḻi* (grain measure) of cooked rice are earmarked ; *T.A.S.* V, pts. i, ii and iii, No. 24, p. 81, ll. 24–25 ; Kiḷimannūr, Tiruvanantapuram Tq. and Dt., Kēr. St. **Dy.** Rulers of Vēṇāḍu, śrī Vīradēva Udayamārttāṇḍavarmma tiruvaḍi, Kollam 343, 1167–68 A.D.

dēvaḍiga (K. *n.*), temple servant ; **text :** . . . . . . ***dēvaḍigaḷu*** *dēvālyake kalu marava horabēku* . . ; **tr.** the **temples servants** should carry loads of stones and woood to the temple ; *S.I.I.* IX, pt. ii, No. 470, p. 485, l. 72 ; Kollūru, Kundapur Tq., Udupi Dt., Karn. St. **Dy.** Saṅgama, Virūpāksha, Ś. 1404 = 1482 A.D.

dēvaḍiyār (T. < Skt. *n.*), female dedicated to the deity ; **text :** . . . . *Tiruvakkarai Āḷuḍaiya nayiṉār kōyil* ***dēvaḍiyār*** *kalattuṭṭi yiṟuttu* . . ; **tr.** the **female dedicated to the deity** Āḷuḍaiya nayiṉār of Tiruvakkarai was exempted from the payment of tax called *kalattuṭṭi* ; *S.I.I.* XVII, No. 219, p. 79, ll. 3–4 ; Tiruvakkarai, Villupuram Tq., S. Arcot Dt., T. Nadu St. **Dy.** Sāḷuva, Narasiṁha, Cy. yr. Śōbhakṛit = 1483 A.D.

dēva gāṇa (K. < Skt.+K. *n.*), oil mills dedicated to the god ; **text :** . . . *Kēśavadēvargge pūjāpunaskārakke* . . . *koṭṭa matta 2 pūdōṁṭa oṁdu* ***dēva gāṇa*** *oṁdumaṁ ekkaṭigarnnālvattu mānasaru irddu barayisida śāsana* ; **tr.** a stone inscription got written by the administrative body of forty members registering grants for the worship and services to the deity Kēśavadēva including 2 *matta* (*mattar*, a land measure) of land, one flower garden and one **oil mill dedicated to the god** . . ; *S.I.I.* IX, pt. i, No. 231, p. 236, ll. 12–16 ; Kolimiguṇḍla, Koilkuntla Tq., Kurnool Dt., A.P. St. **Dy.** Chāḷ. of Kal., Bhūlōkamalla, Ch. Vi. yr. 58 = 1134 A.D.

dēva gey (K. < Skt.+K. *n.*), wet land belonging

to the temple ; **text :** .... *Gauḍokkala dēvageyyiṁ baḍagal* ; **tr.** to the north of the **wet land belonging to the temple** and cultivated by the gauḍa ...; *S.I.I.* IX, pt. i, No. 296, p. 321, l. 65 ; Kurugōḍu, Bellary Tq. and Dt., Karn. St. **Dy.** Kal. of Kal., Sōvidēva, Ś. 1097 = 1176 A.D.

dēvaghāta (T. < Skt. *n.*), natural calamity; **text :** ... *ivviraṇḍuviḷakkiṉukkum vaitta bhūmi* ***dēvaghātam*** ādalil eṉṉaiviḷakkeyerivadāga vaittōm sabhaiyōm; **tr.** as the land granted for two lamps had been destroyed by **natural calamity**, we, the assembly, assigned one oil lamp for burning ...; *S.I.I.* III, No. 48, p. 201, l. 6 ; Tiruvallam, Gudiyattam Tq., N. Arcot Dt., T. Nadu St. **Dy.** Bāṇa, Bāṇa Vidyādhara, in characters of 10th cent. A.D.

dēvagoḷaga (K. < Skt.+K. *n.*), measure of capacity of grains given to the god ; **text :** ... *Kalidēvara naṁdādīvigege gāṇa 1* ***dēvagoḷaga*** *damagoḷagavaṁ dhānyadali kuḷavaṁ Kētayanāyakanu aṟuvattokkalumirddu koṭṭaru*.... ; **tr.** Kētayanāyaka and the body of sixty tenants gave one oil mill and from the produce on land **one measure of capacity of grains to the god** as a pious gift ; *S.I.I.* IX, pt. i, No. 88, p. 59, ll. 23–25 ; Chimnahaḷḷi, Hadagalli Tq., Bellary Dt., Karn. St. **Dy.** Chāḷ. of Kal., Jagadēkamalla, Ś. 956 = 1034 A.D.

dēvakaṉmi (T. < Skt. *n.*), temple servant ; **text**[1]**:** ... *Aṟumoḻidēvaṉāl nel eṇkalamāga* ..... *iddēvar baṇḍārattē koṇḍu .... śeluttuvōmaṉōm iddēvar* ***dēvakaṉmigaḷ****ōm* .... ; **tr.** we the **temple servants** of the god will remit to the temple treasury for a period of one year eight *kalam* (grain measure) of paddy measured by the standard measure named after the royal epithet *Aṟumoḻidēva* ; *S.I.I.* XVII, No. 314, p. 138, ll. 45–51 ; Kāḷahasti, Kalahasti Tq., Chittoor Dt., A.P. St. **Dy.** Chōḷa, Rājēndra I, reg. yr. 4 = 1016 A.D. ; **text**[2] **:** ... *Tiruvaṇṇāmalai Uḍaiyanāyaṉār kōyil* .... *tāṉattōmum* ***dēvakaṉmi*** *kōyilkaṇakkarum .... Umaiyāḻvārkku kalveṭṭikuḍuttapaḍi* .. ; **tr.** as per the stone edict, dedicated to the godess Umaiyāḻvār by the temple officials, **temple servants**, temple accountant etc., of the temple of Tiruvaṇṇāmalai Uḍaiyanāyaṉār ; *S.I.I.* VIII, No. 93, p. 49, l. 2 ; Tiruvaṇṇāmalai, Tiruvannamalai Tq. and Dt., T. Nadu St. **Dy.** Chōḷa, Rājarāja III, reg. yr. 32 = 1248 A.D. ; **text**[3]**:** (damaged) ... *iddēvadāṉam* .... *kallilum śembilum veṭṭikkoḷḷa piḍipāḍu paṇṇi kuḍuttōm* ... . ***dēvakaṉmi****gaḷukku Śēṟṟūr ūṟku śamainda ūrōmum* ..... ; **tr.** we the inhabitants of the village of Śēṟṟūr gave in committed writing to the **temple servants** regarding the creation of *dēvadāṇa* ; *S.I.I.* VIII, No. 171, p. 81, ll. 21–22 ; Kāḷaiyārkōyil, Sivaganga Tq., Ramanathapuram Dt., T. Nadu St. **Dy.** Pāṇḍya, Kulaśēkhara, reg. yr. 37+1 = 1305 A.D.

dēvakarmi (T. < Skt.+T. *n.*), temple servant ; **text :** (badly damaged) ... *sabhaiyum* ***dēvakarmi****gaḷōmum* .. ; **tr.** the members of the *sabhā* (village administrative body) and the **temple**

servants ; *S.I.I.* XIII, No. 260, p. 139, l. 21 ; Tiruppūndurutti, Tanjavur Tq. and Dt., T. Nadu St. **Dy.** Chōḷa, Sundara Chōḷa, reg. yr. 15 = 981 A.D.

dēvakulam (T. < Skt. *n.*), temple ; **text :** . . . *Kandaśēṉaṉ śeyvitta* ***dēvakulam*** . . ; **tr. temple** caused to be constructed by Kandaśēṉaṉ ; *S.I.I.* II, pts. iii, iv and v, No. 72, p. 341, ll. 4–5 ; Vallam, Tanjavur Tq. and Dt., T. Nadu St. **Dy.** Pal. of Kañchi, Mahēndravarman, in characters of the 7th cent. A.D.

dēvaḷa stānikulu (Te. < Skt. *n.*), temple officials; **text :** . . . . *Cheṁnakēśvara* ***dēvaḷasthānikulu*** . . . . *Cheṁnappānu Sthānaṁ Pedōvabayya Pinavōbayyagāriki ichhina* . . . . *dharma śāsana* . . . . . ; **tr.** the edict of charity rercording the pious gift made to Chennappa, Sthānaṁ Pedavōbayya and Pinavōbayya who were **temple officials** of Chennakēśvara ; *I.A.P.* Cuddapah II, No. 135, p. 169, ll. 6–8 ; Pushpagiri, Cuddapah Tq. and Dt., A.P. St. **Dy.** Tuḷuva, Achyutarāya, Ś. 1463 = 1541 A.D.

dēvamāna (K. *n.*), a standard measure for measuring grains in temples ; **text :** . . . . *hērinalli dēvamānavu* . . . ; **tr. a standard measure for measuring grains in temples** as applied to each head load ; *K.I.A.P.*, pt. ii, No. 4, p. 46, l. 24 ; Dākūr, Medak Tq. and Dt., A.P. St. **Dy.** Chāḷ. of Kal., Trailōkyamalla, Ś. 1078 = 1156 A.D.

dēvaṇam piya (Pkt. *n.*), beloved of the gods (a title) ; **text :** . . . . *dēvaṇampiya āṇapayati* . . ; **tr.** the **beloved of the gods** commands ; *Ep. Ind.* III, No. 22, p. 138, l. 1 ; Siddāpura, Molakalmuru Tq., Chitradurga Dt., Karn. St. **Dy.** Maurya, Aśoka, in characters of 3rd cent. B.C.

dēvapolamu (Te. < Skt.+Te. *n.*), field belonging to the temple ; **text :** . . . . ***dēvapolānanu*** *Odayana Bhaṭṭōpādhyala chēta peṭṭi konna kha 5*; **tr.** the **field belonging to the temple** was placed in the care of Odayana Bhaṭṭōpādhya for obtaining 5 *kha* (*khaṁḍuga*, a grain measure) of grain ; *S.I.I.* V, No. 136, p. 52, l. 6 ; Pālakōl, Narasapur Tq., Krishna Dt., A.P. St. **Misc.**, Ś. 1218 = 1296 A.D.

deva putraka (K. < Skt. *n.*), member belonging to a sub caste ; **text :** . . . . . . *dēvara aṁgabhōgakke Kāmiseṭṭiya gāṇavaṁ* . . . . ***dēvaputrakaru*** *salisuvaru*; **tr. members belonging to the sub caste** will suply oil for services to the deity from the oil mill belonging to Kāmiseṭṭi . . .; *S.I.I.* XX, No. 130, p. 168, ll. 8–10 ; Lakshmēśvar, Shirahatti Tq. Dharwar Dt., Karn. St. **Dy.** Chāḷ. of Kal., Sōmēśvara IV, reg. yr. 2 = 1187 A.D.

dēvara boksa (K. < °bokkasa, *n.*), temple treasury; **text :** ***dēvara*** ***boksake*** *pālu 1* . . . ; **tr.** 1 share for the **temple treasury** ; *S.I.I.* IX, pt. ii, No. 607, p. 615, l. 9 ; Hampi, Hospet Tq., Bellary Dt., Karn. St. **Dy.** Tuḷuva, Sadāśiva, Ś. 1465 = 1543 A.D.

dēvaraḍiyāḷ (T. < Skt.+T. *n.*), a female dedicated to a deity; **text :** (badly damaged) . . . *Tiruvaṇṇāmalai uḍaiya nāyaṉārkku innāyaṉār* *dēvaraḍiyāḷ* .... *magaḷ Dēvi* .... ; **tr.** Dēvi, the daughter of the **female dedicated to the deity** Tiruvaṇṇāmalai uḍaiya nāyaṉār ; *S.I.I.* VIII, No. 116, p. 58, l. 2 ; Tiruvaṇṇāmalai, Tiruvannamalai Tq., N. Arcot Dt., T. Nadu St. **Dy.** Chōḷa, Kulōttuṅga I, reg. yr. 2 = 1072 A.D.

dēvara hāne (K. < Skt.+K. *n.*), a measure called *hāne* standardized in temple ; **text :** .... ***dēvara hāne****yalli* ... *prativarshadalli 24 mūḍe akki* .. ; **tr.** 24 *mūḍe* (a grain measure) of rice **measured by the hāne standardized in the temple** ; *S.I.I.* VII, No. 270, p. 139, ll. 32–33 ; Yermaḷ, Udupi Tq. and Dt., Karn. St. **Dy.** Saṅgama, Harihara, Ś. 1324 = 1402 A.D.

dēvaraṁgaḍi (K. < Skt.+K. *n.*), shop belonging to temple ; **text[1] :** .... *aṁgaḍi areyaṁgaḍi* ***dēvaraṁgaḍi*** *mānyadaṁgaḍiyeṁnaduḍisiriyaṁ koṁḍu* ... ; **tr.** collecting taxes without exempting shops, small shops, **shop belonging to the temple**, gifted shops, etc. ; *K.I.* II, No. 21, p. 82, ll. 23–24; Telsang, Athani Tq., Belgaum Dt., Karn. St. **Dy.** Chāḷ. of Kal., Jagadēkamalla, reg. yr. 10 = 1147 A.D.

dēvar kaṇakku (T. < Skt.+T. *n.*), temple accountant; **text :** ..... *Tiruviḍaimarudil nagarattārum tirukkōyil uḍaiyārgaḷum* ***dēvar kaṇakku*** *Marudaṉ Brahma Kuṭṭaṉum* ... *vaitta viḷakku* ... ; **tr.** lamp donated by the administrative body, officials of the temple and Marudaṉ Brahma Kuṭṭaṉ the **temple accountant** at Tiruviḍaimarudūr .... ; *S.I.I.* III, No. 124, p. 260, ll. 1–2 ; Tiruviḍaimarudūr, Kumbhakonam Tq., Tanjavur Dt., T. Nadu St. **Dy.** Chōḷa, Parakēsarivarman, reg. yr. 4 = 975 A.D.

dēvarkanmi (T. < Skt. *n.*), temple servants ; **text[1] :** ... *Tiruviḍaimarudil nagarattōmum* ***dēvar kanmigaḷōmum*** *śādanattiṉṟi mālaikkāraṉ uṇḍuvaruginṟa Viḷanguḍi nilattil Śivapichchaṉ śeyda malligai nondavāṉattukku kāl śeyyum Panmāhēśvarattoṇḍaṉ śeyda malligai nondavānattukku kāl śeyyum nivandamāga śeydu kuḍuttōm* .... ; **tr.** the administrative body and **temple servants** of Tiruviḍaimarudūr granted one quarter *śey* (a land measure) to Śivapichchaṉ for raising a Jasmine garden and quarter *śey* to Panmāhēśvarattoṇḍan for raising a Jasmine garden from the land in the illegal possession of the garland maker at Viḷanguḍi ...; *S.I.I.* XIII, No. 270, p. 143, ll. 6–18 ; Tiruviḍaimarudūr, Kumbhakonam Tq., Tanjavur Dt., T. Nadu St. **Dy.** Chōḷa, Rājakēsarivarman, reg. yr. 17 = 972 A.D. ; **text[2] :** .... *Tiruvottūruḍaiyārkku* .... *nellāyamuṅ kāśāyamuṅkkeykoṇḍu* ...... *śeluttakkaḍavōm ikkōyiṟ* ***dēvarkaṇmi****gaḷōm* .. ; **tr.** the **temple servants** of the temple of Tiruvottūruḍaiyār shall remit to the temple (among many other things), the income from paddy as well as income in cash ..... ; *S.I.I.* VII, No. 99, p. 42, ll. 2, 7–8 ; Tiruvottūr, Cheyyar Tq., N. Arcot Dt., T. Nadu St. **Dy.** Chōḷa, Rājarāja III,

reg. yr. 20 = 1236 A.D.

dēvar nāḻi (T. < Skt.+T. *n.*), liquid measure standardized in the name of the deity ; **text :** (damaged) . . . . . ***dēvar nāḻi****yāl uriy neyyaṭṭi iraṇḍu tirunandā-viḷakkeṟippōmānōm ikkōyil* . . . . *Śivabrāhmaṇarōm* . . . ; **tr.** the Śivabrāhmaṇas of this temple shall burn two perpetual lamps with one *uri* (liquid measure) of ghee measured by the **liquid measure standardized in the name of the deity** ; *S.I.I.* XVII, No. 451, p. 184, ll. 4–5 ; Vēdāraṇyam, Tirutturaippundi Tq., Tanjavur Dt., T. Nadu St. **Dy.** Chōḷa, Kulōttuṅga III, in characters of 12th cent. A.D.

dēvar paṇḍāram (T. < Skt. *n.*), temple treasury ; **text**[1] **:** . . . *iraṇḍu chēriyārumē* ***dēvar paṇḍāra****ttil vaitta nivandam koṇḍu tirumeykāppu iḍuvadāguvam* . . . . . ; **tr.** watch and ward for the temple is to be appointed from the income derived from the endowment kept in the **temple treasury** by the inhabitants of the two streets . . . ; *S.I.I.* III, No. 128, p. 271, ll. 112–13 ; Madras Museum, Chennai Tq. and Dt., T. Nadu St. **Dy.** Chōḷa, Uttamachōḷa, reg. yr. 16 = 987 A.D. ; **text**[2] **:** . . . *id****dēvar paṇḍāra****ttē nūṟu kāśu poliśaikku koṇḍu. ikkāśu nūṟṟālum vanda poliśaikku* . . . . . . *iṟaiyiḻichchi kuḍutta nilamāvadu* . . . . . ; **tr.** the tax free land granted from the interest amount accruing from hundred *kāśu* (coin) borrowed on interest from the **temple treasury** . . . . ; *S.I.I.* III, No. 28, p. 55, l. 8 ; Maṇimaṅgaḷam, Kanchipuram Tq., Chingleput Dt., T. Nadu St. **Dy.** Chōḷa, Rājādhirāja I, reg. yr. 29 = 1047 A.D.

devasavoḷam (K. < Skt.+K. *n.*), each day ; **text :** *Telligēśvaradēvargge* . . . *daṁḍinokkaluṁ taḷadokkaluṁ* ***dēvasavaḷa****veṁṇe gāṇadalli soḷasaveraḍu* ; **tr.** each family in the army cantonment and the township should **each day** measure out two *soḷasa* (a liquid measure) of oil from the oil mills as donation to the god Telligēśvara ; *Ep. Ind.*, XX, No. 12, p. 117, ll. 47, 48–49 ; Beṇachamaṭṭi, Ron Tq., Dharwar Dt., Karn. St. **Dy.** Kal. of Kal., Bijjaṇa, Ś. 1088 = 1167 A.D.

dēvastāna grāma (K. < Skt. *n.*), village belonging to temple ; **text :** . . . *Uravakoṇḍege saluva* . . . ***dēvastāna grāma****gaḷalū idanta nāyindaru* . . . . . ; **tr.** the barbers living in the **villages belonging to the temple** and located within Uravakoṁḍa ; *S.I.I.* IX, pt. ii, No. 625, p. 629, ll. 9–12 ; Gadekallu, Gooty Tq., Anantapur Dt., A.P. St. **Dy.** Tuḷuva, Sadāśiva, Ś. 1469 = 1547 A.D.

dēvasva (K. < Skt. *n.*), property belonging to temple ; **text**[1] **:** . . . *purāṇava hēḷisuva dharmmakke* . . . . *Vināyakadēvara* ***dēvasva****doḷage* . . . *hāneyali 15 mūḍe akki gēṇi bahaṁthā bāḷanu* . . . . *koṭṭaru* . . . . ; **tr.** leased wet land yielding 15 *mūḍe* (a grain measure) measured by *hāne* (a grain measure) of rice, located within the **property belonging to temple** of the god Vināyaka was donated to the the person who gives discourses on *purāṇa* . . . ; *S.I.I.* VII, No. 341, p. 194, ll. 11–13, 20 ; Chauḷikēri,

Udupi Tq. and Dt., Karn. St. **Dy.** Saṅgama, Bukka, Ś. 1298 = 1376 A.D. ; **text**[2] : . . . ***dēvasvada*** *gaḍiyiṁda paḍuvalu* . . . . ; **tr.** to the west of the boundary of the landed **property belonging to the temple** . . . ; *S.I.I.* IX, pt. ii, No. 444, p. 454, l. 17 ; Basarūru, Kundapur Tq., Udupi Dt., Karn. St. **Dy.** Saṅgama, Dēvarāya, Ś. 1356 = 1433 A.D.

dēvatāgrāmālu (Te. *n.*), villages belonging to temple ; **text :** . . . ***dēvatāgrāmāla**ku Ghaṇḍikōta durgavartana* . . . . ; **tr.** the customary grants given from the Ghaṇḍikōṭa fort to the **villages belonging to the temple** ; *I.A.P.* Cuddapah II, No. 135., p. 169, ll. 14–15 ; Pushpagiri, Cuddapah Tq. and Dt., A.P. St. **Dy.** Tuḷuva, Achyutarāya, Ś. 1463 = 1541 A.D.

dēva ugrāṇa (K. < Skt. *n.*), temple store house ; **text :** . . . . *Viṭhalēśvaradēvarige nityavū . . . kelasa . . naḍavadakke* ***dēva ugrāṇa**dallu koḍuva upabatti;* **tr.** additional grant given to the **temple store house** so that work can go on daily in the temple of the god Viṭhalēśvara . . ; *S.I.I.* IV, No. 274, p. 70, ll. 12–15; Hampi, Hospet Tq., Bellary Dt., Karn. St. **Dy.** Achytutarāya, Ś 1452 = 1530 A.D.

dēvi (T. < Skt. *n.*), wife ; **text :** . . . *Tirukkuḍitiṭṭai Perumāḷukku Śiriyavēḷān* ***dēvi*** *Irājādichchi oru nondāviḷakku eriya vaitta īḻakkāśu iruvattañji* ; **tr.** gift of twenty five *īḻakkāśu* (coin minted in northern Śrīlanka) donated by Rājādichchi **wife** of Śiriyavēḷān for burning one perpetual lamp in the temple of the deity Tirukkuḍitiṭṭai Perumāḷ ; *S.I.I.* III, No. 122, p. 258, ll 1–2 ; Tirukkalitaṭṭai, Kumbhakonam Tq., Tanjavur Dt., T. Nadu St. **Dy.** Chōḷa, Sundara Chōḷa II, reg. yr. 14 = 971 A.D.

deyva puttirar (M. < Skt. *n.*), members belonging to a sub caste ; **text :** . . . . . *Kalkkuḷattu Mādēvar kōvilil* ***deyva puttiraril*** *kaṇakku Perumāḷ Tāṇuvaṉ* ; **tr.** Perumāḷ Tāṇuvaṉ a **members belonging to a sub caste** who is the accountant in the temple of Mādēva at Kalkuḷam . . . ; *T.A.S.* V, pts. i, ii and iii, No. 42, p. 147, ll. 9–12 ; Tiruviḍaikkōḍu, Padmanabhapuram Tq. and Dt., Kēr. St. **Misc.**, Kollam 835 = 1660 A.D.

dhaḷa (K. *s. a. daḷa n.*), army ; **text :** . . . *Kāñchīpurādhipati . . . . turagavidyādhara . . .* ***dhaḷa**daṅkakāraṁ* . . . ; **tr.** the lord of the city of Kāñchī, expert in the study of horses and a professional warrior in the **army** ; *S.I.I.* IX, pt. i, No. 30, p. 17, ll. 23–27 ; Kambadūru, Kalyanadurg Tq., Anantapur Dt., A.P. St. **Dy.** Noḷ. Pal., Noḷaṁbādhirāja, Ś 887 = 965 A.D.

dhāḷidu (K. *vb.*), invade ; **text :** . . . . *ariṇipatigaḷaṁ* ***dhāḷiṭṭu*** *kolgumavanīpāḷam Trailōkyamallan Āhavamallaṁ* . . . ; **tr.** Trailōkyamalla Āhavamalla who **invades** and kills enemy kings ; *S.I.I.* IX, pt. i, No. 102, p. 74, l. 6 ; Mailāra, Hadagalli Tq., Bellary Dt., Karn. St. **Dy.** Chāḷ. of Kal., Trailōkyamalla, Ś 968 = 1046 A.D.

dhama (K. < Skt. *dharma, n.*), grant ; **text :** . . . . *nūṟu mūḍe bhattavanū voṁdavasarakke māḍida* ***dhama*** . . . . ; **tr.** one hundred *mūḍe* (grain measure) of paddy was made as a one time **grant** ; *E.C.* (R) IX, Bl. 9, pp. 6–7, ll. 7–8 ; Bēlūru, Belur Tq., Hassan Dt., Karn. St. **Dy.** Ajila, Sōmanātha Birumaṇṇa, Ś 1349 = 1427 A.D.

dhammakaṭṭaḷai (T. < Skt. *n.*), religious custom; **text**[1] : . . . *Mādhavakramavittaṉ pakkal* ***dhammakaṭṭaḷai*** *tuḷai niṟai irubattu aiṅkaḷañju poṉ koṇḍu* . . . ; **tr.** having taken twenty five *kaḷañju* of gold coins weighed by a weighing stone with an impressed as a **religious custom** from Mādhavakramavittan . . . . ; *S.I.I.* III, pts. i & ii, No. 44, p. 95, ll. 12–13 ; Tiruvallam, Chittoor Tq. and Dt., A.P. St. **Dy.** Bāṇa, Mahābalivāṇaraya, Ś. 810 = 888 A.D. ; **text**[2] : . . . *Duggayaṉ Śāttaṉ pakkal yāṅgaḷ koṇḍu kaḍava poṉ* ***dhammakaṭṭaḷai****yāl tuḷai niṟai poṉ iraubadin kaḷañju.* . . . ; **tr.** twenty *kaḷañju* (gold coin) weighed by the weighing stone with an impressed mark was taken from Duggayaṉ Śāttaṉ as per the **religious custom** . . . . ; *S.I.I.* XIII, No. 87, p. 42, ll. 2–3 ; Tiruviḍandai, Chingleput Tq. and Dt., T. Nadu St. **Dy.** Chōḷa, Rājakēsarivarman, reg. yr. 4, in characters of 11th cent. A.D.

dhammam (T. < Pkt. *n.*), charity ; **text** : . . . *gaṇiy Nanda asiriyi kuvaṉke* ***dhammam*** . . . ; **tr.** charity given to the *gaṇiy* (senior Jaina monk) Nanda-siri Kuvaṉ ; *E.T.E.* No. 1, p. 315, ll. 1–2 ; Māṅguḷam, Mangulam Tq., Madurai Dt., T. Nadu. St. **Misc.**, in characters of 3rd cent. B.C.

dhanadateṟe (K. < Skt+K. *n.*), wealth tax; **text** : (damaged) . . . . *Jakkanuṇba nālku mattarkkeyya maneya* ***dhanadateṟe*** . . . . ; **tr.** wealth tax on four *mattar* (land measure) of land being enjoyed by Jakka as also on his house ; *E.C.* VII, Skr. 48, p. 156, l. 26 ; Gauju Agrahāra, Shikaripura Tq., Shimoga Dt., Karn. St. **Misc.**, in characters of 11th cent. A.D.

dhana dhānya (K. < Skt. *n.*), riches and food grains ; **text** : . . . . ***dhana dhānyā****di samasta vastu chayamaṁ sanyāsanaṁ māḍi* . . . ; **tr.** having renounced all materials including **riches, food grains**, etc . . . . ; *S.I.I.* V, No. 856, p. 351, ll. 24–25; Madras Museum, Chennai Tq. and Dt., T. Nadu St. **Dy.** Kal. of Kal., Āhavamalla, in characters of 12th cent. A.D.

dhaṉma chattiram (T. < Skt. *n.*), free feeding house ; **text** : . . . . *Muṇaiyadaraiyanallūru ūr oṉṟum* . . . ***dhaṉma chattira****ttukku* . . . . *aruḷiṇapaḍikku* . . . . ; **tr.** the village Muṇaiyadaraiyanallūr having been granted for the **free feeding house** ; *S.I.I.* VII, No. 469, p. 291, ll. 8–9 ; Achcharapākkam, Madhurantakam Tq., Chingleput Dt., T. Nadu St. **Dy.** Sāḷuva, Narasiṁha, Kali year 4579 = 1478 A.D.

dhaṉma karttar (T. influenced by M. < Skt. *n.*), temple trustee ; **text** : . . . . *Muṟattaṇāṭṭu Kumariyil* . . . . . *Kumari Bhagavati nachchiyār* . . . . *kōyil* ***dhaṉmakarttar*** . . ; **tr.** the temple trustee of the temple of goddess Bhagavati of Kumari in Muṟattānāḍu . . . . . ; *T.A.S.* V, pts. i, ii and iii, No.

66, pp. 195–96, ll. 7–14 ; Kanyākumāri, Kanyakumari Tq. and Dt., T. Nadu St. **Dy.** Nāy. of Mad., Muttuvīrappanāyaka, Kollam 782, Ś. 1529 = 1607 A.D.

dhanmasādanappattaiyam (T. < Skt+T. *n.*), deed of charity ; **text :** .... *Achyutapanāyaka ayyan Tañjāvūr tattārku kudutta* ***dhanmasādanappattaiyam*** ... ; **tr. deed of charity** given to the goldsmiths of Tañjāvūr by Achyutappanāyaka ayyan..... ; *S.I.I.* II, pts. iii, iv and v, No. 97, p. 499, ll. 3–5 ; Tañjāvūr, Tanjavur Tq. and Dt., T. Nadu St. **Dy.** Nāy. of Tañj., Achyutappanāyaka, Ś. 1499 = 1578 A.D.

dhanmāsanam (T. < Skt. *n.*), seat of justice ; **text :** .... *iddhanmam muttāmēy śeluttuvomānōm sabhaiyōmiddhammam muttil* ***dhanmāsana****ttile niśadam aiñkalañju pon panmāhēśvararē manrapperuvadāgavum* .... ; **tr.** we the *sabhai* (administrative assembly) shall have to continue this charity without fail ; if we fail in this charity all the *Māhēśvaras* shall be liable to pay to the **seat of justice** a fine of five *kalañju* of gold per day ..... ; *S.I.I.* III, No. 44, p. 95, l. 13 ; Tiruvallam, Chittoor Tq. and Dt., A.P. St. **Dy.** Bāṇa, Mahābali- vāṇaraya, Ś. 810 = 888 A.D. ; **text**[2] **:** .... ***dhanmāsana****mullitta tān vēndu kōvinukku dandamida ottinōm sabhaiyōm* .... ; **tr.** we, the members of the *sabhai* shall pay a fine to the **seat of justice** including the king ; *S.I.I.* XIII, No. 325, p. 173, l. 16 ; Lalguḍi, Lalgudi Tq., Tiruchirapalli Dt., T. Nadu St. **Dy.** Chōḷa, Rājakēsarivaman, reg. yr. 27 = 898 A.D. ; **text**[3] **:** .... *idukku virōdañchēdārai* ***dhanmāsana****mudalāga* .... *irubbattaiṅkalañju pon manrapperuvāragavum* ... ; **tr.** whoever objects to the implementation of this grant shall pay a fine of twenty five *kalañju* of gold to **the seat of justice** ..... ; *S.I.I.* VII, No. 811, p. 412, ll. 8–10 ; Bāhūr, Pondicherry Tq. and Dt., Puducherry U.T., **Dy.** Rāshtr., Krishna III, reg. yr. 27 = 966 A.D.

dhanmavāriyapperumakkaḷ (T. < Skt.+T. *n.*), members of the charitable administrative board ; **text :** .. ***dhanmavāriyapperumakkaḷ****um ullitta mahāsabhaiyōm* .... *Mahāśāstāvin kōyililē irundu panitta eluttu* .... ; **tr.** document got written while the *mahāsabhā* (administrative body) including the members of the **charitable administrative board** had assembled in the temple of Mahāśāstā .... ; *S.I.I.* III, No. 6, p. 10, l. 6, 8 ; Ukkal, Wandiwash Tq., N. Arcot Dt., T. Nadu St. **Dy.** Chōḷa, Rājarāja I, reg. yr. 17 = 1002 A.D.

dhanurvvidyā śāstra (K. < Skt., *n.*), science of archery ; **text :** ... ***dhanurvvidyā śāstra*** *pravīṇan* ...... *Bīradēvan* ... ; **tr.** Bīradēva who was an expert in the **science of archery** ; *E.C.* VIII, Sgr. 80, p. 288, ll. 26–29 ; Āvinahaḷḷi, Sagara Tq., Shimoga Dt., Karn. St. **Dy.** Chāḷ. of Kal., Vikramāditya VI, Ch. Vi. yr. 19 = 1095 A.D.

dhānya (K. < Skt. *n.*), food grains ; ; **text**[1] **:** .. .... *Kalidēvara naṁdādīvige gāṇa 1 dēvagoḷaga* *damagoḷagavaṁ* ***dhānyadali*** *kuḷavaṁ Kētayanāyakanu aṟuvattokkalumirddu koṭṭaru....*; **tr.** Kētayanāyaka and the body of sixty tenants gave one oil mill, and from the produce on land, one measure of capacity of **food grains** to the god as a pious gift ; *S.I.I.* IX, pt. i, No. 88, p. 59, ll. 23–25 ; Chimnahaḷḷi, Hadagalli Tq., Bellary Dt., Karn. St. **Dy.** Chāḷ. of Kal., Jagadēkamalla, Ś. 956 = 1034 A.D. ; **text**[2] **:** . . . *aramaneyiṁda khāṇa* ***dhānya*** *ettu tuppa .... kuḷa saradiyali teṟuvevū ....*; **tr.** the amount of taxes payble on animal feed, **food grains**, bullocks, ghee and other things to the palace by each family will be regularly paid .... ; *S.I.I.* IX, pt. ii, No. 433, p. 442, ll. 49–51 ; Siṅgānallūru, Coimbatore Tq. and Dt., T. Nadu St. **Dy.** Saṅgama, Dēvarāya, Ś. 1330 = 1408 A.D.

dhānyādāyaṁ (Te. < Skt. *n.*), tax income from food grains ; **text :** ... *chatusīmambuṭṭina sakala suvarṇādāyamu* ***dhānyādāyamu*** . . ; **tr.** all the income in gold and the **tax income from food grains** collected from within the four boundaries .... ; *S.I.I.* XVI, No. 40, p. 43, ll. 40–42 ; Nandalūru, Rajampet Tq., Cuddapah Dt., A.P. St. **Dy.** Sāḷuva, Narasiṁha II, Ś. 1423 = 1501 A.D.

dhānyaṁgaḷ (K. *n.*), food grains ; **text :** . . . *akkasāliyāya uppoḷagāgi dhānyaṁgaḷoḷellaṁ poṁgeraḍu baḷḷavaṁ koḷvaṁtāgi .... koṭṭu koṁḍa poṁgadyāṇa nūṟamūṟu .....* ; **tr.** hundred and three gold coins were the contract amount paid for the right to collect the tax incomes on the blacksmiths, income from salts and all varieties of **food grains** bought at the rate of two *poṁnu* (gold coin) per *baḷḷa* (a grain measure) ..... ; *S.I.I.* IX, pt. i, No. 89, p. 60, ll. 17–20 ; Bāgaḷi, Harapanahalli Tq., Bellary Dt., Karn. St. **Dy.** Chāḷ. of Kal., Jayasiṁha II, Ś. 957 = 1035 A.D.

dhānyamu (Te. < Skt. *n.*), food grains ; **text :** . . . *nānā* ***dhānyamu****nnu tribhāgi lēkhanu rājaku pālu 1 kuḷaku pāḷḷu 2* . . . ; **tr.** of the different varieties of **food grains** 1 share is earmarked for the king and 2 shares for the families ..... ; *S.I.I.* X, No. 753, p. 294, l. 37 ; Dharmavaram, Ongole Tq., Guntur Dt., A.P. St. **Dy.** Rul. Golk, Muhammed Padshah, Ś. 1522 = 1600 A.D.

dharāmara (K. < Skt. *n.*), brāhmaṇa ; **text :** . . .. ***dharāmar****ōtta mōttamarenisuva mahātmara .... mahātme yadeṁteṁdaḍe.* ; **tr.** to describe the greatness of the men who were noble **brāhmaṇas** ; *E.C.* (R) X, Ak. 162, p. 217, ll. 40–41; Taḷalūr, Arasikere Tq., Hassan Dt., Karn. St. **Dy.** Hoy., Ballāḷa, in characters of 12th century A.D.

dharaṇa (K. < Skt. *n.*), silver or gold coin ; **text**[1] **:** .... *pūrvvadalu Śrīmadīśvaradēvargge yāva haḷḷiyalu gadyāṇavāva haḷḷiyalu* ***dharaṇa****vāmārgadiṁdavē gadyāṇadūralli matte gadyāṇa dharaṇadūralli matte dharaṇavāgi . . . koṭṭaru* . . . ; **tr.** the deity Īśvara was granted in accordance with the earlier practice from whichever village tax was collected in the form of *gadyāṇa* (gold coin) and from whichever villages tax was collected in the form of ***dharaṇa*** (**silver or gold coin**), an additional donation of one *gadyāṇa* from the villages where taxation was collected in the form of *gadyāṇa* and an additional ***dharaṇa*** was donated from those villages where taxation was paid in the form of ***dharaṇa*** ; *K.I.* II, No. 30, p. 116, ll. 5–9 ; Belgaum, Belgaum Tq. and Dt., Karn. St. **Dy.** Raṭṭas of Saundatti, Kārtavīrya IV, Ś. 1122 = 1199 A.D. ; **text[2]** : . . . . *innūra eṁbhatavoṁdu varahanu **dharaṇa**ke krayavāgi* . . . . . . ; **tr.** the exchange rate for 281 *varaha* (a coin) was one **dharaṇa** (coin) . . . ; *S.I.I.* IX, pt. ii, No. 582, p. 598, l. 23 ; Lēpākshi, Hindupur Tq., Anantapur Dt., A.P. St. **Dy.** Tuḷuva, Achyutarāya, Ś. 1459 = 1537 A.D.

dharaṇaṁ (Te. < Skt. *n.*), silver or gold coin ; **text** : . . . . . . *Rāmiseṭi Vēpalapariti Tiruvēṅgaḷanāthani naṁdādīpa samārādhanaku suṁkaṁ* . . . *anupu **dharaṇaṁ** samarpiṁchagalavāru*; **tr.** Rāmiseṭi granted (among other things) income from entry tax, income in the **form of silver or gold coin** for burning a perpetual lamp to the god Tiruvēṅgaḷanātha of Vēpalapariti ; *S.I.I.* XVI, No. 142, p. 153, ll. 6–8 ; Vēpalaparti, Kalyanadurga Tq., Ananthpur Dt., A.P. St. **Dy.** Tuḷuva, Sadāśiva, Ś. 1466 = 1545 A.D.

dharaṇa ponnu (K. < Skt.+K. *n.*), gold coin ; **text** : . . . . *Kannayya tanna makkaḷ makkaḷ bara* . . . *varshamprati āneya ponnāṟu gadyāṇamuṁ* . . . . ***dharaṇa ponna*** *Ādityadēvarge* . . . *koṭṭa śāsana* . . . ; **tr.** stone edict registering the annual grant of six gold coins with the figure of an elephant and one **gold coin** donated to the god Ādityadēva by Kannayya to last until the times of his sons and grandsons ; *S.I.I.* IX, pt. i, No. 75, p. 46, ll. 9–12 ; Bāgaḷi, Harapanahalli Tq., Bellary Dt., Karn. St. **Dy.** Chāḷ. of Kal., Āhavamalla, Ś. 909 = 987 A.D.

dharma[1] (K. < Skt., *n.*), merit ; **text[1]** : . . . . . . *eṇṭu mattal gaḷde rājamānaṁ Jinēndra-bhavanakkittōridanārār salippōr avarte **dharma*** . . . . ; **tr.** eight *mattal* (=*mattar*, a land measure) of wet land measured by the royal standard was granted to the Jaina temple and whoever protects this grant would have earned **merit** ; *S.I.I.* XX, No. 9, p. 10, ll. 19–20 ; Āḍūr, Hangal Tq., Dharwar Dt., Karn. St. **Dy.** Chal. of Bād., Kīrttivarmman II, in characters of 7th-8th century A.D. ; **text[2]** : . . . . . *Krushṇadēvarāya mahārāyarige **dharma**vāgabēkeṁdu* . . . *Siṁgappanāyakaru* . . . *silaśāsanavanu pratishṭe māḍisidenu* . . . . . . ; **tr.** I, Siṁgappanāyaka got this stone edict installed in order that **merit** may accrue to the king Kṛishṇadēvarāya ; *E.C.* (R) IX, Bl. 11, p. 8, ll. 19–21, 23–24 ; Bēlūr, Belur Tq., Hassan Dt., Karn. St. **Dy.** Tuḷuva, Kṛishṇadēvarāya, Ś 1443 = 1522 A.D.

dharma[2] (K. < Skt., *n.*), charity ; **text** : . . . *Duggubinnāṇiti taṁna maga svargastanādalli ātaṁge dina 1 kaṁ obba brāhmaṇanu uṁba hāge māḍida*

dharma . . . ; **tr.** an act of **charity** made by Duggubinnāṇiti for the feeding of one brāhmaṇa per day in memory of her deceased son ; *S.I.I.* VII, No. 319, p. 169, ll. 11–13 ; Mūḍakēri, Udupi Tq. and Dt., Karn. St. **Dy.** Saṅgama, Bukka, Ś 1293 = 1371 A.D.

dharma chhatra (K. < Skt. *n.*), charity house, ; **text :** . . . . *Tuḷuvakaheggaḍiti māḍida* ***dharmachhatrada*** *silāsāsanada krama* . . . ; **tr.** stone edict registering the details of the **charity house** established by Tuḷuvakaheggaḍiti ; *S.I.I.* IX, pt. ii, No. 424, p. 431, ll. 8–9 ; Basarūru, Kundapur Tq., Udupi Dt., Karn. St. **Dy.** Saṅgama, Harihara, Ś. 1323 = 1401 A.D.

dharma ḍōṇi (K. < Skt. *n.*), stone trough for free supply of water ; **text :** . . . . ***dharma ḍōṇige*** *nīra etuvanige mōḷe oṁdake yibaḷa uppina lekkadalu biṭu koṭevu* . . . ; **tr.** we granted wages at the rate of two *baḷḷa* (a grain measure) of salt for the person who fills water in the **stone trough for free supply of water** ; *S.I.I.* IX, pt. ii, No. 670, p. 662, ll. 17–18 ; Chatradahaḷḷi, Hadagalli Tq., Bellary Dt., Karn. St. **Dy.** Tuḷuva, Sadāśivarāya, Ś. 1481 = 1559 A.D.

dharmada kaṭṭaḷe (K. < Skt.+K. *n.*), arrangement of temple services ; **text :** . . . . *Kōṭīśvarada dēvaralli . . . naḍasuva* ***dharmada kaṭṭaḷe*** *Kōṭīśvaradēvara nayivēdyakke dina oṁdakkaṁ akki nāḍahāni mūṟaṟa lekka* . . . . ; **tr.** as per the **arrangment of temple service** brought into practice in the temple of Kōṭīśvara, a grant of three *nāḍahāni* (standard grain measure of the territory) of rice per day for the food offerings to the god was made ; *S.I.I.* IX, pt. ii, No. 417, p. 423, ll. 24–25 ; Kōṭēśvara, Kundapur Tq., Udupi Dt., Karn. St. **Dy.** Saṅgama, Harihara, Ś. 1300 = 1377 A.D.

dharma ēta (K. < Skt.+K. *n.*), charity water-lift ; **text :** . . . . *Sōgeya* ***dharma ētakke*** *koṭṭa Daṇāyakapura* . . . . ; **tr.** gift of the village of Daṇāyakapura for the **charity water-lift** at Sōge; *S.I.I.* IX, pt. ii, No. 503, p. 517, ll. 6–7 ; Sōgi, Haḍagalli Tq., Bellary Dt., Karn. St. **Dy.** Tuḷuva, Krishṇadēvarāya, Cy. yr. Dhātu = 1516 A.D.

dharma karttāṁśaṁ (Te. < Skt. *n.*), share of the offering to the god due to the temple trustee; **text :** . . . . *Saṁkrāntula mahōtsavāla* . . . . *padārthalavallanu* ***dharma karttāṁśaṁ*** *chārtubbhāgaṁnu* . . . . *Kaṁdāḷa* . . . . *Śrīraṁgā chāryulayyavāru* . . . . . *anubhaviṁpaṁgalavāru* . . . . ; **tr.** one fourth **share of the offerings** to the god **due to the temple trustee** on occasions of Saṁkrānti festivals was donated to Śrīraṁgāchārya for his enjoyment ; *S.I.I.* XVI, No. 198, p. 205, ll. 5–6, 8 ; Mārkāpūr, Markapur Tq., Kurnool Dt., A.P. St. **Dy.** Tuḷuva, Sadāśiva, Ś. 1476 = 1554 A.D.

dharmasāle (K. < Skt. *n.*), free choultry ; **text :** . . . . *Ahamudakhānanu rāyarige dharmavāga bēkeṁdu kaṭisida* ***dharmasāle*** . . . . ; **tr. free choultry** caused to be constructed by Ahamudakhān for the merit of the king ; *S.I.I.* IX, pt. ii, No. 447, p. 457, ll. 3–4 ; Kamalāpur, Hospet Tq., Bellary Dt., Karn. St. **Dy.** Saṅgama, Dēvarāya, Cy. yr. Siddhārthi = 1439 A.D.

dharmaśāsana (K. < Skt. *n.*), edict recording details of grant ; **text :** . . . . *Kōṭinātha dēvarige koṭṭa* ***dharmaśāsana****da krama* . . . ; **tr. edict recording the details of the grant** made to the god Kōṭinātha ; *S.I.I.* IX, pt. ii, No. 451, p. 460, ll. 4–5 ; Kōṭēśvara, Kundapur Tq., Udupi Dt., Karn. St. **Dy.** Saṅgama, Dēvarāya, Ś. 1369 = 1447 A.D.

dharmasatraṁ (Te. < Skt. *n.*), free feeding house ; **text :** . . . . *Chaṁnayyagāru* . . . . *Tiruvēṅgaḷanāthani Tirumalatirunāḷaku naḍachu varshaku* . . . . *Chaḍupirēla grāmamaṁdu peṭṭa gaṭṭaḍa śēsina* ***dharmasatraṁ*** *Tiṁmarasayyavārikinnu Gōviṁnddayyavārikinnu puṁṇyaṁgānu* . . . . ; **tr.** Chaṁnayya got constructed for the merit of Timmarasayya and Goviṁdayya a **free feeding house** in the village of Chaḍupirēla for the feeding of pilgrims going for the festivals of Tiruvēṅgaḷanātha of Tirumala ; *I.A.P.* Cuddapah II, No. 82, p. 101, ll. 4–8 ; Chiḍipirāla, Kamalapuram Tq., Cuddapah Dt., A.P. St. **Misc.,** Ś. 1442 = 1520 A.D.

dharmavṛiddhi (T. < Skt. *n.*), interest accuring from endowment ; **text :** . . . . (damaged) *Śēndanakkappir̤ān baṭṭa sarvvakratuyājiyār* . . . *Mādēvar vaśam* ***dharmavṛiddhi****yināl polivadāga kuḍutta karuṅkāśu 20* . . . . ; **tr.** Śēndanakkappir̤ān baṭṭa sarvvakratuyājiyār instituted an endowment of 20 *karuṅkāśu* (coin) entrusted to the care of Mādēva; *S.I.I.* XIII, No. 250, p. 133, ll. 13–15 ; Kōyildēvarāyan̤pēṭṭai, Papanasam Tq., Tanjavur Dt., T. Nadu St. **Dy.** Chōḷa, Parāntaka II, reg. yr. 14, in characters of 11th cent. A.D.

dharmma[1] (K. < Skt. *n.*), merit ; **text :** . . . *Chihanapaṭṭiya mūlasthānada Mahādēvarge* ***dharmma****pratipālanaṁ geyda vṛitti Sahalegauḍa biṭṭa yereya matta 13* . . . ; **tr.** 13 *matta* (*mattar*, a land measure) of red soil was granted to the god Mahādēva of the central shrine at Chihanapaṭṭi as an act of religious **merit** by Sahalegauḍa ; *S.I.I.* IX, pt. i, No. 42, p. 25, ll. 12–16 ; Kalkaṁbha, Bellary Tq. and Dt., Karn. St. **Dy.** Noḷ. Pal., Permānaḍidēva, Ś 949 = 1028 A.D.

dharmma[2] (K. < Skt. *n.*), charity ; **text :** . . . *yī* ***dharmmakke*** *āru anukūlavādavarugaḷige anēka śata sahasra puṁṇyaṁgaḷu uṁṭu* . . . . . . ; **tr.** whoever treats this act of **charity** favourably would have earned countless numbers of merits ; *S.I.I.* IV, No. 245, p. 39, l. 32 ; Hampi, Hospet Tq., Bellary Dt., Karn. St. **Dy.** Tuḷuva, Achyutarāya, Ś 1463 = 1541 A.D.

dharmma braya (K. < Skt. *n.*), expenses of charity ; **text :** . . . *Śrīdharabhaṭṭar mahājanakkaṁ prajegaṁ māḍida vyavastheyuṁ* ***dharmma brayad****upabiya mānyada bhūmiya nivēśanada pramāṇaṁ* . . . . ; **tr.** the administrative body and the people were granted by Śrīdharabhaṭṭa land

and house sites for meeting the **expenses of charity** ; *Ep. Ind.*, *XX*, No. 6, p. 67, ll. 14, 15–16; Kōṭavumachagi, Gadag Tq. and Dt., Karn. St. **Dy.** Chāḷ. of Kal., Vikramāditya V, Ś 934 = 1012 A.D.

dharmmadāṉa iṟaiyili (T. *n.*), tax free charitable gift ; **text :** . . . *nañjai puñjai nilattil kaḍamai āyam poṉvari uṭpaṭṭa eppērpaṭṭa varigaḷum uṭpaḍa* . . . . . ***dharmmadāṉa iṟaiyili****yāga Uḍaiyār Tiruvōttūr uḍaiya nāyaṉār tirumuṉbē nāḷoṉṟukku aiñjupēr addhyayanam paṉṉakkaḍavārgaḷāgavum* . . . ; **tr.** taxes, revenue incomes, tax in gold and all other taxes from wet and dry lands were declared as **tax free charitable gift** (and donated), so that five scholars per day may undertake their studies in the presence of the deity Tiruvottūruḍaiya-nāyaṉār ; *S.I.I.* VII, No. 101, pp. 42–43, ll. 3–4 ; Tiruvattūr, Cheyyar Tq., N. Arcot Dt., T. Nadu St. **Dy.** Śambuvarāya, Kulaśēkhara, reg. yr. 23, in characters of 12th cent. A.D.

dharmmādāya (K. < Skt. *n.*), income from religious endowments ; **text :** (fragmentary and incomplete). . . . . *rājayyanavaru koṭṭa* ***dharmmādāya*** . . . ; **tr. income from religious endowments** given by . . . . rājayya ; *E.C.* X, Kōl. 2, p. 1, l. 3 ; Ālahaḷḷi, Kolar Tq. and Dt., Karn. St. **Misc.,** Cy. yr. Āṁgīrasa = 1452 A.D.

dharmmādhikaraṇa (Skt. *n.*), judicial officer; **text**[1] **:** *likhitaṁ chaitad Vāḷabha Kāyastha vaṁśajātēna* ***dharmādhikaraṇa****sthēna bhōgika Vatsarājēna* . . . . ; **tr.** this (inscription) has been written by Vatsarāja belonging to Kāyastha family of Vāḷabha who was a **judicial officer** and held the office of *bhōgika* ; *Ep. Ind.* VI, No. 4, p. 33, ll. 57–58 ; Koṉṉūr, Navalgund Tq., Dharwar Dt., Karn. St. **Dy.** Rāshṭr. Amōghavarsha I, Ś. 782 = 860 A.D. ; **text**[2] **:** *Nāgapuradagrahāra mahājanamuṁ* ***dharmādhikaraṇa****virddu vichārisi* . . . . ; **tr.** the *mahājana* (administrative body) of the brāhmaṇa settlement Nāgapura and the **judicial officer** having met and made enquiries ; *E.C.* VI, Kp. 14, p. 301, ll. 11–12 ; Siṁse, Koppa Tq., Chikkamagaḷūru Dt., Karn. St. **Dy.** Śāntara, Vīraśāntara, Ś. 1089 = 1157 A.D.

dharmmādhyaksha (K. < Skt. *n.*), judicial officer; **text :** ***dharmādhyaksha****ra muṁde* . . . . *Kāḷagavuḍa dibyava hiḍidu geldu koṁḍa jayapatra* . . . . . . ; **tr.** the document of victory awarded to Kāḷagavuḍa when he successfully held fire in his hand as an ordeal in the presence of the **judicial officer** ; *E.C.* VIII, Sor. 387, p. 182, l. 19–20 ; Elevāḷa, Soraba Tq., Shimoga Dt., Karn. St. **Dy.** Sēü of Dēv., Siṅghaṇa, reg. yr. 49 = 1249 A.D.

dharmmakkaṭṭaḷaikal (T. < Skt+T. *n.*), standard weighing stones ; **text :** (damaged) . . . . *poṉ* ***dharmmakkaṭṭaḷai****kallāl tuḷai niṟai muppadiṉ kaḷañju* . . . . ; **tr.** thirty *kaḷañju* of gold weighed by the **standard weighing stone** with a marked impression and called ***dharmmakkaṭṭaḷaikal*** ; *S.I.I.* XXII, pt. i, No. 3, p. 2, l. 3 ; Kāñchīpuram, Kanchipuram Tq., Chingleput Dt., T. Nadu St.

Dy. Chōḷa, Uttamachōḷa, in characters of the 10th cent. A.D.

dharmma karta (Te. < Skt. *n.*), temple trustee; **text :** (badly damaged) . . *Vēṅkaṭēśvarasvāmulu kaṭṭaḷa śēśinadi* ***dharmma karta*** *Sēna Mōdalāri Kṛishṇayyagāriki pratisaṁvatsarakunnu ga 24 varahālu* . . . . ; **tr.** the god Vēṅkaṭēśvarasvmi ordained the payment of 24 *varaha* (a gold coin) every year to the **temple trustee** Sēna Mōdalāri Kṛishṇayyagāru ; *Ep. Ind.* XIX, No. 14, p. 94, ll. 148–50 ; Kandukūru, Madanapalle Tq., Chittoor Dt., A.P. St. **Dy.** Āravīḍu, Veṁkaṭapati, **Ś.** 1535 = 1613 A.D.

dharmma koḍage (K. < Skt.+K. *n.*), grant made for religious purpose ; **text :** (badly damaged) . . . . *koṭa* ***dharmma koḍage*** . . . ; **tr. grant made for religious purpose** ; *E.C.* (R) III, Nj. 277, p. 351, l. 10 ; Dēvanūru, Nanjanagud Tq., Mysore Dt., Karn. St. **Misc., Ś.** 1437 = 1515 A.D.

dharmma mahārāja (Skt. *n.*), righteous king (title) ; **text :** ***dharmma mahārājaḥ*** . . . . *Mānavya sagōtrō* . . . *Kadaṁbāṇām* . . . *Māndhātṛi varmmā* . . . . . ; **tr.** Māndhātṛivarmmā of the Kadamba dynasty who belonged the Mānavyasagōtra and was a **righteous king** ; *Ep. Ind.* VI, No. 2, p. 14, ll. 1, 3–4 ; Kūḍgere, Shikaripur Tq., Shimoga Dt., Karn. St. **Dy.** Kad. of Ban., Māndhātṛivarmmā, reg. yr. 2, in characters of 4th cent. A.D.

dharmma mahārājādhirāja (K. < Skt. *n.*), righteous emperor ; **text :** Nītimārgga Koṁguṇivarmma ***dharmma mahārājādhirāja*** *Kōḷālapuravareśvara* . . . . . ; **tr.** the **righteous emperor** Nītimārgga Koṁguṇivarmmā, the lord of city of Kōḷāla ; *Ep. Ind.* VI, No. 6, p. 43, ll. 1–2 ; Doḍḍahuṇḍi, T. Narasipur Tq., Mysore Dt., Karn. St. **Dy.** W. Gaṅga, Nītimārgga, in characters of 9th cent. A.D.

dharmma pārupatya (K. < Skt.+K. *n.*), management of temple and religious endowments ; **text :** . . . . *Paḍuvakēriyya Tirumala dēvālyasthānada* . . . . . ***dharmma pārupatya****vanu Nallāḷa chakravartti* . . . . . *halaru seṭikāraru sahitavāgi naḍasuvudakke sahāya.vādavaru* . . . ; **tr.** the **halaru seṭikāra** (body of merchants) helped Nallāḷa chakravartti in the **management of the endowments of the temple** of Tirumaladēva of Paḍuvakēri ; *S.I.I.* IX, pt. ii, No. 476, p. 491 ll. 18–21 ; Basarūru, Kundapur Tq., Udupi Dt., Karn. St. **Dy.** Tuḷuva, Narasiṁha, Ś. 1428 = 1506 A.D.

dharmma saṁte (K. < Skt.+K. *n.*), charity fair ; **text :** . . . . . *Māyidēvarasan māḍida dharmmaṁ* . . . . . . ***dharma saṁte*** . . . ; **tr.** this **charity fair** is the pious act of Māyidēvarasa ; *S.I.I.* XX, No. 175, p. 220, ll. 32–33 ; Hirēbēvinūr, Indi Tq., Bijapur Dt., Karn. St. **Dy.** Kal. of Kal., Bhillama, Ś. 1112 = 1190 A.D.

dharmmāsanam (T. < Skt. *n.*), seat of justice ; **text**[1] **:** (damaged) . . . . ***dharmmāsana****ttu niśadi panniru kāṇandaṇḍam* . . . *kuḍuttōm* . . . . ; **tr.** we paid a fine of twelve *kāṇa* (coin) to the **seat of**

justice ; *S.I.I.* III, No. 105, p. 238, ll. 18–19 ; Tiruvoṟṟiyūr, Saidapet Tq., Chingleput Dt., T. Nadu St. **Dy.** Chōḷa, Parāntaka I, reg. yr. 30 = 937 A.D.; **text**[2] : . . . *iddhaṉmattukku iḍaiyūṟu vaṟāmaṟ kākkakkaḍavōmāgavum iḍaiyūru variṟ* ***dharmmāsana****ttile nitta mañjāḍi poṉ maṉṟap peruvadāgavum* . . . . ; **tr.** we are duty bound to see that no harm is done to this act of piety ; in case harm is done we shall pay one *mañjadi* (gold coin) per day to the **seat of justice** . . . . ; *S.I.I.* VII, No. 96, p. 40, ll. 14–15 ; Tiruvattūr, Cheyyar Tq., N. Arcot Dt., T. Nadu St. **Dy.** Chōḷa, Vikramachōḷa, reg. yr. 6+1 = 1124 A.D.

dharmma satram (T. < Skt. *n.*), free feeding house ; **text :** . . . *Periyanāyaṉār maḍattil* ***dharmma satram*** *iḍugeykku viṭṭa Achchiṟupākkam* . . . ; **tr.** village of Achchiṟupākkam donated for establishing a **free feeding house** in the religious institution of the god Periyanāyaṉār ; *S.I.I.* VII, No. 469, p. 291, ll. 6–7 ; Achcharapākkam, Madhurantakam Tq., Chingleput Dt., T. Nadu St. **Dy.** Sāḷuva, Narasiṁha, Kali. 4579 = 1478 A.D.

dharmma vattaḷe (K. < Skt.+K. *n.*), charity deed; **text :** . . . ***dharmma vattaḷe****ya śāsana maryyādeyal tiruva siddhāyaṁ poṁgadyāṇaṁ eṇbattu* ; **tr.** eighty gold coins were remitted as fixed tax in keeping with the custom established through a **charity deed** ; *Ep. Ind.* XV, No. 6, p. 79, ll. 21–22 ; Sūḍi, Ron Tq., Dharwar Dt., Karn. St. **Dy.** Chāḷ. of Kal., Sōmēśvara I, Ś. 973 = 1050 A.D.

dharmma vraya (K. < Skt. *n.*), expenses of charity ; **text :** . . . ***dharmma vraya****kkaṁ upabiyakkaṁ mattar mūnūṟu* . . . . ; **tr.** 300 *mattar* (a land measure) of land for meeting the **expenses of charity** and sundry expenses ; *Ep. Ind.*, XX, No. 6, p. 67, ll. 31–32 ; Kōṭavumachagi, Gadag Tq. and Dt., Karn. St. **Dy.** Chāḷ. of Kal., Vikramāditya V, Ś 934 = 1012 A.D.

dharmmēta (K. < Skt+K. *n.*), charity water-lift ; **text**[1] : . . . . *Kōṭeya keyya sthaḷadoḷage* . . . . *akara khaṁḍikege mattaru ippattu* ***dharmmetakke*** *hattu* . . . ; **tr.** out of the land belonging to the fort 20 *mattar* (a land measure) of land was granted for the school teaching alphabets and 10 *mattar* of land for the **charity water lift** ; *K.I.* II, No. 16, p. 70, ll. 43–44 ; Akkalkōṭ, Akkalkot Tq., Sholapur Dt., Maha. St. **Dy.** Chāḷ. of Kal., Vikramāditya VI, Ch. Vi. yr. 48 = 1124 A.D. ; **text**[2] : (damaged) . . . . *keṟeya keḷagaṇa* ***dharmmēta****da bhāviyiṁ teṁkalu* . . . . . ; **tr.** to the south of the well with a **charity water lift** below the tank ; *S.I.I.* IX, pt. i, No. 367, p. 385, l. 27 ; Chinnatumbaḷam, Adavani Tq., Kurnool Dt., A.P. St. **Dy.** Sēü of Dēv, Jaitugi, Ś. 1151 = 1229 A.D.

dhruva vuṁḍige (K. < Skt.+K. *n.*), permanent grant; **text :** . . . *Kūṭanamaḍuvina aśēsha mahājanaṁgaḷu sabhāstaḷake bijayaṁgeydu tammoḷu sarvaikamatyavāgi haḷḷigaḷanu* ***dhruva vuṁḍige****yāgi hachchikoṁḍa krama* . . . ; **tr.** the details regarding the distribution of villages as **permanent grants** among the members of the administrative body were decided when the *mahājana* (administrative body) met in full quorum in the assembly hall at Kūṭanamaḍuvu ; *E.C.* (R) XII, Tk. 34, p. 365, ll. 2–3 ; Kuṁṭanamaḍuvu, Tarikere Tq., Chikkamagaluru Dt., Karn. St. **Dy.** Hoy., Narasiṁha II, Cy. yr. Vikṛiti = 1230 A.D.

dhūpa (K. < Skt. *n.*), incense ; **text**[1] : . . . . *Aṁgajēśvaradēvaraṁgabhōgakke* ***dhūpa*** *dīpa naivēdyake . . . . . . gadde mattaroṁdu kamma 50* . . . . ; **tr.** one *mattar* (land measure) and 50 *kamma* (land measure) of land donated for the services such as providing **incense**, lamps and food offerings to the god Aṁgajēśvara ; *K.I.* IV, No. 10, p. 30, ll. 63–64 ; Hirēhaḷḷi, Byadagi Tq., Dharwar Dt., Karn. St. **Dy.** Chāḷ. of Kal., Vikramāditya VI, Ch. Vi. yr. 45 = 1121 A.D. ; **text**[2] : . . . . *Tiruvēṁgaḷadēvarige . . . .* ***dhūpa*** *dīpa aṁgaraṁgabhōgake Krushṇarāyaru koṭa śilāśasanada krama* . . . . ; **tr.** the details of the grant as registered in the stone edict and given by Krushṇarāya for offering **incense,** lamps and services to the god Tiruvēṁgaḷadēva ; *S.I.I.* IV, No. 249, p. 41, ll. 13–15 ; Hampi, Hospet Tq., Bellary Dt., Karn. St. **Dy.** Tuḷuva, Kṛishṇadēvarāya, Ś. 1444 = 1522 A.D.

dhura dhare (K. < Skt. *n.*), battle field ; **text :** . . . . ***dhura dhare****yalli . . . Kāḷakritāṁtanenuttā baṇṇikuṁ varavibudha vrajaṁ . . . . Haridēvaseṭṭiyan* . . . ; **tr.** the group of learned persons describe Haridēvaseṭṭi as the very lord of death on the **battle field** ; *K.I.* IV, No. 1, p. 10, ll. 68–69 ; Sātēnahaḷḷi, Hirekerur Tq., Dharwar Dt., Karn. St. **Dy.** Hoy., Ballāḷa II, Ś. 1126 = 1204 A.D.

dhvaja (K. < Skt. *n.*), banner ; **text :** . . . . . . *Banavāsipuraparamēśvara . . . . . vānara****dhvaja*** *. . . . . Kadaṁbavaṁśōdbhava . . . . Māḷayya* . . ; **tr.** Māḷayya of the Kadaṁba dynasty who was lord of the city of Banavāsi and had for his **banner** the figure of Hanumān ; *S.I.I.* IX, pt. i, No. 57, p. 32, l. 7 ; Kaḍabagere, Harapanahalli Tq., Bellary Dt., Karn. St. **Dy.** Rāshṭr., Indra III, Ś. 844 = 922 A.D.

dibya (K. < Skt. *divya, n.*), ordeal by fire ; **text :** *dharmādhyakshara muṁde . . . . Kāḷagavuḍa* ***dibya****va hiḍidu geldu koṁḍa jayapatra* . . . . . ; **tr.** the document of victory scored by Kāḷagavuḍa when he held **fire** in his hand as an **ordeal** in the presence of the judicial officer ; *E.C.* VIII, Sor. 387, p. 182, l. 19–20 ; Elevāḷa, Soraba Tq., Shimoga Dt., Karn. St. **Misc.,** Sēü of Dēv., Siṅghaṇa, reg. yr. 49 = 1249 A.D.

digumati (Te. *n.*), import ; **text :** . . . ***digumati*** *egumati modalaina Paḍanāṭi suṁkhaṁ rēkha gadya 1200* . . . ; **tr.** the **import** and export revenue totalling 1200 *gadya* (*gadyāṇa*, gold coin) from certain ports in Paḍanāḍu ; *S.I.I.* XVI, No. 98, p. 114, l. 3 ; Kāḷahasti, Chandragiri Tq., Chittoor Dt., A.P. St. **Dy.** Tuḷuva, Achyutarāya,

Ś. 1454 = 1532 A.D.

digvijaya (K. < Skt. *n.*), military expedition ; **text:** ... *chakravarti dakshiṇa diśāvarakke* ***digvijayaṁ*** *geydandu* ... ; **tr.** when the emperor was on a **military expedition** in the southern region ; *S.I.I.* IX, pt. i, No. 123, p. 105, l. 13 ; Doṇekallu, Gooty Tq., Anantapur Dt., A.P. St. **Dy.** Chāḷ. of Kal., Traiḷōkyamalla, Ś. 981 = 1059 A.D.

digvijayam (T. < Skt. *n.*), military expedition ; **text :** ... *Irāyar* ***digvijayattukku*** *Gajapatirājyattiṉ pērilēpōyi Udayagiriyum koṇḍu* ... ; **tr.** the emperor having proceeded on a **military expedition** against the kingdom of the Gajapati ruler and having captured Udayagiri ; *S.I.I.* XVII, No. 684, pp. 320–21, ll. 28–29 ; Nāgalāpuram, Tiruvallur Tq., Chingleput Dt., T. Nadu St. **Dy.** Tuḷuva, Kṛishṇadēvarāya, Ś. 1445 = 1524 A.D.

dīkshāgurugaḷ (K. < Skt. *n.*), teacher who administers initiation ; **text :** ... *Bāhubali Siddhāntidēvarē* ***dīkshāgurugaḷ*** ... ; **tr.** Bāhubali Siddhāntidēva is the **teacher who administered initiation** ; *M.A.R.* 1929, No. 14, p. 75, ll. 20–21 ; Haḷēbīḍu, Belur Tq., Hassan Dt., Karn. St. **Misc.**, Ś. 1157 = 1236 A.D.

dīkshāguruḥ (Skt. *n.*), teacher who administers initiation ; **text :** ... *Gauḍarāḍhōllasatpūrvva grāmaśikhāmaṇirGgaṇapatikshmāpāla* ***dīkshāguruḥ*** ... ; **tr.** the **teacher who administered initiation** to the king Gaṇapati who was like a crest jewel of the village Sadgrāma and was the lord Gauḍa; *S.I.I.* X, No. 395, p. 207, l. 79 ; Malkāpuram, Guntur Tq. and Dt., A.P. St. **Dy.** Kākatīya, Gaṇapati, Ś. 1183 = 1261 A.D.

dīkshāsutaṁ (K. < Skt. *n.*), spiritual son ; **text :** .... *Gaṁgarāśipaṁḍitara* ***dīkshāsutaṁ*** *Tribhuvanaśaktipaṁḍitara tammaṁ Vāmajīyar* ...... ; **tr.** Vāmajīyar, the younger brother of Tribhuvanaśaktipaṁḍita and the **spiritual son** of Gaṁgarāśipaṁḍita ; *E.C.* (R) X, Ak. 253, p. 324, ll. 41–42 ; Dēshāṇi, Arasikere Tq., Hassan Dt., Karn. St. **Dy.** Hoy., Nārasiṁha I, Ś. 1061 = 1139 A.D.

dīkshita (K. < Skt. *n.*), male surname ; **text:** .. .. *agrahāradallū sarvvakratugaḷiṁda Muṁmaḍi***dīkshita***rige krayavāgi baṁda vṛittigaḷu* .... ; **tr.** the shares bought from the lands in the *agrahara* by Muṁmaḍi**dīkshita** who had performeld all kinds of sacrifices ; *S.I.I.* IV, No. 245, p. 39, l. 10 ; Hampi, Hospet Tq., Bellary Dt., Karn. St. **Dy.** Tuḷuva, Achyutarāya, Ś. 1463 = 1541 A.D.

diṁba (K. *n.*), mound ; **text :** .... *Guruvanapurada elle kallina baḷiya* ***diṁba****dalli neṭṭa kallu 1* ... ; **tr.** 1 stone slab set up on the **mound** near the boundary stone of Guruvanapura ; *E.C.* (R) V, My. 100, p. 234, ll. 32–33 ; Mysore, Mysore Tq. and Dt., Karn. St. **Dy.** Woḍ. of Mys., Dēvarāja, Ś. 1586 = 1665 A.D.

dinakarakula (K. < Skt. *n.*), solar race ; **text :** .... ***dinakarakula****naṁdanaṁ* .... *Karikālānvyaṁ*

. . . *simhalāñchanam . . . mahāsāmamta Bachharasan* . . . ; **tr.** the feudatory Bachharasa who belonged to the **solar race** and to the lineage of Karikāla and who had the lion emblem as his insignia ; *S.I.I.* IX, pt. i, No. 122, p. 104, ll. 11–13, 17–18 ; Pulakurti, Rāyadurga Tq., Bellary Dt., Karn. St. **Dy.** Chāḷ. of Kal., Trailōkyamalla, Ś. 980 = 1058 A.D.

dinamāna vechcha (K. < Skt. *n.*), daily expenses; **text :** . . . . . . *Tirumaladēvarige namdādīptigū* ***dinamānavechakū*** *Basavarasavoḍeyaru* . . . . *koṭudu* . . . *mūḍabāgila sumka* ; **tr.** the tax income collected at the eastern gateway was donated by Basavarasavoḍeya for the **daily expenses** and for burning a perpetual lamp to the god Tirumaladēva ; *S.I.I.* IX, pt. ii, No. 476, p. 491, ll. 12–13, 14; Basarūru, Kundapur Tq., Udupi Dt., Karn. St. **Dy.** Tuḷuva, Narasimha, Ś. 1428 = 1506 A.D.

dīpa (K. < Skt. *n.*), lamp ; **text :** . . . . *Tiruvēmgaḷa dēvarige* . . . . *dhūpa* ***dīpa*** *amgaramgabhōgake Krushṇarāyaru koṭa śilāśasanada krama*. . . ; **tr.** the details of the grant as registered in the stone edict and give by Krushṇarāya for offering incense, **lamps** and services to the god Tiruvēmgaḷadēva ; *S.I.I.* IV, No. 249, p. 41, ll. 13–15 ; Hampi, Hospet Tq., Bellary Dt., Karn. St. **Dy.** Tuḷuva, Kṛishṇadēvarāya, Ś. 1444 = 1522 A.D.

dīpa kambham (Te. < Skt. *n.*), lamp pillar ; **text:** . . . . *Chandragiri Malikārjunadēvaraku* . . . . . . *Gōpināyaḍu* . . . . ***dīpa kambham*** *peṭitini* . . ; **tr.** I, Gōpināyaḍu have installed **lamp pillar** in the temple of the god Malikārjuna of Chamdragiri ; *S.I.I.* XVI, No. 19, p. 21, ll. 10–11, 15–17 ; Tamballapalle, Madanapalle Tq., Chittoor Dt., A.P. St. **Dy.** Saṅgama, Dēvarāya I, Ś. 1328 = 1406 A.D.

dīpamālākamba (K. *n.*), lamp post for burning a series of lamps ; **text :** . . . . . . *Chemnarāpaṭaaṇada kōṭeyali Chemnarāyasvāmiyavarige* ***dīpamālākambada*** *sēve māḍistarū* . . ; **tr.** donation of a lamp post for the god Chemnarāya in the Chemnarāyapaṭṭaṇa fort ; *E.C.* (R) X, Ch. 4, p. 412, l. 1 ; Channarāyapaṭṭaṇa, Channarayapatna Tq., Hassan Dt., Karn. St. **Dy.** Woḍ. of Mys., Dēvarāya Woḍeya, Ś. 1591 = 1670 A.D.

dīpamāleya kambha (K. < Skt. *n.*), lamp post for burning a series of lamps ; **text :** (damaged) . . . . . . *ā bāḷa sthānakke uḷḷamthā mānya* ***dīpamāleya kambha*** . . . ; **tr.** the **lamp post for burning a series of lamps** in the temple is built in the gift land; *S.I.I.* IX, pt. ii, No. 417, p. 422, l. 11 ; Kōṭēśvara, Kundapur Tq., Udupi Dt., Karn. St. **Dy.** Saṅgama, Harihara, Ś. 1300 = 1377 A.D.

dīpam chamaru (Te. < Skt.+Te. *n.*), supply of oil for lamps ; **text :** *Vijayaramga Chokkanāthanāyanayyavāru* . . . . . *Śamkarāchārya svāmulavāriki* ***dīpam chamaru*** *paḍi 3/4* . . . *ichchi unnāmu*. . . ; **tr.** Vijayaramga Chokkanātha nāyaka granted to the pontiff Śamkarāchārya 3/4 of a *paḍi* (a liquid measure) of **oil to be supplied for the lamp** ; *Ep. Ind.* XVI, No. 12, pp. 94–95, ll. 13–15, 30, 33 ; Jambukēśvaram, Tiruchirapalli Tq. and Dt., T. Nadu St. **Dy.** Āravīḍu, Veṁkaṭa V, Ś. 1632 = 1710 A.D.

dīpāvaḷi (K. *n.*), festival of lights ; **text :** . . . *bādube* ***dīpāvaḷi*** *kārapuṇṇame yenippī mūṟu parvaṁgaḷ* . . . ; **tr.** the three festivals of celebrating minor deities, the **festival of lights**, the festival of full moon day during rainy season ; *S.I.I.* XI, No. 52, p. 42, l. 66 ; Lakkuṇḍi, Gadag Tq. and Dt., Karn. St. **Dy.** Chāḷ. of Kal., Iṟivabeḍeṅga Satyāśraya, Ś. 929 = 1008 A.D.

diramam (T. < Skt. *dramma, n.*), coin denomination; **text :** . . . *kāśu 1 kku āṭṭu iraṇḍu* ***diramaṁ*** *paliśaiyāga polivadāna* ***diramam*** *eṭṭu* . . . ; **tr.** eight **coin denomination** (*diramam*) were endowed fetching an annaul interest of 2 **coin denominations** per 1 *kāśu* ; *S.I.I.* VII, No. 479, p. 296, l. 5 ; Madhurāntakam, Madhurantakam Tq., Chingleput Dt., T. Nadu St. **Dy.** Chōḷa, Vikramachōḷa, reg. yr. 9 = 1127 A.D.

dīrgghikā (K. < Skt. *n.*), rectangular tank; **text :** . . . ***dīrgghikā****nīkamellaṁ daḷitāmbhōjāta rēṇusthagita lalitaṁ* . . . ; **tr.** all the multitudes of **rectangular tank** charmingly powdered with pollen of bursting lotuses ; *Ep. Ind.* XIX, No. 38, p. 229, ll. 12–13 ; Rōṇ, Ron Tq., Dharwar Dt., Karn. St. **Dy.** Kal. of Kal., Saṅkama, Ś. 1102 = 1179 A.D.

diśāvara (K. < Skt. *n.*), region ; **text**[1] **:** . . . *chakravarti dakshiṇa* ***diśāvara****kke digvijayaṁ geydandu* . . . ; **tr.** when the emperor was on a military expedition in the southern **region** ; *S.I.I.* IX, pt. i, No. 123, p. 105, l. 13 ; Doṇekallu, Gooty Tq., Anantapur Dt., A.P. St. **Dy.** Chāḷ. of Kal., Trailōkyamalla, Ś. 981 = 1059 A.D. ; **text**[2] **:** . . . *Sadāśivarāyamahārāyaru sakala****diśāvara****vanēkōttaraṁgeyidu Vidyānagariyalu* . . . . *rājyaṁ geyuttaṁ* . . . ; **tr.** while the emperor Sadāśiva was ruling from Vijayanagari after having brought under his control all the **regions** ; *S.I.I.* IX, pt. ii, No. 640, p. 638, ll. 3–5 ; Bāgaḷi, Harapanahalli Tq., Bellary Dt., Karn. St. **Dy.** Tuḷuva, Sadāśiva, Ś. 1472 = 1550 A.D.

dīva[1] (K. *n.*), fisherman ; **text :** . . . *Basarūṟa* ***dīva****rakēriya tōṭada* . . . . . *sidhāyada kāṭi ga 111* . . . . . . ; **tr.** 111 superior quality of gold coins (*kāṭi ga = kāṭi gadyāṇa*) from the grove in the **fishermen** quarters ; *S.I.I.* IX, pt. ii, No. 456, p. 467, ll. 8–9; Basarūru, Kundapur Tq., Udupi Dt., Karn. St. **Dy.** Saṅgama, Mallikārjuna, Ś. 1374 = 1451 A.D.

dīva[2] (K. *n.*), hunter ; **text :** *kaṇuve kāva* ***dīva****rige aramaneyavara mukhāṁtra viṁgaḍadalū saluvudu* . . . . ; **tr.** the (payment in equal shares for the) **hunters** guarding the valley will be distributed through the palace . . . . . . ; *E.C.* (R) XIII, Tīr. 105, p. 341, ll. 23–25 ; Kavalēdurga, Tirthahalli Tq., Shimoga Dt., Karn. St. **Dy.** Keḷadi Rulers, Vīrabhadra, Ś. 1554 = 1632 A.D.

dīvaḷigai (T. < Skt. *n.*), festival of lights ; **text :** *Ugādi* ***dīvaḷigai****kku Śēnaimudaliyār amuduśeydaruḷum atirasappaḍi 2 ṁ* . . . . ; **tr.** two sweet dishes called *atirasam* presented to the deity as food offering by Śēnaimudaliyār on the occasions of new year's day and the **festival of lights**...... ; *T.D.I.* III, No. 8, p. 24, ll. 2–3 ; Tirumalai, Chandragiri Tq., Chittoor Dt., A.P. St. **Dy.** Tuḷuva, Narasiṁha, Ś. 1428 = 1506 A.D.

dīvaḷige habba (K. *n.*), festival of lights ; **text :** ... *Rāyarasavoḍeyaru* .... *Dēvarāyamahārāyarige* ... *āyushyābhrivriddhi āgabēkeṁdu* .... *māḍida dharmada vivara **dīvaḷige habba*** .... *Śivarātri* .... *Bēnakanachauti modalāgi idda* ... *parvagaḷige* ... *kāṭi ga 30* ... *dharmava māḍi baredu koṭṭa śilāśāsana* .. ; **tr.** in order to ensure a long life for the emperor Dēvarāya, Rāyarasavoḍeya made a grant of 30 *kāṭi ga* (*kāṭi gadyāṇa* = quality gold coin) for the performance of festivals such as the **festival of lights**, Śivarātri, Vināyaka chaturthi, etc. ; *S.I.I.* VII, No. 337, pp. 190–91, ll. 9, 11–13, 21–24 ; Chauḷikēri, Udupi Tq. and Dt., Karn. St. **Dy.** Saṅgama, Dēvarāya, Ś. 1371 = 1449 A.D.

divānakhāna (K. < Urdu, *n.*), administrative office; **text :** (badly damaged) ... *naṁma **divānakhāna***. ... ; **tr.** our **administrative office**...... ; *E.C.* (R) III, Gu. 46, p. 40, l. 8 ; Beḷachalavāḍi, Gundlupet Tq., Mysore Dt., Karn. St. **Dy.** Tuḷuva, Sadāśiva, Ś. 1471 = 1549 A.D.

dīvige (K. < Skt. *n.*), lamp ; **text :** (damaged). . . . ***dīvige**ge soṭige eṇṇeyaṁ biṭṭaru* ... ; **tr.** granted one *soṭige* (liquid measure) of oil for one **lamp** ; *S.I.I.* V, No. 848, p. 346, l. 54 ; Hūli, Saundatti Tq. Belgaum Dt., Karn. St. **Dy.** Chāḷ. of Kal., Vikramāditya VI, Ś. 1019 = 1097 A.D.

divyagāṇa (Te. *n.*), oil mill dedicated to the deity ; **text :** (badly damaged)... *okaṭi **divyagāṇulu*** .... *dhāravosinavi* .... ; **tr.** one oil mill dedicated to the deity was given with the pouring of the water of libation ; *S.I.I.* X, No. 527, p. 285, l. 19 ; Jonnalagaḍḍa, Sattenapalli Tq., Guntur Dt., A.P. St. **Dy.** Kākatīya, Pratāparudradēva, Ś. 1241 = 1319 A.D.

divyakambhamu (Te. < Skt. *n.*), lamp post ; **text :**..... *Dānayanāyaṁkaravāru peṭṭina sommulu śrī Balidēvaraku* .... ***divyakaṁbbhamu** 1*.... ; **tr.** Dānayanāyaṁkara granted to the deity Balidēva, among many other things, one **lamp post** ; *S.I.I.* X, No. 451, p. 243, ll. 103–107, 111–12 ; Mallavōlu, Bandar Tq., Krishna Dt., A.P. St. **Dy.** Kākatīya, Pratāparudradēva, Ś. 1202 = 1280 A.D.

divyaṭiṇḍu (Te. < Skt.+Te. *n.*), torch bearer in the temple ; **text :** .... ***divyaṭiṇḍu** jana 2 ki na 10*. ... ; **tr.** 10 *na* (meaning obscure) for 2 persons who are **torch bearers in the temple** ; *S.I.I.* X, No. 740, p. 386, l. 28 ; Yenikepāḍu, Masulipatnam Tq., Krishna Dt., A.P. St., **Misc.**, in characters of 15th cent. A.D.

doḍa va ga (K. < Skt. = *doḍḍa varaha gadyāṇa*, *n.*), gold coin of higher denomination ; **text :** .. *halara kayyalu kaḍanāgi koṁḍa doḍa va ga 300* ..... *doḍa varaha* .... *ī hoṁnigaṁ bhaḍḍi prativarusha 1 kkaṁ **doḍa va ga** 30* .. ; **tr.** the interest for the loan of 300 *doḍa varaha* of gold coins taken from the *halaru* (an administratrive body) was fixed at **doḍa va ga** (*doḍḍa varaha gadyāṇa* = **gold coin of higher denomination**) 30 per year ; *S.I.I.* VII, No. 364, p. 220, ll. 24–26 ; Maṇigārakēri, Udupi Tq. and Dt., Karn. St. **Dy.** Sāḷuva, Narasiṁha, Ś. 1421 = 1499 A.D.

doḍa varaha (K. wrong for *doḍḍa*°, *n.*), gold coin of higher denomination ; **text**[1] **:** . . . *halara kayyalu kaḍanāgi koṁḍa doḍa va ga 300* . . . ***doḍa varaha*** . . . *ī hoṁnigam bhaḍḍi prativarusha 1 kkaṁ doḍa va ga 30* . . ; **tr.** the interest for the loan of 300 ***doḍa varaha*** of **gold coins of higher denomination** taken from the halaru (an administratrive body) was fixed at *doḍa va ga* (*doḍḍa varaha gadyāṇa* = gold coin of higher denomination) 30 per year ; *S.I.I.* VII, No. 364, p. 220, ll. 24–26 ; Maṇigārakēri, Udupi Tq. and Dt., Karn. St. **Dy.** Sāḷuva, Narasiṁha, Ś. 1421 = 1499 A.D. ; **text**[2] **:** . . . . . ***doḍḍa varaha*** *āṟu nūra aṟuvattu yī hoṁnanu appaṁta kshētragaḷalli koṭṭu tāmrada patragaḷa baresi koṁḍu Pārśvadēvara bhaṁḍāradalli hāki* . ; **tr.** six hundred and sixty **gold coins of higher denomination** having been distributed in designated places and this fact having been registered in copper plate inscription, the latter were deposited in the treasury of the god Pārśvadēva ; *S.I.I.* VII, No. 212, p. 108, ll. 33–35 ; Mūḍabidure, Karkala Tq., Udupi, Dt., Karn. **Dy.** Tuḷuva, Krishṇadēvarāya, Ś. 1437 = 1515 A.D.

doḍḍakere (K. *n.*), a big tank ; **text :** . . . . *chika beṁcheyeṁba kuṁṭe voḍadu khilavāgi yiralāgi nāvu* ***doḍḍakere****yāgi kaṭisi* . . . ; **tr.** the small pond called *chikabeṁche* having breached its bunds and fallen into waste we converted the same into **a big tank** ; *S.I.I.* IV, No. 250, p. 42, l. 3 ; Hampi, Hospet Tq., Bellary Dt., Karn. St. **Dy.** Tuḷuva, Krishṇadēvarāya, Ś. 1443 = 1521 A.D.

doḍḍa varaha gadyāṇa (K. *n.*), gold coin of higher denomination ; **text :** . . . . *5 gaddeyanu biḍāruvāravāgi* . . . . *kaḍaṁgoṁḍadu Bārakūra parivartanake saluva* ***doḍḍa varaha gadyāṇa*** *300* . . . . *yī bāḷige gēṇi aki mu 25* . . ; **tr.** 5 units of wet land were taken on lease by borrowing with 300 **gold coins of higher denomination** which is exchangeable to the equivalent value of coin minted in Bārakūru and the interest for this amount is fixed at 25 *mu* (*muḍi*, a grain measure) of rice from the leased land ; *S.I.I.* VII, No. 390, p. 249, ll. 44–47 ; Hosakēri, Udupi Tq. and Dt., Karn. St. **Misc.,** in characters of 16th cent. A.D.

ḍōḷu (K. *n.*), large purcussion instrument ; **text :** . . . *Dēvalāpurada Vasaṁta Mallikārjunadēvarige yeraḍu* ***ḍōḷu*** . . . ; **tr.** two large purcussion instruments donated to Vasaṁta Mallikārjuna of Dēvalāpura ; *S.I.I.* IX pt. ii, No. 647., p. 643, l. 13 ; Dēvalāpura, Kudligi Tq., Bellary Dt., Karn. St. **Dy.** Tuḷuva, Sadāśiva, Ś. 1474 = 1552 A.D.

doṁmari paṁnu (Te. *n.*), tax on professional jugglers ; **text :** . . . . . *Chālumūla samasta samaya* *pekkaṁḍra paṁpunānu . . . . . ī grāma prajālu ichē* ***doṁmaripaṁnu*** ; **tr.** on the advice of the merchant guild called Chālumūla samasta samaya pekkaṁḍru, the residents of the village donated the **tax on professional jugglers** ; *S.I.I.* XVI, No. 225, pp. 232–33 , ll. 10, 12–13, 19–21 ; Ainavōlu, Guntur Tq. and Dt., A.P. St. **Dy.** Tuḷuva, Sadāśiva, Ś. 1480 = 1558 A.D.

doṇe (K. *n.*), cistern ; **text[1]** : . . . *Bommayya nāyakaru . . . . . hostāgi Hampeya* ***doṇeya*** *tōḍsi barasida śāsana* . . . ; **tr.** stone inscription got engraved by Boṁmayyanāyaka after he got excavated a new **cistern** at Hampe ; *S.I.I.* IX, pt. i, No. 359, p. 376, ll. 11–12 ; Kundurpi, Kalyanadurg Tq., Anantapur Dt., A.P. St. **Dy.** Hoy., Ballāḷa III, Ś. 1262 = 1340 A.D. ; **text[2]** : . . . . . *Tātājōyisara makkaḷu Vellaṁbhaṭṭarige Attivaṭelu Hāigoṁḍana* ***doṇeya*** *gadde kha 110* . . . ; **tr.** Vellaṁbhaṭṭa the son of Tātājōyisa was given wet land of the extent of being sown with 110 *kha* (*khaṁḍuga*, a grain measure) of seeds watered by the **cistern** of Haigoṁḍa in the village of Attivaṭe ; *S.I.I.* IV, No. 254, p. 45, ll. 60, 68 ; Hampi, Hospet Tq., Bellary Dt., Karn. St. **Dy.** Tuḷuva, Kṛishṇadēvarāya, Ś. 1436 = 1514 A.D.

ḍōṇi[1] (K. *n.*), cistern ; **text** : . . . . . *Nārāyaṇadēvargge Posayūralli . . . . . dēvaraṁgabhōgakke biṭṭa* ***ḍōṇi*** *mūṟu*. . . . ; **tr.** gift of three cisterns at the village Posayūru for services to the image of the deity Nārāyaṇadēva ; *S.I.I.* XI, No. 203, p. 258, ll. 4–6 ; Muḷgund, Gadag Tq. and Dt., Karn. St. **Dy.** Chāḷ. of Kal., Vikramāditya VI, in chararacters of 11th-12th cent. A.D.

dōṇi[2] (K. *n.*), boat ; **text** : . . . . ***dōṇi*** *sāsirvvara biṭṭa dharmma . . . . dōṇiyaloṁdu paṇa* . . . ; **tr.** the gift made by the merchant guild doing business in boats was one *paṇa* (a coin) per **boat** ; *S.I.I.* XI, No. 158, p. 202, l. 20 ; Yalicharūr, Gadag Tq. and Dt., Karn. St. **Dy.** Chāḷ. of Kal., Vikramāditya VI, Ch. Vi. yr. 34 = 1109 A.D.

dōṇi sāsirvvaru (K. *n.*), guild of thousand mechants doing business on boats ; **text** : . . . . ***dōṇi sāsirvvara*** *biṭṭa dharmma . . . . dōṇiyaloṁdu paṇa* . . . ; **tr.** the gift made by the **guild of thousand merchants doing business on boats** was one *paṇa* (a coin) per boat ; *S.I.I.* XI, No. 158, p. 202, l. 20 ; Yalicharūr, Gadag Tq. and Dt., Karn. St. **Dy.** Chāḷ. of Kal., Vikramāditya VI, Ch. Vi. yr. 34 = 1109 A.D.

ḍoṁkivaṇa (K. *n.*), a kind of tax ; **text** : . . . *Maruḷēśadēvara nandādīvigege* ***doṁkivaṇa*** *mānenne sahitaṁ biṭṭa gāṇa voṁdu* . . . . ; **tr.** one oil mill along with the oil produced therein as well as income from **a kind of tax called ḍoṁkivaṇa** was granted for burning a perpetual lamp for the god Maruḷēśa ; *K.I.* II, No. 10, p. 32, ll. 37–38 ; Lakkuṁḍi, Gadag Tq. and Dt., Karn. St. **Dy.** Chāḷ. of Kal., Vikramāditya VI, Ch. Vi. yr. 4 = 1079 A.D.

dore (K. < Skt. *n.*), king, ruler ; **text** : . . . . . .

paramārādhyaṁ Mahēśaṁ kuḷavadhu Vijayaśrī nelaṁ pōshya vargaṁ ***doregaḷ*** *vaivāha saṁbaṁdhigaḷ ene negaḻda ...... Baḷḷāḷāvanīśam* ...; **tr. king** Ballāḷa was a great devotee of Lord Śiva whose beloved was the goddess of victory and whose land comprised subjects and for whom all other kings were related by marriages ; *E.C.* (R) IX, Bl. 16, pp. 12–13, ll. 19–20 ; Bēlūru, Belur Tq., Hassan Dt., Karn. St. **Dy.** Hoy., Vishṇuvardhana, Ś. 1039 = 1117 A.D.

dramma (K. *n.*), coin ; **text :** .... *viprara vivāhamumāgappanitaṟoḷellam osage* ***dramma*** *mūṟaṁ tappāde māṇiyoḷeraḍaṁ* ... *śūdragaṇa maduveyoḷandaṁ* .... *Pergeṟegegāyamidendosedu koṭṭar*. .... ; **tr.** the brāhmaṇas of the place granted the following money incomes : three *dramma* (**coin**) for the marriage of the brāhmaṇas, two *drammas* for the ceremoney of sacred thread initiation and one *dramma* for the marriage of the *śūdras* for the maintenance of the big tank ; *K.I.* II, No. 4, pp. 12–13, ll. 6–10; Daṇḍāpur, Dharwar Tq. and Dt., Karn. St. **Dy.** Rāshṭr., Gōvinda IV, Ś. 840 = 918 A.D.

dravatti (T. < Skt. *n.*), a medicine ; **text :** ... *āturaśālai Vīraśōḻanil āṇḍoṉṟil iḍum marundu* ... ... ***dravatti*** *nāḻiyum* .. ; **tr.** in the hospital named after Vīraśōḻa one *nāḻi* (liquid measure) of **medicine** called **dravatti** per year was stored ; *Ep. Ind.* XXI, No. 38, p. 240, ll. 46–47 ; Tirumukkūḍal, Madhurantakam Tq., Chingleput Dt., T. Nadu St. **Dy.** Chōḻa, Vīrarājēndra, in characters of 11th cent. A.D.

dravyadāya (K. < Skt. *n.*), grant in cash ; **text:** . ... *Guṇāḍhyar Kkaṇamageṟeginituṁ* ***dravyadāyamaṁ*** *koṭṭāvarggaḷ* ... ; **tr.** the virtuous **granted all the money** to the Kkaṇamagere tank (for its maintenance) ; *K.I.* II, No. 4, p. 13, l. 11 ; Daṇḍāpur, Dharwar Tq. and Dt., Karn. St. **Dy.** Rāshṭr., Gōvinda IV, Ś. 840 = 918 A.D.

dravyādhikāra (K. < Skt. *n.*), office pertaining to financial matters ; **text :** ..... *chakriya* ..... . ***dravyādhikārakke*** *mudreya mudrāṁguḷikaṁ jagakkavenalāvaṁ Śrīgaṇaṁ pōltapaṁ* .... ; **tr.** who can equal Śrīgaṇa, who was like the very signet ring of the **office pertaining to financial matters** of the emperor ; *S.I.I.* XVIII, No. 111, p. 134, ll. 11–13 ; Hattimattūr, Haveri Tq. and Dt., Karn. St. **Dy.** Chāḷ. of Kal., Vikramāditya VI, Ch. Vi. yr. 40 = 1115 A.D.

dravyam (T. < Skt. *n.*), money ; **text :** ..... *ivaṉ pakkal koṇḍu i* ***dravyamēy*** *kuḍuttu ūrār pakkal* ..... *iṟaiyili poṉ kuḍuttu koṇḍu tiruttina bhūmi* ...... ; **tr.** reclaimed land purchased after giving tax free grant of gold to the *ūrar* (inhabitants of the village) in the form of **money** from him ; *S.I.I.* VII, No. 810, p. 411, ll. 6–7 ; Bāhūr, Puduchchery U.T., **Dy.** Rāshṭr., Kṛishṇa III, reg. yr. 27 = 964 A.D.

dravya mukha (K. < Skt. *n.*), in the form of money ; **text :** ..... *Bhairavadēvara saṁnadhiya* *saṁte kilavāagiralāgi prati huṭṭisi aḷḷu aḍikāsu saha* ***dravyamukha****diṁ dēvara dīpārādhanege . . . biṭṭa dēvadāya . . . .* ; **tr.** for the lamp servivce to the god Bhairavadēva, income in cash collected while re-eastablishing the discontinued market in front of the temple of that god was donated ; *S.I.I.* IX, pt. ii, No. 532, p. 547, ll. 8–10, 13–14 ; Adhamaṉkōṭṭai, Dharmapuri Tq. and Dt., T. Nadu St. **Dy.** Tuḷuva, Achyutarāya, Ś. 1452 = 1530 A.D.

drōhi (K. < Skt. *n.*), traitor ; **text :** . . . . *samasta nakhalaraṁgaḷu svadēśi paradēśiyiṁdaṁ baṁdaṁtaha davaṇa gadyāṇa nūrakke gadyāṇam oṁdaṟōpādiya davaṇa ādidēvarige salauvantāgi koṭṭa śāsana idaṟoḷe virahitaguptavanāru māḍidoḍaṁ . . . . ava dēva****drōhi*** *rāja****drōhi*** *samaya****drōhi*** . . ; **tr.** all the members of the merchant guild granted materaials at the rate of one *gadyāṇa* for every 100 *gadyāṇa* of materials received from either local men or foreigners for Ādidēva. If any one denies or conceals in this matter he shall be a **traitor** to the god, a **traitor** to the king and a **traitor** to the creed ; *E.C.* II, Sb. 459, p. 281, ll. 8–13 ; Śravaṇabeḷagoḷa, Channarayapattana Tq., Hassan Dt., Karn. St. **Misc.,** Cy. yr. Sarvvadhāri = 1288 A.D.

drōṇāmukha (K. < Skt. *n.*), town situated at the end of a valley ; **text :** . . . . *cheluvaṁ taḷeda* ***drōṇāmukha*** *śrēṇiyaneseva nadījāḷadiṁ . . . . . madhya dēśam viśēshaṁ* . . ; **tr.** the central province is unique with a series of beautiful **towns situated at the end of the valley** and with multitude of rivers ; *Ep. Ind.* XIX, No. 38B, p. 229, ll. 15–16 ; Rōṇ, Ron Tq., Dharwar Dt., Karn. St. **Dy.** Kal. of Kal., Saṅkama, Ś. 1102 = 1179 A.D.

drōṇi sāsirvvaru (K. *n.*), guild of thousand mechants doing business on boats ; **text :** . . . *vachanaṁ kaḍeda śilāśāsanamene nuḍidē baṇṇisuve* ***drōṇi sāsirvvaruma*** . . . ; **tr.** I will describe the words uttered by the **guild of thousand merchants doing business on boats,** as words inscribed on stone slabs ; *S.I.I.* XI, No. 158, p. 202, ll. 19–20 ; Yalicharūr, Gadag Tq. and Dt., Karn. St. **Dy.** Chāḷ. of Kal., Vikramāditya VI, Ch. Vi. yr. 34 = 1109 A.D.

du (K. < *duḍḍu, n.*), copper coin ; **text :** . . . . . *maṁgaḷavāra dina ūṭada dadhige* ***du*** *4. . .* ; **tr.** 4 **copper coins** for the curd to be used in the meals on Tuesdays ; *K.I.* III, No. 17, p. 71, l. 68; Bhaṭkal, Bhatkal Tq. and Dt., Karn. St. **Dy.** Hāḍuvaḷḷi Chfs., Channabhairavadēvi, Ś. 1471 = 1549 A.D.

duḍu (K. < *duḍḍu, n.*), money ; **text :** . . . . . . *bhaṁḍāradavarige kāṇike vivara kāsu* ***duḍu*** *muḍupu . . . . ainūru varaha . . .* ; **tr.** a bundle of five hundred *varaha* of **money** to be remitted to the treasury ; *S.I.I.* IV, No. 277, p. 72, l. 5 ; Hampi, Hospet Tq., Bellary Dt., Karn. St. **Dy.** Tuḷuva, Kṛishṇadēvarāya, Ś. 1435 = 1513 A.D.

Duggaipaṭṭi (T. < Skt.+T. *n.*), land belonging to

the godess Durgā ; **text :** . . . . ***Duggaippaṭṭi****yum Piḍāripaṭṭiyum nīkki ivūril nāyaṉārkkuppaṅgu iraṇḍu* . . . ; **tr.** two shares of land to the god after excluding the **land belonging to the goddess Durgā** and the goddess Bhaṭāri ; *S.I.I.* VII, No. 57, p. 24, l. 15 ; Viḷappākkam, Walajapet Tq., N. Arcot Dt., T. Nadu St. **Dy.** Śambuvarāya, Śambuvarāya, reg. yr. 13+1, in characters of 12th cent. A.D.

duguṇa (K. *n.*), twofold ; **text :** . . . *ātana satiyavanī vikhyātey Arundhatige toṇe* . . . . . *Śrī-rāmana Sītege duguṇaṁ* . . . . *Kanakabbe* . . . ; **tr.** his wife Kanakabbe who was world famous was equal to the legendary figure Arundhati and was **twofold** as good as Sītā the wife of Śrīrāma ; *E.C.* VIII, Sgr. 103, p. 300, ll. 34–35 ; Bēsūru, Sagara Tq., Shimoga Dt., Karn. St. **Dy.** Chāḷ. of Kal, Vikramāditya VI, Ch. Vi. yr. 14 = 1089 A.D.

duḷiravaṭa (K. *n.*), a kind of tax ; **text :** . . . . *avasarada Aṁṇamarsaru Tiruvadiya Vīraṭadēvarige koṭṭa dharmaśāsana* . . . . *yī grāmada chatusīmege saluva nañjey puñjey* . . *maravaḍe kuḷavaḍe* . . . . ***duḷiravaṭa*** . . . . *saha sērsi koṭṭevu* . . . ; **tr.** the pious charity endowed by the palace official Aṁṇamarsa to the god Vīraṭadēva of Tiruvaḍi : within the four boundaries of the village, collective income from wet lands, dry lands, *maravaḍe* (tax on fruit yielding trees), *kuḷavaḍe* (land tax), the **tax called *duḷiravaṭa*** etc. ; *S.I.I.* IX, pt. ii, No. 463, p. 475, ll. 2, 7–9 ; Tiruvaḍi, Cuddalore Tq., S. Arcot Dt., T. Nadu St. **Dy.** Sāḷuva, Narasiṁha, Cy. yr. Vikṛiti = 1470 A.D.

duṁdume (K. *n.*), purcussion instrument ; **text :** . . . . . . *suraduṁdumeyeseyuttire surakanneyaroldu* . . . . *suravimānadoḷiraluydaru Kētamalla nāyakanasuvaṁ* . . . ; **tr.** while the divine purcussion instrument was being beaten, divine damsels took with them in a flying chariot the life of Kētamallanāyaka ; *E.C.* (R) X, Chnp. 72, p. 501, ll. 14–15 ; Keṁbāḷu, Channarayapattana Tq., Hassan Dt., Karn. St. **Dy.** Hoy., Ballāḷa II, in characters of 12th-13th cent. A.D.

duṁnē nēla (Te. *n.*), cultivated land ; **text :** . . . . . . *Tippiseṭṭi* . . . . *Thippasamudrāna tāmu tama tallitandrulakuṁ puṁṇyamugānu* . . . . . ***duṁnē nēla*** *dēvabrāhmaṇa vṛittulu peṭṭinavi* . . . ; **tr.** Tippiseṭṭi granted to the gods and brāhmaṇas shares from the **cultivated land** below the tank called Tippasamudra for the merit of his sons and daughters ; *S.I.I.* XVI, No. 9, pp. 8–9, ll. 14–16; Mudivēḍu, Madanapalle Tq., Chittoor Dt., A.P. St. **Dy.** Saṅgama, Harihara II, Cy. yr. Īśvara = 1397 A.D.

duṇḍige (K. *n.*), bracelet ; **text :** . . . . *Indammarasara* ***duṇḍige*** *verisiḻda ponna keyd Eṟeyappan goppisimendu tandu bhagavantara kaigaḷanapikoṭṭu* . . . *kṛitānta sadruśam ripusēneyanaṭṭi* . . . . *asumgoḷe pondida Kesavayya* . . . . . ; **tr.** having taken away by force the **bracelet** of Indamarasa, having brought and putting it into the hands of Bhagavanta with a request that it be plated with gold and be presented to Er̤eyappa, Kēśavayya the very *yama* to enemies fought with the soldiers and died ; *E.C.* (R) III, Nj. 371, p. 415, ll. 12–17 ; Kūgalūru, Nanjanagudu Tq., Mysore Dt., Karn. St. **Dy.** W. Gaṁga, Er̤eyappa, in characters of 10th cent. A.D.

duraushadha (K. < Skt. *n.*), harmful potion ; **text :** . . . . *pati basadakkumintu tamageṁdu* ***duraushadha****vaṁ prayōgipa kritakeyar. . . .* ; **tr.** the unfaithfull wives who administered **harmful potion** to their husbands in order to keep them under their control ; *S.I.I.* XX, No. 248, p. 306, l. 45 ; Saundatti, Saundatti Tq., Belgaum Dt., Karn. St. **Dy.** Raṭṭa Chfs., Lakshmīdēvarasa IV, Ś. 1151 = 1228 A.D.

durga (K. < Skt. *n.*), fort ; **text :** . . . *vīra Kṛishṇarāyaru namage māgaṇi āgi koṭṭa Ādavāniya****durga****ke saluva Kereya Beḷugallu grāmadallu Kṛishṇabhūmi khaṁ. 10. . . .* ; **tr.** black soil land of 10 *khaṁ* (*khaṁḍuga*, a grain measure) of the extent of being sown with 10 *khaṁḍuga* of seeds in the village Kereya Beḷugallu situated in the **fort** in Ādavāni, a province granted to us by Vīra Kṛishṇarāya ; *S.I.I.* IX, pt. ii, No. 498, p. 511, ll. 11–14 ; Cheruvu Belagallu, Kurnool Tq. and Dt., A.P. St. **Dy.** Tuḷuva, Kṛishṇadēvarāya, Ś. 1436 = 1514 A.D.

durgga (K. < Skt. *n.*), fort ; **text :** . . . . *Chalukyō Vallabhēśvaraḥ adhastāduparishṭāchcha* ***durgga****mētadachīkarat . . . .* ; **tr.** the Chalukya emperor got constructed a **fort**ress from the base to the top ; *K.I.* II, No. 2, p. 5, ll. 3, 5 ; Bādāmi, Badami Tq., Bāgalkot Dt., Karn. St. **Dy.** Chal. of Bād., Polekēśi I, Ś. 465 = 543 A.D.

durggādhipati (K. < Skt. *n.*), chief of the fort ; **text :** . . . *Tor̤agaleya* ***durggādhipati*** *Rāmapparāütara makkaḷu Haridāsa Rāütaru Bel̤l̤ūra Prasaṁnna Mādhavadēvara muṁde utsaha maṁṭapa dīpamāleya kaṁbha balipīṭhavanu . . . . nilisidaru* . . . . ; **tr.** Haridāsarāüta son of Rāmapparāüta, the **chief of the fort** of Tor̤agale set up the festival hall, a pillar for lighting a series of lamps and an altar for offering in front of the temple of god Mādhava of Bel̤l̤ūru ; *E.C.* (R) VII, Ng. 91, p. 91, ll. 5–12 ; Bel̤l̤ūru, Nagamangala Tq., Mandya Dt., Karn. St. **Misc.**, Ś. 1441 = 1518 A.D.

durggam (T. < Skt. *n.*), fort ; **text :** (damaged). . . . *Kṛishṇarāyamahārāyar Vijayaṇagarattinum pūrva digvijaya yātraikku yel̤undaruḷi Udayagiri* ***durggam****um sādhittu . . . .* ; **tr.** Kṛishṇarāyamahārāya having proceeded from Vijayanagara on a military expedition to the east and having captured the **fort** of Udayagiri ; *T.D.I.* III, No. 78, p. 176, l. 2 ; Tirumalai, Chandragiri Tq., Chittoor Dt., A.P. St. **Dy.** Tuḷuva, Kṛishṇadēvarāya, Ś. 1437 = 1515 A.D.

durgga varttana (Te. < Skt. *n.*), regular tax levied for the maintenance of the fort ; **text :**

... *Ghaṁḍikōṭaku achēṭi* **durgga varttana** *daṇāyini varttana bēḍige kāṇika .... modalainavi yeṁnigalavu aṁniṁni .... Mōpūri Bhairavēśvaruniki .... dhāravēsi ichchina dharmaśāsanam* ... ; **tr. regular tax** income such as **for the maintenance of the fort**, for the maintenance of the army commander, requisitioned tax, tribute etc. were donated to the god Bhairavēśvara of Mōpūru with the libation of water ; *S.I.I.* XVI, No. 139, p. 151, ll. 15–17, 25, 29 ; Mōpūru, Pulivendla Tq., Cuddapah Dt., A.P. St. **Dy.** Tuḷuva, Sadāśiva, Ś. 1466 = 1545 A.D.

durjana (K. < Skt. *n.*), bad elements ; **text :** . . *kallugaḷanu kittu hākida durjanru yibaru mūvarige takka kaṭṭupāḍu māḍi avara mēḷaṇa lekhada hoṁnanu tegedu guḍige koḍisuvudu* .... ; **tr.** two or three bad elements who had removed the inlaid stones illegally were given punishment and the fine in gold collected from them should be given to the temple ; *S.I.I.* IX, pt. ii, No. 527, p. 543, ll. 3–5 ; Nāgalāpuram, Ponneri Tq., Chingleput Dt., T. Nadu St. **Dy.** Tuḷuva, Kṛishṇadēvarāya, Cy. yr. Sarvvadhāri = 1529 A.D.

dūsiga (K. *n.*), cloth merchant ; **text :** .... *satrakke biṭṭa dhammaventendaḍe* .... ***dūsiga*** *gandhigaraṁgaḍigaḷalli vīsaveraḍuvare* ... ; **tr.** the details of the charitable donation given to the choultry included two and a half *vīsa* (a coin) from each of the shops belonging to **cloth merchants**, incense sellers, etc. ; *K.I.* II, No. 21, p. 82, ll. 21, 27–28 ; Telsangi, Athaṇi Tq., Dharwar Dt., Karn. St. **Dy.** Chāḷ. of Kal, Jagadēkamalla, reg. yr. 10 = 1147 A.D.

dūsiga vasara (K. *n.*), cloth merchant's shop ; **text :** .... ***dūsigavasara****kkamakkasālegaṁ hoṁge haṇaṁ* ... ; **tr.** one *haṇa* (a coin) for one *hoṁnu* (gold coin) on **cloth merchant's shop** and the goldsmith's shop ; *Ep. Ind.* XIX, No. 4A, p. 33, l. 27 ; Kolhāpur, Kolhapur Tq. and Dt., Mahā. St. **Com. gld.** Ś. 1058 = 1135 A.D.

dūtaka (Skt. *n.*), officer in charge of drafting royal charters ; **text :** .... *Chaṁdiyamma Vayamau* ***dūtakau*** ... ; **tr.** Chaṁdiyamma and Vayam were two **officers** who were **in charge of drafting** this **charter** ; *Ep. Ind.* XXIII, No. 33B, p. 222, l. 72 ; Lōhāra, (now deposited in the Central Museum at Nagpur, Mahā. St.), **Dy.** Rāshṭr. Gōvinda III, Ś. 734 = 812 A.D.

duṭṭaragaṇḍa (K. *n.*), hero who punishes bad elements ; **text :** .... *Gaṅgakuḷakamaḷamārtaṇḍaṁ* ***duṭṭaragaṇḍaṁ*** *Nanniya Gaṅgaṁ* ... ; **tr.** the Sun who makes the lotus of the Gaṅga family blossom, the **hero who punishes bad elements** and the truthful Gaṅga ; *E.C.* VII, Sh. 10, p. 20, l. 20 ; Taṭṭakere, Shimoga Tq. and Dt., Karn. St. **Dy.** Chāḷ. of Kal, Vikramāditya VI, Ś. 1001 = 1079 A.D.

dvēdi (K. < Skt. *dvivēdi, n.*), one who is well versed in two vēdas ; **text :** .... *akhila śāstra paṭugaḷ* ***dvēdigaḷ*** *Jātavēdabhaṭṭarnnegaḷdar* ... ;

tr. there flourished Jātavēdabhaṭṭa who was learned in all the kinds of sciences and **who was well versed in two vēdas** ; *S.I.I.* XI, No. 450, p. 31, ll. 22–23 ; Kuruhaṭṭi, Navalgund Tq., Dharwar Dt., Karn. St. **Dy.** Chāḷ. of Kal., Taila II, Ś. 902 = 1080 A.D.

dvīpi lāñchchana (K. *n.*), tiger insignia ; **text :** . . . . *tatō Dvārāvatīnāthāḥ Poysaḷā* ***dvīpi lāñchchhanāḥ*** . . . . . ; **tr.** then followed the lords of the city of Dvārāvati beloging to Poysaḷa family and having the **tiger** for their **insignia** ; *E.C.* (R) IX, Bl. 16, p. 11, l. 3 ; Belūru, Belur Tq., Hassan Dt., Karn. St. **Dy.** Hoy., Vishṇuvardhana, Ś. 1039 = 1117 A.D.

dvisaptati niyōga (K. *n.*), seventy two departments; **text :** . . . . . ***dvisaptati niyōga*** ***Yaugandharāyaṇaṁ*** . . . . . .; **tr.** minister appointed in charge of the **seventy two deopartments** ; *K.I.A.P.*, Gb. 2 (third face), p. 5, ll. 150–53 ; Gulbarga, Gulbarga Tq. and Dt., Karn. St. **Dy.** Chāḷ. of Kal., Sōmēśvara I, Ś. 980 = 1058 A.D.

Note on Editors

Volume Editor

K.V. Ramesh is former Director (Epigraphy) and Joint Director-General, Archaeological Survey of India, and has served as Honorary Director, Oriental Research Institute, University of Mysore. He has also been a member of the editorial board of the Kannada–Kannada dictionary and of the editorial board of the volume I of Kannada–Kannada–English dictionary (Kannada Sahitya Parishat, Bangalore). Author of a number of books in English and Kannada, he is presently the Chairman, Epigraphical Society of India, and Place Names Society of India, and Editor, *Epigraphia Indica.*

General Editor

R.S. Sharma (1919–2011) was Professor Emeritus, Patna University, and the Founder Chairman of Indian Council of Historical Research (ICHR). He also served as Member, University Grants Commission; Secretary and General President of Indian History Congress; and Deputy-chairperson of UNESCO's International Association for the Study of Cultures of Central Asia. He is the author of several works, including *India's Ancient Past* (2005) and *Rethinking India's Past* (2009).